S. Richardson

Clarissa

Or the History of a young Lady

S. Richardson

Clarissa
Or the History of a young Lady

ISBN/EAN: 9783741163166

Manufactured in Europe, USA, Canada, Australia, Japa

Cover: Foto ©ninafisch / pixelio.de

Manufactured and distributed by brebook publishing software (www.brebook.com)

S. Richardson

Clarissa

EACH VOLUME SOLD SEPARATELY.

COLLECTION
OF
BRITISH AUTHORS

TAUCHNITZ EDITION.

VOL. 595.

CLARISSA BY RICHARDSON

IN FOUR VOLUMES.

VOL. 1.

LEIPZIG: BERNHARD TAUCHNITZ.
PARIS: C. REINWALD & Cie, 15, RUE DES SAINTS PÈRES.

This Collection is published with copyright for Continental circulation, but all purchasers are earnestly requested not to introduce the volumes

COLLECTION
OF
BRITISH AUTHORS.
VOL. 595.

CLARISSA BY S. RICHARDSON.

IN FOUR VOLUMES.

VOL. I.

CLARISSA;

or,

THE HISTORY OF A YOUNG LADY:

COMPREHENDING
THE MOST IMPORTANT CONCERNS
OF PRIVATE LIFE; AND PARTICULARLY SHEWING
THE DISTRESSES THAT MAY ATTEND THE
MISCONDUCT BOTH OF PARENTS AND CHILDREN,
IN RELATION TO MARRIAGE.

BY

S. RICHARDSON.

COMPLETE IN FOUR VOLUMES

VOL. I.

LEIPZIG

BERNHARD TAUCHNITZ

1862.

SONNET
TO THE
AUTHOR OF CLARISSA.

O MASTER of the heart! whose magic skill
   The close recesses of the soul can find,
   Can rouse, becalm, and terrify the mind,
Now melt with pity, now with anguish thrill;

Thy moral page while virtuous precepts fill,
   Warm from the heart, to mend the age design'd,
   Wit, strength, truth, decency, are all combin'd
To lead our youth to good, and guard from ill.

O long enjoy what thou so well hast won;
   The grateful tribute of each honest heart,
     Sincere, nor hackneyed in the ways of men:
At each distressful stroke their true tears run;
   And Nature, unsophisticate by Art,
     Owns and applauds the labours of thy pen

PREFACE.

The following History is given in a Series of Letters, written principally in a double, yet separate correspondence;

Between two young ladies of virtue and honour, bearing an inviolable friendship for each other, and writing not merely for amusement, but upon the most *interesting* subjects; in which every private family, more or less, may find itself concerned: and,

Between two gentlemen of free lives; one of them glorying in his talents for stratagem and invention, and communicating to the other, in confidence, all the secret purposes of an intriguing head and resolute heart.

But here it will be proper to observe, for the sake of such as may apprehend hurt to the morals of youth, from the more freely written letters that the gentlemen, though professed libertines as to the female sex, and making it one of their wicked maxims, to keep no faith with any of the individuals of it, who are thrown into their power, are not, however, either infidels or scoffers; nor yet such as think themselves freed from the observance of those other moral duties which bind man to man.

On the contrary, it will be found, in the progress of the work, that they very often make such reflections upon each other, and each upon himself and his own actions, as reasonable beings *must* make, who disbelieve not a future state of rewards and punishments, and who one day propose to reform — One of them actually reforming, and by that means giving an opportunity to censure the freedoms which fall from the gayer pen and lighter heart of the other.

And yet that other, although in unbosoming himself to a select friend, he discovers wickedness enough to entitle him to general detestation, preserves a decency, as well in his images as in his language, which is not always to be found in the works of some of the most celebrated modern writers, whose subjects and characters have less warranted the liberties they have taken.

In the letters of the two young ladies, it is presumed, will be found not only the highest exertion of a reasonable and *practicable* ndship, between minds endowed with the noblest principles of virtue and religion, but occasionally interspersed, such delicacy of sentiments, particularly with regard to the other sex; such instances of impartiality, each freely, as a fundamental principle of their friendship, blaming, praising, and setting right the other, as are strongly to be recommended to the observation of the *younger* part (more especially) of female readers.

The principal of these two young ladies is proposed as an exemplar to her sex. Nor is it any objection to her being so, that she is not in all respects a perfect character. It was not only natural, but it was necessary, that she should have some faults, were it only to shew the reader, how laudably she could mistrust and blame herself, and carry to her own heart, divested of self-partiality, the censure which arose from her own convictions, and that even to the acquittal of those, because revered characters, whom no one else would acquit, and to whose much greater faults her errors were owing, and not to a weak or reproachable heart. As far as is consistent with human frailty, and as far as she could be perfect, considering the people she had to deal with, and those with whom she was inseparably connected, she *is* perfect. To have been impeccable, must have left nothing for the Divine Grace and a Purified State to do, and carried our idea of her from woman to angel. As such is she often esteemed by the man whose *heart* was so corrupt, that he could hardly believe human nature capable of the purity, which, on every trial or temptation, shone out in *hers*.

Besides the four principal persons, several others are introduced, whose letters are characteristic: and it is presumed, that there will be found in some of them, but more especially in those of the chief character among the men, and the second character among the women, such strokes of gaiety, fancy, and humour, as will entertain and divert; and at the same time both warn and instruct.

All the letters are written while the hearts of the writers must be supposed to be wholly engaged in their subjects (the events at the time generally dubious): so that they abound not only with critical situations, but with what may be called *instantaneous* descriptions and reflections (proper to be brought home to the breast of the youthful reader); as also with affecting conversations; many of them written in the dialogue or dramatic way.

"*Much more* lively and affecting, says one of the principal characters, (Vol. IV.) must be the style of those who write in the height of a *present* distress; the mind tortured by the pangs of uncertainty (the events then hidden in the womb of fate); *than* the dry, narrative, unanimated style of a person relating difficulties and dangers surmounted, can be; the relater perfectly at ease; and if himself unmoved by his own story, not likely greatly to affect the reader."

What will be found to be more particularly aimed at in the following work, is — to warn the inconsiderate and thoughtless of the one sex, against the base arts and designs of specious contrivers of the other — to caution parents against the undue exercise of their natural authority over their children in the great article of marriage — to warn children against preferring a man of pleasure to a man of probity, upon that dangerous but too commonly received notion, *that a reformed rake makes the best husband* — but above all, to investigate the highest and most important doctrines not only of morality, but of Christianity, by shewing them thrown into action in the conduct of the *worthy* characters; while the *unworthy*, who set those doctrines at defiance, are condignly, and, as it may be said, consequentially punished.

From what has been said, considerate readers will not enter upon the perusal of the piece before them, as if it were designed *only* to divert and amuse. It will probably be thought tedious to all such as *dip* into it, expecting a *light novel*, or *transitory romance;* and look upon the story in it (interesting as that is generally allowed to be) as its *sole end*, rather than as a vehicle to the instruction.

Different persons, as might be expected, have been of different opinions, in relation to the conduct of the heroine in particular situations; and several very worthy persons have objected to the general catastrophe, and other parts of the History. Whatever is thought material of these shall be taken notice of by way of POSTSCRIPT, at the conclusion of the History; for this work being addressed to the public as a history of *life* and *manners*, those parts of it which are proposed to carry with them the force of an example, ought to be as unobjectionable as is consistent with the *design of the whole*, and with *human nature*.

NAMES OF THE PRINCIPAL PERSONS.

Miss Clarissa Harlowe,	A young lady of great beauty and merit.
Robert Lovelace, Esq.	Her admirer.
James Harlowe, Esq.	Father of Clarissa.
Mrs. Harlowe,	His lady.
James Harlowe,	Their only son.
Arabella	Their elder daughter.
John Harlowe, Esq.	Elder brother of James Harlowe, sen.
Antony Harlowe, Esq.	Third brother.
Roger Solmes, Esq.	An admirer of Clarissa, favoured by her friends.
Mrs. Hervey,	Half-sister of Mrs. Harlowe.
Miss Dolly Hervey,	Her daughter.
Mrs. Judith Norton,	A woman of great piety and discretion, who had a principal share in the education of Clarissa.
Col. Wm. Morden,	A near relation of the Harlowes.
Miss Howe,	The most intimate friend, companion, and correspondent of Clarissa.
Mrs. Howe,	Her mother.
Charles Hickman, Esq.	An admirer of Miss Howe.
Earl of M.	Uncle to Mr. Lovelace.
Lady Sarah Sadleir,	Sisters of Earl of M.
Lady Betty Lawrance,	
Miss Charl. Montague,	Nieces of the same nobleman.
Miss Patty Montague,	
Dr. Lewen,	A worthy divine.
Mr. Elias Brand,	A pedantic young clergyman.
Dr. H.	A humane physician.
Mr. Goddard,	An honest and skilful apothecary.
John Belford, Esq.	Mr. Lovelace's principal intimate and confidant.
Richard Mowbray,	
Thomas Doleman,	Esqrs. libertine friends of Mr. Lovelace.
James Tourville,	
Thomas Belton,	
Mrs. Moore,	A widow keeping a lodging-house at Hampstead.
Miss Rawlins,	A notable young gentlewoman there.
Mrs. Bevis,	A lively young widow of the same place.
Mrs Sinclair,	The pretended name of a private brothel-keeper at London.
Capt. Tomlinson,	The assumed name of a vile pander to the debaucheries of Mr. Lovelace.
Sally Martin,	Assistants of, and partners with, the infamous Sinclair.
Polly Horton,	
Dorcas Wykes,	An artful servant in the vile house.

THE HISTORY OF CLARISSA HARLOWE.

LETTER I.
Miss Anna Howe to Clarissa Harlowe.
Jan. 10.

I am extremely concerned, my dearest friend, for the disturbances that have happened in your family. I know how it must hurt you to become the subject of the public talk: and yet upon an occasion so generally known, it is impossible but that whatever relates to a young lady whose distinguished merits have made her the public care, should engage every body's attention. I long to have the particulars from yourself; and of the usage I am told you receive upon an accident you could not help; and in which, as far as I can learn, the sufferer was the aggressor.

Mr. Diggs, the surgeon, whom I sent for at the first hearing of the rencounter, to inquire, for your sake, how your brother was, told me, that there was no danger from the wound, if there were none from the fever; which it seems had been increased by the perturbation of his spirits.

Mr. Wyerley drank tea with us yesterday; and though he is far from being partial to Mr. Lovelace, as it may be well supposed, yet both he and Mr. Symmes blame your family for the treatment they gave him when he went in person to inquire after your brother's health, and to express his concern for what had happened.

They say, that Mr. Lovelace could not avoid drawing his sword: and that either your brother's unskilfulness or passion left him from the very first pass entirely in his power.

This, I am told, was what Mr. Lovelace said upon it; retreating as he spoke: "Have a care, Mr. Harlowe—your violence puts you out of your defence. You give me too much advantage. For your sister's sake, I will pass by every thing:—if—"

But this the more provoked his rashness, to lay himself open to the advantage of his adversary—who, after a slight wound given him in the arm, took away his sword.

There are people who love not your brother, because of his natural imperiousness and fierce and uncontrolable temper: these say, that the young gentleman's passion was abated on seeing his blood gush plentifully down his arm; and that he received the generous offices of his adversary (who helped him off with his coat and waistcoat, and bound up his arm, till the surgeon could come) with such patience, as was far from making a visit afterwards from that adversary to inquire after his health, appear either insulting or improper.

Be this as it may, every body pities you. So steady, so uniform in your conduct: so desirous, as you always said, of sliding through life to the end of it unnoted; and, as I may add, not wishing to be observed even for your silent benevolence; sufficiently happy in the noble consciousness which attends it: *rather useful than glaring*, your deserved motto; though now to your regret pushed into blaze, as I may say: and yet blamed at home for the faults of others—how must such a virtue suffer on every hand!—Yet it must be allowed, that your present trial is but proportioned to your prudence.

As all your friends without doors are apprehensive that some other unhappy event may result from so violent a contention, in which it seems the families on both sides are now engaged, I must desire you to enable me, on the authority of your own information, to do you occasional justice.

My mother, and all of us, like the rest of the world, talk of nobody but you on this occasion, and of the consequences which may follow from the resentments of a man of Mr. Lovelace's spirit; who, as he gives out, has been treated with high indignity by your uncles. My mother will have it, that you cannot now, with any decency, either see him, or correspond with him. She is a good deal prepossessed by your uncle Antony; who occasionally calls upon us, as you know; and on this rencounter, has represented to her the crime which it would be in a sister to encourage a man who is to wade into her favour (this was his expression) through the blood of her brother.

Write to me therefore, my dear, the whole of your story from the time that Mr. Lovelace was first introduced into your family; and particularly an account of all that passed between him and your sister; about which there are different reports; some people scrupling not to insinuate that the younger sister has stolen a lover from the elder: and pray write in so full a manner as may satisfy those who know not so much of your affairs as I do. If any thing unhappy should fall out from the violence of such spirits as you have to deal with, your account of all things *previous* to it will be your best justification.

You see what you draw upon yourself by excelling all your sex. Every individual of it who knows you, or has heard of you, seems to think you answerable to *her* for your conduct in points so very delicate and concerning.

Every eye, in short, is upon you

with the expectation of an example. I wish to heaven you were at liberty to pursue your own methods: all would then, I dare say, be easy, and honourably ended. But I dread your directors and directresses; for your mother, admirably well qualified as she is to lead, must submit to be led. Your sister and brother will certainly put you out of your course.

But this is a point you will not permit me to expatiate upon: pardon me therefore, and I have done. — Yet, why should I say, pardon me? When your concerns are my concerns? When your honour is my honour? When I love you, as never woman loved another? And when you have allowed of that concern and of that love; and have for years, which in persons so young may be called many, ranked in the first class of your friends,

Your ever grateful and
affectionate,
ANNA HOWE.

Will you oblige me with a copy of the preamble to the clauses in your grandfather's will in your favour; and allow me to send it to my aunt Harman? — She is very desirous to see it. Yet your character has so charmed her, that, though a stranger to you personally, she assents to the preference given you in that will, before she knows the testator's reasons for giving you that preference.

LETTER II.
Miss Clarissa Harlowe to Miss Howe.

Harlowe Place, Jan. 13.

How you oppress me, my dearest friend, with your politeness! I cannot doubt your sincerity; but you should take care that you give me not reason from your kind partiality to call in question your judgment. You do not distinguish that I take many admirable *hints* from you, and have the art to pass them upon you for my own: for in all you do, in all you say, nay, in your very looks (so animated!) you give lessons to one who loves you and observes you as I love and observe you, without knowing that you do — So pray, my dear, be more sparing of your praise for the future, lest after this confession we should suspect that you secretly intend to praise yourself, while you would be thought only to commend another.

Our family has indeed been strangely discomposed. — *Discomposed!* — It has been in *tumults*, ever since the unhappy transaction; and I have borne all the blame; yet should have had too much concern from myself, had I been more justly spared by every one else.

For, whether it be owing to a faulty impatience, having been too indulgently treated to be inured to blame, or to the regret I have to hear those censured on my account whom it is my duty to vindicate; I have sometimes wished, that it had pleased God to have taken me in my last fever, when I had every body's love and good opinion; but oftener that I had never been distinguished by my grandfather as I was: since that distinction has estranged from me my brother's and sister's affections; at least, has raised a jealousy with regard to the apprehended favour of my two uncles, that now and then overshadows their love.

My brother being happily recovered of his fever, and his wound in a hopeful way, although he has not yet ventured abroad, I will be as particular as you desire in the little history you demand of me. But heaven forbid that any thing should ever happen which may require it to be produced for the purpose you mention!

I will begin, as you command, with Mr. Lovelace's address to my sister; and be as brief as possible. I will recite facts only; and leave you to judge of the truth of the report raised that the younger sister has robbed the elder.

It was in pursuance of a conference between Lord M. and my uncle Antony, that Mr. Lovelace [my father and mother not forbidding] paid his respects to my sister Arabella. My brother was then in Scotland, busying himself in viewing the condition of the considerable estate which was left him there by his generous godmother, together with one as considerable in Yorkshire. I was also absent at my *Dairy-house*, as it is called*,

busied in the accounts relating to the estate which my grandfather had the goodness to devise to me; and which once a year are left to my inspection, although I have given the whole into my father's power.

My sister made me a visit there the day after Mr. Lovelace had been introduced; and seemed highly pleased with the gentleman. His birth, his fortune in possession, a clear 2000*l.* a year, as Lord M. had assured my uncle; presumptive heir to that nobleman's large estate: his great expectations from Lady Sarah Sadleir, and Lady Betty Lawrence; who with his uncle interested themselves very warmly (he being the last of his line) to see him married.

"So handsome a man! — O her beloved Clary!" (for then she was ready to love me dearly, from the overflowings of her good humour on his account!) "He was but *too* handsome a man for *her!* — Were she but as amiable as *somebody*, there would be a probability of *holding* his affections! — For he was wild, she heard; *very* wild, very gay; loved intrigue — but he was young; *a man of sense*: would see his error, could she but have patience with his faults, if his faults were not cured by marriage!"

* Her grandfather, in order to invite her to him as often as her other friends would spare her, indulged her in erecting and fitting up a dairy-house in her own taste. When finished, it was so much admired for its elegant simplicity and convenience, that the whole seat (before, of old time, from its situation called *The Grove*) was generally known by the name of the *The Dairy-house*. Her grandfather in particular was fond of having it so called.

Thus she ran on; and then wanted me "to see the charming man," as she called him. — Again concerned, "that she was not handsome enough for him;" with, "a sad thing, that the man should have the advantage of the woman in that particular!" — But then, stepping to the glass, she complimented herself, "that she was very *well:* that there were many women deemed passable who were inferior to herself: that she was always thought comely; and comeliness, let her tell me, having not so much to lose as beauty had, would hold, when that would evaporate or fly off: nay, for that matter, [and again she turned to the glass] her features were not irregular; her eyes not at all amiss." And I remember they were more than usually brilliant at that time. "Nothing, in short, to be found fault with, though nothing very engaging she doubted — was there, Clary?"

Excuse me, my dear, I never was thus particular before; no, not to you. Nor would I now have written thus freely of a sister, but that she makes a merit to my brother of disowning that she ever liked him; as I shall mention hereafter: and then you will always have me give you minute descriptions, nor suffer me to pass by the air and manner in which things are spoken, that are to be taken notice of; rightly observing, that air and manner often express more than the accompanying words.

I congratulated her upon her prospects. She received my compliments with a great deal of self-complacency.

She liked the gentleman still more at his next visit; and yet he made no particular address to her, although an opportunity was given him for it. This was wondered at, as my uncle had introduced him into our family declaredly as a visiter to my sister. But as we are ever ready to make excuses when in good humour with ourselves for the perhaps not unwilful slights of those whose approbation we wish to engage; so my sister found out a reason much to Mr. Lovelace's advantage for his not improving the opportunity that was given him. — It was bashfulness, truly, in him. [Bashfulness in Mr. Lovelace, my dear!]—Indeed, gay and lively as he is, he has not the *look* of an impudent man. But I fancy, it is many, many years ago since he was bashful.

Thus, however, could my sister make it out — "Upon her word she believed Mr. Lovelace deserved not the bad character he had as to women. — He was really, to *her* thinking, a *modest* man. He would have spoken out she believed: but once or twice as he seemed to intend to do so, he was under so *agreeable* a confusion! such a profound respect he seemed to shew her! a perfect *reverence*, she thought: she loved dearly that a man in courtship should shew a reverence to his mistress" — so indeed we all do, I believe: and with reason; since, if I may judge from what I have seen in many families, there is little enough of it shewn afterwards. — And she told my aunt Hervey, that she would be a little less upon the reserve next time he came: "She was not one of those *flirts*, not she, who would give pain to a person that deserved to be well-treated; and the more pain for the greatness of his value for her." — I wish she had not somebody whom I love in her eye.

In his third visit, Bella governed herself by this kind and considerate principle: so that, according to her own account of the matter, the man *might* have spoken out. — But he was still *bashful*: he was not able to overcome this *unseasonable reverence*. So this visit went off as the former.

But now she began to be dissatisfied with him. She compared his general character with this his particular behaviour to her; and having never been courted before, owned herself puzzled how to deal with so odd a lover. "What did the man mean, she wondered? Had not her uncle brought him *declaredly* as a suitor to her? — It could not be bashfulness (now she thought of it) since he might have opened his mind to her *uncle*, if he wanted courage to speak directly to *her*. — Not that she cared much for the man neither: but it was right, surely, that a woman should be put out of doubt *early* as to a man's intentions in such a case as this, from his own mouth. — But, truly, she had begun to think, that he was more solicitous to cultivate her *mamma's* good opinion, than *hers!* — Every body, she owned, admired her mother's conversation; but he was mistaken if he thought respect to her mother *only* would do with *her*. And then, for his own sake, surely he should put it into her power to be complaisant to him, if he gave her reason to approve of him. This distant behaviour, she must take upon her to say, was the more extraordinary, as he continued his visits, and declared himself extremely desirous to cultivate a friendship with the whole family; and as he could have no doubt about her *sense*, if she might take upon her to join her own with the general opinion; he having taken great notice of, and admired many of her *good things* as they fell from her lips. Reserves were painful, she must needs say, to open and free spirits, like hers: and yet she must tell my aunt" (to whom all this was directed) "that she should never forget what she owed to her sex, and to herself, were Mr. Lovelace as unexceptionable in his morals as in his figure, and were he to urge his suit ever so warmly."

I was not of her council. I was still absent. And it was agreed upon between my aunt Hervey and her, that she was to be quite solemn and shy in his next visit, if there were not a peculiarity in his address to her.

But my sister it seems had not considered the matter well. This was not the way, as it proved, to be taken for matters of *mere omission*, with a man of Mr. Lovelace's penetration. Nor with *any* man; since if love has not taken root deep enough to cause it to shoot out into declaration, if an opportunity be fairly given for it, there is little room to expect, that the blighting winds of anger or resentment will bring it forward. Then my poor sister is not naturally good-humoured. This is too well-known a truth for me to endeavour to conceal it, especially from you. She must therefore, I doubt, have appeared to great disadvantage when she aimed to be worse-tempered than ordinary.

How they managed it in their next conversation I know not. One would be tempted to think by the issue, that Mr. Lovelace was ungenerous enough to seek the occasion given *, and to improve it. Yet he thought fit to put the question too:— but, she says, it was not till, by some means, or other (she knew not how) he had wrought her up to such a pitch of displeasure with him, that it was impossible for her to recover herself at the instant. Nevertheless he re-urged his question, as expecting a definitive answer, without waiting for the return of her temper, or endeavouring to mollify her; so that she was under a necessity of persisting in her denial; 'yet gave him reason to think she did not dislike his address, only the manner of it; his court being rather made to her mother than to herself, as if he was sure of *her* consent at any time.'

A good encouraging denial, I must own:— as was the rest of her plea; to wit, "A disinclination to change her state. — Exceedingly happy as she was: she never could be happier!" and such-like *consenting negatives*, as I may call them, and yet not intend a reflection upon my sister: for what can any young creature in the like circumstances say, when she is not sure but a too ready consent may subject her to the slights of a sex that generally values a blessing either more or less as it is obtained with difficulty or ease? Miss Biddulph's answer to a copy of verses from a gentleman, reproaching our sex as acting in disguise, is not a bad one, although *you* perhaps may think it too acknowledging for the female character.

Ungen'rous sex! — to scorn us if we're kind;
And yet upbraid us if we seem *severe!*
Do you, t' encourage us to toll our mind,
Yourselves put off disguise, and be sincere.
You talk of coquetry! — Your own false hearts
Compel our sex to act dissembling parts.

Here I am obliged to lay down my pen. I will soon resume it.

LETTER III.
Miss Clarissa Harlowe to Miss Howe.

Jan. 13, 14.

AND thus, as Mr. Lovelace thought fit to *take it*, had be his answer from my sister. It was with very great regret, as he pretended, [I doubt the man is an hypocrite, my dear] that he acquiesced in it. "So much determinedness; such a noble firmness

---
* See Mr. Lovelace's letter, No. xxxi. in which he briefly accounts for his conduct in this affair.

in my sister, that there was no hope of prevailing upon her to alter sentiments she had adopted on full consideration." He sighed, as Bella told us, when he took his leave of her: " Profoundly sighed; grasped her hand, and kissed it with *such* an ardour — Withdrew with *such* an air of solemn respect — She had him then before her. — She could almost find in her heart, although he had vexed her, to pity him." A good intentional preparative to love, this pity; since, at the time, she little thought that he would not renew his offer.

He waited on my mother after he had taken leave of Bella, and reported his ill success in so respectful a manner, as well with regard to my sister, as to the whole family, and with so much concern that he was not accepted as a relation to it, that it left upon them all (my brother being then, as I have said, in Scotland) impressions in his favour, and a belief that this matter would certainly be brought on again. But Mr. Lovelace going up directly to town, where he stayed a whole fortnight, and meeting there with my uncle Antony, to whom he regretted his niece's cruel resolution not to change her state; it was seen that there was a total end of the affair.

My sister was not wanting to herself on this occasion. She made a virtue of necessity; and the man was quite another man with her. "A vain creature! too well knowing his advantages: yet those not what she had conceived them to be! — Cool and warm by fits and starts; an ague-like lover. A steady man, a man of virtue, a man of morals, was worth a thousand of such gay flutterers. Her sister Clary might think it worth her while perhaps to try to engage such a man: she had patience: she was mistress of persuasion: and indeed, to do the girl justice, had *something*. of a person: but as for *her*, she would not have a man of whose heart she could not be sure for one moment; no, not for the world: and most sincerely glad was she that she had rejected him."

But when Mr. Lovelace returned into the country, he thought fit to visit my father and mother; hoping, as he told them, that however unhappy he had been in the rejection of the wished-for alliance, he might be allowed to keep up an acquaintance and friendship with a family which he should always respect. And then, unhappily, as I may say, was I at home and present.

It was immediately observed, that his attention was fixed on me. My sister, as soon as he was gone, in a spirit of bravery, seemed desirous to promote his address should it be tendered.

My aunt Hervey was there; and was pleased to say, we should make the finest couple in England — if my sister had no objection. — No, indeed! with a haughty toss, was my sister's reply — It would be strange if she had, after the denial she had given him upon full deliberation.

My mother declared, that her only dislike of his alliance with either daughter, was on account of his reputed faulty morals.

My uncle Harlowe, that his daughter Clary, as he delighted to call me from childhood, would reform him, if any woman in the world could.

My uncle Antony gave his approbation in high terms: but referred, as my aunt had done, to my sister.

She repeated her contempt of him; and declared, that were there not another man in England, she would not have him. She was ready, on the contrary, she could assure them, to resign her pretensions under hand and seal, if Miss Clary were taken with his tinsel; and if every one else approved of his address to the girl.

My father indeed, after a long silence, being urged by my uncle Antony to speak his mind, said, That he had a letter from his son, on his hearing of Mr. Lovelace's visits to his daughter Arabella; which he had not shewn to any body but my mother; that treaty being at an end when he received it; — that in this letter he expressed great dislike to an alliance with Mr. Lovelace on the score of his immoralities: that he new indeed there was an old rudge between them; but that, eing desirous to prevent all occasions of disunion and animosity n his family, he would suspend he declaration of his own mind ill his son arrived, and till he had heard his further objections: that he was the more inclined to make his son this compliment, as Mr. Lovelace's general character gave but too much ground for his son's dislike of him; adding, that he had heard (so, he supposed, had every one) that he was a very extravagant man; that he had contracted debts in his travels: and indeed, he was pleased to say, he had the air of a spendthrift.

These particulars I had partly from my aunt Hervey, and partly from my sister; for I was called out as soon as the subject was entered upon. When I returned, my uncle Antony asked me how I should like Mr. Lovelace? Every body saw, he was pleased to say, that I had made a conquest.

I immediately answered, that I did not like him at all: he seemed to have too good an opinion both of his person and parts, to have any great regard to his wife, let him marry whom he would.

My sister particularly was pleased with this answer, and confirmed it to be just; with a compliment to my judgment. — For it was *hers*.

But the very next day Lord M. came to Harlowe Place [I was then absent]; and in his nephew's name made a proposal in form; declaring, that it was the ambition of all his family to be related to ours: and he hoped his kinsman would not have such an answer on the part of the younger sister,' as he had on that of the elder.

In short, Mr. Lovelace's visits

were admitted as those of a man who had not deserved disrespect from our family; but as to his address to me, with a reservation, as above, on my father's part, that he would determine nothing without his son. My discretion as to the rest was confided in: for still I had the same objections as to the man: nor would I, when we were better acquainted, hear any thing but general talk from him; giving him no opportunity of conversing with me in private.

He bore this with a resignation little expected from his natural temper, which is generally reported to be quick and hasty; unused it seems from childhood to check or control. A case too common in considerable families where there is an only son: and his mother never had any other child. But, as I have heretofore told you, I could perceive, notwithstanding this resignation, that he had so good an opinion of himself, as not to doubt, that his person and accomplishments would insensibly engage me: and could that be once done, he told my aunt Hervey, he should hope, from so steady a temper, that his hold in my affections would be durable: while my sister accounted for his patience in another manner, which would perhaps have had more force if it had come from a person less prejudiced: "That the man was not fond of marrying at all: that he might perhaps have half a score of mistresses: and that delay might be as convenient for his *roving*, as for my *well-acted* indifference." — That was her kind expression.

Whatever was his motive for a patience so generally believed to be out of his usual character, and where the object of his address was supposed to be of fortune considerable enough to engage his warmest attention, he certainly escaped many mortifications by it: for while my father suspended his approbation till my brother's arrival, Mr. Lovelace received from every one those civilities which were due to his birth: and although we heard from time to time reports to his disadvantage with regard to morals, yet could we not question him upon them without giving him greater advantages in his own opinion than the situation he was in with us would justify to prudence; since it was much more likely that his address would *not* be allowed of, than that it *would*.

And thus was he admitted to converse with our family almost upon his own terms; for while my friends saw nothing in his behaviour but what was extremely respectful, and observed in him no violent importunity, they seemed to have taken a great liking to his conversation: while I considered him only as a common guest when he came; and thought myself no more concerned in his visits, nor at his entrance and departure, than any other of the family.

But this indifference on my side was the means of procuring him one very great advantage; since upon it was grounded that correspondence by letter which succeeded; — and which, had it been to be begun when the family animosity broke out, would never have been entered into on my part. The occasion was this:

My uncle Hervey has a young gentleman entrusted to his care, whom he has thoughts of sending abroad, a year or two hence, to make the grand tour, as it is called; and finding Mr. Lovelace could give a good account of every thing necessary for a young traveller to observe upon such an occasion, he desired him to write down a description of the courts and countries he had visited, and what was most worthy of curiosity in them.

He consented, on condition that I would *direct* his subjects, as he called it: and as every one had heard his manner of writing commended; and thought his narratives might be agreeable amusements in winter evenings; and that he could have no opportunity particularly to address me in them, since they were to be read in full assembly before they were given to the young gentleman, I made the less scruple to write, and to make observations, and put questions for our further information — Still the less perhaps as I love writing; and those who do, are fond, you know, of occasions to use the pen: and then, having every one's consent, and my uncle Hervey's desire that I would write, I thought that if I had been the only scrupulous person, it would have shewn a particularity that a vain man might construe to his advantage; and which my sister would not fail to animadvert upon.

You have seen some of these letters; and have been pleased with his account of persons, places, and things; and we have both agreed, that he was no common observer upon what he had seen.

My sister herself allowed that the man had a tolerable knack of writing and describing: and my father, who had been abroad in his youth, said, that his remarks were curious, and shewed him to be a person of reading, judgment, and taste.

Thus was a kind of correspondence begun between him and me, with general approbation; while every one wondered at, and was pleased with, his patient veneration of me; for so they called it. However, it was not doubted but he would soon be more importunate, since his visits were more frequent, and he acknowledged to my aunt Hervey a passion for me, accompanied with an awe that he had never known before; to which he attributed what he called his but *seeming* acquiescence with my father's pleasure, and the distance I kept him at. And yet, my dear, this may be his usual manner of behaviour to our sex; for had not my sister at first all his *reverence?*

Meantime, my father, expecting his importunity, kept in readiness the reports he had heard in his disfavour, to charge them upon him then, as so many objections to his address. And it was highly agreeable to me that he did so: it would have been strange if it were not; since the person who could reject Mr. Wyerley's address for the sake of his *free opinions*, must have been inexcusable, had she not rejected another's for his *freer practices*.

But I should own, that in the letters he sent me upon the general subject, he more than once inclosed a particular one, declaring his passionate regards for me, and complaining, with fervour enough, of my reserves: but of these I took not the least notice; for, as I had not written to him at all, but upon a subject so general, I thought it was but right to let what he wrote upon one so particular pass off as if I had never seen it; and the rather, as I was not then at liberty (from the approbation his letters met with) to break off the correspondence, unless I had assigned the true reason for doing so. Besides, with all his respectful assiduities, it was easy to observe, (if it had not been his general character) that his temper is naturally haughty and violent; and I had seen too much of that untractable spirit in my brother to like it in one who hoped to be still more nearly related to me.

I had a little specimen of this temper of his upon the very occasion I have mentioned: for after he had sent me a third particular letter with the general one, he asked me the next time he came to Harlowe Place, if I had not received such a one from him? — I told him I should never answer one so sent; and that I had waited for such an occasion as he had now given me, to tell him so; I desired him therefore not to write again on the subject; assuring him, that if he did, I would return both, and never write another line to him.

You cannot imagine how saucily the man looked; as if, in short, he was disappointed that he had not made a more sensible impression upon me: nor, when he recollected himself (as he did immediately), what a visible struggle it cost him to change his haughty airs for more placid ones. But I took no notice of either; for I thought it best to convince him, by the coolness and indifference with which I repulsed his forward hopes (at the same time intending to avoid the affectation of pride or vanity) that he was not considerable enough in my eyes to make me take over-ready offence at what he said, or at his haughty looks: in other words, that I had not value enough for him to treat him with peculiarity either by smiles or frowns. Indeed he had cunning enough to give me, undesignedly, a piece of instruction, which taught me this caution; for he had said in conversation once, "That if a man could not make a woman in courtship own herself *pleased* with him, it was as *much*, and oftentimes *more* to his purpose, to make her *angry* with him.'

I must break off here, but will continue the subject the very first opportunity. Meantime, I am

Your most affectionate friend and servant,

Cl. Harlowe.

· LETTER IV.

Miss Clarissa Harlowe to Miss Howe.

Jan. 15.

Such, my dear, was the situation Mr. Lovelace and I were in when my brother arrived from Scotland.

The moment Mr. Lovelace's visits were mentioned to him, he, without either hesitation or apology, expressed his disapprobation of them. He found great flaws in his character; and took the liberty to say in so many words, that he wondered how it came into the heads of his uncles to encourage such a man for *either* of his sisters: at the same time returning his thanks to my father for declining his consent till *he* arrived, in such a manner, I thought, as a superior would do, when he commended an inferior for having well performed his duty in his absence.

He justified his avowed inveteracy by common fame, and by what he had known of him at college; declaring, that he had ever hated him; ever should hate him; and would never own *him* for a brother, or me for a sister, if I married him.

That early antipathy I have heard accounted for in this manner.

Mr. Lovelace was always noted for his vivacity and courage; and no less, it seems, for the swift and surprising progress he made in all parts of literature: for diligence in his studies in the hours of study, he had hardly his equal. This it seems was his general character at the university; and it gained him many friends among the more learned; while those who did not love him, feared him, by reason of the offence his vivacity made him too ready to give, and of the courage he shewed in supporting the offence when given; which procured him as many followers as he pleased among the mischievous sort. — No very amiable character, you'll say, upon the whole.

But my brother's temper was not more happy. His native haughtiness could not bear a superiority so visible; and whom we fear more than love, we are not far from hating: and having less command of his passions than the other, he was evermore the subject of his perhaps *indecent* ridicule: so that they never met without quarrelling: and every body, either from love or fear, siding with his antagonist, he had a most uneasy time of it while both continued in the same college. — It was the less wonder therefore that a young man who is not noted for the gentleness of his temper, should resume an antipathy early begun, and so deeply rooted.

He found my sister, who waited but for the occasion, ready to join him in his resentments against the man he hated. She utterly disclaimed all manner of regard for him. "Never liked him at all: — his estate was certainly much encumbered: it was impossible it should be otherwise; so entirely devoted as he was to his pleasures. He kept no house; had no equipage: nobody pretended that he wanted pride: the reason therefore was easy to be guessed at." And then did she boast of, and my brother praise her for, refusing him: and both joined on all occasions to depreciate him, and not seldom *made* the occasions; their displeasure against him causing every subject to run into this, if it began not with it.

I was not solicitous to vindicate him when I was not joined in their reflections. I told them, I did not value him enough to make a difference in the family on his account: and as he was supposed to have given too much cause for their ill opinion of him, I thought he ought to take the consequence of his own faults.

Now and then, indeed, when I observed that their vehemence carried them beyond all bounds of probability in their charges against him, I thought it but justice to put in a word for him. But this only subjected me to reproach, as having a prepossession in his favour which I would not own. — So that when I could not change the subject, I used to retire either to my music, or to my closet.

Their behaviour to him, when they could not help seeing him, was very cold and disobliging; but as yet not directly affrontive. For they were in hopes of prevailing upon my father to forbid his visits. But as there was nothing in his behaviour, that might warrant such a treatment of a man of his birth and fortune, they succeeded not: and then they were very earnest with *me* to forbid them. I asked, what authority I had to take such a step in my father's house; and when my behaviour to him was so distant, that he seemed to be as much the guest of any other person of the family, themselves excepted, as mine? — In revenge, they told me, that it was cunning management between us; and that we both understood one another better than we pretended to do. And at last they gave such a loose to their passions, all of a sudden*, as I may say, that instead of withdrawing, as they used to do when he came, they threw themselves in his way purposely to affront him.

Mr. Lovelace, you may believe, very ill brooked this: but nevertheless contented himself to complain of it to me: in high terms, however, telling me, that but for my sake, my brother's treatment of him was not to be borne.

I was sorry for the merit this gave him in his own opinion with me: and the more, as some of the affronts he received were too flagrant to be excused: but I told him, that I was determined not

---

* The reason of this their more openly shewn animosity is given in Letter xiii.

to fall out with my brother, if I could help it, whatever faults he had: and, since they could not see one another with temper, should be glad that he would not throw himself in my brother's way; and I was sure my brother would not seek *him*.

He was very much nettled at this answer: but said, he must bear his affronts if I would have it so. He had been accused himself of violence in his temper; but he hoped to shew, on *this* occasion, that he had a command of his passions which few young men, so highly provoked, would be able to shew; and doubted not but it would be attributed to a *proper motive* by a person of my generosity and penetration.

My brother had just before, with the approbation of my uncles, employed a person related to a discharged bailiff or steward of Lord M. who had had the management of some part of Mr. Lovelace's affairs (from which he was also dismissed by him) to inquire into his debts, after his companions, into his amours, and the like.

My aunt Hervey, in confidence, gave me the following particulars of what the man said of him.

"That he was a generous landlord: that he spared nothing for solid and lasting improvements upon his estate; and that he looked into his own affairs, and understood them: that he had been very expensive when abroad; and contracted a large debt (for he made no secret of his affairs); yet chose to limit himself to an annual sum, and to decline equipage, in order to avoid being obliged to his uncle and aunts; from whom he might have what money he pleased; but that he was very jealous of their control; had often quarrels with them; and treated them so freely, that they were all afraid of him. However, that his estate was never mortgaged, as my brother had heard it was; his credit was always high; and the man believed, he was by this time near upon, if not quite, clear of the world.

"He was a sad gentleman," he said, "as to women: — if his tenants had pretty daughters, they chose to keep them out of his sight. He believed he kept no particular mistress; for he had heard *newelty*, that was the man's word, was every thing with him. But for his uncles' and aunts' teasings, the man fancied he would not think of marriage: he was never known to be disguised with liquor; but was a great plotter, and a great writer: that he lived a wild life in town, by what he had heard: had six or seven companions as bad as himself; whom now and then he brought down with him; and the country was always glad when they went up again. He would have it, that although passionate, he was good-humoured; loved as well to take a jest as to give one; and would rally himself upon occasion the freest of any man he ever knew."

This was his character from an

enemy; for, as my aunt observed, every thing the man said commendably of him came grudgingly, with a *Must needs say — To do him justice, &c.* while the contrary was delivered with a free good-will. And this character, as a worse was expected, though this was bad enough, not answering the end of inquiring after it, my brother and sister were more apprehensive than before, that his address would be encouraged, since the worst part of it was known, or supposed, when he was first introduced to my sister.

But, with regard to myself, I must observe in his disfavour, that notwithstanding the merit he wanted to make with me for his patience upon my brother's ill-treatment of him, I owed him no compliments for trying to conciliate with *him*. Not that I believe it would have availed any thing if he had made ever such court either to him or to my sister: yet one might have expected from a man of his politeness, and from his pretensions, you know, that he would have been willing to *try*. Instead of which, he shewed such a contempt both of my brother and sister, especially my brother, as was construed into a defiance of them. And for me to have hinted at an alteration in his behaviour to my brother, was an advantage I knew he would have been proud of; and which therefore I had no mind to give him. But I doubted not that having so very little encouragement from *any*-body, his pride would soon take fire, and he would of himself discontinue his visits, or go to town; where, till he became acquainted with our family, he used chiefly to reside: and in this latter case he had no reason to expect, that I would *receive*, much less *answer*, his letters; the occasion which had led me to receive *any* of his being by this time over.

But my brother's antipathy would not permit him to *wait* for such an event; and after several excesses, which Mr. Lovelace still returned with contempt, and a haughtiness too much like that of the aggressor, my brother took upon himself to fill up the doorway once when he came, as if to oppose his entrance: and upon his asking for me, demanded what his business was with his sister?

The other, with a challenging air, as my brother says, told him, he would answer a gentleman *any* question; but he wished that Mr. James Harlowe, who had of late given himself high airs, would remember that he was not *now* at college.

Just then the good Dr. Lewen, who frequently honours me with a *visit of conversation*, as he is pleased to call it, and had parted with me in my own parlour, came to the door; and bearing the words, interposed; both having their hands upon their swords: and telling Mr. Lovelace where I was, he burst by my brother, to come to me; leaving him chafing, he said, like a hunted boar at bay.

This alarmed us all. My father was pleased to hint to Mr. Lovelace, that he wished he would discontinue his visits, for the peacesake of the family: and I, by his command, spoke a great deal plainer.

But Mr. Lovelace is a man not easily brought to give up his purpose, especially in a point wherein he pretends his heart is so much engaged; and no absolute prohibition having been given, things went on for a little while as before: for I saw plainly, that to have denied myself to his visits (which however I declined receiving as often as I could) was to bring forward some desperate issue between the two; since the offence so readily given on one side was brooked by the other only out of consideration to me.

And thus did my brother's rashness lay me under an obligation where I would least have owed it.

The intermediate proposals of Mr. Symmes and Mr. Mullins, both (in turn) encouraged by my brother, induced him to be more patient for a while, as nobody thought me over-forward in Mr. Lovelace's favour; for he hoped that he should engage my father and uncles to approve of the one or the other in opposition to the man he hated. But when he found that I had interest enough to disengage myself from the addresses of those gentlemen, as I had (before he went to Scotland, and before Mr. Lovelace visited here) of Mr. Wyerley's, he then kept no measures: and first set himself to upbraid me for a supposed prepossession, which he treated as if it were criminal; and then to insult Mr. Lovelace in person, at Mr. Edward Symmes's, the brother of the other Symmes, two miles off; and no good Dr. Lewen being there to interpose, the unhappy rencounter followed. My brother was disarmed, as you have heard; and on being brought home, and giving us ground to suppose he was much worse hurt than he really was, and a fever ensuing, every one flamed out; and all was laid at my door.

Mr. Lovelace for three days together sent twice each day to inquire after my brother's health; and although he received rude and even shocking returns, he thought fit on the fourth day to make in person the same inquiries; and received still greater incivilities from my two uncles, who happened to be both there. My father also was held by force from going to him with his sword in his hand, although he had the gout upon him.

I fainted away with terror, seeing every one so violent, and hearing Mr. Lovelace swear that he would not depart till he had made my uncles ask his pardon for the indignities he had received at their hands; a door being held fast locked between him and them. My mother all the time was praying and struggling to withhold my father in the great parlour. Meanwhile my sister, who had treated Mr. Lovelace with virulence, came in to me, and insulted me as fast as I recovered. But when Mr. Lovelace was told how ill I was, he departed; nevertheless vowing revenge.

He was ever a favourite with our domestics. His bounty to them, and having always something facetious to say to each, had made them all of his party; and on this occasion they privately blamed every body else, and reported his calm and gentlemanly behaviour (till the provocations given him ran very high) in such favourable terms, that those reports, and my apprehensions of the consequence of this treatment, induced me to *read a letter* he sent me that night; and, it being written in the most respectful terms (offering to submit the whole to my decision, and to govern himself entirely by my will) to *answer* it some days after.

To this unhappy necessity was owing our renewed correspondence, as I may call it: yet I did not write till I had informed myself from Mr. Symmes's brother, that he was really insulted into the act of drawing his sword by my brother's repeatedly threatening (upon his excusing himself out of regard to me) to brand him if he did not; and, by all the inquiry I could make, that he was again the sufferer from my uncles in a more violent manner than I have related.

The same circumstances were related to my father and other relations by Mr. Symmes; but they had gone too far in making themselves parties to the quarrel either to retract or forgive; and I was forbidden to correspond with him, or to be seen a moment in his company.

One thing however I can say, but that in confidence, because my mother commanded me not to mention it: — that, expressing her apprehension of the consequences of the indignities offered to Mr. Lovelace, she told me, she would leave it to my prudence to do all I could to prevent the impending mischief on *one* side.

I am obliged to break off. But I believe I have written enough to answer very fully all that you have required of me. It is not for a child to seek to clear her own character, or to justify her actions, at the expense of the most revered ones; yet, as I know that the account of all those further proceedings by which I may be affected, will be interesting to so dear a friend (who will communicate to others no more than what is fitting) I will continue to write, as I have opportunity, as minutely as we are used to write to each other. Indeed, I have no delight, as I have often told you, equal to that which I take in conversing with you — by *letter*, when I cannot in *person*.

Meantime I cannot help saying, that I am exceedingly concerned to find, that I am become so much the public talk as you tell me I am. Your kind, your *precautionary* regard for my fame, and the opportunity you have given me to tell my own story previous to any new accident (which heaven avert!) is so like the warm friend I have ever found in my dear Miss Howe, that,

with redoubled obligation, you bind me to be
Your ever grateful and affectionate,
CLARISSA HARLOWE.

COPY OF THE REQUESTED PREAMBLE TO THE CLAUSES IN HER GRANDFATHER'S WILL.
Enclosed in the preceding letter.

As the particular estate I have mentioned and described above, is principally of my own raising: as my three sons have been uncommonly prosperous; and are very rich: the eldest by means of the unexpected benefits he reaps from his new found mines: the second, by what has, as unexpectedly, fallen in to him on the deaths of several relations of his present wife, the worthy daughter by both sides of very honourable families; over and above the very large portion which he received with her in marriage: my son Antony by his East India traffic, and successful voyages: as furthermore my grandson James will be sufficiently provided for by his godmother Lovell's kindness to him; who having no near relations, hath assured me, that she hath, as well by deed of gift as by will, left him both her Scotish and English estates: for never was there a family more prosperous in all its branches, blessed be God therefore; and as my said son James will very probably make it up to my grand-daughter Arabella: to whom I intend no disrespect; nor have reason; for she is a very hopeful and dutiful child: and as my sons John and Antony seem not inclined to a married life; so that my son James is the only one who has children, or is likely to have any — for all these reasons; and because my dearest and beloved grand-daughter Clarissa has been from her infancy a matchless young creature in her duty to me, and admired by all who knew her, as a very extraordinary child: I must therefore take the pleasure of considering her as my own peculiar child; and this without intending offence; and I hope it will not be taken as any, since my son James can bestow his favours accordingly, and in greater proportion, upon his son James, and upon his daughter Arabella: — these, I say, are the reasons which move me to dispose of the above-described estate in the precious child's favour, who is the delight of my old age: and, I verily think, has contributed, by her amiable duty and kind and tender regards, to prolong my life.

Wherefore it is my express will and commandment, and I enjoin my said three sons, John, James, and Antony, and my grandson James, and my grand-daughter Arabella, as they value my blessing, and will regard my memory, and would wish their own last wills and desires to be fulfilled by *their* survivors, that they will not impugn or contest the following bequests and devices of favour of my said grand-daughter Clarissa, although they should not be strictly comformable to law or to the forms thereof; nor suffer them to be controverted or disputed on any pretence whatsoever.

And in this confidence, &c. &c. &c.

LETTER V.
Miss Clarissa Harlowe to Miss Howe.

Jan. 26.

I have been hindered from prosecuting my intention. Neither nights nor mornings have been my own. My mother has been very ill, and would have no other nurse but me. I have not stirred from her bedside (for she kept her bed); and two nights I had the honour of sharing it with her.

Her disorder was a very violent colic. The contentions of these fierce, these masculine spirits, and the apprehension of mischiefs that may arise from the increasing animosity which all *here* have against Mr. Lovelace, and *his* too well-known resenting and intrepid character, she cannot bear. Then the foundations laid, as she dreads, for jealousy and heart-burnings in her own family, late so happy and so united, afflict exceedingly a gentle and sensible mind, which has from the beginning, on all occasions, sacrificed its own inward satisfaction to outward peace. My brother and sister, who used very often to jar, are now so entirely one, and are so much together (*caballing* was the word that dropped from my mother's lips, as if at unawares) that she is very fearful of the consequences that may follow;—to my prejudice, perhaps, is her kind concern; since she sees that they behave to me every hour with more and more shyness and reserve: yet, would she but exert that authority which the superiority of her fine talents gives her, all these family-feuds might perhaps be extinguished in their but-yet beginnings; especially as she may be assured that all fitting concessions shall be made by me, not only as my brother and sister are my elders, but for the sake of so excellent and so indulgent a mother.

For if I may say to you, my dear, what I would not to any other person living, it is my opinion, that had she been of a temper that would have borne less, she would have had ten times less to bear than she has had. No commendation, you'll say, of the generosity of those spirits which can turn to its own disquiet so much condescending goodness.

Upon my word, I am sometimes tempted to think that we may make the world allow for and respect us as we please, if we can but be sturdy in our wills, and set out accordingly. It is but being the *less* beloved for it, that's all: and if we have power to oblige those we have to do with, it will not appear to *us* that we are. Our flatterers will tell us any thing sooner than our faults, or what they know we do not like to hear.

Were there not truth in this observation, is it possible that my brother and sister could make their very failings, their vehemences, of such importance to all the family? "How will my *son*, how will my *nephew*, take this or that measure? What will *he* say to it? Let us consult *him* about it;" are references always previous to every resolution taken by his superiors, whose will ought to be his. Well may he expect to be treated with this deference by every other person, when my father himself, generally so absolute, constantly pays it to him; and the more since his godmother's bounty has given independence to a spirit that was before under too little restraint. — But whither may these reflections lead me! — I know you do not love any of us but my mother and me; and, being above all disguises, make me sensible that you do *not* oftener than I wish. — Ought I then to add force to your dislikes of those whom I wish you to like? — of my father, especially; for he, alas! had some excuse for his impatience of contradiction. He is not *naturally* an ill-tempered man; and in his person and air, and in his conversation too, when not under the torture of a gouty paroxysm, every body distinguishes the gentleman born and educated.

Our sex perhaps must expect to bear a little — *uncourtliness* shall I call it? — from the *husband*, whom as the *lover* they let know the preference their hearts give him to all other men. — Say what they will of generosity being a *manly* virtue; but upon my word, my dear, I have ever yet observed, that it is not to be met with in that sex one time in ten that it is to be found in ours. — But my father was soured by the cruel distemper I have named; which seized him all at once in the very prime of life, in so violent a manner as to take from the most active of minds, as *his* was, all power of activity, and that in all appearance for life. — It imprisoned, as I may say, his lively spirits in himself, and turned the edge of them against his own peace; his extraordinary prosperity adding to his impatiency. Those, I believe, who want the fewest earthly blessings, most regret that they want any.

But my brother! what excuse can be made for his haughty and morose temper? He is really, my dear, I am sorry to have occasion to say it, an ill-tempered young man; and treats my mother sometimes — Indeed he is not dutiful. — But, possessing every thing, he has the vice of age mingled with the ambition of youth, and enjoys nothing — but his own haughtiness and ill-temper, I was going to say. — Yet again am I adding force to your dislikes of some of us. — Once, my dear, it was perhaps in your power to have moulded him as you pleased. — Could you have been my sister! Then had I had a *friend* in a sister. — But no wonder that he does not love you now; who could nip in the bud, and that with a disdain, let me say, too much of kin to his haughtiness, a passion that would not have wanted a fervour worthy of the object; and which possibly would have made him so.

But no more of this. I will prosecute my former intention in my next; which I will sit down to as soon as breakfast is over; dispatching this by the messenger whom you have so kindly sent to inquire after us on my silence. Meantime, I am,

Your most affectionate and obliged
friend and servant,
CL. HARLOWE.

LETTER VI.

Miss Clarissa Harlowe to Miss Howe.

Harlowe Place, Jan. 20.

I WILL now resume my narrative of proceedings here. My brother being in a good way, although you may be sure that his resentments are rather heightened than abated by the galling disgrace he has received, my friends (my father and uncles, however, if not my brother and sister) begin to think that I have been treated unkindly. My mother has been so good as to tell me this since I sent away my last.

Nevertheless I believe they all think that I receive letters from Mr. Lovelace. But Lord M. being inclined rather to support than to blame his nephew, they seem to be so much afraid of Mr. Lovelace, that they do not put it to me whether I do or not; conniving, on the contrary, as it should seem, at the only method left to allay the vehemence of a spirit which they have so much provoked: for he still insists upon satisfaction from my uncles; and this possibly (for he wants not art) as the best way to be introduced again with some advantage into our family. And indeed my aunt Hervey has put it to my mother, whether it were not best to prevail upon my brother to take a turn to his Yorkshire estate (which he was intending to do before) and to stay there till all is blown over.

But this is very far from being his intention: for he has already begun to hint again, that he shall never be easy or satisfied till I am married; and, finding neither Mr. Symmes nor Mr. Mullins will be accepted, has proposed Mr. Wyerley once more, on the score of his great passion for me. This I have again rejected; and but yesterday he mentioned one who has applied to him by letter, making high offers. This is Mr. Solmes; *rich* Solmes you know they call him. But this application has not met with the attention of one single soul.

If none of his schemes of getting me married take effect, he has thoughts, I am told, of proposing to me to go to Scotland, that, as the compliment is, I may put his house there in such order as our own is in. But this my mother intends to oppose for her own sake; because, having relieved her, as she is pleased to say, of the household cares (for which my sister, you know, has no turn) they must again devolve upon her if I go. And if *she* did not oppose it, *I* should; for, believe me, I have no mind to be his housekeeper; and I am sure, were I to go with him, I should be treated rather as a servant than a sister. —Perhaps, not the better because I am his sister. — And if Mr. Lovelace should follow me, things might be worse than they are now.

But I have besought my mother, who is apprehensive of Mr. Lovelace's visits, and for fear of whom my uncles never stir out without arms and armed servants (my brother also being near well enough to go abroad) to procure me permission to be your guest for a fortnight, or so. — Will your mother, think you, my dear, give me leave?

I dare not ask to go to my *dairyhouse*, as my good grandfather would call it: for I am now afraid of being thought to have a wish to enjoy that independence to which his will has entitled me: and as matters are situated, such a wish would be imputed to my regard to the man to whom they have now so great an antipathy. And indeed could I be as easy and happy here as I used to be, I would defy that man and all his sex; and never repent that I have given the power of my fortune into my father's hands.

* * *

Just now, my mother has rejoiced me with the news that my requested permission is granted. Every one thinks it best that I should go to you, except my brother. But he was told that he must not expect to rule in every thing. I am to be sent for into the great parlour, where are my two uncles and my aunt Hervey, and to be acquainted with this concession in form.

You know, my dear, that there is a good deal of solemnity among us. But never was there a family more united in its different branches than ours. Our uncles consider us as their own children, and declare that it is for our sakes they live single. So that they are advised with upon every article relating to us, or that may affect us. It is therefore the less wonder, at a time when they understand that Mr. Lovelace is determined to pay us an *amicable* visit, as he calls it (but which I am sure cannot end amicably) that they should both be consulted upon the permission I had desired to attend you.

* * *

I will acquaint you with what passed at the general leave given me to be your guest. And yet I know that you will not love my brother the better for my communication. But I am angry with him myself, and cannot help it. And besides, it is proper to let you know the terms I go upon, and their motives for permitting me to go.

Clary, said my mother, as soon as I entered the great parlour, your request to go to Miss Howe's for a few days has been taken into consideration, and granted —

Much against my liking, I assure you, said my brother, rudely interrupting her.

Son James! said my father, and knit his brows.

He was not daunted. His arm is in a sling. He often has the mean art to look upon *that*, when any thing is hinted that may be supposed to lead towards the least favour to or reconciliation with Mr. Lovelace. — Let the girl then [I am often the *girl* with him] be prohibited seeing that vile libertine.

Nobody spoke.

Do you hear, sister Clary? taking their silence for approbation of what *he* had dictated; you are not to receive visits from Lord M.'s nephew.

Every one still remained silent.

Do you so understand the licence you have, Miss? interrogated he.

I would be glad, sir, said I, to understand that you are my *brother*; — and that *you* would understand that you are *only* my brother.

O the fond, fond heart! with a sneer of insult, lifting up his hands.

Sir, said I to my father, to your justice I appeal: If I have deserved reflection, let me not be spared. But if I am to be answerable for the rashness —

No more! — No more of either side, said my father. You are not to receive the visits of that Lovelace, though — Nor are you, son James, to reflect upon your sister. She is a worthy child.

Sir, I have done, replied he; — and yet I have *her* honour at heart, as much as the honour of the rest of the family.

And *hence*, sir, retorted I, your unbrotherly reflections upon me!

Well but you observe, miss, said he, that it is not I, but your *father*, that tells you, that you are not to receive the visits of that Lovelace.

Cousin Harlowe, said my aunt Hervey, allow me to say, that your sister Clary's prudence may be confided in.

I am *convinced* it may, joined my mother.

But, aunt, but, madam, (put in my sister) there is no hurt, I presume, in letting my sister know the condition she goes to Miss Howe upon; since, if he gets a knack of visiting her there —

You may be sure, interrupted my uncle Harlowe, he will endeavour to see her there.

So would such an impudent man *here*, said my uncle Antony: and it is better *there* than *here*.

Better *nowhere*, said my father. — I command you (turning to me) on pain of my displeasure, that you see him not at all.

I will not, sir, in any way of encouragement, I do assure you: not at all, if I can properly avoid it.

You know with what indifference, said my mother, she has hitherto seen him. — Her prudence may be trusted to, as my sister Hervey says.

With what *appa*—rent indifference, drolled my brother.

Son James! said my father, sternly.

I have done, sir, said he. But again, in a provoking manner, he reminded me of the prohibition.

Thus ended this conference.

Will you engage, my dear, that the hated man shall not come near your house? — But what an inconsistence is this, when they consent to my going, thinking his visits *here* no otherwise to be avoided! — But if he does come, I charge you never leave us alone together.

As I have no reason to doubt a welcome from your good mother, I will put every thing in order here, and be with you in two or three days.

Meantime, I am
      Your most affectionate and
          obliged
            CLARISSA HARLOWE.

LETTER VII.

Miss Clarissa Harlowe to Miss Howe.

[After her return from her.]

Harlowe Place, Feb. 20.

I beg your excuse for not writing sooner! Alas, my dear, I have sad prospects before me! My brother and sister have succeeded in all their views. They have found out another lover for me; an hideous one! — Yet he is encouraged by every body. No wonder that I was ordered home so suddenly. At an hour's warning! — No other notice, you know, than what was brought with the chariot that was to carry me back. — It was for fear, as I have been informed [an unworthy fear!] that I should have entered into any concert with Mr. Lovelace, had I known their motive for commanding me home; apprehending, 'tis evident, that I should dislike the man they had to propose to me.

And well might they apprehend so; — for who do you think he is? — No other than that *Solmes!* — Could you have believed it? — And they are all determined too; my mother with the rest! — Dear, dear excellence! how could she be thus brought over, when I am assured, that on his first being proposed she was pleased to say, That had Mr. Solmes the *Indies* in possession, and would endow me with them, she would not think him deserving of her Clarissa!

The reception I met with at my return, so different from what I used to meet with on every little absence, (and now I had been from them three weeks) convinced me that I was to suffer for the happiness I had had in your company and conversation, for that most agreeable period. I will give you an account of it.

My brother met me at the door, and gave me his hand when I stepped out of the chariot. He bowed very low: "Pray, Miss, favour me" — I thought it in good humour; but found it afterwards mock respect: and so he led me in great form, I prattling all the way, inquiring of every body's health, (although I was so soon to see them, and there was hardly time for answers) into the great parlour; where were my father, mother, my two uncles, and sister.

I was struck to the heart as soon as I entered, to see a solemnity, which I had been so little used to on the like occasions, in the countenances of every dear relation. They all kept their seats. I ran to my father, and knelt: then to my mother: and met from both a cold salute: from my father a blessing but half pronounced: my mother indeed called me child; but embraced me not with her usual indulgent ardour.

After I had paid my duty to my uncles, and my compliments to my sister, which she received with solemn and stiff form, I was bid to sit down. But my heart was full; and I said it became me to stand, if I *could* stand, upon a reception so awful and unusual. I was forced to turn my face from them, and pull out my handkerchief.

My unbrotherly accuser hereupon stood forth, and charged me with having received no less than *five or six visits* at Miss Howe's from the man they had all so much reason to hate [that was the expression;] notwithstanding the commands I had had to the contrary. And he bid me deny it, if I could.

I had never been used, I said, to deny the truth, nor would I now. I owned I had in the three weeks past seen the person I presumed he meant, *oftener* than five or six times. [Pray bear me, brother, said I, for he was going to flame out.] But he always asked for Mrs. or Miss Howe, when he came.

I proceeded, that I had reason to believe, that both Mrs. Howe and Miss, as matters stood, would much rather have excused his visits; but they had more than once apologized, that having not the same reason my papa had to forbid him their house, his rank and fortune entitled him to civility.

You see, my dear, I made not the pleas I might have made.

My brother seemed ready to give a loose to his passion: my father put on the countenance which always portends a gathering storm: my uncles mutteringly whispered: and my sister aggravatingly held up her hands. While I begged to be heard out;—and my mother said, "Let the *child*," that was her kind word, "be heard."

I hoped, I said, there was no harm done: that it became not me to prescribe to Mrs. or Miss Howe who should be their visitors: that Mrs. Howe was always diverted with the raillery that passed between Miss and him: that I had no reason to challenge *her* guest for *my* visitor, as I should seem to have done had I refused to go into their company when he was with them; that I had never seen him out of the presence of one or both of those ladies; and had signified to him once, on his urging for a few moments' private conversation with me, that unless a reconciliation were effected between my family and his, he must not expect that I would countenance his visits, much less give him an opportunity of that sort.

I told them further, that Miss Howe so well understood my mind, that she never left me a moment while Mr. Lovelace was there: that when he came, if I was not below in the parlour, I would not suffer myself to be called to him: although I thought it would be an affectation which would give him advantage rather than the contrary, if I had left company when he came in; or refused to enter into it when I found he would stay any time.

My brother heard me out with such a kind of impatience as shewed he was resolved to be dissatisfied with me, say what I would. The rest, as the event has proved, behaved as if they *would* have been satisfied, had they not further points to carry by intimidating me. All this made it evident, as I mentioned above, that they themselves expected not my voluntary compliance; and was a tacit confession of the disagreeableness of the person they had to propose.

I was no sooner silent than my *brother* swore, although in my father's presence, (swore, unchecked either by eye or countenance) that for his part, he would *never* be reconciled to that libertine: and that he would renounce me for a sister, if I encouraged the addresses of a man so obnoxious to them all.

A man who had like to have been my brother's murderer, my *sister* said, with a face even bursting with restraint of passion.

My father, with vehemence both of action and voice, [my father has, you know, a terrible voice when he is angry!] told me, that I had met with too much indulgence in being allowed to refuse *this* gentleman, and the *other* gentleman; and it was now *his* turn to be obeyed.

Very true, my *mother* said:— and hoped his will would not now be disputed by a child so favoured.

To shew they were all of a sentiment, my uncle *Harlowe* said, he hoped his beloved niece only wanted to know her father's will, to obey it.

And my uncle *Antony*, in his rougher manner, added, that surely I would not give them reason to apprehend, that I thought my grandfather's favour to me had made me independent of them all. — If I did, he would tell me, the will *could* be set aside, and *should.*

I was astonished, you must needs think. — Whose addresses now, thought I, is this treatment preparative to — Mr. Wyerley's again — or whose? And then, as high comparisons, where *self* is concerned, sooner than low, come into young people's heads; be it for whom it will, this is wooing as the English did for the heiress of Scotland in the time of Edward the Sixth. But that it could be for Solmes, how should it enter into my head?

I did not know, I said, that I had given occasion for this harshness. I hoped I should always have a just sense of every one's favour to me, superadded to the duty I owed as a daughter and a niece: but that I was so much surprised at a reception so unusual and unexpected, that I hoped my papa and mamma would give me leave to retire, in order to recollect myself.

No one gainsaying, I made my silent compliments, and withdrew; — leaving my brother and sister, as I thought, pleased; and as if they wanted to congratulate each other on having occasioned so severe a beginning to be made with me.

I went up to my chamber, and there with my faithful Hannah deplored the determined face which the new proposal it was plain they had to make me wore.

I had not recovered myself when I was sent for down to tea. I begged by my maid to be excused attending; but on the repeated command, went down with as much cheerfulness as I could assume; and had a new fault to clear myself of: for my brother, so pregnant a thing is determined illwill, by intimations equally rude and intelligible, charged my desire of being excused coming down, to sullens, because a certain person had been spoken against, upon whom, as he supposed, my fancy ran.

I could easily answer you, sir, said I, as such a reflection deserves: but I forbear. If I do not find a brother in *you*, you shall have a sister in *me*.

Pretty meekness! Bella whisperingly said; looking at my brother, and lifting up her lip in contempt.

He, with an imperious air, bid me *deserve* his love, and I should be sure to *have* it.

As we sat, my mother, in her admirable manner, expatiated upon brotherly and sisterly love: indulgently blamed my brother and sister for having taken up displeasure too lightly against me; and politically, if I may so say, answered for my obedience to my father's will. — *Then it would be all well,* my father was pleased to say: *Then they should dote upon me*, was my brother's expression: *Love me as well as ever,* was my sister's: and my uncle's, *That I then should be the pride of their hearts.* — But, alas: what a forfeiture of all these must I make?

This was the reception I had on my return from you.

Mr. Solmes came in before we had done tea. My uncle Antony presented him to me, as a gentleman he had a particular friendship for. My uncle Harlowe in terms equally favourable for him. My father said, Mr. Solmes is my friend, Clarissa Harlowe. My mother looked at him, and looked at me, now and then, as he sat near me, I thought with concern. — I at *her*, with eyes appealing for pity. At *him*, when I could glance at him, with disgust little short of affrightment. While my brother and sister Mr. *Solmes*'d him, and *sir*'d him up, at every word. So caressed, in short, by all; — yet such a wretch! — But I will at present only add, my humble thanks and duty to your honoured mother (to whom I will particularly write, to express the grateful sense I have of her goodness to me); and that I am

Your ever obliged
Cl. Harlowe.

LETTER VIII.
Miss Clarissa Harlowe to Miss Howe.

Feb. 24.

They drive on here at a furious rate. The man lives here, I think.

He courts them, and is more and more a favourite. Such terms! such settlements! That's the cry.

O my dear, that I had not reason to deplore the family fault, immensely rich as they all are! But this I may the more unreservedly say to you, as we have often joined in the same concern: I, for a father and uncles; you, for a mother; in every other respect faultless.

Hitherto, I seem to be delivered over to my brother, who pretends as great love to me as ever.

You may believe, I have been very sincere with him. But he affects to rally me, and not to believe it possible, that one so dutiful and so discreet as his sister Clary can resolve to disoblige all her friends.

Indeed, I tremble at the prospect before me; for it is evident that they are strangely determined.

My father and mother industriously avoid giving me opportunity of speaking to them alone. They ask not for my approbation, intending, as it should seem, to *suppose* me into their will. And with them I shall hope to prevail, or with nobody. They have not the *interest* in compelling me, as my brother and sister have: I say less therefore to them, reserving my whole force for an audience with my father, if he will permit me a patient ear. How difficult is it, my dear, to give a negative where both duty and inclination join to make one wish to oblige.

I have already stood the shock of three of this man's particular visits, besides my share in his more general ones; and find it is impossible I should ever endure him. He has but a very ordinary share of understanding; is very illiterate; knows nothing but the value of estates, and how to improve them, and what belongs to land-jobbing and husbandry. Yet am I as one stupid, I think. They have begun so cruelly with me, that I have not spirit enough to assert my own negative.

They had endeavoured, it seems, to influence my good Mrs. Norton before I came home — So intent are they to carry their point! And her opinion not being to their liking, she has been told that she would do well to decline visiting here for the present: yet *she* is the person of all the world, next to my mother, the most likely to prevail upon me, were the measures they are engaged in reasonable measures, or such as she could think so.

My aunt likewise having said that she did not think her niece could ever be brought to like Mr. Solmes, has been obliged to learn another lesson.

I am to have a visit from her to-morrow. And, since I have refused so much as to hear from my brother and sister what the noble settlements are to be, she is to acquaint me with the particulars; and to receive from me my determination: for my father, I am told, will not have patience to *suppose* that I shall stand in opposition to his will.

Meantime it has been signified to me, that it will be acceptable if

I do not think of going to church next Sunday.

The same signification was made me for last Sunday; and I obeyed. They are apprehensive that Mr. Lovelace will be there with design to come home with me.

Help me, dear Miss Howe, to a little of your charming spirit: I never more wanted it.

The man, this Solmes, you may suppose has no reason to boast of his progress with me. He has not the sense to say any thing to the purpose. His courtship indeed is to *them;* and my brother pretends to court me as his proxy, truly! — I utterly to my brother reject his address; but thinking a person so well received and recommended by all my family, entitled to good manners, all I say against him is affectedly attributed to coyness: and he, not being sensible of his own imperfections, believes that my avoiding him when I can, and the reserves I express, are owing to nothing else: for, as I said, all his courtship is to *them;* and I have no opportunity of saying no, to one who asks me not the question. And so, with an air of *mannish* superiority, he seems rather to pity the bashful girl, than to apprehend that he shall not succeed.

Feb. 25.

I have had the expected conference with my aunt.

I have been obliged to hear the man's proposals from her; and have been also told what their motives are for espousing his interest with so much warmth. I am even loth to mention how equally unjust it is for him to make such offers, or for those I am bound to reverence to accept of them. I hate him more than before. One great estate is already obtained at the expense of the relations to it, though distant relations; my brother's I mean, by his godmother: and this has given the hope, however chimerical that hope, of procuring others; and that my own at least may revert to the family. And yet in my opinion the world is but one great family. Originally it was so. What then is this narrow selfishness that reigns in us, but relationship remembered against relationship forgot?

But here, upon my absolute refusal of him upon *any* terms, have I had a signification made me that wounds me to the heart. How can I tell it you? Yet I must. It is, my dear, that I must not for a month to come, or till licence obtained, correspond with *any* body out of the house.

My brother, upon my aunt's report (made, however, as I am informed, in the gentlest manner, and even giving remote hopes, which she had no commission from me to give) brought me, in authoritative terms, the prohibition!

Not to Miss Howe? said I.

No, not to Miss Howe, *madam*, tauntingly: for have you not acknowledged, that Lovelace is a favourite there?

See, my dear Miss Howe! —

And do you think, brother, this is the way —

Do *you* look to that — But your letters will be stopt, I can tell you. — And away he flung.

My sister came to me soon after — Sister Clary, you are going on in a fine way, I understand. But as there are people who are supposed to harden you against your duty, I am to tell you, that it will be taken well if you avoid visits or visitings for a week or two, till further order.

Can this be from those who have authority —

Ask them; ask them, child, with a twirl of her finger. — I have delivered my message. Your father will be obeyed. He is willing to hope you to be all obedience, and would prevent all *incitements* to refractoriness.

I know my duty, said I; and hope I shall not find impossible conditions annexed to it.

A pert young creature, vain and conceited, she called me. I was the only judge, in my own wise opinion, of what was right and fit. She, for her part, had long seen into my specious ways: and now I should shew every body what I was at bottom.

Dear Bella, said I! hands and eyes lifted up — why all this? — Dear, dear Bella! why —

None of your dear, dear Bella's to me. — I tell you, I see through your *witchcrafts* [that was her strange word]. And away she flung; adding, as she went — And so will every body else very quickly, I dare say.

Bless me, said I to myself, what a sister have I! — How have I deserved this?

Then I again regretted my grandfather's too distinguishing goodness to me.

Feb. 25, in the evening.

What my brother and sister have said against me I cannot tell: — but I am in heavy disgrace with my father.

I was sent for down to tea. I went with a very cheerful aspect: but had occasion soon to change it.

Such a solemnity in every body's countenance! My mother's eyes were fixed upon the tea-cups; and when she looked up, it was heavily, as if her eyelids had weights upon them; and then not to me. My father sat half-aside in his elbow-chair, that his head might be turned from me, his hands clasped, and waving, as it were, up and down; his fingers, poor dear gentleman! in motion, as if angry to the very ends of them. My sister sat swelling. My brother looked at me with scorn, having measured me, as I may say, with his eyes as I entered, from head to foot. My aunt was there, and looked upon me as if with kindness restrained, bending coldly to my compliment to her as she sat; and then cast an eye first on my brother, then on my sister, as if to give the reason [so I am willing to construe it] of her unusual stiffness: — Bless me, my dear! that they should choose to intimidate rather than invite a mind, till now, not thought either unpersuadable or ungenerous!

I took my seat. Shall I make

tea, madam, to my mother? — I always used, you know, my dear, to make tea.

No! a very short sentence, in one very short word, was the expressive answer. And she took the canister in her own hand.

My brother bid the footman who attended leave the room; I, said he, will give the water.

My heart was in agitation, I did not know what to do with myself. What is to follow? thought I.

Just after the second dish, out stept my mother — A word with you, sister Hervey! taking her hand. Presently my sister dropt away. Then my brother. And I was left alone with my father.

He looked so very sternly, that my heart failed me as twice or thrice I would have addressed myself to him: nothing but solemn silence on all sides having passed before.

At last, I asked, If it were his pleasure that I should pour him out another dish.

He answered me with the same angry monosyllable, which I had received from my mother before; and then arose, and walked about the room. I arose too, with intent to throw myself at his feet; but was too much overawed by his sternness, even to make such an expression of my duty to him as my heart overflowed with.

At last, as he supported himself, because of his gout, on the back of a chair, I took a little more courage; and approaching him, besought him to acquaint me in what I had offended him

He turned from me, and in a strong voice, Clarissa Harlowe, said he, know that I will be obeyed.

God forbid, sir, that you should not! — I have never yet opposed your will —

Nor I your whimsies, Clarissa Harlowe, interrupted he. — Don't let me run the fate of all who shew indulgence to your sex; to be the more contradicted for mine to you.

My father, you know, my dear, has not (any more than my brother) a kind opinion of our sex; although there is not a more condescending wife in the world than my mother.

I was going to make protestations of duty — No protestations, girl! No words! I will not be prated to! I will be obeyed! I have no child, I *will* have no child, but an obedient one.

Sir, you never had reason, I hope —

Tell me not what I never *had*, but what I *have*, and what I *shall* have.

Good sir, be pleased to hear me — My brother and my sister, I fear —

Your brother and sister shall not be spoken against, girl! — They have a just concern for the honour of my family.

And I hope, sir —

Hope nothing. — Tell me not of *hopes*, but of *facts*. I ask nothing of you but what is in your *power* to comply with, and what it is your *duty* to comply with.

Then, sir, I *will* comply with

it — But yet I hope from your goodness —

No expostulations! no *buts*, girl! no qualifyings! I will be obeyed, I tell you; and cheerfully too! — or you are no child of mine!

I wept.

Let me beseech you, my dear and ever-honoured papa (and I dropt down on my knees) that I may have only yours and my mamma's will, and not my brother's, to obey.

I was going on; but he was pleased to withdraw, leaving me on the floor; saying, that he would not hear me thus by subtilty and cunning aiming to distinguish away my duty; repeating, that he *would* be obeyed.

My heart is too full! — so full, that it may endanger my duty, were I to try to unburden it to you on this occasion: so I will lay down my pen. — But can — Yet, positively, I *will* lay down my pen!

LETTER IX.
Miss Clarissa Harlowe to Miss Howe.

Feb. 26, in the morning.

My aunt, who staid here last night, made me a visit this morning as soon as it was light. She tells me, that I was left alone with my father yesterday, on purpose that he might talk with me on my expected obedience; but that he owned he was put beside his purpose by reflecting on something my brother had told him in my disfavour, and by his impatience but to suppose that such a gentle spirit as mine had hitherto seemed to be, should presume to dispute his will in a point where the advantage of the whole family was to be so greatly promoted by my compliance.

I find by a few words which dropt unawares from my aunt, that they have all an absolute dependence upon what they suppose to be meekness in my temper. But in this they may be mistaken; for I verily think, upon a strict examination of myself, that I have almost as much in me of my father's as of my mother's family.

My uncle Harlowe it seems is against driving me upon extremities: but my brother has engaged, that the regard I have for my reputation, and my principles, will bring me *round to my duty;* that's the expression. Perhaps I shall have reason to wish I had not known this.

My aunt advises me to submit for the present to the interdicts they have laid me under; and indeed to encourage Mr. Solmes's address. I have absolutely refused the latter, let what will (as I have told her) be the consequence. The visiting prohibition I will conform to. But as to that of not corresponding with you, nothing but the menace that our letters shall be intercepted can engage my observation of it.

She believes that this order is from my father, and that my mother has not been consulted upon it. She says, that it is given, as she has reason to think, purely in consideration to me, lest I should mortally offend him; and this from the incitements of *other* people (meaning you and Miss Lloyd, I make no doubt) rather than by my own will. For still, as she tells me, he speaks kind and praiseful things of me.

Here is clemency! Here is indulgence! — And so it is, to prevent a headstrong child, as a good prince would wish to deter disaffected subjects, from running into rebellion, and so forfeiting every thing! But this is all owing to the young man's wisdom, my brother; a plotter without a head, and a brother without a heart.

How happy might I have been with any other brother in the world but James Harlowe; and with any other sister but *his* sister! Wonder not, my dear, that I, who used to chide you for these sort of liberties with my relations, now am more undutiful than you ever was unkind. I cannot bear the thought of being deprived of the principal pleasure of my life; for such is your conversation by person and by letter. And who, besides, can bear to be made the dupe of such low cunning, operating with such high and arrogant passions?

But can you, my dear Miss Howe, condescend to carry on a private correspondence with me? — If you can, there is one way I have thought of, by which it may be done.

You must remember the Green Lane, as we call it, that runs by the side of the wood-house and poultry-yard where I keep my bantams, pheasants, and pea-hens, which generally engage my notice twice a day; the more my favourites because they were my grandfather's, and recommended to my care by him; and therefore brought hither from my Dairy-house since his death.

The lane is lower than the floor of the wood-house, and in the side of the wood-house the boards are rotted away down to the floor for half an ell together in several places. Hannah can step into the lane, and make a mark with chalk where a letter or parcel may be pushed in, under some sticks; which may be so managed as to be an unsuspected cover for the written deposits from either.

* * *

I have been just now to look at the place, and find it will answer. So your faithful Robert may, without coming near the house, and as only passing through the Green Lane which leads to two or three farm-houses [out of livery if you please] very easily take from thence my letters, and deposit yours.

This place is the more convenient, because it is seldom resorted to but by myself or Hannah, on the above-mentioned account; for it is the general store-house for firing; the wood for constant use being nearer the house.

One corner of this being separated off for the roosting-place of my little poultry, either she or I shall never want a pretence to go thither.

Try, my dear, the success of a letter this way; and give me your opinion and advice what to do in this *disgraceful* situation, as I cannot but call it; and what you think of my prospects; and what you would do in my case.

But beforehand I will tell you, that your advice must not run in favour of this Solmes: and yet it is very likely they will endeavour to engage your mother, in order to induce you, who have such an influence over me, to favour him.

Yet, on second thoughts, if you incline to that side of the question, I would have you write your whole mind. Determined as I think I am, and cannot help it, I would at least give a patient hearing to what may be said on the other side. For my regards are not so much engaged [upon my word they are not; I know not myself if they be] to another person as some of my friends suppose: and as you, giving way to your lively vein, upon his last visits, affected to suppose. What preferable favour I may have for him to any other person, is owing more to the usage he has received, and for my sake borne, than to any personal consideration.

I write a few lines of grateful acknowledgment to your good mother for her favours to me in the late happy period. I fear I shall never know such another. I hope she will forgive me that I did not write sooner.

The bearer, if suspected and examined, is to produce *that*, as the only one he carries.

How do needless watchfulness and undue restraint produce artifice and contrivance! I should abhor these clandestine correspondencies, were they not forced upon me. They have so mean, so low an appearance to myself, that I think I ought not to expect that you should take part in them.

But why (as I have also expostulated with my aunt) must I be pushed into a state, which I have no wish to enter into, although I reverence it? — Why should not my brother, so many years older, and so earnest to see me engaged, be first engaged? — And why should not my sister be first provided for?

But here I conclude these unavailing expostulations, with the assurance, that I am, and ever will be,

Your affectionate,
CLARISSA HARLOWE.

LETTER X.
Miss Howe to Miss Clarissa Harlowe.

Feb. 27.

WHAT odd heads some people have! — Miss Clarissa Harlowe to be sacrificed in marriage to Mr. Roger Solmes! — Astonishing!

I must not, you say, *give my advice in favour of this man?* — You now convince me, my dear, that you are nearer of kin than I thought you, to the family that could think of so preposterous a match, or you would never have had the least notion of my advising in his favour.

Ask me for his picture. You

know I have a good hand at drawing an ugly likeness. But I'll see a little further first: for who knows what may happen, since matters are in such a train; and since you have not the courage to oppose so overwhelming a torrent?

You ask me to help you to a little of my spirit. Are you in earnest? But it will not now, I doubt, do you service. — It will not sit naturally upon you. You are your mother's girl, think what you will; and have violent spirits to contend with. Alas! my dear, you should have borrowed some of mine a little sooner; — that is to say, before you had given the management of your estate into the hands of those who think they have a prior claim to it. What though a *father's* — Has not that father two older children? — And do they not both bear more of his stamp and image than you do? — Pray, my dear, call me not to account for this free question, lest your *application* of my meaning, on examination, prove to be as severe as *that*.

Now I have launched out a little, indulge me one word more in the same strain — I will be decent, I promise you. I think you might have known, that AVARICE and ENVY are two passions that are not to be satisfied, the one by *giving*, the other by the envied person's continuing to *deserve* and *excel*. — Fuel, fuel, both, all the world over, to flames insatiate and devouring.

But since ou ask for *my* opinion, you must tell me all you know or surmise of *their* inducements. And if you will not forbid me to make extracts from your letters for the entertainment of my aunt in the little island, who longs to hear more of your affairs, it will be very obliging.

But you are so tender of some people, who have no tenderness for any body but themselves, that I must conjure you to speak out. Remember, that a friendship like ours admits of no reserves. You may trust my impartiality. It would be an affront to your own judgment, if you did not: for do you not *ask* my advice? And have you not taught me that friendship should never give a bias against justice? — Justify them therefore if you can. Let us see if there be any *sense*, whether sufficient *reason* or not, in their choice. At present I cannot (and yet I know a good deal of your family) have any conception how *all* of them, your mother and your aunt Hervey in particular, can join with the rest against judgments given. As to some of the others, I cannot wonder at any thing they do, or attempt to do, where self is concerned.

You ask, why may not your brother be first engaged in wedlock? I'll tell you why: his temper and his arrogance are too well known to induce women he would aspire to, to receive his addresses, notwithstanding his great independent acquisitions, and still greater prospects. Let me tell you, my dear, those acquisitions have given him more pride than reputation. To me he is the most intolerable creature that I ever conversed with. The treatment you blame, he merited from one whom he addressed with the air of a person who presumes that he is about to confer a favour, rather than to receive one. I ever loved to mortify proud and insolent spirits. What, think you, makes me bear Hickman near me, but that the man is humble, and knows and keeps his distance?

As to your question, why your elder sister may not be first provided for? I answer, because she must have no man, but one who has a great and clear estate; that's one thing. Another is, because she has a younger sister. Pray, my dear, be so good as to tell me, what man of a great and clear estate would think of that elder sister, while the younger is single?

You are all too rich to be happy, child. For must not each of you, by the constitutions of your family, marry to be *still* richer? People who know in what their *main* excellence consists, are not to be blamed (are they?) for cultivating and improving what they think most valuable? — Is true happiness any part of your family view? — So far from it, that none of your family but yourself could be happy were they *not* rich. So let them fret on, grumble, and grudge, and accumulate; and wondering what ails them that they have not happiness when they have riches, think the cause is want of more; and so go on heaping up, till Death, as greedy an accumulator as themselves, gathers them into his garner.

Well then, once more I say, do you, my dear, tell *me* what you know of their avowed and general motives; and I will tell *you* more than you will tell *me* of their failings! your aunt Hervey, you say*, has told *you:* why must I ask you to let me know them, when you condescend to ask my advice on the occasion?

That they prohibit your corresponding with *me*, is a wisdom I neither wonder at, nor blame them for: since it is an evidence to me, that they know their own folly: and if they do, is it strange that they should be afraid to trust another's judgment upon it?

I am glad you have found out a way to correspond with me. I approve it much. I shall *more*, if this first trial of it prove successful. But should it *not*, and should it fall into their hands, it would not concern me but for your sake.

We had heard before you wrote, that all was not right between your relations and you at your coming home: that Mr. Solmes visited you, and that with a prospect of success. But I concluded the mistake lay in the person; and that his address was to Miss Arabella. And indeed had she been as good-natured as your plump ones generally are, I should have thought her too good for him by half. This must certainly be the thing, thought I, and my beloved friend is sent for to advise and

* See p. 36.

assist in her nuptial preparations. Who knows, said I to my mother, but that when the man has thrown aside his yellow full-buckled peruke, and his broad-brimmed beaver (both of which I suppose were Sir Oliver's Best of long standing) he may cut a tolerable figure dangling to church with Miss Bell! — The woman, as she observes, *should* excel the man in features: and where can she match so well for a foil?

I indulged this surmise against rumour, because I could not believe that the absurdest people in England could be so *very* absurd as to think of this man for you.

We heard moreover, that you received no visitors. I could assign no reason for this; except that the preparations for your sister were to be private, and the ceremony sudden, for fear this man *should*, as another man *did*, change his mind. Miss Lloyd and Miss Biddulph were with me to inquire what I knew of this; and of your not being at church, either morning or afternoon, the Sunday after your return from us; to the disappointment of a little hundred of your admirers, to use their words. It was easy for me to guess the reason to be what you confirm — Their apprehensions that Lovelace would be there, and attempt to wait on you home.

My mother takes very kindly your compliments in your letter to her. Her words upon reading it were; "Miss Clarissa Harlowe is an admirable young lady: wherever she goes she confers a favour: whomever she leaves, she fills with regret." — And then a little comparative reflection: "O my Nancy, that you had a little of her sweet obligingness!"

No matter. The praise was yours. You are me: and I enjoyed it. The more enjoyed it, because — shall I tell you the truth? — Because I think myself as well as I am — were it but for this reason: that had I twenty brother James's, and twenty sister Bell's, not one of them, nor all of them joined together, would dare to treat me as yours presume to treat you. The person who will bear much shall have much to bear, all the world through: 'tis your own sentiment *, grounded upon the strongest instance that can be given in your own family; though you have so little improved by it.

The result is this, that I am fitter for *this* world than you: you for the *next* than me; — that's the difference. — But long, long, for my sake, and for hundreds of sakes, may it be before you quit us for company more congenial to you and more worthy of you!

I communicated to my mother the account you give of your strange reception; also what a horrid wretch they have found out for you; and the compulsory treatment they give you. It only set her on magnifying her lenity to me on my *tyrannical* behaviour, as she *will* call it [mothers must have their way, you know, my dear] to the man whom she so warmly recommends, against whom it seems

* p. 26.

there can be no just exception; and expatiating upon the complaisance I owe her for her indulgence. So I believe I must communicate to her nothing further — especially as I know she would condemn the correspondence between us, and that between you and Lovelace, as clandestine and undutiful proceedings, and divulge our secret besides: for *duty implicit* is her cry. And moreover she lends a pretty open ear to the preachments of that starch old bachelor your uncle Antony; and for an example to *her* daughter would be more careful how she takes your part, be the cause ever so just.

Yet this is not right policy neither. For people who allow nothing, will be granted nothing: in other words, those who aim at carrying too many points will not be able to carry any.

But can you divine, my dear, what that old preachment-making plump-hearted soul your uncle Antony means by his frequent amblings hither? — There is such smirking and smiling between my mother and him! such mutual praises of economy; and "*That* is my way!" — and "*This* I do!" — and "I am glad it has *your* approbation, sir!" — and "*You* look into every thing, madam!" — "Nothing would be done, if I did not!" — such exclamations against servants! such exaltings of self! and *dear-heart*, and *good lack!* — and '*las a day!* — and now and then their conversation sinking into a whispering accent, if *I* come cross them! — I'll tell you, my dear, I don't above half like it.

Only that these old bachelors usually take as many years to resolve upon matrimony as they can reasonably expect to live, or I should be ready to fire upon his visits; and to recommend Mr. Hickman to my mother's acceptance, as a much more eligible man: for what he wants in years, he makes up in gravity! and if you will not chide me, I will say, that there is a primness in *both* (especially when the man has presumed too much with me upon my mother's favour for him, and is under discipline on that account) as makes them seem near of kin: and then in contemplation of my sauciness, and what they both bear from it, they sigh away! — and seem so mightily to compassionate each other, that if pity be but one remove from love, I am in no danger, while they both are in a great deal, and don't know it.

Now, my dear, I know you will be upon me with your grave airs: so *in for the lamb*, as the saying is, *in for the sheep;* and do you yourself look about you: for I'll have a pull with you by way of being aforehand. Hannibal, we read, always advised to attack the Romans upon their own territories.

You are pleased to say, and upon your word too! that your regards (a mighty quaint word for *affections*) are not so much engaged, as *some of your friends suppose*, to another person. What need you give one to imagine, my dear, that the last month or two has been a period extremely favourable to that *other* person; — whom it has made an obliger of the niece for his patience with the uncles.

But, to pass that by — *so much* engaged! — *How much*, my dear? — Shall I infer? *Some of your friends* suppose *a great deal.* You seem to own *a little.*

Don't be angry. It is all fair: because you have not acknowledged to me that *little.* People, I have heard you say, who affect secrets, always excite curiosity.

But you proceed with a kind of drawback upon your averment, as if recollection had given you a doubt — *you know not yourself, if they be* [so much engaged.] Was it necessary to say this, to me? — and to say it *upon your word too?* — But you know best — yet you don't neither, I believe. For a beginning love is acted by a subtle spirit; and oftentimes discovers itself to a bystander, when the person possessed (why should I not call *possessed?*) knows not it has such a demon.

But further you say, what PREFERABLE *favour you may have for him to any other person, is owing more to the usage he has received, and for your sake borne, than to any personal consideration.*

This is generously said. It is in character. But, O my friend, depend upon it, you are in danger. Depend upon it, whether you know it or not, you are a little in for't. Your native generosity and greatness of mind endanger you: all your friends, by fighting *against* him with impolitic violence, fight *for* him. And Lovelace, my life for yours, notwithstanding all his veneration and assiduities, has seen further than that veneration and those assiduities (so well calculated to your meridian) will let him own he has seen — has seen, in short, that his work is doing for him more effectually than he could do it for himself. And have you not before now said, that nothing is so penetrating as the eye of a lover who has vanity? and who says Lovelace wants vanity?

In short, my dear, it is my opinion, and that from the easiness of his heart and behaviour, that he has seen more than *I* have seen; more than you think *could* be seen — more than I believe you *yourself* know, or else you would let *me* know it.

Already, in order to restrain him from resenting the indignities he has received, and which are daily offered him, he has prevailed upon you to correspond with him privately. I know he has nothing to boast of from *what* you have written: but is not his inducing you to receive his letters, and to answer them, a great point gained? By your insisting that he should keep this correspondence private, it appears that there is *one secret* which you do not wish the world should know: and he is master of that secret. He is indeed *himself*, as I may say, that secret! what an intimacy does this beget for the lover! how is it distancing the parent!

Yet who, as things are situated, can blame you? — Your condescension has no doubt hitherto prevented great mischiefs. It must be continued, for the same reasons, while the cause remains. You are drawn in by a perverse fate against inclination: but custom, with such laudable purposes, will reconcile the inconveniency, and make an inclination — And I would advise you (as you would wish to manage on an occasion so critical with that prudence which governs all your actions) not to be afraid of entering upon a close examination into the true springs and grounds of this your *generosity* to that happy man.

It is my humble opinion, I tell you frankly, that on inquiry it will come out to be love — don't start, my dear! — has not your man himself had natural philosophy enough to observe already to your aunt Hervey, that love takes the deepest root in the steadiest minds? The deuce take his sly penetration, I was going to say: for this was six or seven weeks ago.

I have been tinctured, you know. Nor on the coolest reflection, could I account how and when the jaundice began: but had been over head and ears, as the saying is, but for some of that advice from you which I now return you. Yet my *man* was not half so — so *what*, my dear — to be sure Lovelace is a charming fellow. And were he only — but I will not make you *glow*, as you read — — upon my word I will not. —

Yet, my dear, don't you find at your heart somewhat unusual make it go throb, throb, throb, as you read just here? — If you do, don't be ashamed to own it — it is your *generosity*, my love! that's all. — But, as the Roman augur said, Cæsar, beware of the Ides of March.

Adieu, my dearest friend. — Forgive, and very speedily, by the new-found expedient, tell me, that you forgive

Your ever affectionate
ANNA HOWE.

LETTER XI.

Miss Clarissa Harlowe to Miss Howe.

Wednesday, March 1.

You both nettled and alarmed me, my dearest Miss Howe, by the concluding part of your last. At first reading it, I did not think it necessary, said I to myself, to guard against a critic, when I was writing to so dear a friend. But then recollecting myself, is there not more in it, said I, than the result of a vein so naturally lively? surely I must have been guilty of an inadvertence. Let me enter into the close examination of myself which my beloved friend advises.

I do so; and cannot own any of the *glow*, any of the *throbs* you mention — *upon my word* I will repeat, I cannot. And yet the passages in my letter upon which you are so humorously severe, lay me fairly open to your agreeable raillery. I own they do. And I cannot tell what turn my mind had taken to dictate so oddly to my pen.

But, pray now — is it saying so much, when one, who has no very particular regard to *any* man, says, there are *some* who are preferable to *others?* and is it blameable to say they are the preferable, who are not well used by one's relations; yet dispense with *that* usage out of regard to one's self which they would otherwise resent? Mr. Lovelace, for instance, I may be allowed to say, is a man to be preferred to Mr. Solmes; and that I *do* prefer him to that man: but, surely, this may be said without its being a necessary consequence that I must be in love with him.

Indeed I would not be *in love* with him, as it is called, for the world: first, because I have no opinion of his morals; and think it a fault in which our whole family (my brother excepted) has had a share, that he was permitted to visit us with a hope; which, however being distant, did not, as I have observed heretofore*, entitle any of us to call him to account for such of his immoralities as came to our ears. Next, because I think him to be a vain man, capable of triumphing (secretly at least) over a person whose heart he thinks he has engaged. And, thirdly, because the assiduities and veneration which you impute to him, seem to carry an haughtiness in them, as if he thought his address had a merit in it, that would be more than an

* p. 15, 16, 17, 18.

equivalent to a woman's love. In short, his very politeness, notwithstanding the advantages he must have had from his birth and education, appear to me to be constrained; and with the most remarkably easy and genteel person, something, at times, seems to be behind in his *manner* that is too studiously kept in. Then, good-humoured as he is thought to be in the main to *other people's* servants, and this even to familiarity (although, as you have observed, a familiarity that has dignity *in it* not unbecoming a man of quality), he is apt sometimes to break out into a passion with *his own:* an oath or a curse follows; and such looks from those servants as plainly shew terror; and that they should have fared worse had they not been in my hearing: with a confirmation in the master's looks of a surmise too well justified.

Indeed, my dear, THIS MAN is not THE MAN. I have great objections to him. My heart *throbs* not after him. I *glow* not, but with indignation against myself for having given room for such an imputation. — But you must not, my dearest friend, construe common gratitude into love. I cannot bear that you should. But if ever I should have the misfortune to think it love, I promise you upon my *word*, which is the same as upon my *honour*, that I will acquaint you with it.

You bid me to tell you very speedily, and by the new-found expedient, that I am not displeased with you for your agreeable raillery: I despatch this therefore immediately; postponing to my next the account of the inducements which my friends have to promote with so much earnestness the address of Mr. Solmes.

Be satisfied, my dear, meantime, that I am *not* displeased with you: indeed I am not. On the contrary, I give you my hearty thanks for your friendly premonitions. And I charge you (as I have often done) that if you observe any thing in me so very faulty as would require from you to others in my behalf the palliation of friendly and partial love, you acquaint me with it: for methinks I would so conduct myself as not to give reason even for an *adversary* to censure me: and how shall so weak and so young a creature avoid the censure of *such*, if my *friend* will not hold a looking-glass before me to let me see my imperfections?

Judge me, then, my dear, as any indifferent person (knowing what *you* know of me) would do. I may at first be a little pained; may *glow* a little perhaps to be found less worthy of your friendship than I wish to be; but assure yourself, that your kind correction will give me reflection that shall *amend* me. If it do not, you will have a fault to accuse me of, that will be utterly *inexcusable*: a fault, let me add, that should you *not* accuse me of it (if in your opinion I am guilty) you will not be so much, so *warmly*, my friend as I am yours; since I have never spared *you* on the like occasions.

Here I break off; to begin another letter to you; with the assurance, meantime, that I am, and ever will be,

Your equally affectionate and grateful
CL. HARLOWE.

LETTER XII.

Miss Howe to Miss Clarissa Harlowe.

Thursday morn. March 2.

Indeed you would not be in love with him for the world! — Your servant, my dear. Nor would I have you. For I think, with all the advantages of person, fortune, and family, he is not by any means worthy of you. And this opinion I give as well from the reasons you mention (which I cannot but confirm) as from what I have heard of him but a few hours ago from Mrs. Fortescue, a favourite of Lady Betty Lawrence, who knows him well — but let me congratulate you, however, on your being the first of our sex that ever I heard of, who has been able to turn that lion, love, at her own pleasure into a lap-dog.

Well but, if you have not the throbs and the glows, you have not: and are not in love; good reason why — because you would not be in love; and there's no more to be said — only, my dear, I shall keep a good look-out upon you; and so I hope you will upon yourself: for it is no manner of argument that because you would not be in love, you therefore are not.

— But before I part entirely with this subject, a word in your ear, my charming friend — 'tis only by way of caution, and in pursuance of the general observation, that a stander-by is often a better judge of the game than those that play. — May it not be, that you have had, and have, such cross creatures and such odd heads to deal with, as have not allowed you to attend to the throbs? — Or, if you had them a little now and then, whether having had two accounts to place them to, you have not by mistake put them to the wrong one?

But whether you have a value for Lovelace or not, I know you will be impatient to hear what Mrs. Fortescue has said of him. Nor will I keep you longer in suspense.

An hundred wild stories she tells of him, from childhood to manhood: for, as she observes, having never been subject to contradiction, he was always as mischievous as a monkey. But I shall pass over these whole hundred of his puerile rogueries (although *indicative* ones, as I may say) to take notice as well of some things you are not quite ignorant of, as of others you know not; and to make a few observations upon him and his ways.

Mrs. Fortescue owns, what every body knows, "that he is notoriously, nay, avowedly, a man of pleasure; yet says, that in any thing he sets his heart upon or undertakes, he is the most industrious and persevering mortal under the sun. He rests it seems not above six hours in the twenty-four — any more than you. He delights in writing. Whether at Lord M.'s, or at Lady Betty's, or Lady Sarah's, he has always a pen in his fingers when he retires. One of his companions (confirming his love of writing) has told her, that his thoughts flow rapidly to his pen:" and you and I, my dear, have observed, on more occasions than one, that though he writes even a fine hand, he is one of the readiest and quickest of writers. He must indeed have had early a very docile genius; since a person of his pleasurable turn and active spirit, could never have submitted to take long or great pains in attaining the qualifications he is master of; qualifications so seldom attained by youth of quality and fortune; by such especially of those of either, who, like him, have never known what it was to be controlled.

"He had once it seems the vanity, upon being complimented on these talents (and on his surprising diligence, for a man of pleasure) to compare himself to Julius Cæsar; who performed great actions by day, and wrote them down at night: and valued himself, that he only wanted Cæsar's out-setting, to make a figure among his cotemporaries.

"He spoke this indeed, she says, with an air of pleasantry: for she observed, and so have we, that he has the art of acknowledging his vanity with so much humour, that it sets him above the co tempt which is due to vanity and self-opinion; and at the same time half persuades those who hear him, that he really deserves the exaltation he gives himself."

But supposing it to be true that all his vacant nightly hours are employed in writing, what can be his subjects? If, like Cæsar, his own actions, he must undoubtedly be a very enterprising and very wicked man; since nobody suspects him to have a serious turn: and, decent as he is in his conversation with us, his writings are not probably such as would redound either to his own honour, or to the benefit of others, were they to be read. He must be conscious of this, since Mrs. Fortescue says, "that in the great correspondence by letters which he holds, he is as secret and as careful as if it were of a treasonable nature: yet troubles not his head with politics, though nobody knows the interests of princes and courts better than he is said to do."

That you and I, my dear, should love to write is no wonder. We have always, from the time each could hold a pen, delighted in epistolary correspondences. Our employments are domestic and sedentary; and we can scribble upon twenty innocent subjects, and take delight in them because they *are* innocent; though were they to be seen, they might not much profit or please others. But that such a gay, lively young fellow as this, who rides, hunts, travels, frequents the public entertainments, and has *means* to pursue his pleasures, should be able to set himself down to write for hours together, as you and I have heard him say he frequently does, that is the strange thing.

Mrs. Fortescue says, "that he is a complete master of short-hand writing." By the way, what inducements could such a swift writer as he have to learn short-hand!

She says (and we know it as well as she) "that he has a surprising memory; and a very lively imagination."

Whatever his other vices are, all the world, as well as Mrs. Fortescue, says, "he is a sober man. And among all his bad qualities, *gaming*, that great waster of time as well as fortune, is not his vice:" so that he must have his head as cool, and his reason as clear, as the prime of youth and his natural gaiety will permit; and by his early morning hours, a great portion of time upon his hands, to employ in writing, or worse.

Mrs. Fortescue says, "he has one gentleman who is more his intimate and correspondent than any of the rest." You remember what his dismissed bailiff said of him and of his associates*. I don't find but that man's character of him was in general pretty just. Mrs. Fortescue confirms this part of it, "that all his relations are afraid of him; and that his pride sets him above owing obligations to them. She believes he is clear of the world! and that he will

* P. 21.

4*

continue so:" No doubt from the same motive that makes him avoid being obliged to his relations.

A person willing to think favourably of him would hope, that a *brave*, a *learned*, and a *diligent* man, cannot be *naturally* a *bad* man. — But if he be better than his enemies say he is (and if worse, he is bad indeed) he is guilty of an inexcusable fault in being so careless as he is of his reputation. I think a man can be so but from one of these two reasons: either that he is conscious he deserves the ill spoken of him; or, that he takes a pride in being thought worse than he is. Both very bad and threatening indications; since the first must shew him to be utterly abandoned; and it is but natural to conclude from the other, that what a man is not ashamed to have imputed to him, he will not scruple to be guilty of whenever he has an opportunity.

Upon the whole, and upon all I could gather from Mrs. Fortescue, Mr. Lovelace is a very faulty man. You and I have thought him too gay, too inconsiderate, too rash, too little an hypocrite, to be *deep*. You see he never would disguise his natural temper (haughty as it certainly is) with respect to your brother's behaviour to him. Where he thinks a contempt due, he pays it to the uttermost. Nor has he complaisance enough to spare your uncles.

But were he deep, and ever so deep, you would soon penetrate him, if they would leave you to yourself. His vanity would be your clue. Never man had more: yet, as Mrs. Fortescue observed, "never did man carry it off so happily." There is a strange mixture in it of humorous vivacity: since but for one half of what he says of himself, when he is in the vein, any other man would be insufferable.

* * *

Talk *of the devil*, is an old saying. The lively wretch has made me a visit, and is but just gone away. He is all impatience and resentment at the treatment you meet with; and full of apprehensions too, that they will carry their point with you.

I told him my opinion, that you will never be brought to think of such a man as Solmes; but that it will probably end in a composition, never to have either.

No man, he said, whose fortunes and alliances are so considerable, ever had so little favour from a woman for whose sake he had borne so much.

I told him my mind as freely as I used to do. But who ever was in fault, self being judge? He complained of spies set upon his conduct, and to pry into his life and morals, and this by your brother and uncles.

I told him, that this was very hard upon him; and the more so, as neither his life nor morals perhaps would stand a fair inquiry. He smiled, and called himself *my servant*. — The occasion was too fair, he said, for Miss Howe, who never spared him, to let it pass. But, Lord help the shallow souls of the Harlowes! Would

I believe it? They were for turning plotters upon *him*. They had best take care he did not pay them in their own coin. Their *hearts* were better turned for such works than their *heads*.

I asked him, if he valued himself upon having a head better turned than theirs for *such works*, as he called them?

He drew off: and then ran into the highest professions of reverence and affection for you.

The object so meritorious, who can doubt the reality of his professions?

Adieu, my dearest, my noble friend! — I love and admire you for the generous conclusion of your last more than I can express. Though I began this letter with impertinent raillery, knowing that you always loved to indulge my mad vein; yet never was there a heart that more glowed with friendly love than that of

Your own
ANNA HOWE.

LETTER XIII.
Miss Clarissa Harlowe to Miss Howe.

Wedn. March 1.

I now take up my pen, to lay before you the inducements and motives which my friends have to espouse so earnestly the address of this Mr. Solmes.

In order to set this matter in a clear light, it is necessary to go a little back, and even perhaps to mention some things which you already know: and so you may look upon what I am going to relate as a kind of supplement to my letters of the 15th and 20th of January last *.

In those letters of which I have kept memorandums, I gave you an account of my brother's and sister's antipathy to Mr. Lovelace; and the methods they took (so far as they had then come to my knowledge) to ruin him in the opinion of my other friends. And I told you, that after a very cold yet not a directly affrontive behaviour to him, they all of a *sudden* ** became more violent, and proceeded to personal insults; which brought on at last the unhappy rencounter between my brother and him.

Now you must know, that from the last conversation that passed between my aunt and me, it comes out, that this *sudden* vehemence on my brother's and sister's parts, was owing to stronger reasons than to the college-begun antipathy on his side, or to slighted love on hers; to wit, to an apprehension that my uncles intended to follow my grandfather's example in my favour; at least in a higher degree than they wish they should. An apprehension founded it seems on a conversation between my two uncles and my brother and sister; which my aunt communicated to me in confidence, as an argument to prevail upon me to accept of Mr. Solmes's *noble* settlements: urging, that such a seasonable compliance would frustrate my brother's and sister's views, and

* Letters iv. v.
** See Letter iv. p. 20.

establish me for ever in the love of my father and uncles.

I will give you the substance of this communicated conversation, after I have made a brief introductory observation or two: which, however, I hardly need to make to you, who are so well acquainted with us all, did not the series or thread of the story require it.

I have more than once mentioned to you the darling view some of us have long had of *raising a family*, as it is called: a reflection, as I have often thought, upon our own; which is no inconsiderable or upstart one, on either side: my mother's, especially. — A view too frequently it seems entertained by families which, having great substance, cannot be satisfied without rank and title.

My uncles had once extended this view to each of us three children; urging, that as they themselves intended not to marry, we each of us might be so portioned, and so advantageously matched, as that our posterity, if not ourselves, might make a first figure in our country. — While my brother, as the only son, thought the two girls might be very well provided for by ten or fifteen thousand pounds apiece: and that all the real estates in the family; to wit, my grandfather's, and two uncles', and the remainder of their respective personal estates, together with what he had an expectation of from his godmother, would make such a noble fortune, and give him such an interest, as might entitle him to hope for a peerage. Nothing less would satisfy his ambition.

With this view he gave himself airs very early: "That his grandfather and uncles were his stewards: that no man ever had better: that daughters were but incumbrances and drawbacks upon a family:" and *this* low and familiar expression was often in his mouth, and uttered always with the self-complaisance which an imagined happy thought can be supposed to give the speaker; to wit, "That a man who has sons brings up chickens for his own table, whereas daughters are chickens brought up for the tables of other men." This accompanied with the equally polite reflection, "That to induce people to take them off their hands, the family stock must be impaired into the bargain," used to put my sister out of all patience: and although she now seems to think a *younger* sister only can be an incumbrance, she was then often proposing to me to make a party in our own favour against my brother's *rapacious views*, as she used to call them: while I was for considering the liberties he took of this sort as the effect of a temporary pleasantry; which in a young man not naturally good-humoured, I was glad to see; or as a foible that deserved raillery, but no other notice.

But when my grandfather's will (of the purport of which in my particular favour, until it was opened, I was as ignorant as they) had lopped off one branch of my brother's expectation, he was extremely dissatisfied with me. Nobody indeed was pleased: for although every one loved me, yet being the youngest child, father, uncles, brother, sister, all thought themselves postponed, as to matter of right and power: [Who loves not power?] and my father himself could not bear that I should be made sole, as I may call it, and independent: for such the will, as to that estate and the powers it gave (unaccountably as they all said) made me.

To obviate therefore every one's jealousy, I gave up to my father's management, as you know, not only the estate, but the money bequeathed me (which was a moiety of what my grandfather had by him at his death; the other moiety being bequeathed to my sister); contenting myself to take as from his bounty what he was pleased to allow me, without desiring the least addition to my annual stipend. And then I hoped I had laid all envy asleep: but still my brother and sister (jealous, as now is evident, of my two uncles' favour for me, and of the pleasure I had given my father and them by this act of duty) were every now-and-then occasionally doing me covert ill offices: of which, however, I took the less notice, when I was told of them, as I thought I had removed the cause of their envy; and I imputed every thing of that sort to the petulance they are both pretty much noted for.

My brother's acquisition then took place. This made us all very happy; and he went down to take possession of it: and his absence (on so good an account too) made us still happier. Then followed Lord M.'s proposal for my sister: and this was an additional felicity for the time. I have told you how exceedingly good-humoured it made my sister.

You know how that went off: you know what came on in its place.

My brother then returned; and we were all wrong again: and Bella, as I observed in my letters above-mentioned, had an opportunity to give herself the credit of having refused Mr. Lovelace, on the score of his reputed faulty morals. This united my brother and sister in one cause. They set themselves on all occasions to depreciate Mr. Lovelace, and his *family* too (a family which deserves nothing but respect): and this gave rise to the conversation I am leading to between my uncles and them. of which I now come to give the particulars; after I have observed, that it happened *before* the rencounter, and soon after the inquiry made into Mr. Lovelace's affairs had come out better than my brother and sister hoped it would.*

They were bitterly inveighing against him, in their usual way, strengthening their invectives with some new stories in his disfavour; when my uncle Antony, having given them a patient hearing, declared, "That he thought the gentleman behaved like a gentle-

* See Letter iv. p. 21, 22.

man; his niece Clary with prudence; and that a more honourable alliance for the family, *as he had often told them*, could not be wished for: since Mr. Lovelace had a very good paternal estate; and that, by the evidence of an enemy, all clear. Nor did it appear, that he was so bad a man as he had been represented to be: wild indeed; but it was at a gay time of life: he was a man of sense; and he was sure that his niece would not have him, if she had not good reason to think him reformed, or that there was a likelihood that she could reform him by her example."

My uncle then gave one instance, my aunt told me, as a proof of a generosity in Mr. Lovelace's spirit, which convinced him, that he was not a bad man in nature; and that he was of a temper, he was pleased to say, like my own: which was, that when he (my uncle) had represented to him, that he might, if he pleased, make three or four hundred pounds a year of his paternal estate, more than he did; he answered, "That his tenants paid their rents well: that it was a maxim with his family, from which he would by no means depart, never to rack-rent old tenants, or their descendants; and that it was a pleasure to him, to see all his tenants look fat, sleek, and contented."

I indeed had once occasionally heard him say something like this; and thought he never looked so well as at the time; — except once; and that was in an instance given by him on the following incident.

An unhappy tenant of my uncle Antony came petitioning to my uncle for forbearance, in Mr. Lovelace's presence. When he had fruitlessly withdrawn, Mr. Lovelace pleaded his cause so well, that the man was called in again, and had his suit granted. And Mr. Lovelace privately followed him out, and gave him two guineas, for present relief; the man having declared, that, at the time, he had not five shillings in the world.

On this occasion, he told my uncle (but without any airs of ostentation) that he had once observed an old tenant and his wife in a very mean habit at church; and questioning them about it next day, as he knew they had no hard bargain in their farm, the man said, he had done some very foolish things with a good intention, which had put him behindhand, and he could not have paid his rent, and appear better. He asked him how long it would take him to retrieve the foolish step he acknowledged he had made. He said, perhaps two or three years. "Well then," said he, "I will abate you five pounds a year for seven years, provided you will lay it out upon your wife and self, that you may make a Sunday appearance *like my tenants*. Meantime, take this (putting his hand in his pocket, and giving him five guineas) to put yourselves in present plight; and let me see you next Sunday at church, hand in hand, like an honest and loving couple; and I bespeak you to dine with me afterwards."

Although this pleased me when I heard it, as giving an instance at the same time, not lessening (as my uncle took notice) the yearly value of the farm; yet, my dear, I had no *throbs*, no *glows* upon it! — *Upon my word*, I had not. Nevertheless I own to you, that I could not help saying to myself on the occasion, "Were it ever to be my lot to have this man, he would not hinder me from pursuing the methods I so much delight to take." — With "A pity, that such a man were not *uniformly good*!"

Forgive me this digression.

My uncle went on (as my aunt told me), "That, besides his paternal estate, he was the immediate heir to very splendid fortunes: that, when he was in treaty for his niece Arabella, Lord M. told him (my uncle) what great things he and his two sisters intended to do for him, in order to qualify him for the title, which would be extinct at his lordship's death, and which they hoped to procure for him. That it was with this view that his relations were all so earnest for his marrying: that as he saw not where Mr. Lovelace could better himself; so, truly, he thought there was wealth enough in their own family to build up three considerable ones: that therefore he must needs say, he was the more desirous of this alliance, as there was a great probability, not only from Mr. Lovelace's descent, but from his fortunes, that his niece Clarissa might one day be a peeress of Great Britain: — and upon that prospect [*here was the mortifying stroke*] he should, for his own part, think it not wrong to make such dispositions as should contribute to the better support of the dignity."

My uncle Harlowe, it seems, far from disapproving of what his brother had said, declared, "That there was but one objection to an alliance with Mr. Lovelace; to wit, his faulty morals: especially as so much could be done for Miss Bella, and for my brother too, by my father, and as my brother was actually possessed of a considerable estate by virtue of the deed of gift and will of his godmother Lovell."

Had I known this before, I should the less have wondered at many things I have been unable to account for in my brother's and sister's behaviour to me; and been more on my guard than I imagined there was a necessity to be.

You may easily guess how much this conversation affected my brother at the time. He could not, you know, but be very uneasy to hear *two of his stewards* talk at this rate to his face.

He had from early days, by his violent temper, made himself both feared and courted by the whole family. My father himself, as I have lately mentioned, very often (long before my brother's acquisitions had made him still more assuming) gave way to him as to an only son who was to build up the name, and augment the honour of it. Little inducement therefore had my brother to correct a temper which gave him so much consideration with every body.

"See, sister Bella," said he, in an indecent passion before my uncles, on the occasion I have mentioned — "See how it is! — You and I ought to look about us! — This little syren is in a fair way to *out-uncle*, as she has already *out-grand-fathered* us both!"

From this time (as I now find it plain upon recollection) did my brother and sister behave to me, as to one who stood in their way; and to each other, as having but one interest: and were resolved therefore to bend all their force to hinder an alliance from taking effect, which they believed was likely to oblige them to contract their views.

And how was this to be done, after such a declaration from both my uncles?

My brother found out the way. My sister (as I have said) went hand in hand with him. Between them, the family union was broken, and every one was made uneasy. Mr. Lovelace was received more and more coldly by all: but not being to be put out of his course by slights *only*, personal affronts succeeded; defiances next; then the rencounter: that, as you have heard, did the business: and now, if I do not oblige them, my grandfather's estate is to be litigated with me; and I, who never designed to take advantage of the independency bequeathed me, *am to be as dependent upon my father's will, as a* daughter ought *to be who knows not what is good for herself.* This is the language of the family now.

But if I will suffer myself to be prevailed upon, how happy (as *they* lay it out) shall we all be! — Such presents am I to have, such jewels and I cannot tell what, from every one of the family! Then Mr. Solmes's fortunes are so great, and his proposals so very advantageous (no relation whom he values), that there will be abundant room to raise mine upon them, were the high intended favours of my own relations to be quite out of the question. Moreover, it is now, with this view, found out, that I have qualifications which of *themselves* will be a full equivalent to Mr. Solmes for the settlements he is to make; and still leave *him* under an obligation to me for my compliance. He himself thinks so, I am told — So very poor a creature is he, even in *his* own eyes as well as in *theirs.*

These desirable views answered, how rich, how splendid shall we all three be! And I — what obligations shall I lay upon them all! — And that only by doing an act of duty so suitable to my character and manner of thinking; if indeed I am the generous as well as dutiful creature I have hitherto made them believe I am.

This is the bright side that is turned to my father and uncles, to captivate *them:* but I am afraid, that my brother's and sister's design is to ruin me with them at any rate. Were it otherwise, would they not on my return from you have rather sought to *court* than *frighten* me into measures which their hearts are so much bent to carry? A method they have followed ever since.

Meantime, orders are given to all the servants to shew the highest respect to Mr. Solmes; the *generous* Mr. Solmes is now his character with some of our family! But are not these orders a tacit confession, that they think his own merit will not procure him respect? He is accordingly, in every visit he makes, not only highly caressed by the principals of our family, but obsequiously attended and cringed to by the menials. — And *the noble settlements* are echoed from every mouth.

Noble is the word used to enforce the offers of a man who is mean enough avowedly to *hate*, and wicked enough to propose to rob of their just expectations his own family (every one of which at the same time stands in too much need of his favour) in order to settle all he is worth upon me; and if I die without children, and he has none by any other marriage, upon a family which already abounds. Such are his proposals.

But were there no other motive to induce me to despise the upstart man, is not this unjust one to his family enough? — The *upstart man*, I repeat; for he was not born to the immense riches he is possessed of: riches left by one niggard to another, in injury to the next heir, because that other is a niggard. And should I not be as culpable, do you think, in my *acceptance* of such unjust settlements, as he is in the *offer* of them, if I could persuade myself to be a sharer in them, or suffer a reversionary expectation of possessing them to influence my choice?

Indeed it concerns me not a little, that my friends could be brought to *encourage* such offers on *such* motives as I think a person of conscience should not presume to begin the world with.

But this it seems is the only method that can be taken to disappoint Mr. Lovelace; and at the same time to answer all my relations have to wish for each of us. And *surely* I will not stand against such an accession to the family as may happen from marrying Mr. Solmes: since now a *possibility* is discovered (which such a grasping mind as my brother's can easily turn into a *probability*) that my grandfather's estate will revert to it, with a much more considerable one of the man's own. Instances of estates falling in, in cases far more unlikely than this, are insisted upon: and my sister says, in the words of an old saw, *it is good to be related to an estate.*

While Solmes, smiling no doubt to himself at a hope so remote, by *offers* only, obtains all their interests; and doubts not to join to his own the estate I am envied for; which for the conveniency of its situation between two of his, will it seems be of twice the value to him that it would be of to any other person; and is therefore, I doubt not, a stronger motive with him than the wife.

These, my dear, seem to me the principal inducements of my relations to espouse so vehemently as they do this man's suit. And here, once more, must I deplore the family-fault, which gives those inducements such a force as it will be difficult to resist.

And thus far, let matters with regard to Mr. Solmes and me come out as they will, my brother has succeeded in his views; that is to say, he has, in the first place, got my FATHER to make the cause his own, and to insist upon my compliance as an act of duty.

My MOTHER has never thought fit to oppose my father's will, when once he has declared himself determined.

My UNCLES, stiff, unbroken, highly-prosperous bachelors, give me leave to say (though very worthy persons in the main) have as high notions of a child's duty, as of a wife's obedience; in the last of which, my mother's meekness has confirmed them, and given them greater reason to expect the *first*.

My aunt HEAVEY (not extremely happy in her own nuptials, and perhaps under some little obligation) is got over, and chooses not to open her lips in my favour against the wills of a father and uncles so determined.

This passiveness in my mother and in my aunt, in a point so contrary to their own first judgments, is too strong a proof that my father is absolutely resolved.

Their treatment of my worthy Mrs. NORTON is a sad confirmation of it: a woman deserving of all consideration for her wisdom; and every body thinking so; but who, not being wealthy enough to have due weight in a point against which she has given her opinion, and which they seem bent upon carrying, is restrained from visiting here, and even from corresponding with me, as I am this very day informed.

Hatred to Lovelace, family-aggrandizement, and this great motive *parental authority!*—What a force *united* must they be supposed to have when *singly* each consideration is sufficient to carry all before it!

This is the formidable appearance which the address of this disagreeable man wears at present.

My BROTHER and my SISTER triumph.—*They have got me down*, as Hannah overheard them exult. And so they have (yet I never knew that I was insolently *up*); for now my brother will either lay me under an obligation to comply to my own unhappiness, and so make me an instrument of his revenge upon Lovelace; or, if I refuse, will throw me into disgrace with my whole family.

Who will wonder at the intrigues and plots carried on by undermining courtiers against one another, when a private family, but three of which can possibly have clashing interests, and one of them (as she presumes to think) above such low motives, cannot be free from them?

What at present most concerns me, is the peace of my mother's mind! How can the husband of such a wife (a *good* man too!—But oh! this prerogative of mankind!) be so *positive*, so *unpersuadeable*, to one who has brought into the family, means, which they know so well the value of, that methinks they should value her the more for *their* sake?

They do indeed value her: but I am sorry to say, she has purchased that value by her compliances; yet has merit for which she ought to be venerated; prudence which ought of itself to be conformed to in every thing.

But whither roves my pen? How dare a perverse girl take these liberties with relations so very respectable, and whom she highly respects? What an unhappy situation is that which obliges her, in her *own defence* as it were, to expose *their* failings?

But you, who know how much I love and reverence my mother, will judge what a difficulty I am under, to be obliged to oppose a scheme which *she* has engaged in. Yet I *must* oppose it (to comply is impossible); and must without delay *declare* my opposition, or my difficulties will increase; since, as I am just now informed, a lawyer has been this very day consulted [Would you have believed it?] in relation to settlements.

Were ours a Roman Catholic family, how much happier for me, that they thought a nunnery would answer all their views! — How happy, had not a certain person slighted somebody! — All then would have been probably concluded on between them before my brother had arrived to thwart the match: then had I had a sister, which now I have not; and two brothers; — both aspiring; possibly both titled: while I should only have valued that in either which is above title, that which is truly noble in both!

But by what a long-reaching selfishness is my brother governed! By what remote, exceedingly remote views! Views, which it is in the power of the slightest accident, of a fever, for instance (the seeds of which are always vegetating, as I may say, and ready to burst forth, in his own impetuous temper) or of the provoked weapon of an adversary, to blow up and destroy!

I will break off here. Let me write ever so freely of my friends, I am sure of *your* kind construction: and I confide in your discretion, that you will avoid reading to or transcribing for others, such passages as may have the appearance of treating too freely the parental, or even the fraternal character, or induce others to censure for a supposed failure in duty to the one, or decency to the other,

Your truly affectionate,
Cl. Harlowe.

LETTER XIV.

Miss Clarissa Harlowe to Miss Howe.

Thursday evening, March 2.

On Hannah's depositing my long letter (begun yesterday, but by reason of several interruptions not finished till within this hour) she found and brought me yours of this day. I thank you, my dear, for this kind expedition. These few lines will perhaps be time enough deposited to be taken away by your servant with the other letter: yet they are only to thank you, and to tell you my increasing apprehensions.

I must take or seek the occasion to apply to my mother for her mediation; for I am in danger of having a day fixed, and antipathy taken for bashfulness. — Should not sisters *be* sisters to each other? Should they not make a common cause of it, as I may say, a cause of sex, on such occasions as the present? Yet mine, in support of my brother's selfishness, and no doubt, in concert with him, has been urging in full assembly it seems (and that with an earnestness peculiar to herself when she sets upon any thing) that an absolute day be given me; and if I comply not, to be told, that it shall be to the forfeiture of all my fortunes, and of all their love.

She need not be so officious: my *brother's* interest, without hers, is strong enough; for he has found means to confederate all the family against me. Upon some fresh provocation, or new intelligence concerning Mr. Lovelace (I know not what it is) they have bound themselves, or are to bind themselves, by a signed paper, to one another (The Lord bless me, my dear, what shall I do!] to carry their point in favour of Mr. Solmes, in support of my *father's authority*, as it is called, and against Mr. Lovelace, as a libertine, and an enemy to the family: and if so, I am sure, I may say against *me*. — How impolitic in them all, to join two people in one interest, whom they wish for ever to keep asunder!

What the discharged steward reported of him is surely bad enough: what Mrs. Fortescue said, not only confirms that bad, but gives room to think him still worse: and yet the *something further* which my friends have come at of so heinous a nature (as Betty Barnes tells Hannah) that it proves him to be the worst of men. — But hang the man, I had almost said — What is he to me? What *would* he be — were not this Mr. Sol — O my dear, how I hate the man in the light he is proposed to me!

All of them at the same time are afraid of Mr. Lovelace; yet not afraid to provoke him! — How am I entangled! — to be obliged to go on corresponding with him for *their sakes* — Heaven forbid, that their persisted-in violence should so drive me, as to make it necessary for *my own!*

But surely *they* will yield — Indeed *I* cannot.

I believe the gentlest spirits when provoked (causelessly and cruelly provoked) are the most determined. The reason may be, that not taking up resolutions lightly — their very deliberation makes them the more immoveable. — And then when a point is clear and self-evident, how can one with patience think of entering into an argument or contention upon it? —

An interruption obliges me to conclude myself, in some hurry, as well as fright, what I must ever be,

Yours more than my own,
CLARISSA HARLOWE.

LETTER IV.
Miss Howe to Miss Clarissa Harlowe.

Friday, March 3.

I HAVE both your letters at once. It is very unhappy, my dear, since your friends will have you marry, that a person of your merit should be addressed by a succession of worthless creatures, who have nothing but their presumption for their excuse.

That these presumers appear not in this very unworthy light to some of your friends, is because their defects are not so striking to *them* as to *others*. — And why? shall I venture to tell you? — Because they are nearer their own standard — *Modesty*, after all, perhaps has a concern in it; for how should they think that a *niece* or *sister* of *theirs* [I will not go higher, for fear of incurring your displeasure] should be an angel?

But where indeed is the man to be found (who has the least share of due diffidence) that dares to look up to Miss Clarissa Harlowe with hope, or with any thing but wishes? Thus the bold and forward, not being sensible of their defects, aspire; while the modesty of the really worthy fills them with too much reverence to permit them to explain themselves. Hence your Symmes's, your Byron's, your Mullin's, your Wyerley's (the best of the herd) and your Solmes's, in turn, invade you — Wretches that, looking upon the rest of your family, need not despair of succeeding in an alliance with it — But, to you, what an inexcusable presumption!

Yet I am afraid all opposition will be in vain. You must, you will, I doubt, be sacrificed to this odious man. I know your family. There will be no resisting such baits as he has thrown out. O, my dear, my beloved friend! and are such charming qualities, is such exalted merit, to be sunk in such a marriage! — You must not, your uncle tells my mother, dispute their authority. AUTHORITY! what a full word is that in the mouth of a narrow-minded person, who happened to be born thirty years before one! — Of your uncles I speak; for as to the *parental* authority, that ought to be sacred — But should not parents have *reason* for what they do?

Wonder not, however, at your Bell's unsisterly behaviour in this affair: I have a particular to add to the inducements your insolent brother is governed by, which will account for all her driving. You have already owned, that her *outward eye* was from *the first* struck with the figure and address of the man whom she pretends to despise, and who, 'tis certain, thoroughly despises her: but you have not told me, that still she loves him of all men. Bell has a meanness in her very pride; that meanness rises with her pride, and goes hand in hand with it; and no one is so proud as Bell. She has owned her love, her uneasy days, and sleepless nights, and her revenge grafted upon her love, to her favourite Betty Barnes — To lay herself in the power of a servant's tongue! Poor creature! — But LIKE little souls will find one another out, and mingle, as well as LIKE great ones. This however she told the wench in strict confidence: and thus, by way of the *female round-about*, as Lovelace had the sauciness on such another occasion, in ridicule of our sex, to call it, Betty (pleased to be thought worthy of a secret, and to have an opportunity of inveighing against Lovelace's perfidy, as she would have it to be) told it to one of *her* confidants: that confidant, with like injunctions of secresy, to Miss Lloyd's Harriot — Harriot to Miss Lloyd — Miss Lloyd to *me* — I to you, with leave to make what you please of it.

And now you will not wonder to find Miss Bell an implacable rival rather than an affectionate sister; and will be able to account for the words *witchcraft*, *syren*, and such-like, thrown out against you; and for her driving on for a fixed day for sacrificing you to Solmes: in short, for her rudeness and violence of every kind.

What a sweet revenge will she take, as well upon Lovelace as upon you, if she can procure her rival sister to be married to the man that sister hates; and so prevent her having the man whom she herself loves (whether *she* have hope of him or not,) and whom she suspects her sister loves?

Poisons and poniards have often been set to work by minds inflamed by disappointed love, and actuated by revenge. — Will you wonder then, that the ties of relationship in such a case have no force, and that a sister forgets to be a sister?

Now I know this to be her secret motive (the more grating to her, as her pride is concerned to make her disavow it), and can consider it as joined with her former *envy*, and as strengthened by a brother, who has such an ascendant over the whole family; and whose interest (slave to it as he always was) engaged him to ruin you with every one: both possessed of the ears of all your family, and having it as much in their power as in their will to misrepresent all you say, all you do; such subjects also as the rencounter, and Lovelace's want of morals to expatiate upon: your whole family likewise avowedly attached to the odious man by means of the captivating proposals he has made them: — when I consider all these things, I am full of apprehensions for you. — O my dear, how will you be able to maintain your ground? — I am sure, (alas! I am *too* sure) that they will subdue such a fine spirit as yours, unused to opposition; and (*tell it not in Gath*) you *must* be Mrs. Solmes!

Meantime, it is now easy, as you will observe, to guess from what quarter the report I mentioned to you in one of my former, came, That the younger sister had robbed the elder of her lover *: for Betty whispered it at the time she whispered the rest, that neither Lovelace nor you had done honourably by *her* young mistress — How cruel, my dear, in you to rob the poor Bella of the only lover she ever had!—At the instant too that she was priding herself, that now at last she should have it in her power not only to gratify her own susceptibilities, but to give an example to the *flirts* of her sex ** (my worship's self in her eye) how to govern their man with a silken rein, and without a curb-bridle.

Upon the whole, I have now no doubt of their persevering in favour of the despicable Solmes; and of their dependence upon the gentleness of your temper, and the regard you have for their favour, and for your own reputation. And now I am more than ever convinced of the propriety of the advice I formerly gave you, to keep in your own hands the estate bequeathed to you by your grandfather. — Had you done so, it would have procured you at least an *outward* respect from your brother and sister, which would have made them conceal the envy and ill-will that now are bursting upon you from hearts so narrow.

I must harp a little more upon this string — Do not you observe how much your brother's influence has overtopped yours since he has got into fortunes so considerable, and since you have given some of them an appetite to *continue* in themselves the possession of your estate, unless you comply with their terms?

I know your dutiful, your laudable motives; and one would have thought, that you might have trusted to a father who so dearly loved you. But had you been actually in possession of that estate, and living up to it, and upon it (your youth protected from blighting tongues by the company of your prudent Norton, as you had proposed) do you think that your brother, grudging it to you at the time as he did, and looking upon it as his right as an only son, would have been practising about it, and aiming at it? I told you some time ago, that I thought your trials but proportioned to your prudence *: but you will be more than woman, if you can extricate yourself with honour, having such violent spirits and sordid minds in some, and such tyrannical and despotic wills in others, to deal with. Indeed, all *may* be done, and the world be taught further to admire you for your blind duty and will-less resignation, if you can persuade yourself to be Mrs. Solmes.

I am pleased with the instances you give me of Mr. Lovelace's benevolence to his own tenants, and with his little gift to your uncle's. Mrs. Fortescue *allows* him to be the best of landlords: I

* P. 8.   ** P. 12   * P. 8.

might have told you *that*, had I thought it necessary to put you into some little conceit of him. He has qualities, in short, that may make him a tolerable creature on the other side of fifty: but God help the poor woman to whose lot he shall fall till then! *Women*, I should say, perhaps: since he may break half a dozen hearts before that time.—But to the point I was upon — Shall we not have reason to commend the tenant's grateful honesty, if we are told, that with joy the poor man called out your uncle, and on the spot paid him in part of his debt those two guineas? — But what shall we say of that landlord, who, though he knew the poor man to be quite destitute, could take it; and, saying nothing while Mr. Lovelace staid, as soon as he was gone, tell of it in praise of the poor fellow's honesty? — Were this so, and were not that landlord related to my dearest friend, how should I despise such a wretch?—But perhaps the story is aggravated. Covetous people have every one's ill word: and so indeed they ought; because they are only solicitous to keep that which they prefer to every one's good one. — Covetous indeed would *they* be who deserved *neither*, yet expected *both!*

I long for your next letter. Continue to be as particular as possible. I can think of no other subject but what relates to you and to your affairs: for I am, and ever will be, most affectionately,

Your own
ANNA HOWE.

LETTER XVI.

Miss Clarissa Harlowe to Miss Howe.

[*Her preceding not at that time received.*]

Friday, March 3.

O MY dear friend, I have had a sad conflict! Trial upon trial; conference upon conference! — But what law, what ceremony, can give a man a right to a heart which abhors him more than it does any living creature?

I hope my mother will be able to prevail for me.—But I will recount all, though I sit up the whole night to do it; for I have a vast deal to write; and will be as minute as you wish me to be.

I concluded my last in a fright. It was occasioned by a conversation that passed between my mother and my aunt, part of which Hannah overheard. I need not give you the particulars, since what I have to relate to you from different conversations that have passed between my mother and me in the space of a very few hours, will include them all. I will begin then.

I went down this morning when breakfast was ready with a very uneasy heart, from what Hannah had informed me of yesterday afternoon; wishing for an opportunity, however, to appeal to my mother, in hopes to engage her interest in my behalf, and purposing to try to find one when she retired to her own apartment after breakfast: but, unluckily, there was the odious Solmes sitting asquat between my mother and sister, with *so much* assurance in his looks! — But you know, my dear, that those we love not, cannot do any thing to please us.

Had the wretch kept his seat, it might have been well enough: but the bent and broad-shouldered creature must needs rise, and stalk towards a chair; which was just by that which was set for me.

I removed it to a distance, as if to make way to my own; and down I sat, abruptly I believe; what I had heard all in my head.

But this was not enough to daunt him. The man is a very confident, he is a very bold, staring man! — Indeed my dear, the man is very confident!

He took the removed chair, and drew it so near mine, squatting in it with his ugly weight, that he pressed upon my hoop. — I was so offended (all I had heard, as I said, in my head) that I removed to another chair. I own I had too little command of myself. It gave my brother and sister too much advantage. I dare say they took it. But I did it involuntarily, I think. I could not help it. — I knew not what I did.

I saw that my father was excessively displeased. When angry, no man's countenance ever shews it so much as my father's. Clarissa Harlowe! said he with a big voice — and there he stopped. — Sir! said I, trembling and courtseying (for I had not then sat down again): and put my chair nearer the wretch, and sat down — my face, as I could feel, all in a glow.

Make tea, child, said my kind mamma: sit by me, love: and make tea.

I removed with pleasure to the seat the man had quitted; and being thus indulgently put into employment, soon recovered myself, and in the course of the breakfasting officiously asked two or three questions of Mr. Solmes, which I would not have done, but to make up with my father. — *Proud spirits may be brought to!* whisperingly spoke my sister to me, over her shoulder, with an air of triumph and scorn: but I did not mind her.

My mother was all kindness and condescension. I asked her once, if she were pleased with the tea? she said softly (and again called me *dear*) she was pleased with all I did. I was very proud of this encouraging goodness: and all blew over, as I hoped, between my father and me; for he also spoke kindly to me two or three times.

Small incidents these, my dear, to trouble you with; only as they lead to greater, as you shall hear.

Before the usual breakfast-time was over, my father withdrew with my mother, telling her he wanted to speak to her. Then my sister and next my aunt (who was with us) dropped away.

My brother gave himself some airs of insult, which I understood well enough; but which Mr. Solmes could make nothing of: and at last he arose from *his* seat —Sister, said he, I have a curiosity to shew you. I will fetch it. And away he went shutting the door close after him.

I saw what all this was for. I arose; the man hemming up for a speech, rising, and beginning to set his splay-feet [indeed, my dear, the man in all his ways is hateful to me] in an approaching posture. — I will save my brother the trouble of bringing to me his curiosity, said I. I courtesied — Your servant, sir — the man cried, Madam, madam, twice, and looked like a fool. — But away I went — to find my brother, to save my word — but my brother, indifferent as the weather was, was gone to walk in the garden with my sister. A plain case, that he had left his *curiosity* with me, and designed to show me no other.

I had but just got into my own apartment, and began to think of sending Hannah to beg an audience of my mother (the more encouraged by her condescending goodness at breakfast) when Shorey her woman brought me her commands to attend her in her closet.

My father, Hannah told me, was just gone out of it with a positive angry countenance. Then I as much dreaded the audience as I had wished for it before.

I went down however; but apprehending the subject she intended to talk to me upon, approached her trembling, and my heart in visible palpitations.

She saw my concern. Holding out her kind arms, as she sat, Come kiss me, my dear, said she, with a smile like a sunbeam breaking through the cloud that overshadowed her naturally benign aspect. Why flutters my jewel so?

This preparative sweetness, with her goodness just before, confirmed my apprehensions. My mother saw the bitter pill wanted gilding.

O my mamma! was all I could say; and I clasped my arms round her neck, and my face sunk into her bosom.

My child! my child! restrain, said she, your powers of moving! I dare not else trust myself with you. — And my tears trickled down her bosom, as hers bedewed my neck.

O the words of kindness, all to be expressed in vain, that flowed from her lips!

Lift up your sweet face, my best child, my own Clarissa Harlowe! — O my daughter, best beloved of my heart, lift up a face so ever amiable to me! — Why these sobs? — Is an apprehended duty so affecting a thing, that before I can speak — but I am glad, my love, you can guess at what I have to say to you. I am spared the pains of breaking to you what was a task upon me reluctantly enough undertaken *to* break to you.

Then rising, she drew a chair near her own, and made me sit down by her, overwhelmed as I was with tears of apprehension of what she had to say, and of gratitude for her truly maternal goodness to me — sobs still my only language.

And drawing her chair still nearer to mine, she put her arms round my neck, and my glowing cheek wet with tears, close to her own: Let me talk to you, my child. Since silence is your choice, hearken to me, and *be silent.*

You know, my dear, what I every day forego, and undergo, for the sake of peace. Your papa is a very good man, and means well! but he will not be controlled; nor yet persuaded. You have sometimes seemed to pity *me*, that I am obliged to give up every point. Poor man! his reputation the less for it; *mine* the greater: yet would I not have his credit, if I could help it, at so dear a rate to *him* and to *myself*. You are a dutiful, a prudent, and a *wise* child, [she was pleased to say, in hope, no doubt, to make me so]: you would not add, I am sure, to my trouble! you would not wilfully break that peace which costs your mother so much to preserve. Obedience is better than sacrifice. O my Clary Harlowe, rejoice my heart, by telling me I have apprehended too much! — I see your concern! I see your perplexity! I see your conflict [loosing her arm, and rising, not willing I should see how much she herself was affected]. I will leave you a moment. — Answer me not — [For I was essaying to speak, and had, as soon as she took her dear cheek from mine, dropt down on my knees, my hands clasped, and lifted up in a supplicating manner]. I am not prepared for your irresistible expostulation, she was pleased to say. I will leave you to recollection: and I charge you, on my blessing, that all this my truly maternal tenderness be not thrown away upon you.

And then she withdrew into the next apartment; wiping her eyes as she went from me; as mine overflowed; my heart taking in the whole compass of her meaning. She soon returned, having recovered more steadiness.

Still on my knees, I had thrown my face across the chair she had sat in.

Look up to me, my Clary Harlowe — no sullenness, I hope!

No, indeed, my ever to be revered mamma. — And I arose. I bent my knee.

She raised me. No kneeling to me, but with knees of duty and compliance. Your heart, not your knees, must bend. It is absolutely determined — prepare yourself therefore to receive your *father*, when he visits you by-and-by, as he would wish to receive *you*. But on this one quarter of an hour depends the peace of my future life, the satisfaction of all the family, and your own security from a man of violence: and I charge you *besides*, on my blessing, that you think of being Mrs. Solmes.

There went the dagger to my heart, and down I sunk: and when I recovered, found myself in the arms of my Hannah, my sister's Betty holding open my reluctantly opened palm, my laces cut, my linen scented with hartshorn; and my mother gone. Had I been *less* kindly treated, the hated name still forborne to be mentioned, or mentioned with a little more preparation and reserve, I had stood the horrid sound with less visible emotion — but to be bid, on the blessing of a mother so dearly beloved, so truly reverenced, to think of being Mrs. Solmes — what a denunciation was that!

Shorey came in with a message (delivered in her solemn way); Your mama, miss, is concerned for your disorder; she expects you down again in an hour; and bid me say, that she then hopes every thing from your duty.

I made no reply; for what could I say? And leaning upon my Hannah's arm, withdrew to my own apartment. There you will guess how the greatest part of the hour was employed.

Within that time, my mother came up to me.

I love, she was pleased to say, to come into *this* apartment! — No emotions, child! no flutters! — Am I not your mother? — am I not your fond, your indulgent mother? — do not discompose *me* by discomposing *yourself!* do not occasion *me* uneasiness, when I would give *you* nothing but pleasure. Come, my dear, we will go into your closet.

She took my hand, led the way, and made me sit down by her: and after she had inquired how I did, she began in a strain as if she had supposed I had made use of the intervening space to overcome all my objections.

She was pleased to tell me, that my father and she, in order to spare my natural modesty, had taken the whole affair upon themselves —

Hear me out; and then speak; for I was going to expostulate. You are no stranger to the end of Mr. Solmes's visits —

O madam!

Hear me out, and then speak. — He is not indeed every thing I wish him to be: but he is a man of probity, and has no vices —

No vices, madam! —

Hear me out, child — you have not behaved much amiss to him: we have seen with pleasure that you have not —

O madam, must I not now speak!

I shall have done presently — a young creature of your virtuous and *pious* turn, [she was pleased to say,] cannot surely love a profligate: you love your brother too well, to wish to marry one who had like to have killed him, and who threatened your uncles, and defies us all. You have had your own way six or seven times: we want to secure you against a man so vile. Tell me (I have a *right* to know) whether you prefer this man to all others? — Yet God forbid that I should know you do! for such a declaration would make us all miserable. Yet tell me, are your affections engaged to this man?

I knew what the inference would be, if I had said they were not.

You hesitate — you answer me not — you cannot answer me. — *Rising.* — Never more will I look upon you with an eye of favour —

O madam, madam! kill me not with your displeasure — I would not, I *need* not, hesitate one moment, did I not dread the inference, if I answer you as you wish — yet be that inference what it will, your threatened displeasure will make me speak. And I declare to you, that I know not my own heart, if it be not absolutely free. And pray, let me ask my dearest mamma, in what has my conduct been faulty, that, like a giddy creature, I must be forced to marry, to save me from — from what? Let me beseech you, madam, to be the guardian of my reputation — let not your Clarissa be precipitated into a state she wishes not to enter into with any man! and this upon a supposition that otherwise she shall marry herself, and disgrace her whole family.

Well then, Clary, [passing over the force of my plea] if your heart be free —

O my beloved mamma, let the usual generosity of your dear heart operate in my favour. Urge not upon me the inference that made me hesitate.

I won't be interrupted, Clary — you have seen in my behaviour to you, on this occasion, a truly maternal tenderness; you have observed that I have undertaken this task with some reluctance, because the man is not every thing; and because I know you carry your notions of perfection in a man too high —

Dearest madam, this one time excuse me! — Is there *then* any danger that I should be guilty of an imprudent thing for the man's sake you hint at?

Again interrupted! — am I to be questioned, and argued with? you know this won't do somewhere else. You *know* it won't. What reason, then, ungenerous girl, can you have for arguing with me thus, but because you think from my indulgence to you, you may?

What *can* I say? what *can* I do? what must that cause be that will not bear being argued upon?

Again! Clary Harlowe!

Dearest madam, forgive me: it was always my pride and my pleasure to obey you. But look upon that man — see but the disagreeableness of his person —

Now, Clary, do I see whose person you have in your eye! — Now is Mr. Solmes, I see, but *comparatively* disagreeable; disagreeable only as another man has a much more specious person.

But, madam, are not his manners equally so? — Is not his person the true representative of his mind? — That other man is not, shall not be, any thing to me, release me but from this one man, whom my heart, unbidden, resists.

Condition thus with your father. Will *he* bear, do you think, to be thus dialogued with? Have I not conjured you, as you value my peace — what is it that *I* do not give up? — This very task, because I apprehended you would not be *easily* persuaded, is a task indeed upon me. And will *you* give up nothing? Have you not refused as many as have been offered to you? If you would not have us guess for whom, comply; for comply you must, or be looked upon as in a state of defiance with your whole family.

And saying this, she arose, and went from me. But at the chamber door stopt; and turned back: I will not say below in what a disposition I leave you. Consider of every thing. The matter is resolved upon. As you value your father's blessing and mine, and the satisfaction of all the family, resolve to comply. I will leave you for a few moments. I will come up to you again. See that I find you as I wish to find you; and since *your heart is free*, let your duty govern it.

In about half an hour, my mother returned. She found me in tears. She took my hand: It is my part evermore, said she, to be of the acknowledging side. I believe I have needlessly exposed myself to your opposition, by the method I have taken with you. I first began as if I *expected* a denial and by my indulgence brought it upon myself.

Do not, my dearest mamma! do not say so!

Were the occasion for this debate, proceeded she, to have risen from myself; were it in my power to dispense with your compliance; you too well know what you can do with me.

Would any body, my dear Miss Howe, wish to marry, who sees a wife of such a temper, and blessed with such an understanding as my mother is noted for, not only deprived of all power; but obliged to be even *active* in bringing to bear points of high importance, which she thinks ought not to be insisted upon?

When I came to you a second time, proceeded she, knowing that your opposition would avail you nothing, I refused to hear your reasons: and in this I was wrong too, because a young creature who loves to reason, and *used* to love to be convinced by reason, ought to have all her objections heard: I now therefore, this third time, see you; and am come resolved to hear all you have to say: and let me, my dear, by my patience engage your gratitude; your *generosity*, I will call it; because it is to you I speak, who used to have a mind wholly generous. — Let me, if your heart *be really free*, let me see what it will induce you to do to oblige me: and so as you permit your usual discretion to govern you, I will hear all you have to say; but with this intimation, that say what you will, it will be of no avail elsewhere.

What a dreadful saying is that! but could I engage your pity, madam, it would be somewhat.

You have as much of my pity as of my love. But what is *person*, Clary, with one of your prudence, and *your heart disengaged?*

Should the eye be disgusted, when the heart is to be engaged? — O madam, who can think of marrying when the heart is shocked at the first appearance, and where the disgust must be confirmed by every conversation afterwards?

This, Clary, is owing to your prepossession. Let me not have cause to regret that noble firmness of mind in so young a creature which I thought your glory, and which was my boast in your character. In this instance it would be obstinacy, and want of duty. — Have you not made objections to several —

That was to their *minds*, to their *principles*, madam. — But this man —

Is an honest man, Clary Harlowe. He has a good mind. He is a virtuous man.

He an honest man? *His* a good mind, madam? *He* a virtuous man! —

Nobody denies him these qualities.

Can *he* be an honest man who offers terms that will rob all his own relations of their just expectations — can *his* mind be good —

You, Clary Harlowe, for whose sake he offers so much, are the last person that should make this observation.

Give me leave to say, madam, that a person preferring happiness to fortune, as I do; that want not even what I *have*, and can give up the use of *that*, as an instance of duty —

No more, no more of your merits! — You know you will be a gainer by that cheerful instance of your duty; not a loser. You know you have but *cast your bread upon the waters* — so no more of that! — For it is not understood as a merit by every body, I assure you; though I think it a high one; and so did your father and uncles at the time —

At the *time*, madam! — How unworthily do my brother and sister, who are afraid that the favour I was so lately in —

I hear nothing against your brother and sister — what family feuds have I in prospect, at a time when I hoped most comfort from you all?

God bless my brother and sister in all their *worthy* views! you shall have no family feuds, if I can prevent them. You yourself, madam, shall tell me what I shall bear from them, and I will bear it: but let *my* actions, not *their* misrepresentations (as I am sure by the disgraceful prohibitions I have met with has been the case) speak for me.

Just then, up came my father, with a sternness in his looks that made me tremble. — He took two or three turns about my chamber, though pained by his gout. — And then said to my mother, who was silent as soon as she saw him —

My dear, you are long absent. — Dinner is near ready. What you had to say, lay in a very little compass. Surely, you have nothing to do but to declare *your* will, and *my* will — but perhaps you may be talking of the preparations — let us have you soon down — your daughter in your hand, if worthy of the name.

And down he went, casting his eye upon me with a look so stern, that I was unable to say one word to him, or even for a few minutes to my mother.

Was not this very intimidating, my dear?

My mother, seeing my concern, seemed to pity me. She called me her good child, and kissed me; and told me that my father should not know I had made such opposition. He has kindly furnished us with an excuse for being so long together, said she. — Come, my dear — dinner will be upon table presently — shall we go down? — And took my hand.

This made me start: What, madam, go down to let it be supposed we were talking of *preparations!* — O my beloved mamma, command me not down upon such a supposition.

You see, child, that to stay longer together, will be owning that you are debating about an absolute duty: and that will not be borne. Did not your father himself some days ago tell you, he would be obeyed? I will a third time leave you. I must say something by way of excuse for you: and that you desire not to go down to dinner — that your modesty on the occasion —

O madam! say not my modesty on *such an* occasion: for that will be to give hope —

And design you *not* to give hope? — Perverse girl! — *Rising, and flinging from me;* take more time for consideration! — Since it is necessary, *take* more time — and when I see you next, let me know what blame I have to cast upon myself, or to bear from your father, for my indulgence to you.

She made, however, a little stop at the chamber door; and seemed to expect that I would have besought her to make the gentlest construction for me; for, hesitating, she was pleased to say, I suppose you would not have me make a report —

O madam, interrupted I, whose favour can I hope for, if I lose my mamma's?

To have desired a *favourable* report, you know, my dear, would have been qualifying upon a point that I was too much determined upon to give room for any of my friends to think I have the least hesitation about it. And so my mother went down stairs.

I will deposit thus far; and, as I know you will not think me too minute in my relation of particulars so very interesting to one you honour with your love, proceed in the same way. As matters stand, I don't care to have papers so freely written about me.

Pray let Robert call every day, if you can spare him, whether I have any thing ready or not.

I should be glad if you would not send him empty-handed. What a generosity will it be in you, to write as frequently from friendship, as I am forced to do from misfortune! the letters being taken away will be an assurance that you have them. As I shall write and deposit as I have opportunity, the formality of *super* and *sub* scription will be excused. For I need not say how much I am,

Your sincere and ever affectionate,
CL. HARLOWE.

LETTER XVII.
Miss Clarissa Harlowe to Miss Howe.

My mother on her return, which was as soon as she had dined, was pleased to inform me, that she told my father, on his questioning her about my *cheerful* compliance (for it seems, the *cheerful* was all that was doubted) that she was willing, on so material a point, to give a child whom she had so *much reason to love* (as she condescended to acknowledge were her words) liberty to say all that was in her heart to say, that her compliance might be the freer: letting him know, that when he came up, she was attending to my pleas; for that she found I had rather not marry at all.

She told me, that to this my father angrily said, Let her take care — let her take care — that she give me not ground to suspect her of a preference somewhere else. But if it be to ease *her* heart, and not to dispute *my* will, you may hear her out.

So, Clary, said my mother, I am returned in a temper accordingly: and I hope you will not again, by *your* peremptoriness, shew *me* how I ought to treat you.

Indeed, madam, you did me justice, to say, I have no inclination to marry at all. I have not, I hope, made myself so *very* unuseful in my papa's family as —

No more of your merits, Clary! you have been a good child. You have eased me of all the family cares: but do not now give me more than ever you relieved me from. You have been amply repaid in the reputation your skill and management have given you: but now there is soon to be a period to all those assistances from you. If you marry, there will be a natural, and, if to please us, a desirable period; because your own family will employ all your talents in that way: if you do not, there will be a period likewise, but *not* a natural one — you understand me, child.

I wept.

I have made inquiry already after a housekeeper. I would have had your good Norton; but I suppose you will yourself wish to have the worthy woman with you. If you desire it, that shall be agreed upon for you.

But, why, dearest madam, why am I, the *youngest*, to be precipitated into a state, that I am very far from wishing to enter into with any body?

You are going to question me, I suppose, why your sister is not thought of for Mr. Solmes?

I hope, madam, it will not displease you, if I were?

I might refer you for an answer to your *father*. — Mr. Solmes has reasons for preferring *you* —

And I have reasons, madam, for disliking *him*. And why am I—

This quickness upon me, interrupted my mother, is not to be borne! I am gone, and your father comes, if *I* can do no good with you.

O madam, I would rather die, than—

She put her hand to my mouth. — No peremptoriness, Clary Harlowe: once you declare yourself inflexible, I have done.

I wept for vexation. This is all, all, my brother's doings — his grasping views —

No reflections upon your brother: he has entirely the honour of the family at heart.

I would no more dishonour my family, madam, than my brother would.

I believe it: but I hope you will allow your father, and me, and your uncles, to judge what will do it honour, what dishonour.

I then offered to live single; never to marry at all; or never but with their full approbation.

If you mean to shew your duty, and your obedience, Clary, you must shew it in *our* way, not in *your own*.

I hope, madam, that I have not so behaved hitherto, as to render such a trial of my obedience necessary.

Yes, Clary, I cannot but say that you have hitherto behaved extremely well: but you have had no trials till now: and I hope that now you are called to one, you will not fail in it. Parents, proceeded she, when children are young, are pleased with every thing they do. You have been a good child upon the whole: but we have hitherto rather complied with you than you with us. Now that you are grown up to marriageable years, is the test; especially as your grandfather has made you independent, as we may say, in preference to those who had prior expectations upon that estate.

Madam, my grandfather knew and expressly mentioned in his will his desire, that my father will more than make it up to my sister. I did nothing but what I thought my duty to procure his favour. It was rather a mark of his affection, than any advantage to me. For, do I either seek or wish to be independent? Were I to be queen of the universe, that dignity should not absolve me from my duty to you and to my father. I would kneel for your blessings, were it in the presence of millions — so that —

I am loth to interrupt *you*, Clary; though you could more than once break in upon *me*. You are young and unbroken; but, with all this ostentation of your duty, I desire you to shew a little more deference to me when I am speaking.

I beg your pardon, dear madam, and your patience with me on *such* an occasion as *this*. If I did not speak with earnestness upon it, I should be supposed to have only maidenly objections against a man I never can endure.

Clary Harlowe!

Dearest, dearest madam, permit me to speak what I have to

say this once — It is hard, it is very hard, to be forbidden to enter into the cause of all these misunderstandings, because I must not speak disrespectfully of one who supposes me in the way of his ambition, and treats me like a slave—

Whither, whither, Clary—

My dearest mamma! — My duty will not permit me so far to suppose my father arbitrary, as to make a plea of that arbitrariness to you —

How now, Clary! — O girl! —

Your patience, my dearest mamma: you were pleased to *say*, you would bear me with patience. — PERSON in a man is nothing, because I am supposed to be prudent: so my eye is to be disgusted, and my reason not convinced —

Girl, girl!

Thus are my imputed good qualities to be made my punishment; and I am to be wedded to a *monster* —

[Astonishing! — Can this, Clarissa, be from you?

The man, madam, person and mind, is a monster in my eye.] — And that I may be induced to bear this treatment, I am to be complimented with being indifferent to all men: yet, at other times, and to serve other purposes, be thought prepossessed in favour of a man against whose moral character lie *just* objections. — Confined, as if, like the giddiest of creatures, I would run away with this man, and disgrace my whole family! — O my dearest mamma! who can be patient under such treatment?

Now, Clary, I suppose you will allow *me* to speak. I think I have had patience *indeed* with you. — Could I have thought — but I will put all upon a short issue. Your *mother*, Clarissa, shall shew you an example of that patience you so boldly claim from *her*, without having *any yourself*.

O my dear, how my mother's condescension distressed me at the time! — Infinitely more distressed me than rigour could have done. But she *knew*, she was to be sure *aware*, that she was put upon a harsh, upon an *unreasonable* service, let me say, or she would not, she could not, have had so much patience with me.

Let me tell you then, proceeded she, that all lies in a small compass, as your father said. — You have been hitherto, as you are pretty ready to plead, a dutiful child. You have indeed had no *cause* to be otherwise. No child was ever more favoured. Whether you will discredit all your past behaviour; whether, at a time and upon an occasion, that the highest instance of duty is expected from you (an instance that is to crown all); and when you declare that *your heart is free* — you will give that instance; or whether, having a view to the independence you may claim (for so, Clary, whatever be your motive, it will be judged) and which any man you favour, can assert *for you against* us all; or rather *for himself* in spite of us — whether, I say, you will break with us all; and stand in defiance of a jealous father, needlessly jealous, I will venture to say, of the perogatives of his sex, as to me, and still ten times more jealous of the authority of a father; — this is now the point with us. You know your father has made it a point; and did he ever give up one, he thought he had a right to carry?

Too true, thought I to myself! And now my brother has engaged my father, his fine scheme will *walk alone*, without needing his leading-strings; and it is become my *father's will* that I oppose; not my brother's grasping views.

I was silent. To say the truth, I was just then *sullenly* silent. My heart was too big. I thought it was hard to be thus given up by my mother; and that she should make a will so uncontroulable as my brother's, her will. — My mother, my dear, though I must not say so, was not obliged to marry against *her* liking. My mother loved my father.

My silence availed me still less.

I see, my dear, said she, that you are convinced. Now, my good child, now, my Clary, do I love you! It shall not be known, that you have argued with me at all. All shall be imputed to that modesty which has ever so much distinguished you. You shall have the full merit of your resignation.

I wept.

She tenderly wiped the tears from my eyes, and kissed my cheek — Your father expects you down with a cheerful countenance — but I will excuse your going.

All your scruples, you see, have met with an indulgence truly maternal from me. I rejoice in the hope that you are convinced. This indeed seems to be a proof of the truth of your agreeable declaration, that *your heart is free.*

Did not this seem to border upon *cruelty*, my dear, in so indulgent a mother? — It would be wicked [would it not] to suppose my mother capable of *art?* — But she is put upon it; and obliged to take methods to which her heart is naturally above stooping; and all intended for my good, because she sees that no arguing will be admitted any where else.

I will go down, proceeded she, and excuse your attendance at afternoon tea, as I did to dinner: for I know you will have some little reluctances to subdue. I will allow you those; and also some little natural shynesses — And so you *shall not* come down, if you choose *not* to come down — Only, my dear, do not disgrace my report when you come to supper. And be sure behave as you used to do to your brother and sister; for your behaviour to them will be one test of your cheerful obedience to us. I advise as a friend, you see rather than command as a mother — So adieu, my love. And again she kissed me, and was going.

O my dear mamma, said I, forgive me! — But surely you cannot believe, I can ever think of having that man!

She was very angry, and seemed to be greatly disappointed. She threatened to turn me over to my father and my uncles. — She however bid me (generously bid me) consider, what a handle I gave to my brother and sister, if I thought they had views to serve by making my uncles dissatisfied with me.

I, said she, in a milder accent, have early said all that I thought could be said against the present proposal, on a supposition, that you, who have refused several others (whom I own to be preferable as to person) would *not* approve of it and could I have succeeded, you, Clary, had never heard of it. But if *I* could not, how can *you* expect to prevail? My great ends, in the task I have undertaken, are the preservation of the family peace, so likely to be overturned; to reinstate you in the affections of your father and uncles: and to preserve you from a man of violence. — Your father, you must needs think, will flame out, upon your refusal to comply: your uncles are so thoroughly convinced of the consistency of the measure with their favorite views of aggrandizing the family that they are as much determined as your father — Your aunt Hervey and your uncle Hervey are of the same party. And it is hard, if a father and mother, and uncles and aunt, all conjoined, cannot be allowed to direct your choice — Surely, my dear girl, proceeded she (for I was silent all this time) it cannot be, that you are the *more* averse because the *family views* will be promoted by the match — This, I assure you, is what every body must think, if you comply not. Nor, while the man so obnoxious to us all remains unmarried, and *buzzes* about you, will the strongest asseverations you can make of your resolution and wishes to live single, be in the least regarded. And well you know, that were Mr. Lovelace an angel, and your father had made it a point that you should not have him, it would be in vain to dispute his will. As to the probibition laid upon you (much as I will own against *my* liking) that is owing to the belief that you corresponded by Miss Howe's means with that man; nor do I doubt that you did so.

I answered to every article, in such a manner as I am sure would have satisfied her, could she have been permitted to judge for herself; and I then inveighed with bitterness against the disgraceful prohibitions laid upon me.

They would serve to shew me, she replied, how much in earnest my father was. They might be taken off, whenever I thought fit, and no harm done, nor disgrace received. But if I were to be contumacious, I might thank myself for all that would follow.

I sighed. I wept. I was silent.

Shall I, Clary, said she, shall I tell your father that these prohibitions are as unneccessary as I hoped they would be? That you know your *duty*, and will not offer to controvert his will? What say you, my love?

O madam, what can I say to questions so indulgently put? — I do indeed *know* my duty: no creature in the world is more willing to *practise* it: but, pardon me, dearest madam, if I say, that I must bear these prohibitions, if I am to pay so dear to have them taken off.

Determined and perverse, my dear mamma called me: and after walking twice or thrice in anger about the room, she turned to me; — Your heart *free*, Clarissa! How can you tell me your heart is free? Such extraordinary antipathies to a particular person must be owing to extraordinary prepossessions in another's favour! — Tell me, Clary; and tell me truly — Do you not continue to correspond with Mr. Lovelace?

Dearest madam, replied I, you know my motives: to prevent mischief I answered his letters. The reasons for our apprehensions of this sort are not over.

I own to you, Clary (although now I would not have it known) that I once thought a little qualifying among such violent spirits was not amiss. I did not know but all things would come round again by the mediation of Lord M. and his two sisters: but as they all three think proper to resent for their nephew; and as their nephew thinks fit to defy us all; and as terms are offered on the other hand, that could not be asked, which will very probably prevent your grandfather's estate going out of the family, and may be a means to bring a still greater into it; I see not, that the continuance of your correspondence with him either can or ought to be permitted. I therefore now forbid it to you, as you value my favour.

Be pleased, madam, only to advise me how to break it off with safety to my brother and uncles; and it is all I wish for. Would to heaven, the man so hated had not the pretence to make of having been too violently treated, when he meant peace and reconciliation! It would always have been in my own power to have broke with him. His reputed immoralities would have given me a just pretence at any time to do so. — But, madam, as my uncles and my brother will keep no measures; as he has heard what the view is; and as I have reason to think, that he is only restrained by his regard for me from resenting their violent treatment of him and his family; what can I do? Would you have me, madam, make him desperate?

The law will protect us, child! Offended magistracy will assert itself —

But, madam, may not some dreadful mischief first happen? — The law asserts not itself till it *is* offended.

You have made offers, Clary, if you might be obliged in the point in question — Are you really in earnest, were you to be complied with, to break off all correspondence with Mr. Lovelace? — Let me know this.

Indeed I am; and I will. You, madam, shall see all the letters that have passed between us. You shall see I have given him no encouragement independent of my duty. And when you have seen them, you will be better able to direct me how, on the condition I have offered, to break entirely with him.

I take you at your word, Clarissa — Give me *his* letters; and the copies of *yours*.

I am sure, madam, you will keep the knowledge that I write, and what I write —

No conditions with your mother — surely my prudence may be trusted to.

I begged her pardon; and besought her to take the key of the private drawer in my escritoir, where they lay, that she herself might see, that I had no reserves to my mother.

She did; and took all his letters, and the copies of mine. — Unconditioned with, she was pleased to say; they shall be yours again, unseen by any body else.

I thanked her; and she withdrew to read them; saying, she would return them, when she had.

You, my dear, have seen all the letters that passed between Mr. Lovelace and me, till my last return from you. You have acknowledged, that he has nothing to boast of from them. Three others I have received since, by the private conveyance *I told you of:* the last I have not yet answered.

In these three, as in those you have seen, after having besought my favour, and, in the most earnest manner, professed the ardour of his passion for me; and set forth the indignities done him; the defiances my brother throws out against him in all companies; the menaces, and hostile appearance of my uncles wherever they go; and the methods they take to defame him; he declares, "That neither his own honour, nor the honour of his family (involved as that is in the undistinguishing reflections cast upon him for an unhappy affair which he would have shunned, but could not) permit him to bear these confirmed indignities: that as my inclinations, if not favourable to *him*, cannot be, nor are, to such a man as the newly introduced Solmes, he is interested the more to resent my brother's behaviour; who to every body avows his rancour and malice; and glories in the probability he has, through the address of this Solmes, of mortifying *me*, and avenging himself on *him:* that it is impossible, he should not think himself concerned to frustrate a measure so directly levelled at him, had he not a still higher motive for hoping to frustrate it: that I must forgive him, if he enter into conference with Solmes upon it. He earnestly insists (upon what he has so often proposed) that I will give him leave, in company with my Lord M. to wait upon my uncles, and even upon my father — and he promises patience, if new provocations, absolutely beneath a man to bear, be not given:" which by the way I am far from being able to engage for.

In my answer, I absolutely declare, as I tell him I have often done, "That he is to expect no favour from me against the approbation of my friends: that I am sure their consents for his visiting any of them will never be obtained: that I will not be either so undutiful, or so indiscreet, as to suffer my interests to be separated from the interests of my family, for any man upon earth: that I do not think myself *obliged* to him for the forbearance I desire one flaming spirit to have with others: that in this desire I require nothing of him, but what prudence, justice, and the laws of his country require: that if he has any expectations of favour from me, on that account, he deceives himself; that I have no inclination, as I have often told him, to change my condition: that I cannot allow myself to correspond with him any longer in this clandestine manner: it is mean, low, undutiful, I tell him; and has a giddy appearance, which cannot be excused: that therefore he is not to expect I *will* continue it."

To this, in his last, among other things, he replies, "That if I am actually determined to break off all correspondence with him, he must conclude, that it is with a view to become the wife of a man, whom no woman of honour and fortune can think tolerable. And in that case, I must excuse him for saying, that he shall neither be able to bear the thoughts of losing for ever a person in whom all his present and all his future hopes are centered; nor support himself with patience under the insolent triumphs of my brother upon it. But that nevertheless, he will not threaten either his own life, or that of any other man. He must take his resolutions as such a dreaded event shall impel him, at the time. If he shall know that it will have my consent, he must endeavour to resign to his destiny; but if it be brought about by compulsion, he shall not be able to answer for the consequence.

I will send you these letters for your perusal in a few days. I would inclose them; but that it is possible something may happen, which may make my mother require to re-peruse them — When you see them, you will perceive how he endeavours to hold me to this correspondence.

* * *

In about an hour my mother returned. Take your letters, Clary: I have nothing, she was pleased to say, to tax your discretion with, as to the wording of yours to him: you have even kept up a proper dignity, as well as observed all the rules of decorum; and you have resented, as you ought to resent, his menacing invectives. In a word, I see not that he can form the least expectations from what you have written, that you will encourage the passion he avows for you. But does he not avow his passion? Have you the least doubt about what must be the issue of this correspondence, if continued? And do you yourself think, when you know the avowed hatred of one side, and the declared defiances of the other, that this *can* be, that it *ought to be* a match?

By no means it can, madam; you will be pleased to observe, that I have said as much to him. But now, madam, that the whole correspondence is before you, I beg your commands what to do in a situation so very disagreeable.

One thing I will tell you, Clary — But I charge you, as you would not have me question the generosity of your spirit, to take no advantage of it, either *mentally* or *verbally*; that I am so much pleased with the offer of your keys to me, made in so cheerful and unreserved a manner, and in the prudence you have shewn in your letters, that were it practicable to bring every one, or your father only, into my opinion, I should readily leave all the rest to your discretion, reserving only to myself the direction or approbation of your future letters; and to see, that you broke off the correspondence as soon as possible. But as it is not, and as I know your father would have no patience with you, should it be acknowledged that you correspond with Mr. Lovelace, or that you *have* corresponded with him since the time he prohibited you so to do; I forbid you to continue such a liberty — Yet, as the case is difficult, let me ask you, what you yourself can propose? Your heart, you *say*, is *free*: you own, that you cannot think, as matters are circumstanced, that a match with a man so obnoxious as he now is to us all, is proper to be thought of: what do you propose to do? — What, Clary, are your own thoughts of the matter?

Without hesitation thus I answered — What I humbly propose is this: "That I will write to Mr. Lovelace (for I have not answered his last) that he has nothing to do between my father and me: that I neither *ask* his advice, nor *need* it: but that since he thinks he has some pretence for interfering, because of my brother's avowal of the interest of Mr. Solmes, in displeasure to him, I will assure him (without giving him any reason to impute the assurance to be in the least favourable to himself) that I never will be that man's. And if," proceeded I, "I may be permitted to give him this assurance; and Mr. Solmes, in consequence of it, be discouraged from prosecuting his address; let Mr. Lovelace be satisfied or dissatisfied, I will go no further; nor write another line to him; nor ever see him more, if I can avoid it: and I shall have a good excuse for it, without bringing in any of my family."

Ah! my love! — But what shall we do about the *terms* Mr. Solmes offers? Those are the inducements with every body. He has even given hopes to your brother that he will make exchanges of estates; or at least, that he will purchase the northern one; for you know it must be entirely consistent with the family views, that we increase our interest in this county. Your brother, in short, has given in a plan that captivates us all: and a family so rich in all its branches, and that has its

6*

views to honour, must be pleased to see a very great probability of taking rank one day among the principal in the kingdom.

And for the sake of these views, for the sake of this plan of my brother's, am I, madam, to be given in marriage to a man I never can endure! — O my dear mamma, save me, save me, if you can, from this heavy evil. — I had rather be buried alive, indeed I had, than have that man.

She chid me for my vehemence; but was so good as to tell me, that she would sound my uncle Harlowe, who was then below; and if he encouraged her (or would engage to second her) she would venture to talk to my father herself; and I should hear further in the morning.

She went down to tea, and kindly undertook to excuse my attendance at supper.

But is it not a sad thing, I repeat, to be obliged to stand in opposition to the will of such a mother? Why, as I often say to myself, was such a man as this Solmes fixed upon? The only man in the world, surely, that could offer so much, and deserve so little!

Little indeed does he deserve! — Why, my dear, the man has the most indifferent of characters. Every mouth is opened against him for his sordid ways — A foolish man, to be so base-minded! — when the difference between the obtaining of a fame for generosity, and incurring the censure of being a miser, will not, prudently managed, cost fifty pounds a year!

What a name have you got, at a less expense! and what an opportunity had he of obtaining credit at a very small one, succeeding such a wretched creature as Sir Oliver, in fortunes so vast! — Yet has he so behaved, that the common phrase is applied to him, *That Sir Oliver will never be dead while Mr. Solmes lives.*

The world, as I have often thought, ill-natured as it is said to be, is generally more just in characters (speaking by what it *feels*) than is usually apprehended: and those who complain most of its censoriousness, perhaps should look *inwardly* for the occasion oftener than they do.

My heart is a little at ease, on the hopes that my mother will be able to procure favour for me, and a deliverance from this man; and so I have leisure to moralize. But if I had *not*, I should not forbear to intermingle occasionally these sort of remarks, because you command me never to omit them when they occur to my mind: and not to be able to make them, even in a more affecting situation, when one sits down to write, would shew one's-self more engaged to *self*, and to one's *own* concerns, than attentive to the wishes of a friend. If it be said, that it is *natural* so to be, what makes that *nature*, on occasions where a friend may be obliged, or reminded of a piece of instruction, which (writing down) one's self may be the better for, but a *fault;* which it would set a person above nature to subdue?

LETTER XVIII.
Miss Clarissa Harlowe to Miss Howe.
Sat. March 4.

Would you not have thought that something might have been obtained in my favour, from an offer so reasonable, from an expedient so proper, as I imagine, to put a tolerable end, as *from myself,* to a correspondence I hardly know how otherwise, with safety to some of my family, to get rid of? — But my brother's plan (which my mother spoke of, and of which I have in vain endeavoured to procure a copy, with a design to take it to pieces, and expose it, as I question not there is room to do) joined with my father's impatience of contradiction, are irresistible.

I have not been in bed all night; nor am I in the least drowsy. Expectation, and hope, and doubt (an uneasy state!) kept me sufficiently wakeful. I stepped down at my usual time, that it might not be known I had not been in bed; and gave directions in the family way.

About eight o'clock Shorey came to me from my mother, with orders to attend her in her chamber.

My mother had been weeping, I saw by her eyes: but her aspect seemed to be less tender, and less affectionate, than the day before; and this, as soon as I entered into her presence, struck me with an awe which gave a great damp to my spirits.

Sit down, Clary Harlowe; I shall talk to you by-and-by: and continued looking into a drawer among laces and linen, in a way neither busy nor unbusy.

I believe it was a quarter of an hour before she spoke to me (my heart throbbing with the suspense all the time); and then she asked me coldly what directions I had given for the day?

I shewed her the bill of fare for this day, and to-morrow, if, I said, it pleased her to approve of it.

She made a small alteration in it; but with an air so cold and so solemn, as added to my emotions.

Mr. Harlowe talks of dining out to-day, I think, at my brother Antony's —

Mr. Harlowe! — Not my father! — Have I not then a father? — thought I.

Sit down when I bid you.

I sat down.

You look very sullen, Clary.

I hope not, madam.

If children would always be children — parents — and there she stopped.

She then went to her toilette, and looked in the glass, and gave half a sigh — The other half, as if she would not have sighed could she have helped it, she gently hemmed away.

I don't love to see the girl look so sullen.

Indeed, madam, I am not sullen. — And I arose, and turning from her, drew out my handkerchief; for the tears ran down my cheeks.

I thought, by the glass before me, I saw the *mother* in her softened eye cast towards me: but her words confirmed not the hoped-for tenderness.

One of the most provoking things in the world is, to have people cry for what they can help!

I wish to heaven I could, madam! — and I sobbed.

Tears of penitence and sobs of perverseness are mighty well suited! — You may go up to your chamber. I shall talk with you by-and-by.

I courtesied with reverence.

Mock me not with outward gestures of respect. The heart, Clary, is what I want.

Indeed, madam, you have it. It is not so much mine as my mamma's!

Fine talking! — as somebody says, If words were to pass for duty, Clarissa Harlowe would be the most dutiful child breathing.

God bless that somebody! — be it whom it will, God bless that somebody! — And I courtesied, and pursuant to her last command, was going.

She seemed struck; but was to be angry with me.

So turning from me, she spoke with quickness, Whither now, Clary Harlowe?

You commanded me, madam, to go to my chamber.

I see you are very ready to go out of my presence. — Is your compliance the effect of sullenness, or obedience? — You are very ready to leave me.

I could hold no longer! but threw myself at her feet: O my dearest mamma! Let me know all I am to suffer! Let me know what I am to be! — I *will* bear it, if I *can* bear it: but your displeasure I cannot bear!

Leave me, leave me, Clary Harlowe!—No kneeling!— Limbs so supple; will so stubborn! — Rise, I tell you.

I cannot rise! I will disobey my mamma, when she bids me leave her without being reconciled to me! No sullens, my mamma: no perverseness: but, worse than either: this is direct disobedience! — Yet tear not yourself from me! [wrapping my arms about her as I kneeled: she struggling to get from me; my face lifted up to hers, with eyes running over, that spoke not my heart if they were not all humility and reverence.] You must not, must not, tear yourself from me! [for still the dear lady struggled, and looked this way and that, in a sweet disorder, as if she knew not what to do.] — I will never rise, nor leave you, nor let you go, till you say you are not angry with me.

O thou ever moving child of my heart! [folding her dear arms about my neck, as mine embraced her knees] Why was this task — but leave me! — You have discomposed me beyond expression! Leave me, my dear! — I won't be angry with you — if I can help it — if you will be good.

I arose trembling, and hardly knowing what I did, or how I stood or walked, withdrew to my chamber. My Hannah followed me as soon as she heard me quit my mother's presence, and with salts and spring-water just kept me from fainting; and that was as much as she could do. It was near two hours before I could so far recover myself as to take up my pen, to write to you how unhappily my hopes have ended.

My mother went down to breakfast. I was not fit to appear: but if I had been better, I suppose I should not have been sent for; since the permission for my attending her down, was given by my father (when in my chamber) only on condition that she found me *worthy of the name of daughter.* That, I doubt, I never shall be in *his* opinion, if he be not brought to change his mind as to this Mr. Solmes.

LETTER XIX.

Miss Clarissa Harlowe to Miss Howe.

In answer to Letter XV.

Sat. March 4, 12 o'clock.

Hannah has just now brought me from the usual place your favour of yesterday. The contents of it have made me very thoughtful; and you will have an answer in my gravest style. *I* to have that Mr. Solmes! — No indeed! — I will sooner — But I will write first to those passages in your letter which are less concerning, that I may touch upon this part with more patience.

As to what you mention of my sister's value for Mr. Lovelace, I am not very much surprised at it. She takes such *officious* pains, and it is so much her subject, to have it thought that she never *did,* and never *could* like him, that she gives but too much room to suspect that she does. She never tells the story of their parting, and of her refusal of him, but her colour rises, she looks with disdain upon me, and mingles anger with the airs she gives herself: anger as well as airs, demonstrating, that she refused a man whom she thought worth accepting: where else is the reason either for anger or boast? — Poor Bella! she is to be pitied — she cannot either like or dislike with temper! — Would to heaven she had been mistress of all her wishes! — would to heaven she had!

As to what you say of my giving up to my father's control the estate devised me, my motives at the time, as you acknowledge, were not blameable. Your advice to me on the subject was grounded, as I remember, on your good opinion of me; believing that I should not make a bad use of the power willed me: neither you nor I, my dear, although you now assume the air of a diviner, [pardon me] could have believed *that* would have happened which has happened, as to my *father's* part particularly. You were indeed jealous of my brother's views *against me*; or rather of his predominant love of *himself*; but I did not think so hardly of my brother and sister as you always did. You never loved them; and ill-will has eyes ever open to the faulty side; as goodwill or love is blind even to real imperfections. I will briefly recollect my motives.

I found jealousies and uneasiness arising in every breast, where all before was unity and love: the honoured testator was reflected upon: a second childhood was attributed to him; and I was censured, as having taken advantage of it. All young creatures, thought I, more or less, covet independency; but those who wish most for it, are seldom the fittest to be trusted either with the government of themselves, or with power over others. This is certainly a very high and unusual devise to so young a creature. We should not aim at *all* we have power to do. To take all that good-nature, or indulgence, or good opinion confers, shews a want of moderation, and a graspingness that is unworthy of that indulgence; and are bad indications of the use that may be made of the power bequeathed. It is true, thought I, that I have formed agreeable schemes of making others as happy as myself, by the proper discharge of the stewardship entrusted to me, [Are not all estates stewardships, my dear?] But let me examine myself: is not vanity, or secret love of praise, a principal motive with me at the bottom? — Ought I not to suspect my own heart? If I set up for myself, puffed up with every one's good opinion, may I not be *left* to myself? — Every one's eyes are upon the conduct, upon the visits, upon the visitors, of a young creature of our sex, made independent: and are not such subjected, more than any others, to the attempts of enterprisers and fortune-seekers? — And then, left to myself, should I take a wrong step, though with ever so good an intention, how many should I have to triumph over me, how few to pity me! — The more of the one, and the fewer of the other, for having aimed at excelling.

These were some of my reflections at the time: and I have no doubt, but that in the same situation I should do the very same thing; and that upon the maturest deliberation. Who can command or foresee events? To act up to our best judgments at the time, is all we can do. If I have erred, 'tis to worldly wisdom only that I have erred. If we suffer by an act of duty, or even by an act of generosity, is it not pleasurable on reflection, that the fault is in others, rather than in ourselves? — I had much rather have reason to think others unkind, than that they should have any to think me undutiful.

And so, my dear, I am sure had you.

And now for the *most* concerning part of your letter.

You think I must of necessity, as matters are circumstanced, be Solmes's wife. I will not be very rash, my dear, in protesting to the contrary: but I think it never can, and, what is still more, never *ought* to be! — My temper, I know, is depended upon. But I have heretofore said*, that I have some-

* See Letter lx. p. 39.

thing in me of my father's family, as well as of my mother's. And have I any encouragement to follow too implicitly the example which my mother sets of meekness, and resignedness to the wills of others? Is she not for ever obliged (as she was pleased to hint to me) to be of the *forbearing* side? In my mother's case, your observation, I must own, is verified, that those who will bear much, shall have much to bear*. What is it, as she says, that *she* has not sacrificed to peace? — Yet, has *she* by her sacrifices always found the peace she has deserved to find? Indeed no! — I am afraid the very contrary. And often, and often have I had reason (on her account) to reflect, that we poor mortals, by our over-solicitude to preserve undisturbed the qualities we are *constitutionally* fond of, frequently lose the benefits we propose to ourselves from them: since the designing and encroaching (finding out what we most fear to forfeit) direct their batteries against these our weaker places, and, making an artillery (if I may so phrase it) of our *hopes* and *fears*, play it upon us at their pleasure.

Steadiness of mind, (a quality which the ill-bred and censorious deny to any of our sex) when we are absolutely convinced of being in the right, [otherwise it is not *steadiness*, but *obstinacy*] and when it is exerted in *material* cases, is a quality, which, as my good Dr. Lewen was wont to say, brings great credit to the possessor of it; at the same time that it usually, when *tried* and *known*, raises *such* above the attempts of the meanly machinating. He used therefore to inculcate upon me this steadiness, upon laudable convictions. And why may I not think that I am now put upon a proper exercise of it?

I said above, that I never can be, that I never *ought* to be Mrs. Solmes. — I repeat that I *ought* not: for, surely, my dear, I should not give up to my brother's ambition the happiness of my future life. Surely I ought not to be the instrument of depriving Mr. Solmes's relations of their natural rights and reversionary prospects, for the sake of further aggrandizing a family (although *that* I am of) which already lives in great affluence and splendour; and which might be as justly dissatisfied were all that some of it aim at, to be obtained, that they were not princes, as now they are, that they are not peers [for whenever was an ambitious mind, as you observe in the case of avarice*, satisfied by acquisition?] The less, surely, ought I to give in to these grasping views of my brother, as I myself heartily despise the end aimed at; as I wish not either to change my state, or better my fortunes; and as I am fully persuaded that happiness and riches are *two* things, and very seldom meet together.

Yet I dread, I exceedingly dread, the conflicts I know I must encounter with. It is possible,

* P. 44.

* See Letter x. p. 42.

that I may be more unhappy from the due observation of the good doctor's general precept, than were I to yield the point: since what I call *steadiness* is deemed stubbornness, obstinacy, prepossession, by those who have a right to put what interpretation they please upon my conduct.

So, my dear, were we perfect (which no one can be) we could not be happy in this life, unless those with whom we have to deal (those more especially who have any control upon us) were governed by the same principles. But then does not the good doctor's conclusion recur,—that we have nothing to do, but to choose what is right; to be steady in the pursuit of it; and to leave the issue to Providence?

This, if you approve of my motives (and if you don't, pray inform me), must be my aim in the present case.

But what then can I plead for a palliation to *myself* of my mother's sufferings on *my* account? Perhaps this consideration will carry some force with it — that *her* difficulties cannot last long; only till this great struggle shall be one way or other determined — whereas *my* unhappiness, if I comply, will (from an aversion not to be overcome) be for life. To which let me add, that as I have reason to think, that the present measures are not entered upon with her own natural liking, she will have the less pain, should they want the success which I think in my heart they ought to want

I have run a great length in a very little time. The subject touched me to the quick. My reflections upon it will give you reason to expect from me a perhaps *too* steady behaviour in a new conference, which, I find, I must have with my mother. My father and brother, as she told me, dine at my uncle Antony's; and that, as I have reason to believe, on purpose to give an opportunity for it.

Hannah informs me, that she heard my father high and angry with my mother, at taking leave of her: I suppose for being too favourable to me; for Hannah heard her say, as in tears, "Indeed, Mr. Harlowe, you greatly distress me! — The poor girl does not deserve —" Hannah heard no more, but that he said, he would break somebody's heart — Mine, I suppose — Not my mother's, I hope.

As only my sister dines with my mother, I thought I should have been commanded down: but she sent me up a plate from her table. I continued my writing. I could not touch a morsel. I ordered Hannah, however, to eat of it, that I might not be thought sullen.

Before I conclude this, I will see whether any thing offers from *either* of my private correspondencies, that will make it proper to add to it; and will take a turn in the wood-yard and garden for that purpose.

* * *

I am stopped. Hannah shall deposit this. She was ordered by

my mother (who asked where I was) to tell me, that she would come up and talk with me in my own closet. — She is coming! Adieu, my dear.

LETTER XX.
Miss Clarissa Harlowe to Miss Howe.

Sat. afternoon.

THE expected conference is over: but my difficulties are increased. This, as my mother was pleased to tell me, being the last *persuasory* effort that is to be attempted, I will be as particular in the account of it as my head and my heart will allow me to be.

I have made, said she, as she entered my room, a *short* as well as *early* dinner, on purpose to confer with you: and I do assure you, that it will be the last conference I shall either be permitted or *inclined* to hold with you on the subject, if you should prove as refractory as it is imagined you will prove by some, who are of opinion, that I have not the weight with you which my indulgence deserves. But I hope you will convince as well them as me of the contrary.

Your father both dines and sups at your uncle's, on purpose to give us this opportunity; and according to the report I shall make on his return (which I have promised shall be a very faithful one,) he will take his measures with you.

I was offering to speak — Hear, Clarissa, what I have to tell you, said she, before you speak, unless what you have to say will signify to me your compliance — Say — *Will it?* — If it *will*, you may speak.

I was silent.

She looked with concern and anger upon me — No compliance, I find! — Such a dutiful young creature hitherto! — Will you not, *can* you not, speak as I would have you speak? — Then [rejecting me as it were with her hand] continue silent. — I, no more than your *father*, will bear your *avowed* contradiction.

She paused with a look of expectation, as if she waited for my consenting answer.

I was still silent; looking down; the tears in my eyes.

O thou determined girl! — But say — speak out — Are you resolved to stand in opposition to us all, in a point our hearts are set upon?

May I, madam, be permitted to expostulate? —

To what purpose expostulate with *me*, Clarissa? Your *father* is determined. Have I not told you there is no receding; that the honour as well as the interest of the family is concerned? Be ingenuous: you *used* to be so, even occasionally against yourself: — Who at the long-run *must* submit — *all* of us to *you*; or *you* to *all* of us? If you intend to yield at *last* if you find you cannot conquer, yield *now*, and with a grace — for yield you must, or be none of our child.

I wept. I knew not what to say;

or rather how to express what I had to say.

Take notice, that there are flaws in your grandfather's will: not a shilling of that estate will be yours, if you do not yield. Your grandfather left it to you, as a reward of your duty to *him* and to *us*—You will *justly* forfeit it if—

Permit me, good madam, to say, that if it were *unjustly* bequeathed me, I ought not to wish to have it. But I hope Mr. Solmes will be apprised of these flaws.

This is very pertly said, Clarissa: but reflect, that the forfeiture of that estate through your opposition will be attended with the total loss of your father's favour: and then how destitute must you be: how unable to support yourself; and how many benevolent designs and good actions must you give up!

I must accommodate myself, madam, in the latter case, to my circumstances; *much* only is *required* where *much* is *given*. It becomes me to be thankful for what I have had. I have reason to bless you, madam, and my good Mrs. Norton, for bringing me up to be satisfied with little; with much less, I will venture to say, than my father's indulgence annually confers upon me.—And then I thought of the old Roman and his lentils.

What perverseness! said my mother.—But if you depend upon the favour of either or both of your uncles, vain will be that dependence: *they* will give you up, I do assure you, if your father does, and absolutely renounce you.

I am sorry, madam, that I have had so little merit as to have made no deeper impressions of favour for me in their hearts: but I will love and honour them as long as I live.

All this, Clarissa, makes your prepossession in a certain man's favour the more evident. Indeed your brother and sister cannot go any-whither, but they hear of these prepossessions.

It is a great grief to me, madam, to be made the subject of the public talk: but I hope you will have the goodness to excuse me for observing that the authors of my disgrace within-doors, the talkers of my prepossession without, and the reporters of it from abroad, are originally the same persons.

She severely chid me for this.

I received her rebukes in silence.

You are sullen, Clarissa: I see you are *sullen*.—And she walked about the room in anger. Then turning to me—You can *bear* the imputation of sullenness I see!—You have no concern to clear yourself of it. I was afraid of telling you all I was enjoined to tell you, in case you were to be unpersuadable: but I find that I had a greater opinion of your delicacy, of your gentleness, than I needed to have—It cannot discompose so steady, so inflexible a young creature, to be told, as I now tell you, that the settlements are actually drawn; and that you will be called down in a very few days to hear them read, and to sign them: for it is impossible, if your heart be free, that you can make the least objection to them; except it will be an objection with you, that they are so much in your favour, and in the favour of all our family.

I was speechless, absolutely speechless. Although my heart was ready to burst, yet could I neither weep nor speak.

I am sorry, said she, for your averseness to this match [*match* she was pleased to call it!]: but there is no help. The honour and interest of the family, as your aunt has told you, and as I have told you, are concerned; and you must comply.

I was still speechless.

She folded the *warm statue*, as she was pleased to call me, in her arms; and entreated me, for heaven's sake, and for her sake, to comply.

Speech and tears were lent me at the same time. — You have given me life, madam, said I, clasping my uplifted hands together, and falling on one knee; a happy one, till now, has your goodness, and my *papa's*, made it! O do not, do not, make all the remainder of it miserable!

Your father, replied she, is resolved not to see you, till he sees you as obedient a child as you used to be. You have never been put to a test till now, that deserved to be called a test. This *is*, this *must* be, my last effort with you. Give me hope, my dear child: my peace is concerned: I will compound with you but for *hope:* and yet your father will not be satisfied without an implicit, and even a cheerful obedience — Give me but hope, my child!

To give you hope, my dearest, my most indulgent mamma, is to give you every thing. Can I be honest, if I give a hope that I cannot confirm?

She was very angry. She again called me perverse: she upbraided me with regarding only my own prepossessions, and respecting not either her peace of mind or my own: — "It is a grating thing, said she, for the parents of a child, who delighted in her in all the time of her helpless infancy, and throughout every stage of her childhood; and in every part of her education to womanhood, because of the promises she gave of proving the most grateful and dutiful of children; to find, just when the time arrived which should crown their wishes, that child stand in the way of her own happiness, and her parents' comfort, and refusing an excellent offer, and noble settlements, give suspicions to her anxious friends, that she would become the property of a vile rake and libertine, who, (be the occasion what it will) defies her family, and has actually embrued his hands in her brother's blood.

"I have had a very hard time of it, said she, between your father and you; for, seeing your dislike, I have more than once pleaded for you: but all to no purpose. I am only treated as a too fond mother, who, from motives of a blameable indulgence, encourage a child to stand in opposition to a father's will. I am charged with dividing the family into two parts; I and my youngest daughter, standing against my husband, his two brothers, my son, my eldest daughter, and my sister Hervey. I have been told, that I must be convinced of the fitness as well as advantage to the whole (your brother and Mr. Lovelace out of the question) of carrying the contract with Mr. Solmes, on which so *many* contracts depend, into execution.

"Your father's heart, I tell you once more, is in it: he has declared, that he had rather have no daughter in you, than one he cannot dispose of for your own good: especially as you have owned, that *your heart is free;* and as the general good of his whole family is to be promoted by your obedience. He has pleaded, poor man! that his frequent gouty paroxysms (every fit more threatening than the former) give him no extraordinary prospects, either of worldly happiness or of long days: and he hopes, that you, who have been supposed to have contributed to the lengthening of your *grandfather's* life, will not, by your disobedience, shorten your father's.

This was a most affecting plea, my dear. I wept in silence upon it. I could not speak to it. And my mother proceeded: "What therefore can be *his* motives, Clary Harlowe, in the earnest desire he has to see this treaty perfected, but the welfare and aggrandizement of his family; which already having fortunes to become the highest condition, cannot but aspire to greater distinctions? However slight such views as these may appear to you, Clary, you know, that they are not slight ones to any other of the family: and your father will be his own judge of what is and what is not likely to promote the good of his children. Your abstractedness, child, (*affectation* of abstractedness some call it) savours, let me tell you, of greater particularity, than what we aim to carry: modesty and humility, therefore, will oblige you rather to mistrust yourself of *peculiarity*, than censure views which all the world pursues, as opportunity offers."

I was still silent; and she proceeded — "It is owing to the good opinion, Clary, which your father has of you, and of your prudence, duty, and gratitude, that he engaged for your compliance, in your absence (before you returned from Miss Howe); and that he built and finished contracts upon it, which cannot be made void, or cancelled."

But why then, thought I, did they receive me, on my return from Miss Howe, with so much intimidating solemnity? — To be sure, my dear, this argument, as well as the rest, was obtruded upon my mother.

She went on, "Your father has declared, that your unexpected opposition [*unexpected* she was pleased to call it] and Mr. Lovelace's continued menaces and insults, more and more convince him, that a short day is necessary in order to put an end to all that man's hopes, and to his own apprehensions resulting from the disobedience of a child so favoured. He has therefore actually ordered patterns of the richest silks to be sent for from London —"

I started — I was out of breath — I gasped, at this frightful precipitance — I was going to open with warmth against it. I knew whose the *happy* expedient must be: female minds, I once heard my brother say, that could but be brought to *balance* on the change of their state, might easily be *determined* by the glare and splendour of the nuptial preparations, and the pride of becoming the mistress of a family. — But she hurried on, that I might not have time to express my disgusts at such a communication — to this effect:

"Your father, therefore, my Clary, cannot, either for your sake or his own, labour under a suspense so affecting to his repose. He has even thought fit to acquaint me, on my pleading for you, that it becomes me, as I value my own peace, [*how harsh to such a wife!*] and as I wish, that he do not suspect that I secretly favour the address of a vile rake (a character which all the sex, he is pleased to say, virtuous and vicious, are but too fond of!) to exert my authority over you: and that this I may the less scrupulously do, as you have owned [the old string!] *that your heart is free.*"

Unworthy reflection in my mother's case, surely, this of our sex's valuing a libertine; since she made choice of my father in preference to several suitors of equal fortune, because they were of inferior reputation for morals!

"Your father," added she, "at his going out, told me what he expected from me, in case I found that I had not the requisite influence upon you — It was this — That I should directly separate myself from you, and leave you singly to take the consequence of your double disobedience — I therefore entreat you, my dear Clarissa," concluded she, "and that in the most earnest and condescending manner, to signify to your father, on his return, your ready obedience; and this as well for my sake, as for your own."

Affected by my mother's goodness to me, and by that part of her argument which related to her own peace, and to the suspicions they had of her secretly inclining to prefer the man so hated by *them*, to the man so much *my* aversion, I could not but wish it were possible for me to obey. I therefore paused, hesitated, considered, and was silent for some time. I could see, that my mother hoped that the result of this hesitation would be favourable to her arguments. But then recollecting, that all was owing to the instigations of a brother and sister, wholly actuated by selfish and envious views; that I had not deserved the treatment I had of late met with; that my disgrace was already become the public talk; that the man was Mr. Solmes; and that my aversion to him was too generally known, to make my compliance either creditable to myself or to them: that it would give my brother and sister a triumph over me, and over Mr. Lovelace, which they would not fail to glory in; and which although it concerned me but little to regard on *his* account, yet might be attended with fatal mischiefs — And then Mr. Solmes's disagreeable person; his still more disagreeable manners; his low understanding — Understanding! the glory of a man, so little to be dispensed with in the head and director of a family, in order to preserve to him that respect which a good wife (and that for the justification of her own choice) should pay him herself, and wish every body to pay him — And as Mr. Solmes's *inferiority* in this respectable faculty of the human mind [I must be allowed to say this to you, and no great self-assumption neither] would proclaim to all future, as well as to all present observers, what must have been my mean inducement — All these reflections crowding upon my remembrance; I would, madam, said I, folding my hands, with an earnestness in which my whole heart was engaged, bear the cruellest tortures, bear loss of limb, and even of life, to give *you* peace.

But this man, every moment I would, at your command, think of him with favour, is the more my aversion. You cannot, indeed you cannot, think, how my whole soul resists him! — And to talk of contracts concluded upon; of patterns; of a short day! — Save me, save me, O my dearest mamma, save your child, from this heavy, this insupportable evil!—

Never was there a countenance that expressed so significantly, as my mother's did, an anguish, which she struggled to hide, under an anger she was compelled to assume — till the latter overcoming the former, she turned from me with an up-lifted eye; and stamping — *Strange perverseness!* were the only words I heard of a sentence that she angrily pronounced; and was going. I then, half franticly, I believe, laid hold of her gown — Have patience with me, dearest madam, said I — Do not *you* renounce me totally — If you *must* separate yourself from your child, let it not be with *absolute* reprobation on *your own part!* — My uncles may be hard-hearted — My father may be immoveable — I may suffer from my brother's ambition, and from my sister's envy! — But let me not lose my mamma's love, at least her pity.

She turned to me with benigner rays — You *have* my *love!* you have my *pity!* But, O my dearest girl — I have not *yours*.

Indeed, indeed, madam, you have: and all my reverence, all my gratitude, you have! — But in this *one* point — cannot I be this once obliged? — Will no *expedient* be accepted? Have I not made a very fair proposal as to Mr. Lovelace?

I wish for both our sakes, my dear unpersuadeable girl, that the decision of this point lay with me. But why, when you know it does not, why should you thus perplex and urge me? — To renounce Mr. Lovelace is now but *half* what is aimed at. Nor will any body else believe you in earnest in the offer, if *I* would. While you remain single, Mr. Lovelace will have hopes — and you, in the opinion of others, inclinations.

Permit me, dearest madam, to say, that *your* goodness to me, *your* patience, *your* peace, weigh more with me, than all the rest put together: for although I am to be treated by my brother, and through his instigations, by my father, as a slave in this point, and not as a daughter, yet my mind is not that of a slave. You have not brought me up to be mean.

So, Clary! you are already at defiance with your father! I have had too much cause before to *apprehend* as much — What will this come to? — I, and then my dear mamma sighed — I am forced to put up with many humours —

That you *are*, my ever-honoured mamma, is my grief. And can it be thought, that this very consideration, and the apprehension of what may result from a much *worse* tempered man (a man, who has not half the sense of my father) has not made an impression upon me, to the disadvantage of the married life? Yet 'tis something of an alleviation, if one must bear *undue* control, to bear it from a man of sense. My father, I have heard you say, madam, was for years a very good-humoured gentleman — Unobjectionable in person and manners — But the man proposed to me —

Forbear reflecting upon your father [Did I, my dear, in what I have repeated, and I think they are the very words, reflect upon my father?]: it is not possible, I must say again, and again, were all men *equally* indifferent to you, that you should be thus sturdy in your will. I am tired out with your obstinacy — The most *unpersuadeable* girl — You forget, that I must separate myself from you, if you will not comply. You do not remember, that your father will take you up where I leave you. Once more, however, I will put it to you: — Are you determined to brave your father's displeasure? — Are you determined to defy your uncles? — Do you choose to break with us all, rather than encourage Mr. Solmes? — Rather than give me hope?

Dreadful alternative — But is not my sincerity, is not the integrity of my heart, concerned in my answer? May not my everlasting happiness be the sacrifice? Will not the least shadow of the *hope* you just now demanded from me be driven into absolute and sudden *certainty?* Is it not sought to ensnare, to entangle me in my own desire of obeying, if I could give answers that might be construed into *hope?* — Forgive me, madam: bear with your child's boldness in such a cause as *this!* — Settlements drawn! — Patterns sent for! — An early day! — Dear, dear madam, how can I give hope, and not intend to be this man's?

Ah, girl, never say your *heart is free?* You deceive yourself if you think it is.

Thus to be driven [and I wrung my hands through impatience] by the instigations of a designing, an ambitious brother, and by a sister, that —

How often, Clary, must I forbid your unsisterly reflections? — Does not your father, do not your uncles, does not every body, patronize Mr. Solmes? And let me tell you, ungrateful girl, and unmoveable as ungrateful, let me *repeatedly* tell you, that it is evident to me, that nothing but a love unworthy of your prudence can make a creature late so dutiful, now so sturdy. You may guess what your father's first question on his return will be. He *must* know that I can do nothing with you. I have done my part. Seek *me*, if your mind change before he comes back: you have yet a little more time, as he stays supper. I will no more seek *you*, nor *to* you. — And away she flung.

What could I do but weep?

I am extremely affected on my mother's account — more, I must needs say, than on my own. And indeed, all things considered, and especially, that the measure she is engaged in, is (as I dare say it is) against her own judgment; she *deserves* more compassion than myself. — Excellent woman! What pity, that meekness and condescension should not be attended with the due rewards of those charming graces! — Yet had she not let violent spirits (as I have elsewhere observed with no small regret) find their power over hers, it could not have been thus.

But here, run away with by my pen, I suffer my mother to be angry with me on her own account. She hinted to me, indeed, that I must seek *her*, if my mind *changed;* which is a condition that amounts to a prohibition of attending her: but, as she left me in displeasure, will it not have a very obstinate appearance, and look like a kind of renunciation of her meditation in my favour, if I go not down before my father returns, to supplicate her pity, and her kind report to him?

I will attend her. I had rather all the world should be angry with me than my mamma!

Meantime, to clear my hands from papers of such a nature, Hannah shall deposit this. If two or three letters reach you together, they will but express, from one period to another, the anxieties and difficulties which the mind of your unhappy, but ever affectionate, friend labours under.

CL. H.

LETTER XXI.

Miss Clarissa Harlowe to Miss Howe.

Sat. night.

I have been down. I am to be unlucky in all I do, I think, be my intentions ever so good. I have made matters worse instead of better: as I shall now tell you.

I found my mother and sister together in my sister's parlour. My mother, I fear, by the glow in her fine face (and as the browner, sullener glow in my sister's confirmed) had been expressing herself with warmth against her *unhappier* child: perhaps giving such an account of what had passed, as should clear herself, and convince Bella, and through *her* my brother and uncles, of the sincere pains she had taken with me.

I entered like a dejected criminal, and besought the favour of a private audience. My mother's return, both looks and words, gave but too much reason for my above surmise.

You have, said she [looking at me with a sternness that never sits well on her sweet features] rather a *requesting* than a *concealing* countenance, Clarissa Harlowe. If I am mistaken, tell me so; and I will withdraw with you wherever you will. — Yet whether so, or not, you may say what you have to say before your sister.

My mother, I thought, might have withdrawn with me, as she knows that I have not a friend in my sister.

I come down, madam, said I, to beg of you to forgive me for any thing you may have taken amiss in what passed above respecting your honoured self; and that you will be pleased to use your endeavours to soften my papa's displeasure against me on his return.

Such aggravating looks; such lifting up of hands and eyes; such a furrowed forehead, in my sister!

My mother was angry enough without all that; and asked me, to what purpose I came down, if I were still so untractable.

She had hardly spoken the words, when Shorey came in to tell her, that Mr. Solmes was in the hall, and desired admittance.

Ugly creature! What, at the close of day, quite dark, brought him hither? — But, on second thoughts, I believe it was contrived, that he should be here at supper, to know the result of the conference between my mother and me, and that my father, on his return, might find us together.

I was hurrying away, but my mother commanded me (since I had come down only, as she said, to mock her) not to stir; and at the same time see if I could behave so to Mr. Solmes, as might encourage her to make the favourable report to my father which I had besought her to make.

My sister triumphed. I was vexed to be so caught, and to have such an angry and cutting rebuke given me, with an aspect more like the taunting sister than the indulgent mother, if I may presume to say so: for she herself

7*

seemed to enjoy the surprise upon me.

The man stalked in. His usual walk is by pauses, as if (from the same vacuity of thought which made Dryden's clown whistle) he was telling his steps: and first paid his clumsy respects to my mother; then to my sister; next to me, as if I were already his wife, and therefore to be last in his notice; and sitting down by me, told us in general what weather it was. Very cold he made it; but I was warm enough. Then addressing himself to me; And how do you find it, miss? was his question; and would have taken my hand.

I withdrew it. I believe with disdain enough. My mother frowned. My sister bit her lip.

I could not contain myself: I was never so bold in my life; for I went on with my plea, as if Mr. Solmes had not been there.

My mother coloured, and looked at him, at my sister, and at me. My sister's eyes were opener and bigger than I ever saw them before.

The man understood me. He hemmed, and removed from one chair to another.

I went on, supplicating for my mother's favourable report: Nothing but invincible dislike, said I —

What would the girl be at, interrupted my mother? Why, Clary! Is this a subject! — Is this! — Is this! — Is this a time — And again she looked upon Mr. Solmes.

I am sorry, on reflection, that I put my mamma into so much confusion — To be sure it was very saucy in me.

I beg pardon, madam, said I. But my papa will soon return. And since I am not permitted to withdraw, it is not necessary, I humbly presume, that Mr. Solmes's presence should deprive me of this opportunity to implore your favourable report; and at the same time, if he still visit on my account [looking at him] to convince him, that it cannot possibly be to any purpose —

Is the girl mad? said my mother, interrupting me.

My sister, with the affectation of a whisper to my mother — This is — This is *spite*, madam, [very *spitefully* she spoke the word] because you commanded her to stay.

I only looked at her, and turning to my mother, Permit me, madam, said I, to repeat my request. I have no brother, no sister! If I lose my mamma's favour, I am lost for ever!

Mr. Solmes removed to his first seat, and fell to gnawing the head of his hazel; a carved head, almost as ugly as his own — I did not think the man was so *sensible*.

My sister rose, with a face all over scarlet; and stepping to the table, where lay a fan, she took it up, and, although Mr. Solmes had observed that the weather was cold, fanned herself very violently.

My mother came to me, and angrily taking my hand, led me

out of that parlour into my own; which, you know, is next to it — Is not this behaviour very bold, very provoking, think you, Clary?

I beg your pardon, madam, if it has that appearance to you. But indeed, my dear mamma, there seem to be snares laying for me. Too well I know my brother's drift. With a good word he shall have my consent for all he wishes to worm me out of — Neither he, nor my sister, shall need to take half this pains —

My mother was about to leave me in high displeasure.

I besought her to stay: One favour, but one favour, dearest madam, said I, give me leave to beg of you —

What would the girl?

I see how every thing is working about — I never, never can think of Mr. Solmes. My papa will be in tumults when he is told that I cannot. They will judge of the tenderness of your heart to a poor child who seems devoted by every one else, from the willingness you have already shewn to hearken to my prayers. There will be endeavours used to confine me, and keep me out of your presence, and out of the presence of every one who used to love me. [*This, my dear Miss Howe, is threatened.*] If this be effected; if it be put out of my power to plead my own cause, and to appeal to you, and to my uncle Harlowe, of whom only I have hope; then will every ear be opened against me, and every tale encouraged — It is, therefore, my humble request, that, added to the disgraceful prohibitions I now suffer under, you will not, if you can help it, give way to my being denied *your* ear.

Your listening Hannah has given you this intelligence, as she does many others.

My Hannah, madam, listens not — my Hannah —

No more in Hannah's behalf — Hannah is known to make mischief — Hannah is known — but no more of that bold intermeddler — 'tis true your father threatened to confine you to your chamber, if you complied not, in order the more assuredly to deprive you of the opportunity of corresponding with those who harden your heart against his will. He bid me tell you so, when he went out, if I found you refractory. But I was loth to deliver so harsh a declaration; being still in hope that you would come down to us in a compliant temper. Hannah has overheard this, I suppose; and has told you of it; as also, that he declared he would break your heart, rather than you should break his. And I, now I assure you, that you will be confined, and prohibited making teasing appeals to any of us: and we shall see who is to submit, you to us, or every body to you.

Again I offered to clear Hannah, and to lay the latter part of the intelligence to my sister's echo, Betty Barnes, who had boasted of it to another servant: but I was again bid to be silent on that head.

I should soon find, my mother was pleased to say, that *others* could be as determined as *I* was obstinate: and, once for all, would add, that since she saw that I built upon her indulgence, and was indifferent about involving her in contentions with my father, and his brothers, and with her other children, she would now assure me, that she was as much determined *against* Mr. Lovelace, and *for* Mr. Solmes and the family-schemes, as any body; and would not refuse her consent to any measures that should be thought necessary to reduce a stubborn child to her duty.

I was ready to sink. She was so good as to lend me her arm to support me.

And this, said I, is all I have to hope for from my mamma?

It is. But, Clary, this one further opportunity I give you — go in again to Mr. Solmes, and behave discreetly to him; and let your father find you together, upon *civil* terms at least.

My feet moved [of *themselves*, I think] further from the parlour where he was, and towards the stairs; and there I stopped and paused.

If, proceeded she, you are determined to stand in defiance of us all — then indeed may you go up to your chamber (as you are ready to do) — and God help you!

God help me indeed! for I cannot give hope of what I cannot intend — but let me have your prayers, my dear mamma! — Those shall have mine, who have brought me into all this distress.

I was moving to go up —

And *will* you go up, Clary?

I turned my face to her: my officious tears would needs plead for me: I could not just then speak; and stood still.

Good girl, distress me not thus! — Dear, good girl, do not thus distress me! holding out her hand; but standing still likewise.

What *can* I do, madam? What can I do?

Go in again, my child — go in again, my *dear* child! — repeated she; and let your father find you together.

What, madam, to give *him* hope? — To give hope to Mr. Solmes?

Obstinate, perverse, undutiful Clarissa! with a rejecting hand, and angry aspect; then take your own way, and go up! — But stir not down again, I charge you, without leave, or till your father's pleasure be known concerning you.

She flung from me with high indignation: and I went up with a very heavy heart; and feet as slow as my heart was heavy.

* * *

My father is come home, and my brother with him. Late as it is, they are all shut up together. Not a door opens; not a soul stirs. Hannah, as she moves up and down, is shunned as a person infected.

* * *

The angry assembly is broken up. My two uncles and my aunt Hervey are sent for, it seems, to be here in the morning to breakfast. I shall then, I suppose, know my doom. 'Tis past eleven, and I am ordered not to go to bed.

Twelve o'clock.

This moment the keys of every thing are taken from me. It was proposed to send for me down; but my father said, he could not bear to look upon me. — Strange alteration in a few weeks! — Shorey was the messenger. The tears stood in her eyes when she delivered her message.

You, my dear, are happy—may you always be so—and then I can never be wholly miserable. Adieu, my beloved friend!

CL. HARLOWE.

LETTER XXII.

Miss Clarissa Harlowe to Miss Howe.

Sunday morning, March 5.

HANNAH has just brought me, from the private place in the garden-wall, a letter from Mr. Lovelace, deposited last night, signed also by Lord M.

He tells me in it, "That Mr. Solmes makes it his boast, that he is to be married in a few days to one of the shyest women in England: that my brother explains his meaning; this shy creature, he says, is me; and he assures every one, that his younger sister is very soon to be Mr. Solmes's wife. He tells me of the patterns bespoken which my mother mentioned to me."

Not one thing escapes him that is done or said in this house.

"My sister, he says, reports the same things; and that with such particular aggravations of insult upon *him*, that he cannot but be extremely piqued, as well at the manner, as from the occasion; and expresses himself with great violence upon it.

"He knows not, he says, what my relations' inducements can be, to prefer such a man as Solmes to him. If advantageous settlements be the motive, Solmes shall not offer what he will refuse to comply with.

"As to his estate and family; the first cannot be excepted against: and for the second, he will not disgrace himself by a comparison so odious. He appeals to Lord M. for the regularity of his life and manners ever since he has made his addresses to me, or had hope of my favour."

I suppose, he would have his lordship's signing to this letter to be taken as a voucher for him.

"He desires my leave (in company with my Lord in a pacific manner) to attend my father and uncles, in order to make proposals that *must* be accepted, if they will but see him, and hear what they are: and tells me, that he will submit to any measures that I shall prescribe, in order to bring about a reconciliation.

He presumes to be very earnest with me, "to give him a private meeting some night, in my father's garden, attended by whom I please."

Really, my dear, were you to see his letter, you would think I had given him great encouragement, and that I am in direct treaty with him; or that he is sure that my friends will drive me into a foreign protection; for he has the boldness to offer, in my lord's name, an asylum to me, should I be tyrannically treated in Solmes's behalf.

I suppose it is the way of this sex to endeavour to entangle the thoughtless of ours by bold supposals and offers, in hopes that we shall be too complaisant or bashful to quarrel with them; and, if not checked, to reckon upon our silence, as assents voluntarily given, or concessions made in their favour.

There are other particulars in this letter which I ought to mention to you: but I will take an opportunity to send you the letter itself, or a copy of it.

For my own part I am very uneasy to think how I have been *drawn* on one hand, and *driven* on the other, into a clandestine, in short, into a mere lover-like correspondence, which my heart condemns.

It is easy to see, if I do not break it off, that Mr. Lovelace's advantages, by reason of my unhappy situation, will every day increase, and I shall be more and more entangled. Yet if I do put an end to it, without making it a condition of being freed from Mr. Solmes's addresses — may I, my dear, is it *best* to continue it a little longer, in hopes to extricate myself out of the other difficulty by giving up all thoughts of Mr. Lovelace? — *Whose* advice can I now ask but yours?

All my relations are met. They are at breakfast together. Mr. Solmes is expected. I am excessively uneasy. I must lay down my pen.

* * *

They are all going to church together. Grievously disordered they appear to be, as Hannah tells me. She believes something is resolved upon.

Sunday noon.

What a cruel thing is suspense! — I will ask leave to go to church this afternoon. I expect to be denied: but if I do not ask, they may allege, that my not going is owing to myself.

* * *

I desired to speak with Shorey. Shorey came. I directed her to carry to my mother my request for permission to go to church this afternoon. What think you was the return? Tell her, that she must direct herself to her brother for any favour she has to ask. — So, my dear, I am to be delivered up to my brother!

I was resolved, however, to ask of him this favour. Accordingly, when they sent me up my solitary dinner, I gave the messenger a billet, in which I made it my humble request through him to my father, to be permitted to go to church this afternoon.

This was the contemptuous answer: "Tell her that her request will be taken into consideration *to-morrow.*" — My request to go to church *to-day* to be taken into consideration *to-morrow!*

Patience will be the fittest return I can make to such an insult. But this method will not do with me;

indeed it will not: and yet it is but the beginning, I suppose, of what I am to expect from my brother, now I am delivered up to him.

* * *

On recollection, I thought it best to renew my request. I did. The following is a copy of what I wrote, and what follows that, of the answer sent me.

SIR,

I know not what to make of the answer brought to my request of being permitted to go to church this afternoon. If you designed to shew your pleasantry by it, I hope that will continue: and then my request will be granted.

You know, that I never absented myself, when well, and at home, till the two last Sundays; when I was *advised* not to go. My present situation is such, that I never more wanted the benefit of the public prayers.

I will solemnly engage only to go thither, and back again.

I hope it cannot be thought that I would do otherwise.

My dejection of spirits will give a too just excuse on the score of indisposition for avoiding visits. Nor will I, but by distant civilities, return the compliments of any of my acquaintance. My disgraces, if they are to have an end, need not to be proclaimed to the whole world. I ask this favour, therefore, for my reputation's sake, that I may be able to hold up my head in the neighbourhood, if I live to see an end of the unmerited severities which seem to be designed for

Your unhappy sister,
CLARISSA HARLOWE.

TO MISS CLARISSA HARLOWE.

For a girl to lay so much stress upon going to church, and yet resolve to defy her parents, in an article of the greatest consequence to them, and to the whole family, is an absurdity. You are recommended, miss, to the practice of your *private* devotions. May they be efficacious upon the mind of one of the most pervicacious young creatures that ever was heard of! The *intention* is, I tell you plainly, to mortify you into a sense of your duty. The neighbours you are so solicitous to appear well with, already know that you defy *that*. So, miss, if you have a real value for your reputation, shew it as you ought. It is yet in your own power to establish or impair it.

JA. HARLOWE.

Thus, my dear Miss Howe, has my brother got me into his snares; and I, like a poor silly bird, the more I struggle, am the more entangled.

LETTER XXIII.
Miss Clarissa Harlowe to Miss Howe.

Monday morning, March 6.

They are resolved to break my heart. My poor Hannah is discharged — disgracefully discharged! — Thus it was.

Within half an hour after I had

sent the poor girl down for my breakfast, that bold creature Betty Barnes, my sister's confidant and servant (if a favourite maid and confidant can be deemed a *servant*) came up.

What, miss, will you please to have for breakfast?

I was surprised. What will I have for breakfast, Betty!—How! — What! — How comes it! — Then I named Hannah. I could not tell what to say.

Don't be surprised, miss:—but you'll see Hannah no more in this house.

God forbid!—Is any harm come to Hannah?—What! what is the matter with Hannah?

Why, miss, the short and the long is this: your papa and mamma think Hannah has staid long enough in the house to do mischief; and so she is ordered to *troop* [that was the confident creature's word]; and I am directed to wait upon you in her stead.

I burst into tears. I have no service for you, Betty Barnes; none at all. But where is Hannah? Cannot I speak with the poor girl? I owe her half a year's wages. May I not see the honest creature, and pay her her wages? I may never see her again perhaps: for they are resolved to break my heart.

And they think you are resolved to break theirs: so tit for tat, miss.

Impertinent I called her; and asked her, if it were upon such confident terms that her service was to begin.

I was so very earnest to see the poor maid, that (to *oblige* me, as she said) she went down with my request.

The worthy creature was as earnest to see me; and the favour was granted in presence of Shorey and Betty.

I thanked her when she came up, for her past service to me.

Her heart was ready to break. And she began to vindicate her fidelity and love; and disclaimed any mischief she had ever made.

I told her, that those who occasioned her being turned out of my service, made no question of her integrity: that her dismission was intended for an indignity to me. That I was very sorry to be obliged to part with her, and hoped she would meet with as good a service.

Never, never, wringing her hands, should she meet with a mistress she loved so well. And the poor creature ran on in my praises, and in professions of love to me.

We are all apt, you know, my dear, to praise our benefactors, because they *are* our benefactors; as if every body did right or wrong, as they obliged or disobliged *us*. But this good creature deserves to be kindly treated; so I could have no merit in favouring one whom it would have been ungrateful not to distinguish.

I gave her a little linen, some laces, and other odd things; and instead of four pounds which were due to her, ten guineas: and said if ever I were again allowed to be my own mistress, I would think of her in the first place.

Betty enviously whispered Shorey upon it.

Hannah told me before their faces, having no other opportunity, that she had been examined about letters *to* me, and *from* me: and that she had given her pockets to Miss Harlowe, who looked into them, and put her fingers in her stays, to satisfy herself that she had not any.

She gave me an account of the number of my pheasants and bantams; and I said they should be my own care twice or thrice a day.

We wept over each other at parting. The girl prayed for all the family.

To have so good a servant so disgracefully dismissed, is very cruel: and I could not help saying that these methods might break my heart, but not any other way answer the end of the authors of my disgraces.

Betty, with a very saucy fleer, said to Shorey, there would be a trial of skill about that, she fancied. But I took no notice of it. If this wench thinks that I have robbed her young mistress of a lover, as you say she has given out, she may believe that it is some degree of merit in herself to be impertinent to me.

Thus have I been forced to part with my faithful Hannah. If you can commend the good creature to a place worthy of her, pray do for my sake.

———

LETTER XXIV.

Miss Clarissa Harlowe to Miss Howe.

Monday, near 12 o'clock.

The enclosed letter was just now delivered to me. My brother has carried all his points.

I send you also the copy of my answer. No more at this time can I write!—

Monday, Mar. 6.

By command of your father and mother I write expressly to forbid you to come into their presence, or into the garden when *they* are there: nor when they are *not* there, but with Betty Barnes to attend you; except by particular licence or command.

On their blessings you are forbidden likewise to correspond with the vile Lovelace; as it is well known you did by means of your sly Hannah. Whence her sudden discharge. As was fit.

Neither are you to correspond with Miss Howe; who has given herself high airs of late; and might possibly help on your correspondence with that detested libertine. Nor, in short, with any body without leave.

You are not to enter into the presence of either of your uncles, without their leave first obtained. It is in *mercy* to you, after such a behaviour to your mother, that your father refuses to see you.

You are not to be seen in any apartment of the house you so lately governed as you pleased, unless you are commanded down.

In short, you are strictly to confine yourself to your chamber, except now and then, in Betty Barnes's sight (as aforesaid) you take a morning or evening turn in the garden: and then you are to go directly, and without stopping at any apartment in the way, up and down the back stairs, that the sight of so perverse a young creature may not add to the pain you have given every body.

The hourly threatenings of your fine fellow, as well as your own unheard-of obstinacy, will account to you for all this. What a hand has the best and most indulgent of mothers had with you, who so long pleaded for you, and undertook for you; even when others, from the manner of your setting out, despaired of moving you! — What must your perverseness have been, that *such* a mother can give you up! She thinks it right so to do: nor will take you to favour, unless you make the first steps, by a compliance with your duty.

As for myself, whom perhaps you think hardly of (in very good company if you do, that is my consolation); I have advised, that you may be permitted to pursue your own inclinations (some people need no greater punishment than such a permission), and not to have the house encumbered by one who must give them the more pain for the necessity she has laid them under of avoiding the sight of her, although in it.

If any thing I have written appear severe or harsh, it is still in your power (but perhaps will not always be so) to remedy it; and that by a single word.

Betty Barnes has orders to obey you in all points consistent with her duty to those to whom *you* owe it as well as *she*.

JA. HARLOWE.

TO JAMES HARLOWE, JUNIOR, ESQ.

· SIR,

I WILL only say, that you may congratulate yourself on having *so far* succeeded in all your views, that you may report what you please of me, and I can no more defend myself, than if I were dead. Yet one favour, nevertheless, I will beg of you. It is this — that you will not occasion more severities, more disgraces, than are necessary for carrying into execution your further designs, whatever they be, against

Your unhappy sister,
CLARISSA HARLOWE.

LETTER XXV.
Miss Clarissa Harlowe to Miss Howe.

Tuesday, March 7.

BY my last deposit, you will see how I am driven and what a poor prisoner I am. — No regard had to my reputation. The whole matter is now before you. Can *such* measures be supposed to soften? — But surely they can only mean to try to frighten me into my brother's views! — All my hope is, to be able to weather this point till my cousin Morden comes from Florence; and he is soon expected: yet if they are determined upon a short day I doubt he will not be here time enough to save me.

It is plain by my brother's letter, that my mother has not spared me, in the report she made of the conference between herself and me: yet she was pleased to hint to me, that my brother had views which she would have had me try to disappoint. But indeed she had engaged to give a *faithful* account of what was to pass between herself and me: and it was, doubtless, much more eligible to give up a daughter, than to disoblige a husband, and every other person of the family.

They think they have done every thing by turning away my poor Hannah; but as long as the liberty of the garden, and my poultry visits, are allowed me, they will be mistaken.

I asked Mrs. Betty, if she had any orders to watch or attend me; or whether I was to ask *her* leave whenever I should be disposed to walk in the garden, or to go to feed my bantams? — Lord bless her! what could I mean by such a question! Yet she owned that she had heard, that I was not to go into the garden, when my father, mother, or uncles were there.

However, as it behoved me to be assured on this head, I went down directly, and staid an hour, without question or impediment; and yet a good part of the time, I walked under and in *sight*, as I may say, of my brother's study-window, where both he and my sister happened to be. And I am sure they saw me, by the loud mirth they affected, by way of insult as I suppose.

So this part of my restraint was doubtless a stretch of the authority given him. The enforcing of that, may perhaps come next. But I hope not.

Tuesday night.

Since I wrote the above, I ventured to send a letter by Shorey to my mother. I desired her to give it into her own hand, when nobody was by.

I shall enclose the copy of it. You will see that I would have it thought, that now Hannah is gone, I have no way to correspond out of the house. I am far from thinking all I do right. I am afraid, this is a little piece of art, that is *not* so. But this is an after-thought — the letter went first.

HONOURED MADAM,

HAVING acknowledged to you, that I had received letters from Mr. Lovelace full of resentment, and that I answered them purely to prevent further mischief; and having shewn you copies of my answers which you did not disapprove of, although you thought fit, after you had read them, to forbid me any further correspondence with him; I think it my duty to acquaint you, that another letter from him has since come to my hand, in which he is very earnest with me to permit him to wait on my papa, or you, or my two uncles, in a pacific way, accompanied by Lord M. on which I beg your commands.

I own to you, madam, that had not the prohibition been renewed, and had not Hannah been so suddenly dismissed my service, I should have made the less scruple to have written an answer, and to have commanded her to convey it to him, with all speed, in order to dissuade him from these visits, lest any thing should happen on the occasion that my heart aches but to think of.

And here I cannot but express my grief, that I should have all the punishment, and all the blame, who, as I have reason to think, have prevented great mischief, and have not been the occasion of any. For, madam, could *I* be supposed to govern the passions of *either* of the gentlemen? — Over the one indeed I have had some little influence, without giving him *hitherto* any reason to think he has fastened an obligation upon me for it — Over the other who, madam, has any? — I am grieved at heart, to be obliged to lay so great blame at my brother's door, although my reputation and my liberty are both to be sacrificed to his resentment and ambition. May not, however, so deep a sufferer be permitted to speak out?

This communication being as voluntarily made, as dutifully intended; I humbly presume to hope, that I shall not be required to produce the letter itself. I cannot either in honour or prudence do that, because of the vehemence of his style; for having heard [not, I assure you, by my means, or through Hannah's] of some part of the harsh treatment I have met with, he thinks himself entitled to place it to his own account by reason of speeches thrown out by some of my relations, *equally* vehement.

If I do *not* answer him, he will be made desperate, and think himself justified (though I shall not think him so) in resenting the treatment he complains of; if I *do*, and if, in compliment to me, he forbears to resent what he thinks himself entitled to resent; be pleased, madam, to consider the obligation he will suppose he lays me under.

If I were as strongly prepossessed in his favour as is supposed, I should not have wished this to be considered by you. And permit me, as a still further proof that I am *not* prepossessed, to beg of you to consider, whether, upon the whole, the proposal I made, of declaring for the single life (which I will religiously adhere to) is not the best way to get rid of his pretensions with honour. To renounce him, and not be allowed to aver, that I will never be the other man's, will make him conclude (driven as I am driven) that I am determined in that other man's favour.

If this has not its due weight, my brother's strange schemes must be tried, and I will resign myself to my destiny with all the acquiescence that shall be granted to my prayers. And so leaving the whole to your own wisdom, and whether you choose to consult my papa and uncles upon this humble application or not; or whether I shall be allowed to write an answer to Mr. Lovelace, or not

[And if allowed so to do, I beg your direction, by whom to send it]; I remain,
Honoured madam,
Your unhappy, but ever dutiful daughter,
CL. HARLOWE.

Wednesday morning.

I have just received an answer to the enclosed letter. My mother, you will observe, has ordered me to burn it: but, as you will have it in your safe keeping, and nobody else will see it, her end will be equally answered, as if it were burnt. It has neither date nor superscription.

CLARISSA,

Say not all the blame and all the punishment is yours. I am as much blamed, and as much punished, as you are; yet am more innocent. When your obstinacy is equal to any other person's passion, blame not your brother. We judged right, that Hannah carried on your correspondences. Now she is gone, and you cannot write [we *think* you cannot] to Miss Howe, nor she to you, without our knowledge, one cause of uneasiness and jealousy is over.

I had no dislike to Hannah. I did not tell her so: because somebody was within hearing when she desired to pay her duty to me at going. I gave her a caution, in a raised voice, to take care, wherever she went to live next, if there were any young ladies, how she made parties, and assisted in clandestine correspondences: — but I slid two guineas into her hand. Now was I angry to hear that you were still *more* bountiful to her — So much for Hannah.

I don't know what to write, about your answering that man of violence. What can you think of it, that such a family as ours, should have such a rod held over it? — For my part, I have not owned that I know you *have* corresponded: by your last boldness to me (an astonishing one it was, to pursue before Mr. Solmes the subject that I was forced to break from above stairs!] you may, as far as I know, plead that you had my countenance for your correspondence with him; and so add to the uneasiness between your father and me. You were once all my comfort, Clarissa: you made all my hardship tolerable! — but now! — However, nothing, it is plain, can move you; and I will say no more on that head: for you are under your father's discipline now; and he will neither be prescribed to, nor entreated.

I should have been glad to see the letter you tell me of, as I saw the rest: — you say, both honour and prudence forbid you to shew it me. — O Clarissa! what think you of receiving letters that honour and prudence forbid you to shew to a mother! — But it is not for me to see it, if you would *choose* to shew it me. I will not be in your secret. I will not know that you did correspond. And, as to an answer, take your own methods. But let him know it will be the last you will write. And if you do write, I won't see it: so seal it up (if you do) and give it to Shorey; and she — Yet do not think I give you licence to write.

We will be upon no conditions with him, nor will *you* be allowed to be upon any. Your father and uncles would have no patience were he to come. What have *you* to do to oblige *him* with your refusal of Mr. Solmes? — Will not that refusal be to give *him* hope? and while he has any, can *we* be easy or free from his insults? Were even your brother in *fault*, as that fault cannot be conquered, is a sister to carry on a correspondence that shall endanger her brother? But your father has given his sanction to your brother's dislikes, and they are now your father's dislikes, and my dislikes, your uncles' and every body's, — No matter to *whom* owing.

As to the rest, you have by your obstinacy put it out of my power to do any thing for you. Your father takes upon himself to be answerable for all consequences. You must not therefore apply to me for favour. I shall endeavour to be only an observer; happy, if I could be an unconcerned one! — While I had power, you would not let me use it as I *would* have used it. Your aunt has been forced to engage not to interfere but by your father's direction. You'll have severe trials. If you have any favour to hope for, it must be from the mediation of your uncles. And yet, I believe, they are equally determined: for they make it a principle [alas: they never had children!] that that child, who in marriage is not governed by her parents, is to be given up as a lost creature.

I charge you let not this letter be found. Burn it. There is too much of the *mother* in it, to a daughter so unaccountably obstinate.

Write not another letter to me. I can do nothing for you. But you can do every thing for yourself.

Now, my dear, to proceed with my melancholy narrative.

After this letter, you will believe that I could have very little hopes that an application directly to my father would stand me in any stead! but I thought it became me to write, were it but to acquit myself *to* myself, that I have left nothing unattempted that has the least likelihood to restore me to his favour. Accordingly I wrote to the following effect:

"I presume not, I say, to argue with my papa; I only beg his mercy and indulgence in this *one* point, on which depends my present and perhaps my *future* happiness; and beseech him not to reprobate his child for an aversion which it is not in her power to conquer. I beg, that I may not be sacrificed to projects, and remote contingencies. I complain of the disgraces I suffer in this banishment from his presence, and in being confined to my chamber. In every thing, but this *one* point, I promise implicit duty and resignation to his will. I repeat my offer of a single life; and appeal to him, whether I have ever given him cause to doubt my word. I beg to be admitted to his and to my mamma's presence, and that my conduct may be under their own eye: and this with the more earnestness, as I have too much reason to believe that snares are laid for me; and tauntings and revilings used on purpose to make a handle of my words against me, when I am not permitted to speak in my own defence. I conclude with hoping, that my brother's instigations may not rob an unhappy child of her father."

This is the answer, sent without superscription, and unsealed, although by Betty Barnes, who delivered it with an air, as if she knew the contents.

Wednesday.

I write, perverse girl; but with all the indignation that your disobedience deserves. To desire to be forgiven a fault you own, and yet resolve to persevere in, is a boldness, no more to be equalled, than passed over. It is *my* authority you defy. Your reflections upon a brother, that is an honour to us all, deserve my utmost resentment. I see how light all relationship sits upon *you.* The cause I guess at, too. I cannot bear the reflections that naturally arise from this consideration. Your behaviour to your too indulgent and too fond mother — But, I have no patience — Continue banished from my presence, undutiful as you are, till you know how to conform to my will. Ungrateful creature! Your letter but upbraids me for my past indulgence. Write no more to me, till you can distinguish better; and till you are convinced of your duty to
A justly incensed father.

This angry letter was accompanied with one from my mother, unsealed, and unsuperscribed also. Those who take so much pains to confederate every one against me, I make no doubt obliged her to bear her testimony against the poor girl.

My mother's letter being a repetition of some of the severe things that passed between herself and me, of which I have already informed you, I shall not need to give you the contents — Only thus far, that *she* also praises my brother, and blames me for my freedoms with him.

LETTER XXVI.
Miss Clarissa Harlowe to Miss Howe.

Thursday morn. March 9.

I have another letter from Mr Lovelace, although I had not answered his former.

This man, somehow or other, knows every thing that passes in our family. My confinement; Hannah's dismission; and more of the resentments and resolutions of my father, uncles, and brother, than I can possibly know, and almost as soon as the things happen, which he tells me of. He cannot come at these intelligencies fairly.

He is excessively uneasy upon what he hears; and his expressions, both of love to me, and resentment to them, are very fervent. He solicits me, "to engage my honour to him, never to have Mr. Solmes."

I think I may fairly promise him that I will not.

He begs, "That I will not think he is endeavouring to make to himself a *merit* at any man's expense, since he hopes to obtain my favour on the foot of his *own;* nor that he seeks to *intimidate* me into a consideration for him. But he declares, that the treatment he meets with from my family is of such a nature, that he is perpetually reproached for not resenting it; and that as well by Lord M. and Lady Sarah, and Lady Betty, as by all his other friends: and if he must have no hope from me, he cannot answer for what his despair will make him do."

Indeed, he says, "his relations, the ladies particularly, advise him to have recourse to a *legal* remedy: but how, he asks, can a man of honour go to law for verbal abuses given by people entitled to wear swords?"

You see, my dear, that my mother seems as apprehensive of mischief as myself; and has *indirectly* offered to let Shorey carry my answer to the letter he sent me before.

He is full of the favour of the ladies of his family to me: to whom nevertheless, I am personally a stranger; except that once I saw Miss Patty Montague at Sir Robert Biddulph's.

It is natural, I believe, for a person to be the more desirous of making new friends, in proportion as she loses the favour of old ones: yet had I rather appear amiable in the eyes of my own relations, and in your eyes, than in those of all the world besides. — But these four ladies of his family have such excellent characters, that one cannot but wish to be thought well of by them. Cannot there be a way to find out by Mrs. Fortescue's means, or by Mr. Hickman, who has some knowledge of Lord M. [covertly, however,] what their opinions are of the present situation of things in our family; and of the little likelihood there is, that ever the alliance once approved of by them, can take effect?

I cannot, for my own part, think so well of myself, as to imagine, that they can wish their relation to persevere in his views with regard to me, through such contempts and discouragements. — Not that it would concern me, should they advise him to the contrary. By my Lord's signing Mr. Lovelace's former letter; by Mr. Lovelace's assurances of the continued favour of all his relations; and by the report of others; I seem still to stand high in their favour: but, methinks, I should be glad to have this confirmed to me, as from themselves, by the lips of an indifferent person; and the rather, as they are known to put a value upon their alliance, because of their fortunes and family; and take it amiss (as they have reason) to be included by *ours* in the contempt thrown upon their kinsman.

Curiosity at present is all my motive: nor will there ever, I hope, be a stronger, notwithstanding your questionable *throbs* — Even were the merits of Mr. Lovelace much greater than they are.

* * *

I have answered his letters. If he takes me at my word, I shall need be the less solicitous for the opinions of his relations in my favour: and yet one would be glad to be well thought of by the worthy.

This is the substance of my letter:

"I express my surprise at his knowing (and so early) all that passes here."

I assure him, "That were there not such a man in the world as himself, I would not have Mr. Solmes."

I tell him, "That to return, as I understand he does, defiances for defiances, to my relations, is far from being a proof with me, either of his politeness, or of the consideration he pretends to have for me.

"That the moment I hear he visits any of my friends without their consent, I will make a resolution never to see him more, if I can help it."

I apprise him, "That I am connived at in sending this letter (although no one has seen the contents) provided it shall be the last I will ever write to him: that I had more than once told him, that the single life was my choice; and this before Mr. Solmes was introduced as a visitor in our family: that Mr. Wyerley, and other gentlemen, knew it to be my choice, before himself was acquainted with any of us: that I had never been induced to receive a line from him on the subject, but that I thought he had not acted ungenerously by my brother; and yet had not been so handsomely treated by my friends as he might have expected: but that had he even my friends on his side, I should have very great objections to him, were I to get over my choice of a single life, so really, preferable to me as it is; and that I should have declared as much to him, had I regarded him as *more* than a common visitor. On all these accounts, I desire, that the one more letter, which I will allow him to deposit in the usual place, may be the very *last;* and that only to acquaint me with his acquiescence that it shall be so; at least till happier times."

This last I put in that he may not be quite desperate. But if he take me at my word, I shall be rid of one of my tormentors.

I have promised to lay before you all his letters, and my answers: I repeat that promise: and am the less solicitous for that reason, to amplify upon the contents of either. But I cannot too often express my vexation, to be driven to such straits and difficulties, here at home, as oblige me to answer letters (from a man I had not absolutely intended to encourage, and to whom I had really great objections) filled as *his* are with such warm protestations, and written to me with a spirit of expectation.

For, my dear, you never knew so bold a supposer. As commentators find beauties in an author, to which the author perhaps was a stranger; so he sometimes compliments me in high strains of gratitude for favours, and for a consideration, which I never designed him; insomuch that I am frequently under a necessity of explaining away the attributed goodness to him, which if I shewed, I should have the less opinion of myself.

In short, my dear, like a restiff horse (as I have heard described by sportsmen) he pains one's hands, and half disjoints one's arms, to rein him in. And, when you see his letters, you must form no judgment upon them till you have read my answers. If you do, you will indeed think you have cause to attribute *self-deceit*, and *throbs*, and *glows* to your friend — And yet, at other times, the contradictory creature complains, that I shew him as little favour, and my friends as much inveteracy, as if in the rencounter betwixt my brother and him he had been the aggressor, and as if the catastrophe had been as fatal as it might have been.

If he has a design by this conduct (sometimes complaining of my shyness, at others exulting in my imaginary favours) to induce me at one time to acquiesce with his compliments; at another to be more complaisant for his complaints; and if the contradiction be not the effect of his inattention and giddiness, I shall think him as deep and as artful (too probably, as *practised*) a creature as ever lived; and were I to be sure of it, should hate him, if possible, worse than I do Solmes.

But enough for the present of a creature so very various.

LETTER XXVII.

Miss Howe to Miss Clarissa Harlowe

Thursday night, March 9.

I HAVE not patience with any of the people you are with. I know not what to advise you to do. How do you know, that you are not punishable for being the cause, though to your own loss that the will of your grandfather is not complied with?— Wills are sacred things, child. You see that they, even *they*, think so, who imagine they suffer by a will, through the distinction paid you in it.

I allow of all your noble reasonings for what you did at the time: but since such a charming, such a generous instance of filial duty is to go thus unrewarded, why should you not resume?

Your grandfather knew the family failing. He knew what a noble spirit you had to do good. He himself perhaps [Excuse me, my dear] had done too little in his lifetime; and therefore he put it in your power to make up for the defects of the whole family. Were it to me, I would resume it, indeed I would.

You will say, you cannot do it, while you are with them. I don't know that. Do you think they can use you worse than they do? And is it not your *right?* And do they not make use of your own generosity to oppress you? Your uncle Harlowe is one trustee; your cousin Morden is the other: insist upon your right to your uncle; and write to your cousin Morden about it. This, I dare say, will make them alter their behaviour to you.

Your insolent brother — what has *he* to do to control you? — Were it me [I wish it were me for one month, and no more] I'd shew him the difference. I would be in my own mansion, pursuing my charming schemes, and making all around me happy. I would set up my own chariot. I would visit them when they deserved it. But when my brother and sister gave themselves airs, I would let them know, that I was their sister, and not their servant: and if that did not do, I would shut my gates against them; and bid them go, and be company for each other.

It must be confessed, however, that this brother and sister of yours, judging as such narrow spirits will ever judge, have some reason for treating you as they do. It must have long been a mortification to them (set disappointed love on her side, and avarice on his, out of the question) to be so much eclipsed by a younger sister. Such a sun in a family, where there are none but faint twinklers, how could they bear it! Why, my dear, they must look upon you as a prodigy among them: and prodigies, you know, though they obtain our admiration, never attract our love. The distance between you and them is immense. Their eyes ache to look up at you. What shades does your full day of merit cast upon them! Can you wonder then, that they should embrace the first opportunity that offered to endeavour to bring you down to their level?

Depend upon it, my dear, you will have more of it, and more still, as you bear it.

As to this odious Solmes, I wonder not at your aversion to him. It is needless to say any thing to you, who have so sincere an antipathy to him, to strengthen your dislike: yet, who can resist her own talents? One of mine, as I have heretofore said, is to give an ugly likeness. Shall I indulge it? — I will. And the rather, as in doing so, you will have my opinion in justification of your aversion to him, and in approbation of a steadiness that I ever admired, and must for ever approve of, in your temper.

I was twice in this wretch's company. At one of the times your Lovelace was there. I need not mention to you, who have such a *pretty curiosity* (though at present *only* a curiosity, you know) the unspeakable difference.

Lovelace entertained the company in his lively gay way, and made every body laugh at one of his stories. It was before this creature was thought of for you. Solmes laughed too. It was, however, *his* laugh: for his first three years, at least, I imagine, must have been one continual fit of crying; and his muscles have never yet been able to recover a risible tone. His very smile [you never saw him smile, I believe; never, at least, gave him cause to smile] is so little natural to his features, that it appears in him as hideous as the *grin* of a man in malice.

I took great notice of him, as I do of all the noble lords of the creation, in their peculiarities: and was disgusted, nay, shocked at him, even then. I was glad, I remember, on that particular occasion, to see his strange features recovering their natural gloominess; though they did this but slowly, as if the muscles which contributed to his distortions had turned upon rusty springs.

What a dreadful thing must even the *love* of such a husband be! For my part, were I his wife! (but what have I done to myself, to make but such a supposition?) I should never have comfort but in his absence, or when I was quarrelling with him. A splenetic woman, who must have somebody to find fault with, might indeed be brought to endure such a wretch: the sight of him would always furnish out the occasion, and all her servants, for that reason, and for *that* only, would have cause to bless their master. But how grievous and apprehensive a thing must it be for his wife, had she the least degree of delicacy, to catch herself in having done something to oblige him?

So much for his person: as to the other half of him, he is said to be an insinuating, creeping mortal to any body he hopes to be a gainer by: an insolent, overbearing one, where he has no such views: and is not this the genuine spirit of meanness? He is reported to be spiteful and malicious, even to the whole family of any single person who has once disobliged him; and to his own relations most of all. I am told, that they are none of them such wretches as himself. This may be one reason why he is for disinheriting them.

My Kitty, from one of his domestics, tells me, that his tenants hate him: and that he never had a servant who spoke well of him. Vilely suspicious of their wronging him (probably from the badness of his own heart) he is always changing.

His pockets, they say, are continually crammed with keys: so that when he would treat a guest (a friend he has not out of your family), he is half as long puzzling *which* is *which*, as his niggardly treat might be concluded in. And if it be wine, he always fetches it himself. Nor has he much trouble in doing so; for he has very few visitors — only those, whom business or necessity brings: for a gentleman who can help it, would rather be benighted, than put up at his house.

Yet this is the man they have found out (for considerations as sordid as those he is governed by) for a husband, that is to say, for a lord and master, for Miss Clarissa Harlowe!

But perhaps, he may not be quite so miserable as he is represented. Characters extremely good, or extremely bad, are seldom justly given. Favour for a person will exalt the one, as disfavour will sink the other. But your uncle Antony has told my mother, who objected to his covetousness, that it was intended to *tie him* up, as he called it, to *your own terms;* which would be with a hempen, rather than a matrimonial cord, I dare say. But is not this a plain indication, that even his own recommenders think him a mean creature; and that he must be articled with — perhaps for *necessaries!* But enough, and too much, of such a wretch as this! — You must not have him, my dear — that I am clear in — though not so clear, how you will be able to avoid it, except you assert the independence to which your estate gives you a title.

* * *

Here my mother broke in upon me. She wanted to see what I had written. I was silly enough to read Solmes's character to her.

She owned that the man was not the most desirable of men; and that he had not the happiest appearance: but what, said she, is *person* in a man? And I was chidden for setting you against complying with your father's will. Then followed a lecture upon the preference to be given in favour of a man who took care to discharge all his obligations to the world, and to keep all together, in opposition to a spendthrift or profligate: a fruitful subject you know, whether any particular person be meant by it, or not.

Why will these wise parents by saying too much against the persons they dislike, put one upon defending them? Lovelace is not a spendthrift; owes not obligations to the world; though, I doubt not, profligate enough. Then putting one upon doing *such* but common justice, we must needs be prepossessed, truly! — And so perhaps we are put upon *curiosities* first; that is to say, how *such a one or his friends* may think of one: And then, but too probably, comes in a distinguishing preference, or something that looks exceedingly like it.

My mother charged me at last, to write that side over again. — But excuse me, my good mamma! I would not have the character lost upon any consideration; since my vein ran freely into it: and I never wrote to please myself, but I pleased you. A very good reason why — we have but one mind between us — only that sometimes you are a little too grave, methinks; I, no doubt, a little too flippant in your opinion.

This difference in our tempers, however, is probably the reason that we love one another *so* well, that, in the words of Norris, *no third love* can come in betwixt. Since each, in the other's eye, having something amiss, and each loving the other well enough to bear being told of it (and the rather, perhaps, as neither wishes do mend it;) this takes off a good deal from that rivalry which might encourage a little, if not a great deal, of that latent spleen, which in time might rise into envy, and that into ill-will. So, my dear, if this be the case, let each keep her fault, and much good may do her with it, say I: for there is constitution in both to plead for it: and what an hero or heroine must he or she be, who can conquer a constitutional fault? Let it be *avarice*, as in some I *dare not* name: let it be *gravity*, as in my *best friend*: or let it be *flippancy*, as in — I need not say whom.

It is proper to acquaint you, that I was obliged to comply with my mother's *curiosity* [my mother has her share, her *full* share, of *curiosity*, my dear] and to let her see here-and-there some passages in your letters —

I am broken in upon — But I will tell you by-and-by what passed between my mother and me on this occasion — And the rather, as she had her *girl*, her favourite Hickman, and your Lovelace, all at once in her eye, in her part of the conversation.

* * *

Thus it was.

"I cannot but think, Nancy," said she, "after all, that there is a little hardship in Miss Harlowe's case: and yet (as her mother says) it is a grating thing to have a child, who was always noted for her duty in *smaller* points, to stand in opposition to her parents will, in the *greater*: yea, in the *greatest of all*. And now to middle the matter between both, it is pity, that the man *they* favour has not that sort of merit which a person of a mind so delicate as that of Miss Harlowe might reasonably expect in a husband. — But then, this man is surely preferable to a libertine: to a libertine too, who has had a duel with her own brother: *fathers* and *mothers* must think so, were it *not* for that circumstance — And it is strange if *they* do not know best."

And so they must, thought I, from their experience, if no little dirty views gave *them* also that prepossession in one man's favour, which they are so apt to censure their daughters for having in another's — And if, as I may add in your case, they have no creeping, old, musty uncle Antony's to strengthen their prepossessions, as he does my mother's — Poor, creeping, positive soul! what has such an old bachelor as he to do, to prate about the duties of children to parents; unless he had a notion that parents owe some to their children? But your mother, by her indolent meekness, let me call it, has spoiled all the three brothers.

"But you see, child," proceeded my mother, "what a different behaviour *mine* is to *you.* I recommend to you one of the soberest, yet politest, men in England —"

I think little of my mother's *politest*, my dear. She judges of honest Hickman for her *daughter*, as she would have done, I suppose, twenty years ago, for *herself.*

"Of a good family," continued my mother; "a fine, clear, and improving estate [a prime consideration with my mother, as well as with some other folks, whom you know:] and I *beg*, and I *pray* you to encourage him: at least, not to use him the *worse*, for his being so obsequious to you."

Yes, indeed! To use *him* kindly, that he may treat *me* familiarly — But distance to the men-wretches is best — I say.

"Yet all will hardly prevail upon you to do as I would have you. What would you say, were I to treat you as Miss Harlowe's father and mother treat her?"

"What would I *say*, madam! — That's easily answered. I would *say* nothing. Can you think such usage, and to such a young lady, is to be borne?"

"Come, come, Nancy, be not so hasty: you have heard but one side; and that there is *more* to be said is plain, by your reading to me but parts of her letters. They are her parents. *They* must know best. Miss Harlowe, as fine a child as she is, must have *done* something, must have *said* something (you know how they loved her) to make them treat her thus."

"But if she should be blameless, madam, how does your own supposition condemn *them!*"

Then came up Solmes's great estate; his good management of it — "A little too *near* indeed," was the word! [*O how money-lovers*, thought I, *will palliate!* Yet my mother is a princess in spirit to this Solmes!] "What, strange effects," added she, "have prepossession and love upon young ladies!"

I don't know how it is, my dear; but people take high delight in finding out folks in love. Curiosity *begets* curiosity: I believe that's the thing.

She proceeded to praise Mr. Lovelace's person, and his qualifications natural and acquired: but then she would judge as *mothers* will judge, and as *daughters* are very loth to judge: — But could say nothing in answer to your offer of living single; and breaking with him — if — if — [three or four *if's* she made of one good one, if] *that* could be depended on.

But still '*obedience without reserve*, reason what I will, is the burden of my mother's song: and this, for *my* sake, as well as for *yours.*

I must needs say, that I think duty to parents is a very meritorious excellence: but I bless God I have not your trials. We can all be good when we have no temptation nor provocation to the contrary: — but few young persons (who can help themselves too as you can) would bear what you bear.

I will not mention all that is upon my mind, in relation to the behaviour of your father and uncles, *and the rest of them*, because I would not offend you: but I have now a higher opinion of my own sagacity than ever I had, in that I could never cordially love any one of your family but yourself. I am not *born* to like them. But it is my *duty* to be sincere to my *friend:* and this will excuse her Anna Howe to Miss Clarissa Harlowe.

I ought indeed to have excepted your mother: a lady to be reverenced; and now to be pitied. What must have been her treatment, to be thus subjugated, as I may call it! Little did the good old viscount think, when he married his darling, his only daughter, to so well-appearing a gentleman, and to her own liking too, that she would have been so much kept down. Another would call your father a tyrant, if I must not: all the world that know him, *do* call him so; and if you love your mother, you should not be very angry at the world for taking that liberty.

Yet, after all, I cannot help thinking, that she is the less to be pitied, as she may be said (be the gout, or what will, the occasion of his moroseness) to have long behaved unworthy of her birth and fine qualities, in yielding so much as she yields to encroaching spirits: [you may confine the reflection to your brother, if it will pain you to extend it] and this for the sake of preserving a temporary peace to herself; which was the less worth endeavouring to preserve, as it always produced a strength in the will of others, and was followed by a weakness in her own, which subjected her to an arbitrariness that of course grew, and became established, upon her patience. — And now to give up the most deserving of her children (against her judgment) a sacrifice to the ambition and selfishness of the least deserving! — But I fly from this subject — having, I fear, said too much to be forgiven — and yet much less than is in my heart to say upon the over-meek subject.

Mr. Hickman is expected from London this evening. I have desired him to inquire after Lovelace's life and conversation in town. If he has not inquired, I shall be very angry with him. Don't expect a very good account of either. He is certainly an intriguing wretch, and full of inventions.

Upon my word, I most heartily despise that sex! I wish they would let our fathers and mothers alone; teasing *them* to tease *us* with their golden promises, and protestations, and settlements, and the rest of their ostentatious nonsense. How charmingly might you and I live together, and despise them all! But to be cajoled, wire-drawn, and ensnared, like silly birds, into a state of bondage, or vile subordination; to be courted as princesses for a few weeks, in order to be treated as slaves for the rest of our lives — Indeed, my dear, as you say of Solmes, I cannot endure them! — But for your relations [*friends* no more will I call them, unworthy as they are even of the *other* name!] to take such a wretch's price as that; and to the cutting off all reversions from his own family! — How must a mind but commonly just resist such a measure!

Mr. Hickman shall sound Lord M. upon the subject you recommend. But beforehand, I can tell you what he and what his sisters will say, when they *are* sounded. — Who would not be proud of such a relation as Miss Clarissa Harlowe? Mrs. Fortescue told me, that they are all your very great admirers.

If I have not been clear enough in my advice about what you shall do, let me say, that I can give it in one word: it is only by re-urging you to *resume*. If you do, all the rest will follow.

We are told here, that Mrs. Norton, as well as your aunt Hervey, has given her opinion on the *implicit* side of the question. If she can think, that the part she has had in your education, and your own admirable talents and acquirements, are to be thrown away upon such a worthless creature as Solmes, I could heartily quarrel with her. You may think I say this to lessen your regard for the good woman. And perhaps not wholly without cause, if you do. For, to own the truth, methinks, I don't love her so well as I should do, did you love her so apparently less, that I could be out of doubt, that you loved me better.

Your mother tells you, 'That you will have great trials: that you are under your father's *discipline*.' — The word is enough for me to despise those who gave occasion for its use — ' That it is out of her power to help you!' And again: 'That if you have any favour to hope for, it must be by the mediation of your uncles.' I suppose you will write to the *oddities*, since you are forbid to see them — But can it be, that such a lady, such a sister, such a wife, such a mother, has no influence in her own family? Who, indeed, as you say, if this be so, would marry, that can live single? My choler is again beginning to rise. *Resume*, my dear: — and that is all I will give myself time to say further, lest I offend you when I cannot serve you. — Only this, that I am

Your truly affectionate friend and servant,

ANNA HOWE.

LETTER XXVIII.

Miss Clarissa Harlowe to Miss Howe.

Friday, March 10.

You will permit me, my dear, to touch upon a few passages in your last letter that affect me sensibly.

In the first place, you must allow me to say, low as I am in spirits, that I am very angry with you for your reflections on my relations, particularly on my father and mother, and on the memory of my grandfather. Nor, my dear, does your *own* mother always escape the keen edge of your vivacity. One cannot one's-*self* forbear to write or speak freely of those we love and honour, when grief from imagined hard treatment wrings the heart: but it goes against one to hear any body else take the same liberties. Then you have so very strong a manner of expression where you take a distaste, that when passion has subsided, and I come (upon reflection) to see by *your* severity what I have given occasion for, I cannot help condemning myself.

But least of all can I bear that you should reflect upon my mother. What, my dear, if her meekness should not be rewarded? Is the want of reward, or the want even of a grateful acknowledgment, a reason for us to dispense with what we think our duty? They were my father's lively spirits that first made him an interest in her gentle bosom. They were the same spirits turned inward, as I have heretofore observed*, that made him so impatient when the cruel malady seized him. He always loved my mother: and would not *love* and *pity, excusably,* nay *laudably,* make a good wife (who was an hourly witness of his pangs, when labouring under a paroxysm, and his paroxysms becoming more and more frequent, as well as more

* See p. 87.

and more severe) give up her own will, her own likings, to oblige a husband, thus afflicted, whose love for *her* was unquestionable?—And if so, was it not too natural [human nature is not perfect, my dear] that the husband thus humoured by the wife, should be unable to bear control from any body else; much less contradiction from his children?

If then you would avoid my highest displeasure, you must spare my mother: and surely, you will allow me, with her, to pity, as well as to love and honour my father.

I have no friend but you to whom I can appeal, to whom I dare complain. Unhappily circumstanced as I am, it is but too probable that I *shall* complain, because it is but too probable that I shall have more and more cause given me *for* complaint. But be it your part, if I do, to sooth my angry passions, and to soften my resentments; and this the rather, as you know what an influence your advice has upon me; and as you *must* also know, that the freedoms you take with my friends, can have no other tendency, but to weaken the sense of my duty to them, without answering any good end to myself.

I cannot help owning, however, that I am pleased to have you join with me in opinion of the contempt which Solmes deserves from me. But yet, permit me to say, that he is not *quite* so horrible a creature as you make him: as to his *person,* I mean; for with regard to his *mind*, by all that I have heard, you have done him but justice: but you have such a talent at an ugly likeness, and such a vivacity, that they sometimes carry you out of verisimilitude. In short, my dear, I have known you, in more instances than one, sit down resolved to write all that wit, rather than strict justice, could suggest upon the given occasion. Perhaps it may be thought, that I should say the less on this particular subject, because your dislike of him arises from love to me: but should it not be our aim to judge of ourselves, and of every thing that affects us, as we may reasonably imagine other people would judge of us, and of our actions?

As to the advice you give, to resume my estate, I am determined not to litigate with my father, let what will be the consequence to myself. I may give you, at another time, a more particular answer to your reasonings on this subject: but, at present, will only observe, that it is my opinion, that Lovelace himself would hardly think me worth addressing, were he to know *this* to be my resolution. These *men*, my dear, with all their flatteries, look forward to the *permanent*. Indeed, it is fit they should; for love must be a very foolish thing to look back upon, when it has brought persons born to affluence into indigence, and laid a generous mind under obligation and dependence.

You very ingeniously account for the love we bear to one another, from the *difference* in our tempers. I own, I should not have thought of that. There may, possibly, be something in it: but whether there be, or not, whenever I am cool, and give myself time to reflect, I will love you the better for the correction you give me, be as severe as you will upon me. Spare me not, therefore, my dear friend, whenever you think me in the least faulty. I love your agreeable raillery: you know I always did: nor, however *over*-serious you think me, did I ever think you *flippant*, as you harshly call it. One of the first conditions of our mutual friendship was, that each should say or write to the other whatever was upon her mind, without any offence to be taken: a condition, that is indeed indispensable in friendship.

I knew your mother would be for implicit obedience in a child. I am sorry my case is so circumstanced, that I *cannot* comply. It would be my duty to do so, if I could. You are indeed very happy, that you have nothing but your own agreeable, yet whimsical humours to contend with, in the choice she invites you to make of Mr. Hickman. How happy should I be, to be treated with so much lenity! — I should blush to have *my* mother say, that she *begged* and *prayed* me, and all in vain, to encourage a man so unexceptionable as Mr. Hickman.

Indeed, my beloved Miss Howe, I am ashamed to have your mother say, with *me* in her view, "What strange effects have prepossession and love upon young creatures of our sex!" This touches me the more sensibly, because you yourself, my dear, are so ready to *persuade* me into it.

I should be very blameable to endeavour to hide any the least bias upon my mind from you: and I cannot but say — that this man — this Lovelace — is a man that might be liked well enough, if he bore such a character as Mr. Hickman bears; and even if there were hopes of reclaiming him. And further still I will acknowledge, that I believe it possible that one might be driven, by violent measures, step by step, as it were, into something that might be called — I don't know what to call it — a *conditional kind of liking*, or so. But as to the word *love* — justifiable and charming as it is in some cases (that is to say, in all the *relative*, in all the *social*, and, what is still beyond *both*, in all our *superior* duties, in which it may be properly called *divine*;) it has, methinks, in the narrow, circumscribed, selfish, peculiar sense, in which you apply it to me (the man too so little to be approved for his morals, if all that report says of him be true) no pretty sound with it. Treat me as freely as you will in all other respects, I will love you, as I have said, the better for your friendly freedom: but methinks, that I could be glad, that you would not let this imputation pass so glibly from *your* pen, or *your* lips, as attributable to one of your *own sex*, whether *I* be the person or not: since the *other* must have a *double* triumph, when a person of your delicacy (armed with such contempts of them all, as you would have one think) can give up a friend, with an exultation over her weakness, as a silly, love-sick creature!

I could make some other observations upon the contents of your last two letters; but my mind is not free enough at present. The occasions for the above stuck with me; and I could not help taking the earliest notice of them.

Having written to the end of my second sheet, I will close this letter, and in my next acquaint you with all that has happened here since my last.

LETTER XXIX.

Miss Clarissa Harlowe to Miss Howe.

Saturday, March 11.

I HAVE had such taunting messages, and such repeated avowals of ill offices, brought me from my brother and sister, if I do not comply with their wills, (delivered too with provoking sauciness by Betty Barnes) that I have thought it proper, before I entered upon my intended address to my uncles, in pursuance of the hint given me in my mother's letter, to expostulate a little with *them*. But I have done it in such a manner, as will give you (if you please to take it as you have done some parts of my former letters) great advantage over me. In short, you will have more cause than ever, to declare me far gone in love, if my reasons for the change of my style

In these letters, with regard to Mr. Lovelace, do not engage your more favourable opinion. — For I have thought proper to give them their own way; and since they will have it, that I have a preferable regard for Mr. Lovelace, I give them cause rather to confirm their opinion than doubt it.

These are my reasons, in brief, for the alteration of my style:

In the first place, they have grounded their principal argument for my compliance with their will, upon my acknowledgment that my heart is free; and so, supposing I give up no preferable person, my opposition has the look of downright obstinacy in their eyes; and they argue, that at worst, my aversion to Solmes is an aversion that may be easily surmounted, and *ought* to be surmounted in duty to my father, and for the promotion of family views.

Next, although they build upon this argument in order to silence me, they seem not to believe me, but treat me as disgracefully, as if I were in love with one of my father's footmen: — so that my *conditional* willingness to give up Mr. Lovelace has procured me no favour.

In the next place, I cannot but think, that my brother's antipathy to Mr. Lovelace is far from being well-grounded; the man's inordinate passion for the sex is the crime that is always rung in my ears: and a very great one it is; but does my brother recriminate upon him thus in love to *me?* — No — His whole behaviour shews me, that that is not his principal motive, and that he thinks me rather in his way than otherwise.

It is then the call of justice, as I may say, to speak a little in favour of a man, who, although provoked by my brother, did not do him all the mischief he could have done him, and which my brother had endeavoured to do *him*. It might not be amiss, therefore, I thought, to alarm them a little with an apprehension, that the methods they are taking with me are the very reverse of those they *should* take to answer the end they design by them. And after all, what is the compliment I make Mr. Lovelace, if I *allow* it to be thought, that I do *really* prefer him to such a man as him they terrify me with? Then, my Miss Howe [concluded I] accuses me of a tameness which subjects me to insults from my brother: I will keep that dear friend in my eye; and, for *all* these considerations, try what a little of *her* spirit will do — sit it ever so awkwardly upon me.

In this way of thinking, I wrote to my brother and sister. This is my letter to him.

Treated as I am treated, and, in a great measure, if not *wholly*, by *your* instigations, brother, you must permit me to expostulate with you upon the occasion. It is not my *intention* to displease you in what I am going to write: and yet I must deal freely with you. The occasion calls for it.

And permit me, in the first place, to remind you, that I am your *sister*, and not your *servant*; and that, therefore, the bitter revilings and passionate language brought me from you, upon an occasion in which you have no right to prescribe to me, are neither worthy of my character to bear, nor of yours to offer.

Put the case, that I *were* to marry the man you dislike; and that he were *not* to make a polite or tender husband, is that a reason for you to be an unpolite and disobliging brother? — Why must you, sir, anticipate my misfortunes, were such a case to happen? — Let me tell you plainly, that the man who could treat me as a *wife*, worse than you of late have treated me as a *sister*, must be a barbarous man indeed.

Ask yourself, I pray you, sir, if you would thus have treated your sister Bella, had *she* thought fit to receive the addresses of the man so much hated by you? — If not, let me caution you, my brother, not to take your measures by what you think *will be borne*, but rather by what *ought to be offered*.

How would *you* take it, if you had a brother, who, in a like case, were to act by *you*, as you do by *me?* — You cannot but remember what a laconic answer you gave even to my father, who recommended to you Miss Nelly D'Oily — *You did not like her*, were your words: and that was thought sufficient.

You must needs think, that I cannot but know to *whom* to attribute my disgraces, when I recollect my father's indulgence to me, in permitting me to decline several offers; and to *whom*, that a common cause is endeavoured to be made, in favour of a man whose person and manners are more exceptionable than those of any of the gentlemen I have been permitted to refuse.

I offer not to compare the two men together: nor is there indeed the least comparison to be made between them. All the difference to the *one's* disadvantage, if I *did*, is but in one point — of the greatest importance, indeed — but to whom of *most* importance? — To *myself*, surely, were I to encourage his application: — of the least to *you*. Nevertheless, if you do not, by your strange politics, unite *that man* and *me* as joint sufferers in one cause, you shall find me as much resolved to renounce *him*, as I am to refuse the *other*. I have made an overture to this purpose: I hope you will not give me reason to confirm my apprehensions, that it will be owing to *you* if it be not accepted.

It is a sad thing to have it to say, without being conscious of ever having given you cause of offence, that I have in *you* a brother, but not a friend.

Perhaps you will not condescend to enter into the reasons of your late and present conduct with a foolish sister. But if *politeness*, if *civility*, be not due to that character and to my sex, *justice* is.

Let me take the liberty further to observe, that the principal end of a young man's education at the university, is to teach him to reason justly, and to subdue the violence of his passions. I hope, brother, that you will not give room for anybody who knows us both, to conclude, that the toilet has taught the *one* more of the latter doctrine, than the university has taught the *other*. I am truly sorry to have cause to say, that I have heard it often remarked, that your uncontrolled passions are not a credit to your liberal education.

I hope, sir, that you will excuse the freedom I have taken with you: you have given me too much reason for it, and you have taken much greater with me, *without reason*; so if you are offended, you ought to look at the cause, and not at the effect: — then examining yourself, that cause will cease, and there will not be anywhere a more accomplished gentleman than my brother.

Sisterly affection, I do assure you, sir, (unkindly as you have used *me*) and not the pertness which of late you have been so apt to impute to me, is my motive in this hint. Let me invoke your returning kindness, my *only brother!* And give me cause, I beseech you, to call you my *compassionating friend*. For I am, and ever will be,

Your affectionate sister,
CLARISSA HARLOWE.

This is my brother's answer.

TO MISS CLARISSA HARLOWE.

I KNOW, there will be no end of your impertinent scribble, if I don't write to you. I write therefore. But, without entering into argument with such a conceited and pert preacher and questioner, it is, to forbid you to plague me with your quaint nonsense. I know not what wit in a woman is good for, but to make her overvalue herself, and despise every other person. Yours, Miss Pert, has set you above your duty, and above being taught or prescribed to, either by parents, or anybody else — But go on, Miss: your mortification will be the greater; that's all, child. It *shall*, I assure you, if I can make it so, so long as you prefer that villainous Lovelace (who is justly hated by all your family) to every body. We see by your letter now (what we too justly suspected before) most evidently we see, the hold he has got of your forward heart. But the stronger the hold, the greater must be the force (and you shall have enough of that) to tear such a miscreant from it. In me, notwithstanding your saucy lecturing, and your saucy reflections before, you are sure of a friend, as well as of a brother, if it be not your own fault. But, if you will still think of such a wretch as that Lovelace, never expect either friend or brother in

JA. HARLOWE.

I will now give you a copy of my letter to my sister; with her answer.

In what, my dear sister, have I offended you, that instead of endeavouring to soften my father's anger against me (as I am sure I should have done for you, had my unhappy case been yours) you should, in so hard-hearted a manner, join to aggravate not only *his* displeasure, but my mother's against me. Make but my case your own, my dear Bella; and suppose you were commanded to marry Mr. Lovelace (to whom you are believed to have an antipathy) would you not think it a very grievous injunction? — Yet cannot your dislike to Mr. *Lovelace* be greater than mine is to Mr. *Solmes*. Nor are love and hatred voluntary passions.

My brother may perhaps think it a proof of a *manly* spirit, to shew himself an utter stranger to the gentle passions. We have both heard him boast, that he never loved with distinction; and having predominating passions, and checked in his first attempt, perhaps he never will. It is the less wonder then, raw from the college, so lately himself the *tutored*, that he should set up for a tutor, a prescriber to our gentle sex, whose taste and manners are differently formed: for what, according to his account, are colleges, but classes of tyrants, from the upper-students over the lower, and from them to the tutor? — That *he*, with such *masculine* passions, should endeavour to control and bear down an unhappy sister, in a case where his antipathy, and give me leave to say his ambition, [once you would have allowed the latter to be his fault] can be gratified by so doing, may not be quite so much to be wondered at — but that a sister should give up the cause of a sister, and join with him to set her father and mother against her, in a case that might have been her own. Indeed, my Bella, this is not pretty in you.

There was a time that Mr. Lovelace was thought reclaimable, and when it was far from being deemed a censurable view to hope to bring back to the paths of virtue and honour, a man of his sense and understanding. I am far from wishing to make the experiment: but nevertheless I will say, that if I have *not* a regard for him, the disgraceful methods taken to compel me to receive the addresses of such a man as Mr. Solmes, are enough to induce it.

Do you, my sister, for one moment lay aside all prejudice, and compare the two men in their births, their educations, their persons, their understandings, their manners, their air, and their whole deportments; and in their fortunes too, taking in reversions, and then judge of both; yet, as I have frequently offered, I will live single with all my heart, if that will do.

I cannot thus live in displeasure and disgrace. I would, if I could, oblige all my friends. But will it be *just*, will it be *honest*, to marry a man I cannot endure? If I have not been used to oppose the will of my father, but have always delighted to oblige and obey, judge of the strength of my antipathy, by the painful opposition I am obliged to make, and cannot help it.

Pity then, my dearest Bella, my sister, my friend, my companion, my adviser, as you used to be when I was happy, and plead for

Your ever-affectionate,
CL. HARLOWE.

TO MISS CLARISSA HARLOWE.

LET it be pretty or not pretty in your wise opinion, I shall speak my mind, I will assure you, both of you and your conduct in relation to this detested Lovelace. You are a fond foolish girl with all your wisdom. Your letter shews that enough in twenty places. And as to your cant of living single, nobody will believe you. This is one of your *fetches* to avoid complying with your duty, and the will of the most indulgent parents in the world, as yours have been to you, I am sure — though now they see themselves finely requited for it.

We all, indeed, once thought your temper soft and amiable: but why was it? You never was contradicted before. You had always your own way. But no sooner do you meet with opposition in your wishes to throw yourself away upon a vile rake, but you shew what you are. You cannot love Mr. Solmes! that's the pretence: but sister, sister, let me tell you, that is because Lovelace has got into your fond heart: — A wretch hated, justly hated, by us all; and who has dipped his hands in the blood of your brother. Yet *him* you would make our relation, would you?

I have no patience with you, but for putting the case of my liking such a vile wretch as him. As to the encouragement you pretend he received formerly from all our family, it was before we knew him to be so vile: and the proofs that had such force upon *us*, ought to have had some upon you: — and would, had you not been a foolish, forward girl; as on this occasion every body sees you are.

O how you run out in favour of the wretch! — His birth, his education, his person, his understanding, his manners, his air, his fortune — reversions too taken in to augment the surfeiting catalogue! What a fond string of lovesick praises is here! and yet you would live single — Yes, I warrant! when so many imaginary perfections dance before your dazzled eye! But no more — I only desire, that you will not, while you seem to have such an opinion of your wit, think every one else a fool; and that you can at pleasure, by your whining flourishes, make us all dance after your lead.

Write as often as you will, this shall be the last answer or notice you shall have upon this subject from

ARABELLA HARLOWE.

I had in readiness a letter for each of my uncles, and meeting in the garden a servant of my uncle Harlowe I gave them to him to deliver according to their respective directions. If I am to form a judgment by the answers I have received from my brother and sister, as above, I must not, I doubt, expect any good from those letters. But when I have tried every expedient, I shall have the less to blame myself for, if any thing unhappy should fall out. I will send you copies of both, when I shall see what notice they will be thought worthy of, if of any.

LETTER XXX.
Miss Clarissa Harlowe to Miss Howe.

Sunday night, March 12.

This man, this Lovelace, gives me great uneasiness. He is extremely bold and rash. He was this afternoon at our church — In hopes to see me, I suppose: And yet, if he had such hopes, his usual intelligence must have failed him.

Shorey was at church; and a principal part of her observation was upon his haughty and proud behaviour when he turned round in the pew where he sat, to our family pew. My father and both my uncles were there; so were my mother and sister. My brother happily was not. They all came home in disorder. Nor did the congregation mind any-body but him; it being his first appearance there, since the unhappy rencounter.

What did the man come for, if he intended to look challenge and defiance, as Shorey says he did, and as others, it seems, thought he did, as well as she? Did he come for *my* sake; and, by behaving in such a manner to those present of my family, imagine he was doing me either service or pleasure? — He knows how they hate him: nor will be take pains, would pains do, to obviate their hatred.

You and I, my dear, have often taken notice of his pride; and you have rallied him upon it; and instead of exculpating himself, he has owned it: and by owning it he has thought he has done enough.

For my own part, I thought pride in his case an improper subject for raillery. People of birth and fortune to be proud, is so needless, so mean a vice! If they *deserve* respect, they will have it, without requiring it. In other words, for persons to endeavour to gain respect, by a haughty behaviour, is to give a proof that they mistrust their own merit: to make confession that they *know* that their *actions* will not attract it. — Distinction or quality may be prided in by those to whom distinction or quality is a *new* thing. And then the reflection and contempt which such bring upon themselves by it, is a counterbalance.

Such added advantages too, as this man has in his person and mien: learned also, as they say he is: — *Such* a man to be haughty, to be imperious! — The lines of his own face at the same time condemning him — how wholly inexcusable! — Proud of what? Not of doing well: the only *justifiable* pride. — Proud of *exterior* advantages!—must not one be led by such a *stop short* pride, as I may call it, in him or her who has it, to mistrust the *interior?* Some people may indeed be afraid, that if they did not assume, they would be trampled upon. A very narrow fear, however, since they trample upon themselves, who can fear *this.* But this man must be secure, that humility would be an ornament to him.

He has talents indeed: but those talents and his personal advantages have been snares to him. It is plain they have. And this shews, that, weighed in an equal balance, he would be found greatly wanting.

Had my friends confided, as they did at first, in that discretion which they do not accuse me of being defective in, I dare say I should have found him out: and then should have been as resolute to dismiss *him*, as I was to dismiss others, and as I *am* never to have Mr. *Solmes.* O that they did but know my heart!—It shall sooner burst, than voluntarily, uncompelled, undriven, dictate a measure that shall cast a slur either upon them or upon my sex.

Excuse me, my dear friend, for these grave *soliloquies*, as I may call them. How have I run from reflection to reflection!—But the occasion is recent—they are all in commotion below upon it.

Shorey says, that Mr. Lovelace watched my mother's eye, and bowed to her: and she returned the compliment. He always admired my mother. She would not, I believe, have hated *him*, had she not been *bid* to hate him; and had it not been for the rencounter between him and her only son.

Dr. Lewen was at church; and observing, as every one else did, the disorder into which Mr. Lovelace's appearance had put all our family, was so good as to engage him in conversation, when the service was over, till they were all gone to their coaches.

My uncles had my letters in the morning. They, as well as my father, are more and more incensed against me, it seems. Their answers, if they vouchsafe to answer me, will demonstrate, I doubt not, the unseasonableness of this rash man's presence at our church.

They are angry also, as I understand, with my mother, for returning his compliment. What an enemy is hatred, even to the common forms of civility! which, however, more distinguish the *payer* of a compliment than the *receiver.* But they all see, they say, that there is but one way to put an end to his insults. So I shall suffer: and in what will the rash man have benefited himself, or mended his prospects?

I am extremely apprehensive that this worse than ghost-like appearance of his, bodes some still bolder step. If he come hither (and very desirous he is of my leave to come), I am afraid there will be murder. To avoid that, if there were no other way, I would most willingly be buried alive.

They are all in consultation—

upon my letters, I suppose — So they were in the morning; which occasioned my uncles to be at our church. I will send you the copies of those letters, as I promised in my last, when I see whether I can give you their answers with them. This letter is all — I cannot tell what — the effect of apprehension and displeasure at the man who has occasioned my apprehensions. Six lines would have contained all that is in it to the purpose of my story. CL. H.

[*See p. 140, for Mr. Lovelace's account of his behaviour and intentions in his appearance at their church.*]

LETTER XXXI.
Mr. Lovelace to John Belford, Esq.

Monday, March 13.

IN vain dost thou* and thy compeers press me to go to town, while I am in such an uncertainty as I am in at present with this proud beauty. All the ground I have hitherto gained with her, is entirely owing to her concern for the safety of people whom I have reason to hate.

Write then, thou biddest me, if I will not come: that, indeed, I can do; and as well without a subject as with one. And what follows shall be a proof of it.

* Those gentlemen affected what they called the Roman style (to wit, the *thee* and the *thou*) in their letters: and it was an agreed rule with them, to take in good part whatever freedoms they treated each other with, if the passages were written in that style.

The lady's malevolent brother has now, as I told thee at M. Hall, introduced another man; the most unpromising in his person and qualities, the most formidable in his offers that has yet appeared.

This man has by his proposals captivated every soul of the Harlowes — *Soul!* did I say — There is not a soul among them but my charmer's: and she, withstanding them all, is actually confined, and otherwise maltreated by a father the most gloomy and positive; at the instigation of a brother the most arrogant and selfish — But thou knowest their characters; and I will not therefore sully my paper with them.

But is it not a confounded thing to be in love with one, who is the daughter, the sister, the niece, of a family I must eternally despise? And, the devil of it, that love increasing with her — what shall I call it? — 'Tis not scorn: — 'tis not pride; — 'tis not the insolence of an adored beauty: — but 'tis to *virtue*, it seems, that my difficulties are owing; and I pay for not being a sly sinner, an hypocrite; for being regardless of my reputation; for permitting slander to open its mouth against me. But is it necessary for such a one as I, who have been used to carry all before me, upon my own terms — I, who never inspired a fear, that had not a discernibly predominant mixture of love in it; to be an hypocrite? — Well says the poet:

He who seems virtuous does but act a part;
And shews not his own nature, but his art.

Well, but it seems I must *practise* for this art, if I would succeed with this truly admirable creature; but why *practise* for it? — Cannot I indeed reform? — I have but one vice; — have I, Jack? — Thou knowest my heart, if any man living does. As far as I know it myself, thou knowest it. But 'tis a cursed deceiver; for it has many and many a time imposed upon its master — Master, did I say? That am I not now; nor have I been from the moment I beheld this angel of a woman. Prepared indeed as I was by her character before I saw her: for what a mind must that be, which though not virtuous itself, admires not virtue in another? — My visit to Arabella, owing to a mistake of the sisters, into which, as thou hast heard me say, I was led by the blundering uncle; who was to introduce *me* (but lately come from abroad) to the *divinity*, as I thought; but, instead of her, carried me to a *mere mortal*. And much difficulty had I, so fond and so forward my lady! to get off without forfeiting all with a family that I intended should give me a goddess.

I have boasted that I was once in love before: — and indeed I thought I was. It was in my early manhood - with that quality-jilt, whose infidelity I have vowed to revenge upon as many of the sex as shall come into my power. I believe, in different climes, I have already sacrificed an hecatomb to my Nemesis, in pursuance of this vow. But upon recollecting what I was *then*, and comparing it with what I find myself *now*, I cannot say that I was ever in love before. What was it then, dost thou ask me, since the disappointment had such effects upon me, when I found myself jilted, that I was hardly kept in my senses? — Why, I'll tell thee what, as near as I can remember; for it was a great while ago: — it was — Egad, Jack, I can hardly tell what it was — But a vehement aspiration after a novelty, I think — Those confounded poets, with their terrenely celestial descriptions, did as much with me as the lady: they fired my imagination, and set me upon a desire to become a goddess-maker. I must needs try my new-fledged pinions in sonnet, elegy, and madrigal. I must have a Cynthia, a Stella, a Sacharissa, as well as the best of them: darts and flames, and the devil knows what, must I give to my Cupid. I must create beauty, and place it where nobody else could find it: and many a time have I been at a loss for a *subject*, when my new created goddess has been kinder than it was proper for my plaintive sonnet that she should be.

Then I had a vanity of *another* sort in my passion: I found myself well received among the women in general; and I thought it a pretty *lady-like* tyranny [I was then very young, and very vain!] to single out some *one* of the sex, to make *half a score* jealous. And I can tell thee, it had its effect: for many an eye have I made to sparkle with rival indignation: many a cheek glow; and even many a fan have I caused to be snapped at a sister-beauty; accompanied with reflection perhaps at being seen alone with a wild young fellow who could not be in private with both at once.

In short, Jack, it was more pride than love, as I now find it, that put me upon making such a confounded rout about losing this noble varletess. I thought she loved me at least as well as I believed I beloved her: nay, I had the vanity to suppose she could not help it. My friends were pleased with my choice. They wanted me to be shackled: for early did they doubt my morals as to the sex. They saw, that the dancing, the singing, the musical ladies were all fond of my company: for who [I am in a humour to be vain. I think — for who] danced, who sung, who touched the string, whatever the instrument, with a better grace than thy friend?

I have no notion of playing the hypocrite so egregiously, as to pretend to be blind to qualifications which every one sees and acknowledges. Such praise-begging hypocrisy! Such affectedly disclaimed attributes! Such contemptible praise-traps! — But yet, shall my vanity extend only to *personals*, such as the gracefulness of dress, my debonnaire, and my assurance — Self-taught, self-acquired, these! — For my *parts*, I value not myself upon *them*. Thou wilt say I have no cause. — Perhaps not: but if I had any thing valuable as to intellectuals, those are not my own; and to be proud of what a man is answerable for the abuse of, and has no merit in the right use of, is to strut, like the jay, in borrowed plumage.

But to return to my fair jilt — I could not bear, that a woman, who was the first that had bound me in silken fetters [they were not iron ones, like those I now wear] should prefer a coronet to me: and when the bird was flown, I set more value upon it than when I had it safe in my cage, and could visit it when I pleased.

But now am I *indeed* in love. I can think of nothing, of nobody, but the divine Clarissa Harlowe — *Harlowe?* — How that hated word sticks in my throat — But I shall give her for it the name of love*.

Clarissa! O there's music in the name,
That, soft'ning me to infant tenderness,
Makes my heart spring like the first leaps of life!

But couldst thou have believed that I, who think it possible for me to favour as much as I can be favoured; that I, who for this charming creature think of foregoing the *life of honour* for the *life of shackles*; could adopt those over tender lines of Otway?

I check myself, and leaving the three first lines of the following of Dryden to the family of the whiners, find the workings of the passion in my stormy soul better expressed by the three last:

Love various minds does variously inspire:
He stirs in gentle natures gentle fires;
Like that of incense on the altar laid.
But raging flames tempestuous souls invade:

* Lovelace.

A fire which every windy passion blows;
With pride it mounts, and with revenge
  it glows.

And with revenge it *shall* glow!—For, dost thou think, that if it were not from the hope, that this stupid family are all combined to do my work for me, I would bear their insults?—Is it possible to imagine, that I would be braved as I am braved, threatened as I am threatened, by those who are afraid to see me; and by this brutal brother too, to whom I gave a life [a life, indeed, not worth my taking!]; had I not a greater pride in knowing, that by means of his very spy upon me, I am playing him off as I please; cooling or inflaming his violent passions as may best suit my purposes; permitting so much to be revealed of my life and actions, and intentions, as may give him such a confidence in his double-faced agent, as shall enable me to dance his employer upon my own wires?

This it is that makes my pride mount above my resentment. By this engine, whose springs I am continually oiling, I play them all off. The busy old tarpaulin uncle I make but my ambassador to queen Annabella Howe, to engage her (for example sake to her princessly daughter) to join in their cause, and to assert an authority they are resolved, right or wrong, (or I could do nothing) to maintain.

And what my motive, dost thou ask? No less than this, that my beloved shall find no protection out of my family: for, if I know hers, fly she must, or have the man she hates. This, therefore, if I take my measures right, and my familiar fail me not, will secure her mine in spite of them all; in spite of her own inflexible heart: mine, without condition; without reformation promises; without the necessity of a siege of years, perhaps; and to be even then, after wearing the guise of merit-doubting hypocrisy, at an uncertainty, upon a probation unapproved of—Then shall I have all the rascals and rascalesses of the family come creeping to me: I prescribing to me; and bringing that sordidly imperious brother to kneel at the footstool of my throne.

All my fear arises from the little hold I have in the heart of this charming frost-piece: such a constant glow upon her lovely features: eyes so sparkling: limbs so divinely turned: health so florid: youth so blooming: air so animated—To have an heart so impenetrable: and *I*, the hitherto successful Lovelace, the addresser—How can it be? Yet there are people, and I have talked with some of them, who remember that she was *born*. Her nurse Norton boasts of her maternal offices in her earliest infancy; and in her education *gradatim*. So there is full proof, that she came not from above all at once an angel! how then can she be so impenetrable?

But here's her mistake; nor will she be cured of it—She takes the man she calls her father [her mother had been faultless, had she not been her father's wife]; she takes the men she calls her uncles; the fellow she calls her brother; and the poor contemptible she calls her sister; to *be* her father, to *be* her uncles, her brother, her sister; and that, as such, she owes to some of them reverence, to others respect, let them treat her ever so cruelly! — Sordid ties! — Mere cradle prejudices! For had they not been imposed upon her by nature, when she was in a perverse humour, or could she have chosen her relations, would any of *these* have been among them?

How my heart rises at her preference of them to me, when she is convinced of their injustice to me! convinced, that the alliance would do honour to them all — herself excepted; to whom every one owes honour; and from whom the most princely family might receive it. But how much more will my heart rise with indignation against her, if I find she hesitates but one moment (however persecuted) about preferring me to the man she avowedly hates! But she cannot surely be so mean as to purchase her peace with them at so dear a rate. She cannot give a sanction to projects formed in malice, and founded in a selfishness (and that at her own expense) which she has spirit enough to despise in others; and ought to disavow, that we may not think her a Harlowe.

By this incoherent ramble thou wilt gather, that I am not likely to come up in haste; since I must endeavour first to obtain some assurance from the beloved of my soul, that I shall not be sacrificed to such a wretch as Solmes! Woe be to the fair-one, if ever she be *driven* into my power (for I despair of a voluntary impulse in my favour) and I find a difficulty in obtaining this security.

That her indifference to me is not owing to the superior liking she has for *any* other, is what rivets my chains: but take care, fair-one: take care, O thou most exalted of female minds, and loveliest of persons, how thou debasest thyself by encouraging such a competition as thy sordid relations have set on foot in mere malice to me! — Thou wilt say I rave. And so I do:

Perdition catch my soul, but I do love her.

Else, could I bear the perpetual revilings of her implacable family? — *Else*, could I basely creep about — not her proud father's house — but his paddock — and garden-walls? — Yet (a quarter of a mile distance between us) not hoping to behold the least glimpse of her shadow? — *Else*, should I think myself repaid, amply repaid, if the fourth, fifth, or sixth midnight stroll, through unfrequented paths, and over briery enclosures, affords me a few cold lines: the even *expected* purport only to let me know, that she values the most worthless family, more than she values me; and that she would not write at all, but to induce me to bear insults, which *un-man* me to bear? My lodging in the intermediate way, at a wretched ale-house; disguised like an inmate of it: accommodations equally vile, as those I met with in my Westphalian journey. 'Tis well, that the necessity for all this arises not from scorn and tyranny! but is first imposed upon herself.

But was ever hero in romance (fighting with giants and dragons excepted) called upon to harder trials? — Fortune and family, and reversionary grandeur on my side! such a wretched fellow my competitor? — Must I not be deplorably in love, that can go through these difficulties, encounter these contempts? — By my soul, I am half-ashamed of myself: I, who am perjured too, by priority of obligation, if I am faithful to any woman in the world!

And yet, why say I, I am half-ashamed? — Is it not a glory to love *her* whom every one who sees her, either loves or reveres, or both? Dryden says,

The cause of love can never be assign'd:
'Tis in no face; — but in the lover's mind.

— And Cowley thus addresses beauty as a mere imaginary:

Beauty! thou wild fantastic ape,
Who dost in ev'ry country change thy shape:
Here black; there brown; here tawny; and there white!
Thou flatt'rer, who comply'st with every sight!
Who hast no certain what, nor where.

But both these, had they been her contemporaries, and known her, would have confessed themselves mistaken: and, taking together person, mind, and behaviour, would have acknowledged the *justice* of the universal voice in her favour.

. . . . Full many a lady
I've ey'd with best regard; and many a time
The harmony of their tongues hath into bondage
Brought my too diligent ear. For several virtues
Have I liked several women. Never any
With so full soul, but some defect in her
Did quarrel with the noblest grace she ow'd,
And put it to the foil. But she! — O she!
So perfect and so peerless is created,
Of every creature's best. SHAKESPEARE.

Thou art curious to know, if I have not started a new game? If it be possible for so universal a lover to be confined so long to one object? Thou knowest nothing of this charming creature, that thou canst put such questions to me; or thinkest thou knowest me better than thou dost. All that's excellent in her sex is this lady!— Until by matrimonial, or equal intimacies, I have found her *less than angel*, it is impossible to think of any other. Then there are so many stimulatives to such a spirit as mine in this affair, *besides* love: such a field of stratagem and contrivance, which thou knowest to be the delight of my heart. Then the rewarding end of all! — To carry off such a girl as this, in spite of all her watchful and implacable friends; and in spite of a prudence and reserve that I never met with in any of the sex! — What a triumph! — What a triumph over the whole sex! — And then such a revenge to gratify; which is only at present politically reined in, eventually to break forth with greater fury — Is it possible, thinkest thou, that there can be room for a thought that is not *of* her, and devoted *to* her?

* * *

By the advices I have this moment received, I have reason to think, that I shall have occasion for thee here. Hold thyself in readiness to come down upon the first summons.

Let Belton, and Mowbray, and Tourville, likewise prepare themselves. I have a great mind to contrive a method to send James Harlowe to travel for improvement. Never was there a boobysquire that more wanted it. *Contrive* it, did I say? I have *already* contrived it; could I but put it in execution without being suspected to have a hand in it. This I am resolved upon; if I have not his *sister*, I will have him.

But be this as it may, there is a present likelihood of room for *glorious* mischief. A confederacy had been for *some time* formed against me; but the uncles and the nephew are *now* to be double-servanted [*single* servanted they were before]; and those servants are to be *double* armed when they attend their masters abroad. This indicates their resolute enmity to me, and as resolute favour to Solmes.

The reinforced orders for this hostile apparatus are owing it seems to a visit I made yesterday to their church — A good place I thought to begin a reconciliation in; supposing the heads of the family to be christians, and that they meant something by their prayers. My hopes were to have an invitation (or, at least, to gain a pretence) to accompany home the gloomy sire; and so get an opportunity to see my goddess: for I believe they durst not but be *civil* to me, at least. But they were filled with terror it seems at my entrance; a terror they could not get over. I saw it indeed in their countenances; and that they all expected something extraordinary to follow. — And so it *should* have done, had I been more sure than I am of their daughter's favour. Yet not a hair of any of their stupid heads do I intend to hurt.

You shall all have your directions in writing, if there be occasion. But after all, I dare say there will be no need but to shew your faces in my company.

Such faces never could four men shew — Mowbray's so fierce and so fighting: Belton's so pert and so pimply: Tourville's so fair and so foppish: thine so rough and so resolute: and *I* your leader! — What hearts, although meditating hostility, must those be which we shall not appal? — Each man occasionally attended by a servant or two, long ago chosen for qualities resembling those of his master.

Thus, Jack, as thou desirest, have I written. — Written upon something; upon nothing; upon revenge, which I love; upon love, which I hate, *heartily* hate, because 'tis my master: and upon the devil knows what besides:— for looking back, I am amazed at the length of it. *Thou mayest* read it: *I would not for a king's ransom*—'But so as I do *but* write, thou sayest thou wilt be pleased.

Be pleased then. I *command* thee to be pleased: if not for the writer's or written sake, for thy word's sake. And so in the royal style (for am I not likely to be thy king and thy emperor in the great affair before us?) I bid thee very heartily   Farewell.

LETTER XXXII.
Miss Clarissa Harlowe to Miss Howe.
Tuesday, March 14.

I now send you copies of my letters to my uncles: with their answers. Be pleased to return the latter by the first deposit. I leave them for *you* to make remarks upon. *I* shall make none.

TO JOHN HARLOWE, ESQ.
Sat. March 11.

ALLOW me, my honoured second papa, as in my happy days you taught me to call you, to implore your interest with my papa, to engage him to dispense with a command, which, if insisted upon, will deprive me of my free-will, and make me miserable for my whole life.

For my *whole life!* let me repeat: is that a small point, my dear uncle, to give up? Am not *I* to live with the man? Is any body else? Shall I not therefore be allowed to judge for myself, whether I *can* or *cannot* live happily with him?

Should it be ever so *unhappily*, will it be prudence to complain, or appeal? If it were, to whom could I appeal with *effect* against a husband? And would not the invincible and avowed dislike I have for him at *setting out*, seem to justify any ill usage from him, *in that state*, were I to be ever so observant of him? And if I were to be at all observant of him, it must be from fear, not love.

Once more, let me repeat, that this is not a *small* point to give up: and that it is *for life*. Why, I pray you, good sir, should I be made miserable for *life?* Why should I be deprived of all comfort, but that which the hope that it would be a very short one, would afford me?

Marriage is a very solemn engagement, enough to make a young creature's heart ache, with the *best* prospects, when she thinks seriously of it!—To be given up to a strange man; to be engrafted into a strange family; to give up her very name, as a mark of her becoming his absolute and dependent property; to be obliged to prefer this strange man to father, mother—to every body:—and his humours to all her own—Or to contend perhaps, in breach of a vowed duty, for every innocent instance of free-will—To go nowhither; to make acquaintance; to give up acquaintance; to renounce even the strictest friendships perhaps; all at his pleasure, whether she think it reasonable to do so or not: surely, sir, a young creature ought not to be obliged to make all these sacrifices but for such a man as she can love. — If she be, how sad must be the case! how miserable the life, if to be called *life!*

I wish I could obey you all. What a pleasure would it be to me, if I could! — *Marry first, and love will come after,* was said by one of my dearest friends! but this is a shocking assertion. A thousand things may happen to make that state but barely tolerable, where it is entered into with *mutual affection:* what must it then be, where the husband can have no confidence in the love of his wife; but has reason rather to question it, from the preference he *himself* believes she would have given to somebody else, had she had her own option? What doubts, what jealousies, what want of tenderness, what unfavourable prepossessions will there be, in a matrimony thus circumstanced! How will every look, every action, even the most innocent, be liable to misconstruction! — While, on the other hand, an indifference, a carelessness to oblige, may take place; and fear *only* can constrain even an *appearance* of what ought to be the effect of undisguised love.

Think seriously of these things, dear good sir, and represent them to my father in that strong light which the subject will bear; but in which my sex, and my tender years and inexperience, will not permit me to paint it; and use your powerful interest, that your poor niece may not be consigned to a misery so durable.

I have offered to engage not to marry at all, if that condition may be accepted. What a disgrace is it to me to be thus sequestered from company, thus banished my papa's and mamma's presence; thus slighted and deserted by you, sir, and my other kind uncle! and to be hindered from attending at that public worship, which, were I *out* of the way of my duty, would be most likely to reduce me *into* the right path again! — Is *this* the way, sir; can *this* be thought to be the way to be taken with a free and open spirit? May not this strange method rather harden than convince? I cannot bear to live thus in disgrace: the very servants so lately permitted to be under my own direction, hardly daring to speak to me; my own servant discarded with high marks of undeserved suspicion and displeasure, and my sister's maid set over me.

The matter may be too far pushed. — Indeed it may. — And then, perhaps, every one will be sorry for their parts in it.

May I be permitted to mention an expedient? — "If I am to be watched, banished, and confined; suppose, sir, it were to be at *your* house?" — Then the neighbouring gentry will the less wonder, that the person of whom they used to think so favourably, appeared not at church here; and that she received not their visits.

I hope there can be no objection

to this. You used to love to have me with you, sir, when all went happily with me: and will you not now permit me, in my *troubles*, the favour of your house, till all this displeasure be overblown? Upon my word, sir, I will not stir out of doors, if you require the contrary of me: nor will I see any body, but whom you will allow me to see; provided Mr. Solmes be not brought to persecute me there.

Procure, then, this favour for me; if you cannot procure the still greater, that of a happy reconciliation (which nevertheless I presume to hope for if *you* will be so good as to plead for me); and you will then add to those favours, and to that indulgence, which have bound me, and will for ever bind me, to be

Your dutiful and obliged niece,
CLARISSA HARLOWE.

THE ANSWER.

MY DEAR NIECE, Sunday-night.

IT grieves me to be forced to deny you any thing you ask. Yet it *must* be so; for unless you can bring your mind to oblige us in this one point, in which our promises and honour were engaged before we believed there could be so sturdy an opposition, you must never expect to be what you have been to us all.

In short, niece, we are an *embattled phalanx*. Your reading makes you a stranger to nothing, but what you should be most acquainted with — So you will see by that expression, that we are not to be pierced by your persuasions and invincible persistence. We have agreed *all* to be moved, or *none;* and not to comply without one another. So you know your destiny; and have nothing to do but to yield to it.

Let me tell you, the virtue of obedience lies not in obliging when you can be obliged again — But give up an inclination, and there is some merit in that.

As to your expedient; you shall not come to my house, Miss Clary; though this is a prayer I little thought I ever should have denied you: for were you to keep your word as to seeing nobody but whom we please, yet can you *write* to somebody else, and receive letters from him: this we too well know you can, and have done — more is the shame and the pity!

You offer to live single, miss — *We* wish you married: but because you may not have the man your heart is set upon, why, truly, you will have nobody we shall recommend: and as we know, that somehow or other you correspond with him, or at least did, as long as you could; and as he defies us all, and would not dare to do so, if he were not sure of you in spite of us all (which is not a little vexatious to us, you must think); we are resolved to frustrate him, and triumph over him, rather than that he should triumph over us: that's one word for all. So expect not any advocateship from me: I will not plead for you; and that's enough. From

Your displeased uncle,
JOHN HARLOWE.

P.S. For the rest I refer to my brother Antony.

TO ANTONY HARLOWE, ESQ.

HONOURED SIR, Saturday, March 11.

As you have thought fit to favour Mr. Solmes with your particular recommendation, and was very earnest in his behalf, ranking him (as you told me, upon introducing him to me) among your select friends; and expecting my regards to him accordingly; I beg your patience, while I offer a few things, out of many that I could offer to your serious consideration, on occasion of his *address* to me, if I am to use that word.

I am charged with prepossession in another person's favour. You will be pleased, sir, to remember, that till my brother returned from Scotland, that other person was not absolutely discouraged, nor was I forbid to receive his visits. I believe it will not be pretended, that in birth, education, or personal endowments, a comparison can be made between the two. And only let me ask you, sir, if the one would have been thought of for me, had he not made such offers, as upon my word, I think, *I* ought not in justice to accept of, nor *he* to propose: offers, which if he had not made, I dare say, my *papa* would not have required them of him.

But the one, it seems, has many faults: — Is the other *faultless?* — The principal thing objected to Mr. Lovelace (and a very inexcusable one) is, that he is immoral in his loves — is not the other in his hatreds? — Nay, as I may say, in his loves too (the object only differing), if *the love of money* be *the root of all evil.*

But, sir, if I am prepossessed, what has Mr. Solmes to hope for? — Why should he persevere? What must I think of the man who would wish me to be his wife against my inclination? — And is it not a very harsh thing for my friends to desire to see me married to one I *cannot* love, when they will not be persuaded but that there is one whom I *do* love?

Treated as I am, now is the time for me to speak out or never. — Let me review what it is Mr. Solmes depends upon on this occasion. Does he believe, that the disgrace which I suffer on his account, will give him a merit with me? Does he think to win my esteem, through my uncles' sternness to me; by my brother's contemptuous usage; by my sister's unkindness; by being denied to visit, or be visited; and to correspond with my chosen friend, although a person of unexceptionable honour and prudence, and of my own sex; my servant to be torn from me, and another servant set over me; to be confined, like a prisoner, to narrow and disgraceful limits, in order *avowedly* to mortify me, and to break my spirit; to be turned out of that family management which I loved, and had the greater pleasure in it, because it was an ease, as I thought, to my mamma, and what my sister chose not; and yet, though time hangs heavy upon my hands, to be so put out of my course, that I have as little inclination as liberty to pursue any of my choice delights? — Are these steps necessary to reduce me to a level so low, as to make me a fit wife for this man? — Yet these are all he can have to trust to — and if his reliance is on these measures, I would have him to know, that he mistakes *meekness* and *gentleness* of disposition for *servility* and *baseness* of heart.

I beseech you, sir, to let the natural turn and bent of *his* mind and *my* mind be considered: what are his qualities, by which he would hope to win my esteem? — Dear, dear sir, if I *am* to be compelled, let it be in favour of a man that can read and write — that can *teach* me something: for what a husband must that man make, who can do nothing but command; and needs himself the instruction he should be qualified to give?

I may be conceited, sir; I may be vain of my little reading; of my writing; as of late I have more than once been told I am — But, sir, the more unequal the proposed match, if so; the better opinion I have of myself, the worse I must have of him; and the more unfit are we for each other.

Indeed, sir, I must say, I thought my friends had put a higher value upon me. My brother pretended once, that it was owing to such value, that Mr. Lovelace's address was prohibited. — Can this be; and such a man as Mr. Solmes be intended for me?

As to his proposed settlements, I hope I shall not incur your greater displeasure, if I say, what all who know me have reason to think (and some have upbraided me for), that I *despise* those motives. Dear, dear sir, what are settlements to one who has as much of her own as she wishes for? — Who has more in her own power, as a single person, than it is probable she would be permitted to have at her disposal, as a wife? — Whose expenses and ambition are moderate; and who, if she had superfluities, would rather dispense them to the necessitous, than lay them by her useless? If then such narrow motives have so little weight with me for my *own* benefit, shall the remote and uncertain view of family-aggrandizements, and that in the person of my *brother* and his *descendants*, be thought sufficient to influence me?

Has the behaviour of that brother to me of late, or his consideration for the family (which had so little weight with him, that he could choose to hazard a life so justly precious as an only son's, rather than not gratify passions which he is above attempting to subdue, and, give me leave to say, has been too much indulged in, either with regard to his own good, or the peace of anybody related to him; has his behaviour, I say), deserved of *me* in particular, that I should make a sacrifice of my temporal (and, who knows? of my eternal) happiness, to promote a plan formed upon *chimerical*, at least upon *unlikely* contingencies; as I will undertake to demonstrate, if I may be permitted to examine it?

I am afraid you will condemn my warmth: but does not the occasion require it? To the want of a greater degree of earnestness in my opposition, it seems, it is owing, that such advances have been made as have been made. Then, dear sir, allow something, I beseech you, for a spirit raised and embittered by disgraces, which (knowing my own heart) I am confident to say, are unmerited.

But why have I said so much, in answer to the supposed charge of prepossession, when I have declared to my mamma, as now, sir, I do to you, that if it be not insisted upon that I shall marry any other person, particularly this Mr. Solmes, I will enter into any engagements never to have the other, nor any man else, without their consents; that is to say, without the consents of my father and mother, and of you my uncle, and my elder uncle, and my cousin Morden, as he is one of the trustees for my grandfather's bounty to me?—As to my brother indeed, I cannot say, that his treatment of me has been of late so brotherly, as to entitle him to more than civility from me: and for *this*, give me leave to add, he would be very much my debtor.

If I have not been explicit enough in declaring my dislike to Mr. Solmes (that the *prepossession* which is charged upon me may not be supposed to influence me against him) I do solemnly declare, that were there no such man as Mr. Lovelace in the world, I would not have Mr. Solmes. It is necessary, in some *one* of my letters to my dear friends, that I should write so clearly as to put this matter out of all doubt: and to whom can I better address myself with an explicitness that can admit of no mistake, than to that uncle who professes the highest regard for plain-dealing and sincerity?

Let me then, for these reasons, be still more particular in some of my exceptions to him.

Mr. Solmes appears to me (to all the world indeed) to have a very narrow mind, and no great capacity: he is coarse and indelicate; as rough in his manners as in his person. he is not only narrow, but covetous: being possessed of great wealth, he enjoys it not; nor has the spirit to communicate to a distress of any kind. Does not his own sister live unhappily, for want of a little of his superfluities? And suffers he not his aged uncle, the brother of his own mother, to owe to the generosity of strangers the poor subsistence he picks up from half a dozen families?—You know, sir, my open, free, communicative temper: how unhappy must I be, circumscribed in his narrow, selfish circle! out of which, being withheld by this diabolical parsimony, he dare no more stir, than a conjurer out of his; nor would let me.

Such a man as this, *love!*—Yes, perhaps he may, my grandfather's estate; which he has told several persons (and could not resist hinting the same thing to me, with that sort of pleasure which a low mind takes, when it intimates its own *interest* as a sufficient motive for it to expect *another's favour*) lies so extremely convenient for him, that it would double the value of a considerable part of his own. That estate, and an alliance which would do credit to his obscurity and narrowness, may make him think he *can* love, and induce him to believe he *does:* but at most, it is but a second-place love. Riches were, are, and always will be, his predominant passion. *His* were left him by a miser, on this very account: and I must be obliged to forego all the choice delights of my life, and be as mean as he, or else be quite unhappy. Pardon, sir, this severity of expression — One is apt to say more than one would, of a person one dislikes, when more is said in his favour than he can possibly deserve; and when he is urged to my acceptance with so much vehemence, that there is no choice left me.

Whether these things be perfectly so, or not, while I *think* they are, it is impossible I should ever look upon Mr. Solmes in the light he is offered to me. Nay, were he to be proved ten times better than I have represented him, and sincerely think him; yet would he be still ten times more disagreeable to me than any other man I know in the world. Let me therefore beseech you, sir, to become an advocate for your niece, that she may not be made a victim to a man so highly disgustful to her.

You and my other uncle can do a great deal for me, if you please, with my papa. Be persuaded, sir, that I am not governed by obstinacy in this case; but by aversion; an aversion I cannot overcome: for, if I have but *endeavoured* to reason with myself (out of regard to the duty I owe to my father's will) my heart has recoiled, and I have been averse to myself, for offering but to argue with myself, in behalf of a man who, in the light he appears to me, has no one merit; and who, knowing this aversion, could not persevere as he does, if he had the spirit of a man.

If, sir, you can think the contents of this letter reasonable, I beseech you to support them with your interest: if not — I shall be most unhappy! — Nevertheless, it is but just in me so to write, as that Mr. Solmes may know what he has to trust to.

Forgive, dear sir, this tedious letter; and suffer it to have weight with you; and you will for ever oblige

Your dutiful and affectionate niece,
CL. HARLOWE.

MR. ANTONY HARLOWE TO MISS CL. HARLOWE.

NIECE CLARY,

You had better not write to us, or to any of us. To me, particularly, you had better never to have set pen to paper on the subject whereupon you have written

He that is first in his own cause, saith the wise man, *seemeth just: but his neighbour cometh and searcheth him.* And so, in this respect, I will be your *neighbour;* for I will search your heart to the bottom: that is to say, if your letter be written from your heart. Yet do I know what a task I have undertaken, because of the knack you are noted for at writing: but in defence of a father's authority, in behalf of the good, and honour, and prosperity of a family one comes of, what a hard thing it would be, if one could not beat down all the arguments a *rebel* child (how loth I am to write down that word of Miss Clary Harlowe!) can bring in behalf of her obstinacy!

In the first place, don't you declare (and that contrary to your declarations to your mother; remember that, girl;) that you prefer the man we all hate, and who hates us as bad! — Then what a character have you given of a worthy man! I wonder you dare write so freely of one we all respect — but possibly it may be for that very reason.

How you begin your letter! — Because I value Mr. Solmes as my friend you treat him the worse — That's the plain Dunstable of the matter, miss! — I am not such a fool but I can see that. — And so a noted whoremonger is to be chosen before a man who is a money-lover! — Let me tell you, niece, this little becomes so nice a one as you have been always reckoned. Who, think you, does most injustice, a prodigal man or a saving man? — The one saves his own money; the other spends other people's. But your favourite is a sinner in grain, and upon record.

The devil's in your sex! God forgive me for saying so — the nicest of them will prefer a vile rake and wh—— I suppose I must not repeat the word: — the *word* will offend, when the *vicious* denominated by that word will be chosen! I had not been a bachelor to this time, if I had not seen such a mass of contradictions in you all — such *gnat-strainers* and *camel-swallowers,* as venerable Holy Writ has it.

What names will perverseness call things by! — A prudent man, who intends to be just to every body, is a covetous man! — While a vile, profligate rake is christened with the appellation of a gallant man; and a polite man, I'll warrant you!

It is my firm opinion, Lovelace would not have so much regard for you as he professes; but for two reasons. And what are these? — Why, out of spite to all of us — one of them: the other, because of your independent fortune. I wish your good grandfather had not left what he did so much in your own power, as I may say. But little did he imagine his beloved grand-daughter would have turned upon all her friends as she has done!

What has Mr. Solmes to hope for, if you are prepossessed? Hey-day! Is this *you,* cousin Clary! — Has be then nothing to hope for from your father's, and mother's; and our recommendation? — No, nothing at all, it seems! — O brave! — I should think that *this*, with a dutiful child, as we took you to be, was *enough*. Depending on this your duty, we proceeded: and now there is no help for it: for we will not be balked: neither shall our friend Mr. Solmes, I can tell you that.

If your *estate is convenient for him*, what then? Does that (pert cousin) make it out that he does not love you? He had need to expect some good *with* you, that has so little good to hope for *from* you; mind that. But pray, is not this estate *our* estate, as we may say? Have we not *all* an interest in it, and a prior right, if right were to have taken place? And was it more than a good old man's dotage, God rest his soul! that gave it you before us all? — Well then, ought we not to have a choice who shall have it in marriage with you? And would you have the conscience to wish us to let a vile fellow who hates us all, run away with it? — You bid me weigh what you write: do you weigh this, girl: and it will appear we have more to say for ourselves than you was aware of.

As to your hard treatment, as you call it, thank yourself for that. It may be over when you will: so I reckon nothing upon that. You was not banished and confined till all entreaty and fair speeches were tried with you: mind that. And Mr. Solmes can't help your obstinacy. — Let that be observed too.

As *to being visited, and visiting*; you never was fond of either: so that's a grievance put into the scale to make weight. — As to disgrace, that's as bad to us as to you: so fine a young creature! So much as we used to brag of you — and too besides, this is all in your power, as the rest.

But your heart recoils, when you would persuade yourself to obey your parents — Finely described, is it not? — Too truly described, I own, as you go on. I know, that you may love him if you will. I had a good mind to bid you hate him, then, perhaps you would like him the better: for I have always found a most horrid romantic perverseness in your sex — to *do* and to *love* what you should not, is meat, drink, and vesture, to you all.

I am absolutely of your brother's mind, *that reading and writing*, though not too much for the wits of you young girls, are too much for your judgments. — You say, you *may* be conceited, cousin; you *may be* vain! — And so you *are*, to despise this gentleman as you do. He can read and write as well as *most* gentlemen, I can tell you *that*. Who told you Mr. Solmes cannot read and write? *But you must have a husband who can learn you something!* — I wish you knew but your *duty* as well as you do your talents — that, niece, you have of late days to learn; and Mr. Solmes will therefore find something to instruct you in. I will not show him this letter of yours, though you seem to desire it, lest it should provoke him to be too severe a schoolmaster, when you are his'n.

But now I think of it, suppose you *are* readier at your pen than he — you will make the more useful wife to him: won't you? For who is so good an economist as you? — And you may keep all his accounts, and save yourselves a steward. — And, let me tell you, this is a fine advantage in a family: for those stewards are often sad dogs, and creep into a man's estate before he knows where he is; and not seldom is he forced to pay them interest for his own money.

I know not why a good wife should be above these things. It is better than lying a-bed half the day, and junketting and card-playing all the night, and making yourselves wholly useless to every good purpose in your own families, as is now the fashion among ye — the deuce take ye all that do so, say I! — Only that, thank my stars, I am a bachelor.

Then this is a province you are admirably versed in: you grieve that it is taken from you *here*, you know. So here, miss, with Mr. Solmes you will have something to keep account of, for the sake of you and your children: with the other, perhaps you will have an account to keep too — but an account of what will go over the left shoulder: only what he squanders, what he borrows, and what he owes, and never will pay. Come, come, cousin, you know nothing of the world; a man's a man; and you may have many partners in a handsome man, and costly ones too, who may lavish away all you save. Mr. Solmes therefore for my money, and I hope for yours.

But *Mr. Solmes is a coarse man.* He is not delicate enough for your niceness; because I suppose he dresses not like a fop and a coxcomb, and because he lays not himself out in complimental nonsense, the poison of female minds. He is a man of sense, I can tell you. No man talks more to the purpose to *us:* but you fly him so, that he has no opportunity given him, to express it to *you:* and a man who loves, if he have ever so much sense, looks like a fool; especially when he is despised, and treated as you treated him the last time he was in your company.

As *to his sister;* she threw herself away (as you want to do) against his full warning: for he told her what she had to trust to, if she married where she did marry. And he was as good as his word; and so an honest man ought: offences against warning ought to be smarted for. Take care this be not your case. Mind that.

His *uncle* deserves no favour from *him;* for he would have circumvented Mr. Solmes, and got Sir Oliver to leave to himself the estate he had always designed for him his nephew; and brought him up in the hope of it. *Too ready forgiveness does but encourage offences:* that's your good father's maxim: and there would not be so many headstrong daughters as there are, if this maxim were kept in mind. Punishments are of service to offenders; rewards should be only to the meriting: and I think the former are to be dealt out rigorously, in wilful cases.

As to his love: he shows it but too much for your deservings, as they have been of late; let me tell you that: and this is *his* misfortune; and may in time perhaps be yours.

As *to his parsimony*, which you wickedly call diabolical [a very free word in your mouth, let me tell ye] little reason have *you* of all people for this, on whom he proposes, of his own accord, to settle all he has in the world: a proof, let him love *riches* as he will, that he loves *you* better. But that you may be without excuse on this score, we will tie him up to your own terms, and oblige him by the marriage articles to allow you a very handsome quarterly sum to do what you please with. And this has been told you before; and I have said it to Mrs. Howe (that good and worthy lady) before her proud daughter, that you might hear of it again.

To contradict the charge of prepossession to Lovelace, you offer never to have him without our consents: and what is this saying, but that you will hope on for our consents, and to wheedle and tire us out? Then he will always be in expectation while you are single: and we are to live on at this rate (are we?) vexed by you, and continually watchful about you; and as continually exposed to his insolence and threats. Remember last Sunday, girl! — What might have happened, had your brother and he met? — Moreover, you cannot do with such a spirit as his, 'as you can with worthy Mr. Solmes: the one you make tremble; the other will make you quake — Mind that — and you will not be able to help yourself. And remember, that if there should be any misunderstanding between *one* of them and you, we should all interpose; and with effect, no doubt: but with the *other*, it would be *self-do*, *self-have;* and who would either care or dare to put in a word for you? Nor let the supposition of matrimonial differences frighten you: honeymoon lasts not now-a-days above a fortnight; and Dunmow flitch, as I have been informed, was *never* claimed; though some say *once* it was. Marriage is a queer state, child, whether paired by the parties or by their friends. Out of three brothers of us, you know, there was but one had courage to marry. And why was it, do you think? We were wise by other people's experience.

Don't despise money so much: you may come to know the value of it: that is a piece of *instruction* that you *are to learn;* and which, according to your *own* notions, Mr. Solmes will be *able to teach you.*

I do indeed condemn your *warmth*. I will not *allow for dis-*

graces you bring upon yourself. If I thought them *unmerited*, I would be your advocate. But it was always my notion, that children should not dispute their parents' authority. When your grandfather left his estate to you, though his three sons, and a grandson, and your eldest sister, were in being, we all acquiesced: And why? Because it was our father's doing. Do you imitate that example: if you will not, those who set it you have the more reason to hold you inexcusable. Mind that, cousin.

You mention your brother too scornfully: and, in your letter to him, are very disrespectful; and so indeed you are to your sister, in the letter you wrote to her. Your brother, madam, is your brother; a third older than yourself; and a *man*: and pray be so good as not to forget what is due to a brother, who (next to us three brothers) is the head of the family; and on whom the name depends — as upon your dutiful compliance depends the success of the noblest plan that ever was laid down for the honour of the family you are come of. And pray now let me ask you, if the honour of that will not be an honour to you? — If you don't think so, the more unworthy you. You shall see the plan, if you promise not to be prejudiced against it right or wrong. If you are not besotted to that man, I am sure, you will like it. If you are, were Mr. Solmes an angel, it would signify nothing: for the devil is love, and love is the devil, when it gets into any of your heads. Many examples have I seen of that.

If there were no such man as Lovelace in the world, you would not have Mr. Solmes. — You would not, miss! — Very pretty, truly; — we *see* how your spirit is *embittered* indeed.— Wonder not, since it is come to your *will not's*, that those who have authority over you say, *You shall have the other*. And I am one. Mind that. And if it behoves YOU *to speak out*, miss, it behoves us not to *speak in*. What's *sauce for the goose is sauce for the gander:* take that in your thought too.

I humbly apprehend, that Mr. Solmes *has the spirit of a man, and a gentleman*. I would admonish you therefore not to provoke it. He pities you as much as he loves you. He says, he will convince you of his love by deeds, since he is not permitted by you to express it by words. And all his dependence is upon your generosity hereafter. We hope he *may* depend upon that: we encourage him to think he may. And this heartens him up. So that you may lay his constancy at your parents' and your uncles' doors: and this will be another mark of your duty, you know.

You must be sensible, that you reflect upon your parents, and all of us, when you tell me you cannot in *justice* accept of the settlements proposed to you. This reflection we should have wondered at from you once; but now we don't.

There are many other very

censurable passages in this free letter of yours; but we must place them to the account of your *embittered* spirit. I am glad you mentioned that word, because we should have been at a loss what to have called it. — I should much rather nevertheless have had reason to give it a better name.

I love you dearly still, miss. I think you, though my niece, one of the finest young gentlewomen I ever saw. But upon my conscience, I think you ought to obey your parents, and oblige me, and my brother John: for you know very well, that we have nothing but your good at heart: consistently indeed with the good and honour of *all* of us. What must we think of any one of it, who would not promote the good of the whole? And who would set one part of it against another? — Which God forbid, say I! — You see I am for the good of *all*. What shall *I* get by it, let things go as they will? Do I want any thing of any body for my own sake? — Does my brother John? — Well then, cousin Clary, what would you be at, as I may say?

O but you can't love Mr. Solmes! — But, I say, you know not *what* you can do. You *encourage* yourself in your dislike. You *permit* your heart (little did I think it was such a froward one) to *recoil*. Take it to task, niece; *drive it on* as fast as it *recoils* [we do so in all our sea-fights, and land-fights too, by our sailors and soldiers, or we should not conquer]; and we are all sure you will overcome it. And why? Because you *ought*. So *we* think whatever *you* think: and whose thoughts are to be preferred? You may be *wittier* than we; but, if you are *wiser*, we have lived some of us, let me tell you, to very little purpose thirty or forty years longer than you.

I have written as long a letter as yours. I may not write in so lively, or so polite a style as my niece; but I think I have all the argument on my side: and you will vastly oblige me, if you will show me by your compliance with all our desires, that you think so too. If you do not, you must not expect an advocate, or even a friend, in me, dearly as I love you. For then I shall be sorry to be called

Your uncle,
ANTONY HARLOWE.

Tuesday, two in the morning.

POSTSCRIPT.

You must send me no more letters: but a compliable one you may send. But I need not have forbid you; for I am sure this, by fair argument, is unanswerable — I know it is. I have written day and night, I may say, ever since Sunday morning, only church-time, or the like of that: But this is the last I can tell you, from

ANT. H.

LETTER XXXIII.

Miss Clarissa Harlowe to Miss Howe.

Thursday, March 16.

Having met with such bad success in my application to my relations, I have taken a step that will surprise you. It is no other than writing a letter to Mr. Solmes himself. I sent it; and have his answer. He had certainly help in it. For I have seen a letter of his; as indifferently worded, as poorly spelt. Yet the superscription is of *his* dictating, I dare say; for he is a formal wretch. With these, I shall inclose one from my brother to me, on occasion of mine to Mr. Solmes. I did think that it was possible to discourage the man from proceeding; and if I could have done that, it would have answered all my wishes. It was worth the trial. But you'll see nothing will do. My brother has taken his measures too securely.

TO ROGER SOLMES, ESQ.

Wednesday, March 15.

SIR,

You will wonder to receive a letter from me; and more still at the uncommon subject of it: But the necessity of the case will justify me, at least in my own apprehension; and I shall therefore make no other apology for it.

When you first came acquainted with our family, you found the writer of this one of the happiest creatures in the world; beloved by the best and most indulgent of parents; and rejoicing in the kind favour of two affectionate uncles, and in the esteem of every one.

But how is this happy scene now changed! — You were pleased to cast a favourable eye upon me. You addressed yourself to my friends: your proposals were approved of by them — approved of without consulting me; as if my choice and happiness were of the least signification. Those who had a right to all reasonable obedience from me, insisted upon it without reserve. I had not the felicity to think as they did: almost the first time my sentiments differed from theirs. I besought them to indulge me in a point so important to my future happiness: but, alas, in vain! And then (for I thought it was but honest) I told *you* my mind; and even that my affections were engaged. But, to my mortification and surprise, you persisted, and still persist.

The consequence of all is too grievous for me to repeat: you, who have such free access to the rest of the family, know it too well — too well you know it, either for the credit of your own generosity, or for my reputation. I am used on your account, as I never before was used, and never before was thought to deserve to be used; and this was the hard, the impossible condition of their returning favour, that I must prefer a man *to* all others, that *of* all others I cannot prefer.

Thus distressed, and made unhappy, and all for your sake, and through your cruel perseverance, I write, sir, to demand of you the peace of mind you have robbed me of: to demand of you the love of so many dear friends, of which you have deprived me; and, if you have the generosity that should distinguish a man, and a gentleman, to adjure you not to continue an address that has been attended with such cruel effects to the creature you profess to esteem.

If you really value me, as my friends would make me believe, and as you have declared you do, must it not be a mean and selfish value? A value that can have no merit with the unhappy object of it, because it is attended with effects so grievous to her? It must be for *your own sake* only, not for *mine*. And even in this point you must be mistaken; for, would a prudent man wish to marry one who has not a heart to give? Who cannot esteem him? Who therefore must prove a bad wife? — And how cruel would it be to make a poor creature a bad wife, whose pride it would be to make a good one?

If I am capable of judging, our tempers and inclinations are vastly different. Any other of my sex will make you happier than I can. The treatment I meet with, and the obstinacy, as it is called, with which I support myself under it, ought to convince you of this; were I *not* able to give so good a reason for this my supposed perverseness, as that I cannot consent to marry a man whom I cannot value.

But if, sir, you have not so much generosity in your value for me, as to desist for *my own* sake, let me conjure you, by the regard due to *yourself*, and to your own future happiness, to discontinue your suit, and place your affections on a worthier object: for why should you make *me* miserable and *yourself* not happy? By this means you will do all that is now in your power to restore to me the affection of my friends; and, if that can be, it will leave me in as happy a state as you found me in. You need only to say, that you see there are no hopes, as you will perhaps complaisantly call it, of succeeding with me (and indeed, sir, there cannot be a greater truth); and that you will therefore no more think of me; but turn your thoughts another way.

Your compliance with this request will lay me under the highest obligation to your generosity, and make me ever

Your well-wisher, and humble servant,
CLARISSA HARLOWE.

TO MISS CLARISSA HARLOWE.
These most humbly present.

DEAREST MISS,

YOUR letter has had a very contrary effect upon me, to what you seem to have expected from it. It has doubly convinced me of the excellency of your mind, and of the honour of your disposition. Call it *selfish*, or what you please, I must persist in my suit; and happy shall I be, if by patience and perseverance, and a steady and unalterable devoir, I may at last overcome the difficulty laid in my way.

As your good parents, your uncles, and other friends, are absolutely determined you shall never have Mr. Lovelace, if they can help it; and as I presume no other person is in the way; I will contentedly wait the issue of this matter. And forgive me, dearest miss; but a person should sooner persuade me to give up to him my estate, as an instance of my generosity, because *he* could not be happy without it, than I would a much more valuable treasure, to promote the felicity of another, and make his way easier to circumvent myself.

Pardon me, dear miss; but I must persevere, though I am sorry you suffer on my account, as you are pleased to think; for I never before saw the woman I could love: and while there is any hope, and that you remain undisposed of to some happier man, I must and will be

Your faithful and obsequious admirer,

March 16. ROGER SOLMES.

MR. JAMES HARLOWE TO MISS CL. HARLOWE.

March 16.

WHAT a fine whim you took into your head, to write a letter to Mr. Solmes, to persuade him to give up his pretensions to you! — Of *all* the pretty romantic flights you have delighted in, this was certainly one of the most extraordinary. But to say nothing of what fires us all with indignation against you (your owning your prepossession in a villain's favour; and your impertinence to me, and your sister, and your uncles; one of which has given it you home, child); how can you lay at Mr. Solmes's door the usage you so bitterly complain of? — You know, little fool as you are, that it is your fondness for Lovelace that has brought upon you all these things; and which would have happened whether Mr. Solmes had honoured you with his addresses or not.

As you must needs know this to be true, consider, pretty witty miss, if your fond love-sick heart can let you consider, what a fine figure all your expostulations with us, and charges upon Mr. Solmes, make! — With what propriety do you *demand* of *him* to restore to you your former happiness (as you call it, and *merely* call it; for if you thought our favour so, you would restore it to yourself), since it is in your own power to do so? therefore, Miss Pert, none of your pathetics, except in the right place. Depend upon it, whether you have Mr. Solmes, or not, you shall never have your heart's delight, the vile rake Lovelace, if our parents, if our uncles, if I can hinder it: no! you fallen angel, you shall not give your father and mother such a *son*, nor me such a *brother*, in giving yourself that profligate wretch for a *husband*. And so set your heart at rest, and lay aside all thoughts of him, if ever you expect forgiveness, reconciliation, or a kind opinion, from any of your family; but especially from him, who, at present, styles himself

Your brother,
JAMES HARLOWE.

P. S. I know your knack at letter-writing. If you send me an answer to this, I will return it unopened; for I will not argue with your perverseness in so plain a case. — Only once for all, I was willing to put you right as to Mr. Solmes; whom I think to blame to trouble his head about you.

LETTER XXXIV.
Mr. Lovelace to John Belford, Esq.

Friday, March 17.

I RECEIVE, with great pleasure, the early and cheerful assurances of your loyalty and love. And let our principal and most trusty friends named in my last know that I do.

I would have thee, Jack, come down, as soon as thou canst. I believe I shall not want the others so soon. Yet they may come down to Lord M's. I will be there, if not to receive them, to satisfy my lord, that there is no new mischief in hand, which will require his second intervention.

For thyself, thou must be constantly with me: not for my *security*: the family dare do nothing but bully: they bark only at a distance: but for my *entertainment*: that thou mayest, from the Latin and the English classics, keep my love-sick soul from drooping.

Thou hadst best come to me here, in thy old corporal's coat: thy servant out of livery; and to be upon a familiar foot with thee, as a distant relation, to be provided for by thy interest above — I mean not in heaven, thou mayest be sure. Thou wilt find me at a little alehouse; they call it an inn: the White Hart; most terribly wounded (but by the weather only) the sign: — in a sorry village; within five miles from Harlowe Place. Every body knows Harlowe Place; for, like Versailles, it is sprung up from a dunghill, within every elderly person's remembrance. Every poor body, particularly, knows it. But that only for a few years past, since a certain angel has appeared there among the sons and daughters of men.

The people here at the Hart are poor, but honest, and have gotten it into their heads, that I am a man of quality in disguise; and there is no reining in their officious respect. Here is a pretty little smirking daughter; seventeen six days ago. I call her my rose-bud. Her grandmother (for there is no mother) a good neat old woman, as ever filled a wicker chair in a chimney-corner, has besought me to be merciful to her.

This is the right way with me. Many and many a pretty rogue had I spared, whom I did *not* spare, had my power been acknowledged, and my mercy in time implored. But the *Debellare superbos* should be my motto, were I to have a new one.

This simple chit (for there is a simplicity in her thou wouldst be highly pleased with: all humble; all officious; all innocent — I love her for her humility, her officiousness, and even for her *innocence*), will be pretty amusement to thee; while I combat with the weather, and dodge and creep about the walls and purlieus of Harlowe Place. Thou wilt see in her mind all that her superiors have been taught to 'conceal, in order to render themselves less natural, and of consequence less pleasing.

But I charge thee, that thou do not (what I would not permit myself to do for the world — I charge thee, that thou do not) crop my rose-bud. She is the only flower of fragrance, that has blown in this vicinage for ten years past; or will for ten years to come: for I have looked backward to the *have-been's*, and forward to the *will-be's*; having but too much leisure upon my hands in my present waiting.

I never was so honest for so long together since my matriculation. It behoves me so to be — some way or other, my recess at this little inn may be found out; and it will then be thought that my rose-bud has attracted me. A report in my favour, from simplicities so amiable, may establish me; for the grandmother's relation to my rose-bud may be sworn to; and the father is an honest poor man: has no joy, but in his rose-bud. — O Jack! spare thou therefore (for I shall leave thee often alone with her, spare thou) my rose-bud! — Let the rule I never departed from, but it cost me a long regret, be observed to my rose-bud! — never to ruin a poor girl, whose simplicity and innocence were all she had to trust to; and whose fortunes were too low to save her from the rude contempts of worse minds than her own, and from an indigence extreme: such a one willouly pine in secret; and at last, perhaps, in order to refuge herself from slanderous tongues and virulence, be induced to tempt some guilty stream, or seek her end in the knee-encircling garter, that, per-adventure, was the first attempt of abandoned love. — No defiances will my rose-bud breathe; no *self* dependent, *thee* doubting watchfulness (indirectly challenging thy inventive machinations to do their worst) will she assume. Unsuspicious of her danger, the lamb's throat will hardly shun thy knife! — O be not thou the butcher of my lambkin!

The less be thou so, for the reason I am going to give thee — The gentle heart is touched by love: her soft bosom heaves with a passion she has not yet found a name for. I once caught her eye following a young carpenter, a widow neighbour's son, living [to speak in her dialect] *at the little white house over the way;* a gentle youth he also seems to be, about three years older than herself:

playmates from infancy, till his eighteenth and her fifteenth year furnished a reason for a greater distance in show, while their hearts gave a better for their being nearer than ever — for I soon perceived the love reciprocal. A scrape and a bow at first seeing his pretty mistress; turning often to salute her following eye; and, when a winding lane was to deprive him of her sight, his whole body turned round, his hat more reverently d'offed than before. This answered (for, unseen, I was behind her) by a low courtesy, and a sigh, that Johnny was too far off to hear! — Happy whelp! said I to myself. — I withdrew; and in tript my rose-bud, as if satisfied with the dumb show, and wishing nothing beyond it.

I have examined the little heart. She has made me her confidant. She owns, she could love Johnny Barton very well: and Johnny Barton has told her, he could love her better than any maiden he ever saw — but, alas! it must not be thought of. Why not be thought of? — She don't know! — And then she sighed: but Johnny has an aunt, who will give him an hundred pounds, when his time is out; and her father cannot give her but a few things, or so, to set her out with; and though Johnny's mother says, she knows not where Johnny would have a prettier, or notabler wife, yet — and then she sighed again — what signifies talking? — I would not have Johnny be unhappy and poor for me! — For what good would that do *me*, you know, sir!

What would I give [by my soul, my angel will indeed reform me, if her friends' implacable folly ruin us not both! — What would I give] to have so innocent and so good a heart, as either my rose-bud's, or Johnny's!

I have a confounded mischievous one — by *nature* too, I think. — A good motion now and then rises from it: but it dies away presently — A love of intrigue — An invention for mischief — A triumph in subduing — Fortune encouraging and supporting — And a constitution — What signifies palliating? But I believe I had been a rogue, had I been a plough-boy.

But the devil's in this sex! Eternal misguiders. Who, that has once trespassed with them, ever recovered his virtue? And yet where there is not virtue, which nevertheless we free-livers are continually plotting to destroy, what is there even in the ultimate of our wishes with them? — *Preparation* and *expectation* are in a manner every thing: *reflection* indeed may be something, if the mind be hardened above feeling the guilt of a past *trespass*: but the *fruition*, what is there in that? And yet that being the end, nature will not be satisfied without it.

See what grave reflections an innocent subject will produce! It gives me some pleasure to think, that it is not out of my *power* to reform: but then, Jack, I am afraid I must keep better company than I do at present — for we certainly harden one another. But be not cast down, my boy; there will be time enough to give the whole fraternity warning to choose another leader: and I fancy thou wilt be the man.

Meantime, as I make it my rule, whenever I have committed a very capital enormity, to do some good by way of atonement; and as I believe I am a pretty deal indebted to that score: I intend, before I leave these parts [successfully shall I leave them I hope, or I shall be tempted to double the mischief by way of revenge, though not to my rose-bud any] to join an hundred pounds to Johnny's aunt's hundred pounds, to make one innocent couple happy. — I repeat therefore, and for half-a-dozen more *therefores* — Spare thou my rose-bud.

An interruption — Another letter anon; and both shall go together.

LETTER XXXV.

Mr. Lovelace to John Belford, Esq.

I HAVE found out by my *watchful spy* almost as many of my charmer's motions, as of those of the rest of her relations. It delights me to think how the rascal is caressed by the uncles and nephew; and let into *their* secrets; yet proceeds all the time by *my* line of direction. I have charged him, however, on forfeiture of his present weekly stipend, and my future favour, to take care, that neither my beloved, nor any of the family, suspect him; I have told him that he may indeed watch her egresses and regresses; but that only to keep off other servants from her paths, yet not to be seen by her himself.

The dear creature has tempted him, he told *them*, with a bribe [*which she never offered*] to convey a letter [*which she never wrote*] to Miss Howe; *he believes*, with one inclosed (*perhaps to me*): but he declined it: and he begged they would take no notice of it to *her*. This brought him a stingy shilling; great applause; and an injunction followed it to all the servants, for the strictest lookout, lest she should contrive some way to send it — And, about an hour after, an order was given him to throw himself in her way; and (expressing his concern for denying her request) to tender his service to her, and to bring them her letter; which it will be *proper for him to report* that she has refused to give him.

Now seest thou not, how many good ends this contrivance answers?

In the first place, the lady is secured by it, against her own knowledge, in the liberty allowed her of taking her private walks in the garden: for *this attempt* has confirmed them in their belief, that now they have turned off her maid, she has no way to send a letter out of the house: if she had, she would not have run the risque of tempting a fellow who had not been in her secret — So that she can prosecute unsuspectedly her correspondence with me, and Miss Howe.

In the next place, it will perhaps afford me an opportunity of a private interview with her, which I am meditating, let her take it as she will; having found out by my *spy* (who can keep off every body else) that she goes every morning and evening to a woodhouse remote from the dwelling-house, under pretence of visiting and feeding a set of bantam-poultry, which were produced from a breed that was her grandfather's, and of which for that reason she is very fond; as also of some other curious fowls brought from the same place. I have an account of all her motions here. — And as she has owned to me in one of her letters that she corresponds privately with Miss Howe, I presume it is by this way.

The interview I am meditating, will produce her consent, I hope, to other favours of the like kind: for, should she not choose the place in which I am expecting to see her, I can attend her any where in the rambling, Dutch-taste garden, whenever she will permit me that honour: for my implement, *hight Joseph Leman*, has procured me the opportunity of getting two keys made to the garden door (one of which I have given him, for reasons good); which door opens to the haunted coppice, as tradition has made the servants think it; a man having been found hanging in it about twenty years ago: and Joseph, upon proper notice, will leave it unbolted.

But I was obliged previously to give him my honour, that no mischief should happen to any of my adversaries, from this liberty: for the fellow tells me, he loves all his masters: and, only that he knows I am a man of honour; and that my alliance will do credit to the family; and after prejudices are overcome, every body will think so; or he would not for the world act the part he does.

There never was a rogue, who had not a salvo to himself for being so. — What a praise to *honesty*, that every man pretends to it, even at the instant that he knows he is pursuing the methods that will perhaps prove him a knave to the whole world, as well as to his own conscience!

But what this stupid family can mean, to make all this necessary, I cannot imagine. MY REVENGE and my LOVE are uppermost by turns. If the latter succeed not, the gratifying of the former will be my only consolation: and, by all that's good, they shall feel it; although for it I become an exile from my native country for ever.

I will throw myself into my charmer's presence. I have twice already attempted it in vain. I shall then see what I may depend upon from her favour. If I thought I had no prospect of that, I should be tempted to carry her off. — That would be a rape worthy of a Jupiter!

Clarissa. I.   11

But all gentle shall be my movements: all respectful, even to reverence, my address to her — Her hand shall be the only witness to the pressure of my lip — my trembling lip: I *know* it will tremble, if I do not *bid* it tremble. As soft my sighs, as the sighs of my gentle rose-bud. By *my* humility will I invite *her* confidence: the loneliness of the place shall give me no advantage: to dissipate her fears, and engage her reliance upon my honour for the future, shall be my whole endeavour: but little will I complain of, not at all will I threaten, those who are continually threatening me: but yet with a view to act the part of Dryden's Lion; to secure my love, or to let loose my vengeance upon my hunters.

What though his mighty soul his grief
contains?
He meditates revenge who least complains:
And like a lion slumb'ring in his way,
Or sleep dissembling, while he waits his
prey,
His fearless foes within his distance
draws;
Constrains his roaring, and contracts his
paws;
Till at the last, his time for fury found,
He shoots with sudden vengeance from
the ground:
The prostrate vulgar passes o'er, and
spares:
But, with a lordly rage, his hunters tears.

LETTER XXXVI.

Miss Clarissa Harlowe to Miss Howe.

Saturday, March 18.

I HAVE been frighted out of my wits — Still am in a manner out of breath — Thus occasioned — I went down, under the usual pretence, in hopes to find something from you. Concerned at my disappointment, I was returning from the woodhouse, when I heard a rustling as of somebody behind a stack of wood. I was extremely surprised: but still more, to behold a man coming from behind the furthermost stack. O, thought I, at that moment, the sin of a prohibited correspondence!

In the same point of time that I saw him, he besought me not to be frighted: and still nearer approaching me, threw open a horseman's coat: and who should it be but Mr. Lovelace! — I could not scream out (yet attempted to scream, the moment I saw a man; and again, when I saw who it was); for I had no voice: and had I not caught hold of a prop which supported the old roof, I should have sunk.

I had hitherto, as you know, kept him at a distance: and now, as I recovered myself, judge of my first emotions, when I recollected his character from every mouth of my family; his enterprising temper; and found myself alone with him, in a place so near a bye-lane, and so remote from the house.

But his respectful behaviour soon dissipated these fears, and gave me others; lest we should be seen together, and information of it given to my brother: the consequences of which, I could readily think, would be, if not further mischief, an imputed assignation, a stricter confinement, a forfeited correspondence with you, my beloved friend, and a pretence for the most violent compulsion: and neither the one set of reflections, nor the other, acquitted him to me for his bold intrusion.

As soon therefore as I could speak, I expressed with the greatest warmth my displeasure; and told him, that he cared not how much he exposed me to the resentment of all my friends, provided he could gratify his own impetuous humour. I then commanded him to leave the place that moment; and was hurrying from him, when he threw himself in the way at my feet, beseeching my stay for one moment; declaring, that he suffered himself to be guilty of this rashness, as I thought it, to avoid one much greater:— for, in short, he could not bear the hourly insults he received from my family, with the thoughts of having so little interest in my favour, that he could not promise himself that his patience and forbearance would be attended with any other issue than to lose me for ever, and be triumphed over and insulted upon it.

This man, you know, has very ready knees. You have said, that he ought, in small points, frequently to offend, on purpose to shew what an address he is master of.

He ran on, expressing his apprehensions that a temper so gentle and obliging, as he said mine was, to every body but him (and a dutifulness so exemplary inclining me to do my part to others, whether they did theirs or not by me) would be wrought upon in favour of a man set up in part to be revenged upon myself, for my grandfather's envied distinction of me; and in part to be revenged upon him, for having given life to one, who would have taken his; and now sought to deprive him of hopes dearer to him than life.

I told him he might be assured, that the severity and ill-usage I met with would be far from effecting the proposed end: that although I could, with great sincerity, declare for a single life (which had always been my choice); and particularly, that if ever I married, if they would not insist upon the man I had an aversion to, it should not be with the man they disliked —

He interrupted me here: he hoped I would forgive him for it; but he could not help expressing his great concern, that, after so many instances of his passionate and obsequious devotion —

And pray, sir, said I, let me interrupt you in my turn; — why don't you assert, in still plainer words, the obligation you have laid me under by this your boasted devotion? Why don't you let me know, in terms as high as your implication, that a perseverance I have not wished for, which has set all my relations at variance with me, is a merit that throws upon me the guilt of ingratitude for not answering it as you seem to expect?

I must forgive him, he said, if

11*

he, who pretended only to a comparative merit (and otherwise thought no man living could deserve me) had presumed to hope for a greater share in my favour, than he had hitherto met with, when such men as Mr. Symmes, Mr. Wyerley, and now, lastly, so vile a reptile as this Solmes, however discouraged by myself, were made his competitors. As to the perseverance I mentioned, it was impossible for him *not* to persevere: but I must needs know, that were *he* not in being, the terms Solmes had proposed were such, as would have involved me in the same difficulties with my relations that I now laboured under. He therefore took the liberty to say, that my favour to him, far from increasing those difficulties, would be the readiest way to extricate me from them. They had made it impossible [he told me, with too much truth] to oblige them any way, but by sacrificing myself to Solmes. They were well apprised besides of the difference between the two: one, whom they hoped to manage as they pleased; the other, who could and would protect me from every insult; and who had *natural* prospects much superior to my brother's *foolish* views of a title.

How comes this man to know so well all our foibles? But I more wonder, how he came to have a notion of meeting me in this place?

I was very uneasy to be gone; and the more as the night came on apace. But there was no getting from him, till I had heard a great deal more of what he had to say.

As he hoped, that I would one day make him the happiest man in the world, he assured me, that he had so much regard for my fame, that he would be as far from advising any step that was likely to cast a shade upon my reputation (although that step was to be ever so much in his own favour), as I would be to follow such advice. But since I was not to be permitted to live single, he would submit it to my consideration, whether I had any way but *one* to avoid the intended violence to my inclinations — My father so jealous of his authority: both my uncles in my father's way of thinking: my cousin Morden at a distance: my uncle and aunt Hervey awed into *insignificance*, was his word: my brother and sister inflaming every one: Solmes's offers captivating: Miss Howe's mother rather of a party with them, from motives respecting example to her own daughter.

And then he asked me, if I would receive a letter from Lady Betty Lawrence, on this occasion, for Lady Sarah Sadleir, he said, having lately lost her only child, hardly looked into the world, or thought of it further than to wish him married, and preferably to all the women in the world with me.

To be sure, my dear, there is a great deal in what the man said — I may be allowed to say this without an imputed *glow* or *throb,*

— But I told him nevertheless, that although I had great honour for the ladies he was related to, yet I should not choose to receive a letter on a subject that had a tendency to promote an end I was far from intending to promote: that it became me, ill as I was treated at present, to *hope* every thing, to *bear* every thing, and to *try* every thing: when my father saw my steadfastness, and that I would die rather than have Mr. Solmes, he would perhaps recede —

Interrupting me, he represented the unlikelihood there was of that, from the courses they had entered upon; which he thus enumerated: — their engaging Mrs. Howe against me in the first place, as a person I might have thought to fly to, if pushed to desperation: — my brother continually buzzing in my father's ears, that my cousin Morden would soon arrive, and then would insist upon giving me possession of my grandfather's estate, in pursuance of the will; which would render me independent of my father: — their disgraceful confinement of me: — their dismissing so suddenly my servant, and setting my sister's over me: — their engaging my mother, contrary to her own judgment, against me: these, he said, were all so many flagrant proofs that they would stick at nothing to carry their point: and were what made him inexpressibly uneasy.

He appealed to me, whether ever I knew my father recede from any resolution he had once fixed; especially, if he thought either his prerogative, or his authority, concerned in the question. His acquaintance with our family, he said, enabled him to give several instances (but they would be too grating to me) of an arbitrariness that had few examples, even in the families of princes: an arbitrariness, which the most excellent of women, my mother, too severely experienced.

He was proceeding, as I thought, with reflections of this sort; and I angrily told him, I would not permit my father to be reflected upon; adding, that his severity to me, however unmerited, was not a warrant for me to dispense with my duty to him.

He had no pleasure, he said, in urging any thing that could be *so* construed; for, however well-warranted *he* was to make such reflections from the provocations they were continually giving him, he knew how offensive to *me* any liberties of this sort would be. — And yet he must own, that it was painful to *him*, who had youth and passions to be allowed for as well as others; and who had always valued himself upon speaking his mind, to curb himself, under such treatment. Nevertheless, his consideration for me would make him confine himself in his observations, to facts that were too flagrant, and too openly avowed to be disputed. It could not therefore *justly* displease, he would venture to say, if he made this natural inference from the premises, that if such were my father's behaviour to a *wife*, who disputed not the imaginary prerogative he was so unprecedently fond of asserting, what room had a *daughter* to hope, that he would depart from an *authority* he was so earnest, and so much more concerned to maintain? — Family interests at the same time engaging; an aversion, however causelessly received, stimulating; my brother's and sister's resentments and selfish views co-operating; and my banishment from their presence depriving me of all *personal* plea or entreaty in my own favour.

How unhappy, my dear, that there is but too much reason for these observations, and for this inference; made, likewise, with more coolness and respect to my family than one would have apprehended from a man so much provoked, and of passions so high, and generally thought uncontrolable!

Will you not question me about *throbs* and *glows* if, from such instances of a command over his fiery temper, for my sake, I am ready to infer, that were my friends capable of a reconciliation with him, he might be affected by arguments apparently calculated for his present and future good? Nor is it a very bad indication, that he has such moderate notions of that very high prerogative in husbands, of which we in our family have been accustomed to hear so much.

He represented to me, that my present disgraceful confinement was known to all the world: that neither my sister nor brother scrupled to represent me as an obliged and favoured child in a state of actual rebellion: — that, nevertheless, every body who knew me was ready to justify me for an aversion to a man whom every body thought utterly unworthy of *me*, and more fit for my *sister:* that unhappy as he was, in not having been able to make any greater impression upon me in his favour, all the world gave me to him: — nor was there but one objection made to him, by his very enemies (his birth, his fortunes, his prospects all unexceptionable, and the latter splendid); and that objection, he thanked God, and my example, was in a fair way of being removed for ever: since he had seen his error, and was heartily sick of the courses he had followed; which, however, were far less enormous than malice and envy had represented them to be. But of this he should say the less, as it were much better to justify himself by his actions, than by the most solemn asseverations and promises. And then complimenting my *person*, he assured me (for that he always *loved* virtue, although he had not followed its rules as he ought) that he was still more captivated with the graces of my *mind:* and would frankly own, that till he had the honour to know *me*, he had never met with an inducement sufficient to enable him to overcome an unhappy kind of prejudice to matrimony; which had made him before inpenetrable to the wishes and recommendations of all his relations.

You see, my dear, he scruples not to speak of himself, as his enemies speak of him. I can't say, but his openness in these particulars gives a credit to his other professions. I should easily, I think, detect an hypocrite: and *this* man particularly, who is said to have allowed himself in great liberties, were he to pretend to *instantaneous* lights and convictions — at his time of life too — habits, I am sensible, are not so easily changed. You have always joined with me in remarking, that he will speak his mind with freedom, even to a degree of unpoliteness sometimes; and that his very treatment of my family is a proof that he cannot make a mean court to any body for interest sake — What pity, where there are such laudable traces, that they should have been so mired, and choaked up, as I may say! — We have heard, that the man's head is better than his heart: but do you really think Mr. Lovelace can have a *very* bad heart? Why should not there be something in *blood* in the human creature, as well as in the ignobler animals? None of his family are exceptionable — but himself, indeed. The characters of the ladies are admirable — but I shall incur the imputation I wish to avoid. Yet what a look of censoriousness does it carry in an unsparing friend, to take one to task for doing that justice, and making those charitable inferences, in favour of a particular person, which one ought without scruple to do, and to make, in the behalf of any other man living?

He then again pressed me to receive a letter of offered protection from Lady Betty. He said, that people of birth stood a little too much upon punctilio; as people of virtue also did (but indeed birth, worthily lived up to, was virtue: a decent punctilio the same; the origin of both one) [how came this notion from him!] — Else, Lady Betty would write to *me:* but she would be willing to be first apprised, that her offer would be well received — as it would have the appearance of being made against the liking of one part of my family; and which nothing would induce her to make, but the degree of unworthy persecution which I actually laboured under, and had reason further to apprehend.

I told him, that however greatly I thought myself obliged to Lady Betty Lawrence, if this offer came from herself; yet it was easy to see to what it led. It might look like vanity in me perhaps to say, that this urgency in him on this occasion, wore the face of art, in order to engage me into measures from which I might not easily extricate myself. I said, that I should not be affected by the splendour of even a royal title. *Goodness*, I thought, was *greatness:* that the excellent characters of the ladies of his family weighed more with me, than the consideration that they were sisters to Lord M. and daughters of an earl: that he would not have found encouragement from me, had my friends been *consenting* to his address, if he had only a *mere* relative merit to those ladies; since in that case, the very reasons that made me admire *them*, would have been so many objections to their *kinsman*.

I then assured him, that it was with infinite concern, that I had found myself drawn into an epistolary correspondence with him; especially since that correspondence had been prohibited: — and the only agreeable use I could think of making of this unexpected and undesired interview, was, to let him know that I should from henceforth think myself obliged to discontinue it. And I hoped, that he would not have the *thought* of engaging me to carry it on by menacing my relations.

There was light enough to distinguish, that he looked very grave upon this. He so much valued my *free* choice, he said, and my *unbiassed* favour (scorning to set himself upon a footing with Solmes in the compulsory methods used in that man's behalf) that he should hate himself, were he capable of a view of intimidating me by so very poor a method. But, nevertheless, there were two things to be considered: first, that the continual outrages he was treated with; the spies set over him, one of which he had detected; the indignities all his family were likewise treated with; as also myself; avowedly in malice to him, or he should not presume to take upon himself to resent for me, without my leave [the artful wretch saw he would have laid open here, had he not thus guarded] — all these considerations called upon him to shew a proper resentment: and he would leave it to me to judge, whether it would be reasonable for him, as a man of spirit, to bear such insults, if it were not for my sake. I would be pleased to consider, in the next place, whether the situation I was in (a prisoner in my father's house, and my whole family determined to compel me to marry a man unworthy of me; and that speedily, and whether I consented or not) admitted of delay in the preventive measures he was desirous to put me upon, *in the last resort only*. Nor was there a necessity, he said, if I were actually in Lady Betty's protection, that I should be his, if, afterwards, I should see any thing objectible in his conduct.

But what would the world conclude would be the end, I demanded, were I, in the last resort, as he proposed, to throw myself into the protection of *his* friends, but that it was with such a view?

And what less did the world think *now*, he asked, than that I was confined that I *might not?* You are to consider, madam, you have not now an option; and to whom it is owing that you have not; and that you are in the power of those (parents why should I call them?) who are determined, that you shall *not* have an option. All I propose is, that you will embrace such a protection; — but not till you have tried every way, to avoid the necessity for it.

And give me leave to say, proceeded he, that if a correspondence on which I have founded all my hopes, is, at this critical conjuncture, to be broken off; and if you are resolved not to be *provided against* the worst; it must be plain to me, that you will at last yield to that worst — worst to *me* only — it cannot be to *you* — and *then!* [and he put his hand clenched to his forehead] how shall I bear the supposition? — *Then* will you be that Solmes's!—But, by all that's sacred, neither he, nor your brother, nor your uncles, shall enjoy their triumph — perdition seize my soul, if they shall!

The man's vehemence frightened me: yet in resentment, I would have left him; but throwing himself at my feet again, Leave me not thus — I beseech you, dearest madam, leave me not thus in despair. I kneel not, repenting of what I have vowed in such a case as that I have supposed. I revow it, at your feet! — *and so he did.* But think not it is by way of menace, or to intimidate you to favour me. If your heart inclines you [and then he arose] to obey your father (your *brother* rather) and to have Solmes; although I shall avenge myself on those who have insulted me, for their insults to myself and family; yet will I tear out my heart from this bosom (if possible with my own hands) were it to scruple to give up its ardours to a woman capable of such a preference.

I told him, that he talked to me in very high language; but he might assure himself, that I never would have Mr. Solmes (yet that this I said not in favour to him), and I had declared as much to my relations, were there not such a man as himself in the world.

Would I declare, that I would still honour him with my correspondence? — He could not bear, that, hoping to obtain *greater* instances of my favour, he should forfeit the *only* one he had to boast of.

I bid him forbear rashness or resentment to any of my family, and I would, for some time at least, till I saw what issue my present trials were likely to have, proceed with a correspondence, which, nevertheless, my heart condemned —

And his spirit him, the impatient creature said, interrupting me, for bearing what he did; when he considered, that the necessity of it was imposed upon him, not by my will (for then would he bear it cheerfully, and a thousand times more) but by creatures — and there he stopt.

I told him plainly that he might thank himself (whose indifferent character, as to morals, had given such a handle against him) for all. It was but just, that a man should be spoken evil of, who set no value upon his reputation.

He offered to vindicate himself: but I told him, I would judge him by his own rule — by his *actions*, not by his *professions*.

Were not his enemies, he said, so powerful, and so determined; and had they not already shewn their intentions in such high acts of even *cruel* compulsion; but would leave me to my choice, or to my desire of living single; he would have been content to undergo a twelvemonth's probation, or more: but he was confident that one month would either complete all their purposes, or render them abortive: and I best knew what hopes I had of my *father's* receding — he did not know him, if I had *any*.

I said, I would try every method, that either my duty or my influence upon any of them should suggest, before I would put myself into any other protection: and if nothing else would do, would resign the envied estate; and that I dared to say *would*.

He was contented, he said, to abide that issue. He should be far from wishing me to embrace any other protection, but, as he had frequently said, in the last necessity. But, dearest creature, catching my hand with ardour, and pressing it to his lips, if the yielding up that estate will do — resign it; — and be mine — and I will corroborate, with all my soul, your resignation!

This was not ungenerously said: but what will not these men say to obtain belief, and a power over one? I made many efforts to go; and now it was so dark, that I began to have great apprehensions. I cannot say from his behaviour: indeed, he has a good deal raised himself in my opinion by the personal respect, even to reverence, which he paid me during the whole conference; for although he flamed out once, upon a supposition that Solmes might succeed, it was upon a supposition that would excuse passion, if any thing could, you know, in a man pretending to love with fervour: although it was so levelled, that I could not avoid resenting it.

He recommended himself to my favour at parting, with great earnestness, yet with as great submission; not offering to condition any thing with me; although he hinted his wishes for another meeting: which I forbad him ever attempting again in the same place. — And I will own to you, from whom I should be really blameable to conceal any thing, that his arguments (drawn from the disgraceful treatment I meet with) of what I *am* to expect, make me begin to apprehend, that I shall be under an obligation to be either the one man's, or the other's — and if so, I fancy, I shall not incur your blame, were I to say, *which* of the two it must be. You have said, which it must *not* be. But, O my dear, the single life is by far the most eligible to me: *indeed* it is. And I hope yet to be permitted to make that option.

I got back without observation: but the apprehension that I should not, gave me great uneasiness; and made me begin my letter in a greater flutter than he gave me cause to be in, except at the first seeing him; for then indeed my spirits failed me; and it was a particular felicity, that, in such a fright, and alone with him, I fainted not away.

I should add, that having reproached him with his behaviour the last Sunday at church, he solemnly assured me, that it was not what had been represented to me: that he did not *expect* to see me there: but hoped to have an opportunity to address himself to my father, and to be permitted to attend him home. But that the good Dr. Lewen had persuaded him not to attempt speaking to any of the family, at that time; observing to him the emotions into which his presence had put every body. He intended no pride, or haughtiness of behaviour, he assured me; and that the attributing such to him was the effect of that ill-will which he had the mortification to find insuperable: adding that when he bowed to my mother, it was a compliment he intended generally to every one in the pew, as well as to *her*, whom he sincerely venerated.

If he may be believed (and I should think he would not have come purposely to defy my family, yet expect favour from me) one may see, my dear, the force of hatred, which misrepresents all things: — yet why should Shorey (except officiously to please her principals) make a report in his disfavour? He told me, that he would appeal to Dr. Lewen for his justification on this head; adding, that the whole conversation between the Doctor and him turned upon his desire to attempt to reconcile himself to us all, in the *face of the church*; and upon the Doctor's endeavouring to dissuade him from making such a public overture, till he knew how it would be accepted. But to what purpose his appeal, when I am debarred from seeing that good man, or any one who would advise me what to do in my present difficult situation!

I fancy, my dear, however, that there would hardly be a guilty person in the world, were each *suspected* or *accused* person to tell his or her own story, and be allowed any degree of credit.

I have written a very long letter.

To be so particular as you require in subjects of conversation, it is impossible to be short.

I will add to it only the assurance, that I am, and ever will be,
Your affectionate and faithful
friend and servant,
CLARISSA HARLOWE.

You'll be so good, my dear, as to remember, that the date of your last letter to me was the 9th.

LETTER XXXVII.

Miss Howe to Miss Clarissa Harlowe.

Sunday, March 19.

I beg your pardon, my dearest friend, for having given you occasion to remind me of the date of my last. I was willing to have before me as much of the workings of your *wise* relations as possible; being verily persuaded, that one side or the other would have yielded by this time: and then I should have had some degree of certainty to found my observations upon. And indeed what can I write that I have not already written? — You know, that I can do nothing but rave at your stupid persecutors: and that you don't like. I have advised you to resume your own estate: that you won't do. You cannot bear the thoughts of having their Solmes: and Lovelace is resolved you shall be his, let who will say to the contrary. I think you must be either the one man's or the other's. Let us see what their next step will be.

As to Lovelace, while he tells his own story (having also behaved so handsomely on his intrusion in the woodhouse; and intended so well at church) who can say, that the man is in the *least* blameworthy? — *Wicked people:* to combine against so *innocent* a man! — But, as I said, let us see what *their next* step will be, and what course *you* will take upon it; and then we may be the more enlightened.

As to your change of style to your uncles, and brother and sister, since they were so fond of attributing to you a regard for Lovelace, and would not be persuaded to the contrary; and since you only strengthened their arguments against yourself by denying it; you did but just as I would have done, in giving way to their suspicions, and trying what that would do — but if — but if — pray, my dear, indulge me a little — you *yourself* think it was necessary to apologize to *me* for that change of style to *them* — and till you will speak out like a friend to her *unquestionable* friend, I must tease you a little — let it run therefore; for it will run —

If, then, there be not a reason for this change of style, which you have not thought fit to give me, be so good as to watch, as I once before advised you, how the cause for it will come on — why should it be permitted to steal upon you, and you know nothing of the matter?

When we get a great cold, we are apt to puzzle ourselves to find out when it began, or how we got it; and when that is accounted for, down we sit contented, and let it have its course; or, if it be very troublesome, take a sweat, or use other means to get rid of it — so my dear, before the malady you wot of, yet wot *not* of, grows so importunate, as that you must be obliged to sweat it out, let me advise you to mind how it comes on. For I am persuaded, as surely as that I am now writing to *you*, that the indiscreet violence of your friends on one hand, and the insinuating address of Lovelace on the other, (if the man be not a greater fool than any body thinks him) will effectually bring it to this, and do all his work for him.

But let it — if it must be Lovelace or Solmes, the choice cannot admit of debate. Yet if all be true that is reported, I should prefer almost any of your other lovers to either; unworthy as *they* also are. But who can be worthy of a Clarissa?

I wish you are not *indeed* angry with me for harping so much on one string. I must own, that I should think myself inexcusable so to do (the rather, as I am bold enough to imagine it a point out of all doubt from fifty places in your letters, were I to labour the proof) if you would ingenuously own —

Own what? you'll say. Why, my Anna Howe, I hope you don't think that I am already in love! —

No, to be sure! how can your Anna Howe have such a thought? — What then shall we call it? You have helped me to a phrase. — A *conditional kind of liking!* — that's it. — O my friend! did I not know how much you despise prudery; and that you are too young, and too lovely, to be a prude —

But avoiding such hard names, let me tell you one thing, my dear (which nevertheless I have told you before); and that is *this;* that I shall think I have reason to be highly displeased with you, if, when you write to me, you endeavour to keep from me any secret of your heart.

Let me add, that if you would clearly and explicitly tell me, how far Lovelace *has*, or has *not*, a hold in your affections, I could better advise you what to do, than at present I can. You, who are so famed for *prescience*, as I may call it: and than whom no young lady ever had stronger pretensions to a share of it; have had, no doubt, reasonings in your heart about him, supposing you *were* to be oneday his [no doubt but you have had the same in Solmes's case; whence the ground for the hatred of the one: and for the *conditional liking* of the other]: will you tell me, my dear, what you have thought of Lovelace's *best* and of his *worst?* — How far eligible for the *first;* how far rejectible for the *last?* — Then weighing both parts in opposite scales, we shall see which is likely to preponderate; or rather which *does* preponderate. Nothing less than the knowledge of the inmost recesses of your heart, can satisfy my love and my friendship. Surely, you are not afraid to trust *yourself* with a secret of this nature: if you are, then you may the *more* allowably doubt *me.* But I dare say, you will not own either. — Nor is there, I hope, cause for either.

Be pleased to observe one thing, my dear, that whenever I have given myself any of those airs of raillery, which have seemed to make you look about you (when, likewise, your case may call for a more serious turn from a sympathizing friend) it has not been upon those passages which are written, though perhaps not intended, with such explicitness [don't be alarmed, my dear!] as leaves little cause of doubt: but only when you affect reserve: when you give new words for common things: when you come with your *curiosities*, with your *conditional likings*, and with your PRUDE-encies [mind how I spell the word] in a case that with every other person defies all prudence. — Overt acts of treason all these, against the sovereign friendship we have avowed to each other!

Remember, that you found *me* out in a moment. You challenged me. I owned directly, that there was only my pride between the man and me; for I could not endure, I told you, to think it in the power of any fellow living to give me a moment's uneasiness. And then my man, as I have elsewhere said, was not such a one as yours: so I had reason to impute full as much to my own inconsideration, as to his *power* over me: nay, *more*. But still more to *yours*. For you reasoned me out of the *curiosity* first: and when the liking was brought to be *conditional* — why then, you know, I *throbbed* no more about him.

O! *pray now*, as you say, now I have mentioned that my fellow was not such a charming fellow as yours, let Miss Biddulph, Miss Lloyd, Miss Campion, and me, have your opinion, how far *figure* ought to engage us: with a view to your own case however — *mind that* — as Mr. Tony says — and whether *at all*, if the man be vain of it; since, as you observe in a former, that vanity is a *stop short pride* in such a one, that would make one justly doubt the *worthiness of his interior*. You, our pattern, so lovely in feature, so graceful in person, have none of it; and have therefore with the *best* grace always held, that it is not excusable even in a woman.

You must know, that this subject was warmly debated among us in our last conversation; and Miss Lloyd wished me to write to you upon it for your opinion; to which in every debated case, we always paid the greatest deference. I hope you will not be so much engrossed by your more weighty cares, as not to have freedom of spirits enough to enter upon the task. — You know how much we all admire your opinion on such topics; which ever produces something new and instructive, as you handle the subjects. And pray tell us to what you think it owing, that your man seems so careful to adorn that self-adorned person of his; yet so manages, that one cannot for one's heart think him a coxcomb? — Let this question, and the above tasks, divert, and not displease you, my dear — one subject, though ever so important, could never yet engross your capacious mind. If they *should* displease you, you must recollect the many instances of my impertinence which you have forgiven, and then say, "This is a mad girl: but yet I love her!— And she is my own."

ANNA HOWE.

LETTER XXXVIII.

Miss Clarissa Harlowe to Miss Howe.

Monday, March 20.

Your last so sensibly affects me, that I must postpone every other consideration, however weighty, to reply to it: and this I will do very distinctly, and with all the openness of heart which our mutual friendship demands.

But let me observe in the first place, *gratefully* observe, that if I have in *fifty passages* of my letters given you such *undoubted* proofs of my value for Mr. Lovelace, that you have spared me for the sake of my *explicitness*, it is acting by me with a generosity worthy of yourself.

But lives the man, think you, who is so very bad, that he does not give even a doubting mind reason at *one* time to be better pleased with him than at *another?* And when that reason offers, is it not just to express one's self accordingly? I would do the man who addresses me as much justice, as if he did *not* address me: it has such a look of tyranny, it appears so ungenerous, methinks, in our sex, to use a man worse for his respect to us (no other cause for disrespect occurring), that I would not by any means be that person who should do so.

But although I may intend no more than justice, it will perhaps be difficult to hinder those who know the man's views, from construing it as a partial favour: and especially if the eager-eyed observer has been formerly touched herself, and would triumph that her friend had been no more able to escape than she. Noble minds, emulative of perfection (and yet the passion properly directed, I do not take to be an *imperfection* neither), may be allowed a little generous envy, I think.

If I meant by this a reflection, by way of revenge, it is but a revenge, my dear, in the *soft* sense of the word. I love, as I have told you, your pleasantry. Although at the time your reproof may pain me a little; yet on recollection, when I find in it more of the cautioning friend, than of the satirising observer, I shall be all gratitude upon it. All the business will be this; I shall be sensible of the pain in the present letter perhaps; but I shall thank you in the next, and ever after.

In this way, I hope, my dear, you will account for a little of that sensibility which you will find above, and perhaps still more, as I proceed. — You frequently remind me, by an excellent *example*, your own to *me*, that I must not spare *you*.

I am not conscious that I have written any thing of this man, that has not been more in his dispraise than in his favour. Such *is* the man, that I think I must have been faulty, and ought to take myself to account, if I had not: but if you think otherwise, I will not put you upon *labouring the proof*, as you call it. My conduct must then have a faulty *appearance* at least, and I will endeavour to rectify it. But of this I assure you, that whatever interpretation my words were capable of, I *intended not* any reserve to you. I wrote my heart at the time: — if I had had thoughts of disguising it, or been conscious, that there was *reason* for doing so, perhaps I had not given you the opportunity of remarking upon my *curiosity* after his relations' esteem for me; nor upon my *conditional liking*, and such-like. All I intended by the first, I believe, I honestly told you at the time: to that letter I therefore refer, whether it make for me, or against me: and by the other, that I might bear in mind, what it became a person of my sex and character to *be* and to *do*, in such an unhappy situation, where the imputed love is thought an undutiful, and therefore a criminal passion; and where the supposed object of it is a man of faulty morals too. And I am sure you will excuse my desire of appearing at those times the person I ought to be; had I no other view in it but to merit the continuance of your good opinion.

But that I may acquit myself of having reserves — O, my dear, I must here break off! —

LETTER XXXIX.
Miss Clarissa Harlowe to Miss Howe.
Monday, March 20.

This letter will account to you, my dear, for my abrupt breaking off in the answer I was writing to yours of yesterday; and which, possibly, I shall not be able to finish, and send you till to-morrow or next day; having a great deal to say to the subjects you put to me in it. What I am now to give you are the particulars of another effort made by my friends, through the good Mrs. Norton.

It seems they had sent to her yesterday, to be here this day, to take their instructions, and to try what *she* could do with me. It would, at least, I suppose they thought have this effect; to render me inexcusable with *her*, or to let *her* see, that there was no room for the expostulations she had often wanted to make in my favour to my mother.

The declaration that my heart was *free*, afforded them an argument to prove obstinacy and perverseness upon me; since it could be nothing else that governed me in my opposition to their wills, if I had no particular esteem for another man: and now, that I have given them reason (in order to obviate this argument), to suppose that I *have* a preference to another, they are resolved to carry their schemes into execution as soon as possible. And in order to this, they sent for this good woman, for whom they know I have even a filial regard.

She found assembled my father and mother, my brother and sister, my two uncles, and my aunt Hervey.

My brother acquainted her with all that had passed since she was last permitted to see me; with the contents of my letters avowing my regard for Mr. Lovelace (as they all interpreted them); with the substance of their answers to them; and with their resolutions.

My mother spoke next; and delivered herself to this effect, as the good woman told me.

After reciting how many times I had been indulged in my refusals of different men, and the pains she had taken with me, to induce me to oblige my whole family in one instance out of five or six, and my obstinacy upon it: "O my good Mrs. Norton," said the dear lady, "could you have thought, that *my* Clarissa and *your* Clarissa was capable of so determined an opposition to the will of parents so indulgent to her? But see what *you* can do with her. The matter is gone too far to be receded from on our parts. Her father had concluded every thing with Mr. Solmes, not doubting her compliance. Such noble settlements, Mrs. Norton, and such advantages to the whole family! In short, she has it in her power to lay an obligation upon us all. Mr. Solmes, knowing she has good principles, and hoping by his patience *now*, and good treatment *hereafter*, to engage her gratitude, and by degrees her love, is willing to overlook all!

[*Overlook* all, my dear! Mr. Solmes to *overlook* all! There's a word!].

"So, Mrs. Norton, if you are convinced, that it is a child's duty to submit to her parents' authority, in the most important point as well as in the least, I beg you will try *your* influence over her: *I* have none: her *father* has none: her *uncles* neither: although it is her apparent interest to oblige us all; for, on that condition, her grandfather's estate is not half of what, living and dying, is purposed to be done for her. If any body can prevail with her, it is *you;* and I hope you will *heartily* enter upon this task."

My arrogant brother told her, she was sent for to expostulate with his *sister*, and not with *them*. And *this*, Goody Norton [she is always *goody* with him!] you may tell her, that the treaty with Mr. Solmes is concluded: that nothing but her compliance with her duty is wanting; of consequence, that there is no room for *your* expostulation, or *hers* either.

Be assured of this, Mrs. Norton, said my father, in an angry tone, that we will not be baffled by her. We will not appear like fools in this matter, and as if we had no authority over our own daughter. We will not, in short, be bullied out of our child by a cursed rake, who had like to have killed our only son! — And so she had better make a merit of her obedience: for comply she shall, if I live; independent as she thinks my father's indiscreet bounty has made her of me, her father. Indeed, since that, she has never been what she was before. An unjust bequest! — And it is likely to prosper accordingly! — But if she marry that vile Lovelace, I will litigate every shilling with her: tell her so; and that the will *may* be set aside, and *shall*.

My uncles joined, with equal heat.

My brother was violent in his declarations.

My sister put in with vehemence, on the same side.

My aunt Hervey was pleased to say, there was no article so proper, for parents to govern in, as this of marriage: and it was very fit, mine should be obliged.

Thus instructed, the good woman came up to me. She told me all that had passed, and was very earnest with me to comply; and so much justice did she to the task imposed upon her, that I more than once thought, that her own opinion went with theirs. But when she saw what an immoveable aversion I had to the man, she lamented with me their determined resolution: and then examined into the sincerity of my declaration, that I would gladly compound with them by living single. Of this being satisfied, she was so convinced that this offer, which, carried into execution, would exclude Lovelace effectually, *ought* to be accepted, that she would go down (although I told her, it was what I had tendered over-and-over to no purpose) and undertake to be guarantee for me on that score.

She went accordingly; but soon returned in tears: being used harshly for urging this alternative: — they had a *right* to my obedience upon their own terms, they said: my proposal was an artifice, only to gain time: nothing but marrying Mr. Solmes should do: they had told me so before: they should not be at rest till it was done; for they knew what an interest Lovelace had in my heart: I had as good as owned it in my letters to my uncles, and brother and sister, although I had most disingenuously declared otherwise to my mother. I depended, they said, upon *their* indulgence, and my *own power* over them: they would not have banished me from their presence, if they had not known that their consideration for *me* was greater than mine for *them*. And they *would* be obeyed, or I never should be restored to their favour, let the consequence be what it would.

My brother thought fit to tell the good woman, that her whining nonsense did but harden me. There was a perverseness, he said, in female minds, a tragedy-pride, that would make a romantic young creature, such a one as me, risk any thing to obtain pity. I was of an age, and a turn [the insolent said] to be fond of a lover-like distress: and my grief (which she pleaded) would never break my heart: I should sooner break that of the best and most indulgent of mothers. He added, that she might once more go up to me: but that, if she prevailed not, he should suspect, that the man they all hated had found a way to attach *her* to his interest.

Every body blamed him for this unworthy reflection, which greatly affected the good woman. But nevertheless he said, and nobody contradicted him, that if she could not prevail upon her *sweet child* [as it seems she had fondly called me], she had best withdraw to her own home, and there tarry till she was sent for; and so leave her *sweet child* to her father's management.

Sure nobody ever had so insolent, so hard-hearted a brother, as I have! So much resignation to be expected from me! So much arrogance, and to so good a woman, and of so fine an understanding, to be allowed in him!

She nevertheless told him, that however she might be ridiculed for speaking of the sweetness of my disposition, she must take upon her to say, that there never was a sweeter in the sex: and that she had ever found, that by mild methods, and gentleness, I might at any time be prevailed upon, even in points against my own judgment and opinion.

My aunt Hervey hereupon said, It was worth while to consider what Mrs. Norton said: and that she had sometimes allowed *herself* to doubt, whether I had been *begun* with by such methods as generous tempers are only to be influenced by, in cases where their hearts are supposed to be opposite to the will of their friends.

She had both my brother and sister upon her for this: who referred to my mother, whether she had not treated me with an indulgence that had hardly any example.

My mother said, she must own, that no indulgence had been wanting from *her*: but she must need say, and had *often* said it, that the reception I met with on my return from Miss Howe, and the manner in which the proposal of Mr. Solmes was made to me (which was such as left nothing to my choice), and before I had had an opportunity to converse with him, were not what she had by any means approved of.

She was silenced, you will guess by whom, — with, — My dear! my dear! — you have *ever* something to say, something to palliate, for this rebel of a girl! — Remember her treatment of you, of me! — Remember, that the wretch, whom we so justly hate, would not dare to persist in his purposes, but for her encouragement of *him*, and obstinacy to *us*. — Mrs. Norton (angrily to her) go up to her once more — and if you think gentleness will do, you have a commission to be gentle. — If it will not, never make use of that plea again.

Ay, my good woman, said my mother, try *your* force with her. My sister Hervey and I will go up to her, and bring her down in our hands, to receive her father's blessing, and assurances of every body's love, if she will be prevailed upon: and, in that case, we will all love you the better for your good offices.

She came up to me, and repeated all these passages with tears: but I told her, that after what had passed between us, she could not hope to prevail upon me to comply with measures so wholly my brother's; and so much to my aversion. — And then folding me to her maternal bosom, I leave you, my dearest miss, said she — I leave you, because I *must!* — But let me beseech you to do nothing rashly; nothing unbecoming your character. If all be true that is said, Mr. Lovelace cannot deserve you. If you *can* comply, remember it is your *duty* to comply. They take not, I own, the right method with so generous a spirit. But remember, that there would not be any merit in your compliance, if it were *not* to be against your own liking. Remember also, what is expected from a character so extraordinary as yours: remember it is in your power to unite or disunite your whole family for ever. Although it should at *present* be disagreeable to you to be thus compelled, your prudence, I dare say, when you consider the matter seriously, will enable you to get over all prejudices against the one, and all prepossessions in favour of the other: and then the obligation you will lay all your family under, will be not only meritorious in you, with regard to *them*, but in a few months, very probably highly satisfactory, as well as reputable to *yourself.*

Consider, my dear Mrs. Norton, said I, *only* consider, that it is not a small thing that is insisted upon; nor for a short duration; it is for my *life:* consider too, that all this is owing to an over-bearing brother, who governs every body. Consider how desirous I am to oblige them, if a *single life*, and breaking all correspondence with the man they hate because my brother hates him, will do it.

I consider every thing, my dearest miss: and, added to what I have said, do *you* only consider, that if, by pursuing your *own* will, and rejecting *theirs*, you *should* be unhappy, you will be deprived of all that consolation which those have, who have been directed by their *parents*, although the event prove not answerable to their wishes.

I *must* go, repeated she: — your brother will say (and she wept) that I harden you by my *whining nonsense.* 'Tis indeed hard, that so much regard should be paid to the *humours* of one child; and so little to the inclination of another. But let me repeat, that it is your *duty* to acquiesce, if you *can* acquiesce: your father has given your brother's schemes *his* sanction; and they are now *his.* Mr. Lovelace, I doubt, is not a man that will justify *your* choice so much as he will *their* dislike. It is easy to see that your brother has a *view* in discrediting you with all your friends, with your uncles in particular: but for that very reason, you should comply, if possible, in order to disconcert his ungenerous measures. I will pray for you; and that is all I can do for you. I must now go down, and make a report, that you are resolved never to have Mr. Solmes — Must I? — Consider, my dear Miss Clary — *Must* I?

Indeed you must! — But of this I do assure you, that I will do nothing to disgrace the part you have had in my education. I will bear every thing that shall be short of forcing my hand into *his* who never can have any share in my heart. I will try by patient duty, by humility, to overcome them. But death will I choose, in any shape, rather than that man.

I dread to go down, said she, with so determined an answer: they will have no patience with me. — But let me leave you with one observation, which I beg of you always to bear in mind: —

"That persons of prudence, and distinguished talents, like yours, seem to be sprinkled through the world, to give credit, by their example, to religion and virtue. When such persons *wilfully* err, how great must be the fault! how ungrateful to that God, who blessed them with such talents! what a loss likewise to the world! what a wound to virtue! — But this, I hope, will never be to be said of Miss Clarissa Harlowe!"

I could give her no answer, but by my tears. And I thought, when she went away the better half of my heart went with her.

I listened to hear what reception she would meet with below: and found it was just such a one as she had apprehended.

Will she, or will she *not*, be Mrs. Solmes? None of your whining, circumlocutions, Mrs. Norton! — [You may guess who said this] *Will* she, or will she *not*, comply with her parents' will?

This cut short all she was going to say.

If I *must* speak so briefly, miss will sooner die, than have —

Any body but Lovelace! interrupted my brother. — This, madam, this, sir, is your meek daughter! This is Mrs. Norton's *sweet child!* — Well, goody, you may return to your own habitation. I am empowered to forbid you to have any correspondence with this perverse girl for a month to come, as you value the favour of our whole family, or of any individual of it.

And saying this, uncontradicted by any body, he himself showed her to the door — No doubt, with all that air of cruel insult, which the haughty rich can put on to the unhappy low, who have not pleased them.

So here, my dear Miss Howe, I am deprived of the advice of one of the most prudent and conscientious women in the world, were I to have ever so much occasion for it.

I might indeed write (as I presume, under your cover), and receive *her* answers to what I should write. But should such a correspondence be charged upon her, I know she would not be guilty of a falsehood for the world; nor even of an equivocation: and should she own it after this prohibition, she would forfeit my mother's favour for ever. And in my dangerous fever, some time ago, I engaged my mother to promise me, that, if I died before I could do anything for the good woman, she would set her above want for the rest of her life, should her eyes fail her, or sickness befal her, and she could not provide for herself, as she now so prettily does by her fine needleworks.

What measures will they fall upon next?—Will they not recede when they find that it must be a rooted antipathy, and nothing else, that could make a temper not naturally inflexible, so sturdy?

Adieu, my dear. Be you happy! To *know* that it is in your power to be so, is all that seems wanting to make you so.

CL. HARLOWE.

LETTER XL.
Miss Clarissa Harlowe to Miss Howe.

[In continuation of the subject in letter xxxviii.]

I WILL now, though midnight (for I have no sleep in my eyes), resume the subject I was forced so abruptly to quit; and will obey yours, Miss Lloyd's, Miss Campion's, and Miss Biddulph's call, with as much temper as my divided thoughts will admit. The dead stillness of this solemn hour will, I hope, contribute to calm my disturbed mind.

In order to acquit myself of so heavy a charge as that of having reserves to so dear a friend, I will acknowledge (and I thought I had over and over) that it is owing to my particular situation, if Mr. Lovelace appears to me in a tolerable light: and I take upon me to say, that had they opposed to him a man of sense, of virtue, of generosity; one who enjoyed his fortune with credit; who had a tenderness in his nature for the calamities of others, which would have given a moral assurance, that he would have been still less wanting in grateful returns to an obliging spirit: — had they opposed such a man as this to Mr. Lovelace, and been as earnest to have me married, as now they are, I do not know myself, if they would have had reason to tax me with that invincible obstinacy which they lay to my charge: and this, whatever had been the *figure* of the man; since the *heart* is what the women should judge by in the choice we make, as the best security for the party's good behaviour in every relation of life.

But situated as I am, thus persecuted and driven; I own to you, that I have now-and-then had a little more difficulty than I wished for, in passing by Mr. Lovelace's tolerable qualities, to keep up my dislike to him for his others.

You say, I must have argued with myself in his favour, and in his disfavour, on a supposition, that I might possibly be one day his. I own that I have: and thus called upon by my dearest friend, I will set before you both parts of the argument.

And first, *what occurred to me in his favour.*

At his introduction into our family, his negative virtues were insisted upon; — he was no gamester; no horse-racer; no foxhunter; no drinker: my poor aunt Hervey had, in confidence, given us to apprehend much disagreeable evil (especially to a wife of the least delicacy) from a wine lover: and common sense instructed us, that sobriety in a man is no small point to be secured, when so many mischiefs happen daily from excess. I remember, that my sister made the most of this favourable circumstance in his character while she had any hopes of him.

He was never thought to be a niggard: not even ungenerous: nor when his conduct came to be inquired into, an extravagant, a squanderer: his pride [so far was it a laudable pride] secured him from that. Then he was ever ready to own his errors. He was no jester upon sacred things: poor Mr. Wyerley's fault; who seemed to think, that there was wit in saying bold things, which would shock a serious mind. His conversation with *us* was always unexceptionable; even chastely so; which, be his actions what they would, shewed him capable of being influenced by *decent* company; and that he might probably therefore be a *led* man, rather than a *leader*, in other company. And one late instance, so late as last Saturday evening, has raised him not a little in my opinion, with regard to this point of good (and at the same time, of manly) behaviour.

As to the advantage of birth, that is of his side, above any man who has been found out for me. If we may judge by that expression of his, which you were pleased with at the time; "that upon *true* quality, and *hereditary* distinction, if good sense were not wanting, honour sat as easy as his glove;" that, with *as* familiar an air, was his familiar expréssion; "while none but the prosperous upstart MUSHROOMED into rank (another of his peculiars) was arrogantly proud of it."—If, I say, we may judge of him by this, we shall conclude in his favour, that he knows what sort of behaviour is to be expected from persons of birth, whether he act up to it or not. Conviction is half way to amendment.

His fortunes in possession are handsome; in expectation, splendid: so nothing need be said on that subject.

But it is impossible, say some, that he should make a tender or kind husband. Those who are for imposing upon me such a man as Mr. Solmes, and by methods so violent, are not entitled to make this objection. But now, on this subject, let me tell you how I have argued with myself—For still you must remember, that I am upon the extenuating part of his character.

A great deal of the treatment a wife may expect from him, will possibly depend upon herself. Perhaps she must *practise* as well as *promise* obedience, to a man so little used to control; and must be careful to oblige. And what husband expects not this?—The *more* perhaps if he had not reason to assure himself of the preferable love of his wife before she became such. And how much easier and pleasanter to obey the man of her choise, if he should be even unreasonable sometimes, than one she would not have had, could she have avoided it? Then I think, as the men were the framers of the matrimonial office, and made *obedience* a part of the woman's vow, she ought not, even in *policy*, to shew him, that she can break through *her* part of the contract (however lightly she may think of the instance), lest *he* should take it into his head (himself his judge), to think as lightly of other points, which she may hold more important — But indeed no point so solemnly vowed can be slight.

Thus principled, and *acting* accordingly, what a wretch must that husband be, who could treat such a wife brutally! — Will Lovelace's *wife* be the only person, to whom he will not pay the grateful debt of civility and good manners? He is allowed to be brave: who ever knew a brave man, if a man of *sense*, an universally base man? And how much the gentleness of our sex, and the manner of our training up and education, make us need the protection of the brave, and the countenance of the generous, let the general approbation which we are all so naturally inclined to give to men of that character, testify.

At worst, will he confine me prisoner to my chamber? Will he deny me the visits of my dearest friend, and forbid me to correspond with her? Will he take from me the mistressly management, which I had not faultily discharged? Will he set a servant over me, with licence to insult me? Will he, as he has not a *sister*, permit his cousins Montague, or would either of those ladies *accept* of a permission, to insult and tyrannize over me? — It cannot be. — Why then, think I often, do you tempt me. O my cruel friends, to try the difference?

And then has the secret pleasure intruded itself, to be able to reclaim such a man to the paths of virtue and honour: to be a *secondary* means, if I were to be his, of saving him, and preventing the mischiefs so enterprising a creature might otherwise be guilty of, if he be such a one.

When I have thought of him in these lights (and that as a man of sense he will sooner see his errors, than another) I own to you, that I have had some difficulty to avoid taking the path they so violently endeavour to make me shun: and all that command of my passions which has been attributed to me as my greatest praise, and in so young a creature, as my distinction, has hardly been sufficient for me.

And let me add, that the favour of his relations (all but himself unexceptionable) has made a good deal of additional weight, thrown into the same scale.

But now in his disfavour. When I have reflected upon the prohibition of my parents: the giddy appearance, disgraceful to our sex, that such a preference would have, that there is no manner of likelihood, inflamed by the rencounter, and upheld by art and ambition on my brother's side, that ever the animosity will be got over, that I must therefore be at perpetual variance with all my own family: that I must go to *him*, and to *his*, as an obliged and half-fortuned person: that his aversion to them all is as strong as theirs to him: that his whole family are hated for his sake; they hating ours in return: that he has a very immoral character as to women: that knowing this, it is a high degree of impurity to think of joining in wedlock with such a man: that he is young, unbroken, his passions unsubdued: that he is violent in his temper, yet artful; I am afraid vindictive too: that such an husband might unsettle me in all my own principles, and hazard my future hopes: that his own relations, two excellent aunts, and an uncle, from whom he has such large expectations, have no influence upon him: that what tolerable qualities he has, are founded more in pride than in virtue: that allowing, as he does, the excellency of moral precepts, and believing the doctrine of future rewards and punishments, he can live as if he despised the one, and defied the other: the probability that the taint arising from such free principles, may go down into the manners of posterity: that I, knowing these things, and the importance of them, should be more inexcusable than one who knows them not; since an error *against* judgment is worse, infinitely worse, than an error *in* judgment:—reflecting upon these things, I cannot help conjuring you, my dear, to pray *with* me, and to pray *for* me, that I may not be pushed upon such indiscreet measures, as will render me inexcusable to myself: for that is the test, after all. The world's opinion ought to be but a secondary consideration.

I have said in his praise, that he is extremely ready to *own his errors*: but I have sometimes made a great drawback upon this article, in his disfavour; having been ready to apprehend, that this ingenuousness may possibly be attributable to two causes, neither of them, by any means, creditable to him. The one, that his vices are so much his masters, that he *attempts* not to conquer them; the other, that he may think it policy, to give up *one half* of his character, to save the *other*, when the *whole* may be blameable: by this means, silencing by acknowledgment the objections he cannot answer; which may give him the praise of ingenuousness, when he can obtain no other; and when the *challenged* proof might bring out, upon discussion, other evils. These, you will allow, are severe constructions; but every thing his enemies say of him cannot be false.

I will proceed by-and-by.

* * *

Sometimes we have both thought him one of the most undesigning *merely* witty men we ever knew; at other times one of the deepest creatures we ever conversed with. So that when in one visit we have imagined we fathomed him, in the next he has made us ready to give him up as impenetrable. This impenetrableness, my dear, is to be put among the shades in his character.—Yet, upon the whole, you have been so far of his party, that you have contested, that his principal fault is overfrankness, and too much regardlessness of appearances, and that he is too giddy to be very artful: you would have it, that at *the time* he says any thing good, he means what he speaks; that his variableness and levity are constitutional, owing to sound health, and to a soul and body [that was your observation] fitted for and pleased with each other. And hence you concluded, that could this *consentaneousness* [as you called it] of corporal and animal faculties be pointed by discretion; that is to say, could his vivacity be confined within the *pale* of *but* moral obligations; he would be far from being rejectible as a companion for life.

But I used then to say, and I still am of opinion, that he wants a *heart:* and if he does, he wants every thing. A wrong *head* may be convinced, may have a right turn given it; but who is able to give a *heart*, if a heart be wanting! Divine Grace, working a miracle, or next to a miracle, can only change a bad heart. Should not one fly the man who is but *suspected* of such a one? What, O what, do parents do, when they endeavour to force a child's inclination, but make her think better than otherwise she would think of a man obnoxious to themselves, and perhaps whose char- acter will not stand examination?

I have said, that I think Mr. Lovelace a vindictive man: upon my word, I have sometimes doubted, whether his perseverance in his addresses to me has not been the more obstinate, since he has found himself so disagreeable to my friends. From that time I verily think he has been the more fervent in them; yet courts them not, but sets them at defiance. For this indeed he pleads disinterestedness [I am sure he cannot politeness]; and the more plausibly, as he is apprised of the ability they have to make it worth his while to court them. 'Tis true he has declared, and with too much reason (or there would be no bearing him), that the lowest submissions on his part would not be accepted; and to oblige me, has offered to seek a reconciliation with them, if I would give him hope of success.

As to his behaviour at church, the Sunday before last, I lay no stress upon that, because I doubt there was too much *outward pride* in his *intentional humility*, or Shorey, who is not his enemy, could not have mistaken it.

I do not think him so deeply learned in human nature, or in ethics, as some have thought him. Don't you remember how he stared at the following trite observations, which every moralist could have furnished him with? Complaining as he did, in a half-menacing strain, of the obloquies raised against him — "That if he were innocent, he should despise the obloquy: if not, revenge would not wipe off his guilt."—"That nobody ever thought of turning a sword into a sponge!"—"That it was in his own power by reformation of an error laid to his charge by an enemy, to make that enemy one of his best friends; and (which was the noblest revenge in the world) *against his will;* since an enemy would not *wish* him to be without the faults he taxed him with."

But the *intention*, he said, was the wound.

How so, I asked him, when *that* cannot wound without the *application?* "That the adversary only held the sword: he himself pointed it to his breast:—and why should he mortally resent that malice, which be might be the better for as long as he lived?" — What could be the reading he has been said to be master of, to wonder, as he did, at these observations?

But, indeed, he must take pleasure in revenge; and yet holds others to be inexcusable for the same fault. He is not, however, the only one who can see how truly blameable those errors are in another, which they hardly think such in themselves.

From these considerations; from these *over-balances;* it was, that I said, in a former, that I would not be in love with this man for the world: and it was going further than prudence would warrant, when I was for compounding with you, by the words *conditional*

liking; which you so humorously rally.

Well but, methinks you say, what is all this to the purpose? This is still but reasoning; but if you *are* in love, you *are:* and love, like the vapours, is the deeper rooted for having no sufficient cause assignable for its hold. And so you call upon me again, to have no reserves, and so forth.

Why then, my dear, if you will have it, I think that, with all his preponderating faults, I like him better than I ever thought I should like him; and, those faults considered, better perhaps than *I* ought to like him. And I believe, it is possible for the persecution I labour under, to induce me to like him still more — Especially while I can recollect to his advantage our last interview, and as every day produces stronger instances of *tyranny,* I will call it, on the other side. — In a word, I will frankly own (since you cannot think any thing I say too explicit) that were he *now* but a moral man, I would prefer him to all the men I ever saw.

So that this is but *conditional liking* still, you'll say. — Nor, I hope, is it more. I never was in *love* as it is called; and whether this be *it,* or not, I must submit to *you.* But will venture to think it, if it be, no such *mighty* monarch, no such unconquerable power, as I have heard it represented; and it must have met with greater encouragement than I think I have given it, to be absolutely unconquerable—Since I am persuaded, that I could yet, without a *throb*, most willingly give up the *one* man to get rid of the *other*.

But now to be a little more serious with you: if, my dear, my particularly unhappy situation had driven (or *led* me, if you please) into a *liking* of the man; and if that liking *had*, in your opinion, inclined me to *love* him; should *you*, whose mind is susceptible of the most friendly impressions; who have such high notions of the delicacy which ought to be observed by our sex in these matters; and who actually *do* enter so deeply into the distresses of one you love—should *you* have pushed so far that unhappy friend on so very nice a subject?—Especially, when I aimed not (as you could *prove by fifty* instances, it seems) to guard *against being found out*. Had you rallied me by word of mouth in the manner you do, it might have been more in character; especially, if your friend's distresses had been surmounted; and if she had affected prudish airs in revolving the subject: but to sit down to *write* it, as methinks I see you, with a gladdened eye, and with all the archness of exultation — Indeed, my dear (and I take notice of it, rather for the sake of your own generosity, than for my sake; for, as I have said, I love your raillery), it is not so *very* pretty; the delicacy of the subject, and the delicacy of your own mind, considered.

I lay down my pen here, that you may consider of it a little, if you please.

* * *

I RESUME, to give you my opinion of the force which *figure* or *person* ought to have upon our sex: and this I shall do both *generally* as to the other sex, and *particularly* as to this man: whence you will be able to collect how far my friends are in the right, or in the wrong, when they attribute a good deal of prejudice in favour of one man, and in disfavour of the other, on the score of figure. But, first, let me observe, that they see abundant reason, on comparing Mr. Lovelace and Mr. Solmes together, to believe that this *may* be a consideration with me; and therefore they believe it *is*.

There is certainly something very plausible and attractive, as well as creditable to a woman's *choice* in *figure*. It gives a favourable impression at first sight, in which we wish to be confirmed: and if, upon further acquaintance, we find reason so to be, we are pleased with our judgment, and like the person the better, for having given us cause to compliment our own sagacity, in our first-sighted impressions. But nevertheless, it has been generally a rule with me, to suspect a fine figure, both in man and woman; and I have had a good deal of reason to approve my rule: — with regard to *men* especially; who ought to value themselves rather upon their intellectual than personal qualities. For, as to our sex, if a fine woman should be led by the opinion of the world, to be vain and conceited upon her form and features; and that to such a degree, as to have neglected the more material and more *durable* recommendations: the world will be ready to excuse her; since a pretty fool, in all she says, and in all she does, will please, we know not why.

But who would grudge this pretty fool her short day! Since, with her summer's sun, when her butterfly flutters are over, and the winter of age and sorrow arrives, she will feel the just effects of having neglected to cultivate her better faculties: for then like another Helen, she will be unable to bear the reflection even of her own glass; and being sunk into the insignificance of a *mere old woman*, she will be entitled to the contempts which follow that character. While the *discreet matron*, who carries up [we will not, in such a one's case, say *down*] into advanced life, the ever amiable character of virtuous prudence, and useful experience, finds solid veneration take place of airy admiration, and more than supply the want of it.

But for a *man* to be vain of his person, how effeminate! If such a one happens to have genius, it seldom strikes deep into intellectual subjects. His outside usually runs away with him. To adorn, and perhaps, *intending* to adorn, to render ridiculous, that person, takes up all his attention. All he does is *personal*; that is to say, for himself: all he admires, *is* himself: and in spite of the correction of the stage, which so often and so justly exposes a coxcomb, he usually dwindles down, and sinks into that character; and, of consequence, becomes the scorn of one sex, and the jest of the other.

This is generally the case of your fine figures of men, and of those who value themselves on dress and outward appearance: whence it is, that I repeat, that *mere person* in a man, is a despicable consideration. But if a man, *besides* figure, has learning, and such talents as *would* have distinguished him, whatever were his form; then indeed *person* is an addition: and if he has not run too egregiously into self-admiration, and if he has preserved his morals, he is truly a valuable being.

Mr. Lovelace has certainly taste; and, as far as I am able to determine, he has judgment in most of the politer arts. But although he has a humorous way of carrying it off, yet one may see, that he values himself not a little, both on his person and his parts, and even upon his *dress*; and yet he has so happy an ease in the latter that it seems to be the least part of his study. And as to the former, I should hold myself inexcusable, if I were to add to his vanity by shewing the *least regard* for what is too evidently so much *his*.

And now, my dear, let me ask you; have I come up to your expectations? If I have not, when my mind is more at ease, I will endeavour to please you better. For, methinks, my sentences drag; my style creeps; my imagination is sunk; my spirits serve me not only to tell you, that whether I have more or less, I am wholly devoted to the commands of my dear Miss Howe.

P. S. The insolent Betty Barnes has just now fired me anew, by reporting to me the following expressions of the hideous creature Solmes — "That he is sure of the coy girl; and that *with little labour to himself*." — "That be I ever so averse to him beforehand, he can depend upon my principles; and it will be a pleasure to him to see by what pretty degrees I shall come to." — Horrid wretch!! "That it was Sir Oliver's observation, who knew the world perfectly well, that *fear* was a better security than *love*, for a woman's good behaviour to her husband; although, for his part, to such a fine creature truly he would try what love would do; for a few weeks at least: being unwilling to believe what the old Knight used to aver, that fondness spoils more wives than it makes good."

What think you, my dear, of such a wretch as this! tutored, too, by that old surly *mysogynist*, as he was deemed, Sir Oliver? —

LETTER XLI.
Miss Clarissa Harlowe to Miss Howe.

Tuesday, March 21.

How willingly would my dear mother shew kindness to me, were she permitted! None of this persecution should I labour under, I am sure, if that regard were paid to her prudence and fine understanding, which they so well deserve. Whether owing to her, or to my aunt, or to both, that a new trial was to be made upon me, I cannot tell; but this morning her Shorey delivered into my hand the following condescending letter.

MY DEAR GIRL,

FOR so I must still call you; since *dear* you may be to me, in every sense of the word — We have taken into particular consideration some hints that fell yesterday from your good Norton, as if we had not, at Mr. Solmes's first application, treated you with that condescension, wherewith we have in all other instances treated you. If it even *had been so*, my dear, you were not excusable to be wanting in *your* part, and to set yourself to oppose your father's will in a point into which he had entered too far, to recede with honour. But all yet may be well. On your single will, my child, depends all our happiness.

Your father permits me to tell you, that if you now at last comply with his expectations, all past disobligations shall be buried in oblivion, as if they had never been: but withal, that this is the last time that that grace will be offered you.

I hinted to you, you must remember*, that patterns of the richest silks were sent for. They are come. And as they *are* come, your father, to shew how much he is determined, will have me send them up to you. I could have

* See p. 95.

wished they might not have accompanied this letter — But there is no great matter in *that*. I must tell you, that your delicacy is not to be quite so much regarded, as I had once thought it deserved to be.

These are the newest, as well as richest, that we could procure; answerable to our station in the world; answerable to the fortune, additional to your grandfather's estate, designed you; and to the noble settlements agreed upon.

Your father intends you six suits (three of them dressed suits) at his own expense. You have an entire new suit; and one besides, which I think you never wore but twice. As the new suit is rich, if you choose to make that one of the six, your father will present you with an hundred guineas in lieu.

Mr. Solmes intends to present you with a set of jewels. As you have your grandmother's and your own, if you choose to have the former new set, and to make them serve, his present will be made in money: a very round sum — which will be given in full property to yourself; besides a fine annual allowance for pin-money, as it is called. So that your objection against the spirit of a man you think worse of than it deserves, will have no weight; but you will be more independent than a wife of less discretion than we attribute to you, perhaps *ought* to be. You know full well, that I, who first and last brought a still larger fortune into the family than you will carry to Mr. Solmes, had not a provision made me of near this that we have made for you — Where people marry to their liking, terms are the least things stood upon — Yet should I be sorry if you cannot (to oblige us all) overcome a dislike.

Wonder not, Clary, that I write to you thus plainly and freely upon this subject. Your behaviour hitherto has been such, that we have had no opportunity of entering minutely into the subject with you. Yet, after all that has passed between you and me in conversation, and between you and your uncles by letter, you have no room to doubt what is to be the consequence. — Either, child, we must give up *our* authority, or you *your* humour. You cannot expect the one. We have all the reason in the world to expect the other. You know I have told you more than once, that you must resolve to have Mr. Solmes, or never to be looked upon as our child.

The draught of the settlements you may see whenever you will. We think there can be no room for objection to any of the articles. There is still more in them in our family's favour, than was stipulated at first, when your aunt talked of them to you. More so, indeed, than we could have asked. If, upon perusal of them, you think any alteration necessary, it shall be made. — Do, my dear girl, send to me within this day or two, or rather *ask* me, for the perusal of them.

As a certain person's appearance at church so lately, and what he gives out every where, make us extremely uneasy, and as that uneasiness will continue while you are single, you must not wonder that a short day is intended. This day fortnight we design it to be, if you have no objection to make that I shall approve of. But if you determine as we would have you, and signify it to us, we shall not stand with you for a week or so.

Your sightliness of person may perhaps make some think this alliance disparaging. But I hope you will not put such a personal value upon yourself: if you do, it will indeed be the less wonder that *person* should weigh with you (however weak the consideration!) in another man.

Thus we parents, in justice, ought to judge, that our two daughters are *equally* dear and valuable to us: if so, why should *Clarissa* think that a disparagement, which *Arabella* would not (nor *we* for her) have thought any, had the address been made to her? — You will know what I mean by this, without my explaining myself further.

Signify to us, now, therefore, your compliance with our wishes. And then there is an end of your confinement. An act of oblivion, as I may call it, shall pass upon all your former refractoriness: and you will once more make us happy in you, and in one another. You may, in this case, directly come down to your father and me, in his study; where we will give you our opinions of the patterns, with our hearty forgiveness and blessings.

Come, be a good child, as you used to be, my Clarissa. I have (notwithstanding your past behaviour, and the hopelessness which some have expressed in your compliance) undertaken this one time more for you. Discredit not my hopes, my dear girl! I have promised never more to interfere between your *father* and *you*, if this my most earnest application succeed not. I expect you down, love. Your father expects you down. But be sure don't let him see any thing uncheerful in your compliance. If you come, I will clasp you to my fond heart, with as much pleasure as ever I pressed you to it in my whole life. You don't know what I have suffered within these few weeks past; nor ever will be able to guess, till you come to be in my situation; which is that of a fond and indulgent mother, praying night and day, and struggling to preserve, against the attempts of more ungovernable spirits, the peace and union of her family.

But you know the terms. Come not near us, if you resolve to be undutiful; but this, after what I have written, I hope you cannot be.

If you come directly, and, as I said, *cheerfully*, as if your heart were in your duty) and you told me it was *free*, you know), I shall then, as I said, give you the most tender proofs, how much I am

Your truly affectionate mother.

Think for me, my dearest friend,

how I must be affected by this letter; the contents of it is so surprisingly terrifying, yet so sweetly urged! — O why, cried I to myself, am I obliged to undergo this severe conflict between a command that I cannot obey, and language so condescendingly moving! — Could I have been sure of being struck dead at the altar before the ceremony had given the man I hate a title to my vows, I think I could have submitted to have been led to it. But to think of living *with* and living *for* a man one abhors, what a sad thing is that!

And then, how could the glare of habit and ornament be supposed any inducement to one, who has always held, that the principal view of a good wife in the adorning of her person, ought to be, to *preserve* the affection of her husband, and to *do credit* to his choice; and that she should be even fearful of attracting the eyes of *others?* — In this view, must not the very richness of the patterns add to my disgusts? — Great encouragement indeed to think of adorning one's self to be the wife of Mr. *Solmes!*

Upon the whole, it was not possible for me to go down upon the prescribed condition. Do you think it was? — And to *write*, if my letter would have been *read*, what could I write that would be admitted, and after what I had written and said to so little effect?

I walked backward and forward. I threw down with disdain the patterns. Now to my closet retired I; then quitting it, threw myself upon the settee; then upon this chair; then upon that; then into another — I knew not what to do! — And while I was in this suspense, having again taken up the letter to re-peruse it, Betty came in, reminding me, by order, that my papa and mamma waited for me in my father's study.

Tell my mamma, said I, that I beg the favour of seeing her here for one moment; or to permit me to attend her any where by herself.

I listened at the stairs-head — You see, my dear, how it is, cried my father, very angrily; all your condescension (as your indulgence heretofore) is thrown away. *You blame your son's violence,* as you call it [*I had some pleasure in hearing this*]; but nothing else will do with her. You shall not see her alone. Is my presence an exception to the bold creature?

Tell her, said my mother to Betty, she knows upon what terms she may come down to us. Nor will I see her upon any other.

The maid brought me this answer. I had recourse to my pen and ink; but I trembled so, that I could not write, nor knew I what to say, had I had steadier fingers. At last Betty brought me these lines from my father.

UNDUTIFUL AND PERVERSE CLARISSA,

No condescension, I see, will move you. Your mother shall *not* see you; nor will I. Prepare however to obey. You know our pleasure.

Your uncle Antony, your brother, and your sister, and your favourite Mrs. Norton, shall see the ceremony performed privately at your uncle's chapel. And when Mr. Solmes can introduce you to us, in the temper we wish to behold you in, we may perhaps forgive *his* wife, although we never can, in any *other* character, our perverse daughter. As it will be so privately performed, clothes and equipage may be provided afterwards. So prepare to go to your uncle's for an early day in next week. We will not see you till all is over; and we will have it over the sooner, in order to shorten the time of your deserved confinement, and our own trouble in contending with such a rebel, as you have been of late. I will hear no pleas, I will receive no letter, nor expostulation. Nor shall you hear from me any more till you have changed your name to my liking. This from

Your incensed father.

If this resolution be adhered to, then will my father never see me more! — For I will never be the wife of that Solmes — I will die first! —

Tuesday evening.

He, this Solmes, came hither soon after I had received my father's letter. He sent up to beg leave to wait upon me — I wonder at his assurance! —

I said to Betty, who brought me this message, let him restore an unhappy creature to her father and mother, and then I may hear what he has to say. But, if my friends will not see *me* on *his* account, I will not see *him* upon his own.

I hope, miss, said Betty, you will not send me down with this answer. He is with your papa and mamma.

I am driven to despair, said I I cannot be used worse. I will not see him.

Down she went with my answer. She pretended, it seems, to be loth to repeat it: so was *commanded* out of her affected reserves, and gave it in its full force.

O how I heard my father storm! They were all together, it seems, in his study. My brother was for having me turned out of the house that moment, to Lovelace, and my evil destiny. My mother was pleased to put in a gentle word for me: I know not what it was: but thus she was answered. — My dear, this is the most provoking thing in the world in a woman of your good sense! — To love a rebel, as well as if she were dutiful. What encouragement for duty is this? — Have I not loved her as well as ever you did? And *why* am I changed? Would to the Lord, your sex knew how to distinguish! It is plain that she relies upon her power over you. The fond mother ever made a hardened child!

She was pleased, however, to blame Betty, as the wench owned, for giving my answer its full force. But my father praised her for it. The wench says, that he would have come up in his wrath, at my refusing to see Mr. Solmes, had not my brother and sister prevailed upon him to the contrary.

I wish he had! — And, were it not for his own sake, that he had killed me!

Mr. Solmes condescended [I am mightily obliged to him, truly!] to plead for me.

They are all in tumults! How it will end, I know not — I am quite weary of my life — So happy, till within these few weeks! — So miserable now!

Well, indeed, might my mother say, that I should have severe trials *.

P. S. The *idiot* [such a one am I treated like!] is *begged*, as I may say, by my brother and sister. They have desired, that I may be consigned over entirely to their management. If it be granted [it *is* granted, on my father's part, I understand, but not *yet* on my mother's], what cruelty may I not expect from their envy, jealousy, and ill-will! — I shall soon see, by its effects, if I am to be so consigned — This is a written intimation privately dropt in my woodhouse-walk, by my cousin Dolly Hervey. The dear girl longs to see me, she tells me: but is forbidden till she see me as Mrs. Solmes, or as consenting to be his. I will take example by *their* perseverance! — Indeed I will!

* P. 112.

LETTER XLII.

Miss Clarissa Harlowe to Miss Howe.

An angry dialogue, a scolding-bout rather, has passed between my sister and me. Did you think I could scold, my dear?

She was sent up to me, upon my refusal to see Mr. Solmes — Let loose upon me, I think! — No intention on their parts to conciliate! It seems evident that I am given up to my brother and her, by general consent.

I will do justice to every thing she said against me, which carried any force with it. As I ask for your approbation or disapprobation of my conduct, upon the facts I lay before you, I should think it the sign of a very bad cause, if I endeavoured to mislead my judge.

She began with representing to me the danger I had been in, had my father come up, as he would have done, had he not been hindered — by Mr. *Solmes*, among the rest. She reflected upon my Norton, as if she encouraged me in my perverseness. She ridiculed me for my supposed esteem for Mr. Lovelace. — Was surprised that the *witty*, the *prudent*, nay, the *dutiful* and pi—ous [so she sneeringly pronounced the word] Clarissa Harlowe, should be so strangely fond of a profligate man that her parents were forced to lock her up, in order to hinder her from running into his arms. "Let me ask you, my dear, said she, how you now keep your account of the disposition of your time? *How many hours* in the *twenty-four* do you devote to your needle? How many to your prayers? How many to letter-writing? And how many to love? — I doubt, I doubt, my little dear, [was her arch expression], the latter article is like Aaron's rod, and swallows up all the rest! — Tell me; is it not so?"

To these I answered, that it was a double mortification to me to owe my safety from the effects of my father's indignation to a man I could never thank for any thing. I vindicated the good Mrs. Norton with a warmth that was due to her merit. With equal warmth I resented her reflections upon me on Mr. Lovelace's account. As to the disposition of my time in the twenty-four hours, I told her it would better have become her to pity a sister in distress, than to exult over her — Especially, when I could too justly attribute to the disposition of some of her wakeful hours no small part of that distress.

She raved extremely at this last hint: but reminded me of the gentle treatment of all my friends, my mother's in particular, before it came to this: she said, that I had discovered a spirit they never had expected: that, if they had *thought* me such a championess, they would hardly have ventured to engage with me: but that now, the short and the long was, that the matter had gone too far to be given up: that it was become a contention between *duty* and *wilfulness;* whether a parent's authority were to yield to a daughter's obstinacy, or the contrary: that I must therefore bend or break, that was all, child.

I told her, that I wished the subject were of such a nature, that I could return her pleasantry with equal lightness of heart: but that, if Mr. Solmes had such merit in every body's eyes, in *hers* particularly, why might he not be a *brother* to me, rather than a *husband?*

O child, said she, methinks you are as pleasant to the full as I am: I begin to have some hopes of you now. But do you think I will rob my sister of her humble servant? Had he first addressed himself to me, something might have been said: but to take my younger sister's refusal! No, no, child; it is not come to that neither! besides, that would be to leave the door open in your heart for you know who, child; and we would fain bar him out, if possible. In short [and then she changed both her tone and her looks] had I been as forward as somebody, to throw myself into the arms of one of the greatest profligates in England, who had endeavoured to support his claim to me through the blood of my brother, then might all my family join together to save me from such a wretch, and to marry me as fast as they could, to some worthy man, who might *opportunely* offer himself. And now, Clary, all's out, and make the most of it.

Did not this deserve a severe return? Do, say it did, to justify my reply. — Alas! for my poor sister! said I — The man was not *always* so great a profligate. How true is the observation, *that unrequited love turns to deepest hate!*

I thought she would have beat me. But I proceeded — I have heard often of my brother's danger, and my brother's murderer. When so little ceremony is made with me, why should I not speak out? — Did he not seek to kill the other, if he could have done it? Would my brother have given Lovelace *his* life, had it been in his power? — The *aggressor* should not *complain*. — And, as to opportune offers, would to Heaven some one had offered *opportunely* to somebody! It is not my fault, Bella, the *opportune* gentleman don't come!

Could *you*, my dear, have shewn more spirit? I expected to feel the weight of her hand. She did come up to me, with it held up: then speechless with passion, ran down half way of the stairs, and came up again.

When she could speak — God give me patience with you!

Amen, said I: but you see, Bella, how ill you bear the retort you provoke. Will you forgive me; and let me find a sister in you, as *I* am sorry, if you have reason to think me unsisterly, in what I have said?

Then did she pour upon me with greater violence; considering my gentleness as a triumph of temper over her. She was resolved, she said, to let every body know how I took the wicked Lovelace's part against my brother.

I wished, I told her, I could make the plea for *myself*, which she might for *herself*; to wit, that my anger was more inexcusable than my judgment. But I presumed she had some other view in coming to me, than she had hitherto acquainted me with. Let me, said I, but know (after all that has passed) if you have any thing to propose that I *can* comply with; any thing that can make my *only* sister once more my friend?

I had before, upon her ridiculing me on my supposed character of *meekness*, said, that, although I wished to be thought *meek*, I would not be *abject;* although *humble* not *mean:* and here, in a sneering way, she cautioned me on that head.

I replied, that her pleasantry was much more agreeable than her anger. But I wished she would let me know the end of a visit that had hitherto (*between* us) been so unsisterly.

She desired to be informed in the name of *every body*, was her word, what I was determined upon? And whether to comply or not? — One word for all: my friends were not to have patience with so perverse a creature for ever.

This then I told her I would do: absolutely break with the man they were all so determined against: upon condition, however, that neither Mr. Solmes, nor any other, were urged to me with the force of a command.

And what was this, more than I had offered before? What, but ringing my changes upon the same bells, and neither receding nor advancing one tittle?

If I knew what other proposals I could make, I told her, that would be acceptable to them all, and free me from the address of a man so disagreeable to me, I *would* make them. I had indeed before offered, never to marry without my father's consent—

She interrupted me, that was because I depended upon my whining tricks to bring my father and mother to what I pleased.

A *poor* dependence! I said:— *she* knew those who would make that dependence vain—

And *I should* have brought them to my own beck, very probably, and my uncle Harlowe too, as also my aunt Hervey, had I not been forbidden their sight, and thereby hindered from playing my pug's tricks before them.

At least, Bella, said I, you have hinted to me to *whom* I am obliged, that my father and mother, and every body else, treat me thus harshly. But surely you make them all very weak. Indifferent persons judging of us two from what *you* say, would either think *me* a very artful creature, or *you* a very spiteful one—

You are *indeed* a very artful one, for that matter, interrupted she in a passion: one of the artfullest I ever knew! And then followed an accusation so low! so unsisterly!— That I half-bewitched people by my insinuating address: that nobody could be valued or respected, but must stand like ciphers wherever I came. How often, said she, have I and my brother been talking upon a subject, and had every body's attention, till *you* came in, with your bewitching *meek* pride, and *humble* significance? And then have we either been stopped by references to Miss Clary's opinion, forsooth; or been forced to stop ourselves, or must have talked on unattended to by every body.

She paused. Dear Bella, proceed!

She indeed seemed only gathering breath.

And so I *will*, said she — Did you not bewitch my grandfather? Could any thing be pleasing to him, that you did not say or do? How did he use to hang, till he slabbered again, poor doting old man! on your silver tongue! Yet what did *you* say, that *we* could not have said? What did *you* do, that we did not endeavour to do? — And what was all this for? Why, truly, his last will shewed what effect your *smooth* obligingness had upon him!— To leave the *acquired part* of his estate from the next heirs, his own sons, to a grandchild; to his *youngest* grandchild! a *daughter* too!— To leave the family pictures from his sons to you, because you could *tiddle* about them, and, though you now neglect their examples, could wipe and clean them with your dainty hands! The family-plate too, in such quantities, of two or three generations standing, must not be changed, because his *precious* child *, humouring his old *fal-lal* tricks; curling, like a serpent, taste, admired it, to make it all about your mamma; and making her own. her cry to deny you any thing

This was too low to move me: your little obstinate heart was set O my poor sister! said I: not to upon!—
be able, or at least willing, to distinguish between art and nature! Obstinate heart, Bella!
If I *did* oblige, I was happy in it: Yes, obstinate heart! For did I looked for no further reward: you ever give up any thing? Had my mind is above art, from the you not the art to make them dirty motives you mention. I wish think all was right you asked, with all my heart my grandfather though my brother and I were had not thus distinguished me: frequently refused favours of no he saw my brother likely to be greater import?
amply provided for *out* of the family, as well as *in* it: he desired granted. I seldom asked favours that *you* might have the greater for *myself*, but for *others*.
share of my father's favour for it; I was a reflecting creature for and no doubt but you *both* will. this.
You know, Bella, that the estate All you speak of, Bella, was a my grandfather bequeathed *me* long time ago. I cannot go so far was not half the real estate he back into our childish follies. left. Little did I think of how *long*

What's all that to an estate in *standing* this your *late-shewn* antipossession, and left you with such pathy is.
distinctions, as gave you a reputation of greater value than the *saucy meekness;* such a *best manner;* and such venom in words!—
estate itself?

Hence my misfortune, Bella, in O Clary! Clary! thou wert always your envy, I doubt!—But have a *two-faced* girl!
I not given up that possession in Nobody thought I had two faces, the best manner I could— when I gave up all into my fa-

Yes, interrupting me, she hated ther's management; taking from me for that *best manner.* Specious little witch! she called me: pocket-money, without a shilling your *best manner*, so full of art addition to my stipend, or desiand design, had never been seen ring it—
through, if you, with your blan- Yes, cunning creature!—And dishing ways, had not been put that was another of your *fetches!*
out of sight, and reduced to positive declarations!—Hindered father (as no doubt you thought from playing your little, whining it would) to tell you, that, since

* Alluding to his words in the preamble to the clauses in his will. See p. 35. tiful a thing, he would keep entire,

for your use, all the produce of the estate left you, and be but your steward in it; and that you should be entitled to the same allowances as before? Another of your *hook-in's*, Clary! — So that all your extravagancies have been supported gratis.

My extravagancies, Bella! — But did my father ever give me any thing he did not give you?

Yes, indeed; I got more by that means, than I should have had the conscience to ask. But I have still the greater part to shew! But *you!* what have *you* to shew! — I dare say, not fifty pieces in the world!

Indeed I have not!

I believe you! — Your mamma Norton, I suppose — But mum for that!—

Unworthy Bella! — The good woman, although low in circumstance, is great in mind! Much greater than those who would impute meanness to a soul incapable of it.

What then have you done with the sums given you from infancy to squander? — Let me ask you [affecting archness] has, has, has Lovelace, has your rake, put it out at interest for you?

O that my sister would not make me blush for her! It *is*, however, out at interest! — And I hope it will bring me interest upon interest! — Better than to lie useless in my cabinet.

She understood me, she said. Were I a man, she should suppose I was aiming to carry the county — Popularity! A crowd to follow me with their blessings as I went to and from church, and nobody else to be regarded, were agreeable things. House-top-proclamations! I *hid not my light under a bushel*, she would say that for me. But was it not a little hard upon me, to be kept from blazing on a Sunday? — And to be hindered from my charitable ostentations?

This, indeed, Bella, is cruel in *you*, who have so largely contributed to my confinement.— But go on. You'll be out of breath by-and-by. I cannot wish to be *able* to return this usage.— *Poor* Bella! and I believe I smiled a little too contemptuously for a sister to a sister.

None of your saucy contempts [rising in her voice]: none of your *poor Bella's*, with that air of superiority in a younger sister.

Well then, *rich* Bella? courtesying — that will please you better — And it is due likewise to the hoards you boast of.

Look-ye, Clary, holding up her hand, if you are not a little more abject in your *meekness*, a little more *mean* in your *humility*, and treat me with the respect due to an elder sister — you shall find —

Not that you will treat me worse than you *have done*, Bella! — That cannot be, unless you were to let fall your uplifted hand upon me— And that would less become you to *do*, than me to *bear*.

Good, meek creature; but you were upon your overtures just now! — I shall surprise every body by tarrying so long. They will think some good may be done with you.—And supper will be ready.

A tear would stray down my cheek — How happy have I been, said I, sighing, in the supper-time conversations, with all my dear friends in my eye, round their hospitable board!

I met only with insult for this — Bella has not a *feeling* heart. The highest joy in this life she is not capable of: but then she saves herself many griefs, by her impenetrableness — Yet, for ten times the pain that such a sensibility is attended with, would I not part with the pleasure it brings with it.

She asked me, upon my turning from her, if she should say any thing below of my *compliances?*

You may say, that I will do every thing they would have me do, if they will free me from Mr. Solmes's address.

This is all you desire at present, *creeper on! insinuator!* [what words she has!] But will not t'other man flame out, and roar most horribly, upon the snatching from his paws a prey he thought himself sure of?

I must let you talk in your own way, or we shall never come to a point. I shall not matter his *roaring*, as you call it. I will promise him, that, if I ever marry any other man, it shall not be till *he* is married. And if he be not satisfied with such a condescension, I shall think he *ought*: and I will give any assurances, that I will neither correspond with him, nor see him. Surely this will do.

But I suppose then you will have no objection to see and converse, on a civil foot, with Mr. Solmes — as your father's friend, or so?

No! I must be permitted to retire to my apartment whenever he comes. I would no more converse with the one, than correspond with the other. That would be to make Mr. Lovelace guilty of some rashness, on a belief, that I broke with him, to have Mr. Solmes.

And so, that wicked wretch is to be allowed such a control over you, that you are not to be civil to your father's friends, at his own house, for fear of incensing *him!* — When this comes to be represented, be so good as to tell me, what it is you expect from it?

Every thing, I said, or *nothing*, as she was pleased to represent it. — Be so good as to give it your interest, Bella, and say, further, "That I will by any means I can, in the law or otherwise, make over to my father, to my uncles, or even to my brother, all I am entitled to by my grandfather's will, as a security for the performance of my promises. And as I shall have no reason to expect any favour from my father, if I break them, I shall not be worth any body's having. And further still, unkindly as my brother has used me, I will go down to Scotland privately, as his housekeeper [I now see I may be spared here], if he will promise to treat me no worse than he would do an hired one. — Or I will go to Florence, to my cousin Morden, if his stay in Italy will admit of it. In *either case*, it may be given out, that I am gone to the *other;* or to the world's end. I care not whither it is said I am gone, or do go."

Let me ask you, child, if you will give your pretty proposal in writing?

Yes, with all my heart. And I stept to my closet, and wrote to the purpose I have mentioned; and, moreover, the following lines to my brother.

MY DEAR BROTHER,

I HOPE I have made such proposals to my sister, as will be accepted. I am sure they will, if you please to give them your sanction. Let me beg of you, for God's sake, that you will. I think myself very unhappy in having incurred your displeasure. No sister can love a brother better than I love you. Pray do not put the worst, but the best construction upon my proposals, when you have them reported to you. Indeed I mean the best. I have no subterfuges, no arts, no intentions, but to keep to the letter of them. You shall yourself draw up every thing into writing, as strong as you can; and I will sign it: and what the *law* will not do to enforce it, my *resolution* and my *will* shall: so that I shall be worth nobody's address, that has not my papa's consent: nor shall any person, nor any consideration induce me to revoke it. You can do more than any body to reconcile my parents and uncles to me. Let me owe this desirable favour to your brotherly interposition, and you will for ever oblige

Your afflicted sister,
CL. HARLOWE.

And how do you think Bella employed herself while I was writing! — Why, playing gently upon my harpsichord: and *humming* to it, to shew her unconcernedness.

When I approached her with what I had written, she arose with an air of levity — Why, love, you have not written already! — You have, I protest! — O what a ready pen-woman! — And may I read it?

If you please. And let me beseech you, my dear Bella, to back these proposals with your good offices: and [folding my uplifted hands; tears, I believe, standing in my eyes] I will love you as never sister loved another.

Thou art a strange creature, said she; there is no withstanding thee.

She took the proposals and letter; and having read them, burst into an affected laugh: How wise ones may be taken in! — Then you did not know, that I was jesting with you all this time! — And so you would have me carry down this pretty piece of nonsense?

Don't let me be surprised at your seeming unsisterliness, Bella. I hope it is *but* seeming. There can be *no* wit in such jesting as this.

The folly of the creature! — How natural is it for people, when they set their hearts upon any thing, to think every body must see with their eyes! — Pray, dear child, what becomes of your father's authority *here?* — Who *stoops* here, the *parent,* or the *child?* — How does *this* square with the engagements actually agreed upon between your father and Mr. Solmes? What security, that your rake will not follow you to the world's end? — Nevertheless, that you may not think that I stand in the way of a reconciliation on such fine terms as these, I will be your messenger this once, and hear what my papa will say to it; although beforehand I can tell you, these proposals will not answer the principal end.

So down she went. But, it seems, my aunt Hervey and my uncle Harlowe were gone away: and as they have all engaged to act in concert, messengers were dispatched to my uncle and aunt to desire them to be here to breakfast in the morning.

Tuesday night, 10 o'clock.

I am afraid I shall not be thought worthy —

Just as I began to fear I should not be thought worthy of an answer, Betty rapped at my door, and said, if I were not in bed, she had a letter for me. I had but just done writing the above dialogue, and stept to the door, with the pen in my hand — Always writing, miss! said the bold wench: it is admirable how you can get away what you write — But the Fairies, they say, are always at hand to help lovers. — She retired in so much haste, that had I been disposed, I could not take the notice of this insolence which it deserved.

I inclose my brother's letter. He was resolved to let me see, that I should have nothing to expect from his kindness. But surely he will not be permitted to carry every point. The assembling of my friends to-morrow is a good sign: and I will hope something from that, and from proposals so reasonable. And now I will try if any repose will fall to my lot for the remainder of this night.

TO MISS CLARA HARLOWE.

Inclosed in the preceding.

YOUR proposals will be considered by your father and mother, and all your friends, to-morrow morning. What trouble does your shameful forwardness give us all! I wonder you have the courage to write to me, upon whom you are so continually emptying your *whole female quiver.* I have no patience with you, for reflecting upon me as the aggressor in a quarrel which owed its beginning to my consideration for you.

You have made such confessions in a villain's favour, as ought to cause all your relations to renounce you for ever. For my part, I will not believe any woman in the world, who promises against her *avowed* inclination. To put it out of your *power* to ruin yourself is the only way left to prevent your ruin. I did not intend to write; but your *too-kind* sister has prevailed upon me. As to your going into Scotland, that day of grace is over. Nor would I advise, that you should go to *grandfather-up* your cousin Morden. Besides, that worthy gentleman might be involved in some fatal dispute, upon your account; and then be called the *aggressor*.

A fine situation you have brought yourself to, to propose to hide yourself from your rake, and to have falsehoods told, to conceal you! — Your confinement, at this rate, is the happiest thing that could befal you. Your bravo's behaviour at church, looking out for you, is a sufficient indication of his power over you, had you *not* so shamelessly acknowledged it.

One word for all — Your parents and uncles may do as they will: but if, for the honour of the family, I cannot carry this point, I will retire to Scotland, and never see the face of any one of it more.

JA. HARLOWE.

There's a brother! — There's flaming duty to a father, and mother, and uncles! — But he sees himself valued, and made of consequence; and he gives himself airs accordingly! — Nevertheless, as I said above, I will hope better things from those who have not the interest my brother has to keep open these unhappy differences.

LETTER XLIII.

Miss Clarissa Harlowe to Miss Howe.

Wednesday, March 22.

WOULD you not have thought, my dear Miss Howe, as well as I, that my proposal must have been accepted: and that my brother, by the last article of his unbrotherly letter (where he threatens to go to Scotland if it should be hearkened to) was of opinion that it *would*.

For my part, after I had read the unkind letter over and over, I concluded, upon the whole, that a reconciliation upon terms so disadvantageous to myself, as hardly any other person in my case, I dare say, would have proposed, must be the result of this morning's conference. And in that belief I had begun to give myself new trouble in thinking (this difficulty over) how I should be able to pacify Lovelace on that part of my engagement, by which I undertook to break off all correspondence with him, unless my friends should be brought by the interposition of his powerful friends, and any offers they might make (which it was rather *his* part to suggest, than *mine* to intimate) to change their minds.

Thus was I employed, not very agreeably, you may believe, because of the vehemence of the tempers I had to conflict with; when breakfasting-time approached, and my judges began to arrive.

And oh! how my heart fluttered on hearing the chariot of the one, and then of the other, rattle through the court-yard, and the hollow sounding footstep giving notice of each person's stepping out, to take his place on the awful bench which my fancy had formed for them and my other judges!

That, thought I, is my aunt Hervey's! That my uncle Harlowe's! Now comes my uncle

Antony! And my imagination made a fourth chariot for the odious Solmes, although it happened that he was not there.

And now, thought I, are they all assembled: and now my brother calls upon my sister to make *her* report! Now the hard-hearted Bella interlards her speech with invective! Now has she concluded her report! Now they debate upon it!—Now does my brother flame! Now threaten to go to Scotland! Now is he chidden, and now soothed!

And then I ran through the whole conference in my imagination, forming speeches for this person and that, *pro* and *con*. till all concluded, as I flattered myself, in an acceptance of my conditions, and in giving directions to have an instrument drawn to tie me up to my good behaviour: while I supposed all agreed to give Solmes a wife every way more worthy of him, and with *her* the promise of my grandfather's estate, in case of my forfeiture, or dying unmarried, on the righteous condition he proposes to entitle himself to it with me.

And now, thought I, am I to be ordered down to recognize my own proposals. And how shall I look upon my awful judges? How shall I stand the questions of some, the set surliness of others, the returning love of one or two? How greatly shall I be affected!

Then I wept: then I dried my eyes: then I practised at my glass for a look more cheerful than my heart.

And now [as any thing stirred] is my sister coming to declare the issue of all! Tears gushing again, my heart fluttering as a bird against its wires; drying my eyes again and again to no purpose.

And thus, my dear, [excuse the fanciful prolixity] was I employed, and such were my thoughts and imaginations, when I found a very different result from the hopeful conference.

For about ten o'clock up came my sister, with an air of cruel triumph, waving her hand with a light flourish—

Obedience without reserve is required of you, Clary. My papa is justly incensed, that you should *presume* to dispute his will, and to make conditions with him. He knows what is best for you: and as you own matters are gone a great way between this hated Lovelace and you, they will believe nothing you say; except you will give the one *only* instance, that will put them out of doubt of the sincerity of your promises.

What, child, are you surprised?—Cannot you speak?—Then, it seems, you had expected a different issue, had you?—Strange that you could!—With all your acknowledgments and confessions, so creditable to your *noted prudence!*—

I was indeed speechless for some time: my eyes were even fixed, and ceased to flow. But upon the hard-hearted Bella's proceeding with her airs of insult, Indeed I *was* mistaken, said I; indeed I was!—For in you, Bella,

I expected, I hoped for a sister —

What! interrupted she, with all your mannerly flings, and your despising airs, did you expect that I was capable of telling stories for you? — Did you think, that when I was asked my own opinion of the sincerity of your declarations, I could not tell them, *how far matters had gone between you and your fellow?* — When the intention is to bend that stubborn will of yours to your duty, do you think I would deceive them? — Do you think I would encourage them to call you down, to contradict all that I should have *invented* in your favour?

Well, well, Bella; I am the less obliged to you; that's all. I was willing to think, that I had still a brother and sister. But I find I am mistaken.

Pretty Mopsa-eyed soul! — was her expression! — And was it willing to think it had still a *brother* and *sister?* And why don't you go on, Clary? [mocking my half-weeping accent] I thought too I had a *father,* and *mother, two uncles,* and an *aunt: but I am mis — taken, that's all* — Come, Clary, say this, and it will in part be true, because you have thrown off their authority, and because you respect one vile wretch more than them all.

How have I deserved this at your hands, sister? — But I will only say, I pity you.

And with that disdainful air too, Clary! — None of that bridled neck! None of your scornful pity, girl — I beseech you!

This sort of behaviour is natural to you, surely, — Bella! — What *new* talents does it discover in you! — But proceed — If it be a pleasure to you, proceed, Bella. And since I must not pity *you*, I will pity *myself*: for nobody else will.

Because you don't, said she —

Hush, Bella, interrupting her, *because I don't deserve it* — I know you were going to say so. I will say as you say in every thing; and that's the way to please you.

Then say, Lovelace is a villain. So I will, when I think him so. Then you don't think him so? Indeed I don't. *You* did not always, Bella.

And what, Clary, mean you by that? [bristling up to me] — Tell me what you mean by that reflection?

Tell me why you call it a reflection? — What did I say?

Thou art a provoking creature — But what say you to two or three duels of that wretch's?

I can't tell what to say, unless I knew the occasions.

Do you justify duelling at all? I do not: neither can I help his duelling.

Will you go down, and humble that stubborn spirit of yours to your mamma?

I said nothing.

Shall I conduct your ladyship down? [offering to take my declined hand.]

What! not vouchsafe to answer me?

I turned from her in silence.

What! turn your back upon me

too! — Shall I bring up your mamma to you, love? [following me, and taking my struggling hand] What! not speak yet! Come, my sullen, silent dear, speak one word to me — You must say *two* very soon to Mr. Solmes, I can tell you that.

Then [gushing out into tears, which I could not hold in longer] they shall be the last words I will ever speak.

Well, well [insultingly wiping my averted face with her handkerchief, while her other hand held mine in a ridiculing tone] I am glad any thing will make thee speak: then you think you may be brought to speak the *two* words — only they are to be the last! — How like a gentle *lovyer* from its tender bleeding heart was that!

Ridiculous Bella!

Saucy Clary! [changing her sneering tone to an imperious one] But do you think you can humble yourself to go down to your mamma?

I am tired with such stuff as this. Tell me, Bella, if my mamma will condescend to see me?

Yes, if you can be dutiful at last.

I can. I will.

But what call you dutiful?

To give up my own *inclinations* — That's something more for you to tell of — in obedience to my parents' commands; and to beg I may not be made miserable with a man that is fitter for *any body* than for me.

For *me*, do you mean, Clary?

Why not? since you have put the question. You have a better opinion of him than I have. My friends, I hope, would not think him too good for *me*, and not good enough for *you*. But cannot you tell me, Bella, what is to become of me, without insulting over me thus? — If I must be thus treated, remember, that if I am guilty of any rashness, the usage I meet with will justify it.

So, Clary, you are contriving an *excuse*, I find, for somewhat that we have not doubted has been in your head a great while.

If it were so, you seemed resolved, for your part, and so does my brother for *his*, that I shall not want one. — But indeed, Bella, I can bear no longer this repetition of the worst part of yesterday's conversation: I desire I may throw myself at my father's and mother's feet, and hear from them what their sentence is. I shall at least avoid, by that means, the unsisterly insults I meet with from you.

Hey-day! what, is this you? Is it you, my meek sister Clary?

Yes, it is I, Bella; and I will claim the protection due to a child of the family, or to know why I am to be thus treated, when I offer only to preserve to myself the liberty of *refusal*, which belongs to my sex; and, to please my parents, would give up my *choice*. I have contented myself till now to take *second-hand* messengers, and *first-hand* insults: you are but my sister: my brother is not my sovereign, and while I have a father and mother living,

I will not be thus treated by a brother and sister, and their servants, all setting upon me, as it should seem to make me desperate, and to do a rash thing. I will know in short, sister Bella, *why* I am to be constrained thus! — What is intended by it? — And whether I am to be considered as a *child* or a *slave*?

She stood aghast all this time, partly with real, partly with affected surprise.

And is it *you*? Is it *indeed* you? — Well, Clary, you amaze me! But since you are so desirous to refer yourself to your father and mother, I will go down, and tell them what you say. Your friends are not yet gone, I believe: they shall assemble again; and then you may come down, and plead your own cause in person.

Let me then. But let my *brother* and *you* be absent. You have made yourselves too much *parties* against me, to sit as my judges. And I desire to have none of yours or his interpositions. I am sure you could not have represented what I proposed fairly: I am *sure* you could not. Nor is it possible you should be *commissioned* to treat me thus.

Well, well, I'll call up my brother to you. — I will indeed. — He shall justify himself, as well as me.

I desire not to see my brother, except he will come *as* a brother, laying aside the authority he has unjustly assumed over me.

And so, Clary, it is nothing to him, or to me, is it, that our sister shall disgrace her whole family?

As how, Bella, disgrace it? — The man whom you thus freely treat, is a man of birth and fortune: he is a man of parts, and nobly allied. — He was once thought worthy of you; and I wish to Heaven you had had him. I am sure it was not my fault you had not, although you treat me thus!

This set her into a flame! I wish I had forborn it. O how the poor Bella raved: I thought she would have beat me once or twice: and she vowed, her fingers itched to do so — But I was not worth her *anger*: yet she flamed on.

We were heard to be high. — And Betty came up from my mother to command my sister to attend her. — She went down accordingly, threatening me with letting every one know what a violent creature I had shewn myself to be.

Wednesday noon, March 22.

I HAVE as yet heard no more of my sister: and have not courage enough to insist upon throwing myself at the feet of my father and mother, as I thought in my heat of temper I should be able to do. And I am now grown as calm as ever; and were Bella to come up again, as fit to be played upon as before.

I am indeed sorry that I sent her from me in such disorder. But my father's letter threatening me with my uncle Antony's house and chapel, terrifies me strangely; and by their silence I am afraid some new storm is gathering.

But what shall I do with this Lovelace? I have just now, by the unsuspected hole in the wall (*that I told you of in my letter by Hannah*) got a letter from him — So uneasy is he for fear I should be prevailed upon in Solmes's favour; so full of menaces, if I am; so resenting the usage I receive [for, how I cannot tell; but he has undoubtedly intelligence of all that is done in the family]; such protestations of inviolable faith and honour; such vows of reformation; such pressing arguments to escape from this disgraceful confinement — O my dear, what shall I do with this Lovelace?

LETTER XLIV.

Miss Clarissa Harlowe to Miss Howe.

Wednesday, 12 o'clock.

My aunt Hervey is but just gone from me. She came up to me with my sister. They would not trust my aunt without this ill-natured witness. When she entered my chamber, I told her, that this visit was a high favour to a poor prisoner in her hard confinement. I kissed her hand. She, kindly saluting me, said, Why this distance to your aunt, my dear, who loves you so well?

She owned, that she came to expostulate with me, for the peace-sake of the family: for that she could not believe it possible, if I did not conceive myself unkindly treated, that I, who had ever shewn such a sweetness of temper, as well as manners, should be thus resolute, in a point so *very near* to my father, and all my friends. My mother and she were both willing to impute my resolution to the manner I had been begun with; and to my supposing that my brother had originally more of a hand in the proposals made by Mr. Solmes, than my father or other friends. In short, fain would my aunt have furnished me with an excuse to come off my opposition; Bella all the while humming a tune, and opening this book and that, without meaning; but saying nothing.

After having shewed me, that my opposition could not be of signification, my father's honour being engaged, my aunt concluded with enforcing upon me my duty, in stronger terms than I believe she would have done (the circumstances of the case considered) had not my sister been present.

It would be but repeating what I have so often mentioned, to give you the arguments that passed on both sides. — So I will only recite what she said, that carried with it a new face.

When she found me inflexible, as she was pleased to call it, she said, for her part she could not but say, that if I were not to have either Mr. Solmes or Mr. Lovelace, and yet, to make my friends easy, *must* marry, she should not think amiss of Mr. Wyerley. What did I think of Mr. Wyerley?

Ay, Clary, put in my sister, what say you to Mr. Wyerley?

I saw through this immediately. It was said on purpose, I doubted not, to have an argument against me of absolute prepossession in Mr. Lovelace's favour: since Mr. Wyerley everywhere avows his value, even to veneration, for me; and is far less exceptionable, both in person and mind, than Mr. Solmes: and I was willing to turn the tables, by trying how far Mr. Solmes's terms might be dispensed with; since the same terms could not be expected from Mr. Wyerley.

I therefore desired to know, whether my answer, if it should be in favour of Mr. Wyerley, would release me from Mr. Solmes? — For I owned, that I had not the aversion to *him*, that I had to the other.

Nay, she had no commission to propose such a thing. She only knew, that my father and mother would not be easy till Mr. Lovelace's hopes were entirely defeated.

Cunning creature! said my sister.

And this, and her joining in the question before, convinced me, that it was a designed snare for me.

Don't you, dear madam, said I, put questions that can answer no end, but to support my brother's schemes against me. — But are there any hopes of an end to my sufferings and disgrace, without having this hated man imposed upon me? Will not what I have offered be accepted? I am sure it *ought* — I will venture to say that.

Why, niece, if there be *not* any such hopes, I presume you don't think yourself absolved from the duty due from a child to her parents?

Yes, said my sister, I do not doubt but it is Miss Clary's aim, if she does not fly to her Lovelace, to get her estate into her own hands, and go to live at *the Grove*, in that independence upon which she builds all her perverseness. And, dear heart! my little love, how will you then blaze away! Your mamma Norton, your oracle, with your poor at your gates, mingling so *proudly* and so *meanly* with the ragged herd! Reflecting, by your ostentation, upon all the ladies in the country, who do not as you do. This is known to be your scheme! and the poor *without*-doors, and Lovelace *within*, with one hand building up a name, pulling it down with the other! — O what a charming scheme is this! — But let me tell you, my pretty little flighty one, that your father's *living* will shall control your grandfather's *dead* one; and that estate will be disposed of as your fond grandfather would have disposed of it, had he lived to see such a change in his favourite. In a word, miss, it will be kept out of your hands, till my father sees you discreet enough to have the management of it, or till you can *dutifully*, by law, tear it from him.

Fie, Miss Harlowe! said my aunt: this is not pretty to your sister.

O madam, let her go on. This is nothing to what I have borne from Miss Harlowe. She is either commissioned to treat me ill by her *envy*, or by an *higher* authority, to which I must submit. — As to revoking the estate, what hinders, if I pleased? I know my power; but have not the least thought of exerting it. Be pleased to let my father know, that whatever be the consequence to myself, were he to turn me out of doors (which I should rather he would do, than to be confined and insulted as I am) and were I to be reduced to indigence and want, I would seek no relief that should be contrary to his will.

For that matter, child, said my aunt, were you to marry, you must do as your *husband* will have you. If that husband be Mr. Lovelace, he will be glad of any opportunity of further embroiling the families. And, let me tell you, niece, if he had the respect for you which he pretends to have, he would not throw out defiances as he does. He is known to be a very revengeful man; and were I *you*, Miss Clary, I should be afraid he would wreak upon me that vengeance, though I had not offended him, which he is continually threatening to pour upon the family.

Mr. Lovelace's threatened vengeance is in *return* for threatened vengeance. It is not every body will bear insult, as, of late, I have been forced to bear it. O how my sister's face shone with passion!

But Mr. Lovelace, proceeded I, as I have said twenty and twenty times, would be quite out of the question with me, were I to be generously treated!

My sister said something with great vehemence: but only raising my voice, to be heard, without minding her, I'ray, madam (provokingly interrogated I) was he not known to have been as wild a man, when he was at *first* introduced into our family, as he *now* is said to be? Yet *then*, the common phrases of *wild oats*, and *black oxen*, and such like, were qualifiers; and marriage, and the wife's discretion, were to perform wonders — But (turning to my sister) I find I have said too much.

O thou wicked reflecter! — And what made *me* abhor him, think you, but the proof of those villainous freedoms that ought to have had the same effect upon you, were you but half so good a creature as you pretend to be.

Proof, did you say Bella! I thought that you had not *proof?* — But *you know best.*

Was not this very spiteful, my dear?

Now, Clary, said she, would I give a thousand pounds to know all that is in thy little rancorous and reflecting heart, at this moment.

I might let you know for a much less sum, and not be afraid of being worse treated than I have been.

Well, young ladies, I am sorry to see passion run so high between you. You know, niece, (to me) you had not been confined thus to your apartment, could your mother by condescension, or your father by authority, have been able to move you. But how can you expect, when there must be a concession on *one* side, that it should be on

14*

theirs? If *my* Dolly, who has not the hundredth part of your understanding, were thus to set herself up in absolute contradiction to my will, in a point so material, I should not take it well of her — indeed I should not.

I believe not, madam: and if Miss Hervey had just such a brother, and just such a sister [you *may* look, Bella!] and if both were to aggravate her parents, as my brother and sister do mine — Then, perhaps, you might use her as I am used: and if she hated the man you proposed to her, and with as much reason as I do Mr. Solmes —

And loved a rake and libertine, miss, as you do Lovelace, said my sister —

Then might she [continued I, not minding her] beg to be excused from obeying. But yet if she did, and would, give you the most solemn assurances, and security besides, that she would never have the man you disliked, against your consent — I dare say, Miss Hervey's father and mother would sit down satisfied, and not endeavour to force her inclinations.

So! — [said my sister, with uplifted hands] *father* and *mother* now come in for their share.

But if, child, replied my aunt, I know she *loved a rake*, and suspected that she sought only to gain time, in order to wire-draw me into a consent —

I beg pardon, madam, for interrupting you; but if Miss Hervey could *obtain* your consent, what further would be to be said?

True, child; but she never should.

Then, madam, it never would be.

That I doubt, niece.

If you do, madam, can you think confinement and ill usage is the way to prevent the apprehended rashness?

My dear, this sort of intimation would make one but too apprehensive, that there is no trusting to yourself, when one knows your inclination.

That apprehension, madam, seems to have been conceived before this intimation, or the least cause for it, was given. Why else the disgraceful confinement I have been laid under? — Let me venture to say, that my sufferings seem to be rather owing to a concerted design to intimidate me [*Bella held up her hands*], (knowing there were too good grounds for my opposition) than to a doubt of my conduct; for, when they were inflicted first, I had given no *cause* of doubt: nor should there now be room for any, if my discretion might be trusted to.

My aunt, after a little hesitation, said, But, consider, my dear, what confusion will be perpetuated in your family, if you marry this hated Lovelace?

And let it be considered, what misery to me, madam, if I marry that hated Solmes?

Many a young creature has thought she could not love a man, with whom she has afterwards been very happy. Few women, child, marry their first loves.

That may be the reason there are so few happy marriages.

But there are few first impressions *fit* to be encouraged.

I am afraid so too, madam. I have a very indifferent opinion of light and first impressions. But, as I have often said, all I wish for is, to have leave to live *single*.

Indeed you must not, miss. Your father and mother will be unhappy till they see you married, and out of Lovelace's reach. —I am told that you propose to condition with him (so far are matters gone between you) never to have *any* man, if you have not *him*.

I know no better way to prevent mischief on all sides, I freely own it — And there is not, if *he* be out of the question, another man in the world I can think favourably of. Nevertheless, I would give all I have in the world, that he were married to some other person — Indeed I would, Bella, for all you put on that smile of incredulity.

May be so, Clary: but I will smile for all that.

If *he* be out of the question! repeated my aunt — so, Miss Clary, I see how it is — I will go down — [Miss Harlowe, shall I follow you? —] and I will endeavour to persuade your father to let my sister herself come up: and a happier event may then result.

Depend upon it, madam, said my sister, this will be the case: my mother and she will be both in tears; but with this different effect: my mother will come down softened and cut to the heart; but will leave her favourite hardened, from the advantages she will think she has over my mother's tenderness — why, madam, it is for this very reason the girl is not admitted into her presence.

Thus she ran on as she went down stairs.

LETTER XLV.

Miss Clarissa Harlowe to Miss Howe.

My heart fluttered with the hope and the fear of seeing my mother, and with the shame and the grief of having given her so much uneasiness. But it needed not: she was not permitted to come. But my aunt was so good as to return; yet not without my sister: and, taking my hand, made me sit down by her.

She came, she must own, *officiously*, she said, this *once* more; though against the opinion of my father: but knowing and dreading the consequence of my opposition, she could not *but* come.

She then set forth to me my friends' expectations from me; Mr. Solmes's riches (three times as rich he came out to be, as any body had thought him) the settlements proposed; Mr. Lovelace's bad character; their aversion to him; all in a very strong light; but not in a stronger than my mother had before placed them in. My mother, surely, could not have given the particulars of what had passed between herself and me: if she had, my aunt would not have repeated many of the same sentiments, as you will find she did, that had been still more strongly urged, without effect, by her venerable sister.

She said it would break the heart of my father to have it imagined, that he had not a power over his child; and that, as *he* thought, for my own good: a child too, whom they had always doated upon! — Dearest, dearest miss, concluded she, clasping her fingers, with the most condescending earnestness, let me beg of you, for *my* sake, for *your own* sake, for a *hundred* sakes, to get over this averseness, to give up your prejudices, and make every one happy and easy once more. — I would kneel to you, my dearest niece — nay, I *will* kneel to you! —

And down she dropt, and I with her, kneeling to her, and beseeching her not to kneel; clasping my arms about her, and bathing her worthy bosom with my tears.

O rise! rise! my beloved aunt, said I: you cut me to the heart with this condescending goodness.

Say then, my dearest niece, say then, that you will oblige all your friends! — If you love us, I *beseech* you do —

How can I promise what I can sooner choose to die than perform? —

Say then, my dear, you will *consider* of it. Say you will but *reason* with yourself. Give us but hopes. Don't let me entreat, and *thus* entreat, in vain. For still she kneeled, and I by her. What a hard case is mine! — Could I but *doubt*, I know I could conquer. — That which is an inducement to my friends, is none at all to me — how often, my dearest aunt, must I repeat the same thing? — Let me but be single — cannot I live single? Let me be sent, as I have proposed, to Scotland, to Florence; any whither: let me be sent a slave to the Indies: any whither — any of these I will consent to. But I cannot, *cannot* think of giving my vows to a man I cannot endure.

Well then, rising, (Bella silently, with uplifted hands, reproaching my supposed perverseness) I see nothing can prevail with you to oblige us.

What *can* I do, my dearest aunt Hervey? What *can* I do? Were I capable of giving a hope I meant not to enlarge, then could I say, I would *consider* of your kind advice. But I would rather be thought *perverse* than *insincere*. Is there, however, no *medium?* Can *nothing* be thought of? Will *nothing* do, but to have a man who is the *more* disgustful to me, because he is unjust in the very articles he offers?

Whom now, Clary, said my sister, do you reflect upon? Consider that.

Make not invidious applications of what I say, Bella. It may not be looked upon in the same light by every one. The *giver* and the *accepter* are principally answerable, in an unjust donation. While I think of it in this light, I should be inexcusable to be the latter. But why do I enter upon a *supposition* of this nature? — My heart, as I have often, often said, recoils at the *thoughts* of the man, in every light — Whose father, but mine, agrees upon articles where there is no prospect of a liking? Where the direct contrary is avowed, all along avowed, without the least variation, or *shadow* of a change of sentiment? — But it is not my father's doing originally. O my cruel, cruel brother, to cause a measure to be forced upon me, which he would not behave tolerably under were the like to be offered to him!

The girl is got into her altitudes, Aunt Hervey, said my sister. You see, madam, she spares nobody. Be pleased to let her know what she has to trust to. Nothing is to be done with her. Pray, madam, pronounce her doom.

My aunt retired to the window, weeping, with my sister in her hand: I cannot, indeed I cannot, Miss Harlowe, said she, softly (but yet I heard every word she said): there is great hardship in her case. She is a noble child after all. What pity things are gone so far! — But Mr. Solmes ought to be told to desist.

O madam, said my sister, in a kind of loud whisper, are *you* caught too by the little siren? — My mother did well not to come up! — I question whether my father himself, after his first indignation, would not be turned round by her. Nobody but my brother can do any thing with her, I am sure.

Don't think of your brother's coming up, said my aunt, still in a low voice — He is too furious. I see no obstinacy, no perverseness in her manner! If your brother comes, I will not be answerable for the consequences: for I thought twice or thrice she would have gone into fits.

O madam, she has a strong heart; — and you see there is no prevailing with her, though you were upon your knees to her.

My sister left my aunt musing at the window, with her back towards us; and took that opportunity to insult me still more barbarously: for, stepping to my closet, she took up the patterns which my mother had sent me up, and bringing them to me, she spread them upon the chair by me; and, offering one, and then another, upon her sleeve and shoulder, thus she ran on, with great seeming tranquillity, but whisperingly, that my aunt might not hear her. *This*, Clary, is a pretty pattern enough: but *this* is quite *charming!* I would advise you to make your appearance in it. And *this*, were I you, should be my wedding night-gown — and *this* my second dressed suit; won't you give orders, love, to have your grandmother's jewels new set? — Or will you think to show away in the new ones Mr. Solmes intends to present to you? He talks of laying out two or three thousand pounds in presents, child! Dear heart! — How gorgeously will you be arrayed! — What! silent, my dear! Mamma Norton's *sweet dear!* What! silent still? — But, Clary, won't you have a velvet suit? It would cut a great figure in a country church, you know: and the weather may bear it for a month yet to come. Crimson velvet, suppose! Such a fine complexion as yours, how it would be set off by it! What an agreeable blush would it give you; — high ho! (mocking me; for I sighed to be thus fooled with) And do you sigh, love? — Well then, as it will be a solemn wedding, what think you of *black* velvet, child? — Silent still, Clary! — Black velvet, so fair as you are, with those charming eyes, gleaming through a wintry cloud, like an April sun! — Does not Lovelace tell you they are charming eyes! — How lovely will you appear to every one! — What! silent still, love! — But about your laces, Clary! —

She would have gone on still further, had not my aunt advanced towards us, wiping her eyes — What! whispering, ladies! You seem so easy and so pleased, Miss Harlowe, with your private conference, that I hope I shall carry down good news.

I am only giving her my opinion of her pattern, *here*. — Unasked indeed; but she seems, by her silence, to approve of my judgment.

O Bella! said I, that Mr. Lovelace had not taken you at your word! — You had before now been exercising your judgment on your own account: and *I* had been happy as well as *you!* Was it my fault, I pray you, that it was not so? —

O how she raved!

To be so ready to *give*, Bella, and so loth to *take*, is not very fair in you.

The poor Bella descended to call names.

Why, sister, said I, you are as angry as if there were more in the hint than possibly might be designed. My wish is sincere, for both our sakes! — for the whole family's sake! — And what is there in it? — Do not, do not, dear Bella, give me cause to suspect, that I have found a reason for your unkind behaviour to me; and which till now was wholly unaccountable from sister to sister —

Fie, fie, Clary! said my aunt.

My sister was more and more outrageous.

O how much fitter, said I, to be a *jest*, than a *jester!* — But now, Bella, turn the glass to you, and see how poorly sits the robe upon your own shoulders, which you have been so unmercifully fixing upon mine!

Fie, fie, Miss Clary, repeated my aunt.

And fie, fie, likewise, good madam, to Miss Harlowe, you would say, were you to have heard her barbarous insults!

Let us go, madam, said my sister, with great violence; let us leave the creature to swell till she bursts with her own poison — the last time I will ever come nearer, in the mind I am in!

It is so easy a thing, returned I, were I to be mean enough to follow an example that is so censurable in the setter of it, to vanquish such a teasing spirit as yours with its own blunt weapons, that I am amazed you will provoke me! — Yet, Bella, since you *will* go (for she had hurried to the door), forgive me. I forgive you. And you have a double reason to do so, both from eldership, and from the offence so studiously given to one in affliction. But may *you* be happy, though *I* never shall! May *you* never have half the trials *I* have had! Be *this* your comfort, that you cannot have a sister to treat *you* as you have treated *me!* — And so God bless you!

O thou art a — and down she flung without saying what.

Permit me, madam, said I to my aunt, sinking down, and clasping her knees with my arms, to detain you one moment — not to say any thing about my poor sister — she is her own punisher — only to thank you for all your condescending goodness to me. I only beg of you not to impute to obstinacy the immoveableness I have shewn to so tender a friend; and to forgive me every thing I have said or done amiss in your presence; for it has not proceeded from inward rancour to the poor Bella. But I will be bold to say, that neither she, nor my brother, nor even my father himself, knows what a heart they have set a bleeding.

I saw, to my comfort, what effect my sister's absence wrought for me. — Rise, my noble-minded niece! — charming creature! — [those were her kind words] kneel not to me! — Keep to yourself what I now say to you. — I admire you more than I can express — and if you can forbear claiming your estate, and can resolve to avoid Lovelace, you will continue to be the greatest miracle I ever knew at your years — but I must hasten down after your sister — These are my last words to you: "Conform to your father's will, if you possibly can. How meritorious will it be in you to do so! Pray to God to *enable* you to conform. You don't know what may be done."

Only, my dear aunt, one word, *one* word more (for she was going) — speak all you can for my dear Mrs. Norton. She is but low in the world: should ill health overtake her, she may not know how to live without my mamma's favour. I shall have no means to help her; for I will want necessaries before I will assert my right: and I do assure you, she has said so many things to me in behalf of my submitting to my father's will, that her arguments have not a little contributed to make me resolve to avoid the extremities which, nevertheless, I pray to God they do not at last force upon me. And yet they deprive me of her advice, and think unjustly of one of the most excellent of women.

I am glad to hear you say this: and take *this*, and *this*, and *this*, my charming niece (for so she called me almost at every word; kissing me earnestly, and clasping her arms about my neck): and God protect you and direct you! But you *must* submit: indeed you *must*. Some *one day* in a month from *this* is all the choice that is left you.

And this, I suppose, was the doom my sister called for; yet not worse than what had been pronounced upon me before.

She repeated these last sentences louder than the former. "And remember, miss," added she, "it is your *duty* to comply." — And down she went, leaving me with my heart full, and my eyes running over.

The very repetition of this fills me with almost equal concern to that which I felt at the time.

I must lay down my pen. Mistinesses, which give to my deluged eye the appearance of all the colours in the rainbow, will not permit me to write on.

Wednesday, five o'clock.

I WILL now add a few lines — my aunt, as she went down from me, was met at the foot of the stairs by my sister, who seemed to think she had staid a good while after her: and hearing her last words prescribing to me implicit duty, praised her for it, and exclaimed against my obstinacy. Did you ever hear of such perverseness, madam? said she: could you have thought, that *your* Clarissa, and *every body's* Clarissa, was such a girl? — And who, as *you* said, *is* to submit, her *father* or *she?*

My aunt said something in answer to her, compassionating me, as I thought, by her accent: but I heard not the words.

Such a strange perseverance in a measure so unreasonable! — But my brother and sister are continually misrepresenting all I say and do; and I am deprived of the opportunity of defending myself! — My sister says,* that had they thought me such a championess, they would not have engaged with me: and now, not knowing how to reconcile my supposed obstinacy with my general character and natural temper, they seem to hope to tire me out, and resolve to vary their measures accordingly. My brother, you see,** is determined to carry his point, or to abandon Harlowe Place, and never to see it more. — So they are to lose a son, or to conquer a daughter — the perversest and most ungrateful that ever parents had! — This is the light he places things in: and has undertaken, it seems, to subdue me, if *his* advice be followed. It will be *further* tried; of *that* I am convinced; and what will be their next measure, who can divine?

I shall dispatch with this my answer to yours of Sunday last, begun on Monday;*** but which is not yet quite finished. It is too long to copy: I have not time for it. In it I have been very free

* See p. 196.
** In his Letter, p. 204.
*** See Letter xi.

with you, my dear, in more places than one. I cannot say, that I am pleased with all I have written — yet will not now alter it. — My mind is not at ease enough for the subject. — Don't be angry with me. Yet, if you can excuse one or two passages, it will be because they were written by

Your
CLARISSA HARLOWE.

LETTER XLVI.

Miss Howe to Miss Clarissa Harlowe.

Wednesday night, March 22.

ANGRY! — What should I be angry for? I am mightily pleased with your freedom, as you call it. I only wonder at your patience with me; that's all. I am sorry I gave you the trouble of so long a letter upon the occasion*, notwithstanding the pleasure I received in reading it.

I believe you did *not* intend reserves to me: for two reasons I believe you did not: first, because you *say* you did not: next, because you have not *as yet* been able to convince *yourself* how it is to be with you; and persecuted as you are, how so to separate the effects that sprung from the two causes [*persecution* and *love*] as to give to each its particular due. But this I believe I hinted to you once before; and so will say no more upon this subject at present.

Robin says you had but just deposited your last parcel when he took it: for he was there but half an hour before, and found nothing. He had seen my impatience, and loitered about, being willing to bring me something from you, if possible.

My cousin Jenny Fynnett is here, and desires to be my bedfellow to-night. So I shall not have an opportunity to sit down with that seriousness and attention which the subjects of yours require. For she is all prate, you know, and loves to set *me* a prating; yet comes upon a very grave occasion — to procure my mother to go with her to her grandmother Larkin, who has been long bed-ridden; and at last has taken it into her head that she is mortal, and therefore will make her will; a work she was till now extremely averse to: but it must be upon condition that my mother, who is her distant relation, will go to her, and advise her as to the particulars of it: for she has an high opinion, as every one else has, of my mother's judgment in all matters relating to wills, settlements, and such-like notable affairs.

Mrs. Larkin lives about seventeen miles off; and as my mother cannot endure to lie out of her own house, she proposes to set out early in the morning, that she may be able to get back again at night. So, to-morrow I shall be at your devotion from day-light to day-light; nor will I be at home to any body.

As to the impertinent man, I have put him upon escorting the

---

* See Letter xxxvii. for the occasion: and Letters xxxviii. xl., for the freedoms Clarissa apologizes for.

two ladies, in order to attend my mother home at night. Such expeditions as these, and to give us women a little air of vanity and assuredness at public places, is all that I know these dangling fellows are good for.

I have hinted before, that I could almost wish my mother and Mr. Hickman would make a match of it: and here I repeat my wishes. What signifies a difference of fifteen or twenty years; especially when the lady has spirits that will make her young a long time, and the lover is a *mighty* sober man? — I think verily, that I could like him better for a papa than for a nearer relation: and they are *strange* admirers of one another.

But allow me a perhaps still better (and, as to *years*, more suitable and happier) disposal; for the *man* at least. — What think you, my dear, of compromising with your friends, by rejecting *both* your men, and encouraging my parader? — If your liking of one of the two go no further than *conditional*, I believe it will do. A rich thought, if it obtain your approbation! In this light, I should have a prodigious respect for Mr. Hickman; more by half than I can have in the other. The vein is opened — shall I let it flow? How difficult to withstand constitutional foibles!

Hickman is certainly a man more in your taste than any of those who have hitherto been brought to address you. He is mighty sober, mighty grave, and all that. Then you have told me, that he is your favourite. But that is because he is my mother's perhaps. The man would certainly rejoice at the transfer, or he must be a greater fool than I take him to be.

O but your fierce lover would knock him o'the head — I forgot that! — What makes me incapable of seriousness when I write about this Hickman? — Yet the man so good a sort of man in the main? — But who is perfect? This is one of my foibles. And it is something for you to chide me for.

You believe me to be very happy in my prospects in relation to him: because you are so very unhappy in the foolish usage you meet with, you are apt (as I suspect) to think *that* tolerable which otherwise would be far from being so. I dare say, you would not, with all your grave airs, like him for yourself; except, being addressed by Solmes and him, you were obliged to have one of them. — I have given you a test. Let me see what you will say to it.

For my own part, I confess to you, that I have great exceptions to Hickman. *He* and *wedlock* never yet once entered into my head at one time. Shall I give you my free thoughts of him? — Of his *best* and his *worst;* and that as if I were writing to one who knows him not? — I think I will. Yet it is impossible I should do it gravely. The subject won't bear to be so treated in my opinion. We are not come so far as that yet, if ever we shall: and to do it in another strain ill becomes my present real concern for you.

* * *

HERE I was interrupted on the honest man's account. He has been here these two hours — courting the mother for the daughter, I suppose — Yet she wants no courting neither; 'tis well one of us does: else the man would have nothing but halcyon; and be remiss and saucy of course.

He was going. His horses at the door. My mother sent for me down, pretending to want to say something to me.

Something she said when I came that signified nothing — evidently, for no reason called me, but to give me an opportunity to see what a fine bow her man could make; and that he might wish me a good night. She knows I am not over ready to oblige him with my company, if I happen to be otherwise engaged. I could not help an air a little upon the fretful, when I found she had nothing of moment to say to me, and when I saw her intention.

She smiled off the visible fretfulness, that the man might go away in good humour with himself.

He bowed to the ground, and would have taken my hand, his whip in the other. I did not like to be so companioned: I withdrew my hand, but touched his elbow with a motion, as if from his low bow I had supposed him falling, and would have helped him up — A sad slip it might have been! said I.

A mad girl! smiled it off my mother.

He was put quite out; took his horse bridle, stumped back, back, back, bowing, till he run against his servant. I laughed. He mounted his horse. I mounted up stairs, after a little lecture. — And my head is so filled with him, that I must resume my intention, in hopes to divert you for a few moments.

Take it then — his *best* and his *worst*, as I said before.

Hickman is a sort of fiddling, busy, yet, to borrow a word from you, *unbusy* man: has a great deal to do, and seems to me to dispatch nothing. Irresolute and changeable in every thing, but in teasing me with his nonsense; which yet, it is evident, he must continue upon my mother's interest more than upon his own hopes; for none have I given him.

Then I have a quarrel against his face, though in his person, for a well-thriven man, tolerably genteel — not to his features so much neither; for what, as you have often observed, are features in a man? — But Hickman, with strong lines, and big cheek and shin bones, has not the manliness in his aspect, which Lovelace has with the most regular and agreeable features.

Then what a set and formal mortal he is in some things! — I have not been able yet to laugh him out of his long bib and beads. Indeed, that is, because my mother thinks they become him; and I would not be so free with him, as to own I should *choose* to have him leave it off. If he did, so particular is the man, he would certainly, if left to himself, fall into a King William's cravat, or some such antique chin-cushion, as by the pictures of that prince one sees was then the fashion.

As to his dress in general, he cannot indeed be called a sloven, but sometimes he is too gaudy, at other times too plain, to be uniformly elegant. And for his manners, he makes such a bustle with them, and about them, as would induce one to suspect that they are more strangers than familiars to him. You, I know, lay this to his fearfulness of disobliging or offending. Indeed your *over-doers* generally give the offence they endeavour to avoid.

The man however is honest: is of family: has a clear and good estate; and may one day be a baronet, an't please you. He is humane and benevolent, tolerably generous, as people say, and as *I* might say too, if I would accept of his bribes; which he offers in hopes of having them all back again, and the *bribed* into the bargain. A method taken by all corrupters, from old Satan to the lowest of his servants. Yet, to speak in the language of a person I am bound to honour, he is deemed a *prudent* man; that is to say, a *good manager*.

Then I cannot but confess, that now I like not any body better, whatever I did once.

He is no fox-hunter: he keeps a pack indeed; but prefers not his hounds to his fellow creatures. No bad sign for a wife, I own. He loves his horse; but dislikes racing in a gaming way, as well as all sorts of gaming. Then he is sober; modest: they *say*, virtuous; in short, has qualities that mothers would be fond of in a husband for their daughters; and for which perhaps their daughters would be the happier could they judge as well for themselves as experience possibly may teach *them* to judge for their *future* daughters.

Nevertheless, to own the truth, I cannot say I love the man; nor, I believe, ever shall.

Strange! that these sober fellows cannot have a decent sprightliness, a modest assurance with them! Something debonnaire; which need not be separated from that awe and reverence, when they address a woman, which should shew the ardour of their passion, rather than the sheepishness of their nature; for who knows not that love delights in taming the lion-hearted? That those of the sex, who are most conscious of their own defect in point of courage, naturally *require*, and therefore as naturally *prefer*, the man who has most of it, as the most able to give them the requisite protection? That the greater their own cowardice, as it would be called in a man, the greater is their delight in subjects of heroism? As may be observed in their reading; which turns upon difficulties encountered, battles fought, and enemies overcome, four or five hundred by the prowess of one single hero, the *more* improbable the *better:* in short, that *their* man should be a hero to every one living but themselves; and to them know no bound to his humility. A woman has some glory in subduing a heart no man living can appal: and hence too often the bravo, assuming the hero, and making himself pass for one, succeeds as only a hero should.

But as for honest Hickman, the good man is so *generally* meek, as I imagine, that I know not whether I have any *preference* paid me in his obsequiousness. And then, when I rate him, he seems to be so naturally fitted for rebuke, and so much expects it, that I know not how to disappoint him, whether he just then deserve it or not. I am sure he has puzzled me many a time, when I have seen him look penitent for faults he has not committed, whether to pity or laugh at him.

You and I have often *retrospected* the faces and minds of grown people; that is to say, have formed images from their present appearances, outside and in, (as far as the manners of the persons would justify us in the latter) what sort of figures they made when boys and girls. And I'll tell you the lights in which HICKMAN, SOLMES, and LOVELACE, our three heroes, have appeared to me, supposing them boys at school.

Solmes I have imagined to be a little sordid pilfering rogue, who would purloin from every body, and beg every body's bread and butter from him; while, as I have heard a reptile brag, he would in a winter morning spit upon his thumbs, and spread his own with it, that he might keep it all to himself.

Hickman, a great overgrown, lank-haired, chubby boy, who would be hunched and punched by every body: and go home with his finger in his eye, and tell his mother.

While Lovelace I have supposed a curl-pated villain, full of fire, fancy, and mischief; an orchard robber, a wall climber, a horse rider, without saddle or bridle, neck or nothing: a sturdy rogue, in short, who would kick and cuff, and do no right, and take no wrong of any body; would get his head broke, then a plaster for it, or let it heal of itself; while he went on to do more mischief, and if not to get, to deserve broken bones. And the same dispositions have grown up with them, and distinguish them as *men*, with no very material alteration.

Only that all men are monkeys more or less, or else that you and I should have such baboons as these to choose out of, is a mortifying thing, my dear.

I am sensible, that I am a little out of season in treating thus ludicrously the subject I am upon, while you are so unhappy; and if my manner does not divert you, as my flightiness used to do, I am inexcusable both to you, and to my own heart: which, I do assure you, nothwithstanding my seeming levity, is wholly in your case.

As this letter is entirely whimsical, I will not send it until I can accompany it with something more solid, and better suited to your unhappy circumstances: that is to say, to the present subject of our correspondence. To-morrow, as I told you, will be wholly my own, and of consequence yours. Adieu, therefore, till then.

LETTER XLVII.
Miss Howe to Miss Clarissa Harlowe.

Thursday morn. 7 o'clock.

My mother and cousin are already gone off in our chariot and four, attended by their doughty 'squire on horseback, and he by two of his own servants, and one of my mother's. They both love parade when they go abroad, at least in compliment to one another; which shews, that each *thinks* the other does. Robin is your servant and mine, and nobody's else — and the day is all my own.

I must begin with blaming you, my dear, for your resolution not to litigate for your right, if occasion were to be given you. Justice is due to ourselves, as well as to every body else. Still more must I blame you for declaring to your aunt and sister, that you will *not*: since (as they will tell it to your father and brother) the declaration must needs give advantage to spirits who have so little of that generosity for which you are so much distinguished.

There never was a spirit in the world that would insult where it *dared*, but it would creep and cringe where it dared *not*. Let me remind you of a sentence of your own, the occasion for which I have forgotten: "That little spirits will always accommodate themselves to the temper of those they would work upon: will fawn upon a sturdy tempered person: will insult the meek:" — and another given to Miss Biddulph, upon an occasion you cannot forget: — "If we assume a dignity in what we say and do, and take care not to disgrace by arrogance our own assumption, every body will treat us with respect and deference."

I remember that you once made an observation, which you said you was obliged to Mrs. Norton for, and she to her father, upon an excellent preacher, who was but an indifferent liver: "That to excel in theory, and to excel in practice, generally required different talents; which did not always meet in the same person." Do you, my dear, (to whom theory and practice are the same thing in almost every laudable quality) apply the observation to yourself, in this particular case, where resolution is required, and where the performance of the will of the defunct is the question — no more to be dispensed with by *you*, in whose favour it was made, than by any body else who have only themselves in view by breaking through it.

I know how much you despise riches in the main: but yet it behoves you to remember, that in one instance you yourself have judged them valuable — "In that they put it into our power to *lay* obligations; while the want of that power puts a person under a necessity of receiving favours — receiving them perhaps from grudging and narrow spirits, who know not how to confer them with that grace, which gives the principal merit to a beneficent action." — Reflect upon this, my dear, and see how it agrees with the declaration you have made to your aunt and sister, that you would not resume your estate, were you to be turned out of doors, and reduced to indigence and want. Their very fears that you *will* resume, point out to you the *necessity* of resuming upon the treatment you meet with.

I own, that (at first reading) I was much affected with your mother's letter sent with the patterns. A strange measure however from a mother! for *she* did not intend to insult you; and I cannot but lament that so sensible and so fine a woman should stoop to so much art as that letter is written with: and which also appears in some of the conversations you have given me an account of. See you not in her passiveness what boisterous spirits can obtain from gentler, merely by teasing and ill-nature?

I know the pride they have always taken in calling you an Harlowe — *Clarissa Harlowe*, so *formal* and so *set*, at every word, when they are grave or proudly solemn. — Your mother has learnt it of them — and as in *marriage*, so in *will*, has been taught to bury her own superior name and family in theirs. I have often thought that the same spirit governed them, in this piece of affectation, and others of the like nature (as *Harlowe* Place, and so-forth, though not the elder brother's or paternal seat), as governed the tyrant Tudor*, who marrying Elizabeth, the heiress of the house of York, made himself a title to a throne, which he would not otherwise have had (being but a base descendant of the Lancaster line); and proved a gloomy and vile husband to her; for no other cause, than because she had laid him under obligations which his pride would not permit him to own. — Nor would the unprincely wretch marry her till he was in possession of the crown, that he might not be supposed to owe it to her claim.

You have chidden me, and again will, I doubt not, for the liberties I take with some of your relations. But, my dear, need I tell *you*, that pride in *ourselves* must, and for ever will, provoke contempt, and bring down upon us abasement from *others?* — Have we not, in the case of a celebrated bard, observed, that those who aim at *more* than their due, will be refused the honours they may justly claim? — I am very loth to offend you; yet I cannot help speaking of your relations, as well as of others, as I think they deserve. *Praise* or *dispraise* is the reward or

* Henry VII.

punishment which the world confers or inflicts on *merit* or *demerit*; and, for my part, I neither can nor will confound them in the application. I despise them all but your mother: indeed I do: and as for her—but I will spare the good lady for your sake — and one argument, indeed, I think may be pleaded in her favour, in the present contention — she who has for so many years, and with such absolute resignation, borne what she has borne, to the sacrifice of her own will, may think it an easier task than another person can imagine it, for her daughter to give up *hers*. But to think to whose instigation all this is originally owing — God forgive me; but with such usage I should have been with Lovelace before now! Yet remember, my dear, that the step which would not be wondered at from such an hasty-tempered creature as me, would be inexcusable in such a considerate person as you.

After your mother has been thus drawn in against her judgment, I am the less surprised, that your aunt Hervey should go along with her; since the two sisters never separate. I have enquired into the nature of the obligation which Mr. Hervey's indifferent conduct in his affairs has laid him under — it is only, it seems, that your brother has paid off for him a mortgage upon one part of his estate, which the mortgagees was about to foreclose; and taken it upon himself. A small favour (as he has ample security in his hands) from kindred to kindred: but such a one, it is plain, as has laid the whole family of the Herveys under obligation to the ungenerous lender, who has treated him, and his aunt too (as Miss Dolly Hervey has privately complained) with the less ceremony ever since.

Must I, my dear, call such a creature your *brother?* — I believe I must — because he is your *father's* son. There is no harm, I hope, in saying that.

I am concerned, that you ever wrote at all to him. It was taking too much notice of him: it was adding to his self significance: and a call upon him to treat you with insolence. — A call which you might have been assured he would not fail to answer.

But such a pretty master as this to run riot against such a man as Lovelace, who had taught him to put his sword into his scabbard, when he had pulled it out by accident! — These in-door insolents, who, turning themselves into bugbears, frighten women, children, and servants, are generally cravens among men. Were he to come fairly cross me, and say to my face some of the free things which I am told he has said of me behind my back, or that (as by your account) he has said of our sex, I would take upon myself to ask him two or three questions; although he were to send me a challenge likewise.

I repeat, you know that I will speak my mind, and *write* it too. He is not *my* brother. Can you say, he is *yours?* — So, for your life, if you are just, you can't be angry with me: for would you side with a *false brother* against a *true friend?* A brother may *not* be a friend: but a friend will be *always* a brother — *mind that*, as your uncle *Tony* says!

I cannot descend so low, as to take very particular notice of the epistles of those poor souls, whom you call *uncles*. Yet I love to divert myself with such grotesque characters too. But I know *them* and love *you*; and so cannot make the jest of them which their absurdities call for.

You chide me, my dear*, for my freedoms with relations still nearer and dearer to you, than either uncles or brother or sister. You had better have permitted me (uncorrected) to have taken my own way. Do not those freedoms naturally arise from the subject before us? And from *whom* arises that subject, I pray you? Can you for one quarter of an hour put yourself in my place, or in the place of those who are still more indifferent to the case than I can be — if you *can* — but although I have you not often at advantage, I will not push you.

Permit me, however, to subjoin, that well may your father love your mother, as you say he does. A wife who has no will but his! but were there not, think you, some struggles between them at first, gout out of the question? — Your mother, when a maiden, had as I have heard (and it is very likely) a good share of those lively spirits which she liked in your father. She has none of them now. How came they to be dissipated? — Ah! my dear! — She has been too long resident in Trophonius's cave, I doubt.*

Let me add one reflection upon this subject, and so entitle myself to your correction for all at once. — It is upon the conduct of those wives (for you and I know more than *one* such) who can suffer themselves to be out-blustered and out-gloomed of their own wills, instead of being fooled out of them by acts of tenderness and complaisance. — I wish, that it does not demonstrate too evidently, that, with some of the sex, insolent control is a more efficacious subduer than kindness or concession. Upon my life, my dear, I have often thought that many of us are mere babies in matrimony: perverse fools, when too much indulged and humoured; creeping slaves, when treated harshly. But shall it be said, that *fear* makes us more gentle obligers than *love?* — Forbid it, honour! forbid it, gratitude! forbid it, justice! that any woman of sense should give occasion to have this said of her!

Did I think you would have any manner of doubt, from the style or contents of this letter, whose saucy pen it is that has run on at this rate, I would write my name at length; since it comes too much from my heart to disavow it: but at present the initials shall serve; and I will go on again directly.

A. H.

* See Letter xxviii.

* Spectator, Vol. VIII. No. 599.

LETTER XLVIII.

Miss Howe to Miss Clarissa Harlowe.

Thursday morn. (10 o'clock) March 23.

I WILL postpone, or perhaps pass by, several observations which I had to make on other parts of your letters; to acquaint you, that Mr. Hickman, when in London, found an opportunity to inquire after Mr. Lovelace's town life and conversation.

At the Cocoa-tree, in Pall-mall, he fell in with two of his intimates, the one named Belton, the other Mowbray; both very free of speech, and probably as free in their lives: but the waiters paid them great respect, and on Mr. Hickman's inquiry after their characters, called them men of fortune and honour.

They began to talk of Mr. Lovelace of their own accord; and upon some gentlemen in the room asking when they expected him in town, answered, that very day. Mr. Hickman (as they both went on praising Lovelace) said, he had indeed heard that Mr. Lovelace was a very fine gentleman — and was proceeding, when one of them interrupting him, said — Only, sir, the finest gentleman in the world; that's all.

And he then led them on to expatiate more particularly on his qualities, which they were very fond of doing: but said not one single word in behalf of his morals — *mind that* also in your uncle's style.

Mr. Hickman said, that Mr. Lovelace was very happy, as he understood, in the esteem of the ladies; and smiling, to make them believe he did not think amiss of it, that he pushed his good fortune as far as it would go.

Well put, Mr. Hickman! thought I; equally grave and sage — thou seemest not to be a stranger to their dialect, as I suppose this is. But I said nothing; for I have often tried to find out this *mighty* sober man of my mother's; but hitherto have only to say, that he is either very moral or very cunning.

No doubt of it, replied one of them; and out came an oath, with a who would not? — That he did as every young fellow would do.

Very true! said my mother's puritan — but I hear he is in treaty with a fine lady —

So he was, Mr. Belton said — the devil fetch her! [vile brute!] for she engrossed all his time — but that the lady's family ought to be — something — [Mr. Hickman desired to be excused repeating what — though he had repeated what was worse] and might dearly repent their usage of a man of his family and merit.

Perhaps they may think him too wild, cried Hickman: and their's is, I hear, a very sober family —

SOBER: said one of them: a good honest word, Dick! — Where the devil has it lain all this time? — D—me if I have heard of it in this sense ever since I was at college! And then we bandied it about among twenty of us as an obsolete.

These, my dear, are Mr. Lovelace's companions: you'll be pleased to take *notice of that!*

Mr. Hickman said, this put him out of countenance.

I stared at him, and with such a meaning in my eyes as he knew how to take; and so he was out of countenance again.

Don't you remember, my dear, who it was that told a young gentleman designed for the gown, who owned that he was apt to be too easily put out of countenance when he came into free company; "That it was a bad sign; that it looked as if his morals were not proof; but that his good disposition seemed rather the effect of accident and education, than of such a choice as was founded upon principle?" And don't you know the lesson the very same young lady gave him, "To endeavour to stem and discountenance vice, and to glory in being an advocate in all companies for virtue;" particularly observing, "That it was natural for a man to shun, or to give up, what he was ashamed of!" Which she should be sorry to think *his* case on this occasion: adding, "that vice was a coward, and would hide its head when opposed by such a virtue as had presence of mind, and a full persuasion of its own rectitude to support it." The lady, you may remember, modestly put her doctrine into the mouth of a worthy preacher, Dr. Lewen, as she uses to do when she has a mind not to be thought to be what she is at so early an age; and that it may give more weight to any thing *she hit upon, that might appear tolerable,* was her modest manner of speech.

Mr. Hickman, upon the whole, professed to me, upon his *second recovery*, that he had no reason to think well of Mr. Lovelace's morals, from what he heard of him in town: yet his two intimates talked of his being *more regular* than he *used to be*: that he had made a very good resolution, *that* of old Tom Wharton was the expression, that he would never *give* a challenge, nor *refuse* one; which they praised in him highly: that, in short, he was a very brave fellow, and the most agreeable companion in the world: and would one day make a great figure in his country: since there was nothing he was not capable of —

I am afraid that this last assertion is too true. And this, my dear, is all that Mr. Hickman could pick up about him: and is it not enough to determine such a mind as yours, if not *already* determined?

Yet it must be said too, that if there be a woman in the world that can reclaim him, it is you. And, by your account of his behaviour in the interview between you, I own I have some hope of him. At least, this I will say, that all the arguments he then used with you, seem to be just and right, and if you *are* to be his — but no more of that: he cannot, after all, deserve you.

LETTER XLIX.

Miss Howe to Miss Clarissa Harlowe.

Thursday afternoon, March 23.

An unexpected visitor has turned the course of my thoughts, and changed the subject I had intended to pursue. The only one for whom I would have dispensed with my resolution not to see any body all the dedicated day: a visitor, whom, according to Mr. Hickman's report from the expectations of his libertine friends, I supposed to be in town. — Now, my dear, have I saved myself the trouble of telling you, that it was your too agreeable rake. Our sex is said to love to trade in surprises: yet have I, by my promptitude, surprised myself out of mine. I had intended, you must know, to run twice the length, before I had suffered you so much as to guess who, and whether man or woman, my visitor was: but since you have the discovery at so cheap a rate, you are welcome to it.

The end of his coming was to engage my interest with my *charming friend;* and as he was sure that I knew all your mind, to acquaint him what he had to trust to.

He mentioned what had passed in the interview between you: but could not be satisfied with the result of it, and with the little satisfaction he had obtained from you; the malice of your family to him increasing, and their cruelty to you not abating. His heart, he told me, was in tumults, for fear you should be prevailed upon in favour of a man despised by every body.

He gave me fresh instances of indignities cast upon himself by your uncles and brother; and declared, that if you suffered yourself to be forced into the arms of the man for whose sake he was loaded with undeserved abuses, you should be one of the youngest, as you would be one of the loveliest widows in England: and that he would moreover call your brother to account for the liberties he takes with his character to every one he meets with.

He proposed several schemes, for you to choose some one of them, in order to enable you to avoid the persecutions you labour under. One I will mention: that you will resume your estate; and if you find difficulties that can be no otherwise surmounted, that you will, either avowedly or privately, as he had proposed to you, accept of Lady Betty Lawrence's or Lord M.'s assistance to instate you in it. He declared, that if you did, he would leave you absolutely to your own pleasure afterwards, and to the advice which your cousin Morden on his arrival should give you, whether to encourage his address or not, as you should be convinced of the sincerity of the reformation which his enemies make him so much want.

I had now a good opportunity to sound him, as you wished Mr. Hickman would Lord M. as to the continued or diminished favour of the ladies, and of his lordship, towards you, upon their being acquainted with the animosity of your relations to them, as well as to their kinsman. I laid hold of the opportunity, and he satisfied me, by reading some passages of a letter he had about him, from Lord M. That an alliance with you, and that on the foot of your own single merit, would be the most desirable event to them that could happen: and so far to the purpose of your wished inquiry does his lordship go in this letter, that he assures him, that whatever you suffer in fortune from the violence of your relations on *his* account, he and Lady Sarah and Lady Betty will join to make it up to him. And yet that the reputation of a family so splendid, would, no doubt, in a case of such importance to the honour of both, make them prefer a general consent.

I told him, as you yourself, I knew, had done, that you were extremely averse to Mr. Solmes; and that, might you be left to your own choice, it would be the single life. As to himself, I plainly said, that you had great and just objections to him on the score of his careless morals: that it was surprising, that men who gave themselves the liberties he was said to take, should presume to think, that whenever they took it into their heads to marry, the most virtuous and worthy of their sex were to fall to their lot: that as to the resumption, it had been very strongly urged by myself, and would be still further urged; though you had been hitherto averse to that measure: that your chief reliance and hopes were upon your cousin Morden: and that to suspend or gain time till he arrived, was, as I believed, your principal aim.

I told him, that with regard to the mischief he threatened, neither the act nor the menace could serve any turn but theirs who persecuted you; as it would give them a pretence for carrying into effect their compulsory projects; and that with the approbation of all the world; since he must not think the public would give its voice in favour of a violent young man, of no extraordinary character as to morals, who should seek to rob a family of eminence of a child so valuable; and who threatened, if he could not obtain her in preference to a man chosen by themselves,' that he would avenge himself upon them all by acts of violence.

I added, that he was very much mistaken, if he thought to intimidate *you* by such menaces: for that, though your disposition was all sweetness, yet I knew not a steadier temper in the world than yours; nor one more inflexible (as your friends had found, and would still further find, if they continued to give occasion for its exertion) whenever you thought yourself in the right; and that you were ungenerously dealt with in matters of too much moment to be indifferent about. Miss Clarissa Harlowe, Mr. Lovelace, let me tell you, said I, timid as her foresight and prudence may make her in some cases, where she apprehends dangers to those she loves, is above fear in points where her honour and the true dignity of her sex are concerned. — In short, sir, you must not think to frighten Miss Clarissa Harlowe into such a mean or unworthy conduct as only a weak or unsteady mind can be guilty of.

He was so very far from intending to intimidate you, he said, that he besought me not to mention one word to you of what had passed between us; that what he had hinted at, which carried the air of a menace, was owing to the fervor of his spirits, raised by his apprehensions of losing all hope of you for ever: and on a supposition, that you were to be actually forced into the arms of a man you hated: that were this to be the case, he must own, that he should pay very little regard to the world, or its censures: especially as the menaces of some of your family now, and their triumph over him afterwards, would both provoke and warrant all the vengeance he could take.

He added, that all the countries in the world were alike to him, but on your account. So that whatever he should think fit to do, were you lost to *him*, he should have nothing to apprehend from the laws of this.

I did not like the determined air he spoke this with: he is certainly capable of great rashness.

He palliated a little this fierceness (which by the way I warmly censured) by saying, that while you remain single, he will bear all the indignities that shall be cast upon him by your family. But would you throw yourself, if you were still further driven, into any *other* protection, if not Lord M.'s, or that of the ladies of his family, into my mother's*, suppose; or would you go to London to private lodgings, where he would never visit you, unless he had your leave (and from whence you might make your own terms with your relations); he would be entirely satisfied; and would, as he had said before, wait the effect of your cousin's arrival, and your free determination as to his own fate. — Adding, that he knew the family so well, and how much fixed they were upon their measures, as well as the absolute dependence they had upon your temper and principles, that he could not but apprehend the worst, while you remained in their power, and under the influence of their persuasion and menaces.

We had a great deal of other discourse: but as the reciting of the rest would be but a repetition of many of the things that passed between you and him in the inter-

* Perhaps it will be unnecessary to remind the reader, that although Mr. Lovelace proposes (as above) to Miss Howe, that her fair friend should have recourse to the protection of Mrs. Howe, if further driven; yet he had artfully taken care, by means of his agent in the Harlowe family, not only to inflame the family against her, but to deprive her of Mrs. Howe's, and of every other protection, being from the first resolved to reduce her to an absolute dependence upon himself. See Letter xxxl.

view between you in the woodhouse, I refer myself to your memory on that occasion *.

And now, my dear, upon the whole, I think it behoves you to make yourself independent: all then will fall right. This man is a violent man. I should wish, methinks, that you should not have either him or Solmes. You will find, if you get out of your brother's and sister's way, what you *can* or *cannot* do with regard to either. If your relations persist in their foolish scheme, I think I will take his hint, and, at a proper opportunity, sound my mother. Meantime, let me have your clear opinion of the resumption, which I join with Lovelace in advising. You can but see how your demand will work. To *demand* is not to *litigate*. But be your resolution what it will, do not by any means repeat to them, that you will not assert your right. If they go on to give you provocation, you may have sufficient reason to change your mind: and let them expect that you *will* change it. They have not the generosity to treat you the better for disclaiming the power they know you have. That, I think, need not now be told you. I am, my dearest friend, and will be ever,

Your most affectionate and faithful
ANNA HOWE.

* See Letter xxxvi

LETTER L.

Miss Clarissa Harlowe to Miss Howe.

Wedn. night, March 22.

ON the report made by my aunt and sister of my *obstinacy*, my assembled relations have taken an *unanimous* resolution (as Betty tells me it is) against me. This resolution you will find signified to me in the enclosed letter from my brother, just now brought me. Be pleased to return it when perused. I may have occasion for it in the altercations between my relations and me.

MISS CLARY,

I AM commanded to let you know, that my father and uncles having heard your aunt Hervey's account of all that has passed between her and you: having heard from your sister what sort of treatment she has had from you: having recollected all that has passed between your mother and you: having weighed all your pleas and proposals: having taken into consideration their engagements with Mr. Solmes; that gentleman's patience, and great affection for you; and the little opportunity you have given yourself to be acquainted either with his merit or his proposals: having considered two points more; to wit, the wounded authority of a father, and Mr. Solmes's continual entreaties (little as you have deserved regard from him) that you may be freed from a confinement to which he is desirous to attribute your perverseness to him [averse-

ness I should have said, but let it go] be being unable to account otherwise for so strong a one, supposing you told truth to your mother when you asserted that your heart *was free;* and which Mr. Solmes is willing to believe, though nobody else does — for all these reasons, it is resolved, that you shall go to your uncle Antony's: and you must accordingly prepare yourself so to do. You will have but short notice of the day, for obvious reasons.

I will honestly tell you the motive for your going: it is a double one; first, that they may be sure that you shall not correspond with any body they do not like (for they find from Mrs. Howe, that, by some means or other, you *do* correspond with her daughter; and through her perhaps with somebody else): and next, that you may receive the visits of Mr. Solmes; which you have thought fit to refuse to do here; by which means you have deprived yourself of the opportunity of knowing *whom* and *what* you have hitherto refused.

If after one fortnight's conversation with Mr. Solmes, and after you have heard what your friends shall further urge in his behalf, unhardened by clandestine correspondences, you shall convince them that Virgil's *amor omnibus idem* (for the application of which I refer you to the Georgic as translated by Dryden) is verified in you, as well as in the rest of the animal creation; and that you cannot, or will not, forego your prepossession in favour of the *moral*, the *virtuous*, the *pious* Lovelace (I would please you if I could!) it will then be considered, whether to humour you, or to renounce you for ever.

It is hoped, that as you *must* go, you will go cheerfully. Your uncle Antony will make every thing at his house agreeable to you. But indeed he won't promise, that he will not, at *proper times*, draw up the bridge.

Your visitors, besides Mr. Solmes, will be myself, if you permit me that honour, Miss Clary; your sister, and, as you behave to Mr. Solmes, your aunt Hervey and your uncle Harlowe; and yet the two latter will hardly come neither, if they think it will be to hear your *whining vocatives.* — Betty Barnes will be your attendant: and I must needs tell you, miss, that we none of us think the worse of the faithful maid for your dislike of her: although Betty, who would be glad to oblige you, laments it as a misfortune.

Your answer is required, whether you *cheerfully* consent to go? And your indulgent mother bids me remind you from her, that a fortnight's visits from Mr. Solmes are all that is meant at present.

I am, as you shall be pleased to deserve,

Your's, &c.
JAMES HARLOWE, JUN.

So here is the master-stroke of my brother's policy, called upon to consent to go to my uncle Antony's, *avowedly* to receive Mr.

Solmes's visits! — A chapel! — A moated house! — Deprived of the opportunity of corresponding with you! — or of any possibility of escape, should violence be used to compel me to be that odious man's!*

Late as it was when I received this insolent letter, I wrote an answer to it directly, that it might be ready for the writer's time of rising. I enclose the rough draught of it. You will see by it how much his vile hint from the Georgic, and his rude one of my *whining vocatives*, have set me up. Besides, as the command to get ready to go to my uncle's is in the name of my father and uncles, it is but to shew a piece of the art they accuse me of, to resent the vile hint I have so much reason to resent in order to palliate my refusal of preparing to go to my uncle's; which refusal would otherwise be interpreted an act of rebellion by my brother and sister: for it seems plain to me, *that they will work but half their ends, if they do not deprive me of my father's and uncle's favour, even although it were possible for me to comply with their own terms.*

You might have told me, brother, in three lines, what the determination of my friends was; only, that then you would not have had room to display your pedantry by so detestable an allusion or reference to the Georgic. Give me leave to tell you, sir, that if *humanity* were a branch of your studies at the university, it has not found a genius in you for mastering it. Nor is either my sex or myself, though a sister, I see, entitled to the least decency from a brother, who has studied, as it seems, rather to cultivate the malevolence of his natural temper, than any tendency which one would have hoped his parentage, if not his education, might have given him to a tolerable politeness.

I doubt not, that you will take amiss my freedom: but as you have deserved it from me, I shall be less and less concerned on that score, as I see you are more and more intent to shew your wit at the expense of justice and compassion.

The time is indeed come that I can no longer bear those contempts and reflections which a brother least of all men is entitled to give. And let me beg of you one favour, officious sir; — it is *this*, that you will not give yourself any concern about a husband for *me*, till I shall have the forwardness to propose a wife to *you*. Pardon me, sir; but I cannot help thinking, that could I have the art to *get my father* of my side, I should have as much right to prescribe for you as you have for me.

As to the communication you make me, I must take upon me to say, that although I will receive,

---

* These violent measures, and the obstinate perseverance of the whole family in them, will be the less wondered at, when it is considered, that all the time they were but as so many puppets danced upon Mr. Lovelace's wires, as he boasts. Letter xxxi.

as becomes me, any of my father's commands; yet, as this signification is made by a brother, who has shown of late so much of an unbrotherly animosity to me (for no reason in the world that I know of, but that he believes he has in me *one* sister too many for his interest) I think myself entitled to conclude, that such a letter as you have sent me is all your own — and of course to declare, that, while I *so* think it, I will not willingly, nor even without violence, go to any place, avowedly to receive Mr. Solmes's visits.

I think myself so much entitled to resent your infamous hint, and this as well for the sake of my sex, as for my own, that I ought to declare, as I do, that I will not receive any more of your letters, unless commanded to do so by an authority I never will dispute, except in a case where I think my *future* as well as *present* happiness concerned — and were such a case to happen, I am sure my father's harshness will be less owing to himself than to you; and to the specious absurdities of your ambitious and selfish schemes. — Very true, sir!

One word more, provoked as I am, I will add: that had I been thought as really obstinate and perverse as of late I am said to be, I should not have been so disgracefully treated as I have been — lay your hand upon your heart, brother, and say, by whose instigations — and examine what I have done to deserve to be made thus unhappy, and to be obliged to style myself
   Your injured sister,
     CL. HARLOWE.

When, my dear, you have read my answer to my brother's letter, tell me what you think of me? — It *shall go!*

LETTER LI.

Miss Clarissa Harlowe to Miss Howe.

Thursday morning, March 23.

My latter has set them *all* in tumults: for, it seems, none of them went home last night; and they all were desired to be present to give their advice, if I should refuse compliance with a command thought so reasonable as it seems this is.

Betty tells me, that at first, my father, in a rage, was for coming up to me himself, and for turning me out of his doors directly. Nor was he restrained, till it was hinted to him, that that was no doubt my wish, and would answer all my perverse views. But the result was, that my brother (having really, as my mother and aunt insisted, taken wrong measures with me) should write again in a more *moderate* manner: for nobody else was permitted or cared to write to such a *ready scribbler.* And I having declared that I would not receive any more of his letters, without command from a superior authority, my mother was to give it *hers:* and accordingly has done so in the following lines, written on the superscription of his letter to me: which letter also follows, together with my reply.

CLARY HARLOWE,

RECEIVE and read this, with the temper that becomes your sex, your character, your education, and your duty: and return an answer to it, directed to your brother.

CHARLOTTE HARLOWE.

TO MISS CLARISSA HARLOWE.

Thursday morning.

ONCE more I write, although imperiously prohibited by a younger sister. Your mother will have me do so, that you may be destitute of all defence, if you persist in your *pervicacy*. Shall I be a *pedant*, miss, for this word? She is willing to indulge in you the least appearance of that delicacy for which she once, as well as every body else, admired you — before you knew Lovelace: I cannot, however, help saying *that:* and she, and your aunt Hervey, will have it — [they would fain favour you, if they could] that I may have provoked from you the answer they nevertheless own to be so exceedingly *unbecoming*. I am now learning, you see, to take up the softer language, where you have laid it down. This then is the case:

They *entreat*, they *pray*, they *beg*, they *supplicate* [will either of these do, Miss Clary?] that you will make no scruple to go to your uncle Antony's: and fairly I am to tell you, for the very purpose mentioned in my last — or, 'tis presumable, they need not *entreat*, *beg*, *pray*, *supplicate*. Thus much is promised to Mr. Solmes, who is your advocate, and very uneasy that you should be under constraint, supposing that your dislike to him arises from that. And, if he finds that you are not to be moved in his favour, when you are absolutely freed from what you call a *control*, he will forbear thinking of you, whatever it costs him. He loves you too well: and in *this* I really think his understanding, which you have reflected upon, is to be questioned.

Only for one fortnight, therefore, permit his visits. Your education [you tell me of *mine*, you know] ought to make you incapable of rudeness to any body. He will not, I hope, be the first man, myself excepted, whom you ever treated rudely, purely because he is esteemed by us all. I am, what you have a mind to make me, friend, brother, or servant — I wish I could be still *more* polite, to so polite, so delicate a sister. JA. HARLOWE.

You must still write to *me*, if you condescend to reply. Your mother will not be permitted to be disturbed with your nothing-meaning vocatives! — *Vocatives* once more, Madam Clary, repeats the *pedant*, your brother!

TO JAMES HARLOWE, JUN. ESQ.

Thursday, March 23.

PERMIT me, my ever-dear and honoured papa and mamma, in this manner to surprise you into an *audience* (presuming this will be read to you) since I am denied the honour of writing to you directly. Let me beg of you to believe, that nothing but the most unconquerable dislike could make me stand against your pleasure. What are riches, what are settlements, to happiness? Let me not thus cruelly be given up to a man my very soul is averse to. Permit me to repeat, that I cannot *honestly* be his. Had I a slighter notion of the matrimonial duty than I have, perhaps I might. But when I am to bear all the misery, and that for *life;* when my *heart* is less concerned in this matter than my *soul;* my *temporary*, perhaps, than my *future* good; why should I be denied the liberty of *refusing?* That liberty is all I ask.

It were easy for me to give way to hear Mr. Solmes talk for the mentioned fortnight, although it is impossible for me, say what he would, to get over my dislike to him. But the moated house, the chapel there, and the little mercy my brother and sister, who are to be there, have hitherto shewn me, are what I am extremely apprehensive of. And why does my brother say, my restraint is to be taken off (and that too at Mr. Solmes's desire) when I am to be a still closer prisoner than before; the bridge threatened to be drawn up; and no dear papa and mamma near me, to appeal to, in the last resort?

Transfer not, I beseech you, to a brother and sister your own authority over your child — to a brother and sister, who treat me with unkindness and reproach; and, as I have too much reason to apprehend, misrepresent my words and behaviour: or greatly favoured as I used to be, it is impossible I should be sunk so low in your opinions, as I unhappily am!

Let but this my hard, my disgraceful confinement be put an end to. Permit me, my dear mamma, to pursue my needleworks in your presence, as one of your maidens; and you shall be witness, that it is not either wilfulness or prepossession that governs me. Let me not, however, be put out of your own house. Let Mr. Solmes come and go, as my papa pleases: let me but stay or retire when he comes, as I can; and leave the rest to Providence.

Forgive me, brother, that thus, with an appearance of art, I address myself to my father and mother, to whom I am forbidden to approach, or to write. Hard it is to be reduced to such a contrivance! Forgive likewise the plain dealing I have used in the above, with the nobleness of a gentleman, and the gentleness due from a brother to a sister. Although of late you have given me but little room to hope either for your favour or compassion; yet having not deserved to forfeit *either,* I presume to claim *both:* for I am confident it is at present much in your power, although but my brother (my honoured parents both, I bless God, in being) to give peace to the greatly disturbed mind of

Your unhappy sister,
CL. HARLOWE.

Betty tells me, my brother has taken my letter all in pieces; and has undertaken to write such an answer to it, as shall confirm the *wavering*—So, it is plain, that I should have moved somebody by it, but for this hard-hearted brother—God forgive him!

LETTER LII.

Miss Clarissa Harlowe to Miss Howe.

Thursday night, March 23.

I SEND you the boasted confutation letter, just now put into my hands—My brother and sister, my uncle Antony and Mr. Solmes, are, I understand, exulting over the copy of it below, as an unanswerable performance.

TO MISS CLARISSA HARLOWE.

ONCE again, my inflexible sister, I write to you. It is to let you know, that the pretty piece of art you found out to make me the vehicle of your whining pathetics to your father and mother, has not had the expected effect.

I do assure you, that your behaviour has not been misrepresented—nor need it. Your mother, who is solicitous to take all opportunities of putting the most favourable constructions upon all you do, has been forced, as you well know, to give you up, upon full trial: no need then of the expedient of pursuing your needleworks in her sight. She cannot bear your whining pranks: and it is for *her* sake, that you are not permitted to come into her presence—nor will be, but upon her own terms.

You had like to have made a simpleton of your aunt Hervey yesterday: she came down from you, pleading in your favour; but when she was asked, what concession she had brought you to? she looked about her, and knew not what to answer. So your mother, when surprised into the beginning of your cunning address to her and to your father, under my name (for I had begun to read it, little suspecting such an *ingenious* subterfuge) and would then make me read it through, wrung her hands, Oh! her dear child, her dear child, must not be so compelled!—But when she was asked, whether she would be willing to have for her son-in-law the man who bids defiance to her whole family; and who had like to have murdered her son? And what concessions she had gained from her dear child to merit this tenderness? And that for one who had apparently deceived her in assuring her that her heart *was free?* —Then could she look about her, as her sister had done before: then was she again brought to herself, and to a resolution to assert her authority [Not to *transfer* it, witty presumer!] over the rebel who of late has so ingratefully struggled to throw it off.

You seem, child, to have a high notion of the matrimonial duty; and I'll warrant, like the rest of your sex (one or two, whom I have the honour to know, excepted) that you will go to church to pro-

mise what you will never think of
afterwards. But, *sweet* child! as
your *worthy* mamma Norton calls
you, think a little less of the *matrimonial* (at least, till you come into
that state) and a little more of the
filial duty.

How can you say, you are to
bear *all the misery*, when you give
so large a share of it to your
parents, to your uncles, to your
aunt, to myself, and to your sister;
who all, for eighteen years of your
life, loved you so well?

If of late I have not given you
room to hope for my favour or
compassion, it is because of late
you have not deserved either. I
know what you mean, little reflecting fool, by saying it is much
in my power, although *but* your
brother (a very slight degree of
relationship with you) to give you
that peace which you can give
yourself whenever you please.

The liberty of *refusing*, pretty
miss, is denied you, because we
are all sensible, that the liberty of
choosing, to every one's dislike,
must follow. The vile wretch you
have set your heart upon speaks
this plainly to every body, though
you won't. He says you are *his*,
and shall be *his*, and he will be the
death of any man who robs him of
his PROPERTY. So, miss, we have a
mind to try this point with him.
My father supposing he has the
right of a father in his child, is absolutely determined not to be
bullied out of that right. And
what must that child be, who
prefers the rake to a father?

This is the light in which this
whole debate ought to be taken.
Blush, then, delicacy, that cannot
bear the poet's *amor omnibus
idem!* — Blush, then, purity! Be
ashamed, virgin modesty! And, if
capable of conviction, surrender
your whole will to the will of the
honoured pair, to whom you owe
your being: and beg of all your
friends to forgive and forget the
part you have of late acted.

I have written a longer letter,
than ever I designed to write to
you, after the insolent treatment
and prohibition you have given
me: and, now I am commissioned
to tell you, that your friends are
as weary of confining you, as you
are of being confined. And therefore you must prepare yourself to
go in a very few days, as you have
been told before, to your uncle
Antony's; who, notwithstanding
your apprehensions, will draw up
his bridge when he pleases; will
see what company he pleases in
his own house; nor will he de-
molish his chapel to cure you of
your foolish late commenced antipathy to a place of divine worship.
— The more foolish, as, if we intended to use force, we could have
the ceremony pass in your chamber, as well as any where else.

Prejudice against Mr. Solmes
has evidently blinded you, and
there is a *charitable* necessity to
open your eyes: since no one but
you thinks the gentleman so contemptible in his *person*; nor, for a
plain country gentleman, who has
too much solid sense to appear
like a coxcomb, justly blameable
in his *manners* — And as to his

temper, it is necessary you should speak upon fuller knowledge, than at present it is plain you can have of him.

Upon the whole, it will not be amiss, that you prepare for your speedy removal, as well for the sake of your own conveniency, as to shew your readiness, in *one* point, at least, to oblige your friends; one of whom you may, if you please to deserve it, reckon, though *but* a brother,

JAMES HARLOWE.

P. S. If you are disposed to see Mr. Solmes, and to make some excuses to him for your past conduct, in order to be able to meet him *somewhere else* with the less concern to yourself for your freedoms with him; he shall attend you where you please.

If you have a mind to read the settlements, before they are read *to* you for your signing, they shall be sent you up—Who knows, but they will help you to some fresh objections?—Your heart is *free*, you know — It *must* — For, did you not tell your mother it was? And will the *pious* Clarissa fib to her mamma?

I desire no reply. The case requires none. Yet I will ask you, have you, miss, no more proposals to make?

I was so vexed when I came to the end of this letter (the postscript to which, perhaps, might be written after the others had seen the letter) that I took up my pen, with an intent to write to my uncle Harlowe about resuming my own estate, in pursuance of your advice: but my heart failed me, when I recollected, that I had not one friend to stand by or support me in my claim; and that it would but the more incense them, without answering any good end. O that my cousin were but come!

Is it not a sad thing, beloved as I thought myself so lately by every one, that now I have not one person in the world to plead for me, to stand by me, or who would afford me refuge, were I to be under the necessity of seeking for it!—I who had the vanity to think I had as many friends as I saw faces, and flattered myself too, that it was not altogether unmerited, because I saw not my Maker's image, either in man, woman, or child, high or low, rich or poor, whom, comparatively, I loved not as myself. — Would to heaven, my dear, that you were married! Perhaps, then, you could have induced Mr. Hickman to afford me protection, till these storms were over-blown. But then this might have involved *him* in difficulties and dangers; and that I would not have done for the world.

I don't know what to do, not I! — God forgive me, but I am very impatient! I wish — but I don't know what to wish, without a sin! — Yet I wish it would please God to take me to his mercy!—I can meet with none here — What a world is this? — What is there in it desirable? The good we hope for, so strangely mixed, that one knows not what to wish for! And one half of mankind tormenting the other, and being tormented themselves in tormenting! — For here in this my particular case, my relations cannot be happy, though they make me unhappy! — Except my brother and sister, indeed, — and they seem to take delight in and enjoy the mischief they make.

But it is time to lay down my pen, since my ink runs nothing but gall.

LETTER LIII.

Miss Clarissa Harlowe to Miss Howe.

Friday morning, 6 o'clock.

MRS. Betty tells me, there is now nothing talked of but of my going to my uncle Antony's. She has been ordered, she says, to get ready to attend me thither: and, upon my expressing my averseness to go, had the confidence to say, that having heard me often praise the *romanticness* of the place, she was astonished (her hands and eyes lifted up) that I should set myself against going to a house so much in *my taste*.

I asked if this was her own insolence, or her young mistress's observation?

She half-astonished *me* by her answer; that it was hard she could not say a *good* thing, without being robbed of the merit of it.

As the wench looked as if she really thought she had said a good thing, without knowing the boldness of it, I let it pass. But, to say the truth, this creature has surprised me on many occasions with her smartness: for, since she has been employed in this controlling office, I have discovered a' great deal of wit in her assurance, which I never suspected before. This shews, that insolence is her talent; and that fortune, in placing her as a servant to my sister, had not done so kindly by her as nature: for that she would make a better figure as her *companion*. And indeed I can't help thinking sometimes, that I myself was better fitted by *nature* to be the servant of *both*, than the *mistress* of the *one*, or the *sister* of the *other*. And within these few months past, *fortune* has acted by me, as if she were of the same mind.

Friday, 10 o'clock.

GOING down to my poultry-yard, just now, I heard my brother and sister and that Solmes laughing and triumphing together. The high yew hedge between us, which divides the yard from the garden, hindered them from seeing me.

My brother, as I found, had been reading part, or the whole perhaps, of the copy of his last letter — Mighty prudent, and consistent you'll say, with their views to make me the wife of a man from whom they conceal not what, were I to be such, it would be kind in them to endeavour to conceal, out of regard to my future peace! — But I have no doubt, that they hate me heartily.

Indeed you was up with her there, brother, said my sister. You need not have bid her not to write to you. I'll engage, with all her wit, she'll never pretend to answer it.

Why, indeed, said my brother, with an air of college-sufficiency, with which he abounds (for he thinks nobody writes like himself), I believe I have given her a choke-pear. What say you, Mr. Solmes?

Why, sir, said he, I think it is unanswerable. But will it not exasperate her more against me?

Never fear, Mr. Solmes, said my brother, but we'll carry our point, if she do not tire *you* out first. We have gone too far in this method to recede. Her cousin Morden will soon be here: so all must be over before that time, or she'll be made independent of us all.

There, Miss Howe, is the reason given for their Jehu-driving.

Mr. Solmes declared that he was determined to persevere while my brother gave him any hopes, and while my father stood firm.

My sister told my brother, that he *hit me charmingly* on the reason why I ought to converse with Mr. Solmes: but that he should not be so smart upon the *sex*, for the faults of *this perverse girl.*

Some lively, and I suppose, witty answer, my brother returned: for he and Mr. Solmes laughed outrageously upon it, and Bella, laughing too, called him a naughty man: but I heard no more of what they said; they walking on into the garden.

If you think, my dear, that what I have related did not again fire me, you will find yourself mistaken when you read at this place the inclosed copy of my letter to my brother; struck off — while the iron was redhot.

No more call me meek and gentle, I beseech you.

TO MR. JAMES HARLOWE.

SIR, Friday morning.

IF, notwithstanding your prohibition, I should be silent, on occasion of your last, you would, perhaps, conclude, that I was consenting to go to my uncle Antony's upon the condition you mention. My father must do as he pleases with his child. He may turn me out of his doors, if he thinks fit, or give *you* leave to do it: but (loth as I am to say it) I should think it very hard to be carried by force to any body's house when I have one of *my own* to go to.

Far be it from me, notwithstanding yours and my sister's provocations, to think of taking my estate into my own hands, without my father's leave: but why, if I must not stay any longer here, may I not be permitted to go thither? I will engage to see nobody they would not have me see, if this favour be permitted. *Favour* I call it, and am ready to receive and acknowledge it as such, although my grandfather's will has made it matter of right.

You ask me, in a very unbrotherly manner, in the postscript to your letter, if I have not some new proposals to make? I HAVE (since you put the question) three or four; *new ones* all, I think; though I will be bold to say, that,

16*

submitting the case to any one person whom *you* have not set against me, my *old* ones ought not to have been rejected. I *think* this: why then should I not *write* it? — Nor have you any more reason to storm at your *sister* for telling it you (since you seem in your letter to make it your boast how you turned my mother and my aunt Hervey against me) than I have to be angry with my *brother*, for treating me as no brother ought to treat a sister.

These, then, are my new proposals.

That, as above, I may not be hindered from going to reside (under such conditions as shall be prescribed to me, which I will most religiously observe) at my grandfather's late house. I will not again in this place call it *mine*. I have reason to think it a great misfortune, that ever it was so — *Indeed* I have.

If this be not permitted, I desire leave to go for a month, or for what time shall be thought fit, to Miss Howe's. I dare say her mother will consent to it, if I have my father's permission to go.

If this, neither, be allowed, and I am to be turned out of my father's house, I beg I may be suffered to go to my aunt Hervey's, where I will inviolably observe her commands, and those of my father and mother.

But if this, neither, is to be granted, it is my humble request, that I may be sent to my uncle Harlowe's, instead of my uncle Antony's. I mean not by this any disrespect to my uncle Antony: but his moat, with his bridge threatened to be drawn up, and perhaps the chapel there, terrify me beyond expression, notwithstanding your *witty* ridicule upon me for that apprehension.

If this likewise be refused, and if I *must* be carried to the moated house, which used to be a delightful one to me, let it be promised me, that I shall not be compelled to receive Mr. Solmes's visits there; and then I will as cheerfully go, as ever I did.

So, here, sir, are my new proposals. And if none of them answer your end, as each of them tends to the exclusion of that ungenerous *persister's* visits, be pleased to know, that there is no misfortune I will not submit to, rather than yield to give my hand to the man to whom I can allow no share in my heart.

If I write in a style different from my usual, and different from what I wished to have occasion to write, an impartial person, who knew what I have accidentally, within this hour past, heard from your mouth, and my sister's, and a third person's (particularly the reason you give for driving on at this violent rate; to wit, my cousin Morden's soon expected arrival) would think I have but too much reason for it. Then be pleased to remember, sir, that when my *whining vocatives* have subjected me to so much scorn and ridicule, it is time, were it but to *imitate* example so excellent as *you* and my sister set me, that I should endeavour to assert my character in order to be thought *less an alien,* and *nearer of kin to you both,* than either of you of late have seemed to suppose me.

Give me leave, in order to *empty my female quiver* at once, to add, that I know no other reason which you can have for forbidding me to reply to you, after you have written what you pleased to me, than that you are conscious you cannot answer to reason and to justice the treatment you give me.

If it be otherwise, I, an unlearned, unlogical girl, younger by near a third than yourself, will venture (so assured am I of the justice of my cause) to put my fate upon an issue with *you:* with *you,* sir, who have had the advantage of an academical education; whose mind must have been strengthened by observation, and learned conversation, and who, pardon my going so *low,* have been accustomed to give *choke-pears* to those you vouchsafe to write against.

Any impartial person, your late tutor, for instance, or the pious and worthy Dr. Lewen, may be judge between us: and if either give it against me, I will promise to resign to my destiny: provided, if it be given against you, that my father will be pleased only to allow of my negative to the person so violently sought to be imposed upon me.

I flatter myself, brother, that you will the readier come into this proposal, as you seem to have a *high* opinion of your talents for argumentation: and not a *low* one of the cogency of the arguments contained in your last letter. And as I can possibly have no advantage in a contention with you, if the justice of my cause affords me not any (as you have no opinion it will); it behoves you, methinks, to shew to an impartial moderator, that *I* am wrong, and *you* not so.

If this be accepted, there is a necessity for its being carried on by the pen; the facts to be stated, and agreed upon by both; and the decision to be given, according to the force of the arguments each shall produce in support of their side of the question: for, give me leave to say, I know too well the *manliness* of your temper, to offer at a *personal* debate with you.

If it be not accepted, I shall conclude, that you cannot defend your conduct towards me; and shall only beg of you, that, for the future, you will treat me with the respect due to a sister from a brother who would be thought as polite as learned.

And now, sir, if I have seemed to shew some spirit, not quite foreign to the relation I have the honour to bear to *you,* and to my *sister;* and which may be deemed not altogether of a piece with that part of my character, which once, it seems, gained me every one's love; be pleased to consider to *whom,* and to *what* it is owing; and that this part of that character was not dispensed with, till it subjected me to that scorn, and to those insults, which a brother, who has been *so tenacious of an independence voluntarily* given up by me, and who has appeared *so* exalted upon it, ought not to have shewn to *any body*, much less to a *weak* and *defenceless* sister: who is, notwithstanding, an affectionate and respectful one, and would be glad to shew herself to be so upon all future occasions; as she has in every action of her past life, although of late she has met with such unkind returns.

CL. HARLOWE.

See, my dear, the force, and volubility, as I may say, of passion; for the letter I send you, is my first draught, struck off without a blot or erasure.

Friday, 3 o'clock.

As soon as I had transcribed it, I sent it down to my brother by Mrs. Betty.

The wench came up soon after, all aghast, with a *Laud, miss!* What *have* you done? — What *have* you written? For you have set them all in a *joyful* uproar!

* * *

My sister is but this moment gone from me: she came up all in a flame; which obliged me abruptly to lay down my pen: she ran to me —

O spirit! said she; tapping my neck a little *too* hard. And is it come to this at last! —

Do you beat me, Bella?

Do you call this beating you? Only tapping your shoulder *thus*, said she; tapping again more gently — this is what we *expected* it would come to — you want to be independent — my father has lived too long for you! —

I was going to speak with vehemence: but she put her handkerchief before my mouth, very rudely — You have done enough with your pen, mean listener as you are! But, *know*, that neither your independent scheme, nor any of your visiting ones, will be granted you. Take your course, perverse one: call in your rake to help you to an *independence* upon your parents, and a *dependence* upon him! — Do so! — Prepare this moment — resolve what you will take with you — to-morrow you go — depend upon it to-morrow you go! — No longer shall you stay here, watching and creeping about to hearken to what people say — 'tis determined, child! — You go to-morrow — my brother would have come up to tell you so; but I persuaded him to the contrary — for I know not what had become of you, if he had — such a letter! such an insolent, such a conceited *challenger!* — O thou vain creature! But prepare yourself, I say — to-morrow you go — my brother will accept of your bold challenge; but it must be *personal;* and at my uncle Antony's — or perhaps at Mr. Solmes's —

Thus she ran on, almost foaming with passion till, quite out of patience, I said, No more of your violence, Bella — had I known in what a way you designed to come up, you should not have found my chamber-door open. — Talk to your *servant* in this manner. Unlike you, as I bless God I am, I am nevertheless your sister — and let me tell you, that I won't go to-morrow, nor next day, nor next day to that—except I am dragged away by violence.

What! not if your father or your mother command it — *girl?* said she, intending another word, by her pause and manner before it came out.

Let it come to *that*, Bella; then I shall know what to say. But it shall be from their own mouths, if I do — not from yours, nor your Betty's — and say another word to me, in this manner, and be the consequence what it may, I will force myself into their presence; and demand what I have done to be used thus!

Come along, child! Come along, meekness — taking my hand, and leading me towards the door — demand it of them now — you'll find both your despised parents together! — What! does your heart fail you? — for I resisted, being thus insolently offered to be led, and pulled my hand from her.

I want not to be led, said I; and since I can plead your invitation, I *will* go; and was hastening to the stairs accordingly in my passion — but she got between me and the door, and shut it —

Let me first, bold one, said she, apprise them of your visit — for your own sake let me — for my brother is with them. But yet opening the door again, seeing me shrink back — Go, if you will! — Why don't you go? — Why don't you go, miss? — following me to my closet, whither I retired, with my heart full, and pulled the sash-door after me; and could no longer hold in my tears.

Nor would I answer one word to her repeated aggravations, nor to her demands upon me to open my door (for the key was on the inside); nor so much as turn my head towards her, as she looked through the glass at me. And at last, which vexed her to the heart, I drew the silk curtain, that she should not see me, and down she went muttering all the way.

Is not this usage enough to provoke a rashness never before thought of?

As it is but too probable that I may be hurried away to my uncle's without being able to give you previous notice of it; I beg that as soon as you shall hear of such a violence, you would send to the usual place, to take back such of your letters as may not have reached my hands, or to fetch any of mine that may be there.

May you, my dear, be always happy, prays your
     CLARISSA HARLOWE.

I have received your four letters. But am in such a ferment, that I cannot at present write to them.

LETTER LIV.

Miss Clarissa Harlowe to Miss Howe.

Friday night, March 24.

I HAVE a most provoking letter from my sister. I might have supposed, she would resent the contempt she brought upon herself in my chamber. Her conduct surely

TO MISS CLARISSA HARLOWE.

I AM to tell you, that your mother has begged you off for the morrow: but that you have effectually done your business with her, as well as with every body else.

In your proposals, and letter to your brother, you have shewn yourself so silly, and so wise; so young, and so old; so gentle, and so obstinate; so meek, and so violent; that never was there so mixed a character.

We all know *of whom* you have borrowed this new spirit. And yet the seeds of it must be in your heart, or it could not all at once shew itself so rampant. It would be doing Mr. Solmes a spite to wish him such a *shy, un-shy* girl; another of your contradictory qualities — I leave you to make out what I mean by it.

Here, miss, your mother will not let you remain! she cannot have any peace of mind while such a rebel of a child is so near her: your aunt Hervey will not take a charge which all the family put together cannot manage: your uncle Harlowe will not see you at his house, till you are married — so, thanks to your own stubbornness, you have nobody that will receive you but your uncle Antony. — Thither you must go in a very few days; and when there, your brother will settle with you, in my presence, all that relates to your modest challenge: — for it *is* accepted, I assure you. Dr. Lewen will possibly be there, since you make choice of him. Another gentleman likewise, were it but to convince you, that he is another sort of man than you have taken him to be. Your two uncles will *possibly* be there too, to see that the *poor, weak,* and *defenceless* sister has fair play. So, you see, miss, what company your smart challenge will draw together.

Prepare for the day. You'll soon be called upon. Adieu, mamma Norton's *sweet child!*

ARAB. HARLOWE.

I transcribed this letter, and sent it to my mother, with these lines:

A very few words, my ever-honoured mamma!

IF my sister wrote the inclosed by my father's direction, or yours, I must submit to the usage she gives me in it, with this *only* observation, that it is short of the personal treatment I have received from her. If it be of her own head — why then, madam — but I *knew*, that when I was banished from your presence — yet, till I know if she has or has not authority for this usage, I will only write further, that I am

Your very unhappy child,
CL. HARLOWE.

This answer I received in an open slip of paper; but it was wet in one place. I kissed the place; for I am sure it was blistered, as I may say, by a mother's tear! —

She must (I *hope* she must) have written it reluctantly.

To apply for protection, where authority is defied, is bold. Your sister, who would not in *your* circumstances have been guilty of *your* perverseness, may allowably be angry at you for it. However, we have told her to moderate her *zeal* for our insulted authority. See, if you can deserve another behaviour, than that you complain of; which cannot, however, be so grievous to *you*, as the *cause* of it is to

Your more unhappy mother.

How often must I forbid you any address to me!

Give me, my dearest Miss Howe, your opinion, what I *can*, what I *ought* to do. Not what you would do (pushed as I am pushed) in *resentment* or *passion* — since, so instigated, you tell me, that you should have been with somebody before now — and steps taken in passion hardly ever fail of giving cause for repentance: but acquaint me with what you think cool judgment, and after-reflection, whatever were to be the event, will justify.

I doubt not your *sympathizing* love: but yet you cannot possibly feel indignity and persecution so very sensibly as the immediate sufferer feels them — are *fitter* therefore to advise me, than I am myself.

I will here rest my cause. Have I, or have I not suffered or borne enough? And if they will still persevere; if that strange persister against an antipathy so strongly avowed, will *still* persist, say, What can I do? — What can I do? — What course pursue? — Shall I fly to London, and endeavour to hide myself from Lovelace, as well as from all my own relations, till my cousin Morden arrives? Or shall I embark for Leghorn in my way to my cousin? Yet my sex, my youth, considered, how full of danger is this last measure! — And may not my cousin be set out for England, while I am getting thither? — What *can* I do? — Tell me, tell me, my dearest Miss Howe [for I dare not trust myself] tell me, what I can do.

Eleven o'clock at night.

I have been forced to try to compose my angry passions at my harpsichord; having first shut close my doors and windows, that I might not be heard below. As I was closing the shutters of the windows, the distant whooting of the bird of Minerva, as from the often-visited wood-house, reminded me of that charming ODE TO WISDOM, which does honour to our sex, as it was written by one of it. I made an essay, a week ago, to set the three last stanzas of it, as not unsuitable to my unhappy situation; and after I had reperused the ode, those were my lesson; and I am sure, in the solemn address they contain to the all-wise and all-powerful Deity, my heart went with my fingers.

I inclose the ode, and my effort with it. The subject is solemn: my circumstances are affecting; and I flatter myself, that I have not been quite unhappy in the performance. If it obtain your approbation, I shall be out of doubt: and should be still more assured, could I hear it tried by your voice and finger.

ODE TO WISDOM.
BY A LADY.

The solitary bird of night
 Through the thick shades now wings his flight,
And quits the time-shook tow'r;
 Where shelter'd from the blaze of day,
 In philosophic gloom he lay,
Beneath his ivy bow'r.

With joy I hear the solemn sound,
Which midnight echoes waft around,
 And sighing gales repeat.
Fav'rite of Pallas! I attend,
And, faithful to thy summons, bend
 At wisdom's awful seat.

She loves the cool, the silent eve,
Where no false shows of life deceive,
 Beneath the lunar ray.
Here folly drops each vain disguise;
Nor sport her gaily colour'd dyes,
 As in the beam of day.

O Pallas! queen of ev'ry art,
That glads the sense, and mends the heart,
 Bless'd source of purer joys!
In ev'ry form of beauty bright,
That captivates the mental sight
 With pleasure and surprise;

To thy unspotted shrine I bow:
Attend thy modest suppliant's vow,
 That breathes no wild desires;
But, taught by thy unerring rules,
To shun the fruitless wish of fools,
 To nobler views aspires.

Not fortune's gem, ambition's plume,
Nor Cytherea's fading bloom,
 Be objects of my prayer:
Let avarice, vanity, and pride,
Those envied glittering toys divide,
 The dull rewards of care.

To me thy better gifts impart,
Each moral beauty of the heart,
 By studious thought refin'd:
For wealth, the smiles of glad content;
For power, its amplest, best extent,
 An empire o'er my mind.

When fortune drops her gay parade,
When pleasure's transient roses fade,
 And wither in the tomb,
Unchang'd is thy immortal prize;
Thy ever-verdant laurels rise
 In undecaying bloom.

By thee protected, I defy
The coxcomb's sneer, the stupid lie
 Of ignorance and spite:
Alike contemn the leaden fool,
And all the pointed ridicule
 Of undiscerning wit.

From envy, hurry, noise, and strife,
The dull impertinence of life,
 In thy retreat I rest:
Pursue thee to the peaceful groves,
Where Plato's sacred spirit roves,
 In all thy beauties drest.

He bad Ilyssus' tuneful stream
Convey the philosophic theme
 Of perfect, fair, and good:
Attentive Athens caught the sound,
And all her list'ning sons around
 In awful silence stood:

Reclaim'd her wild licentious youth,
Confess'd the potent voice of truth,
 And felt its just control.
The passions ceas'd their loud alarms,
And virtue's soft persuasive charms
 O'er all their senses stole.

Thy breath inspires the poet's song,
The patriot's free, unbiass'd tongue,
 The hero's gen'rous strife;
Thine are retirement's silent joys,
And all the sweet engaging ties
 Of still, domestic life.

No more to fabled names confin'd,
To thee supreme all perfect mind,
 My thoughts direct their flight.
Wisdom's thy gift and all her force
From thee deriv'd, eternal source
 Of intellectual light!

O send her sure, her steady ray,
To regulate my doubtful way,
 Thro' life's perplexing road:
The mists of error to controul,
And thro' its gloom direct my soul
 To happiness and good.

Beneath her clear discerning eye
The visionary shadows fly
Of folly's painted show.
She sees thro' ev'ry fair disguise,
That all but VIRTUE's solid joys,
Is vanity and woe.

LETTER LV.

Miss Clarissa Harlowe to Miss Howe.

Friday, midnight.

I HAVE now a calmer moment. Envy, ambition, high and selfish resentment, and all the violent passions, are now, most probably, asleep all around me; and shall not my own angry ones give way to the silent hour, and subside likewise?—They *have* given way to it; and I have made use of the gentler space to re-peruse your last letters. I will touch upon some passages in them. And that I may the less endanger the but just recovered calm, I will begin with what you write about Mr. Hickman.

Give me leave to say, that I am sorry you cannot yet persuade yourself to think better, that is to say *more justly*, of that gentleman, than your whimsical picture of him shews you do; or, at least, than the humourousness of your natural vein would make one *think* you do.

I do not imagine, that you *yourself* will say, he sat for the picture you have drawn. And yet, upon the whole, it is not greatly to his disadvantage. Were I at ease in my mind, I would venture to draw a much more amiable and just likeness.

If Mr. Hickman has not that assurance which some men have, he has that humanity and gentleness which many want: and which, with the infinite value he has for you, will make him one of the properest husbands in the world for a person of your vivacity and spirit.

Although you say I would not like him myself, I do assure you, if Mr. Solmes were such a man as Mr. Hickman in person, mind, and behaviour, my friends and I had never disagreed about him, if they would not have permitted me to live single; Mr. Lovelace (having such a character as he has) would have stood no chance with me. This I can the more boldly aver, because I plainly perceive, that of the two passions, *love* and *fear*, this man will be able to inspire one with a much greater proportion of the *latter*, than I imagine is compatible with the *former*, to make a happy marriage.

I am glad you own, that you like no one better than Mr. Hickman. In a little while, I make no doubt, you will be able, if you challenge your heart upon it, to acknowledge, that you like not any man so well: especially, when you come to consider, that the very faults you find in Mr. Hickman, admirably fit him to make *you* happy: that is to say, if it be necessary to your happiness, that you should have *your own will in every thing*.

But let me add one thing; and that is this:—you have such a sprightly turn, that, with your admirable talents, you would make any man in the world, who loved you, look like a fool, except he were such a one as Lovelace.

Forgive me, my dear, for my frankness: and forgive me also, for so soon returning to subjects so immediately relative to myself, as those I now must touch upon.

You again insist (strengthened by Mr. Lovelace's opinion) upon my *assuming* my own estate [I cannot call it *resuming*, having never been in possession of it]: and I have given you room to expect, that I will consider this subject more closely than I have done before. — I must however own, that the reasons which I had to offer against taking your advice, were so obvious, that I thought you would have seen them yourself, and been determined by them, against your own hastier counsel. — But since this has not been so, and that both you and Mr. Lovelace call upon me to assume my own estate, I will enter briefly into the subject.

In the first place, let me ask you, my dear, supposing I were *inclined* to follow your advice, whom have I to support me in my demand? My uncle Harlowe is one of my trustees — he is against me. My cousin Morden is the other — he is in Italy, and very probably may be set against me too.

My brother has declared, that they are resolved to carry their point before he arrives: so that, as they drive on, all will probably be decided before I can have an answer from him, were I to write: and, confined as I am, were the answer to come in time, and they did not like it, they would keep it from me.

In the next place, parents have great advantages in every eye over the child, if she dispute their pleasure in the disposing of her: and so they ought: since out of *twenty* instances, perhaps *two* could not be produced, when *they* were not in the right, the *child* in the wrong.

You would not, I am sure, have me accept of Mr. Lovelace's offered assistance in such a claim. If I would embrace any *other* person's, who else would care to appear for a child against parents, ever, till of late, so affectionate? — But were such a protector to be found, what a length of time would it take up in a course of litigation? The will and the deeds have flaws in them, they say. My brother sometimes talks of going to reside at *the Grove:* I suppose, with a design to make ejectments necessary, were I to offer at assuming; or, where I to marry Mr. Lovelace, in order to give him all the opposition and difficulty the law would help him to give.

These cases I have put to myself, for argument-sake: but they are all out of the question, although anybody *were* to be found who would espouse my cause: for I do assure you, I would sooner beg my bread, than litigate for my right with my father: since I am convinced, that whether the parent do his duty by the child or not, the child cannot be excused from doing hers to him. And to go to law with my *father*, what a sound has that? You will see, that I have mentioned my wish (as an alternative, and as a favour) to be permitted, if I *must* be put out of his house, to go thither: but not one step further can I go. And you see how this is resented.

Upon the whole, then, what have I to hope for, but a change in my father's resolution? — And is there any probability of *that;* such an ascendancy as my brother and sister have obtained over every body; and such an interest to pursue the enmity they have now openly avowed against me?

As to Mr. Lovelace's approbation of your assumption-scheme, I wonder not at it. He very probably penetrates the difficulties I should have to bring it to effect, without *his* assistance. Were I to find myself as free as I would wish myself to be, perhaps Mr. Lovelace would stand a worse chance with me, than his vanity may permit him to imagine; notwithstanding the pleasure you take in rallying me on his account. How know you, but all that appears to be specious and reasonable in his offers; such as, standing his chance for my favour, after I became *independent*, as I may call it [by which I mean no more, than to have the liberty of refusing for my husband a man whom it hurts me but to think of in that light]; and such as his not visiting me but by my leave: and till Mr. Morden come; and till I am satisfied of reformation; — how know you, I say, that he gives not himself these airs purely to stand better in *your* opinion as well as *mine*, by offering of his own accord conditions which he must needs think would be insisted on, were the case to happen?

Then am I utterly displeased with him. To threaten as be threatens; yet to pretend, that it is not to intimidate me; and to beg of you *not to tell me*, when he must know you *would*, and no doubt *intended* that you *should*, is so meanly artful! — The man must think he has a frighted fool to deal with. — I, to join hands with such a man of violence! my own brother the man whom he threatens! — And what has Mr. Solmes done to him? — Is *he* to be blamed, if he thinks a person would make a wife worth having, to endeavour to obtain her? — O that my friends would but leave me to my own way in this one point! For have I given the man encouragement sufficient to ground these threats upon? Were Mr. Solmes a man to whom I could be but *indifferent*, it might be found, that to have the merit of a *sufferer* given him from such a flaming spirit, would very little answer the views of that spirit. It is my fortune to be treated as a fool by my brother: but Mr. Lovelace shall find — Yet I will let *him* know my mind, and then it will come with a better grace to your knowledge.

Meantime, give me leave to tell you, that it goes against me, in my cooler moments, unnatural as my brother is to me, to have you, my dear, who are my other self, write such very severe reflections upon him, in relation to the advantage Lovelace had over him. He is not indeed *your* brother: but remember, that you write to *his* sister. — Upon my word, my dear Miss Howe, you dip your pen in gall whenever you are offended: and I am almost ready to question, when I read some of your expressions against *others* of my relations as well as him (although *in my favour*) whether you are so thoroughly warranted by *your own* patience, as you think yourself, to call other people to account for *their* warmth. Should we not be particularly careful to keep clear of the faults we censure? — And yet I am so angry both at my brother and sister, that I should not have taken this liberty with my dear friend, notwithstanding I know you *never* loved them, had you not made so light of so shocking a transaction, where a brother's life was at stake: when his credit in the eye of the mischievous sex has received a still deeper wound than he *personally* sustained; and when a revival of the same wicked resentments (which may end more fatally) is threatened.

His credit, I say, in the eye of the *mischievous sex:* — Who is not warranted to call it so, when it is reckoned among the men such an extraordinary piece of self-conquest (as the two libertines his companions gloried) to resolve never to give a challenge; and among whom duelling is so fashionable a part of brutal bravery, that the man of *temper*, who is, mostly, I believe, the *truly* brave man, is often at a loss so to behave in some cases as to avoid incurring either a mortal guilt, or a general contempt?

To enlarge a little upon this subject, may we not infer, that those who would be guilty of throwing these contempts upon a man of temper, who would rather pass by a verbal injury, than to imbrue his hands in blood, know not the measure of true magnanimity? nor how much nobler it is to *forgive*, and even how much more *manly* to *despise*, than to *resent* an injury? Were I a man, methinks, I should have too much scorn for a person, who could wilfully do me a mean wrong, to put a value upon *his* life, equal to what I put upon *my own*. What an absurdity, because a man had done me a *small* injury, that I should put it in his power (at least, to an *equal* risk) to do me, and those who love me, an irreparable one? — Were it not a *wilful* injury, nor *avowed* to be so, there could not be *room* for resentment.

How willingly would I run away from myself, and what most concerns myself, if I could! This digression brings me back again to the occasion of it — and that to the impatience I was in, when I ended my last letter, for my situation is not altered. I renew therefore my former earnestness, as the new day approaches, and will bring with it perhaps new trials, that you will (as undivestedly as possible of favour or resentment) tell me what you would have me do:—for, if I am obliged to go to my uncle Antony's, all, I doubt, will be over with me. Yet how to avoid it—that's the difficulty!

I shall deposit this the first thing. When you have it, lose no time, I pray you, to advise (lest it be too late)

Your ever obliged
Cl. Harlowe.

LETTER LVI.

Miss Howe to Miss Clarissa Harlowe.

Saturday, March 25.

What can I advise you to do, my noble creature? Your merit is your crime. You can no more change *your* nature, than your persecutors can *theirs*. Your distress is owing to the vast disparity between you and them. What would you have of them? Do they not act in character?—And to whom? To an alien. You are not one of them. They have two dependencies in their hope to move you to compliance.—Upon their *impenetrableness* one [I'd give it a more proper name, if I dared]; the other, on the regard you have always had for your *character* [have they not heretofore owned as much?] and upon your apprehensions from *that* of Lovelace, which would discredit you, should you take any step by his means to extricate yourself. Then they know, that resentment and unpersuadableness are not natural to you; and that the anger they have wrought you up to, will subside, as all *extraordinaries* soon do; and that once married, you will make the best of it.

But surely your *father's* son and eldest daughter have a view (by communicating to so narrow a soul all they know of your just aversion to him) to entail unhappiness for life upon you, were you to have the man who is already more nearly related to them, than ever he can be to you, although the shocking compulsion should take place.

As to that wretch's perseverance, those only, who know not the man, will wonder at it. He has not the least delicacy. His principal view in marriage is not to the mind. How shall those beauties be valued, which cannot be comprehended? Were you to be his, and shew a visible want of tenderness to him, it is my opinion, he would not be much concerned at it. I have heard you well observe, from your Mrs. Norton, that a person who has any *over-ruling* passion, will compound by giving up twenty *secondary* or *under-satisfactions*, though more laudable ones, in order to have *that* gratified.

I'll give you the substance of a conversation [no fear you can be made to like him worse than you do already] that passed between Sir Harry Downeton and this Solmes, but three days ago, as Sir Harry told it but yesterday to my mother and me. It will confirm to you that what your sister's insolent Betty reported he should say, of governing by *fear*, was not of her own head.

Sir Harry told him, he wondered he should wish to obtain you so much against your inclination as every body knew it would be, if he did.

He mattered not that, he said! coy maids made the fondest wives [a sorry fellow!] It would not at all grieve him to see a pretty woman make wry faces, if she gave him cause to vex her. And your estate, by the convenience of its situation, would richly pay him for all he could bear with your shyness.

He should be sure, he said, after a while, of your complaisance, if not of your love: and in that should be happier than nine parts in ten of his married acquaintance.

What a wretch is this!

For the rest, your known virtue would be as great a security to him, as he could wish for.

She will look upon you, said Sir Harry, if she be forced to marry you, as Elizabeth of France did upon Philip II. of Spain, when he received her on his frontiers as her husband, who *was* to have been but her father-in-law: that is, with fear and terror, rather than with complaisance and love: and you will perhaps be as surly to her, as that old monarch was to *his* young bride.

Fear and terror, the wretch, the horrid wretch! said, looked pretty in a bride as well as in a wife: and, laughing [yes, my dear, the hideous fellow laughed immoderately, as Sir Harry told us, when he said it] it should be his care to perpetuate the occasion for that fear, if he could not think he had the *love*. And, truly, he was of opinion, that if LOVE and FEAR must be separated in matrimony, the man who made himself *feared*, fared best.

If my eyes would carry with them the execution which the eyes of the basilisk are said to do, I would make it my first business to *see* this creature.

My mother, however, says, it would be a prodigious merit in you, if you could get over your aversion to him. Where, asks she [as you have been asked before] is the praiseworthiness of obedience, if it be only paid in instances where we give up nothing?

What a fatality, that you have no better an option — either a *Scylla* or a *Charybdis*.

Were it not you, I should know how (barbarously used as you are used) to advise you in a moment. But such a noble character to suffer from a (supposed) rashness and indiscretion of such a nature, would, as I have heretofore observed, be a wound to the sex.

While I was in hope, that the asserting of your own independence would have helped you, I was pleased, that you had one resource, as I thought: but now, that you have so well proved, that such a step would not avail you, I am entirely at a loss what to say.

I will lay down my pen and think.

  *   *   *

I have considered, and considered again; but, I protest, I know no more what to say now, than before. Only this: that I am young, like yourself; and have a much weaker judgment, and stronger passions, than you have.

I have heretofore said, that you have offered as much as you ought, in offering to live single. If you were never to marry, the estate they are so loth should go out of their name, would, in time, I suppose, revert to your brother: and *he* or *his* would have it, perhaps, much more certainly this way, than by the precarious reversions which Solmes makes them hope for. Have you put this into their odd heads, my dear? — The tyrant word AUTHORITY, as they use it, can be the only objection against this offer.

One thing you must consider, that, if you leave your parents, your duty and love will not suffer you to justify yourself by an appeal against them; and so you'll have the world against you. And should Lovelace continue his wild life, and behave ungratefully to you, will not his baseness seem to justify their cruel treatment of you, as well as their dislike of him?

May heaven direct you for the best! — I can only say, that, for my own part, I would do any thing, go any whither, rather than be compelled to marry the man I hate; and (were he such a man as Solmes) must always hate — nor could I have borne what you have borne, if from father and uncles, not from brother and sister.

My mother will have it, that after they have tried their utmost efforts to bring you into their measures, and find them ineffectual, they will recede. But I cannot say I am of her mind. She does not own she has any other authority for this, but her own conjecture. I should otherwise have hoped, that your uncle Antony and she had been in one secret, and that favourable to you: woe be to one of them at least [to your uncle to be sure I mean] if they should be in *any* *other*.

You must, if possible, avoid being carried to that uncle's. The man, the parson, your brother and sister present! — they'll certainly there marry you to the wretch. Nor will your newly-raised spirit support you in your resistance on such an occasion. Your meekness will return; and you will have nothing for it but tears [tears despised by them all] and ineffectual appeals and lamentations: — and these tears, when the ceremony is *profaned*, you must suddenly dry up; and endeavour to dispose yourself to such an humble frame of mind, as may induce your new-made lord to forgive all your past declarations of aversion.

In short, my dear, you must

then blandish him over with a confession, that all your past behaviour was maidenly reserve only: and it will be *your* part to convince him of the truth of his impudent sarcasm, *that the coyest maids make the fondest wives*. Thus will you enter the state with a high sense of obligation to his *forgiving goodness:* and if you will not be kept to it by that *fear*, by which he proposes to govern, I am much mistaken.

Yet, after all, I must leave the point undetermined, and only to be determined, as you find they recede from their avowed purpose, or resolve to remove you to your uncle Antony's. But I must repeat my wishes, that something may fall out, that *neither* of these men may call you *his!* — And may you live single, my dearest friend, till some man shall offer, that may be as worthy of you, as man *can* be!

But yet, methinks, I would not, that you, who are so admirably qualified to adorn the married state, should be always single. You know, I am incapable of flattery; and that I always speak and write the sincerest dictates of my heart. Nor can you, from what you must know of your own merit (taken only in a comparative light with others) doubt my sincerity. For why should a person who delights to find out and admire every thing that is praiseworthy in *another*, be supposed ignorant of like perfections in *herself*, when she could not so much admire them *in* another, if she had them

not herself? And why may not I give *her* those praises, which she would give to any other, who had but half of her excellencies? — Especially when she is incapable of pride and vainglory; and neither despises *others* for the want of her fine qualities, nor over-values *herself* upon them? — *Over*-values, did I say! — How can that be?

Forgive me, my beloved friend. My admiration of you (increased, as it is, by every letter you write) will not always be held down in silence; although, in order to avoid offending you, I generally endeavour to keep it from flowing to my pen, when I write to you, or to my lips, whenever I have the happiness to be in your company.

I will add nothing (though I could an hundred things on account of your latest communications) but that I am

Your ever affectionate and faithful,

ANNA HOWE.

I hope I have pleased you with my dispatch. I wish I had been able to please you with my requested advice.

LETTER LVII.

Miss Clarissa Harlowe to Miss Howe.

Sunday Morning, March 26.

How soothing a thing is praise from those we love! — Whether conscious or not of deserving it, it cannot but give us great delight, to see ourselves stand high in the opinion of those whose favour we are ambitious to cultivate. An ingenuous mind will make this further use of it, that if it be sensible that it does not *already* deserve the charming attributes, it will hasten (before its friend finds herself mistaken) to obtain the graces it is complimented for: and this it will do, as well in honour to itself, as to preserve its friend's opinion, and justify her judgment. May this be always my aim! — And then you will not only give the *praise* but the *merit;* and I shall be more worthy of that friendship, which is the only pleasure I have to boast of.

Most heartily I thank you for the kind dispatch of your last favour. How much am I indebted to you! and even to your honest servant! — Under what obligations does my unhappy situation lay me!

But let me answer the kind contents of it, as well as I may.

As to getting over my disgusts to Mr. Solmes, it is impossible to be done; while he wants generosity, frankness of heart, benevolence, manners, and every qualification that distinguishes the worthy man. O, my dear! what a degree of patience, what a greatness of soul, is required in the wife, not to despise a husband who is more ignorant, more illiterate, more low-minded than herself! — The wretch, vested with prerogatives, who will claim rule in virtue of them (and not to *permit* whose claim will be as disgraceful to the *prescribing* wife as to the *governed* husband); how shall such a husband as this be borne, were he, for reasons of *convenience* and *interest*, even to be our choice? But, to be compelled to have such a one, and that compulsion to arise from motives as unworthy of the *prescribers* as of the *prescribed*, who can think of getting over an aversion so justly founded? How much easier to bear the temporary persecutions I labour under, *because* temporary, than to resolve to be *such* a man's for *life?* Were I to comply, must I not leave my relations, and go to him? A *month* will decide the one perhaps: but what a *duration of woe* will the other be! — Every day, it is likely, rising to witness some new breach of an altar-vowed duty!

Then, my dear, the man seems already to be meditating vengeance against me for an aversion I cannot help: for yesterday my saucy gaoleress assured me, that all my opposition would not signify that *pinch of snuff*, holding out her genteel finger and thumb: that I *must* have Mr. Solmes: that therefore I had not best carry my jest too far; for that Mr. Solmes was a man of spirit, and had told her, that as I should surely be his, I acted very impoliticly; since, if he had not more *mercy* [that was *her* word; I know not if it were *his*] than I had, I might have cause to repent the usage I gave him to the last day of my life.

But enough of this man, who, by what you repeat from Sir Harry Downeton, has all the insolence of his sex, without any one quality to make that insolence tolerable.

I have received two letters from Mr. Lovelace, since his visit to you, which make three that I have not answered. I doubt not his being very uneasy; but in his last he complains in high terms of my silence; not in the still small voice, or rather style of an humble lover, but in a style like that which would probably be used by a slighted protector. And his pride is again touched, that like a *thief*, or *eves-dropper*, he was forced to dodge about in hopes of a letter, and return five miles (and then to an inconvenient lodging) without any.

His letters, and the copy of mine to him, shall soon attend you: till when, I will give you the substance of what I wrote him yesterday.

I take him severely to task for his freedom in threatening me, through you, with a visit to Mr. Solmes, or to my brother. I say, "That, surely, I must be thought to be a creature fit to bear *any thing;* that violence and menaces from some of my *own family* are not enough for me to bear, in order to make me avoid *him;* but that I must have them from him too, if I oblige those whom it is both my *inclination* and *duty* to oblige in every thing that is reasonable, and in my power."

"Very extraordinary, I tell him, that a violent spirit shall threaten to do a rash and unjustifiable thing, which concerns *me* but a little and himself a great deal, if I do not something *as* rash, my character and sex considered, to divert him from it.

"I even hint, that, however it would affect *me*, were any mischief to happen on my account, yet there are persons, as far as I know, who in my case would not think there would be reason for *much* regret, were such a committed rashness as he threatens Mr. Solmes with to rid her of *two* persons whom had she never known she had never been unhappy."

This is plain dealing, my dear, and I suppose he will put it into still plainer English for me.

I take his pride to task, on his disdaining to watch for my letters; and for his *eves-dropping* language: and say, "That, surely, he has the less reason to think so hardly of his situation, since his faulty morals are the cause of all; and since faulty morals deservedly level all distinction, and bring down rank and birth to the *Canaille*, and to the necessity which he so much regrets, of appearing (if I must descend to his language) as an *eves-dropper* and a *thief*. And then I forbid him ever to expect another letter from me that is to subject him to such disgraceful hardships.

"As to the solemn vows and protestations he is so ready, upon all occasions, to make, they have the less weight with me, I tell him, as they give a kind of demonstration, that he himself, from his own character, thinks there is *reason* to make them. *Deeds* are to me the only evidence of *intentions.* And I am more and more convinced of the necessity of breaking off a correspondence with a person whose addresses I see it is impossible either to expect my friends to encourage, or him to deserve that they should.

"What therefore I repeatedly desire is, that since his birth, alliances, and expectations, are such as will at any time, if his immoral character be not an objection, procure him at least equal advantages in a woman whose taste and inclinations moreover might be better adapted to his own: I insist upon it, as well as advise it, that he give up all thoughts of me: and the rather, as he has all along (by his threatening and unpolite behaviour to my friends, and whenever he speaks of them) given me reason to conclude, that there is more malice to *them* than regard to *me* in his perseverance."

This is the substance of the letter I have written to him.

The man, to be sure, must have the penetration to observe, that my correspondence with him hitherto is owing more to the severity I meet with than to a very high value for him. And so I would have him think. What a *worse* than Moloch deity is that, which expects an offering of reason, duty, and discretion, to be made to its shrine!

Your mother is of opinion, you say, that *at last* my friends will relent. Heaven grant that they may. But my brother and sister have such an influence over every body, and are so determined; so pique themselves upon subduing me, and carrying their point; that I despair that they will: — and yet, if they do not, I frankly own, I would not scruple to throw myself upon any not disreputable protection, by which I might avoid my present persecutions on one hand, and not give Mr. Lovelace advantage over me on the other — that is to say, were there manifestly *no other* way left me: for if there *were,* I should think the leaving my father's house, without his consent, one of the most inexcusable actions I could be guilty of, were the protection to be ever so unexceptionable; and this notwithstanding the independent fortune willed me by my grandfather. And indeed I have often reflected with a degree of indignation and disdain upon the thought of what a low, selfish creature that child must be, who is to be reined in only by the hopes of what a parent can or will do for her.

But, notwithstanding all this, I owe it to the sincerity of friendship to confess, that I know not what I *should* have done, had your advice been conclusive any way. Had you, my dear, been witness to my different emotions as I read your letter, when in one place you advise me of my danger if I am carried to my uncle's; in another, when you own you could not bear what I bear, and would do any thing rather than marry the man you hate; yet, in another, represent to me my reputation suffering in the world's eye; and the necessity I should be under to justify my conduct at the expense of my friends, were I to take a rash step: in another, insinuate the *dishonest* figure I should be forced to make in so compelled a matrimony; endeavouring to cajole, fawn upon, and play the hypocrite with a man to whom I have an aversion, who would have reason to *believe* me an hypocrite, as well from my former avowals, as from the sense he *must* have (if common sense he has) of his own demerits: — The necessity you think there would be for me, the more averse I really was, to seem the. fonder of him: a fondness (were I capable of so much dissimulation) that would be imputable to disgraceful motives; as it would be visible that love, either of person or mind, could be neither of them — then his undoubted, his even constitutional narrowness; his too probable jealousy and unforgivingness, bearing in mind my declared aversion, and the unfeigned despights I took all opportunities to do him, in order to discourage his address; a preference avowed against him from the *same* motive; with the pride he professes to take in curbing and sinking the spirits of a woman he had acquired a right to tyrannize over: had you, I say, been witness of my different emotions as I read; now leaning this way, now that; now perplexed; now apprehensive; now angry at one, then at another; now resolving; now doubting: — you would have seen the power you have over me; and would have had reason to believe, that, had you given your advice in any determined or positive manner, I had been ready to have been concluded by it. So, my dear, you will find, from these acknowledgments, that you must justify me to those laws of friendship, which require undisguised frankness of heart, although your justification of me in that particular will perhaps be at the expense of my prudence.

But, upon the whole, this I do repeat — that nothing but the *last* extremity shall make me abandon my father's house, if they will permit me to stay; and if I can, by any means, by any honest pretences, but keep off my evil destiny in it till my cousin Morden arrives. As one of my trustees, *his* is a protection into which I may, without discredit, throw myself, if my other friends should remain determined. And this (although they seem too well aware of it) is all my hope; for, as to Lovelace, were I to be sure of his tenderness, and even of his reformation, must not the thoughts of embracing the offered protection of his family, be the same thing in the world's eye as accepting of his own? — Could I avoid receiving his visits at his own relations? Must I not be his, whatever (on seeing him in a *nearer* light) I should find him out to be? For you know, it has always been my observation, that very few people in courtship see each other as they are. Oh! my dear, how wise have I endeavoured to be! how anxious to choose and to avoid every thing, *precautiously*, as I may say, that might make me happy or unhappy; yet all my wisdom now, by a strange fatality, likely to become foolishness!

Then you tell me, in your usual kindly-partial manner, what is expected of *me* more than would be of some others. This should be a lesson to me. Whatever my motives were, the world would not know them: to complain of a brother's unkindness, *that*, indeed, I might do: differences between brothers and sisters, where interests clash, but too commonly arise: but where the severe father cannot be separated from the faulty brother; who could bear to lighten herself by loading a father? — Then, in this particular case, must not the hatred Mr. Lovelace expresses to every one of my family (although in return for *their* hatred of *him*) shock one extremely? Must it not shew, that there is something implacable, as well as highly unpolite, in his temper? — And what creature can think of marrying so as to be out of all hopes ever to be on happy terms with her own nearest and dearest relations?

But here, having tired myself, and I dare say you, I will lay down my pen.

* * *

Mr. Solmes is almost continually here: so is my aunt Hervey: so are my two uncles. Something is working against me, I doubt.

What an uneasy state is suspense! — When a naked sword too, seems hanging over one's head!

I hear nothing but what this confident creature Betty throws out in the wantonness of office. Now it is, why, miss, don't you look up your things? You'll be called upon, depend upon it, before you are aware. Another time she intimates darkly, and in broken sentences (as if on purpose to tease me) what *one* says, what *another;* with their inquiries how I dispose of my time? And my brother's insolent question comes frequently in, whether I am not writing a history of my sufferings?

But I am now used to her pertness: and as it is only through that that I can hear of any thing intended against me, before it is to be put in execution; and as, when she is most impertinent, she pleads a commission for it, I bear with her: yet, now and then, not without a little of the heart-burn.

I will deposit thus far. Adieu, my dear, CLARISSA HARLOWE.

Written on the cover, after she went down, with a pencil.

On coming down, I found your second letter of yesterday's date.* I have read it; and am in hopes that the enclosed will in a great measure answer your mother's expectations of me.

My most respectful acknowledgments to her for it, and for her very kind admonitions.

You'll read to her what you please of the enclosed.

* See the next Letter.

LETTER LVIII.

Miss Howe to Miss Clarissa Harlowe.

Sat. March 25.

I FOLLOW my last of this date by command. I mentioned in my former my mother's opinion of the merit you would have if you could oblige your friends against your own inclination. Our conference upon this subject was introduced by the conversation we had had with Sir Harry Downeton; and my mother thinks it of so much importance, that she enjoins me to give you the particulars of it. I the rather comply, as I was unable in my last to tell what to advise you to; and as you will in this recital have my mother's opinion at least, and perhaps in *her's* what the *world's* would be, were it only to know what she knows, and not so much as I know.

My mother argues upon this case in a most discouraging manner for all such of our sex as look forward for happiness in marriage with the *man of their choice.*

Only, that I know she has a side view to her daughter; who, at the same time that she now prefers no one to another, values not the man her mother most regards of one farthing, or I should lay it more to heart.

What is there in it, says she, that all this bustle is about? Is it such a mighty matter for a young woman to give up her inclinations to oblige her friends?

Very well, my mamma, thought I! Now may you ask this — at FORTY you may — but what would you have said at SIXTEEN is the question?

Either, said she, the lady must be thought to have very violent inclinations [and what nice young creature would have that supposed?] which she *could* not give up; or a very stubborn will, which she *would* not; or, thirdly, have parents she was indifferent about obliging.

You know my mother now-and-then argues very notably; always very warmly at least. I happen often to differ from her; and we both think so well of our own arguments, that we very seldom are so happy as to convince one another. A pretty common case, I believe, in all *vehement* debatings. She says, I am *too witty;* Anglicè, *too pert:* I, that she is *too wise;* that is to say, being likewise put into English, *not so young as she has been:* in short, is grown so much into *mother* that she has forgotten she ever was a *daughter*. So, generally, we call another cause by consent — yet fall into the old one half a dozen times over, *without* consent — quitting and resuming, with half angry faces, forced into a smile, that there might be some room to piece together again: but go to bed, if bed-time, a little sullen nevertheless: or, if we speak, her silence is broken with an ah! Nancy! you are so lively! so quick! I wish you were less like your papa, child.

I pay it off with thinking, that my mother has no reason to disclaim *her* share in her Nancy: and if the matter go off with greater severity on her side than I wish for, then her favourite Hickman fares the worse for it next day.

I know I am a saucy creature. I know, if I do not say so you will *think* so. So no more of this just now. What I mention it for, is to tell you, that on this serious occasion I will omit, if I can, all that passed between us that had an air of flippancy on my part, or quickness on my mother's, to let you into the *cool* and the *cogent* of the conversation.

"Look through the families," said she, "which we both know, where the man and the woman have been said to marry for love; which (at the time it is so called) is perhaps no more than a passion begun in folly or thoughtlessness, and carried on from a spirit of perverseness and opposition [here we had a parenthetical debate, which I omit]; and see if they appear to be happier than those whose principal inducement to marry has been convenience, or to oblige their friends; or even whether they are generally *so* happy: for *convenience* and *duty*, where observed, will afford a permanent, and even an *increasing* satisfaction (as well at the time as upon the reflection) which seldom fail to reward themselves: while *love*, if love *be* the motive, is an idle passion," [*idle in* ONE SENSE *my mother cannot say: for love is as busy as a monkey, and as mischievous as a school-boy*] — "It is a fervor that, like all other *fervors*, lasts but a little while after marriage; a bow over-strained, that soon returns to its natural bent.

"As it is founded generally upon mere *notional* excellencies, which were unknown to the persons themselves till attributed to either by the other: one, two, or three months, usually sets all right on both sides; and then with opened eyes they think of each other — just as every body else thought of them before.

"The lover's *imaginaries* [her own notable word!] are by that time gone off; nature and old habits (painfully dispensed with or concealed) return; disguises thrown aside, all the moles, freckles, and defects in the minds of *each* discover themselves; and 'tis well if each do not sink in the opinion of the other as much below the common standard as the blinded imagination of both had set them above it. And now the fond pair, who knew no felicity out of each other's company, are so far from finding the never-ending variety each had proposed in an unrestrained conversation with the other (when they seldom were together, and always parted with something *to say*, or on recollection, when parted, wishing they *had* said); that they are continually on the wing in pursuit of amusements out of themselves; and those, concluded my sage mamma, [did you think her wisdom so *very* modern?] will perhaps be the livelier to each in which the other has no share."

I told my mother, that if *you* were to take any rash step, it would be owing to the indiscreet violence of your friends. I was afraid, I said, that these reflections upon the conduct of people in the married state, who might set out with better hopes, were but too well grounded: but that this must be allowed me, that if children weighed not these matters so thoroughly as they ought, neither did parents make those allowances for youth, inclination, and inexperience, which had been found necessary to be made for themselves at their children's time of life.

I remembered a letter, I told her, hereupon, which you wrote a few months ago, personating an anonymous elderly lady (in Mr. Wyerley's day of plaguing you) to Miss Drayton's mother, who, by her severity and restraints, had like to have driven the young lady into the very fault against which her mother was most solicitous to guard her. And I dared to say, she would be pleased with it.

I fetched the first draught of it, with which, at my request, you obliged me at the time; and read the whole letter to my mother. But the following passage she made me read twice. I think you once told me you had not a copy of this letter.

"Permit me, madam, [says the personated grave writer] to observe, that if persons of your experience would have young people look *forward*, in order to be wiser and better by their advice, it would be kind in them to look *backward*, and allow for their children's youth and natural vivacity; in other words, for their lively hopes, unabated by time, unaccompanied by reflection, and unchecked by disappointment. Things appear to us all in a very different light at our entrance upon a favourite party, or tour; when, with golden prospects, and high expectations, we rise vigorous and fresh like the sun beginning its morning course; from what they do, when we sit down at the end of our views, tired, and preparing for our journey homeward: for then we take into our *reflection* what we had left out in *prospect*, the fatigues, the checks, the hazards, we had met with: and make a true estimate of pleasures, which from our raised expectations must necessarily have fallen miserably short of what we had promised ourselves at setting out. — Nothing but experience can give us a strong and efficacious conviction of this difference: and when we would inculcate the fruits of *that* upon the minds of those we love, who have not lived long enough to find those fruits; and would hope, that our *advice* should have as much force upon *them* as *experience* has upon *us*; and which, perhaps, *our parents*' advice had not upon *ourselves* at our daughters' time of life; should we not proceed by patient reasoning and gentleness, that we may not harden where we would convince? For, madam, the tenderest and most generous minds, when harshly treated, become generally the most inflexible. If the young lady knows her *heart* to be right, however defective her *head* may be for want of age and experience, she will be apt to be very tenacious. And if she believes her friends to be wrong, although perhaps they may be only so in their methods of treating her, how much will every *unkind* circumstance on the parent's part, or *heedless* one on the child's, though ever so slight in itself, widen the difference! The parent's *prejudice* in disfavour will confirm the daughter's in favour of the same person; and the best reasonings in the world on either side will be attributed to that prejudice. In short, neither of them will be convinced: a perpetual opposition ensues: the parent grows impatient; the child desperate: and, as a too natural consequence, that falls out which the mother was most afraid of, and which possibly had not happened, if the child's passions had been only *led*, not *driven*."

My mother was pleased with the whole letter; and said, it *deserved* to have the success it met with. But asked me what excuse could be offered for a young lady capable of making such reflections (and who at her time of life could so well assume the character of one of riper years) if she should rush into any fatal mistake herself?

She then touched upon the moral character of Mr. Lovelace; and how reasonable the aversion of your relations is to a man who gives himself the liberties he is said to take; and who indeed himself denies not the accusation; having been heard to declare, that he will do all the mischief he can to the sex, in revenge for the ill usage and broken vows of his first love, at a time when he was *too young* [his own expression it seems] to be insincere.

I replied, that I had heard every one say, that the lady meant really used him ill; that it affected him so much at the time, that he was forced to travel upon it; and to drive her out of his heart ran into courses which he had ingenuousness himself to condemn: that, however, he had denied that he had thrown out such menaces against the sex when charged with them by me in your presence; and declared himself incapable of so unjust and ungenerous a resentment against *all* for the perfidy of *one*.

You remember this, my dear; as I do your innocent observation upon it, that you could believe his solemn asseveration and denial: "For surely," said you, "the man who would resent, as the highest indignity that could be offered to a gentleman, the imputation of a *wilful* falsehood, would not be guilty of one."

I insisted upon the extraordinary circumstances in your case, particularizing them. I took notice, that Mr. Lovelace's morals were at one time no objections with your relations for Arabella: that then much was built upon his family, and more upon his parts and learning, which made it out of doubt that he might be reclaimed by a woman of virtue and prudence: [and pray forgive me for mentioning it] I ventured to add, that although your family might be good sort of folks, as the world went, yet nobody imputed to any of them but to you a *very* punctilious concern for religion or piety — therefore were they the less intitled to object to defects of that kind in others. Then, what an odious man, said I, have they picked out, to supplant in a lady's affections one of the finest figures of a man, and one noted for his brilliant parts, and other accomplishments, whatever his morals may be!

Still my mother insisted, that there was the greater merit in your obedience on that account; and urged, that there hardly ever was a very handsome and a very sprightly man who made a tender and affectionate husband: for that they were generally such Narcissus's, as to imagine every woman ought to think as highly of them as they did of themselves.

There was no danger from that consideration *here*, I said, because the lady had still greater advantages, both of person and mind, than the man; graceful and elegant as he must be allowed to be beyond most of his sex.

She cannot endure to hear me praise any man but her favourite Hickman: upon whom, nevertheless, she generally brings a degree of contempt which he would escape, did she not lessen the little merit he has, by giving him, on all occasions, more than I think he can deserve, and entering him into comparisons in which it is impossible but he must be a sufferer. And now [preposterous partiality!] she thought, for *her* part, that Mr. Hickman, bating that his *face* indeed was not so smooth, nor his complexion quite so good, and saving that he was not so presuming and so bold (which ought to be no fault with a modest woman) equalled Mr. Lovelace *at any hour of the day*.

To avoid entering further into such an *incomparable* comparison, I said, I did not believe, had they left you to your own way, and treated you generously, that you would have had the thought of encouraging any man whom they disliked.

Then, Nancy, catching me up, the excuse is less — for, if so, must there not be more of *contradiction* than *love* in the case?

Not so, neither, madam: for I know Miss Clarissa Harlowe would prefer Mr. Lovelace to all men, if morals —

IF, Nancy! — That *if* is every thing. — Do you really think she loves Mr. Lovelace?

What would you have had me to say, my dear? — I won't tell you what I *did* say: but had I not said what I *did* who would have believed me?

Besides, I *know* you love him! — Excuse me, my dear: yet if you deny it, what do you but reflect upon yourself, as if you thought you *ought not* to allow yourself in what you cannot help doing?

Indeed, madam, said I, the man is worthy of any woman's love [*if, I could say*] — but her parents —

Her parents, Nancy — [you know, my dear, how my mother, who accuses her daughter of quickness, is evermore interrupting one!]

May take wrong measures, said I —

Cannot do wrong — they have reason I'll warrant.

By which they may provoke a young woman, said I, to do rash things, which otherwise she would not do.

But if it *be* a rash thing [returned she] should she do it? A prudent daughter will not wilfully err, because her parents err, if they were to err: if she *do*, the world which blames the parents will not acquit the child. All that can be said in extenuation of a daughter's error in this case, arises from a kind consideration which Miss Clary's letter to Lady Drayton pleads for, to be paid to *her* daughter's youth and inexperience. And will such an admirable young person as Miss Clarissa Harlowe, whose prudence, as we see, qualifies her to be an adviser of persons much older than herself, take shelter under so poor a covert?

Let her know, Nancy, what I say: and I charge you to represent further to her, that let her dislike one man and approve of another ever so much, it will be expected of a young lady of her unbounded generosity and greatness of mind, that she should *deny herself* when she can *oblige all her family* by so doing — no less than ten or a dozen perhaps the nearest and dearest to her of all the persons in the world, an indulgent father and mother at the head of them. It may be *fancy* only on her side; but parents look deeper: and will not Miss Clarissa Harlowe give up her *fancy* to her parents' *judgment?*

I said a great deal upon this *judgment* subject: all that you could wish I should say; and all that your extraordinary case allowed me to say. And my mother was so sensible of the force of it, that she charged me not to write to you any part of my answer to what she said; but only what she herself had advanced; lest, in so critical a case, it should induce you to take measures which might give us both reason (me for giving it, you for following it) to repent it as long as we lived.

And thus, my dear, have I set my mother's arguments before you. And the rather as I cannot myself tell what to advise you to do — you know best your own heart; and what that will let you do.

Robin undertakes to deposit this very early, that you may have an opportunity to receive it by your first morning airing.

Heaven guide and direct you for the best, is the incessant prayer of

Your ever-affectionate

ANNA HOWE.

LETTER LIX.

Miss Clarissa Harlowe to Miss Howe.

Sunday afternoon.

I AM in great apprehensions. Yet cannot help repeating my humble thanks to your mother and you, for your last favour. I hope her kind end is answered by the contents of my last. Yet I must not think it enough to acknowledge her goodness to me with a pencil only, on the cover of a letter sealed up. A few lines give me leave to write with regard to my anonymous letter to Lady Drayton. If I did *not* at that time tell you, as I believe I *did*, that my excellent Mrs. Norton gave me her assistance in that letter, I now acknowledge that she did.

Pray let your mother know this, for two reasons: one, that I may not be thought to arrogate to myself a discretion which does not belong to me: the other that I may not suffer by the severe but just inference she was pleased to draw; *doubting* my faults upon me, if I myself should act unworthy of the advice I was supposed to give.

Before I come to what most nearly affects me, I must chide you once more for the severe, the *very* severe things you mention of our family, to the disparagement of their MORALS. Indeed, my dear, I wonder at you! — A slighter occasion might have passed me, after I have written to you so often to so little purpose on this topic. But, affecting as my own circumstances are, I cannot pass by without animadversion, the reflection I need not repeat in words.

There is not a worthier woman in England than my mother. Nor is my father that man you sometimes make him. Excepting in one point, I know not any family which lives more up to their duty than the principals of ours. A little too *uncommunicative* for their great circumstances — that is all. — Why, then, have they not reason to insist upon unexceptionable morals in a man whose sought-for relationship to them, by a marriage in their family, they have certainly a right either to allow of or to disallow.

Another line or two, before I am engrossed by my own concerns — upon your treatment of Mr. Hickman. Is it, do you think, generous to revenge upon an innocent person the displeasure you receive from another quarter, where I doubt you are a trespasser too? — But one thing I could tell him; and you had not best provoke me to it: it is this, that no woman uses ill the man she does not absolutely reject, but she has it in her heart to make him amends, when her tyranny has had its run, and he has completed the measure of his services and patience. My mind is not enough at ease to push this matter further.

I will now give you the occasion of my present apprehensions. I had reason to fear, as I mentioned in mine of this morning, that a storm was brewing. Mr.

Solmes came home from church this afternoon with my brother. Soon after, Betty brought me up a letter, without saying from whom. It was in a cover, and directed by a hand I never saw before; as if it were supposed that I would not receive and open it, had I known from whom it came.

These are the contents:

TO MISS CLARISSA HARLOWE.

DEAREST MADAM, Sunday, March 26.

I THINK myself a most unhappy man, in that I have never yet been able to pay my respects to you with youre consent, for one halfe-hour. I have something to communicat to you that concernes you much, if you be pleased to admit me to youre speech. Youre honour is concerned in it, and the honour of all youre familly. It relates to the designes of one whom you are said to valew more than he desarves; and to some of his reprobat actions; which I am reddie to give you convincing proofes of the truth of. I may appear to be interested in it: but neverthelesse, I am reddie to make oathe, that every tittle is true: and you will see what a man you are sed to favour. But I hope not so, for your owne honour.

Pray, madam, vouchsafe me a hearing, as you valew your honour and familly: which will oblidge, dearest miss,

Your most humble and most faithful servant, ROGER SOLMES.

I waite below *for* the hope of admittance.

I have no manner of doubt, that this is a poor device to get this man into my company. I would have sent down a verbal answer; but Betty refused to carry any message which should prohibit his visiting me. So I was obliged either to see him or to write to him. I wrote therefore an answer, of which I shall send you the rough draught. And now my heart aches for what may follow from it: for I hear a great hurry below.

TO ROGER SOLMES, ESQ.

SIR,

WHATEVER you have to communicate to me, which concerns my honour, may as well be done by writing as by word of mouth. If Mr. Lovelace is any of *my* concern, I know not that *therefore* he ought to be *yours:* for the usage I receive on *your* account [I *must* think it so?] is so harsh, that were there not such a man in the world as Mr. *Lovelace,* I would not wish to see Mr. *Solmes,* no, not for one halfhour, in the way he is pleased to be desirous to see me. I never can be in any danger from Mr. Lovelace (and of consequence cannot be affected by any of your discoveries) if the proposal I made be accepted. You have been acquainted with it, no doubt. If not, be pleased to let my friends know, that if they will rid *me* of my apprehensions of one gentleman, I will rid them of *theirs* of another: and then, of what consequence to *them* or to *me* will it be, whether Mr. Lovelace be a good man or a bad? And if not to *them*, nor to *me*, I see not how it can be of any to *you*. But if *you* do, I have nothing to say to that; and it will be a Christian part, if you will expostulate with him upon the errors you have discovered, and endeavour to make him as good a man as, no doubt, you are *yourself*, or you would not be so ready to detect and expose *him*.

Excuse me, sir: but after my former letter to you, and your ungenerous perseverance; and after this attempt to avail yourself at the expense of another man's character, rather than by your own proper merit, I see not that you can blame any asperity in her whom you have so largely contributed to make unhappy.

CL. HARLOWE.

Sunday night.

My father was for coming up to me in great wrath it seems; but was persuaded to the contrary. My aunt Hervey was permitted to send me this that follows.— Quick work, my dear!

TO MISS CLARISSA HARLOWE.

NIECE,

EVERY body is now convinced, that nothing is to be done with you by way of gentleness or persuasion. Your mother will not permit you to stay in the house: for your father is so incensed by your strange letter to his friend, that she knows not what will be the consequence if you do. So, you are commanded to get ready to go to your uncle Antony's without delay.

Your uncle thinks he has not deserved of you such an unwillingness as you shew to go to his house.

You don't know the wickedness of the man for whose sake you think it worth while to quarrel with all your friends.

You must not answer me. There will be no end of that.

You know not the affliction you give to every body; but to none more than to

Your affectionate aunt,
DOROTHY HERVEY.

Forbid to write to my aunt, I took a bolder liberty. I wrote a few lines to my mother, beseeching her to procure me leave to throw myself at my father's feet and her's, if I *must* go (nobody else present) to beg pardon for the trouble I had given them both, and their blessings; and to receive their commands as to my removal, and the time for it, from their own lips.

"What new boldness this!— Take it back; and bid her learn to obey," was my mother's angry answer, with my letter returned unopened.

But that I might omit nothing that had an appearance of duty, I wrote a few lines to my father himself, to the same purpose; begging, that he would not turn me out of his house without his blessing. But this, torn in two pieces, and unopened, was brought me up again by Betty, with an air, one hand held up, the other extended, the torn letter in her open palm; and a see here!— What a sad thing is this? — Nothing will do but duty, miss! — Your papa said, let her tell me of *deeds!* — I'll receive no *words* from her: and so he tore the letter, and flung the pieces at my head.

So desperate my case, I was resolved not to stop even at this repulse. I took my pen, and addressed myself to my uncle Harlowe, inclosing that which my mother had returned unopened, and the torn unopened one sent to my father; having first hurried off a transcript for you.

My uncle was going home, and it was delivered to him just as he stepped into his chariot. What may be the fate of it therefore I cannot know till to-morrow.

The following is a copy of it.

TO JOHN HARLOWE, ESQ.

MY DEAR AND EVER-HONOURED UNCLE,

I HAVE nobody now but you, to whom I can apply with hope, so much as to have my humble addresses, opened and read. My aunt Hervey has given me commands which I want to have explained; but she has forbid me writing to *her.* Hereupon I took the liberty to write to my father and mother: you will see, sir, by the torn one, and by the other (both unopened) what has been the result. This, sir, perhaps you already know: but, as you know not the *contents* of the disgraced letters, I beseech you to read them both, that you may be a witness for me, that they are not filled either with complaints or expostulations, nor contain any-thing undutiful. Give me leave to say, sir, that if deafeared anger will neither grant *me* a hearing, nor *what I write* a perusal, some time hence the hard-heartedness may be regretted. I beseech you, dear, good sir, to let me know what is meant by sending me to my uncle Antony's house, rather than to your's, or to my aunt Hervey's, or elsewhere? If it be for what I apprehend it to be, life will not be supportable upon the terms. I beg also to know WHEN I am to be turned out of doors! — My heart strongly gives me, *that if once I am compelled to leave this house, I never shall see it more.*

It becomes me, however, to declare, that I write not this through perverseness, or in resentment. God knows my heart, I do not! But the treatment I apprehend I shall meet with, if carried to my other uncle's, will, in all probability, give the finishing stroke to the distresses, the undeserved distresses I will be bold to call them, of

Your once highly favoured,
But now unhappy,
CL. HARLOWE.

LETTER LX.

Miss Clarissa Harlowe to Miss Howe.

Monday morning, March 27.

THIS morning early my uncle Harlowe came hither. He sent up the inclosed very tender letter. It has made me wish I *could* oblige him. You will see how Mr. Solmes's ill qualities are glossed over in it. What blemishes does affection hide! — But perhaps they may say to me, what faults does antipathy bring to light!

Be pleased to send me back this letter of my uncle by the first return.

Sunday night, or rather Monday morning.

I MUST answer you, though against my own resolution. Every body loves you, and you know they do. The very ground you walk upon is dear to most of us. But how can we resolve to see you? There is no standing against your looks and language. It is our love makes us decline to see you. How can we, when you are resolved *not* to do what we are resolved you *shall* do? I never, for my part, loved any creature as I loved you from your infancy till now. And indeed, as I have often said, never was there a young creature so deserving of our love. But what is come to you now! Alas! alas! my dear kinswoman, how you fail in the trial!

I have read the letters you inclosed. At a proper time I may shew them to my brother and sister. But they will receive nothing from you at present.

For my part, I could not read your letter to me without being unmanned. How can you be so unmoved yourself, yet be so able to move every body else? How could you send such a letter to Mr. Solmes? Fie upon you! How strangely are you altered!

Then to treat your brother and sister as you did, that they don't care to write to you or to see you!

Don't you know where it is written, that *soft answers turn away wrath?* But if you will trust to your sharp pointed wit you may wound: yet a club will beat down a sword: and how can you expect that they who are hurt by you will not hurt you again? Was this the way you used to take to make us all adore you as we did? — No, it was your gentleness of heart and manners that made every body, even strangers, at first sight treat you as a lady, and call you a lady, though not born one, while your elder sister had no such distinctions paid her. If you *were* envied, why should you sharpen envy, and file up its teeth to an edge?— You see I write like an impartial man, and as one that loves you still.

But since you have displayed your talents, and spared nobody, and moved every body, without being moved, you have but made us stand the closer and firmer together. This is what I likened to an *embattled phalanx* once before. Your aunt Hervey forbids your writing, for the same reason that I must not countenance it. We are all afraid to see you, because we know we shall be made as so many fools. Nay, your mother is so afraid of you, that once or twice, when she thought you was coming to force yourself into her presence, she shut the door, and locked herself in, because she knew she must not see you upon *your* terms, and you are resolved you will not see her upon *hers*

Resolve but to oblige us all, my dearest Miss Clary, and you shall see how we will clasp you every one by turns to our rejoicing hearts. If the one man has not the wit, and the parts, and the person of the other, no one breathing has a worse heart than that other: and is not the love of all your friends, and a sober man (if he be not so polished) to be preferred to a debauchee, though ever so fine a man to look at? You have such talents, that you will be adored by the one: but the other has as much advantage in those respects as you have yourself, and will not set by them one straw: for husbands are sometimes jealous of their authority with witty wives. You will have in one a man of virtue. Had you not been so rudely affronting to him, he would have made your ears tingle with what he could have told you of the other.

Come, my dear niece, let me have the honour of doing with you what nobody else yet has been able to do. Your father, mother, and I, will divide the pleasure, and the *honour* I will again call it, between us; and all past offences shall be forgiven; and Mr. Solmes, we will engage, shall take nothing amiss hereafter of what has passed.

He knows, he says, what a jewel that man will have who can obtain your favour; and he will think light of all he has suffered, or shall suffer, in obtaining you.

Dear, sweet creature, oblige us: and oblige us with a grace. It *must* be done, whether with a grace or not. I do assure you it *must*. You must not conquer father, mother, uncles, every body: depend upon that.

I have sat up half the night to write this. You do not know how I am touched at reading yours, and writing this. Yet will I be at Harlowe Place early in the morning. So, upon reading this, if you will oblige us all, send me word to come up to your apartment: and I will lead you down, and present you to the embraces of every one; and you will then see, you have more of a brother and sister in them both than of late your prejudices will let you think you have. This from one who used to love to style himself,

Your paternal uncle,
JOHN HARLOWE.

In about an hour after this kind letter was given me, my uncle sent up to know, if he should be a welcome visitor upon the terms mentioned in his letter? He bid Betty bring him down a verbal answer: a written one, he said, would be a bad sign: and he bid her therefore not bring a letter. But I had just finished the inclosed transcription of one I had been writing. She made a difficulty to carry it; but was prevailed upon to oblige me by a token which these Mrs. Betty's cannot withstand.

DEAR AND HONOURED SIR,

How you rejoice me by your condescending goodness! — So

kind, so paternal a letter! — so soothing to a wounded heart! and of late what I have been so little used to! — How am I affected with it! Tell me not, dear sir, of my way of writing: your letter has more moved me than I have been able to move *any body!* — It has made me wish, with all my heart, that I could entitle myself to be visited upon your own terms; and to be led down to my father and mother by so good and so kind an uncle.

I will tell you, dearest sir, what I will do to make my peace. I have no doubt that Mr. Solmes, upon consideration, would greatly prefer my sister to such a strange averse creature as me. His chief, or one of his chief motives in his address to me, is, as I have reason to believe, the contiguity of my grandfather's estate to his own. I will resign it; for ever I will resign it: and the resignation must be good, because I will never marry at all. I will make it over to my sister, and her heirs for ever. I shall have no heirs but my brother and her; and I will receive, as of my father's bounty, such an annuity (not in lieu of the estate, but as *of* his bounty) as he shall be pleased to grant me, if it be ever so small: and whenever I disoblige him, he to withdraw it, at his pleasure.

Will not this be accepted? — Surely it must — surely it will! — I beg of you, dearest sir, to propose it; and second it with your interest. This will answer every end. My sister has a high opinion of Mr. Solmes. I never can have *any* in the light he is proposed to me. But as my sister's husband, he will be always intitled to my respect, and shall have it.

If this be accepted, grant me, sir, the honour of a visit; and do me then the inexpressible pleasure of leading me down to the feet of my honoured parents, and they shall find me the most dutiful of children; and to the arms of my brother and sister, and they shall find me the most obliging and most affectionate of sisters.

I wait, sir, for your answer to this proposal, made with the whole heart of

Your dutiful and most obliged niece,

Cl. Harlowe.

Monday noon.

I hope this will be accepted: for Betty tells me, that my uncle Antony and my aunt Hervey are sent for; and not Mr. Solmes; which I look upon as a favourable circumstance. With what cheerfulness will I assign over this envied estate! — What a much more valuable consideration shall I part with it for! — The love and favour of all my relations! That love and favour, which I used for eighteen years together to rejoice in, and be distinguished by! — And what a charming pretence will this afford me of breaking with Mr. Lovelace! And how easy will it possibly make him to part with *me!*

I found this morning in the usual place a letter from him, in answer I suppose to mine of Friday, which

I deposited not till Saturday. But I have not opened it; nor will I, till I see what effect this new offer will have.

Let me but be permitted to avoid the man I *hate:* and I will give up with cheerfulness the man I *could prefer.* To renounce the one, were I really to value him as much as you seem to imagine, can give but a *temporary* concern, which *time* and *discretion* will alleviate. . This is a sacrifice which a child owes to parents and friends, if they insist upon its being made. But the other, to marry a man one *cannot endure,* is not only a dishonest thing as to the man, but it is enough to make a creature who wishes to be a *good wife* a bad or indifferent one, as I once wrote to the man himself: and then she can hardly be either a *good mistress* or a *good friend,* or any thing but a discredit to her family, and a bad example to all around her.

Methinks I am both, in the *suspense* I am in at present to deposit this, because it will be leaving you in one as *great:* but having been prevented by Betty's officiousness twice, I will now go down to my little poultry; and if I have an opportunity, will leave it in the usual place, where I hope to find something from you.

LETTER LXI.
Miss Clarissa Harlowe to Miss Howe.

Monday afternoon, March 27.

I have deposited my narrative down to this day noon; but I hope soon to follow it with another letter, that I may keep you as little a while as possible in that suspense which I am so much affected by at this moment: for my heart is disturbed at every foot I hear stir, and at every door below that I hear open or shut.

They have been all assembled some time, and are in close debate I believe: but can there be room for long debate upon a proposal, which, if accepted, will so effectually answer all their views? — Can they insist a moment longer upon my having Mr. Solmes, when they see what sacrifices I am ready to make to be freed from his addresses? — O but I suppose the struggle is, first, with Bella's nicety, to persuade her to accept of the estate and of the husband; and next with her pride, to take her *sister's refusals,* as she once phrased it! — Or, it may be, my brother is insisting upon equivalents for his reversion in the estate: and these sort of things take up but too much the attention of some of our family. To these, no doubt, one or both, it must be owing, that my proposal admits of so much consideration.

I want, methinks, to see what Mr. Lovelace, in his letter, says. But I will deny myself *this* piece of curiosity till that which is raised by my present suspense is answered. — Excuse me, my dear, that I thus trouble you with my uncertainties: but I have no employment, nor heart, if I had, to pursue any other but what my pen affords me.

Monday evening.

Would you believe it? — Betty, by anticipation, tells me, that I am to be refused. I am "a vile, artful creature. Every body is too good to me. My uncle Harlowe has been *taken-in*, that's the phrase. They knew how it would be, if he either wrote to me or saw me. He has, however, been made ashamed to be so wrought upon. A pretty thing truly in the eye of the world would it be, were they to take me at my word! It would look as if they had treated me thus hardly, as *I* think it, for this very purpose. My *peculiars*, particularly Miss Howe, would give it that turn; and I myself could mean nothing by it, but to see if it would be accepted in order to strengthen my own arguments against Mr. Solmes. It was amazing, that it could admit of a moment's deliberation, that any thing could be *supposed* to be done in it. It was equally against law and equity: and a fine security Miss Bella would have, or Mr. Solmes, when I could resume it when I would!—My *brother* and *she* my heirs! O the artful creature! — *I* to resolve to live single, when Lovelace is so *sure* of me — and everywhere declares as much! — and can whenever he pleases, if my husband, claim under the will! — Then the insolence — the confidence — [as Betty mincingly told me, that *one* said; you may easily guess who] that she, who was so justly in disgrace for downright rebellion, should pretend to prescribe to the whole family! — nor should name a husband for her elder sister! — What a triumph would her obstinacy go away with, to delegate her commands, not as from a prison, as she called it, but as from her throne, to her elders and betters; and to her father and mother too! — Amazing, perfectly amazing, that any body could argue upon such a proposal as this! It was a master-stroke of *finesse* — it was ME in perfection — surely my uncle Harlowe will never again be so taken in!"

All this was the readier told me, because it was against me, and would teaze and vex me. But as some of this fine recapitulation implied, that somebody spoke up for me, I was curious to know who it was: but Betty would not tell me, for fear I should have the consolation to find that *all* were not against me.

But do you not see, my dear, what a sad creature she is whom you honour with your friendship? — You could not doubt your influence over me: why did you not let me know myself a little better? Why did you not take the friendly liberty I have always taken with you, and tell me my faults, and what a specious hypocrite I am? For if my brother and sister could make such discoveries, how is it possible that faults so enormous [you could see *others*, you thought, of a *more* secret nature!] could escape your penetrating eye?

Well, but now, it seems, they are debating how and by whom to answer me: for they know not, nor *are* they to know, that Mrs. Betty has told me all these fine things. One desires to be excused, it seems: another chooses not to have any thing to say to me: another has enough of me: and of writing to so ready a scribbler there will be no end.

Thus are those imputed qualifications, which used so lately to gain me applause, now become my crimes: so much do disgust and anger alter the property of things.

The result of their debate, I suppose, will somehow or other be communicated to me by-and-by. But let me tell you, my dear, that I am made so desperate, that I am afraid to open Mr. Lovelace's letter, lest, in the humour I am in, I should do something (if I find it not exceptionable) that may give me repentance as long as I live.

Monday night.

This moment the following letter is brought me by Betty.

MISS CLARISSA-ONE, Monday, five o'clock.

Your fine new proposal is thought unworthy of a particular answer. Your uncle Harlowe is ashamed to be so taken in. Have you no new fetch for your uncle Antony? Go round with us, child, now your hand's in. But I was bid to write only one line, that you might not complain, as you did of your worthy sister, for the freedoms you provoked: it is this; — prepare yourself. To-morrow you go to my uncle Antony's. That's all, child.

JAMES HARLOWE.

I was vexed to the heart at this: and immediately, in the warmth of resentment, wrote the inclosed to my uncle Harlowe, who it seems stays here this night.

TO JOHN HARLOWE, ESQ.

HONOURED SIR,   Monday night.

I FIND I am a very sad creature, and did not know it. I wrote not to my brother. To *you*, sir, I wrote. From *you* I hope the honour of an answer. No one reveres her uncle more than I do. Nevertheless, I will be bold to say, that the distance, great as it is, between uncle and niece, excludes not such a hope: and I think I have not made a proposal that deserves to be treated with scorn.

Forgive me, sir — my heart is full. Perhaps one day you may think you have been *prevailed upon* (for that is plainly the case!) to join to treat me — as I do not deserve to be treated. If *you* are ashamed, as my brother hints, of having expressed any returning tenderness to me, God help me! I see I have no mercy to expect from any body! But, sir, from your pen let me have an answer; I humbly implore it of you — till my brother can recollect what belongs to a sister, I will take from *him* no answer to the letter I wrote to *you*, nor any commands whatever.

I move every body! — This, sir, is what you are pleased to mention: — but whom have I moved? — One person in the family has more moving ways than I have, or he could never so undeservedly have made every body ashamed to shew tenderness to a poor distressed child of the same family.

Return me not this with contempt, or torn, or unanswered, I beseech you. My father has a title to do that or any thing by his child: but from no other person in the world of your sex, sir, ought a young creature of mine (while she preserves a supplicating spirit) to be so treated.

When what I have before written in the humblest strain has met with such strange constructions, I am afraid that this unguarded scrawl will be very ill received. But I beg, sir, you will oblige me with one line, be it ever so harsh, in answer to my proposal. I still think it ought to be attended to. I will enter into the most solemn engagements to make it valid by a perpetual single life. In a word, any thing I *can* do, I *will* do, to be restored to all your favours. More I cannot say, but that I am, very undeservedly,

A most unhappy creature.

Betty scrupled again to carry this letter; and said she should have anger; and I should but have it returned in scraps and bits.

I must take that chance, said I: I only desire that you will deliver it as directed.

Sad doings! very sad! she said, that young ladies should so violently set themselves against their duty.

I told her, she should have the liberty to say what she pleased, so she would but be my messenger that one time — And down she went with it.

I bid her, if she could, slide it into my uncle's hand, unseen; at least unseen by my brother or sister, for fear it should meet, through *their* good offices, with the fate she had bespoken for it.

She would not undertake for that, she said.

I am now in expectation of the result. But having so little ground to hope for either favour or mercy, I opened Mr. Lovelace's letter.

I would send it to you, my dear (as well as those I shall inclose) by this conveyance: but not being able at present to determine in what manner I shall answer it, I will give myself the trouble of abstracting it here, while I am waiting for what may offer from the letter just carried down.

"He laments, as usual, my ill opinion of him, and readiness to believe every thing to his disadvantage. He puts into plain English, as I supposed he would, my hint, that I might be happier, if, by any rashness he might be guilty of to Solmes, he should come to an untimely end himself."

He is concerned, he says, "That the violence he had expressed on his extreme apprehensiveness of losing me, should have made him guilty of any thing I had so much reason to resent."

He owns, "That he is passionate: all good-natured men, he says, are so; and a sincere man cannot hide it." But appeals to me, "Whether, if any occasion in the world could excuse the rashness of his expressions, it would not be his present dreadful situation, through my indifference, and the malice of his enemies."

He says, "He has more reason than ever, from the contents of my last, to apprehend, that I shall be prevailed upon by force, if not by fair means, to fall in with my brother's measures; and sees but too plainly, that I am preparing him to expect it."

"Upon this presumption, he supplicates, with the utmost earnestness, that I will not give way to the malice of his enemies.

"Solemn vows of reformation, and everlasting truth and obligingness, he makes; all in the style of desponding humility: yet calls it a cruel turn upon him, to impute his protestations to a consciousness of the necessity there is for making them from his bad character.

"He despises himself, he solemnly protests, for his past follies: he thanks God he has seen his error; and nothing, but my more particular instructions, is wanting to perfect his reformation.

"He promises, that he will do every thing that I shall think he can do with honour, to bring about a reconciliation with my father; and even will, if I insist upon it, make the first overtures to my brother, and treat him as his own brother, because he is mine, if he will not by new affronts revive the remembrance of the past.

"He begs, in the most earnest and humble manner, for one half-hour's interview; undertaking by a key, which he owns he has to the garden-door, leading into the *coppice*, as we call it (if I will but unbolt the door) to come into the garden at night, and wait till I have an opportunity to come to him, that he may re-assure me of the truth of all he writes, and of the affection, and, if needful, protection, of all his family.

"He presumes not, he says, to write by way of menace to me: but, if I refuse him this favour, he knows not (so desperate have some strokes in my letter made him) what his despair may make him do."

He asks me, "Determined, as my friends are, and far as they have already gone, and declare they will go, what can I propose to do, to avoid having Mr. Solmes, if I am carried to my uncle Antony's unless I resolve to accept of the protection he has offered to procure me; or except I will escape to London, or elsewhere, while I *can* escape?"

He advises me, "To sue to *your* mother, for her private reception of me; only till I can obtain possession of my own estate, and procure my friends to be reconciled to me; which he is sure they will be desirous to *be*, the moment I am out of their power."

He apprises me [it is still my wonder, how he comes by his intelligence!] "That my friends have written to my cousin Morden to represent matters to him in their own partial way; nor doubt they to influence him on their side of the question.

"That all this shows I have

but *one* way; if none of my own friends or intimates will receive me.

"If I will transport him with the honour of my choice of this *one* way, settlements shall be drawn, with proper blanks, which I shall fill up as I please. Let him but have my commands from my own mouth, all my doubts and scruples from my own lips; and only a repetition, that I will not, on any consideration, be Solmes's wife, and he shall be easy. But, after such a letter as I have written, nothing but an interview can make him so." He beseeches me, therefore, "To unbolt the door, *as that very night;* or, if I receive not this time enough, *this night;* — and he will in a disguise that shall not give a suspicion who he is, if he should be seen, come to the garden door, in hopes to open it with his key; nor will he have any other lodging than in the coppice both nights; watching every wakeful hour for the propitious unbolting, unless he has a letter with my orders to the contrary, or to make some other appointment."

This letter was dated yesterday: so he was there last night, I suppose: and will be there this night; and I have not written a line to him: and now it is too late, were I determined *what* to write.

I hope he will not go to Mr. Solmes:—I hope he will not come hither.—If he do either, I will break with him for ever.

What have I to do with such headstrong spirits? I wish I had never—But what signifies wishing?—I am strangely perplexed—But I need not have told you this, after such a representation of my situation.

LETTER LXII.

Miss Clarissa Harlowe to Miss Howe.

Tuesday morning, 7 o'clock.

My uncle has vouchsafed to answer me. These that follow are the contents of his letter; but just now brought me, although written last night—Late I suppose.

MISS CLARY,   Monday night.

Since you are grown such a bold challenger, and teach us all our duty, though you will not practise your own, I *must* answer you. Nobody wants your estate from you. Are *you*, who refuse every body's advice, to prescribe a husband to your *sister?* Your letter to Mr. Solmes is inexcusable. I blamed you for it before. Your parents *will* be obeyed. It is fit they *should.* Your mother has nevertheless prevailed to have your going to your uncle Antony's put off till Thursday: yet owns you deserve not that, or any other favour from her. I will receive no more of your letters. You are too artful for me. You are an ungrateful and unreasonable child: must you have your will paramount to every body's? How are you altered!

Your displeased uncle,
JOHN HARLOWE.

To be carried away on Thursday—To the moated house—

To the chapel — To Mr. Solmes! How can I think of this! — They will make me desperate.

Tuesday morning, 8 o'clock.

I have another letter from Mr. Lovelace. I opened it with the expectation of its being filled with bold and free complaints, on my not writing to prevent his two nights watching, in weather not extremely agreeable. But, instead of complaints, he is "full of tender concern lest I may have been prevented by indisposition, or by the closer confinement which he has frequently cautioned me that I may expect."

He says, "He had been in different disguises loitering about our garden and park-wall, all the day on Sunday last; and all Sunday night was wandering about the coppice, and near the back-door. It rained; and he has got a great cold, attended with feverishness, and so hoarse, that he has almost lost his voice."

Why did he not flame out in his letter? — Treated as I am treated by my friends, it is dangerous to be laid under the sense of an obligation to an addresser's patience; especially when such a one suffers in health for my sake.

"He had no shelter, he says, but under the great overgrown ivy, which spreads wildly round the heads of two or three oaklings; and that was soon wet through."

You remember the spot. You and I, my dear, once thought ourselves obliged to the natural shade which those ivy-covered oaklings afforded us, in a sultry day.

I can't help saying, I am sorry he has suffered for my sake — but 'tis his own seeking.

His letter is dated last night at eight: "and indisposed as he is, he tells me, that he will watch till ten, in hopes of my giving him the meeting he so earnestly requests. And after that, he has a mile to walk to his horse and servant; and four miles then to ride to his inn."

He owns, "That he has an intelligencer in our family; who has failed him for a day or two past: and not knowing how I do, or how I may be treated, his anxiety is increased."

This circumstance gives me to guess who this intelligencer is: Joseph Leman; the very creature employed and confided in, more than any other, by my brother.

This is not an honourable way of proceeding in Mr. Lovelace. Did he learn this infamous practice of corrupting the servants of other families at the French court, where he resided a good while?

I have been often jealous of this Leman in my little airings and poultry-visits. Doubly obsequious as he was always to me, I have thought him my brother's spy upon me; and although he obliged me by his hastening out of the garden and poultry-yard, whenever I came into either, have wondered, that from *his reports* my liberties of those kinds have not been abridged.* So, possibly, this man may be bribed by both, and yet betray both. Worthy

* Mr. Lovelace accounts for this, letter xxxv.

views want not such obliquities as these on either side. An honest mind must rise into indignation both at the traitor-maker and the traitor.

"He presses with the utmost earnestness for an interview. He would not presume, he says, to disobey my last personal commands, that he should not endeavour to attend me again in the wood-house. But says, he can give me such reasons for my permitting him to wait upon my father or uncles, as he hopes will be approved by me: for he cannot help observing, that it is no more suitable to my own spirit than to his, that he, a man of fortune and family, should be obliged to pursue such a clandestine address, as would only become a vile fortune-hunter. But, if I will give my consent for his visiting me like a man, and a gentleman, no ill-treatment shall provoke him to forfeit his temper.

"Lord M. will accompany him, if I please: or, Lady Betty Lawrence will first make the visit to my mother, or to my aunt Hervey, or even to my uncles, if I choose it. And such terms shall be offered, as *shall* have weight upon them.

"He begs, that I will not deny him making a visit to Mr. Solmes. By all that's good, he vows, that it shall not be with the least intention either to hurt or affront him; but only to set before him, calmly, and rationally, the consequences that may possibly flow from so fruitless a perseverance, as well as the ungenerous folly of it, to a mind so noble as mine. He repeats his own resolution to attend my pleasure, and Mr. Morden's arrival and advice, for the reward of his own patience.

"It is impossible, he says, but one of these methods *must* do. Presence, he observes, even of a disliked person, takes off the edge of resentments which absence whets, and makes keen.

"He therefore most earnestly repeats his importunities for the supplicated interview." He says, "He has business of consequence in London: but cannot stir from the inconvenient spot where he has for some time resided, in disguises unworthy of himself, until he can be absolutely certain, that I shall not be prevailed upon, either by force or otherwise; and until he finds me delivered from the insults of my brother. Nor ought this to be an indifferent point to one, for whose sake all the world reports me to be used unworthily. — But *one* remark, he says, he cannot help making; That did my friend's know the little favour I show him, and the very great distance I keep him at, they would have no reason to confine me on his account: and *another*, that they *themselves* seem to think him entitled to a different usage, and expect that he receives it; when, in truth, what he meets with from me is exactly what they wish him to meet with, excepting in the favour of the correspondence I honour him with; upon which, he says, he puts the highest value, and for the sake of which he has submitted to a thousand indignities.

"He renews his professions of reformation: he is convinced, he says, that he has already run a long and dangerous course; and that it is high time to think of returning: it *must be* from proper convictions, he adds, that a person who has lived too gay a life, resolves to reclaim, before age or sufferings come upon him.

"All generous spirits, he observes, hate compulsion. Upon this observation he dwells; but regrets, that he is likely to owe all his hopes to this compulsion; this *injudicious* compulsion, he justly calls it; and none to my esteem for him. Although he presumes upon some merit — In his implicit, regard to my will — In the bearing the daily indignities offered not only to him, but to his relations, by my brother — In the nightly watchings, and risks which he runs, in all weathers; and which his present indisposition makes him mention, or he had not debased the nobleness of his passion for me, by such a selfish instance."

I cannot but say, I am sorry the man is not well.

I am afraid to ask you, my dear, what *you* would have done, thus situated. But what I *have* done, I *have* done. In a word, I wrote, "That I would, if possible, give him a meeting to-morrow night, between the hours of nine and twelve, by the ivy summer-house, or in it, or near the great cascade, at the bottom of the garden; and would unbolt the door, that he might come in by his own key. But that, if I found the meeting impracticable, or should change my mind, I would signify as much by another line: which he must wait for until it were dark."

Tuesday, 11 o'clock.

I AM just returned from depositing my billet. How diligent is this man! It is plain he was in waiting: for I had walked but a few paces, after I had deposited it, when, my heart misgiving me, I returned, to have taken it back, in order to reconsider it as I walked, and whether I should, or should not, let it go. But I found it gone.

In all probability, there was but a brick wall, of a few inches thick, between Mr. Lovelace and me, at the very time I put the letter under the brick!

I am come back dissatisfied with myself. But I think, my dear, there can be no harm in meeting him. If I do *not*, he may take some violent measures. What he knows of the treatment I meet with in malice to him, and with the view to frustrate all his hopes, may make him desperate. His behaviour last time I saw him, under the disadvantages of time and place, and surprised as I was, gives me no apprehension of any thing but discovery. What he requires is not unreasonable, and cannot affect my future choice and determination: it is only to assure him from my own lips, that I never will be the wife of a man I hate. If I have not an opportunity to meet him without hazard or detection, he must once more bear the disappointment. All his trouble, and mine too, is owing to his faulty character. This, although I hate tyranny and arrogance in all shapes, makes me think less of the risks he runs, and the fatigues he undergoes, than otherwise I should do; and still less, as my sufferings (derived from the same source) are greater than his.

Betty confirms the intimation, that I must go to my uncle's on Thursday. She was sent on purpose to direct me to prepare myself for going, and to help me to get every thing up in order for my removal.

LETTER LXIII.

Miss Clarissa Harlowe to Miss Howe.

Tuesday, 3 o'clock, March 28.

I HAVE mentioned several times the pertness of Mrs. Betty to me; and now having a little time upon my hands, I will give you a short dialogue that passed just now between us. It may, perhaps, be a little relief to you from the dull subjects with which I am perpetually teazing you.

As she attended me at dinner, she took notice, that nature is satisfied with a very little nourishment: and thus she complimentally proved it — For, miss, said she, you eat nothing; yet never looked more charmingly in your life.

As to the former part of your speech, Betty, said I, you observe well; and I have often thought, when I have seen how healthy the children of the labouring poor *look*, and *are*, with empty stomachs, and hardly a good meal in a week, that God Almighty is very kind to his creatures, in this respect, as well as in all others, in making *much* not necessary to the support of life; when three parts in four of His creatures, if it were, would not know how to obtain it. It puts me in mind of two proverbial sentences, which are full of admirable meaning.

What, pray, miss, are they? I love to hear you talk, when you are so sedate as you seem now to be.

The one is to the purpose we are speaking of; *Poverty is the mother of health:* and let me tell you, Betty, if I had a better appetite, and were to encourage it, with so little rest, and so much distress and persecution, I don't think I should be able to preserve my reason.

There's no inconvenience but has its convenience, said Betty, giving me proverb for proverb. But what is the other, madam?

That the *pleasures of the mighty are obtained by the tears of the poor:* it is but reasonable, therefore, methinks, that the plenty of the one should be followed by distempers; and that the indigence of the other should be attended with that health, which makes all its other discomforts light on the comparison. And hence a third proverb, Betty, since you are an admirer of proverbs: *Better a bare foot than none at all;* that is to say, than not to be able to walk.

She was mightily taken with what I said: See, returned she, what a fine thing scholarship is!—I, said she, had always, from a girl, a taste of reading, though it were but in *Mother Goose*, and concerning the *Fairies* [and then she took genteely a pinch of snuff]: could but my parents *have let go as fast as I pulled*, I should have been a very happy creature.

Very likely, you would have made great improvements, Betty: but as it is, I cannot say, but since I had the favour of your attendance in this *intimate* manner, I have heard smarter things from you, than I have heard at table from some of my brother's fellow-collegians.

Your servant, dear miss; dropping me one of her best courtesies: so fine a judge as you are!—It is enough to make one very proud. Then with another pinch—I cannot indeed but say, bridling upon it, that I have heard famous scholars often and often say very silly things: things I should be ashamed myself to say—But I thought they did it out of humility, and in condescension to those who had not their learning.

That she might not be too proud, I told her, I would observe, that the liveliness or quickness she so happily discovered in herself, was not so much an honour to her, as what she owed to her *sex;* which as I had observed in many instances, had great advantages over the other, in all the powers that related to imagination: and hence, Mrs. Betty, you'll take notice, as I have of late had opportunity to do, that your own talent at repartee and smartness, when it has *something to work upon*, displays itself to more advantage, than could well be expected from one whose friends, to speak in your own phrase, could not *let go so fast as you pulled*.

The wench gave me a proof of the truth of my observation, in a manner still more alert than I had expected: if, said she, our sex have so much advantage in *smartness*, it is the less to be wondered at, that *you*, miss, who have had such an education, should outdo all the men, and *women* too, that come near you.

Bless me, Betty, said I, what a proof do you give me of your wit and your courage at the same time! This is outdoing yourself. It would make young ladies less proud, and more apprehensive, were they generally attended by such smart servants, and their mouths permitted to be unlocked upon them as yours has been lately upon me.—But, take away, Mrs. Betty.

Why, Miss, you have eat nothing at all — I hope you are not displeased with your dinner for any thing I have said.

No, Mrs. Betty, I am pretty well used to your freedoms now, you know. — I am not displeased in the main, to observe, that, were the succession of modern fine ladies to be extinct, it might be supplied from those whom they place in the next rank to themselves, their chambermaids and confidantes. Your young mistress has contributed a great deal to this quickness of yours. She always preferred your company to mine. As *you pulled, she let go*; and so, Mrs. Betty, you have gained by *her* conversation what I have lost.

Why, Miss, if you come to that, nobody says better things than Miss Harlowe. I could tell you one, if *I pleased*, upon my observing to her, that you lived of late upon air, and had no stomach to any thing; yet looked as charmingly as ever.

I dare say, it was a very good-natured one, Mrs. Betty! Do you then *please* that I shall hear it?

Only this, Miss, *That your stomachfulness had swallowed up your stomach*; and, *That obstinacy was meat, drink, and cloth to you*.

Ay, Mrs. Betty; and did she say this? — I hope she laughed when she said it, as she does at all her *good things*, as she calls them. It was very smart, and very witty. I wish my mind were so much at ease, as to aim at being witty too. But if you admire such sententious sayings, I'll help you to another; and that is, *Encouragement and approbation make people show talents they were never suspected to have*; and this will do for both mistress and maid: and another I'll furnish you with, the contrary of the former, that will do only for me; that *Persecution and discouragement depress ingenuous minds, and blunt the edge of lively imaginations*. — And hence may my *sister's* brilliancy and my stupidity be both accounted for. *Ingenuous*, you must know, Mrs. Betty, and *ingenious*, are two things; and I would not arrogate the latter to myself.

Lord, Miss, said the foolish girl, you know a great deal for your years. — You are a very learned young lady! — What pity —

None of your *pities*, Mrs. Betty. I know what you'd say. But tell me, if you can, is it resolved that I shall be carried to my uncle Antony's on Thursday?

I was willing to reward myself for the patience she had made me exercise, by getting at what intelligence I could from her.

Why, Miss, seating herself at a little distance (excuse my sitting down) with the snuff-box tapped very smartly, the lid opened, and a pinch taken with a dainty finger and thumb, the other three fingers distendedly bent, and with a fine flourish — I cannot but say, that it is my opinion, you will certainly go on Thursday; and this *noles foless*, as I have heard my young lady say in FRENCH.

Whether I am *willing*, or *not willing*, you mean, I suppose, Mrs. Betty?

You have it, Miss.

Well but, Betty, I have no mind to be turned out of doors so suddenly. Do you think I could not be permitted to tarry one week longer?

How can I tell, Miss?

O Mrs. Betty, you can tell a great deal, if *you please*. But here I am forbid writing to any one of my family; none of it now will come near *me;* nor will any of it permit me to see *them:* how shall I do to make known my request, to stay here a week or fortnight longer?

Why, Miss, I fancy, if you were to show a compliable temper, your friends would show a compliable one too. But would you expect favours and grant none?

Smartly put, Betty! But who knows what may be the result of my being carried to my uncle Antony's?

Who knows, Miss! — Why any body may guess what will be the result.

As how, Betty?

As how! repeated the pert wench, why, Miss, you will stand in your own light, as you have hitherto done: and your parents, as such good parents *ought,* will be obeyed.

If, Mrs. Betty, I had not been used to your *oughts,* and to have my duty laid down to me by your oraculous wisdom, I should be apt to stare at the liberty of your speech.

You seem angry, Miss. I hope I take no unbecoming liberty.

If thou really thinkest thou dost not, thy ignorance is more to be pitied, than thy pertness resented. I wish thou wouldst leave me to myself.

When young ladies fall out with their *own* duty, it is not much to be wondered at, that they are angry at any body who do *theirs.*

That's a very pretty saying, Mrs. Betty! — I see plainly what thy duty is in thy *notion*, and am obliged to those who taught it thee.

Every body takes notice, Miss, that you can say very cutting words in a cool manner, and yet not call names, as I have *known some* gentlefolks as well as others do when in a passion. But I wish you had permitted 'Squire Solmes to see you: he would have told you such stories of 'Squire Lovelace, as would have turned your heart against him for ever.

And know you any of the particulars of those sad stories?

Indeed I don't; but you'll hear all at your uncle Antony's, I suppose; and a great deal more perhaps than you will like to hear.

Let me hear what I will, I am determined against Mr. Solmes, were it to cost me my life.

If you are, miss, the Lord have mercy on you! For what with this letter of your's to 'Squire Solmes, whom they so much value, and what with their antipathy to 'Squire Lovelace, whom they hate, they will have no patience with you.

What will they do, Betty? They won't kill me? What *will* they do?

Kill you! No! — but you will not be suffered to stir from thence, till you have complied with your duty. And *no pen and ink* will be allowed you as here; where they are of opinion you make no good use of it: nor would it be allowed here only as they intend so soon to send you away to your uncle's. Nobody will be permitted to see you, or to correspond with you.

290   THE HISTORY OF

What further will be done, I can't say; and, if I could, it may not be proper. But you may prevent it all, by one word: and I wish you would, miss. All then would be easy and happy. And, if I may speak my mind, I see not why one man is not as good as another: why, especially, a sober man is not as good as a rake.

Well, Betty, said I, sighing, all thy impertinence goes for nothing. But I see I am destined to be a very unhappy creature. Yet I will venture upon one request more to them.

And so, quite sick of the pert creature and of myself, I retired to my closet, and wrote a few lines to my uncle Harlowe, notwithstanding his prohibition; in order to get a reprieve from being carried away so soon as Thursday next, if I must go. And this, that I might, if complied with, suspend the appointment I have made with Mr. Lovelace; for my heart misgives me as to meeting him; and that more and more; I know not why. Under the superscription of the letter, I wrote these words: 'Pray, dear sir, be pleased to give this a reading.''

This is the copy of what I wrote:

HONOURED SIR,   Tuesday afternoon.

LET me this once be heard with patience, and have my petition granted. It is only, that I may not be hurried away so soon as next Thursday.

Why should the poor girl be turned out of doors so suddenly, so disgracefully? Procure for me, sir, one fortnight's respite. In that space of time, I hope you will all relent. My mamma shall not need to shut her door in apprehension of seeing her disgraced child. I will not presume to think of entering her presence, or my papa's, without leave. One fortnight's respite is but a *small favour* for them to grant, except I am to be refused every thing I ask; but it is of the *highest import* to my peace of mind. Procure it for me, therefore, dear sir; and you will exceedingly oblige

Your dutiful, though greatly afflicted niece,

CL. HARLOWE.

I sent this down: my uncle was not gone: and he now stays to know the result of the question put to me in the enclosed answer which he has given to mine.

YOUR going to your uncle's was absolutely concluded upon for next Thursday. Nevertheless, your mother, seconded by Mr. Solmes, pleaded so strongly to have you indulged, that your request for a delay will be complied with, upon one condition; and whether for a fortnight, or a shorter time, that will depend upon yourself. If you refuse this condition, your mother declares, she will give over all further intercession for you. — Nor do you deserve this favour, as you put it upon our yielding to you, not you to us.

This condition is, that you admit of a visit from Mr. Solmes for one hour, in company of your brother, your sister, or your uncle Antony; choose which you will.

If you comply not, you go next Thursday to a house which is become strangely odious to you of late, whether you get ready to go or not. Answer therefore directly to the point. No evasion. Name your day and hour. Mr. Solmes will neither eat you, nor drink you. Let us see, whether *we* are to be complied with in *any thing* or not. JOHN HARLOWE.

After a very little deliberation, I resolved to comply with this condition. All I fear is, that Mr. Lovelace's intelligencer may inform him of it; and that his apprehensions upon it may make him take some desperate resolution: especially as now (having more time given me here) I think to write to him to suspend the interview he is possibly so sure of. I sent down the following to my uncle.

HONOURED SIR,

ALTHOUGH I see not what end the proposed condition can answer, I comply with it. I wish I could with every thing expected of me. If I must name one, in whose company I am to see the gentleman, and that *one* not my mamma, whose presence I could wish to be honoured by on the occasion, let my uncle, if he pleases, be the *person*. If I must name the *day* (a long day, I doubt, will not be permitted me) let it be next Tuesday. The *hour*, four in the afternoon. The *place*, either the ivy summer-house, or in the little parlour I used to be permitted to call mine.

Be pleased, sir, nevertheless, to prevail upon my mamma, to vouchsafe me her presence on the occasion. I am, sir,
Your ever dutiful
CL. HARLOWE.

A reply is just sent me. I thought it became my averseness to this meeting, to name a distant day: but I did not expect they would have complied with it. So here is one week gained!

This is the reply:

You have done well to comply. We are willing to think the best of every slight instance of duty from you. Yet have you seemed to consider the day as an evil day, and so put it far off. This nevertheless is granted you, as no time need to be lost, if you are as generous *after* the day, as we are condescending *before* it. Let me advise you, not to harden your mind; nor take up your resolution beforehand. Mr. Solmes has more awe, and even terror, at the thoughts of seeing you, than you can have at the thoughts of seeing him. *His* motive is *love;* let not *yours* be *hatred.* My brother Antony will be present, in hopes you will deserve well of *him*, by behaving well to the friend of the family. See you use him as such. Your mother had permission to be there, if she thought fit: but says, she would not for a thousand pounds, unless you would encourage her beforehand as she wishes to be encouraged. One hint I am to give you mean time. It is this: *to make a discreet use of your pen and ink.* Methinks a young creature of niceness should be less ready to write to one man, when she is designed to be another's.

This compliance, I hope, will produce greater; and then the peace of the family will be restored: which is what is heartily wished by
   Your loving uncle,
    JOHN HARLOWE.

Unless it be to the purpose our hearts are set upon, you need not write again.

This man have *more terror at seeing me, than I can have at seeing him!* — How can that be? If he had half as much, he would not wish to see me! — HIS *motive love!* — Yes indeed! Love of himself! He knows no other; for love, that deserves the name, seeks the satisfaction of the beloved object more than its own. — Weighed in this scale, what a profanation is this man guilty of!

Not to take up my resolution beforehand! — That advice comes too late.

But I must *make a discreet use of my pen.* That, I doubt, as they have managed it, in the sense they mean it, is as much out of my power as the other.

But *to write to one man, when I am designed for another!* — What a shocking expression is that!

Repenting of my appointment with Mr. Lovelace *before* I had this favour granted me, you may believe I hesitated not a moment to revoke it *now* that I had gained such a respite. Accordingly, I wrote, "that I found it inconvenient to meet him, as I had intended: that the risque I should run of a discovery, and the mischiefs that might flow from it, could not be justified by any end that such a meeting could answer: that I found one certain servant more in my way, when I took my morning and evening airings, than any other: that the person who might reveal the secrets of a family to *him*, might, if opportunity were given him, betray me, or him, to those whom it was his duty to serve: that I had not been used to a conduct so faulty, as to lay myself at the mercy of servants: and was sorry he had measures to pursue that made steps necessary in his own opinion, which, in mine, were very culpable, and which no end could justify: that things drawing towards a crisis between my friends and me, an interview could avail nothing; especially as the method by which this correspondence was carried on, was not suspected, and he could write all that was in his mind to write: that I expected to be at liberty to judge of what was proper and fit upon this occasion: especially as he might be assured, that I would sooner choose death, than Mr. Solmes."

      Tuesday night.

I HAVE deposited my letter to

Mr. Lovelace. Threatening as things look against me, I am much better pleased with myself for declining the interview than I was before. I suppose he will be a little out of humour upon it, however: but as I reserved to myself the liberty of changing my mind; and as it is easy for him to imagine there may be reasons for it *within doors*, which he cannot judge of *without*; besides those I have suggested, which of themselves are of sufficient weight to engage his acquiescence; I should think it strange, if he acquiesces not on this occasion, and that with a cheerfulness, which may shew me, that his last letter is written from his heart: for if he be really so much concerned at his past faults, as he pretends, and has for some time pretended, must he not, of course, have corrected, in some degree, the impetuosity of his temper? The first step to reformation, as I conceive, is to subdue sudden gusts of passion, from which frequently the greatest evils arise, and to learn to bear disappointments. If the irascible passions cannot be overcome, what opinion can we have of the person's power over those to which bad habit, joined to *greater* temptation, gives stronger force?

Pray, my dear, be so kind, as to make enquiry by some safe hand, after the disguises Mr. Lovelace assumes at the inn he puts up at in the poor village of *Neal*, he calls it. If it be the same I take it to be, I never knew it was considerable enough to have a name; nor that it has an inn in it.

As he must, to be so constantly near us, be much there, I would be glad to have some account of his behaviour; and what the people think of him. In such a length of time, he must by his conduct either give scandal, or hope of reformation. Pray, my dear, humour me in this enquiry. I have reasons for it, which you shall be acquainted with another time, if the result of the enquiry discover them not.

LETTER LXIV.

Miss Clarissa Harlowe to Miss Howe.

Wednesday morning, nine o'clock.

I AM just returned from my morning walk, and already have received a letter from Mr. Lovelace in answer to mine deposited last night. He must have had pen, ink, and paper with him; for it was written in the coppice; with this circumstance: on one knee, kneeling with the other. *Not* from reverence to the written to, however, as you'll find!

Well are we instructed early to keep these men at distance. An undesigning open heart, where it is loth to disoblige, is easily drawn in, I see, to oblige more than ever it designed. It is too apt to govern itself by what a bold spirit is encouraged to *expect* of it. It is very difficult for a good natured young person to give a negative where it disesteems not.

Our hearts may harden and contract, as we gain experience,

and when we have smarted perhaps for our easy folly: and so they *ought*, or we should be upon very unequal terms with the world.

Excuse these grave reflections. This man has vexed me heartily, I see his gentleness was *art:* fierceness, and a temper like what I have been too much used to at home, are *nature* in him. Nothing, I think, shall ever make me forgive him; for surely, there can be no good reason for his impatience on an expectation given with reserve, and revocable. — *I* so much to suffer *through* him; yet, to be treated as if I were obliged to bear insults *from* him! —

But here you will be pleased to read his letter; which I shall inclose.

TO MISS CLARISSA HARLOWE.

Good God!

What is *now* to become of me! — How shall I support this disappointment! — No new cause! — On one knee, kneeling with the other, 1 write! — My feet benumbed with midnight wanderings through the heaviest dews, that ever fell: my linen dripping with the hoar frost dissolving on it! — Day but just breaking — sun not risen to exhale — may it never rise again! — Unless it bring healing and comfort to a benighted soul! In proportion to the joy you had inspired (ever lovely promiser!) in such proportion is my anguish!

O my beloved creature! — But are not your very excuses confessions of excuses inexcusable? I know not what I write! — *That* servant in your way!* By the great God of heaven, that servant *was not, dared not, could not* be in your way! — Curse upon the cool caution that is pleaded to deprive me of an expectation so transporting!

And *are things drawing towards a crisis between your friends and you?* — Is not this a reason for me to expect, the *rather* to expect, the promised interview?

Can *I write all that is in my mind*, say you? — Impossible! — Not the hundredth part of what is in my mind, and in my apprehension, can I write!

O the wavering, the changeable sex! — But can Miss Clarissa Harlowe —

Forgive me, madam! — I know not what I write!

Yet, I must, I do insist upon your promise — or that you will condescend to find better excuses for the failure — or convince me, that stronger reasons are imposed upon *you*, than those you offer. — A promise *once* given (upon *deliberation* given) the *promised* only can dispense with; — except in cases of a very apparent necessity imposed upon the *promiser;* which leaves no power to perform it.

The first promise you ever made me! life and death perhaps depending upon it — my heart desponding from the barbarous methods resolved to be taken with you in malice to me!

* See p. 292.

You would sooner choose death than Solmes (how my soul spurns the competition!) O my beloved creature, what are these but words? — *Whose* words? — Sweet and ever adorable — what? — Promise breaker — must I call you? — How shall I believe the asseveration (your *supposed duty* in the question! Persecution so flaming! Hatred to me so strongly avowed!) after this instance of your so lightly dispensing with your promise?

If, my dearest life! you would prevent my distraction, or, at least, distracted consequences, renew the promised hope! — My fate is indeed upon its crisis.

Forgive me, dearest creature, forgive me! — I know I have written in too much anguish of mind!--Writing this, in the same moment that the just dawning light has imparted to me the heavy disappointment.

I dare not re-peruse what I have written. — I *must* deposit it — it may serve to show you my distracted apprehension that this disappointment is but a prelude to the greatest of all. — Nor, having here any other paper, am I able to write again if I would on this gloomy spot (gloomy is my soul; and all nature round me partakes of my gloom!) — I trust it therefore to your goodness — if its fervor excite your displeasure rather than your pity, you wrong my passion; and I shall be ready to apprehend, that I am intended to be the sacrifice of more miscreants than one! [have patience with me, dearest creature! — I mean Solmes and your brother only]. But if, exerting your usual generosity, you will excuse and *re-appoint*, may that God, whom you profess to serve, and who is the God of *truth* and of *promises*, protect and bless you, for both; and for restoring to himself, and to hope,

Your ever adoring,
yet almost desponding
LOVELACE.

Ivy-cavern, in the coppice —
day but just breaking.

This is the answer I shall return.

Wednesday morning.

I AM amazed, sir, at the freedom of your reproaches. Pressed and teazed, against convenience and inclination to give you a private meeting, am *I* to be thus challenged and upbraided, and my sex reflected upon, because I thought it prudent to change my mind? — A liberty I had reserved to myself when I made the *appointment*, as you call it. I wanted not instances of your impatient spirit to other people: yet may it be happy for me, that I have this new one: which shows, that you can as little spare *me*, when I pursue the dictates of my own reason, as you do *others*, for acting up to theirs. Two motives you must be governed by in this excess. The one *my easiness;* the other *your own presumption*. Since you think you have found out the *first*, and have shown so much of the *last* upon it, I am too much alarmed, not to wish and desire, that your letter of

this day may conclude all the trouble you have had from, or for,
Your humble servant,
CL. HARLOWE.

I believe, my dear, I may promise myself your approbation, whenever I write or speak with spirit, be it to whom it will. Indeed, I find but too much reason to exert it, since I have to deal with people who govern themselves in their conduct to me, not by what is fit or decent, right or wrong but by what they think my temper will bear. I have, till very lately, been praised for mine; but it has always been by those who never gave me opportunity to return the compliment to them. Some people have acted, as if they thought forbearance on *one side* absolutely necessary for them and me to be upon good terms together; and in this case have ever taken care rather to *owe* that obligation than to *lay* it. You have hinted to me, that resentment is not natural to my temper, and that therefore it must soon subside: it may be so with respect to my relations; but not to Mr. Lovelace, I assure you.

Wednesday noon, March 29.

We cannot always answer for what we *can* do: but to convince you, that I can keep my above resolution, with regard to Mr. Lovelace, angry as my letter is, and three hours as it is since it was written, I assure you, that I repent it not; nor will soften it, although I find it is not taken away.

And yet I hardly ever before did any thing in anger, that I did not repent in half an hour; and question myself in *less* than that time, whether I were right or wrong.

In this respite till Tuesday, I have a little time to look about me, as I may say, and to consider of what I *have* to do, and *can* do. And Mr. Lovelace's insolence will make me go very home with myself. Not that I think I can conquer my aversion to Mr. Solmes. I am sure I cannot. But, if I absolutely break with Mr. Lovelace, and give my friends convincing proofs of it, who knows but they will restore me to their favour, and let their views in relation to the other man go off by degrees? — Or, at least, that I may be safe till my cousin Morden arrives: to whom I think I will write; and the rather, as Mr. Lovelace has assured me, that my friends have written to him to make good their side of the question.

But, with all my courage, I am exceedingly apprehensive about the Tuesday next, and of what may result from my stedfastness; for stedfast I am sure I shall be. They are resolved, I am told, to try every means to induce me to comply with what they are determined upon. And I am resolved to do all I can to avoid what they would force me to do. A dreadful contention between parents and child! — Each hoping to leave the other without excuse, whatever the consequence may be.

What can I do? Advise me, my dear. Something is strangely wrong somewhere! to make parents, the most indulgent till now, seem cruel in a child's eye; and a daughter, till within these few weeks, thought unexceptionably dutiful, appear, in their judgment, a rebel! — O my ambitious and violent brother! What may he have to answer for to both!

Be pleased to remember, my dear, that your last favour was dated on Saturday. This is Wednesday: and none of mine have been taken away since. Don't let me want *your* advice. My situation is extremely difficult. — But I am sure you love me still: and not the less on *that* account. Adieu, my beloved friend.

CL. HARLOWE.

LETTER LXV.

Miss Howe to Miss Clarissa Harlowe.

Thursday morning, day-break, March 30.

AN accident, and not remissness, has occasioned my silence.

My mother was sent for on Sunday night by her cousin Larkin, whom I mentioned in one of my former, and who was extremely earnest to see her.

This poor woman was always afraid of death, and was one of those weak persons who imagine that the making of their will must be an undoubted forerunner of it.

She had always said, when urged to the necessary work, that whenever she made it, she should not live long after; and one would think, imagined she was under an obligation to prove her words: for, though she had been long bed-rid, and was, in a manner, worn out before, yet she thought herself better, till she was persuaded to make it: and from that moment, remembering what she used to prognosticate (her *fears helping on what she feared*, as is often the case, particularly in the small-pox) grew worse; and had it in her head once to burn her will, in hopes to grow better upon it.

She sent my mother word, that the doctors had given her over: but that she could not die till she saw her. I told my mother, that if she wished her a chance for recovery, she should not, for *that* reason, go. But go she would; and, what was worse, would make me go with her; and that, at an hour's warning; for she said nothing of it to me, till she was rising in the morning *early*, resolving to return *at night*. Had there been more time for argumentation, to be sure I had not gone; but as it was, there was a kind of necessity that my preparation to obey her, should, in a manner, accompany her command. — A command so much out of the way, on such a solemn occasion! And this I represented: but to no purpose: there never was such a contradicting girl in the world — *my* wisdom always made *her* a fool! — But she *would* be obliged *this time*, proper or improper.

I have but one way of accounting for this sudden whim of my

mother; and that is this — She had a mind to accept of Mr. Hickman's offer to escort her! — And I verily believe [I wish I were quite sure of it] had a mind to oblige him with *my* company — as far as I know, to keep me out of *worse.*

For, would you believe it? — As sure as you are alive, she is afraid for her favourite Hickman, because of the long visit your Lovelace, though so much by accident, made me in her absence, last time she was at the same place. I hope, my dear, *you are* not jealous too. But indeed I now-and-then, when she teazes me with praises which Hickman cannot deserve, in return fall to praising those qualities and personalities in Lovelace, which the other never will have. Indeed I do love to teaze a little bit, that I do. — My mamma's girl — I had like to have said.

As you know she is as passionate, as I am pert, you will not wonder to be told, that we generally fall out on these occasions. She flies from me, at the long run. It would be undutiful in me to leave her *first* — and then I get an opportunity to pursue our *correspondence.*

For, now I am rambling, let me tell you, that she does not much favour *that;* — for *two* reasons, I believe: — one that I don't show her all that passes between us; the other, that she thinks I harden your mind against your *duty*, as it is called. And with *her,* for a reason at *home,* as I have hinted more than once, parents cannot do wrong; children cannot oppose, and be right. This obliges me now-and-then to *steal* an hour, as I may say, and not let her know how I am employed.

You may guess from what I have written, how averse I was to comply with this unreasonable stretch of motherly authority — but it came to be a *test of duty;* so I was obliged to yield, though with a full persuasion of being in the right.

I have always your reproofs upon these occasions: in your late letters stronger than ever. A good reason why, you'll say, because more deserved than ever. I thank you kindly for your correction. I hope to make *correction* of it — but let me tell you, that your stripes, whether deserved or not, have made me sensible deeper than the skin — but of this another time.

It was Monday afternoon before we reached the old lady's house. That fiddling, parading fellow [you know who I mean] made us wait for him two hours! and I to go a journey I disliked, only for the sake of having a little more tawdry upon his housings; which he had hurried his sadler to put on, to make him look fine, being to escort his dear Mrs. Howe and her fair daughter. I told him, that I supposed he was afraid, that the double solemnity in the case (that of the visit to a dying woman, and that of his own countenance) would give him the appearance of an *undertaker;* to avoid which, he ran into as bad an extreme, and I doubted would be taken for a *mountebank*.

The man was confounded. He took it as strongly as if his conscience gave assent to the justice of the remark; otherwise he would have borne it better; for he is used enough to this sort of treatment. I thought he would have cried. I have heretofore observed, that on *this* side of the contract, he seems to be a mighty meek sort of creature. — And though I should like it in him *hereafter*, perhaps, yet I can't help despising him a little in my heart for it *now*. I believe, my dear, we all love your blustering fellows best; could we but direct the bluster, and bid it roar when, and at whom we pleased.

The poor man looked at my mother. She was so angry (my airs upon it, and my opposition to the journey, having all helped) that for half the way she would not speak to me. And when she did, it was, I wish I had not brought you! You know not what it is to condescend. It is *my* fault, not Mr. *Hickman*'s, that you are here so much against your will. Have you no eyes for this side of the chariot?

And then he fared the better from *her*, as he always does, for faring worse from *me*: for there was, how do you *now*, sir? And how do you *now*, Mr. Hickman? as he ambled now on this side of the chariot, now on that, stealing a prim look at me; *her* head half out of the chariot, kindly smiling as if married to the man but a fortnight herself: while I always saw something to divert myself on the side of the chariot where the honest man was not, were it but old Robin at a distance, on his Roan Keffel.

Our courtship-days, they say, are our best days. Favour destroys courtship. Distance increases it. Its essence is distance. And to see how familiar these men wretches grow upon a smile; what an awe they are struck into when we frown; who would not make them stand off? Who would not enjoy a power, that is to be so short-lived?

Don't chide me one bit for this, my dear. It is in nature. I can't help it. Nay, for that matter, I love it, and wish not to help it. So spare your gravity, I beseech you, on this subject. I set not up for a perfect character. The man will bear it. And what need *you* care? My mother overbalances all he suffers: and if he thinks himself unhappy, he ought never to be otherwise.

Then did he not deserve a fit of the sullens, think you, to make us lose our dinner for his parade, since in so short a journey my mother would not bate, and lose the opportunity of coming back that night, had the old lady's condition permitted it? To say nothing of being the cause, that my mamma was in the glout with her poor daughter all the way.

At our alighting I gave him another dab; but it was but a little one. Yet the manner and the air, made up (as I intended they should) for that defect. My mother's hand was kindly put into his, with a simpering altogether bridal; and with another how do you now, sir? — All his plump muscles were in motion, and a double charge of care and obsequiousness fidgeted up his whole form, when he offered to me his officious palm. My mother, when I was a girl, always bid me hold up my head. I just then remembered her commands, and was dutiful — I never held up my head so high. With an averted supercilious eye, and a rejecting hand, half flourishing — I have no need of help, sir! — You are in my way.

He ran back as if on wheels: with a face excessively mortified: I had thoughts else to have followed the too gentle touch, with a declaration, that I had as many hands and feet as himself. But this would have been telling him a piece of news, as to the latter, that I hope he had not the presumption to guess at.

* * *

We found the poor woman, as we thought, at the last gasp. Had we come *sooner*, we could not have got away, as we intended, that night. You see I am for excusing the man all I can; and yet, I assure you, I have not so much as a *conditional liking* to him. My mother sat up most part of the night, expecting every hour would have been her poor cousin's last. I bore her company till two.

I never saw the approaches of death in a grown person before; and was extremely shocked. Death, to one in health, is a very terrible thing. We pity the person for what *she* suffers: and we pity ourselves for what *we* must some time hence in like sort suffer; and so are *doubly* affected.

She held out till *Tuesday* morning, eleven. As she had told my mother that she had left her an executrix, and her and me rings and mourning; we were employed all that day in matters of the will [by which, by the way, my cousin Jenny Fynnet is handsomely provided for]; so that it was Wednesday morning early, before we could set out on our return.

It is true, we got home (having no housings to stay for) by noon: but though I sent Robin away before he dismounted (who brought me back a whole packet, down to the same Wednesday noon) yet was I really so fatigued, and shocked, as I must own, at the hard death of the old lady; my mother likewise (who has no reason to dislike this world) being indisposed from the same occasion; that I could not set about writing time enough for Robin's return that night.

But having recruited my spirits, my mother having also had a good night, I arose with the dawn, to write this, and get it dispatched time enough for your breakfast airing; that your suspense might be as short as possible.

* * *

I will soon follow this with another. I will employ a person directly to find out how Lovelace behaves himself at his inn. Such a busy spirit must be traceable.

But, perhaps, my dear, you are indifferent *now* about him or his employments; for this request was made before he *mortally* offended you. Nevertheless, I will have enquiry made. The result, it is very probable, will be of use to confirm you in your present unforgiving temper. — And yet, if the *poor* man [shall I pity him for *you*, my dear?] should be deprived of the greatest blessing any man on earth can receive, and to which he has the presumption, with so little merit, to aspire; he will have run great risks; caught great colds; hazarded fevers; sustained the highest indignities; braved the inclemencies of skies, and all for — *nothing!* — Will not this move your *generosity* (if nothing else) in his favour! — Poor Mr. Lovelace! —

I would occasion no throb; nor half throb; no flash of sensibility, like lightning darting in, and as soon suppressed, by a discretion that no one of the sex ever before could give such an example of. — I *would not*, I say; and yet, for a trial of *you* to *yourself*, rather than as an impertinent overflow of raillery in your friend, as moneytakers try a suspected guinea by the *sound*, let me on such a supposition, sound *you* by repeating, *Poor Mr. Lovelace!* —

And now, my dear, how is it with you? How do you now, as my mother says to Mr. Hickman, when her pert daughter has made him look sorrowful?

LETTER LXVI.

Mr. Hickman to Mrs. Howe.

MADAM, Wednesday, March 29.

IT is with infinite regret that I think myself obliged, by pen and ink, to repeat my apprehensions, that it is impossible for me ever to obtain a share in the affections of your beloved daughter. O that it were not too evident to every one, as well as to myself, even to our very servants, that my love for her, and my assiduities, expose me rather to her scorn [forgive me, madam, the hard word!] than to the treatment due to a man whose proposals have met with your approbation, and who loves her above all the women in the world.

Well might the merit of my passion be doubted, if like Mr. Solmes to the truly admirable Miss Clarissa Harlowe. I could continue my addresses to Miss Howe's distaste. Yet what will not the discontinuance cost me!

Give me leave, nevertheless, dearest, worthiest lady, to repeat what I told you, on Monday night, at Mrs. Larkin's, with a hearteven bursting with grief, that I wanted not the treatment of that day to convince me, that I am not, nor ever can be, the object of Miss Howe's voluntary favour. What hopes can there be, that a lady will ever esteem as a husband, the man, whom as a lover, she despises? Will not every act of obligingness from such a one, be construed an unmanly tameness of spirit, and entitle him the more to her disdain? — My heart is full: forgive me if I say, that Miss Howe's treatment of me does no credit either to her education, or fine sense.

Since then it is too evident, that she cannot esteem me; and since, as I have heard it justly observed by the excellent Miss Clarissa Harlowe, that love is not a voluntary passion; would it not be ungenerous to subject the dear daughter to the displeasure of a mother so justly fond of her; and you, madam, while you are so good as to interest yourself in my favour, to uneasiness? And why, were I to be even sure, at last, of succeeding by means of your kind partiality to me, should I wish to make the best-beloved of my soul unhappy; since mutual must be our happiness, or misery for life the consequence to both?

My best wishes will for ever attend the dear, the ever dear lady! May her nuptials be happy! They must be so, if she marry the man she can honour with her love. Yet I will say, that whoever be the happy, the thrice happy man, he never can love her with a passion more ardent and more sincere than mine.

Accept, dear madam, of my most grateful thanks for a distinction that has been the only support of my presumption in the address I am obliged, as utterly hopeless, to discontinue. A distinction, on which (and not on my own merits) I had entirely relied; but which, I find, can avail me nothing. To the last hour of my life, it will give me pleasure to think, that had your favour, your recommendation, been of sufficient weight to conquer what seems to be an invincible aversion, I had been the happiest of men.

I am, dear madam, with inviolable respect,
Your ever obliged and
faithful humble servant,
CHARLES HICKMAN.

LETTER LXVII.

Mrs. Howe to Charles Hickman, Esq.

Thursday, March 30.

I CANNOT but say, Mr. Hickman, but you have cause to be dissatisfied — to be out of humour — to be displeased — with Nancy — But, upon my word; but indeed — What shall I say? — Yet this I will say, that you *good* young gentlemen know nothing at all of our sex. Shall I tell you — But why should I? And yet I will say, that if Nancy did not think well of you in the main, she is too generous to treat you so freely as she does. — Don't you think she has courage enough to tell me, she would not see you, and to refuse at any time seeing you, as she knows on what account you come, if she had not something in her head favourable to you? — Fie! that I am forced to say thus much in writing, when I have hinted it to you twenty and twenty times by word of mouth?

But if you are so indifferent, Mr. Hickman — if you think you can part with her for her skittish tricks — if *my* interest in your favour — why, Mr. Hickman, I must tell you, that my Nancy is worth bearing with. If she be *foolish* — what is that owing to? — Is it not to her *wit?* Let me tell you, sir, you cannot have the convenience without the inconvenience. What workman loves not a sharp tool to work with? But is there not more danger from a sharp tool, than from a blunt one? And what workman will throw away a sharp tool, because it may cut his fingers? Wit may be likened to a sharp tool. And there is something very pretty in wit, let me tell you. Often and often have I been forced to smile at her arch turns upon me, when I could have beat her for them. And pray, don't I bear a great deal from her? — And why? Because I love her. And would you not wish me to judge of your love for her by my own? And would not you bear with her? — Don't you love her (what though with another sort of love?) as well as I do? I do assure you, sir, that if I thought you did not — well, but it is plain that you don't — and is it plain that you don't? — Well, then, you must do as you think best.

Well might the merit of your passion be doubted, you say, if, like Mr. Solmes — Fiddle-faddle! — Why, you are a captious man, I think! — Has Nancy been so plain in her repulses of you as Miss Clary Harlowe has been to Mr. Solmes? — Does Nancy love any man better than you, although she may not shew so much love to you as you wish for? — if she did, let me tell you, she would have let us all hear of it. — What idle comparisons then!

But it may be you are tired out. It may be you have seen somebody else — it may be you would wish to change mistresses with that gay wretch Mr. Lovelace. It may be too, that, in that case, Nancy would not be sorry to change lovers. — The *truly admirable* Miss Clarissa Harlowe? And the *excellent* Miss Clarissa Harlowe! — Good lack! — But take care, Mr. Hickman, that you do not praise any woman living, let her be as admirable and as excellent as she will, above your own mistress. No polite man will do that, surely. And take care, too, that you do not make her or me think you are in earnest in your anger — just though it may be, as anger only — I would not for a thousand pounds, that Nancy should know that you can so easily part with her, if you have the love for her which you declare you have. Be sure, if you are not absolutely determined, that you do not so much as whisper the contents of this your letter to your own heart, as I may say.

Her treatment of you, you say, does no credit either to her education or fine sense. Very home put, truly! Nevertheless, so say I. But is not hers the disgrace more than yours? I can assure you, that every body blames her for it. And *why* do they blame her? — Why? Because they think you merit better treatment at her hands: and is not this to your credit? Who but pities *you*, and blames *her?* Do the servants, who, as you observe, see her skittish airs, disrespect you for them? Do they not, at such times, look concerned for you? Are they not then doubly officious in their respects and services to you? — I have observed with pleasure, that they are.

But you are afraid you shall be thought tame, perhaps, when married. That you shall not be thought *manly* enough, I warrant! — And this was poor Mr. Howe's fear. And many a tug did this lordly fear cost us both, God knows! — Many more than needed, I am sure: — and more than ought to have been, had he known how to *bear and forbear;* as is the duty of those who pretend to have most sense, the woman or the man?

Well, sir, and now what remains, if you really love Nancy so well as you say you do? — Why, I leave that to you. You may, if you please, come to breakfast with me in the morning. But with no *full heart*, nor resenting looks, I advise you; except you can brave it out. That have I, when provoked, done many a time with my *husband*, but never did I get any thing by it with my *daughter!* much less will you. Of which, for your observation, I thought fit to advise you.

As from
Your friend,
ANNABELLA HOWE.

LETTER LXVIII.

Miss Howe to Miss Clarissa Harlowe.

Thursday morning.

I WILL now take some notice of your last favour. But being so far behind-hand with you, must be brief.

In the first place, as to your reproofs, thus shall I discharge myself of that part of my subject. Is it likely, think you, that I should avoid deserving them now-and-then, occasionally, when I admire the manner in which you give me our rebukes, and love you the better for them? And when you are so well *entitled* to give them? For what faults can *you* possibly have, unless your relations are so kind as to find you a *few* to keep their *many* in countenance? — But they are as kind to *me* in this, as to *you;* for I may venture to affirm, that any one who should read *your* letters, and would say you were *right*, would not on reading *mine* condemn me for being *quite wrong*.

Your resolution not to leave your father's house is right — if you can stay in it, and avoid being Solmes's wife.

I think you answered Solmes's letter, as *I* should have answered it. — Will you not compliment me and yourself at once, by saying, *that* was right?

You have, in your letters to your uncle and the rest, done all that you ought to do. You are wholly guiltless of the consequence, be it what it will. To offer to give up your estate! — That would not I have done! You see this offer staggered them: they took time to consider of it. They made my heart ache in the time they took. I was afraid they would have taken you at your word: and so, but for shame, and for fear of Lovelace, I dare say they would. You are too noble for them. This, I repeat, is an offer *I* would not have made. Let me beg of you, my dear, never to repeat the temptation to them.

I freely own to you, that their usage of you upon it, and Lovelace's different treatment of you * in his letter received at the same time, would have made *me* his, past redemption. The deuce take the man I was going to say, for not having had so much regard to his character and morals, as would have entirely justified such a step in a CLARISSA, persecuted as she is!

I wonder not at your appointment with him. I may further touch upon some part of this subject by-and-by.

Pray — pray — I pray you now, my dearest friend, contrive to send your Betty Barnes to me! — Does the Coventry Act extend to women, know ye? — The *least* I will do, shall be, to send her home well soused in and dragged through our deepest horsepond. I'll engage, if I get her hither, that she will keep the anniversary of her deliverance as long as she lives.

I wonder not at Lovelace's saucy answer, saucy as it really is.** If he loves you as he ought, he must be vexed at so great a disappointment. The man must have been a detestable hypocrite, I think, had he not shewn his vexation. Your expectations of such a

* See p. 283—285.
** See p. 294—295.

Christian command of temper in him, in a disappointment of this nature especially, are too early by almost half a century in a man of his constitution. But nevertheless I am very far from blaming you for your resentment.

I shall be all impatience to know how this matter ends between you and him. But a *few inches of brick-wall* between you so lately; and now such *mountains?* — And you think to hold it? — May be so!

You see, you say, that the temper he shewed in his preceding letter was not *natural* to him. And did you before think it *was?* Wretched creepers and insinuators! Yet when opportunity serves, as insolent encroachers! — This very Hickman, I make no doubt, would be as saucy as your Lovelace, if he dared. He has not half the arrogant bravery of the other, and can better hide his horns; that's all. But whenever he has the power, depend upon it, he will *butt* at one as valiantly as the other.

If ever I should be persuaded to have him, I shall watch how the obsequious lover *goes-off;* and how the imperative husband *comes upon him;* in short, how he *ascends*, and how I *descend*, in the matrimonial wheel, never to take my turn again, but by fits and starts, like the feeble struggles of a sinking state for its dying liberty.

All good-natured men are passionate, says Mr. Lovelace. A pretty plea to a beloved object in the plenitude of her power! As much as to say, "Greatly as I value you, madam, I will not take pains to curb my passions to oblige you."—Methinks I should be glad to hear from Mr. Hickman such a plea for good-nature as this.

Indeed, we are too apt to make allowances for such tempers as *early* indulgence has made uncontroulable; and therefore habitually evil. But if a boisterous temper, when under *obligation*, is to be thus allowed for, what, when the tables are turned, will it expect? You know a husband, who, I fancy, had some of these early allowances made for him: and you see that neither himself nor any body else is the happier for it.

The suiting of the tempers of two persons who are to come together, is a great matter: and yet there should be boundaries fixed between them, by consent as it were, beyond which neither should go: and each should hold the other to it; or there would probably be encroachment in both. To illustrate my assertion by a very high, and by a more manly (as some would think it) than womanly instance—If the boundaries of the three estates that constitute our political union were not known, and occasionally asserted, what would become of the prerogatives and privileges of each? The two branches of the legislature would encroach upon each other; and the executive power would swallow up both.

But if two persons of discretion, you'll say, come together —

Ay, my dear, that's true: but, if none but persons of discretion were to marry — and would it not surprise you if I were to advance, that the persons of discretion are generally single? — Such persons are apt to consider too much, to resolve. — Are not you and I complimented as such? — And would either of us marry, if the fellows, and our friends, would let us alone?

But to the former point; — had Lovelace made his addresses to me (unless indeed I had been taken with a liking for him *more* than *conditional*) I would have forbid him, upon the first *passionate* instance of his *good-nature*, as he calls it, ever to see me more; "thou must bear with me, honest friend, might I have said [had I condescended to say any thing to him] an hundred times more than this: — be gone therefore! — I bear with no passions that are predominant to that thou hast pretended for me!"

But to one of your mild and gentle temper, it would be all one, were you married, whether the man were a Lovelace or a Hickman in his spirit. — You are so obediently principled, that perhaps you would have told a mild man that he must not *entreat*, but *command;* and that it was beneath him not to exact from you the obedience you had so solemnly vowed to him at the altar. — I know of old, my dear, your meek regard to that little piddling part of the marriage vow which some prerogative-monger foisted into the office, to make that a *duty*, which he knew was not a *right*.

Our way of training up, you say, makes us need the protection of the brave. Very true: and how extremely brave and gallant is it, that this brave man will free us from all insults but those which will go nearest to our hearts; that is to say, his own!

How artfully has Lovelace, in the abstract you give me of one of his letters, calculated to your meridian! *Generous spirits hate compulsion!* — He is certainly a deeper creature by much than once we thought him. He knows, as you intimate, that his own wild pranks cannot be concealed; and so owns just enough to palliate (because it teaches you not to be surprised at) any new one that may come to your ears; and then, truly, he is, however faulty, a mighty *ingenuous* man: and by no means an *hypocrite*: a character the most odious of all others, to our sex, in a lover, and the least to be forgiven, were it only because, when detected, it makes us doubt the justice of those praises which we are willing to believe he thought to be our due.

By means of this supposed *ingenuity*, Lovelace obtains a praise, instead of a merited dispraise; and, like an absolved confessionaire, wipes off as he goes along one score, to begin another: for an eye favourable to him will not see his faults through a magnifying glass; nor will a woman, willing to *hope the best*, forbear to impute to ill-will and prejudice all that charity can make so imputable. And if she even give credit to such of the unfavourable imputations as may be too flagrant to be doubted, she will be very apt to take in the *future hope*, which he inculcates, and which to question would be to question her own power, and perhaps *merit:* and thus may a woman be inclined to make a *slight*, even a *fancied* merit, atone for the most *glaring* vice.

I have a reason, a new one, for this preachment upon a text you have given me. But, till I am better informed, I will not explain myself. If it come out, as I shrewdly suspect it will, the man, my dear, is a devil; and you must rather think of — I protest I had like to have said *Solmes* than him.

But let this be as it will, shall I tell you, how, after all his offences, he may creep in with you again?

I will. Thus then: it is but to claim for himself the *good-natured character:* and this, granted, will blot out the fault of *passionate* insolence: and so he will have nothing to do, but this hour to accustom you to insult; the next, to bring you to forgive him, upon his submission: the consequence must be, that he will by this teazing break your resentment all to pieces: and then, a little *more* of the insult, and a little *less* of the submission, on his part, will go down, till nothing else but the *first* will be seen, and not a bit of the *second:* you will then be afraid to provoke so offensive a spirit; and at last will be brought so *prettily* and so *audibly*, to pronounce the little reptile word OBEY, that it will do one's heart good to hear you. The *Muscovite* wife then takes place of the *managed* mistress. — And if you doubt the progression, be pleased, my dear, to take your mother's judgment upon it.

But no more of this just now. Your situation is become too critical to permit me to dwell upon these sort of topics. And yet this is but an *affected levity* with me. My heart, as I have heretofore said, is a sincere sharer in all your distresses. My sun-shine darts but through a drizzly cloud. My eye, were you to see it, when it seems to you so *gladdened*, as you mentioned in a former, is *more* than ready to overflow, even at the very passages perhaps upon which you impute to me the *archness* of *exultation*.

But now the unheard-of cruelty and perverseness of some of your friends [*relations*, I should say — I am always blundering thus!] the strange determinedness of others; your present quarrel with Lovelace; and your approaching interview with Solmes, from which you are right to apprehend a great deal; are such considerable circumstances in your story, that it is fit they should engross all my attention.

You ask me to advise you how to behave upon Solmes's visit. I *cannot* for my life. I know they expect a great deal from it: you had not else had your long day complied with. All I will say is, that if Solmes cannot be prevailed for, now, that Lovelace has so much offended you, he never will. When the interview is over, I doubt not but that I shall have reason to say, that all you did, that all you said, was right, and could not be better; yet, if I don't think so, I won't say so; that I promise you.

Only let me advise you to pull up a spirit, even to your uncle, if there be occasion. Resent the vile and foolish treatment you meet with, in which he has taken so large a share, and make him ashamed of it, if you can.

I know not, upon recollection, but this interview may be a good thing for you, however designed. For when Solmes sees (if that be to *be* so) that it is impossible he should succeed with you; and your relations see it too; the one must, I think, recede, and the other come to terms with you, upon offers, that it is my opinion, will go hard enough with you to comply with; when the *still* harder are dispensed with.

There are several passages in your last letters, as well as in your former, which authorize me to say this. But it would be unseasonable to touch this subject further just now.

But, upon the whole, I have no patience to see you thus made the sport of your brother's and sister's cruelty: for what, after *so much* steadiness on your part, in *so many* trials, can be their hope? *Except indeed it be to drive you to extremity, and to ruin you in the opinion of your uncles, as well as father.*

I urge you by all means to send out of their reach all the letters and papers you would not have them see. Methinks, I would wish you to deposit likewise a parcel of clothes, linen, and the like, before your interview with Solmes; lest you should not have an opportunity for it afterwards. Robin shall fetch it away on the first orders, by day or by night.

I am in hopes to procure from my mother, if things come to extremity, leave for you to be privately with us.

I will condition to be good-humoured, and even *kind*, to use favourite, if she will shew me an indulgence that shall make me serviceable to mine.

This alternative has been a good while in my head. But as your foolish uncle has so strangely attached my mother to their views, I cannot promise that I shall succeed as I wish.

Do not absolutely despair, however. What though the contention will be between *woman* and *woman?* I fancy I shall be able to manage it, by the help of a little *female perseverance.* Your quarrel with Lovelace, if it continue, will strengthen my hands. And the offers you made in your answer to your uncle Harlowe's letter of Sunday night last, *duly dwelt upon*, must add force to my pleas.

I depend upon your forgiveness of all the perhaps unseasonable flippancies of your naturally too lively, yet most sincerely sympathizing,

ANNA HOWE.

LETTER LXIX.

Miss Clarissa Harlowe to Miss Howe.

Friday, March 31.

You have very kindly accounted for your silence. People in misfortunes are always in doubt. They are too apt to turn even unavoidable accidents into slights and neglects; especially in those whose favourable opinion they wish to preserve.

I am sure I ought evermore to exempt my Anna Howe from the supposed possibility of her becoming one of those who bask only in the sunshine of a friend: but nevertheless her friendship is too precious to me, not to doubt my own merits on the one hand, and not to be anxious for the preservation of it, on the other.

You so generously give me liberty to chide you that I am afraid of taking it, because I could sooner mistrust my own judgment, than that of a beloved friend, whose ingenuousness in acknowledging an *imputed* error seems to set her above the commission of a *wilful* one. This makes me half afraid to ask you, if you think you are not too cruel, too *ungenerous* shall I say? In your behaviour to a man who loves you so dearly, and is so worthy and so sincere a man?

Only it is by You, or I should be ashamed to be outdone in that true magnanimity, which makes one thankful for the wounds given by a true friend. I believe I was guilty of a petulance, which nothing but my uneasy situation can excuse; if *that* can. I am almost afraid to beg of you, and yet I repeatedly *do*, to give way to that charming spirit, whenever it rises to your pen, which smiles, yet goes to the quick of my fault. What patient shall be afraid of a probe in so delicate a hand? — I say, I am almost afraid to pray you to give way to it, for fear you should, for that very reason, restrain it. For the edge may be taken off, if it does not make the subject of its raillery wince a little. *Permitted* or *desired* satire may be apt, in a generous satirist, mending as it raillies, to turn too soon into panegyric. Yours is intended to instruct; and though it bites, it pleases at the same time: no fear of a wound's rankling or festering by so delicate a point as you carry; not envenomed by *personality*, not intending to expose, or ridicule, or exasperate. The most admired of our moderns know nothing of this art: why? because it must be founded in good-nature, and directed by a right heart. The *man*, not the *fault*, is generally the subject of *their* satire: and were it to be *just*, how should it be *useful*; how should it answer any good purpose; when every gash (for their weapon is a broadsword, not a lancet) lets in the air of public ridicule, and exasperates where it should heal? Spare me not therefore because I am your friend. For *that* very reason spare me not. I may *feel* your edge, fine as it is. I may be pained: you would lose your end if I were not: but after the first sensibility (as I have said more than once before) I will love you the better, and my amended heart shall be all yours: and it will then be more worthy to be yours.

You have taught me what to say to, and what to think of, Mr. Lovelace. You have, by agreeable anticipation, let me know how it is probable he will apply to me to be excused. I will lay every thing before you that shall pass on the occasion, if he *do* apply, that I may take your advice, when it can come in time; and when it cannot, that I may receive your correction, or approbation, as I may happen to merit either. — Only one thing must be allowed for me; that whatever course I shall be *permitted* or be *forced* to steer, I must be considered as a person out of her own direction. Tost to and fro by the high winds of passionate control (and, as I think, unreasonable severity), I behold the desired port, the *single state*, into which I would fain steer; but am kept off by the foaming billows of a brother's and sister's envy, and by the raging winds of a supposed invaded authority; while I see in Lovelace, the rocks on one hand, and in Solmes, the sands on the other; and tremble, lest I should split upon the former, or strike upon the latter.

But you, my better pilot, to what a charming hope do you bid me aspire, if things come to extremity! — I will not, as you caution me, too much depend upon your success with your mother in my favour; for well I know her high notions of implicit duty in a child: but yet I will *hope* too; because her seasonable protection may save me perhaps from a greater rashness: and in this case she shall direct me in all my ways: I will do nothing but by her orders, and by her advice and yours: Lot see any body: not write to any body: nor shall any living soul, but by her direction and yours, know where I am. In any cottage place me, I will never stir out, unless, disguised as your servant, I am now and then permitted an evening walk with you: and this private protection to be granted for no longer time than till my cousin Morden comes; which, as I hope, cannot be long.

I am afraid I must not venture to take the hint you give me, to deposit some of my clothes; although I will some of my linen, as well as papers.

I will tell you why — Betty had for some time been very curious about my wardrobe, whenever I took out any of my things before her.

Observing this, I once, on taking one of my garden airings, left my keys in the locks; and on my return surprised the creature with her hand upon the keys, as if shutting the door.

She was confounded at my sudden coming back. I took no notice: but, on her retiring, I found my clothes were not in the usual order.

I doubted not, upon this, that her curiosity was owing to the orders she had received; and being afraid they would abridge me of my airings, if their suspicions were not obviated, it has ever since been my custom (among other contrivances) not only to leave my keys in the locks; but to employ the wench now and then in taking out my clothes, suit by suit, on pretence of preventing their being rumpled or creased, and to see that the flowered silver suit did not tarnish; sometimes declaredly to give myself employment, having little else to do: with which employment (superadded to the delight taken by the low as well as by the high of our sex in seeing fine clothes) she seemed always, I thought, as well pleased as if it answered one of the offices she had in charge.

To this, and to the confidence they have in a spy so diligent, and to their knowing, that I have not one confidante in a family in which nevertheless I believe every servant loves me; nor have attempted to make one; I suppose, I owe the freedom I enjoy of my airings: and perhaps (finding I make no movements towards going away) they are the more secure, that I shall at last be prevailed upon to comply with their measures: since they must think, that, otherwise, they give me provocation enough to take some rash step in order to free myself from a treatment so disgraceful; and which [God forgive me, if I judge amiss] *I am afraid my brother* and sister would not be sorry to drive me to take.

If therefore such a step should become necessary (which I yet hope will not) I must be contented to go away with the clothes I shall have on at the time. My custom to be dressed for the day, as soon as breakfast is over, when I have had no household employments to prevent me, will make such a step (if I am forced to take it) less suspected. And the linen I shall deposit, in pursuance of your kind hint, cannot be missed.

This custom, although a prisoner (as I may too truly say), and neither visited nor visiting, I continue. We owe to ourselves, and to our *sex*, you know, to be always neat; and never to be surprised in a way we should be pained to be seen in.

Besides, people in adversity (which is the state of trial of every good quality) should endeavour to preserve laudable customs, that, if sunshine return, they may not be losers by their trial.

Does it not, moreover, manifest a firmness of mind, in an unhappy person, to keep hope alive? To *hope* for better days, is half to *deserve* them: for could we have just ground for such a hope, if we did not resolve to deserve what that hope bids us aspire to? — Then who shall befriend a person who forsakes herself?

These are reflections by which I sometimes endeavour to support myself.

I know you don't despise my *grave airs*, although (with a view no doubt to irradiate my mind in my misfortunes) you rally me upon them. Every body has not your talent of introducing serious and important lessons, in such a happy manner as at once to delight and instruct.

What a multitude of contrivances may not young people fall upon, if the mind be not engaged by acts of kindness and condescension! I am not used by my friends of late as I always used their servants.

When I was entrusted with the family management, I always found it right, as well in policy as generosity, to repose a trust in them. Not to seem to expect or depend upon justice from them, is in a manner to bid them take opportunities, whenever they offer, to be unjust.

Mr. Solmes (to expatiate a little on this low, but not unuseful subject) in his more trifling solicitudes would have had a sorry key-keeper in me. Were I mistress of a family, I would not either take to myself, or give to servants, the pain of keeping those I had reason to suspect. People low in station have often minds not sordid. Nay, I have sometimes thought, that (even take number for number) there are more *honest low people*, than *honest high*. In the one, honesty is their *chief* pride. In the other, the love of power, of grandeur, of pleasure, mislead; and that and their ambition induce a paramount pride, which too often swallows up the more laudable one.

Many of the former would scorn to deceive a confidence. But I have seen, among the most ignorant of their class, a susceptibility of resentment, if their honesty has been suspected: and have more than once been forced to put a servant *right*, whom I have heard say, that, although she valued herself upon her *honesty*, no master or mistress should suspect her for nothing.

How far has the comparison I had in my head, between my friends' treatment of *me*, and my treatment of their *servants*, carried me!—But we always allowed ourselves to expatiate on such subjects, whether low or high, as might tend to enlarge our minds, or mend our management, whether notional or practical, and whether such expatiating respected our present, or might respect our probable future situations.

What I was principally leading to, was to tell you, how ingenious I am in my contrivances and pretences to blind my gaoleress, and to take off the jealousy of her principals on my going down so often into the garden and poultry-yard. People suspiciously treated are never I believe at a loss for invention. Sometimes I want *air*, and am better the moment I am out of my chamber.—Sometimes *spirits;* and then my bantams and pheasants or the cascade divert me; the former, by their inspiriting liveliness; the latter, more solemnly, by its echoing dashings, and hollow murmurs.—Sometimes solitude is of all things my wish; and the awful silence of the night, the spangled element, and the rising and setting sun, how promotive of contemplation!—Sometimes, when I intend nothing, and expect no letters, I am officious to take Betty with me; and at others, bespeak her attendance when I know she is otherwise employed, and cannot give it me.

These more capital artifices I branch out into lesser ones, without number. Yet *all* have not only the face of truth, but are real truth; although not my principal motive. How prompt a thing is *will!*—What impediments does *dislike* furnish!—How swiftly, through every difficulty, do we move with the one!—How tardily with the other!—Every trifling obstruction weighing us down, as if lead were fastened to our feet!

Friday morning, eleven o'clock.

I have already made up my parcel of linen. My heart ached all the time I was employed about it: and still aches, at the thoughts of its being a necessary precaution.

When the parcel comes to your hands, as I hope it safely will, you will be pleased to open it. You will find in it two parcels sealed up; one of which contains the letters you have not yet seen; being those written since I left you: in the other are all the letters and copies of letters that have passed between you and me since I was last with you; with some other papers on subjects so much above me, that I cannot wish them to be seen by any body whose indulgence I am not so sure of, as I am of yours. If my judgment ripen with my years, perhaps I may review them.

Mrs. Norton used to say, from her reverend father, that youth was the time of life for *imagination* and *fancy* to work in: then, were a writer to lay by his works till *riper years* and *experience* should direct the fire rather to *glow*, than to *flame out;* something between both might perhaps be produced that would not displease a judicious eye.

In a third division, folded up separately, are all Mr. Lovelace's letters written to me since he was forbidden this house, and copies of my answers to them. I expect that you will break the seals of this parcel, and when you have perused them all, give me your free opinion of my conduct.

By the way, not a line from that man! — Not *one* line! — Wednesday I deposited mine. It remained there on Wednesday night. What time it was taken away yesterday, I cannot tell: for I did not concern myself about it, till towards night; and then it was not there. No return at ten this day. I suppose he is as much out of humour, as I. — With all my heart!

He may be mean enough, perhaps, if ever I should put it into his *power*, to avenge himself for the trouble he has had with me. — But that now, I dare say, I never shall.

I see what sort of a man the encroacher is. And I hope we are equally sick of one another. — My heart is *vexedly* easy, if I may so describe it. — *Vexedly* — because of the apprehended interview with Solmes, and the consequences it may be attended with: or else I should be *quite easy;* for I have not *deserved* the usage I receive: and could I be rid of Solmes, as I presume I am of Lovelace, *their* influence over my father, mother, and uncles, against me, could not hold.

The five guineas tied up in one corner of a handkerchief under the linen, I beg you will let pass as an acknowledgment for the trouble I give your trusty servant. You must not chide me for this. You know I cannot be easy unless I have my way in these little matters.

I was going to put up what little money I have, and some of my ornaments; but they are portable, and I cannot forget them. Besides, should they (suspecting me) desire to see any of the jewels, and were I not able to produce them, it would amount to a demonstration of an intention which would have a guilty appearance to them.

Friday, one o'clock, in the wood-house.

No letter yet from this man! I have luckily deposited my parcel, and have your letter of last night. If Robert take this without the parcel, pray let him return immediately for it. But he cannot miss it, I think; and must con-

clude that it is put there for him to take away. You may believe, from the contents of yours, that I shall immediately write again.
CLARISSA HARLOWE.

LETTER LXI.
Miss Howe to Miss Clarissa Harlowe.
Thursday night, March 30.

The fruits of my inquiry after your abominable wretch's behaviour and baseness at the paltry alehouse, which he calls an inn, prepare to hear.

Wrens and sparrows are not too ignoble a quarry for this villanous gos-hawk!— His assiduities; his watchings; his nightly risks; the inclement weather he journeys in; must not be all placed to your account. He has opportunities of making every thing light to him of that sort. A sweet pretty girl, I am told — Innocent till he went thither — Now! (ah! poor girl!) who knows what?

But just turned of seventeen! — His friend and brother rake (a man of humour and intrigue), as I am told, to share the social bottle with. And sometimes another disguised rake or two. No sorrow comes near their hearts. Be not disturbed, my dear, at his hoarseness! His pretty Betsy, his Rosebud, as the vile wretch calls her, can *hear* all he says.

He is very fond of her. They say she is innocent even yet — Her father, her grandmother, believe her to be so. He is to fortune her out to a young lover! — Ah! the poor young lover! — Ah! the poor simple girl!

Mr. Hickman tells me, that he heard in town, that he used to be often at plays, and at the Opera, with women; and every time with a different one — Ah! my sweet friend! — But I hope he is nothing to you, if all this were truth — But this intelligence, in relation to this poor girl, will do his business, if you had been ever so good friends before.

A vile wretch! Cannot such purity in pursuit, in view, restrain him? But I leave him to you! — There can be no hope of him. More of a fool, than of such a man. Yet I wish I may be able to snatch the poor young creature out of his villanous paws. I have laid a scheme to do so; if indeed she be hitherto innocent and heart free.

He appears to the people as a military man, in disguise, secreting himself on account of a duel fought in town; the adversary's life in suspense. They believe he is a great man. His friend passes for an inferior officer; upon a foot of freedom with him. He, accompanied by a third man, who is a sort of subordinate companion to the second. The wretch himself with but one servant.

O my dear! how pleasantly can these devils, as I must call them, pass their time, while our gentle bosoms heave with pity for their supposed sufferings for us!

* * *

I have sent for this girl and her father; and am just now informed that I shall see them. I will sift them thoroughly. I shall soon find out such a simple thing as this, if he has not corrupted her already — and if he has, I shall soon find that out too. — If more art than nature appears either in her or her father, I shall give them both up — but depend upon it, the girl's undone.

He is said to be fond of her. He places her at the upper end of his table. He sets her a-prattling. He keeps his friend at a distance from her. She prates away. He admires for nature all she says. Once was heard to call her charming little creature! An hundred has he called so no doubt. He puts her upon singing. He praises her wild note. — O, my dear, the girl's undone! — must be undone! — The man you know is LOVELACE.

Let 'em bring Wyerley to you, if they will have you married — any body but Solmes and Lovelace be yours! — So advises

Your
ANNA HOWE.

My dearest friend, consider this alehouse as his garrison: him as an enemy: his brother rakes as his assistants and abettors. Would not your brother, would not your uncles, tremble, if they knew how near them he is as they pass to and fro? — I am told, he is resolved you shall not be carried to your uncle Antony's. — What can you do with or without such an enterprising — Fill up the blank I leave. — I cannot find a word bad enough.

LETTER LXXI.

Miss Clarissa Harlowe to Miss Howe.

Friday, three o'clock.

You incense, alarm, and terrify me, at the same time — hasten, my dearest friend, hasten to me, what further intelligence you can gather about this vilest of men.

But never talk of innocence, of simplicity and this unhappy girl together. Must she not know, that such a man as that, dignified in his very aspect; and no disguise able to conceal his being of condition; must mean too much, when he places her at the upper end of his table, and calls her by such tender names? Would a girl, modest as simple, above seventeen, be set a singing at the pleasure of such a man as that? A stranger, and professedly in disguise! — Would her father and grandmother, if honest people, and careful of their simple girl, permit such freedoms?

Keep his friend at distance from her! — To be sure his *designs* are villanous, if they have not been already effected.

Warn, my dear, if not too late, the unthinking father of his child's danger. There cannot be a father in the world who would sell his child's virtue. No mother! — The poor thing!

I long to hear the result of your intelligence. You shall *see* the simple creature you tell me. — Let me know what sort of a girl she is. — A *sweet pretty girl!* you say. A *sweet* pretty *girl*, my dear! — They are sweet pretty words from your pen. But are they yours or *his* of her? — If she be so simple, if she have ease and nature in her manner, in her speech, and warbles prettily her *wild notes*, such a girl as that must engage such a profligate wretch (as now indeed I doubt this man is), accustomed, perhaps, to town women, and their confident ways. Must *deeply*, and for a *long season*, engage him: since perhaps when her innocence is departed, she will endeavour by heart to supply the loss of the natural charms which now engage him.

Fine hopes of such a wretch's reformation! I would not, my dear, for the world, have any thing to say — but I need not make resolutions. I have not opened, nor will I open, his letter. — A sycophant creature! — with his hoarsenesses — got perhaps by a midnight revel, singing to his wild-note singer, and only increased in the coppice!

To be already on a foot! — In *his* esteem, I mean: for myself I despise him. I hate myself almost for writing so much about *him*, and of such a simpleton as *this sweet pretty girl*, as you call her: but no one can be either *sweet* or *pretty* that is not modest, that is not virtuous.

And now, my dear, I will tell you how I came to put you upon this inquiry.

This vile *Joseph Leman* had given a hint to *Betty*, and she to *me*, as if Lovelace would be found out to be a very bad man, at a place where he had been lately seen in disguise. But he would see further, he said, before he told her more; and she promised *secrecy*, in hope to get at *further intelligence*. I thought it could be no harm, to get you to inform yourself and me of what could be gathered*. And now I see his enemies are but too well war-

* It will be seen in Letter xxxiv. that Mr. Lovelace's motive for sparing his Rosebud was twofold. First, because his pride was gratified by the grandmother's desiring him to spare her granddaughter. "Many a pretty rogue" says he, "had I spared, whom I did not spare, had my power been acknowledged, and my mercy in time implored. But the *debellare superbos* should be my motto were I to have a new one."

His other motive will be explained in the following passage, in the same. "I never was so honest, for so long together," says he, "since my matriculation. It *behoves me* so to be. Some way or other my recess (at this little inn) may be found out, and it then will be thought that my Rosebud has attracted me. A report in my favour from simplicities so amiable, may establish me," &c.

Accordingly, as the reader will hereafter see, Mr. Lovelace finds, by the *effects*, his expectations from the contrivance he set on foot by means of his agent Joseph Leman (who plays, as above, upon Betty Barnes) fully answered, though he could not know what passed on the occasion between the two ladies.

This explanation is the more necessary to be given, as several of our readers (through want of due attention) have attributed to Mr. Lovelace, on his behaviour to his Rosebud, a greater merit than was due to him; and moreover imagined, that it was improbable that a man, who was capable of acting so generously (as they supposed) in *this* instance, should be guilty of any *atrocious* vileness. Not considering that love, pride, and revenge, as he owns in Letter xxxi. were ingredients of equal force in his composition, and that resistance was a stimulus to him.

ranted in their reports of him: and, if the ruin of this poor young creature be his aim, and if he had not known her but for his visits to Harlowe Place, I shall have reason to be doubly concerned for her; and doubly incensed against so vile a man.

I think I hate him worse than I do Solmes himself.

But I will not add one more word about him; after I have told you, that I wish to know as soon as possible what further occurs from your inquiry. I have a letter from him; but shall not open it till I do: and then, if it come out, as I dare say it will, I will directly put the letter unopened into the place I took it from, and never trouble myself more about him. Adieu, my dearest friend.

CL. HARLOWE.

LETTER LXII.

Miss Howe to Miss Clarissa Harlowe.

Friday noon, March 31.

JUSTICE obliges me to forward this after my last on the wings of the wind, as I may say. I really believe the man is innocent. Of this one accusation I think he must be acquitted; and I am sorry I was so forward in dispatching away my intelligence by halves.

I have seen the girl. She is really a very pretty, a very neat, and, what is still a greater beauty, a very innocent young creature. He who could have ruined such an undesigning home-bred, must have been indeed infernally wicked. Her father is an honest simple man; entirely satisfied with his child, and with her new acquaintance.

I am almost afraid for your heart, when I tell you, that I find, now I have got to the bottom of this inquiry, something noble come out in this Lovelace's favour.

The girl is to be married next week; and this promoted and brought about by him. He is resolved, her father says, to make one couple happy, and wishes he could make more so [*there's for you, my dear!*] And having taken a liking also to the young fellow whom she professes to love, he has given her an hundred pounds: the grandmother actually has it in her hands, to answer to the like sum given to the youth by one of his own relations: while Mr. Lovelace's companion, attracted by the example, has given twenty-five guineas to the father, who is poor, towards clothes to equip the pretty rustic.

Mr. Lovelace and his friend, the poor man says, when they first came to his house, affected to appear as *persons of low degree;* but now he knows the one (but mentioned it in confidence) to be Colonel Barrow, the other Captain Sloane. The Colonel, he owns, was at first very *sweet upon his girl:* but upon her grandmother's begging of him to spare her innocence, he vowed, that he would never offer any thing but good counsel to her. He kept his word; and the pretty fool acknowledged, that she could never have been better instructed by the minister himself from the *Bible book!* — The girl pleased me so well, that I made her visit to me worth her while.

But what, my dear, will become of us now? — Lovelace not only reformed, but turned preacher; — What will become of us now? — Why, my sweet friend, your *generosity* is now engaged in his favour — Fie upon this *generosity!* I think in my heart that it does as much mischief to the noble-minded as *love* to the ignobler. — What before was only a *conditional liking*, I am now afraid will turn to *liking unconditional.*

I could not endure to change my invective into panegyric all at once, and so soon. We, or such as I at least, love to keep ourselves in countenance for a rash judgment, even when we know it to be rash. Every body has not your generosity in confessing a mistake. It requires a greatness of soul frankly to do it. So I made still further inquiry after his life and manners, and behaviour there, in hopes to find something bad: but all uniform!

Upon the whole, Mr. Lovelace comes out with so much advantage from this inquiry, that were there the least room for it, I should suspect the whole to be *a plot set on foot to wash a blackamore white.* Adieu, my dear.

ANNA HOWE.

LETTER LXXIII.

Miss Clarissa Harlowe to Miss Howe.

Saturday, April 1.

HASTY censurers do indeed subject themselves to the charge of variableness and inconsistency in judgment: and so they ought: for, if you, even you, my dear, were so loth to own a mistake, as in the instance before us you pretend you were. I believe I should not have loved you so well as I really do love you. Nor could you, in that case, have so frankly thrown the reflection I hint at upon yourself, had not your mind been one of the most ingenuous that ever woman boasted.

Mr. Lovelace has faults enow to deserve very severe censure, although he be not guilty of this. If I were upon such terms with him as he could wish me to be, I should give him a hint, that this treacherous Joseph Leman cannot be *so much* attached to him as perhaps he thinks him to be. If he were, he would not have been so ready to report to his disadvantage (and to Betty Barnes too) this slight affair of the pretty rustic. Joseph has engaged Betty to secrecy; promising to let her, and her young master too, know more when he knows the whole of the matter: and this hinders her from mentioning it, as she is nevertheless eager to do, to my sister or brother. And then she does not choose to disoblige Joseph: for although she pretends to look above him, she listens, I believe, to some love stories he tells her.

Women having it not in their power to *begin* a courtship, some of them very frequently, I believe, lend an *ear* where their *hearts* incline not.

But to say no more of these low people, neither of whom I think tolerably of; I must needs own, that as I should for ever have despised this man, had he been capable of such a vile intrigue in his way to Harlowe Place, and as I believed he *was* capable of it, it has indeed (I own it has) proportionably engaged my *generosity*, as you call it, in his favour: perhaps *more than I may have reason to wish it had*. And, rally me as you will, pray tell me fairly, my dear, would it not have had such an effect upon you?

Then the *real* generosity of the act. — I protest, my beloved friend, if he would be good for the rest of his life from this time, I would forgive him a great many of his past errors, were it only for the demonstration he has given in this that he is *capable* of so good and bountiful a manner of thinking.

You may believe I made no scruple to open his letter, after the receipt of your second on this subject; nor shall I of answering it, as I have no reason to find fault with it. — An article in his favour procured him, however, so much the easier (I must own) by way of amends for the undue displeasure I took against him, though he knows it not.

It is lucky enough that this matter was cleared up to me by your friendly diligence so soon: for had I written before it was, it would have been to reinforce my dismission of him; and perhaps I should have mentioned the very motive; for it affected me more than I think it ought: and then, what an advantage would that have given him, when he could have cleared up the matter so happily for himself?

When I send you this letter of his, you will see how very humble he is: what *acknowledgments* of *natural* impatience: what confession of faults, as you prognosticated.

A very different appearance, I must own, all these make, now the story of the pretty rustic is cleared up, to what they would have made, had it not.

You will see how he accounts to me, "that he could not, by reason of indisposition, come for my letter in person:" and the forward creature labours the point, as if he thought I should be uneasy that he did not. I am indeed sorry he should be ill on my account; and I will allow, that the suspense he has been in for some time past must have been vexatious enough to so impatient a spirit. But all is owing originally to himself.

You will find him in the presumption of being forgiven, "full of contrivances and expedients for my escaping the threatened compulsion."

I have always said, that next to being without fault, is the acknowledgment of a fault; since no amendment can be expected where an error is defended: but you will see in this very letter, an haughtiness even in his submissions. 'Tis true, I know not where to find fault as to the expression; yet cannot I be satisfied, that his humility *is* humility; or even an humility upon such conviction as one should be pleased with.

To be sure, he is far from being a polite man: yet is not directly and characteristically, as I may say, *unpolite*. But *his* is such a sort of politeness, as has by a carelessness founded on very early indulgence, and perhaps on too much success in riper years, and an arrogance built upon both, grown into assuredness, and, of course, I may say, into indelicacy.

The distance you recommend at which to keep these men, is certainly right in the main: familiarity destroys reverence: but with whom? Not with those, surely, who are prudent, grateful, and generous.

But it is very difficult for persons, who would avoid running into one extreme to keep clear of another. Hence Mr. Lovelace, perhaps, thinks it the mark of a great spirit to humour his pride, though at the expense of his politeness: but can the man be a deep man, who knows not how to make such distinctions as a person of but moderate parts cannot miss?

He complains heavily of my "readiness to take mortal offence at him, and to dismiss him for ever: it is a *high* conduct, he says, he must be frank enough to tell me; a conduct that must be very far from contributing to allay his apprehensions of the possibility that I may be persecuted into my relations' measures in behalf of Mr. Solmes."

You will see how he puts his present and his future happiness, "with regard to both worlds, entirely upon me." The ardour with which he vows and promises, I think the heart only can dictate: how else can one guess at a man's heart?

You will also see, "that he has already heard of the interview I am to have with Mr. Solmes;" and with what vehemence and anguish he expresses himself on the occasion. — I intend to take proper notice of the ignoble means he stoops to, to come at his early intelligence out of our family. If persons pretending to principle bear not their testimony against unprincipled actions, what check can they have?

You will see, "how passionately he presses me to oblige him with a few lines before the interview between Mr. Solmes and me takes place, if (as he says) it *must* take place, to confirm his hope, that I have no view, in my present displeasure against *him*, to give encouragement to *Solmes*. An apprehension, he says, that he must be excused for repeating; especially as the interview is a favour granted to that man which I have refused to him; since, as he infers, were it not with such an expectation, why should my *friends* press it?"

* * *

I have written, and to this effect: "That I had never intended to write another line to a man, who could take upon himself to reflect upon my sex and myself, for having thought fit to make use of my own judgment.

"I tell him that I have submitted to this interview with Mr. Solmes, purely as an act of duty to shew my friends that I will comply with their commands as far as I can; and that I hope, when Mr. Solmes himself shall see how determined I am, he will cease to prosecute a suit in which it is impossible he should succeed with my consent.

"I assure him, that my aversion to Mr. Solmes is too sincere to permit me to doubt myself on this occasion. But, nevertheless, he must not imagine that my rejecting of Mr. Solmes is in favour to him. That I value my freedom and independency too much, if my friends will but leave me to my own judgment, to give them up to a man so uncontrollable, and who shews me beforehand what I have to expect from him, were I in his power.

"I express my high disapprobation of the methods he takes to come at what passes in a private family: the pretence of corrupting other people's servants by way of reprisal for the spies they have set upon him I tell him is a very poor excuse; and no more than an attempt to justify one meanness by another.

"There is, I observe to him, a *right* and a *wrong* in every thing, let people put what glosses they please upon their actions. To condemn a deviation, and to follow it by as great a one, what, I ask him, is this, but propagating a general corruption? A stand must be made by somebody, turn round the evil as many as may, or virtue will be lost: *and shall it not be I*, a worthy mind would ask, that shall make this stand?

"I leave him to judge, whether *his* be a worthy one, tried by this rule: and whether, knowing the impetuosity of his own disposition, and the improbability there is that my father and family will ever be reconciled to him, I ought to encourage his hopes?

"These spots and blemishes, I further tell him, give me not earnestness enough for any sake but *his own*, to wish him in a juster and nobler train of thinking and acting; for that I truly despise many of the ways he allows himself in; our minds are therefore infinitely different: and as to his professions of reformation, I must tell him, that profuse acknowledgments, without amendment, are but to me as so many anticipating concessions, which he may find much easier to make than either to defend himself or amend his errors.

"I inform him that I have been lately made acquainted" [and so I have by Betty, and she by my brother] "with the weak and wanton airs he gives himself of declaiming against matrimony. I severely reprehend him on this occasion: and ask him with what view he can take so witless, so despicable a liberty, in which only the most abandoned of men allow themselves, and yet presume to address me?

"I tell him, that if I am obliged to go to my uncle Antony's, it is not to be inferred, that I must therefore *necessarily* be Mr. Solmes's wife: since I may not be so sure perhaps that the same exceptions lie so strongly against my quitting a house to which I shall be forcibly carried, as if I left my father's house; and, at the worst, I may be able to keep them in suspense till my cousin Morden comes, who will have a right to put me in possession of my grandfather's estate if I insist upon it."

This, I doubt, is somewhat of an artifice; which can only be excusable, as it is principally designed to keep him out of mischief. For I have but little hope, if carried thither, whether sensible or senseless, if I am left to the mercy of my brother and sister, but they will endeavour to force the solemn obligation upon me. Otherwise, were there but any prospect of avoiding this, by delaying (or even by taking things to make me ill, if nothing else would do) till my cousin comes, I hope I should not think of leaving even my uncle's house. For I should not know how to square it to my own principles, to dispense with the duty I owe to my father, wherever it should be his will to place me.

But while you give me the charming hope, that, in order to avoid one man, I shall not be under the necessity of throwing myself upon the friends of the other, I think my case not absolutely desperate.

* * *

I see not any of my family, nor hear from them in any way of kindness. This looks as if they themselves expected no great matters from that Tuesday's conference which makes my heart flutter every time I think of it.

My uncle Antony's presence on the occasion I do not much like; but I had rather meet him than my brother or sister: yet my uncle is very impetuous. I can't think Mr. Lovelace can be much more so; at least he cannot *look* anger as my uncle, with his harder features, can. These sea-prospered gentlemen, as my uncle has often made me think, not used to any but elemental control, and even ready to buffet that, bluster often as violently as the winds they are accustomed to be angry at.

I believe Mr. Solmes will look as much like a fool as I shall do, if it be true, as my uncle Harlowe writes, and as Betty often tells me, that he is as much afraid of seeing me as I am of seeing him.

Adieu, my happy, thrice happy Miss Howe, who have no hard terms affixed to your duty!—Who have nothing to do but to fall in with a choice your mother has made for you, to which you have not, nor can have, a just objection: except the forwardness of our sex, as our free censurers would perhaps take the liberty to say, makes it one, that the choice was your mother's at first hand. Perverse nature, we know, loves not to be prescribed to; although youth is not so well qualified, either by sedateness or experience, to choose for itself.

To *know* your own happiness, and that it is *now*, nor to leave it to *after-reflection* to look back upon the *preferable past* with a heavy and self-accusing heart, that you did not choose it when you might have chosen it, is all that is necessary to complete your felicity!—And this power is wished you by

Your
CLARISSA HARLOWE.

LETTER LXXIV.

Miss Howe to Miss Clarissa Harlowe.

Saturday, April 1.

I OUGHT yesterday to have acknowledged the receipt of your parcel: Robin tells me, that the Joseph Leman, whom you mention as the traitor, saw him. He was in the poultry-yard, and spoke to Robin over the bank which divides that from the Green-Lane. "What brings you hither, Mr. Robert?—But I can tell. Hie away as fast as you can."

No doubt but their dependence upon this fellow's vigilance, and upon Betty's, leaves you more at liberty in your airings than you would otherwise be. But you are the only person I ever heard of, who in such circumstances had not some faithful servant to trust little offices to. A poet, my dear, would not have gone to work for an Angelica, without giving her her Violetta, her Cleanthe, her Clelia, or some such pretty named confidante — an old nurse at the least.

I read to my mother several passages of your letters. But your last paragraph in your yesterday's quite charmed her. You have won her heart by it she told me. And while her fit of gratitude for it lasted, I was thinking to make my proposal, and to press it with all the earnestness I could give it, when Hickman came in, making his legs, and stroaking his cravat and ruffles.

I could most freely have *ruffled* him for it. As it was — Sir, said I, saw you not some of the servants? — Could not one of them have come in before you?

He begged pardon: looked as if he knew not whether he had best keep his ground or withdraw: — till my mother, his fast friend, interposed — Why, Nancy, we are not upon particulars.—Pray, Mr. Hickman, sit down.

By your le—ave, good madam, to me. You know his drawl, when his muscles give him the respectful hesitation —

Ay, ay, pray sit down, honest man, if you are weary — but by my *mamma*, if you please. I desire my hoop may have its full circumference. All they're good for, that I know, is to clean dirty shoes, and to keep fellows at a distance.

Strange girl! cried my mother, displeased; but with a milder turn, ay, ay, Mr. Hickman, sit down by me; I have no such *forbidding* folly in my dress.

I looked serious: and in my heart was glad this speech of hers was not made to your uncle Antony.

My mother, with the true widow's freedom, would mighty prudently have led into the subject we had been upon; and would have had read to him, I question not, that very paragraph in your letter which is so much in his favour. He was highly obliged to dear Miss Harlowe, she would assure him; that she *did* say—

But I asked him, if he had any news by his last letters from London—a question which he always understands to be a *subject changer*; for otherwise I never put it. And so if he be *but* silent, I am not angry with him that he answers it not.

I choose not to mention my proposal before him, till I know how it will be relished by my mother. If it be not well received, perhaps I may employ *him* on the occasion. Yet I don't like to owe him an obligation, if I could help it. For men who have his views in their heads, do so parade it, so strut about, if a woman condescend to employ them in her affairs, that one has no patience with them.

However, if I *find* not an opportunity this day, I will make one to-morrow.

I shall not open either of your sealed up parcels, but in *your* presence. There is no need. Your conduct is out of all question with me: and by the extracts you have given me from his letters and your own, I know all that relates to the present situation of things between you.

I was going to give you a little flippant hint or two. But since you wish to be thought superior to all our sex in the command of yourself; and since indeed you deserve to be thought so, I will spare you. You are, however, at times, more than half inclined to speak out. That you do not, is only owing to a little bashful struggle between you and *yourself*, as I may say. When that is quite got over, I know you will favour me undisguisedly with the result.

I cannot forgive your taking upon you (at so extravagant a rate too) to pay my mother's servant. Indeed I *am*, and I *will be*, angry with you for it. A year's wages at once well nigh! only as, unknown to my mother, I make it better for the servants according to their merits — how it made the man stare! — And it may be his ruin too, as far as I know. If he should buy a ring, and marry a sorry body in the neighbourhood with the money, one would be loth, a twelvemonth hence, that the poor old fellow should think he had reason to wish the bounty never conferred.

I MUST *give you your way in these things*, you say. — And I know there is no contradicting you: for you were ever putting too great a value upon little offices done for *you*, and too little upon the great ones you do for *others*. The satisfaction you have in doing so, I grant it, repays you. But why should you, by the nobleness of your mind, throw reproaches upon the rest of the world? Particularly upon your own family—and upon ours too?

If, as I have heard you say, it is a good rule to *give words the hearing*, *but to form our judgments of men and things by DEEDS ONLY*, what shall we think of one, who seeks to find palliatives in *words* for narrowness of heart in the very persons her *deeds* so silently, yet so forcibly reflect upon? Why blush you not, my dear friend, to be thus singular?—When you meet with another person whose mind is like your own, then display your excellencies as you please: but till then, for pity's sake, let your heart and your spirit suffer a little contraction.

I intended to write but a few lines; chiefly to let you know your parcels are come safe. And accordingly I began in a large hand; and I am already come to the end of my second sheet. But I could write a quire without hesitation upon a subject so copious and so beloved as is your praise.—Not for *this* single instance of your generosity; since I am really angry with you for it; but for the benevolence exemplified in the whole tenor of your life and actions; of which this is but a common instance. Heaven direct you in your own arduous trials is all I have room to add; and make you as happy as you think to be

Your own
ANNA HOWE.

LETTER LXXV.
Miss Clarissa Harlowe to Miss Howe.

Sunday night, April 2.

I HAVE many new particulars to acquaint you with, that shew a great change in the behaviour of my friends to me. I did not think we had so much art among us as I find we have. I will give these particulars to you as they offered.

All the family was at church in the morning. They brought good Dr. Lewen with them, in pursuance of a previous invitation. And the doctor sent up to desire my permission to attend me in my own apartment.

You may believe it was easily granted.

So the doctor came up.

We had a conversation of near an hour before dinner: but, to my surprise, he waved every thing that would have led to the subject I supposed he wanted to talk upon. At last, I asked him, if it were not thought strange I should be so long absent from church? He made me some handsome compliments upon it: but said, for his part, he had ever made it a rule, to avoid interfering in the private concerns of families, unless desired to do so.

I was prodigiously disappointed: but supposing that he was thought too just a man to be made a judge in this cause, I led no more to it: nor, when he was called down to dinner, did he take the least notice of leaving me behind him there.

But this was not the first time

since my confinement that I thought it a hardship not to dine below. And when I parted with him on the stairs, a tear would burst its way; and he hurried down: his own good-natured eyes glistening; for he saw it. — Nor trusted he his voice, lest the accent I suppose should have discovered his concern: departing in silence, though with his usual graceful obligingness.

I hear that he praised me, and my part in the conversation that passed between us. — To shew them, I suppose, that it was not upon the interesting subjects which I make no doubt he was desired not to enter upon.

He left me so dissatisfied, yet so perplexed with this new way of treatment, that I never found myself so much disconcerted, and out of my train.

But I was to be more so. This was to be a day of puzzle to me. *Pregnant* puzzle, if I may so say: for there must great meaning lie behind it.

In the afternoon, all but my brother and sister went to church with the good doctor, who left his compliments for me. I took a walk in the garden: my brother and sister walked in it too, and kept me in their eye a good while, on purpose, as I thought, that I might see how gay and good-humoured they were together. At last they came down the walk that I was coming up, hand-in-hand, lover-like.

Your servant, miss — your servant, sir — passed between my brother and me.

Is it not cold-ish, sister Clary! in a kinder voice than usual, said my sister, and stopped. — I stopped and courtesied low to her half-courtesy. — I think not sister, said I.

She went on. I courtesied without return; and proceeded, turning to my poultry-yard.

By a shorter turn, arm-in-arm, they were there before me.

I think, Clary, said my brother, you must present me with some of this breed for Scotland.

If you please, brother.

I'll choose for you, said my sister.

And while I fed them, they pointed to half a dozen: yet intending nothing by it, I believe, but to shew a deal of love and good humour to each other before me.

My uncles next, (at their return from church) were to do me the honour of *their* notice. They bid Betty tell me, they would drink tea with me in my own apartment. Now, thought I, I shall have the subject of next Tuesday, enforced upon me.

But they contradicted the order for tea, and only my uncle Harlowe came up to me.

Half-distant, half-affectionate, at his entering my chamber, was the air he put on to his *daughter-niece,* as he used to call me; and I threw myself at his feet, and besought his favour.

None of these discomposures, child. None of these apprehensions. You will now have every body's favour. All is coming about, my dear. I was impatient to see you. I could no longer deny myself this satisfaction. He then raised me, and kissed me, and called me charming creature.

But he waved entering into any interesting subject. All will be well now. All will be right.—No more complainings! Every body loves you!—I only came to make my earliest court to you! [were his condescending words] and to sit and talk of twenty and twenty fond things, as I used to do.— And let every past disagreeable thing be forgotten, as if nothing had happened.

He understood me as beginning to hint at the disgrace of my confinement—no disgrace, my dear, can fall to your lot: your reputation is too well established.—I longed to see you, repeated he—I have seen nobody half so amiable since I saw you last.

And again he kissed my cheek, my glowing cheek; for I was impatient, I was vexed, to be thus, as I thought, played upon: and how could I be thankful for a visit, that (it now was evident) was only a too *humble* artifice, to draw me in against the next Tuesday, or to leave me inexcusable to them all?

O my cunning brother!—this is *his* contrivance. And then my anger made me recollect the triumph in his and my sister's fondness for each other, as practised before me; and the mingled indignation flashing from their eyes, as arm-in-arm they spoke to me, and the forced condescension playing upon their lips when they called me Clary and sister.

Do you think I could, with these reflections, look upon my uncle Harlowe's visit as the favour he seemed desirous I should think it to be?—Indeed I could not; and seeing him so studiously avoid all recrimination, as I may call it, I gave into the affectation; and followed him in his talk of indifferent things: while he seemed to admire this thing and that, as if he had never seen them before; and now-and-then condescendingly kissed the hand that wrought some of the things he fixed his eyes upon; not so much to admire them, as to find subjects to divert what was most in *his* head and in *my* heart.

At his going away—how can I leave you here by yourself, my dear? You, whose company used to enliven us all. You are expected down, indeed: but I protest I have a good mind to surprise your father and mother!—If I thought nothing would arise that would be disagreeable—my dear! my love! [O the dear artful gentleman! How could my uncle Harlowe so dissemble?] What say you? Will you give me your hand? Will you see your father? Can you stand his displeasure, on first seeing the dear creature who has given him and all of us so much disturbance? Can you promise future—

He saw me rising in my temper—nay, my dear, interrupting himself, if you cannot be all resignation, I would not have you think of it.

My heart, struggling between duty and warmth of temper, was full. You know, my dear, I never could bear to be dealt meanly with! — How — how *can* you, sir! You my papa-uncle — how *can* you, sir! — The poor girl! — For I could not speak with connexion.

Nay, my dear, if you cannot be all duty, all resignation — better stay where you are. — But after the instance you have given —

Instance I have given! — What instance, sir?

Well, well, child, better stay where you are, if your past confinement hangs so heavy upon you — but now there will be a sudden end to it — adieu, my dear! — Three words only — let your compliance be sincere! — And love me as you used to love me — your grandfather did not do so much for you as I will do for you.

Without suffering me to reply, he hurried away, as I thought, like one who had been employed to act a part against his will, and was glad it was over.

Don't you see, my dear Miss Howe, how they are all determined? — Have I not reason to dread next Tuesday?

Up presently after came my sister: — to observe, I suppose, the way I was in.

She found me in tears.

Have you not a Thomas à Kempis, sister? with a stiff air.

I have, madam.

Madam! — How long are we to be at this distance, Clary?

No longer, my dear Bella, if you allow me to call you sister. And I took her hand.

No fawning neither, girl!

I withdrew my hand as hastily as you may believe I should have done had I, in feeling for one of your parcels under the wood, been bitten by a viper.

I beg pardon, said I — too-too ready to make advances, I am always subjecting myself to contempts.

People who know not how to keep a middle behaviour, said she, must evermore do so.

I will fetch you the Kempis, sister. I did. Here it is. You will find excellent things, Bella, in that little book.

I wish, retorted she, you had profited by them.

I wish *you* may, said I. *Example* from a sister older than one's self, is a fine thing.

Older! Saucy little fool! — And away she flung.

What a captious old woman will my sister make, if she lives to be one! — demanding the reverence, perhaps, yet not aiming at the merit; and ashamed of the years that only can entitle her to the reverence.

It is plain, from what I have related, that they think they have got me at some advantage by obtaining my consent to this interview: but if it were *not*, Betty's impertinence just now would make it evident. She has been complimenting me upon it; and upon the visit of my uncle Harlowe. She says, the difficulty now is more than half over with me. She is sure I would not see Mr. Solmes but to have him. Now shall she be soon better employed than of late she has been. All hands will be at work. She loves dearly to have weddings go forward! — Who knows whose turn will be next?

I found in the afternoon a reply to my answer to Mr. Lovelace's letter. It is full of promises, full of vows of gratitude, of *eternal* gratitude is his word, among others still more hyperbolic. Yet Mr. Lovelace, the *least* of any man whose letters I have seen, runs into those elevated absurdities. I should be apt to despise him for it if he did. Such language looks always to me, as if the flatterer thought to *find* a woman a fool, or hoped to *make* her one.

"He regrets my indifference to him; which puts all the hope he has in my favour upon the shocking usage I receive from my friends.

"As to my charge upon him of unpoliteness and uncontrolableness — what [he asks] can he say? — Since being unable absolutely to vindicate himself, he has too much ingenuousness to attempt to do so: yet is struck dumb by my harsh construction, that his acknowledging temper is owing more to his carelessness to defend himself than to his inclination to amend. He had never *before* met with the objections against his morals which I had raised, *justly* raised: and he was resolved to obviate them. What is it, he asks, that he has promised, but reformation by my example? And what occasion for the promise, if he had not faults, and those very great ones, to reform? He hopes acknowledgment of an error is no bad sign, although my severe virtue has interpreted it into one.

"He believes I may be right (*severely* right, he calls it) in my judgment against making reprisals in the case of the intelligence he receives from my family: he cannot charge himself to be of a temper that leads him to be inquisitive into any body's private affairs: but hopes that the circumstances of the case, and the strange conduct of my friends, will excuse him; especially when so much depends upon his knowing the movements of a family so violently bent, by measures right or wrong, to carry their point against me in malice to him. People, he says, who act like angels, ought to have angels to deal with. For his part, he has not yet learned the difficult lesson of returning *good for evil*: and shall think himself the less encouraged to learn it by the treatment I have met with from the very persons who would trample upon him as they do upon me, were he to lay himself under their feet.

"He excuses himself for the liberties he owns he has heretofore taken in ridiculing the marriage state. It is a subject, he says, that he has not of late treated so lightly. He owns it to be so trite, so beaten a topic with all libertines and witlings; so frothy, so empty, so nothing-meaning, so worn-out a theme, that he is heartily ashamed of himself ever to have made it *his*. He condemns it as a stupid reflection upon the laws and good order of society, and upon a man's own ancestors: and in himself, who has some reason to value himself upon his descent and alliances, more censurable than in those who have not the same advantage to boast of. He promises to be more circumspect than ever, both in his words and actions, that he may be more and more worthy of my approbation; and that he may give an assurance beforehand, that a foundation is laid in his mind for my example to work upon with equal reputation and effect to us both: — if he may be so happy to call me his.

"He gives me up as absolutely lost if I go to my uncle Antony's; the close confinement; the moated house; the chapel; the implacableness of my brother and sister, and their power over the rest of the family, he sets forth in strong lights; and plainly says, that he must have a struggle to prevent my being carried thither."

Your kind, your generous endeavours to interest your mother in my behalf, will, I hope, prevent those harsher extremities to which I might be otherwise driven. And to you I will fly, if permitted, and keep all my promises of not corresponding with any body, not seeing any body, but by your mother's direction and yours. I will close and deposit at this place. It is not necessary to say how much I am

Your ever affectionate and
obliged
CL. HARLOWE.

LETTER LXXV.

Miss Clarissa Harlowe to Miss Howe.

I AM glad my papers are safe in your hands. I will make it my endeavour to deserve your good opinion that I may not at once disgrace your judgment and my own heart.

I have another letter from Mr. Lovelace. He is extremely apprehensive of the meeting I am to have with Mr. Solmes to-morrow. He says, "that the airs that wretch gives himself on the occasion add to his concern; and it is with infinite difficulty that he prevails upon himself not to make him a visit to let him know what he may expect, if compulsion be used towards me in his favour. He assures me that Solmes has actually talked with tradesmen of new equipages, and names the people in town with whom he has treated: that he has even" [was there ever such a horrid wretch!] "allotted this and that apartment in his house for a nursery and other offices."

How shall I bear to hear such a creature talk of love to me? I shall be out of all patience with him. Besides, I thought that he did not dare to make or talk of these impudent preparations. — So inconsistent as such are with my brother's views — but I fly the subject.

Upon this confidence of Solmes, you will less wonder at that of Lovelace, "in pressing me in the name of all his family to escape from so determined a violence as is intended to be offered to me at my uncle's: that the forward contriver should propose Lord M.'s chariot and six to be at the stile that leads up to the lonely coppice adjoining to our paddock. You will see how audaciously he mentions settlements ready drawn; horsemen ready to mount, and one of his cousins Montague to be in the chariot, or at the George in the neighbouring village waiting to accompany me to Lord M.'s, or to Lady Betty's or Lady Sarah's, or to town, as I please; and upon such orders, or conditions, and under such restrictions as to himself as I shall prescribe."

You will see how he threatens, "to watch and way-lay them, and to *rescue* me, as he calls it, by an armed force of friends and servants, if they attempt to carry me against my will to my uncle's: and this whether I give my consent to the enterprise or not: — since he shall have no hopes if I am once there."

O my dear friend! who can think of these things, and not be extremely miserable in her apprehensions!

This mischievous sex! What had I to do with any of them, or they with me? — I had deserved this, were it by my own seeking, by my own giddiness, that I had brought myself into this situation — I wish with all my heart — but how foolishly we are apt to wish when we find ourselves unhappy, and know not how to help ourselves!

On your mother's goodness, however, is my reliance. If I can but avoid being precipitated on either hand till my cousin Morden arrives, a reconciliation must follow, and all will be happy.

I have deposited a letter for Mr. Lovelace, in which "I charge him, as he would not disoblige me for ever, to avoid any rash step, any visit to Mr. Solmes, which may be followed by acts of violence." I re-assure him, that I will sooner die than be that man's wife.

"Whatever be my usage, whatever shall be the result of the apprehended interview, I insist upon it that he presume not to offer violence to any of my friends; and express myself highly displeased, that he should presume upon such an interest in my esteem, as to think himself entitled to dispute my father's authority in my removal to my uncle's; although I tell him, that I will omit neither prayers nor contrivance, even to the making of myself ill, to avoid going."

To-morrow is Tuesday! How soon comes upon us the day we dread! — O that a deep sleep of twenty-four hours would seize my faculties! — But then the next day would be Tuesday, as to all the effects and purposes for which I so much dread it. If this reach you before the event of the so much apprehended interview can be known, pray for

Your
CLARISSA HARLOWE.

LETTER LXXVI.
Miss Clarissa Harlowe to Miss Howe.

Tuesday morning, six o'clock.

THE day is come!—I wish it were happily over. I have had a wretched night. Hardly a wink have I slept, ruminating upon the approaching interview. The very distance of time to which they consented, has added solemnity to the meeting which otherwise it would not have had.

A thoughtful mind is not a blessing to be coveted unless it had such a happy vivacity with it as yours: a vivacity, which enables a person to enjoy the *present*, without being over anxious about the *future*.

Tuesday, eleven o'clock.

I have had a visit from my aunt Hervey. Betty, in her alarming way, told me I should have a lady to breakfast with me, whom I little expected; giving me to believe it was my mother. This fluttered me so much, on hearing a lady coming up stairs, supposing it was she (and not knowing how to account for her motives in such a visit, after I had been so long banished from her presence) that my aunt, at her entrance, took notice of my disorder; and after her first salutation,

Why, miss, said she, you seem surprised.—Upon my word, you thoughtful young ladies have strange apprehensions about nothing at all. What, taking my hand, can be the matter with you? —Why, my dear, tremble, tremble, tremble at this rate? You'll not be fit to be seen by any body. Come, my love, kissing my cheek, pluck up a courage. By this needless flutter on the approaching interview, when it is over, you will judge of your other antipathies, and laugh at yourself for giving way to so apprehensive an imagination.

I said, that whatever we strongly imagined, was in its effects at the time, *more* than imaginary, although to others it might not appear so: that I had not rested one hour all night: that the impertinent set over me, by giving me room to think my mother was coming up, had so much disconcerted me, that I should be very little qualified to see any body I disliked to see.

There was no accounting for these things, she said. Mr. Solmes last night supposed he should be under as much agitation as I could be.

Who is it, then, madam, that so reluctant an interview on *both* sides, is to please?

Both of you, my dear, I hope, after the first flurries are over. The most apprehensive beginnings, I have often known, make the happiest conclusions.

There can but be one happy conclusion to the intended visit;

and that is, that both sides may be satisfied it will be the last.

She then represented, how unhappy it would be for me, if I did not suffer myself to be prevailed upon: she pressed me to receive Mr. Solmes as became my education: and declared, that his apprehensions on the expectation he had of seeing me were owing to his love and his awe; intimating that true love is ever accompanied by fear and reverence; and that no blustering, braving lover could deserve encouragement.

To this I answered, that constitution was to be considered: that a man of spirit would act like one, and could do nothing meanly: that a creeping mind would creep in every thing, where it had a view to obtain a benefit by it: and insult, where it had power, and nothing to expect: that this was not a point now to be determined with me: that I had said as much as I could possibly say on this subject: that this interview was imposed upon me by those, indeed, who had a right to impose it: but that it was sorely against my will complied with; and for this reason, that there was *aversion*, not *wilfulness*, in the case; and so nothing could come of it, but a pretence, as I much apprehended, to use me still more severely than I had been used.

She was then pleased to charge me with prepossession, and prejudice. She expatiated upon the duty of a child. She imputed to me abundance of fine qualities; but told me, that, in this case, that of persuadeableness was wanting to crown all. She insisted upon the *merit* of obedience, although my will were *not* in it. From a little hint I gave of my still greater dislike to see Mr. Solmes on account of the freedom I had treated him with, she talked to me of his forgiving disposition; of his infinite respect for me; and I cannot tell what of this sort.

I never found myself so fretful in my life: and so I told my aunt; and begged her pardon for it. But she said it was well disguised then; for she saw nothing but little tremors, which were usual with young ladies when they were to see their admirers for the *first* time; and this might be called so with respect to me; since it was the first time I had consented to see Mr. Solmes in that light—But that the *next*—

How, madam, interrupted I—Is it then imagined, that I give this meeting on that foot?

To be sure it is, child.

To be sure it is, madam! Then I do yet desire to decline it.—I will not, I cannot, see him, if he expects me to see him upon those terms.

Niceness, punctilio — Mere punctilio, niece!—Can you think that your appointment (day, place, hour) and knowing what the intent of it was, is to be interpreted away as a mere ceremony, and to mean nothing?—Let me tell you, my dear, your father, mother, uncles, every body, respect this appointment as the first act of your compliance with their wills:

and therefore recede not, I desire you; but make a merit of what cannot be avoided.

O the hideous wretch! — Pardon me, madam — *I* to be supposed to meet such a man as *that*, with such a view! and *he* to be armed with such an expectation! — But it cannot be that he expects it, whatever *others* may do. — It is plain he cannot, by the fear he tells you all, he shall have to see me. If his *hope* were so audacious, he could not *fear* so much.

Indeed, he *has* this hope; and justly founded too. But his fear arises from his reverence, as I told you before.

His *reverence!* — his unworthiness! — 'Tis so apparent, that even he himself sees it, as well as every body else. Hence his offers to purchase me! Hence it is, that settlements are to make up for acknowledged want of merit!

His *unworthiness*, say you! — Not so fast, my dear. Does not this look like setting a high value upon yourself? — We all have exalted notions of your merit, niece; but nevertheless, it would not be wrong, if you were to arrogate less to yourself; though more were to be your due than your friends attribute to you.

I am sorry, madam, it should be thought arrogance in me, to suppose I am not worthy of a better man than Mr. Solmes, both as to person and mind: and as to fortune, I thank God I despise all that can be insisted upon in his favour from so poor a plea.

She told me, it signified nothing to talk: I knew the expectation of every one.

Indeed I did not. It was impossible I could think of such a strange expectation, upon a compliance made only to show I would comply in all that was in my power to comply with.

I might easily, she said, have supposed, that every one thought I was beginning to oblige them all, by the kind behaviour of my brother and sister to me in the garden, last Sunday; by my sister's visit to me afterwards in my chamber (although *both more stiffly received by me*, than were either wished or expected); by my uncle Harlowe's affectionate visit to me the same afternoon, not indeed *so very gratefully received* as I used to receive his favours: — but this he kindly imputed to the displeasure I had conceived at my confinement, and to my intention to come off by degrees, that I might keep myself in countenance for my past opposition.

See, my dear, the low cunning of that Sunday management, which then so much surprised me! And see the reason why Dr. Lewen was admitted to visit me, yet forbore to enter upon a subject about which I thought he came to talk to me! — For it seems there was no occasion to dispute with me on the point I was to be *supposed* to have conceded to. — See, also, how unfairly my brother and sister must have represented their pretended kindness, when (though they had an end to answer by ap-

pearing kind) their antipathy to me seems to have been so strong, that they could not help insulting me by their arm-in-arm lover-like behaviour to each other; as my sister afterwards likewise did, when she came to borrow my Kempis.

I lifted up my hands and eyes! I cannot, said I, give *this* treatment a name! The *end* so unlikely to be answered by *means* so low! I know *whose* the whole is! He that could get my uncle Harlowe to contribute his part, and procure the acquiescence of the rest of my friends to it, must have the power to do any thing with them against me.

Again my aunt told me, that talking and invective, now I had given the expectation, would signify nothing. She hoped I would not show every one that they had been too forward in their constructions of my desire to oblige them. She could assure me, that it would be worse for me, if *now* I receded, than if I had never advanced.

Advanced, madam! How can you say *advanced?* Why, this is a trick upon me! A poor low trick! Pardon me, madam, I don't say you have a hand in it. — But, my dearest aunt, tell me, will not my mother be present at this dreaded interview? Will she not so far favour me? Were it but to qualify —

Qualify, my dear, interrupted she — your mother, and your uncle Harlowe would not be present on this occasion for the world —

O then, madam, how can they look upon my consent to this interview as an *advance?*

My aunt was displeased at this home push. Miss Clary, said she, there is no dealing with you. It would be happy for you, and for every body else, were your obedience as ready as your wit. I will leave you —

Not in anger, I hope, madam, interrupted I — All I meant was, to observe, that let the meeting issue as it may, and as it *must* issue, it cannot be a disappointment to *any body.*

O miss! you seem to be a very determined young creature. Mr. Solmes will be here at your time; and remember once more, that upon the coming afternoon depends the peace of your whole family, and your own happiness.

And so saying, down she hurried.

Here I will stop. In what way I shall resume, or when, is not left to me to conjecture; much less determine. I am excessively uneasy! — No good news from your mother, I doubt! — I will deposit thus far, for fear of the worst.

Adieu, my best, rather, my *only* friend!

CL. HARLOWE.

LETTER LXXVII.
Miss Clarissa Harlowe to Miss Howe.

Tuesday evening; and continued through the night.

WELL, my dear, I am alive, and here! But how long I shall be either here, or alive, I cannot say. I have a vast deal to write; and perhaps shall have little time for it. Nevertheless, I must tell you how the saucy Betty again discomposed me, when she came up with this Solmes's message; although, as you will remember from my last, I was in a way before that wanted no additional surprises.

Miss! Miss! Miss! cried she, as fast as she could speak, with her arms spread abroad, and all her fingers distended, and held up, will you be pleased to walk down into your own parlour? — There is every body, I will assure you, in full *congregation!* — And there is Mr. Solmes, as fine as a lord, with a charming white peruke, fine laced shirt and ruffles, coat trimmed with silver, and a waistcoat standing an end with lace! — Quite handsome, believe me! — You never saw such an alteration! — Ah! Miss, shaking her head, 'tis pity you have said so much against him! But you know how to come off for all that! — I hope it will not be too late!

Impertinence! said I — Wert thou bid to come up in this fluttering way? — And I took up my fan and fanned myself.

Bless me! said she, how soon these fine young ladies will be put into *flusterations!* — I meant not either to offend or frighten you, I am sure. —

Every body there, do you say? — Who do you call every body? —

Why, miss, holding out her left palm opened, and with a flourish, and a saucy leer, patting it with the fore finger of the other, at every mentioned person, there is your papa! — There is your mamma! — There is your uncle Harlowe! — There is your uncle Antony! — Your aunt Hervey! — *My* young lady! — and my young master! — And Mr. Solmes, with the air of a great courtier, standing up, because he named you: — Mrs. Betty, said he [then the ape of a wench bowed and scraped, as awkwardly as I suppose the person did whom she endeavoured to imitate] pray give my humble service to miss, and tell her, I wait her commands.

Was not this a wicked wench? — I trembled so, I could hardly stand. I was spiteful enough to say, that her young mistress, I supposed, bid her put on these airs, to frighten me out of a capacity of behaving so calmly as should procure me my uncle's compassion.

What a way do you put yourself in, miss! said the insolent. — Come, dear madam, taking up my fan, which I had laid down, and approaching me with it, fanning, shall I —

None of thy impertinence! — But say you, *all* my friends are below with him? And am I to *appear* before them *all?*

I can't tell if they'll stay when you come. I think they seemed to be moving when Mr. Solmes gave me his orders. — But what answer shall I carry to the 'squire?

Say I can't go! — But yet when 'tis over 'tis over! — Say, I'll wait upon — I'll attend — I'll come presently — say any thing; I care not what — but give me my fan, and fetch me a glass of water —

She went, and I fanned myself all the time; for I was in a flame; and hemmed, and struggled with myself all I could; and, when she returned, drank the water; and finding no hope. presently of a quieter heart, I sent her down, and followed her with precipitation; trembling so, that, had I not hurried, I question if I could have gone down at all. — O my dear, what a poor, passive machine is the body when the mind is disordered!

There are two doors to *my* parlour, as I used to call it. As I entered at one, my friends hurried out at the other. I just saw the gown of my sister, the last who slid away. My uncle Antony went out with them; but he staid not long, as you shall hear; and they all remained in the next parlour, a wainscot partition only parting the two. I remember them both in one: but they were separated in favour of us girls for each to receive her visitors in at her pleasure.

Mr. Solmes approached me as soon as I entered, cringing to the ground, a visible confusion in every feature of his face. After half a dozen choaked up madams, — he was very sorry — he was very much concerned — it was his misfortune — and there he stopped being unable presently to complete a sentence.

This gave me a little more presence of mind. Cowardice in a foe begets courage in one's self — I see that plainly now — yet perhaps, at bottom, the new made bravo is a greater coward than the other.

I turned from him, and seated myself in one of the fire-side chairs, fanning myself. I have since recollected, that I must have looked very saucily. Could I have had any *thoughts* of the man, I should have despised myself for it. But what can be said in the case of an aversion so perfectly sincere?

He hemmed five or six times, as I had done above; and these produced a sentence — That I could not but see his confusion. This sentence produced two or three or more. I believe my aunt had been his tutoress; for it was his awe, his reverence for so superlative a lady [I assure you!] and he hoped — he hoped — three times he hoped before he told me what — at last it came out, that I was too generous (generosity, he said, was my character) to despise him for such — for such — for such — *true* tokens of his love.

I do indeed see you under some confusion, sir; and this gives me hope, that although I have been compelled, as I may call it, to give way to this interview, it may be attended with happier effects than I had apprehended from it.

He had hemmed himself into more courage.

You could not, madam, imagine any creature so blind to your merits, and so little attracted by them, as easily to forego the interest and approbation he was honoured with by your worthy family, while he had any hope given him, that one day he might, by his perseverance and zeal, expect your favour.

I am but too much aware, sir, that it is upon the interest and approbation you mention, that you build such hope. It is impossible otherwise, that a man, who has any regard for his *own* happiness, would persevere against such declarations as I have made, and think myself obliged to make, in justice to you, as well as to myself.

He had seen many instances, he told me, and had heard of more, where ladies had seemed as averse, and yet had been induced, some by motives of compassion, others by persuasion of friends, to change their minds; and had been very happy afterwards; and he hoped this might be the case here.

I have no notion, sir, of compliment, in an article of such importance as this: yet I am sorry to be obliged to speak my mind so plainly, as I am going to do.—Know then, that I have an invincible objection, sir, to your address. I have avowed them with an earnestness that I believe is without example. Because I believe it is without example, that any young creature, circumstanced as I am, was ever treated as I have been treated on your account.

It is hoped, madam, that your consent may in time be obtained —*that* is the hope; and I shall be a miserable man if it cannot.

Better, sir, give me leave to say, you were miserable by yourself, than that you should make two so.

You may have heard, madam, things to my disadvantage. No man is without enemies. Be pleased to let me know *what* you have heard, and I will either own my faults, and amend; or I will convince you that I am basely *bespattered:* and once I understand you overheard something that I should say, that gave you offence: unguardedly, perhaps; but nothing but what showed my value, and that I would persist so long as I could have hope.

I have indeed heard many things to your disadvantage: — and I was far from being pleased with what I overheard fall from your lips: but as you were not any thing to me, and never could be, it was not for me to be concerned about the one or the other.

I am sorry, madam, to hear this. I am sure you should not tell me of any fault, that I would be unwilling to correct in myself.

Then, sir, correct *this* fault—do not wish to have a young creature compelled in the most material article of her life, for the sake of motives she despises; and in behalf of a person she cannot value: one that has, in her own right, sufficient to set her above all your offers, and a spirit that craves no more than what it *has*, to make itself easy and happy.

I don't see, madam, how you

22*

would be happy, if I were to discontinue my address: for —

That is nothing to you, sir, interrupted I: do you but withdraw your pretensions: and if it be thought fit to start up another man for my punishment, the blame will not lie at your door. You will be entitled to my thanks; and most heartily will I thank you.

He paused, and seemed a little at a loss: and I was going to give him still stronger and more personal instances of my plain dealing; when in came my uncle Antony.

So, niece, so! — Sitting in state like a queen, giving audience! *haughty* audience! — Mr. Solmes, why stand you thus humbly? — Why this distance, man? I hope to see you upon a more intimate footing before we part.

I arose, as soon as he entered — and approached him with a bent knee: Let me, sir, reverence my uncle, whom I have not for so long time seen! — Let me, sir, bespeak your favour and compassion.

You will have the favour of every body, niece, when you know how to deserve it.

If ever I deserved it, I deserve it now. — I have been hardly used! — I have made proposals that ought to be accepted, and such as would not have been *asked* of me. What have I done, that I must be banished and confined thus disgracefully? That I must not be allowed to have any free will in an article that concerns my present and future happiness? —

Miss Clary, replied my uncle, you have had your will in every thing till now; and this makes your parents' wills sit so heavy upon you.

My will, sir! Be pleased to allow me to ask, what was my will till now, but my father's will, and yours and my uncle Harlowe's will? — Has it not been my pride to obey and to oblige? — I never asked a favour, that I did not first sit down and consider, if it were *fit* to be granted. And now, to show my obedience, have I not offered to live single? — Have I not offered to divest myself of my grandfather's bounty, and to cast myself upon my father's; and that to be withdrawn, whenever I disoblige him? Why, dear good sir, am I to be made unhappy in a point so concerning to my happiness?

Your grandfather's estate is not wished from you. You are not desired to live a single life. You know *our* motives, and we guess at *yours*. And, let me tell you, well as we love you, we should much sooner choose to follow you to the grave, than that *yours* should take place.

I will engage never to marry any man, without my father's consent, and yours, sir, and every body's. Did I ever give you any cause to doubt my word? — And here I will take the solemnest oath that can be offered me —

That is the matrimonial one, interrupted he, with a big voice — And to this gentleman — It shall, it shall, cousin Clary! — And the more you oppose it, the worse it shall be for you.

This, and before the man, who seemed to assume courage upon it, highly provoked me.

Then, sir, you shall sooner follow me to the grave *indeed.* — I will undergo the cruelest death — I will even consent to enter into the awful vault of my ancestors, and have that bricked up upon me, rather than consent to be miserable for life. And Mr. Solmes, turning to him, take notice of what I say; *this* or *any* death, I will sooner undergo [that will quickly be over] than be yours, and for *ever* unhappy!

My uncle was in a terrible rage upon this. He took Mr. Solmes by the hand, shocked as the man seemed to be, and drew him to the window — Don't be surprised, Mr. Solmes, don't be concerned at *this.* We know, and rapt out a sad oath, what women will say in their wrath: the wind is not more boisterous, nor more changeable; and again he swore to that. — If you think it worth your while to wait for such an ungrateful girl as this, I'll engage she'll *veer about;* I'll engage she *shall.* And a third time violently swore to it.

Then coming up to me (who had thrown myself very much disordered by my vehemence, into the most distant window) as if he would have beat me; his face violently working, his hands clenched, and his teeth set — Yes, yes, yes, hissed the poor gentleman, you shall, you shall, you shall, cousin Clary, be Mr. Solmes's wife; we will see that you shall; and this in one week at furthest — and then a fourth time he confirmed it! — Poor gentleman! how he swore!

I am sorry, sir, said I, to see you in such a passion. All this, I am but too sensible, is owing to my brother's instigation; who would not himself give the instance of duty that is sought to be exacted from me. It is best for me to withdraw. I shall but provoke you further, I fear; for although I would gladly obey you if I could, yet this is a point determined with me; and I cannot so much as *wish* to get it over.

How could I avoid making these strong declarations, the man in presence?

I was going out at the door I came in at; the gentlemen looking upon one another, as if referring to each other what to do, or whether to engage my stay, or suffer me to go; and whom should I meet at the door but my brother, who had heard all that had passed!

He bolted upon me so unexpectedly, that I was surprised. He took my hand, and grasped it with violence: Return, pretty miss, said he; return, if you please. You shall not yet be *bricked up.* — Your *instigating* brother shall save you from that! — O thou fallen angel, said he, peering up to my downcast face — such a sweetness *here!* — and such an obstinacy *there!* — tapping my neck — O thou true woman! — though so young! — But you shall not have your rake: remember that: in a loud whisper, as if he would be decently indecent before the man. You shall be redeemed, and this worthy gentleman, raising his voice, will be so good as to redeem you from ruin—and hereafter you will bless him, or have reason to bless him, for his *condescension;* that was the brutal brother's word!

He had led me up to meet Mr. Solmes, whose hand he took, as he held mine. Here, sir, said he, take the rebel daughter's hand; I give it you now: she shall confirm the gift in a week's time, or will have neither father, mother, nor uncles, to boast of.

I snatched my hand away.

How now, miss! —

And how now, sir! — What right have *you* to dispose of my hand? — If you govern every body else, you shall not govern me; especially in a point so immediately relative to myself, and in which you neither have, nor ever shall have, any thing to do.

I would have broken from him; but he held my hand too fast.

Let me go, sir! — Why am I thus treated? — You *design*, I doubt not, with your unmanly gripings, to hurt me, as you do; but again I ask, wherefore is it that I am to be thus treated by you?

He tossed my hand from him with a whirl, that pained my very shoulder. I wept, and held my other hand to the part.

Mr. Solmes blamed him. So did my uncle.

He had no patience, he said, with such a perverse one; and to think of my reflections upon himself, before he entered. He had only given me back the hand I had not deserved he should touch. It was one of my arts to pretend to be pained.

Mr. Solmes said, he would sooner give up all his hopes of me, than that I should be used unkindly: and he offered to plead in my behalf to them both; and applied himself with a bow, as if for my approbation of his interposition.

Interpose not, Mr. Solmes, said I, to save me from my brother's violence. I cannot wish to owe an obligation to a man whose ungenerous perseverance is the occasion of *that* violence, and of all my disgraceful sufferings.

How generous in you, Mr. Solmes, said my brother, to interpose so kindly in behalf of such an immoveable spirit! I beg of you to persist in your address — the unnatural brother called it *address!* — For all our family's sake, and for *her* sake too, if you love her, persist! — Let us save her, if possible, from ruining herself. Look at her person! [And he gazed at me, from head to foot, pointing at me, as he referred to Mr. Solmes] think of her fine qualities! — All the world confesses them, and we all gloried in her till now. She is worth saving; and, after two or three more struggles, she will be yours, and take my word for it, will reward your patience. Talk not, therefore, of giving up your hopes, for a little whining folly. She has entered upon a parade, which she knows not how to quit with a *female grace*. You have only her pride and her obstinacy to encounter: and, depend upon it, you will be as happy a man in a fortnight, as a married man can be.

You have heard me say, my dear, that my brother has always taken a liberty to reflect upon our sex, and upon matrimony! — He would not, if he did not think it *wit* to do so! — Just as poor Mr. Wyerley, and others, whom we both know, profane and ridicule scripture; and all to evince their pretensions to the same pernicious talent, and to have it thought they are too wise to be religious.

Mr. Solmes, with a self-satisfied air, presumptuously said, he would suffer every thing, to *oblige* my family, and to *save* me: and doubted not to be amply rewarded, could he be so happy as to succeed at last.

Mr. Solmes, said I, if you have any regard for your own happiness (mine is out of the question with you: you have not generosity enough to make *that* any part of your scheme) prosecute no further your *address*, as my brother calls it. It is but *just* to tell you, that I could not bring my heart so much as to *think* of you, without the utmost disapprobation, *before* I was used as I have been: — and can you suppose I am such a slave, such a poor slave, as to be brought to change my mind by the violent usage I have met with?

And you, sir, turning to my brother, if you think that *meekness* always indicates *tameness;* and that there is no *magnanimity* without *bluster;* own yourself mistaken for once: for you shall have reason to judge from henceforth, that a generous mind is not to be forced; and that —

No more, said the imperious wretch, I charge you, lifting up his hands and eyes. Then turning to my uncle, Do you hear, sir? This is your once faultless niece! This is your favourite!

Mr. Solmes looked as if he knew not what to think of the matter; and had I been left alone with him, I saw plainly I could have got rid of him easily enough.

My uncle came to me, looking up also to my face, and down to my feet: And is it possible this can be *you?* All this violence from *you*, Miss Clary?

Yes, it *is* possible, sir — and, I will presume to say this vehemence on my side is but the natural consequence of the usage I have met with, and the rudeness I am treated with, even in your presence, by a brother, who has no more right to control me, than I have to control him.

This usage, cousin Clary, was not till all other means were tried with you.

Tried! to what end, sir? — Do I contend for any thing more than a mere negative? You *may*, sir, [turning to Mr. Solmes] *possibly* you may be induced the *rather* to persevere thus ungenerously, as the usage I have met with for your sake, and what you have now seen offered to me by my brother will show you what I *can* bear, were my evil destiny ever to make me yours.

Lord, madam, cried Solmes [all this time distorted into twenty different attitudes, as my brother and my uncle were blessing themselves, and speaking only to each other by their eyes, and by their working features; Lord, madam] what a construction is this!

A fair construction, sir, interrupted I: for he that can see a person whom he pretends to value, thus treated, and approve of it, must be capable of treating her thus himself. And that you *do* approve of it, is evident, by your declared perseverance, when you know I am confined, banished, and insulted, in order to make me consent to be what I never *can* be. — And this, let me tell you, as I have often told others, not from motives of obstinacy, but aversion.

Excuse me, sir, turning to my uncle — To you, as to my father's brother, I owe duty. I beg *your* pardon, that I cannot obey you: but as for my *brother;* he is *but* my brother; he shall not constrain me: and [turning to the unnatural wretch — I will call him wretch] knit your brows, sir, and frown as you will, I will ask you, Would *you,* in my case, make the sacrifices I am willing to make, to obtain every one's favour? If *not,* what right have you to treat me thus; and to procure me to be treated as I have been for so long a time past?

I had put myself by this time into great disorder: they were silent, and seemed by their looks to want to talk to one another, (walking about in violent disorders too) between whiles. I sat down fanning myself (as it happened, against the glass) and I could perceive my colour go and come; and being sick to the very heart, and apprehensive of fainting, I rung.

Betty came in. I called for a glass of water, and drank it: but nobody minded me. I heard my brother pronounce the words, Art! female art! to Solmes; which, together with the apprehension that he would not be welcome, I suppose kept *him* back. Else I could see the man was affected. And (still fearing I should faint) I arose, and taking hold of Betty's arm, Let me hold by you, Betty, said I: let me withdraw. And moved with trembling feet towards the door, and then turned about, and made a courtsey to my uncle — Permit me, sir, said I, to withdraw.

Whither go you, niece? said my uncle: we have not done with you yet. I charge you depart not. Mr. Solmes has something to open to you, that will astonish you — And you *shall* hear it.

Only, sir, by your leave, for a few minutes into the air, I will return, if you command it. I will hear all that I am to bear: that it may be over *now* and *for ever* — You will go with me, Betty?

And then without any further prohibition, I retired into the garden; and there, casting myself upon the first seat, and throwing Betty's apron over my face, leaning against her side, my hands between hers, I gave way to a violent burst of grief, or passion, or both; which, as it seemed, saved my heart from breaking, for I was sensible of an immediate relief.

I have already given you specimens of *Mrs.* Betty's impertinence. I shall not, therefore, trouble you with more; for the wench, notwithstanding this my distress, took great liberties with me, after she saw me a little recovered, and as I walked further into the garden; insomuch that I was obliged to silence her by an absolute prohibition of saying another word to me; and then she dropped behind me sullen and gloomy.

It was near an hour before I was sent for in again. The messenger was my cousin Dolly Hervey, who, with an eye of compassion and respect (for Miss Hervey always loved me, and calls herself my scholar, as you know) told me, my company was desired.

Betty left us.

Who commands my attendance, Miss Hervey? said I — Have you not been in tears, my dear?

Who can forbear tears? said she.

Why, what is the matter, cousin Dolly? — Sure, nobody is entitled to weep in this family, but *me!*

Yes, *I* am, madam, because I love you.

I kissed her; and is it for me, my sweet cousin, that you shed tears? — There never was love lost between us: but tell me, what is designed to be done with me, that I have this kind instance of your compassion for me?

You must take no notice of what I tell you, said the dear girl: but my mamma has been weeping for you, too, with me; but durst not let any body see it: O my Dolly, said my mamma, there never was so set a malice in man as in your cousin James Harlowe. They will ruin the flower and ornament of their family.

As how, Miss Dolly? — Did she not explain herself? — As how, my dear?

Yes; she said, Mr. Solmes would have given up his claim to you; for he said, you hated him, and there were no hopes; and your mamma was willing he should; and to have taken you at your word, to renounce Mr. Lovelace, and to live single: my mamma was for it too; for they heard all that passed between you and uncle Antony, and cousin James; saying, it was impossible to think of prevailing upon you to have Mr. Solmes. Uncle Harlowe seemed in the same way of thinking; at least, my mamma says he did not say any thing to the contrary. But your papa was immoveable, and was angry at your mamma and mine upon it: and hereupon your brother, your sister, and my uncle Antony, joined in, and changed the scene entirely. In short, she says, that Mr. Solmes had great matters engaged to him. He owned, that you were the finest young lady in England, and he would be content to be but little beloved, if he could *not*, after marriage, engage your heart, for the sake of having the honour to call you his but for one twelvemonth — I suppose he would break your heart in the next — for he is a cruel hearted man, I am sure.

My friends may break my heart, cousin Dolly; but Mr. Solmes will never have it in his power to break it.

I do not know that, madam: you will have good luck to avoid having him, by what I can find; for my mamma says, they are all now of one mind, herself excepted: and she is forced to be silent, your papa and brother are both so outrageous.

I am got above minding my brother, cousin Dolly: he is *but* my brother. But to my father I owe duty and obedience, if I could comply.

We are apt to be fond of any body that will side with us, when oppressed or provoked. I always loved my cousin Dolly; but now she endeared herself to me ten times more, by her soothing concern for me. I asked what *she* would do, were she in my case?

Without hesitation she replied, have Mr. Lovelace without doubt, and take up her own estate, if she were me; and there would be an end to it. — And Mr. Lovelace, she said, was a fine gentleman; Mr. Solmes was not worthy to *buckle his shoes.*

Miss Hervey told me further, that her mother was desired to come to me, to fetch me in; but she excused herself. I should have all my friends, she said, she believed, sit in judgment upon me.

I wish it had been so. But, as I have been told since, neither my father nor my mother would trust themselves with seeing me: the one it seems for passion-sake; my mother for tender considerations.

By this time we entered the house. Miss Hervey accompanied me into the parlour, and left me, as a person devoted, I then thought.

Nobody was there. I sat down, and had leisure to weep; reflecting upon what my cousin Dolly had told me.

They were all in my sister's parlour adjoining: for I heard a confused mixture of voices, some louder than others, which drowned the more compassionating accents.

Female accents I could distinguish the drowned ones to be. O my dear! what a hard-hearted sex is the other! Children of the same parents, how came they by their cruelty? — Do they get it by travel? — Do they get it by conversation with one another? — Or how do they get it? — Yet my sister, too, is as hard-hearted as any of them. But this may be no exception neither: for she has been thought to be masculine in her air and her spirit. She has then, perhaps, a soul of the *other* sex in a body of *ours.* — And so, for the honour of *our own*, will I judge of every woman for the future, who, imitating the rougher manners of men, acts unbeseeming the gentleness of her own sex.

Forgive me, my dear friend, for breaking into my story by these reflections. Were I rapidly to pursue my narration, without thinking, without reflecting, I believe I should hardly be able to keep in my right mind: since vehemence and passion would then be always uppermost; but while I *think* as I write, I cool, and my hurry of spirits is allayed.

I believe I was above a quarter of an hour enjoying my own comfortless contemplations, before any body came in to me; for they seemed to be in full debate. My aunt looked in first; O my dear, said she, are you there? and withdrew hastily to apprise them of it.

And then (as agreed upon I suppose) in came my uncle Antony, crediting Mr. Solmes with the words, *Let me lead you in, my dear friend,* having hold of his hand; while the new-made beau awkwardly followed, but more edgingly, as I may say, setting his feet mincingly, to avoid treading upon his leader's heels. Excuse me, my dear, this seeming levity; but those we do not love, appear in every thing ungraceful to us.

I stood up. My uncle looked very surly. — Sit down! — sit down, girl, said he — and drawing a chair near me, he placed his *dear* friend in it, whether he would or not, I having taken my seat. And my uncle sat on the other side of me.

Well, niece, taking my hand, we shall have very little more to say to you than we have already said, as to the subject that is so distasteful to you — unless, indeed, you have better considered of the matter — and first, let me know if you have?

The matter wants no consideration, sir.

Very well, very well, *madam!* said my uncle, withdrawing his hands from mine: could I ever have thought of this from you?

For God's sake, dearest madam, said Mr. Solmes, folding his hands — and there he stopped.

For God's sake, *what*, sir? — How came God's sake, and your sake, I pray you, to be the same?

This silenced *him*. My uncle could *only* be angry; and that he was before.

Well, well, well, Mr. Solmes, said my uncle, no more of supplication. You have not *confidence* enough to expect a woman's favour.

He then was pleased to hint what great things he had designed to do for me; and that it was more for *my* sake, after he returned from the Indies, than for the sake of any *other* of the family, that he had resolved to live a single life. — But now, concluded he, that the perverse girl despises all the great things it was once as much in my will, as it is in my power, to do for her, I will change my measures.

I told him, that I most sincerely thanked him for all his kind intentions to me: but that I was willing to resign all claim to any *other* of his favours than kind looks, and kind words.

He looked about him this way and that.

Mr. Solmes looked pitifully down.

But both being silent, I was sorry, I added, that I had too much reason to say a very harsh thing, as it might be thought; which was, that if he would but be pleased to convince my brother and sister, that he was absolutely determined to alter his generous purposes towards me, it might possibly procure me better treatment from both, than I was otherwise likely to have.

My uncle was very much displeased. But he had not the opportunity to express his displeasure, as he seemed preparing to do; for in came my brother in exceeding great wrath; and called me several vile names. His success hitherto, in his devices against me, had set him above keeping even decent measures.

Was this my spiteful construction? he asked — Was this the interpretation I put upon his brotherly care of me, and concern for me, in order to prevent my ruining myself?

It *is*, indeed, it *is*, said I: I know no other way to account for your late behaviour to me: and before your face, I repeat my request to my uncle, and I will make it to my other uncle whenever I am permitted to see him, that they will confer all their favours upon you and upon my sister; and only make me happy (it is all I wish for!) — in their kind looks, and kind words.

How they all gazed upon one another! — But could I be less peremptory before the man?

And, as to *your* care and concern for me, sir, turning to my brother; once more I desire it not. You are *but* my brother. My father and mother, I bless God, are both living; and were they *not*, you have given me abundant reason to say, that you are the very last person I would wish to have any concern for me.

How, niece! And is a brother, an *only* brother, of so little consideration with you, as this comes to? And ought he to have no concern for his sister's honour, and the family's honour?

My honour, sir! — I desire none of his concern for that! It never was endangered till it had his undesired concern! — Forgive me, sir — but when my brother knows how to act like a brother, or behave like a gentleman, he may deserve more consideration from me than it is possible for me now to think he does.

I thought my brother would have beat me upon this: but my uncle stood between us.

Violent girl, however, he called me — Who, said he, who would have thought it of her?

Then was Mr. Solmes told that I was unworthy of his pursuit.

But Mr. Solmes warmly took my part: he could not bear, he said, that I should be treated so roughly.

And so very much did he exert himself on this occasion, and so patiently was his warmth received by my brother, that I began to suspect, that it was a contrivance to make me think myself obliged to him; and that this might perhaps be one end of the pressed-for interview.

The very suspicion of this low artifice, violent as I was thought to be before, put me still more out of patience; and my uncle and my brother again praising his wonderful generosity, and his noble return of good for evil, You are a happy man, Mr. Solmes, said I, that you can so *easily* confer obligations upon a whole family, except upon one ungrateful person of it, whom you seem to intend *most* to oblige; but who being made unhappy by your favour, desires not to owe to *you* any protection from the violence of a brother.

Then was I a rude, an ungrateful, and unworthy creature.

I own it all — all, all you can call me, or think me, brother, do I own. I own my unworthiness with regard to this gentleman. I take your word for his abundant merit, which I have neither leisure nor inclination to examine into — it may perhaps be as great as your own — but yet I cannot thank him for his mediation: for who sees not, looking at my uncle, that this is giving himself a merit with every body at my expense?

Then turning to my brother, who seemed surprised into silence by my warmth, I must also acknowledge, sir, the favour of your superabundant care for me. But I discharge you of it; at least, while I have the happiness of nearer and dearer relations. You have given me no reason to think better of *your* prudence, than of my *own*. I am independant of *you*, sir, though I never desire to be so of my father: and although I wish for the good opinion of my uncles, it is *all* I wish for from them: and this, sir, I repeat *to make you and my sister easy*.

Instantly almost came in Betty, in a great hurry, looking at me as spitefully, as if she were my *sister*: Sir, said she to my brother, my master desires to speak with you this moment at the door.

He went to that which led into my sister's parlour; and this sentence I heard thundered from the mouth of one who had a right to all my reverence: Son James, let the rebel be this moment carried away to my brother's — this very moment — she shall not stay one hour more under my roof!

I trembled; I was ready to sink. Yet, not knowing what I did, or said, I flew to the door, and would have opened it: but my brother pulled it to, and held it close by the key — O my papa! — my dear papa! said I, falling upon my knees, at the door — admit your child to your presence! — Let me but plead my cause at your feet! — O reprobate not thus your distressed daughter!

My uncle put his handkerchief to his eyes: Mr. Solmes made a still more grievous face than he had before. But my brother's marble heart was untouched.

I will not stir from my knees, continued I, without admission.

At this door I beg it! — O let it be the door of mercy! and open it to me, honoured sir, I beseech you! — But this once, this once! although you were afterwards to shut it against me for ever!

The door was endeavoured to be opened on the inside, which made my brother let go the key on a sudden; and I pressing against it (all the time remaining on my knees) fell flat on my face into the other parlour; however without hurting myself. But, every body was gone, except Betty, who I suppose was the person that endeavoured to open the door. She helped to raise me up; and when I was on my feet, I looked round that apartment, and seeing nobody there, re-entered the other, leaning upon her; and then threw myself into the chair which I had sat in before; and my eyes overflowed, to my great relief: while my uncle Antony, my brother, and Mr. Solmes, left me, and went to my other relations.

What passed among them, I know not: but my brother came in by the time I had tolerably recovered myself, with a settled and haughty gloom upon his brow — Your father and mother command you instantly to prepare for your uncle Antony's. You need not be solicitous about what you shall take with you. You may give Betty your keys — take them, Betty, if the perverse one has them about her, and carry them to her mother. She will take care to send every thing after you that you shall want — but another night you will not be permitted to stay in this house.

I don't choose to give my keys to any body, except to my mother and into her own hands. You see how much I am disordered. It may cost me my life, to be hurried away so suddenly. I beg to be indulged till next Monday at least.

That will not be granted you. So prepare for this very night. And give up your keys. Give them to me, miss. I'll carry them to your mother!

Excuse me, brother. Indeed I won't.

Indeed you must. Have you any thing you are afraid should be seen by your mother?

Not if I am permitted to attend her.

I'll make a report accordingly. He went out.

In came Miss Dolly Hervey: I am sorry, madam, to be the messenger — but your mamma insists upon your sending up all the keys of your cabinet, library, and drawers.

Tell my mother, that I yield them up to her commands: tell her, I make no conditions with my mother: but if she find nothing she shall disapprove of, I beg that she will permit me to tarry here a few days longer. — Try, my Dolly [the dear girl sobbing with grief]; try, if your gentleness cannot prevail for me.

She wept still more, and said, It is sad, very sad, to see matters thus carried!

She took the keys, and wrapped

her arms about me; and begged me to excuse her for her message; and would have said more; but Betty's presence awed her, as I saw.

Don't pity me, my, dear, said I. It will be imputed to you as a fault. You see who is by.

The insolent wench scornfully smiled: One young lady pitying another in things of this nature, looks promising in the youngest, I must needs say.

I bid her be gone from my presence.

She would most gladly go, she said, were she not to stay about me by my mother's order.

It soon appeared for what she staid; for I offering to go up stairs to my apartment when my cousin went from me with the keys, she told me she was commanded (to her very great regret, she must own) to desire me not to go up at present.

Such a bold face, as she, I told her, should not binder me.

She instantly rang the bell, and in came my brother, meeting me at the door.

Return, return, miss — no going up yet.

I went in again, and throwing myself upon the window seat, wept bitterly.

Shall I give you the particulars of a ridiculously spiteful conversation that passed between my brother and me, in the time that he (with Betty) was in office to keep me in the parlour while my closet was searching? — But I think I will not. It can answer no good end.

I desired several times, while he staid, to have leave to retire to my apartment: but was denied. The search, I suppose, was not over.

Bella was one of those employed in it. They could not have a more diligent searcher. How happy it was they were disappointed!

But when my sister could not find the *cunning creature's* papers, I was to stand another visit from Mr. Solmes — preceded now by my aunt Hervey, sorely against her will, I could see that; accompanied by my uncle Antony, in order to keep her steady, I suppose.

But being a little heavy (for it is now past two in the morning) I will lie down in my clothes, to indulge the kind summons, if it will be indulged.

3 o'clock, Wednesday Morning.

I could not sleep — only dozed away one half-hour.

My aunt Hervey accosted me thus — O my dear child, what troubles do you give to your parents, and to every body! — I wonder at you!

I am sorry for it, madam.

Sorry for it, child! — *Why* then so very obstinate? — Come, sit down, my dear. I will sit next you; taking my hand.

My uncle placed Mr. Solmes on the other side of me: himself over-against me, almost close to me. Was I not finely beset, my dear?

Your brother, child, said my aunt, is too passionate — his zeal for *your* welfare pushes him on a little too vehemently.

Very true, said my uncle: but no more of this. We would now be glad to see if milder means will do with you — though, indeed, they were tried before.

I asked my aunt, if it were necessary, that that gentleman should be present?

There is a reason that he should, said my aunt, as you will hear by-and-by. — But I must tell you, first, that, thinking you was a little too angrily treated by your brother, your mother desired me to try what gentler means would do upon a spirit so generous as we used to think yours.

Nothing can be done, madam, I must presume to say, if this gentleman's address be the end.

She looked upon my uncle, who bit his lip; and looked upon Mr. Solmes, who rubbed his cheek; and shaking her head, Good, dear creature, said she, be calm. Let me ask you, if something would have been done, had you been more gently used, than you seem to think you have been?

No, madam, I cannot say it would, in this gentleman's favour. You know, madam, you know, sir, to my uncle, I ever valued myself upon my sincerity: and once indeed had the happiness to be valued for it.

My uncle took Mr. Solmes aside. I heard him say, whisperingly, She must, she shall, still be yours. — We'll see who'll conquer, parents or child, uncles or niece. I doubt not to be witness to all this being got over, and many a good-humoured jest made of this high phrenzy!

I was heartily vexed.

Though we cannot find out, continued he, yet we *guess*, who puts her upon this obstinate behaviour. It is not natural to her, man. Nor would I concern myself so much about her, but that I know what I say to be true, and intend to do great things for her.

I will hourly pray for that happy time, whispered as audibly Mr. Solmes. I never will revive the remembrance of what is now so painful to me.

Well, but niece, I am to tell you, said my aunt, that the sending up your keys, without making any conditions, has wrought for you what nothing else could have done. That, and the not finding any thing that could give them umbrage, together with Mr. Solmes's interposition —

O, madam, let me not owe an obligation to Mr. Solmes. I cannot repay it, except by my *thanks;* and *those* only on condition that he will decline his suit. To my thanks, sir [turning to him] if you have a heart capable of humanity, if you have any esteem for me for my *own* sake, I beseech you to entitle yourself! — I beseech you, do! —

O madam, cried he, believe, believe, believe me, it is impossible. While you are single, I *will* hope. While that hope is encouraged by so many worthy friends, I *must* persevere. I must not slight *them*, madam, because you slight *me*.

I answered him only with a look; but it was of high disdain: and turning from him— But what favour, dear madam [to my aunt] has the instance of duty you mention procured me?

Your mother and Mr. Solmes, replied my aunt, have prevailed, that your request to stay here till Monday next shall be granted, if you will promise to go cheerfully then.

Let me but choose my own visitors, and I will go to my uncle's house with pleasure.

Well, niece, said my aunt, we must wave this subject, I find. We will now proceed to another, which will require your utmost attention. It will give you the reason why Mr. Solmes's presence is requisite—

Ay, said my uncle, and shew you what sort of a man somebody is. Mr. Solmes, pray favour us, in the first place, with the letter you received from your anonymous friend.

I will, sir. And out he pulled a letter-case, and, taking out a letter, It is written in answer to one, sent to the person. It is superscribed, *To Roger Solmes, Esq.* It begins thus: *Honoured Sir—*

I beg your pardon, sir, said I: but what, pray, is the intent of reading this letter to me?

To let you know what a vile man you are thought to have set your heart upon, said my uncle in an audible whisper.

If, sir, it be suspected, that I have set my heart upon any other, why is Mr. Solmes to give himself any further trouble about me?

Only hear, niece, said my aunt; only hear what Mr. Solmes has to read and to say to you on this head.

If, madam, Mr. Solmes will be pleased to declare, that he has no view to serve, no end to promote, for himself, I will hear any thing he shall read. But if the contrary, you must allow me to say, that it will abate with me a great deal of the weight of whatever he shall produce.

Hear it but read, niece, said my aunt—

Hear it read, said my uncle. You are so ready to take part with—

With any body, sir, that is accused anonymously, and from interested motives.

He began to read; and there seemed to be a heavy load of charges in this letter against the poor criminal: but I stopped the reading of it, and said, It will not be *my* fault, if this vilified man be not as indifferent to me, as one whom I never saw. If he be otherwise at present, which I neither own nor deny, it proceeds from the strange methods taken to prevent it. Do not let one cause unite him and me, and we shall not be united. If my offer to live single be accepted, he shall be no more to me than *this* gentleman.

Still — Proceed, Mr. Solmes — hear it out, niece, was my uncle's cry.

But to what purpose, sir! said I — Has not Mr. Solmes a *view* in this? And, besides, can any thing worse be said of Mr. Lovelace, than I have heard said for several months past?

But this, said my uncle, and what Mr. Solmes can tell you besides, amounts to the *fullest proof* —

Was the unhappy man, then, so freely treated in his character before, *without* full proof? I beseech you, sir, give me not *too good* an opinion of Mr. Lovelace; as I *may* have, if such pains be taken to make him guilty, by one who means not his reformation by it; nor to do good, if I may presume to say so in this case, to any body but himself.

I see very plainly, girl, said my uncle, your prepossession, your fond prepossession, for the person of a man without morals.

Indeed, my dear, said my aunt, you too much justify all our apprehensions. Surprising! that a young creature of virtue and honour should thus esteem a man of a quite opposite character!

Dear madam, do not conclude against me too hastily. I believe Mr. Lovelace is far from being so good as he ought to be: but if every man's private life were searched into by *prejudiced people*, set on for that purpose, I know not whose reputation would be safe. I love a virtuous character, as much in man, as in woman. I think it as requisite and as meritorious in the one as in the other. And, if left to myself, I would prefer a person of such a character to royalty without it.

Why then, said my uncle —

Give me leave, sir — but I may venture to say, that many of those who have escaped censure, have not merited applause.

Permit me to observe, further, that Mr. Solmes himself may not be absolutely faultless. I never heard of his virtues. Some vices I have heard of. — Excuse me, Mr. Solmes, I speak to your face — the text about *casting the first stone* affords an excellent lesson.

He looked down; but was silent.

Mr. Lovelace may have vices *you* have not. You may have others, which *he* has not. — I speak not this to defend him, or to excuse you. No man is bad, no one is good, in *every thing*. Mr. Lovelace, for example, is said to be implacable, and to hate my friends: that does not make me value him the more: but give me leave to say, that *they* hate him as much. Mr. Solmes has his antipathies, likewise; very *strong* ones, and those to his *own relations;* which I don't find to be the other's fault; for he lives well with *his* — yet he may have as bad: — worse, pardon me, he cannot have, in my poor opinion: for what must be the man who *hates his own flesh?*

You know not, madam; ⎫ all in
You know not, niece;   ⎬ one
You know not, Clary;   ⎭ breath.

I may not, nor do I desire to know, Mr. Solmes's reasons. It concerns not me to know them: but the world, even the impartial part of it, accuses him. If the world is unjust or rash, in *one* man's case, why may it not be so in *another's?* That's all I mean by it. Nor can there be a greater sign of want of merit, than where a man seeks to pull down another's character, in order to build up his own.

The poor man's face was all this time overspread with confusion, twisted, as it were, and all awry, neither mouth nor nose standing in the middle of it. He looked, as if he were ready to cry! and had he been capable of pitying me, I had certainly tried to pity him.

They all three gazed upon one another in silence.

My aunt, I saw (at least I thought so) looked as if she would have been glad she might have appeared to approve of what I said. She but feebly blamed me, when she spoke, for not hearing what Mr. Solmes had to say. He himself seemed not now very earnest to be heard. My uncle said, there was no talking to me. And I should have absolutely silenced both gentlemen, had not my brother come in again to their assistance.

This was the strange speech he made at his entrance, his eyes flaming with anger: This prating girl has struck you all dumb, I perceive. Persevere, however, Mr. Solmes. I have heard every word she has said: and I know no other method of being even with her, than after she is yours, to make her as sensible of your power, as she now makes you of her insolence.

Fie, cousin Harlowe! said my aunt — could I have thought a brother would have said this to a gentleman, of a *sister?*

I must tell you, madam, said he, that *you* give the rebel courage. You yourself seem to favour too much the arrogance of her sex in her; otherwise she durst not have thus stopped her uncle's mouth by reflections upon him; as well as denied to hear a gentleman tell her the danger she is in from a libertine, whose protection, as she has plainly hinted, she intends to claim against her family.

Stopped my uncle's mouth by reflections upon him, Sir! said I, how can that be! How *dare* you to make such an application as this!

My aunt wept at his reflection upon her. — Cousin, said she to him, if *this* be the thanks I have for my trouble, I have done: your father would not treat me thus — and I *will* say, that the hint you gave was an unbrotherly one.

Not more unbrotherly than all the rest of his conduct to me, of late, madam, said I. I see by this specimen of his violence, how every body has been brought into his measures. Had I any the least apprehension of ever being in Mr. Solmes's power, this *might* have affected me. But you see, sir, to Mr. Solmes, what a conduct is thought necessary to enable you

23*

to arrive at your ungenerous end. You see how my brother *courts* for you!

I disclaim Mr. Harlowe's violence, madam, with all my soul. I will never remind you—

Silence, worthy sir, said I; I will take care you never shall have the opportunity.

Less violence, Clary, said my uncle. Cousin James, you are as much to blame as your sister.

In then came my sister. Brother, said she, you kept not your promise. You are *thought* to be to blame within, as well as here. Were not Mr. Solmes's generosity and affection to the girl *well* known, what you have said would be inexcusable. My father desires to speak with you; and with you, aunt; and with you, uncle; and with you, Mr. Solmes, if you please.

They all four withdrew into the next apartment.

I stood silent, as not knowing presently how to take this intervention of my sister's. But she left me not long at a loss— O thou perverse thing, said she [poking out her angry face at me, when they were all gone, but speaking spitefully low] — what trouble do you give to us all!

You and my brother, Bella, said I, give trouble to yourselves; yet neither you nor he have any business to concern yourselves about me.

She threw out some spiteful expressions, still in a low voice, as if she chose not to be heard without; and I thought it best to oblige her to raise her tone a little, if I could. If I *could*, did I say? It is easy to make a passionate spirit answer all one's views upon it.

She accordingly flamed out in a raised tone: and this brought my cousin Dolly in to us. Miss Harlowe, your company is desired.

I will come presently, cousin Dolly.

But again provoking a severity from me which she could not bear, and calling me names; in once more came Dolly, with another message that her company was desired.

Not mine, I doubt, Miss Dolly, said I.

The sweet-tempered girl burst out into tears, and shook her head.

Go in before me, child, said Bella [vexed to see her concern for me], with thy sharp face like a new moon: what dost thou cry for? Is it to make thy keen face look still keener?

I believe Bella was blamed, too, when she went in; for I heard her say, The *creature* was so provoking, there was no keeping a resolution.

Mr. Solmes, after a little while, came in again by himself, to take leave of me: full of scrapes and compliments; but too well tutored and encouraged, to give me hope of his declining his suit. He begged me not to impute to him any of the severe things to which he had been a sorrowful witness. He besought my compassion, as he called it.

He said, the result was, that he

had still hopes given him; and although discouraged by me, he was resolved to persevere, while I remained single. — And such long and such painful services he talked of, as never before were heard of.

I told him, in the strongest manner, what he had to trust to.

Yet still he determined to persist. — While I was no man's else, he must hope.

What! said I, will you still persist, when I declare, as I now do, that my affections are engaged? — And let my brother make the most of it.

He knew my principles, and adored me for them. He doubted not, that it was in his power to make me happy: and he was sure I would not want the will to be so.

I assured him, that were I to be carried to my uncle's, it should answer no end; for I would never see him; nor receive a line from him; nor hear a word in his favour, whoever were the person who should mention him to me.

He was sorry for it. He must be miserable, were I to hold in that mind. But he doubted not, that I might be induced by my father and uncles to change it —

Never, never, he might depend upon it.

It was richly worth his patience, and the trial.

At my *expense!* — At the price of all my *happiness*, sir?

He hoped I should be induced to think otherwise.

And then would he have run into his fortune, his settlements, his affection — vowing that never man loved a woman with so sincere a passion, as he loved me.

I stopped him as to the first part of his speech: and to the second, of the sincerity of his passion. What then, sir, said I, is your love to one, who must assure you, that never young creature looked upon man with a more sincere disapprobation, than I look upon you? and tell me, what argument can you urge, that this *true* declaration answers not beforehand?

Dearest madam, what can I say? — On my knees I beg —

And down the ungraceful wretch dropped on his knees.

Let me not kneel in vain, madam: let me not be thus despised. — And he looked most odiously sorrowful.

I have kneeled too, Mr. Solmes: often have I kneeled: and I will kneel again — even to *you*, sir, will I kneel, if there be so much merit in kneeling; provided you will not be the implement of my cruel brother's undeserved persecution.

If all the services, even to worship you, during my whole life — you, madam, invoke and expect mercy: yet shew none —

Am I to be cruel to myself, to shew mercy to you; take my estate, sir, with all my heart, since you are such a favourite in this house! — Only leave me *myself* — the mercy you ask for, do you shew to others.

If you mean to my relations, madam — unworthy as they are,

all shall be done that you shall prescribe.

Who, I, sir, to find you bowels you naturally have not? I to purchase their happiness by the forfeiture of *my own?* What I ask you for, is mercy to myself: that, since you seem to have some power over my relations, you will use it in my behalf. Tell them that you see I cannot conquer my aversion to you; tell them, if you are a wise man, that you too much value your own happiness, to risk it against such a determined antipathy: tell them, that I am unworthy your offers: and that in mercy to yourself, as well as to me, you will not prosecute a suit so impossible to be granted.

I will risk all consequences, said the fell wretch, rising with a countenance whitened over, as if with malice, his hollow eyes flashing fire, and biting his under lip, to shew he could be *manly.* Your hatred, madam, shall be no objection with me: and I doubt not in a few days to have it in my power to shew you —

You have it in your power, sir —

He came well off — *to shew you* more generosity, than, noble as you are said to be to others, you shew to me.

The man's face became his anger: it seems formed to express the passion.

At that instant, again came in my brother — Sister, sister, sister, said he, with his teeth set, act on the termagant part you have so newly assumed — most wonderfully well does it become you. It is but a short one, however. Tyranness in your turn, accuse others of your own guilt — but leave her, Mr. Solmes: her time is short. You'll find her humble and mortified enough very quickly — then, how like a little tame fool will she look, with her conscience upbraiding her, and begging of you [with a whining voice, the barbarous brother spoke] to forgive and forget!

More he said, as he flew out, with a glowing face, upon Shorey's coming in to recal him on his violence.

I removed from chair to chair, excessively frighted and disturbed at this brutal treatment.

The man attempted to excuse himself, as being sorry for my brother's passion.

Leave me, leave me, sir, fanning — or I shall faint. And indeed I thought I should.

He recommended himself to my favour with an air of assurance; augmented, as I thought, by a distress so visible in me; for he even snatched my trembling, my struggling hand; and ravished it to his odious mouth.

I flung from him with high disdain: and he withdrew, bowing and cringing; self-gratified, and enjoying, as I thought, the confusion he saw me in.

The wretch is now, methinks, before me; and now I see him awkwardly striding backward, as he retired, till the edge of the opened door, which he ran against, remembered him to turn his welcome back upon me.

Upon his withdrawing, Betty brought me word, that I was permitted to go up to my own chamber: and was bid to consider of every thing: for my time was short. Nevertheless, she believed I might be permitted to stay till Saturday.

She tells me, that although my brother and sister were blamed for being so *hasty* with me, yet when they made *their* report, and my uncle Antony *his*, of *my* provocations, they were all more determined than ever in Mr. Solmes's favour.

The wretch himself, she tells me, pretends to be more in love with me than before; and to be rather delighted than discouraged with the conversation that passed between us. He ran on, she says, in raptures, about the grace wherewith I should dignify his board; and the like sort of stuff, either of *his* saying, or of *her* making.

She closed all with a Now is your time, miss, to submit with a grace, and to make your own terms with him: — else, I can tell you, were I Mr. Solmes, it should be worse for you: and who, miss, of *our* sex, proceeded the saucy creature, would admire a rakish gentleman, when she might be admired by a sober one to the end of the chapter?

She made this further speech to me on quitting my chamber — You have had amazing good luck, miss, I must tell you, to keep your writings concealed so cunningly, you must needs think I know that you are always at your pen: and as you endeavour to hide that knowledge from me, I do not think myself obliged to keep your secret. But I love not to aggravate. I had rather reconcile by much. Peace-making is my talent, and ever was. And had I been as much your foe, as you imagine, you had not perhaps been here now. But this, however, I do not say to make a merit with you, miss: for, truly, it will be the better for you the sooner every thing is over with you. And better for me, and for every one else; that's certain. Yet one hint I must conclude with; that your pen and ink (soon as you are to go away) will not be long in your power, I do assure you, miss. And then, having lost *that* amusement, it will be seen, how a mind so active as yours will be able to employ itself.

This hint alarms me so much, that I shall instantly begin to conceal, in different places, pens, ink, and paper; and to deposit some in the ivy summer-house, if I can find a safe place there; and, at the worst, I have got a pencil of black, and another of red lead, which I use in my drawings; and my patterns shall serve for paper, if I have no other.

How lucky it was, that I had got away my papers! They made a strict search for them; that I can see, by the disorderly manner they have left all things in: for you know that I am such an observer of method, that I can go to a bit of ribband, or lace, or edging, blindfold. The same in my books: which they have strangely disordered and mismatched; to look behind them, and in some of them, I suppose. My clothes too are rumpled not a little. No place has escaped them. To your hint, I thank you, are they indebted for their disappointment.

The pen, through heaviness and fatigue, dropt out of my fingers, at the word *indebted*. I resume it to finish the sentence; and to tell you, that I am,

Your for ever obliged and
affectionate
CL. HARLOWE.

LETTER LXXVIII.
Miss Clarissa Harlowe to Miss Howe.

Wednesday, 11 o'clock, April 5.

I MUST write as I have opportunity; making use of my concealed stores: for my pens and ink (all of each that they could find) are taken from me; as I shall tell you more particularly by-and-by.

About an hour ago I deposited my long letter to you; as also, in the usual place, a billet to Mr. Lovelace, lest his impatience should put him upon some rashness; signifying, in four lines, "that the interview was over; and that I hoped my steady refusal of Mr. Solmes would discourage any further applications to me in his favour."

Although I was unable (through the fatigue I had undergone, and by reason of sitting up all night, to write to you; which made me lie longer than ordinary this morning) to deposit my letter to you sooner; yet I hope you will have it in such good time, as that you will be able to send me an answer to it this night, or in the morning early; which, if ever so short, will inform me, whether I may depend upon your mother's indulgence or not. This it behoves me to know as soon as possible; for they are resolved to hurry me away on Saturday next at furthest; perhaps to-morrow.

I will now inform you of all that happened previous to their taking away my pen and ink, as well as of the manner in which that act of violence was committed; and this as briefly as I can.

My aunt, who (as well as Mr. Solmes, and my two uncles) lives here, I think, came up to me, and said, she would fain have me hear what Mr. Solmes had to say of Mr. Lovelace — only that I might be apprised of some things, that would convince me what a vile man he is, and what a wretched husband he must make. I might give them what degree of credit I pleased; and take them with abatement for Mr. Solmes's interestedness, if I thought fit. But it might be of use to me, were it but to question Mr. Lovelace indirectly upon some of them that related to *myself.*

I was indifferent, I said, about what he could say of me; as I was sure it could not be to my disadvantage: and as *he* had no reason to impute to me the forwardness which my unkind friends had so causelessly taxed me with.

She said, that he gave himself high airs on account of his family; and spoke as despicably of ours as if an alliance with *us* were beneath him.

I replied, that he was a very unworthy man, if it were true, to speak slightingly of a family, which was as good as his own, 'bating that it was not allied to the peerage: that the dignity itself, I thought, conveyed more shame than honour to descendants, who had not merit to adorn, as well as to be adorned by it: that my brother's absurd pride, indeed, which made him every where declare, he would never marry but to *quality*, gave a disgraceful preference against ours: but that were I to be assured, that Mr. Lovelace was capable of so mean a pride as to insult us, or value himself on such an accidental advantage, I should think as despicably of his sense, as every body else did of his morals.

She insisted upon it, that he had taken such liberties; and offered to give some instances, which, she said, would surprise me.

I answered, that were it ever so certain that Mr. Lovelace had taken such liberties, it would be but common justice (so much hated as he was by all our family, and so much inveighed against in all companies by them) to inquire into the provocation he had to say what was imputed to him; and whether the value some of my friends put upon the riches they possess (throwing perhaps contempt upon every other advantage, and even discrediting *their own* pretensions to family, in order to depreciate *his*) might not provoke him to like contempts. Upon the whole, madam, said I, can you say, that the inveteracy lies not as much on *our* side, as on *his?* Can *he* say any thing of *us* more disrespectful than *we* say of *him?*—And as to the suggestion, so often repeated, that he will make a bad husband, is it possible for him to use a wife worse than I am used; particularly by my brother and sister?

Ah, niece! ah, my dear! how firmly has this wicked man attached you!

Perhaps not, madam. But really great care should be taken by fathers and mothers, when they would have their daughters of *their* minds in these particulars, not to say things that shall necessitate the child, in honour and generosity, to take part with the man her friends are averse to. But, waving all this, as I have offered to renounce him for ever, I see not why he should be mentioned to me, nor why I should be wished to hear any thing about him.

Well, but still, my dear, there can be no harm to let Mr. Solmes tell you what Mr. Lovelace has said of *you*. Severely as you have treated Mr. Solmes, he is fond of attending you once more: he begs to be heard on this head.

If it be proper for me to hear it, madam —

It *is*, eagerly interrupted she, very proper.

Has what he has said of *me*, madam, convinced *you* of Mr. Lovelace's baseness?

It has, my dear: and that you ought to abhor him for it.

Then, dear madam, be pleased to let me hear it from *your* mouth: there is no need that I should see Mr. *Solmes*, when it will have double the weight from *you*. What, madam, has the man dared to say of *me?*

My aunt was quite at a loss.

At last, Well, said she, I see how you are attached. I am sorry for it, miss. For I do assure you it will signify nothing. You must be Mrs. Solmes, and that in a very few days.

If consent of heart, and assent of voice, be necessary to a marriage, I am sure I never can, nor ever will, be married to Mr. Solmes. And what will any of my relations be answerable for, if they force my hand into his, and hold it there till the service be read; I perhaps insensible, and in fits, all the time!

What a romantic picture of a forced marriage have you drawn, niece! Some people would say, you have given a fine description of your own obstinacy, child.

My brother and sister would: but you, madam, distinguish, I am sure, between obstinacy and aversion.

Supposed aversion may owe its rise to *real* obstinacy, my dear.

I know my own heart, madam. I wish *you* did.

Well, but see Mr. Solmes once more, niece. It will oblige, and make for you, more than you imagine.

What should I see him for, madam — Is the man fond of hearing me declare my aversion to him? — Is he desirous of having me more and more incense my friends against myself? — *O my cunning, my ambitious brother!*

Ah, my dear! — with a look of pity, as if she understood the meaning of my exclamation — but must that necessarily be the case?

It must, madam, if they will take offence at me for declaring my steadfast detestation of Mr. Solmes as a husband.

Mr. Solmes is to be pitied, said she. He adores you. He longs to see you once more. He loves you the better for your cruel usage of him yesterday. He is in raptures about you.

Ugly creature, thought I! — He in raptures!

What a cruel wretch must he be, said I, who can enjoy the distress to which he so largely contributes! — But I see, I see, madam, that I am considered as an animal to be baited, to make sport for my brother and sister, and Mr. Solmes. They are all, all of them, wanton in their cruelty. — *I*, madam, see the man! — the man so incapable of pity! — Indeed I will not see him if I can help it. — Indeed I will not.

What a construction does your

lively wit put upon the admiration, Mr. Solmes expresses of you! — Passionate as you were yesterday, and contemptuously as you treated him, he dotes upon you for the very severity by which he suffers. He is not so ungenerous a man as you think him: nor has he an unfeeling heart. — Let me prevail upon you, my dear (as your *father* and *mother* expect it of you) to see him once more, and hear what he has to say to you.

How can I consent to see him again, when yesterday's interview was interpreted by you, madam, as well as by every other, as an encouragement to him? When I myself declared, that if I saw him a *second* time by my own consent, it might be so taken? — And when I am determined never to encourage him?

You might spare your reflections upon *me*, miss. I have no thanks either from one side or the other.

And away she flung.

Dearest madam! said I, following her to the door —

But she would not hear me further; and her sudden breaking from me occasioned a hurry to some mean listener; as the slipping of a foot from the landing-place on the stairs discovered to me.

I had scarcely recovered myself from this attack, when up came Betty — Miss, said she, your company is desired below stairs in your own parlour.

By whom, Betty?

How can I tell, miss? — Perhaps by your sister, perhaps by your brother — I know they won't come up stairs to your apartment again.

Is Mr. Solmes gone, Betty?

I believe he is, miss — would you have him sent for back? said the bold creature.

Down I went: and to whom should I be sent for but to my brother and Mr. Solmes! The latter standing sneaking behind the door, so that I saw him not till I was mockingly led by the hand into the room by my brother. And then I started as if I had beheld a ghost.

You are to sit down, Clary.

And what then, brother?

Why then, you are to put off that scornful look, and hear what Mr. Solmes has to say to you.

Sent for down to be baited again! thought I.

Madam, said Mr. Solmes, as if in haste to speak, lest he should not have an opportunity given him, [and indeed he judged right] Mr. Lovelace is a declared *marriage hater*, and has a design upon your honour, if ever —

Base accuser! said I, in a passion, snatching my hand from my brother, who was insolently motioning to give it to Mr. Solmes; he has not! — he dares not! — But *you* have, if endeavouring to force a free mind be to dishonour it!

O thou violent creature! said my brother — but not gone yet — for I was rushing away.

What mean you, sir /struggling

vehemently to get away] to detain me thus against my will?

You shall not go, violence! clasping his unbrotherly arms about me.

Then let not Mr. Solmes stay. — Why hold you me thus? He shall not for *your own* sake, if I can help it, see how barbarously a brother can treat a sister who deserves not evil treatment.

And I struggled so vehemently to get from him, that he was forced to quit my hand! which he did with these words — Begone then, fury! — How strong is will! — There is no holding her.

And up I flew to my chamber, and locked myself in, trembling and out of breath.

In less than a quarter of an hour up came Betty. I let her in upon her tapping, and asking (half out of breath too) for admittance.

The Lord have mercy upon us; said she. — What a *confusion of a house* is this; — [hurrying up and down, fanning herself with her handkerchief] Such angry masters and mistresses! — Such an obstinate young lady! — Such an humble lover! — Such enraged uncles! — Such — O dear! — dear! what a topsy-turvy house is this! — And all for what, trow? — Only because a young lady *may* be happy, and will *not*? — Only because a young lady *will* have a husband, and will *not* have a husband? What hurly-burlies are here, where all used to be peace and quietness!

Thus she ran on to herself, while I sat as patiently as I could (being assured that her errand was not designed to be a welcome one to me) to observe when her soliloquy would end.

At last, turning to me — I must do as I am bid. I can't help it — don't be angry with me, miss. But I must carry down your pen and ink: and that this moment.

By whose order?

By your papa's and mamma's.

How shall I know that?

She offered to go to my closet: I stept in before her: Touch it if you dare.

Up came my cousin Dolly — Madam! — madam! said the poor weeping good-natured creature, in broken sentences — you must — indeed you must — deliver to Betty — or to me — your pen and ink.

Must I, my sweet cousin? Then I will to you; but not to this bold body. And I gave my standish to her.

I am sorry, very sorry, said she, to be the messenger: but your papa will not have you in the same house with him: he is resolved you shall be carried away to-morrow, or Saturday at furthest. And therefore your pen and ink are taken away, that you may give nobody notice of it.

And away went the dear girl, very sorrowful, carrying down with her my standish, and all its furniture, and a little parcel of pens beside, which having been seen when the great search was made, she was bid to ask for. As it happened, I had not diminished it, having hid half a dozen crowquills in as many different places. It was lucky; for I doubt not they had numbered how many were in the parcel.

Betty ran on, telling me, that my mother was now as much incensed against me as any body — that my doom was fixed — that my violent behaviour had not left one to plead for me — that Mr. Solmes bit his lip, and muttered, and *seemed to have more in his head than could come out at his mouth;* that was her phrase.

And yet she also hinted to me, that the cruel wretch took pleasure in seeing me: although so much to my disgust — and so wanted to see me again. Must he not be a savage, my dear?

The wench went on — that my uncle Harlowe said, that now *he* gave me up — that he pitied Mr. Solmes — yet hoped he would not think of this to my detriment hereafter; that my uncle Antony was of opinion, that I ought to smart for it; *and*, for *her* part — and then, as one of the family, she gave her opinion of the same side.

As I have no other way of hearing any thing that is said or intended below, I bear sometimes more patiently than I otherwise should do with her impertinence. And indeed she seems to be in all my brother's and sister's councils.

Miss Hervey came up again, and demanded an half-pint ink-bottle which they had seen in my closet.

I gave it her without hesitation. If they have no suspicion of my being able to write, they will perhaps let me stay longer than otherwise they would.

This, my dear, is now my situation.

All my dependence, all my hopes, are in your mother's favour. But for that, I know not *what* I might do: for who can tell what will come next?

LETTER LXXIX.

Miss Clarissa Harlowe to Miss Howe.

Wednesday, four o'clock in the afternoon.

I am just returned from depositing the letter I so lately finished, and such of Mr. Lovelace's letters as I had not sent you. My long letter I found remaining there. — So you will have both together.

I am concerned, methinks, it is not with you. — But your servant cannot always be at leisure. However, I will deposit as fast as I write. I must keep nothing by me now: and when I write, lock myself in, that I may not be surprised now they think I have no pen and ink.

I found in the usual place another letter from this diligent man: and by its contents a confirmation that nothing passes in this house but he knows it; and that almost as soon as it passes. For this letter must have been written before he could have received my billet; and deposited, I suppose, when that was taken away; yet he compliments me in it upon asserting myself (as he calls it) on that occasion to my uncle and to Mr. Solmes.

"He assures me, however, that they are more and more determined to subdue me.

"He sends me the compliments of his family; and acquaints me with their earnest desire to see me amongst them. Most vehemently does he press for my quitting this house while it is in my power to get away: and again begs leave to order his uncle's chariot and six to attend my commands at the stile leading to the coppice adjoining to the paddock.

"Settlements to my own will he again offers. Lord M. and Lady Sarah, and Lady Betty to be guarantees of his honour and justice. But if I choose not to go to either of those ladies, nor yet to make him the happiest of men so soon as it is nevertheless his hope that I will, he urges me to withdraw to my own house, and to accept of my Lord M. for my guardian and protector till my cousin Morden arrives. He can contrive to give me easy possession of it, and will fill it with his female relations on the first invitation from me; and Mrs. Norton or Miss Howe may be undoubtedly prevailed upon to be with me for a time. There can be no pretence for litigation, he says, when I am once in it. Nor, if I choose to have it so, will he appear to visit me, nor presume to mention marriage to me till all is quiet and easy; till every method I shall prescribe for a reconciliation with my friends is tried; till my cousin comes; till such settlements are drawn as he shall approve of for me; and that I have unexceptionable proofs of his own good behaviour."

As to the disgrace a person of my character may be apprehensive of upon quitting my father's house, he observes (too truly I doubt), "that the treatment I meet with is in every one's mouth: yet that the public voice is in my favour: my friends themselves, he says, *expect* that I will do myself what he calls this justice: why else do they confine me? He urges, that, thus treated, the independence I have a right to will be my sufficient excuse, going but from their house to my own, if I choose that measure; or in order to take possession of my own, if I do not: that all the disgrace I *can* receive they have already given me: that his concern and his family's concern in my honour will be equal to my own, if he may be so happy ever to call me his: and he presumes, he says, to aver, that no family can better supply the loss of my own friends to me than his, in whatever way I shall do them the honour to accept of his and their protection.

"But he repeats, that, in all events, he will oppose my being carried to my uncle's; being well assured that I shall be lost to him for ever if once I enter into that house." He tells me, "that my brother and sister, and Mr. Solmes, design to be there to receive me: that my father and mother will not come near me till the ceremony is actually over; and that then they will appear, in order to try to reconcile me to my odious husband, by urging upon me the obligations I shall be supposed to be under from a double duty."

How, my dear, am I driven on one side, and invited on the other! — This last intimation is but a too probable one. All the steps they take seem to tend to this! and, indeed, they have declared almost as much.

He owns, "that he has already taken his measures upon this intelligence. — But that he is so desirous for *my sake* (I must suppose, he says, that he owes them no forbearance *for their own*) to avoid coming to extremities, that he has suffered a person, whom they do not suspect, to acquaint them with his resolutions, as, if come at by accident, if they persist in their design to carry me by violence to my uncle's, in hopes that they may be induced from the fear of mischief which may ensue to *change* their measures: and yet he is aware that he has exposed himself to the greatest risks by having caused this intimation to be given them; since, if he cannot benefit himself by their fears, there is no doubt but they will doubly guard themselves against him upon it."

What a dangerous enterpriser, however, is this man!

"He begs a few lines from me by way of answer to this letter, either this evening or to-morrow morning. If he be not so favoured, he shall conclude, from what he knows of the fixed determination of my relations, that I shall be under a closer restraint than before: and he shall be obliged to take his measures according to that presumption."

You will see by this abstract, as well as by his letter preceding this (for both run in the same strain), how strangely forward the difficulty of my situation has brought him in his declarations and proposals, and in his threatenings too: which, but for that, I would not take from him.

Something, however, I must speedily resolve upon, or it will be out of my power to help myself.

Now I think of it, I will inclose his letter (so might have spared the abstract of it) that you may the better judge of all his proposals and intelligence, and lest it should fall into other hands. I cannot forget the contents, although I am at a loss what answer to return.*

I cannot bear the thoughts of throwing myself upon the protection of his friends: — but I will not examine his proposals closely till I hear from you. Indeed I have no *eligible* hope but in your mother's goodness. *Her's* is a protection I could more *reputably* fly to than to that of any other person: and from her's should be ready to return to my father's (for the breach then would not be irre-

---

* She accordingly incloses Mr. Lovelace's letter. But as the most material contents of it are given in her abstract it is omitted.

parable, as it would be if I fled to his family): to *return*, I repeat, on such terms as shall secure but my *negative*, not my *independence:* I do not aim at that (so shall lay your mother under the less difficulty): although I have a right to be put into possession of my grandfather's estate, if I were to insist upon it:— such a right, I mean, as my brother exerts in the estate left *him;* and which nobody disputes.— God forbid that I should ever think myself freed from my father's *reasonable* control, whatever right my grandfather's will has given me! He, good gentleman, left me that estate as a reward of my duty, and not to set me above it, as has been justly hinted to me: and this reflection makes me more fearful of not answering the intention of so valuable a bequest.— O that my friends knew but my heart!— Would but think of it as they used to do!— For once more I say, if it deceive me not, it is not altered, although theirs are!

Would but your mother permit you to send her chariot, or chaise, to the by-place where Mr. Lovelace proposes Lord M.'s shall come (provoked, intimidated, and apprehensive as I am), I would not hesitate a moment what to do. Place me any where, as I have said before—in a cot, in a garret; any where — disguised as a servant — or let me pass as a servant's sister — so that I may but escape Mr. Solmes on one hand, and the disgrace of refuging with the family of a man at enmity with my own on the other, and I shall be in some measure happy! — Should your good mother refuse me, what refuge, or whose, can I fly to?— Dearest creature, advise your distressed friend.

* * *

I broke off here — I was so excessively uneasy, that I durst not trust myself with my own reflections: I therefore went down to the garden, to try to calm my mind, by shifting the scene. I took but one turn upon the filbert-walk, when Betty came to me. Here, miss, is your papa — here is your uncle Antony! — here is my young master — and my young mistress coming to take a walk in the garden; and your papa sends me to see where you are, for fear he should meet you.

I struck into an oblique path, and got behind the yew hedge, seeing my sister appear; and there concealed myself till they were gone past me.

My mother, it seems, is not well. My poor mother keeps her chamber — should she be worse, I should have an additional unhappiness, in apprehension that my reputed undutifulness had touched her heart.

You cannot imagine what my emotions were behind the yew hedge, on seeing my father so near me. I was glad to look at him through the hedge as he passed by: but I trembled in every joint, when I heard him utter *these* words: Son James, to you, and to Bella, and to you, brother, do I wholly commit this matter. That I was meant I cannot doubt. And yet why was I so affected; since I may be said to have been given up to the cruelty of my brother and sister for many days past?

* * *

While my father remained in the garden, I sent my dutiful compliments to my mother, with inquiry after her health, by Shorey, whom I met accidentally upon the stairs; for none of the servants, except my gaoleress, dare to throw themselves in my way. I had the mortification of such a return, as made me repent my message, though not my concern for her health. "Let her not inquire after the disorders she occasions," was her harsh answer. "I will not receive any compliments from her."

Very, *very* hard, my dear! Indeed it is very hard.

* * *

I have the pleasure to hear that my mother is already better. A colicky disorder, to which she is too subject. It is hoped it is gone off — God send it may! — Every evil that happens in this house is owing to me!

This good news was told me, with a circumstance very unacceptable; for Betty said, she had orders to let me know, that my garden walks and poultry visits were suspected: and that both will be prohibited, if I stay here till Saturday or Monday.

Possibly this is said by order, to make me go with less reluctance to my uncle's.

My mother bid her say, if I expostulated about these orders, and about my pen and ink, "that reading was more to the purpose at present than writing: that by the one I might be taught my duty; that the other, considering whom I was believed to write to, only stiffened my will: that my needle-works had better be pursued than my airings, which were observed to be taken in all weathers."

So, my dear, if I do not resolve upon something soon, I shall neither be able to avoid the intended evil, nor have it in my power to correspond with you.

Wednesday night.

ALL is in a hurry below stairs. Betty is in and out like a spy. Something is working, I know not what. I am really a good deal disordered in body as well as mind. Indeed I am quite heart-sick.

I will go down, though 'tis almost dark, on pretence of getting a little air and composure. Robert has my two former, I hope, before now: and I will deposit this, with Lovelace's inclosed, if I can, for fear of another search.

I know not what I shall do! — All is so strangely busy! — Doors clapt to — going out of one apartment, hurryingly, as I may say, into another. Betty, in her alarming way, staring, as if of frighted importance; twice with me in half an hour; called down in haste by Shorey the last time; leaving me with still *more* meaning in her looks and gestures — yet possibly nothing in all this worthy of my apprehensions —

Here again comes the creature, with her deep-drawn affected sighs, and her *O dears! O dears!*

* * *

More dark hints thrown out by the saucy creature. But she will not explain herself. "Suppose this pretty business ends in murder!" she says, "I may rue my opposition as long as I live, for aught she knows. Parents will not be *baffled* out of their children by impudent gentlemen; nor is it fit they should. It may come home to me when I least expect it."

These are the gloomy and perplexing hints this impertinent throws out. Probably they arise from the information Mr. Lovelace says he has secretly permitted them to have (from his vile double-faced agent, I suppose!) of his resolution to prevent my being carried to my uncle's.

How *justly*, if so, may this exasperate them! — How am I driven to and fro, like a feather in the wind, at the pleasure of the rash, the selfish, and the headstrong! and when I am as averse to the proceedings of the one as I am to those of the other! For although I was induced to carry on this unhappy correspondence, as I think I ought to call it, in hopes to prevent mischief; yet indiscreet measures are fallen upon by the rash man, before I, who am so much concerned in the event of the present contentions, can be consulted: and between his violence on one hand, and that of my relations on the other, I find myself in danger from both.

O my dear! what is worldly wisdom but the height of folly? — I, the meanest, at least the youngest, of my father's family, to thrust myself in the gap between such uncontrollable spirits! — To the interception perhaps of the designs of Providence, which may intend to make these hostile spirits their own punishers. — If so, what presumption! — Indeed, my dear friend, I am afraid I have thought myself of too much consequence. But, however this be, *it is good, when calamities befal us, that we should look into ourselves, and fear.*

If I am prevented depositing this and the inclosed (as I intend to try to do, late as it is) I will add to it as occasion shall offer. Mean time, believe me to be

Your ever affectionate and grateful
CL. HARLOWE.

Under the superscription, written with a pencil after she went down.

"My two former are not yet taken away — I am surprised — I hope you are well — I hope all is right betwixt your mother and you."

LETTER LXXX.

Miss Howe to Miss Clarissa Harlowe.

Thursday morning, April 6.

I have your three letters. Never was there a creature more impatient on the most interesting uncertainty than I was, to know the event of the interview between you and Solmes.

It behoves me to account to my dear friend, in her present unhappy situation, for every thing that may have the least appearance of negligence or remissness on my part. I sent Robin in the morning early, in hopes of a deposit. He loitered about the place till near ten to no purpose; and then came away; my mother having given him a letter to carry to Mr. Hunt's, which he was to deliver before three, when only, in the day-time, that gentleman is at home; and to bring her back an answer to it. Mr. Hunt's house, you know, lies wide from Harlowe Place. Robin but just saved his time: and returned not till it was too late to send him again. I could only direct him to set out before day this morning; and if he got any letter, to ride as for his life to bring it to me.

I lay by myself: a most uneasy night I had through impatience; and being discomposed with it, lay longer than usual. Just as I was risen, in came Kitty from Robin with your three letters. I was not a quarter dressed; and only slipt on my morning gown; proceeding no further till I had read them all through, long as they are: and yet I often stopped to rave aloud (though by myself) at the devilish people you have to deal with.

How my heart rises at them all! How poorly did they design to trick you into an encouragement of Solmes, from the extorted interview! — I am very, very angry at your aunt Hervey — to give up her own judgment so tamely! — And, not content to do so, to become such an *active* instrument in their hands! — But it is so like the world! — So like my mother too! — Next to her own child, there is not any body living she values so much as she does you: — yet it is — Why should we embroil ourselves, Nancy, with the affairs of other people?

Other people! — How I hate the poor words, where friendship is concerned, and where the protection to be given may be of so much consequence to a friend, and of so little detriment to one's self?

I am delighted with your spirit, however. I expected it not from you. Nor did they, I am sure. Nor would *you*, perhaps, have exerted it, if Lovelace's intelligence of Solmes's nursery offices had not set you up. I wonder not that the wretch is said to love you the better for it. What an honour would it be to him to have such a wife? And he can be even with you when you are so. He must indeed be a savage, as you say. — Yet he is less to blame for his perseverance than those of your own family whom most you reverence for theirs.

24*

It is well, as I have often said, that I have not such provocations and trials; I should perhaps long ago have taken your cousin Dolly's advice — yet dare I not to touch that key. I shall always love the good girl for her tenderness to you.

I know not what to say to Lovelace; nor what to think of his promises, nor of his proposals to you. 'Tis certain that you are highly esteemed by all his family. The ladies are persons of unblemished honour. My Lord M. is also (as men and peers go) a man of honour. I could tell what to advise any other person in the world to do but you. So much expected from you! — Such a shining light! — Your quitting your father's house, and throwing yourself into the protection of a family, however honourable, that has a man in it, whose person, parts, declarations, and pretensions, will be thought to have engaged your warmest esteem; — methinks I am rather for advising that you should get privately to London; and not to let either him, or any body else but me, know where you are, till your cousin Morden comes.

As to going to your uncle's, that you must not do, if you can help it. Nor must you have Solmes, that's certain: not only because of his unworthiness in every respect, but because of the aversion you have so openly avowed to him, which every body knows and talks of, as they do of your approbation of the other. For your reputation-sake, therefore, as well as to prevent mischief, you must either live single, or have Lovelace.

If you think of going to London, let me know; and I hope you will have *time* to allow me a further concert as to the manner of your getting away, and thither, and how to procure proper lodgings for you.

To obtain this *time*, you must palliate a little, and come into some seeming compromise, if you cannot do otherwise. Driven as you are driven, it will be strange if you are not obliged to part with a few of your admirable punctilios.

You will observe, from what I have written, that I have not succeeded with my mother.

I am extremely mortified and disappointed. We have had very strong debates upon it. But, besides the narrow argument of *embroiling ourselves with other people's affairs*, as above mentioned, she will have it, that it is your duty to comply. She says, she was *always* of opinion that daughters should implicitly submit to the will of their parents in the great article of marriage; and that she governed herself accordingly in marrying my father, who at first was more the choice of her parents than her own.

This is what she argues in behalf of her favourite Hickman, as well as for Solmes in your case.

I must not doubt but my mother always governed herself by this principle — because she *says* she did. I have likewise another reason to believe it; which you shall have, though it may not become me to give it — that they did not live so very happily together as one would hope people might do who married preferring each other at the time to the rest of the world.

Somebody shall fare never the better for this double-meant policy of my mother, I do assure you. Such retrospection in her arguments to him, and to his address, it is but fit that *he* should suffer for *my* mortification in failing to carry a point upon which I had set my whole heart.

Think, my dear, if in any way I can serve you. If you allow of it, I protest I will go off privately with you, and we will live and die together. Think of it: improve upon my hint, and command me.

A little interruption. — What is breakfast to the subject I am upon?

* * *

London, I am told, is the best hiding-place in the world. I have written nothing but what I will stand to at the word of command. Women love to engage in knight-errantry now and then, as well as to encourage it in the men. But in your case, what I propose will not seem to have any thing of that nature in it. It will enable me to perform what is no more than a duty in serving and comforting a dear and worthy friend, who labours under undeserved oppression: and you will *ennoble*, as I may say, your Anna Howe, if you allow her to be your companion in affliction.

I will engage, my dear, we shall not be in town together one month, before we surmount all difficulties: and this without being beholden to any men-fellows for their protection.

I must repeat what I have often said, that the authors of your persecutions would not have presumed to set on foot their selfish schemes against you, had they not depended upon the gentleness of your spirit: though now, having gone so far, and having engaged *old* AUTHORITY in it [chide me if you will!] neither *he* nor *they* know how to recede.

When they find you out of their reach, and know that I am with you, you'll see how they'll pull in their odious horns.

I think, however, that you should have written to your cousin Morden the moment they had begun to treat you disgracefully.

I shall be impatient to hear whether they will attempt to carry you to your uncle's. I remember that Lord M.'s dismissed bailiff reported of Lovelace, that he had six or seven companions as bad as himself; and that the country was always glad when they left it.* He actually *has*, as I hear, such a knot of them about him now. And, depend upon it, he will not suffer them quietly to carry you to your uncle's: and whose must you be, if he succeeds in taking you from them?

I tremble for you, but upon *sup-*

* p. 31.

posing what may be the consequence of a conflict upon this occasion. Lovelace owes some of them vengeance. This gives me a double concern, that my mother should refuse her consent to the protection I had set my heart upon procuring for you.

My mother will not breakfast without me. A quarrel has its conveniencies sometimes. Yet too much love, I think, is as bad as too little.

* * *

We have just now had another pull. Upon my word, she is *excessively* — what shall I say? — *unpersuadeable* — I must let her off with that soft word.

Who was the old Greek that said, *he* governed Athens; his *wife*, him; and his *son*, her?

It was not my mother's fault [I am writing to *you*, you know] that she did not govern my *father*. But I am but a *daughter!* — Yet I thought I was not quite so powerless when I was set upon carrying a point as I find myself to be.

Adieu, my dear! — Happier times must come — and that quickly too. — The strings cannot long continue thus overstrained. They must break or be relaxed. In either way, the certainty must be preferable to the suspense.

One word more!

I think in my conscience you must take one of these two alternatives; either to consent to let us go to London together privately [in which case, I will procure a vehicle, and meet you at your appointment at the stile to which Lovelace proposes to bring his uncle's chariot], or to put yourself into the protection of Lord M. and the ladies of his family.

You have another, indeed; and that is, if you are absolutely resolved against Solmes, to meet and marry Lovelace directly.

Whichsoever of these you make choice of, you will have this plea, both to yourself and to the world, that you are concluded by the same uniform principle that has governed your whole conduct ever since the contention between Lovelace and your brother has been on foot: that is to say, that you have chosen a lesser evil in hope to prevent a greater.

Adieu! and Heaven direct for the best my beloved creature, prays

Her
Anna Howe.

LETTER LXXXI.

Miss Clarissa Harlowe to Miss Howe.

Thursday, April 6.

I thank you, my dearest friend for the pains you have taken in accounting so affectionately for my papers not being taken away yesterday; and for the kind protection you would have procured for me, if you could.

This kind protection was what I wished for: but my wishes, raised at first by your love, were rather governed by my despair of other refuge [having before cast about, and not being able to determine, what I *ought* to do, and what I *could* do, in a situation so unhappy] than by a reasonable hope: for why indeed should any body embroil themselves for others, when they can avoid it?

All my consolation is, as I have frequently said, that I have not, by my own inadvertence or folly, brought myself into this sad situation. If I *had*, I should not have dared to look up to any body with the expectation of protection or assistance, nor to you for excuse of the trouble I give you. But nevertheless we should not be angry at a person's not doing that for ourselves, or for our friend, which she thinks she ought *not* to do; and which she has it in her option either to *do*, or to *let it alone*. Much less have you a right to be displeased with so prudent a mother for not engaging herself so warmly in my favour as you wished she would. If my own aunt can give me up, and that against her judgment, as I may presume to say; and if my father and mother, and uncles, who once loved me so well, can join so strenuously against me; can *I* expect, or ought *you*, the protection of your mother, in *opposition* to them?

Indeed, my dear love, [permit me to be *very* serious] I am afraid I am singled out (either for my own faults, or for the faults of my family, or perhaps for the faults of both) to be a very unhappy creature!—*signally* unhappy! For see you not how irresistibly the waves of affliction come tumbling down upon me?

We have been till within these few weeks, every one of us, too happy. No crosses, no vexations, but what we gave ourselves from the *pamperedness*, as I may call it, of our own wills. Surrounded by our heaps and stores, hoarded up as fast as acquired, we have seemed to think ourselves out of the reach of the bolts of adverse fate. I was the pride of all my friends, proud *myself* of *their* pride, and glorying in my standing. Who knows what the justice of Heaven may inflict, in order to convince us that we are not out of the reach of misfortune; and to reduce us to a better reliance than what we have hitherto presumptuously made?

I should have been very little the better for the *conversation-visits* which the good Dr. Lewen used to honour me with, and for the principles *wrought* (as I may say) into my earliest mind by my pious Mrs. Norton, founded on her reverend father's experience, as well as on her own, if I could not thus retrospect and argue, in such a strange situation as we are in. *Strange* I may well call it; for don't you see, my dear, that we seem all to be *impelled*, as it were, by a perverse fate, which none of us are able to resist?—And yet all arising (with a strong appearance of self-punishment) from ourselves? Do not my parents see the hopeful children, from whom they expected a perpetuity of worldly happiness to their branching family, now grown up to answer the *till* now distant hope, setting their angry faces against each other, pulling up by the roots, as I may say, that hope which was ready to be carried into a probable certainty?

Your partial love will be ready to acquit me of *capital* and *intentional* faults: — but oh, my dear! my calamities have humbled me enough to make me turn my gaudy eye inward; to make me look into myself. — And what have I discovered there? — Why, my dear friend, more *secret* pride and vanity than I could have thought had lain in my unexamined heart.

If *I* am to be singled out to be the *punisher* of myself and family, who so lately was the *pride* of it, pray for me, my dear, that I may not be left wholly to myself; and that I may be enabled to support my character, so as to be *justly* acquitted of wilful and premeditated faults. The will of Providence be resigned to in the rest: as *that* leads, let me patiently and unrepiningly follow! — I shall not live always!—May but my *closing* scene be happy!

But I will not oppress you, my dearest friend, with further reflections of this sort. I will take them all into myself. Surely I have a mind that has room to them. My afflictions are too sharp to last long. The crisis is at hand. Happier times you bid me hope for. I *will* hope.

* * *

But yet I cannot but be impatient at times, to find myself thus driven, and my character so depreciated and sunk, that were all the *future* to be happy, I should be ashamed to shew my face in public, or to look up. And all by the instigation of a selfish brother and envious sister. —

But let me stop: let me reflect! — Are not these suggestions the suggestions of the *secret* pride I have been censuring? Then *already* so impatient! But this moment so resigned, so much better disposed for reflection! Yet 'tis hard, 'tis *very* hard, to subdue an embittered spirit! — in the instant of its trial too! — O my cruel brother! — But now it rises again. — I will lay down a pen I am so little able to govern. — And I will try to subdue an impatience, which (if my afflictions are sent me for corrective ends) may otherwise lead me into still more punishable errors. —

* * *

I will return to a subject which I cannot fly from for ten minutes together — called upon especially as I am, by your three alternatives stated in the conclusion of your last.

As to the first; to wit, *your advice for me to escape to London* — let me tell you, that the other hint or proposal which accompanies it perfectly frightens me — surely, my dear (happy as you are, and indulgently treated as your mother treats you) you cannot mean what you propose! What a wretch must I be, if, for *one* moment only, I could lend an ear to such a proposal as this! — *I*, to be the occasion of making such a mother's (perhaps *shortened*) life unhappy to the last hour of it! — *Ennoble* you, my dear creature! how must such an enterprise (the rashness *public*, the motives, were they excusable, *private*) debase you! — But I will not dwell upon the subject — for your *own* sake I will not.

As to your second alternative, *to put myself into the protection of Lord M. and of the ladies of that family*, I own to you (as I believe I have owned before) that although to do this would be the same thing in the eye of the world as putting myself into Mr. Lovelace's protection, yet I think I would do it rather than be Mr. Solmes's wife, if there were evidently no other way to avoid being so.

Mr. Lovelace, you have seen, proposes to contrive a way to put me into possession of my own house; and he tells me, that he will soon fill it with the ladies of his family, as my visitors; — upon my invitation, however, to them. A very inconsiderate proposal I think it to be, and upon which I cannot explain myself to him. What an exertion of independency does it chalk out for me! How, were I to attend to *him* (and not to the natural consequences to which the following of his advice would lead me) might I be drawn by *gentle* words into the perpetration of the most *violent* acts! — For how could I gain possession, but either by legal litigation, which, were I *inclined* to have recourse to it, (as I never can be) must take up time; or by forcibly turning out the persons whom my father has placed there, to look after the gardens, the house, and the furniture — persons entirely attached to himself, and who, as I know, have been lately instructed by my brother?

Your third alternative, *to meet and marry Mr. Lovelace directly;* a man with whose morals I am far from being satisfied — a step that could not be taken with the least hope of ever obtaining pardon from or reconciliation with any of my friends; and against which a thousand objections rise in my mind — *that is not to be thought of*.

What appears to me upon the fullest deliberation the most eligible, if I *must* be thus driven, is the escaping to London. But I would forfeit all my hopes of happiness in this life, rather than you should go away with me, as you rashly, though with the kindest intention, propose. If I could get safely thither, and be private, methinks I might remain absolutely independent of Mr. Lovelace, and at liberty either to make proposals to my friends, or, should they renounce me, (and I had no other or better way) to make terms with him; supposing my cousin Morden, on his arrival, were to join with my other relations. But they would *then* perhaps indulge me in my choice of a single life, on giving him up: the renewing to them this offer, when at my own liberty, will at least convince them that I was in earnest when I made it first: and, upon my word, I *would* stand to it, dear as you seem to think, when you are disposed to rally me, it would cost me, *to* stand to it.

If, my dear, you can procure a vehicle for us *both*, you can perhaps procure one for me *singly;* but can it be done without embroiling *yourself* with your mother, or *her* with our family? — Be it coach, chariot, chaise, waggon, or horse, I matter not, provided you appear not to have a hand in my withdrawing. Only, in case it be one of the two latter, I believe I must desire you to get me an ordinary gown and coat, or habit, of some servant; having no concert with any of our own: the more ordinary the better. They may be thrust into the woodhouse: where I can put them on; and then slide down from the bank that separates the wood-yard from the green lane.

But, alas! my dear, this, even *this* alternative, is not without difficulties, which to a spirit so little enterprising as mine, seem in a manner insuperable. These are my reflections upon it.

I am afraid, in the first place, that I shall not have time for the requisite preparations for an escape.

Should I be either detected in those preparations, or pursued and overtaken in my flight, and so brought back, then would they think themselves doubly warranted to compel me to have their Solmes: and, conscious of an intended fault, perhaps, I should be the less able to contend with them.

But were I even to get safely to London, I know nobody there but by name, and those the tradesmen to our family, who no doubt would be the first written to, and engaged to find me out. And should Mr. Lovelace discover where I was, and he and my brother meet, what mischiefs might ensue between them, whether I were willing or not to return to Harlowe Place?

But supposing I could remain there concealed, to what might not my youth, my sex, and unacquaintedness with the ways of that great, wicked town, expose me! — I should hardly dare to go to church for fear of being discovered. People would wonder how I lived. Who knows but I might pass for a kept mistress; and that, although nobody came to me, yet, that every time I went out, it might be imagined to be in pursuance of some assignation?

You, my dear, who alone would know where to direct to me, would be watched in all your steps, and in all your messages; and your mother, at present not highly pleased with our correspondence, would then have reason to be *more* displeased; and might not differences follow between her and you, that would make me very unhappy were I to know them? And this the more likely, as you take it so unaccountably (and, give me leave to say, so ungenerously) into your head, to revenge yourself upon the innocent Mr. Hickman, for all the displeasure your mother gives you?

Were Lovelace to find out my place of abode, that would be the same thing in the eye of the world as if I had actually gone off with him: for would he, do you think, be prevailed upon to forbear visiting me? And then his unhappy character (a foolish man!) would be no credit to any young creature desirous of concealment. Indeed the world, let me escape whither and to whomsoever I could, would conclude *him* to be the contriver of it.

These are the difficulties which arise to me on revolving this scheme; which, nevertheless, might appear surmountable to a more enterprising spirit in my circumstances. If you, my dear, think them surmountable in any one of the cases put [and to be sure I can take no course but what must have some difficulty in it] be pleased to let me know your free and full thoughts upon it.

Had you, my dear friend, been married, then should I have had no doubt but that you and Mr. Hickman would have afforded an asylum to a poor creature more than half lost in her own apprehension for want of one kind protecting friend!

You say I should have written to my cousin Morden the moment I was treated disgracefully: but could I have believed that my friends would not have softened by degrees when they saw my antipathy to their Solmes?

I had thoughts indeed several times of writing to my cousin: but by the time an answer could have come, I imagined all would have been over, as if it had never been: so from day to day, from week to week, I hoped on: and, after all, I might as reasonably fear (as I have heretofore said) that my cousin would be brought to side against me, as that some of those I have named would.

And then to appeal to a *cousin* [I must have written with *warmth* to engage him] against a *father;* this was not a desirable thing to set about. Then I had not, you know, one soul on my side; my mother herself against me. To be sure my cousin would have suspended his judgment till he could have arrived. He might not have been in haste to come, hoping the malady would cure itself: but *had* he written, his letters probably would have run in the qualifying style; to persuade me to submit, or *them* only to relax.

Had his letters been more on *my* side than on *theirs*, they would not have regarded them: nor perhaps *himself*, had he come and been an advocate for me: for you see how strangely determined they are; how they have over-awed or got in every body; so that no one dare open their lips in my behalf. And you have heard that my brother pushes his measures with the more violence, that all may be over with me before my cousin's expected arrival.

But you tell me, that in order to gain time, I must *palliate;* that I must seem to compromise with my friends:" but how *palliate?* how *seem* to compromise? You would not have me endeavour to make them believe that I will consent to what I never intend to consent to!

You would not have me try to gain time with a view to *deceive!*

To *do evil that good may come of it* is forbidden: and shall I do evil, yet know not whether good may come of it or not?

Forbid it, Heaven! that Clarissa Harlowe should have it in her thought to *serve*, or even to *save* herself at the expense of her sincerity, and by a *studied* deceit!

And is there, after all, no way to escape one great evil, but by plunging myself into another? What an ill-fated creature am I! — Pray for me, my dearest friend! — My mind is at present so much disturbed, that I can hardly pray for myself.

LETTER LXXXII.
Miss Clarissa Harlowe to Miss Howe.
Thursday night.

THE alarming hurry I mentioned under my date of last night, and Betty's saucy dark hints, come out to be owing to what I guessed they were; that is to say, to the private intimation Mr. Lovelace contrived our family should have of his insolent resolution [*insolent* I must call it] to prevent my being carried to my uncle's.

I saw at the time that it was as *wrong* with respect to answering his own view as it was *insolent:* for could he think, as Betty (I suppose from her betters) justly observed, that parents would be insulted out of their right to dispose of their own child by a violent man whom they hate; and who could have no pretension to dispute that right with them, unless what he had from *her* who had none over herself? And how must this insolence of his, aggravated as my brother is able to aggravate it, exasperate them against me?

The rash man has indeed so far gained his point, as to intimidate them from attempting to carry me away: but he has put them upon a surer and a more desperate measure: and this has driven me also into one as desperate; the consequence of which, although he could not foresee it*, may perhaps too well answer his great end, little as he deserves to have it answered.

In short, I have done, as far as I know, the most rash thing that ever I did in my life.

But let me give you the motive, and then the action will follow of course.

About six o'clock this evening, my aunt (who stays here all night; on my account, no doubt) came up, and tapped at my door, for I was writing; and had locked myself in. I opened it; and she entering, thus delivered herself:

I come once more to visit you, my dear; but sorely against my will, because it is to impart to you matters of the utmost concern to you and to the whole family.

What, madam, is now to be done with me? said I, wholly attentive.

* She was mistaken in this. Mr. Lovelace did foresee this consequence. All his contrivances led to it, and the whole family, as he boasts, unknown to themselves, were but so many puppets danced by his wires. See p. 137.

You will not be hurried away to your uncle's, child; let that comfort you. — They see your aversion to go. — You will not be obliged to go to your uncle Antony's.

How you revive me, madam! This is a cordial to my heart!

I little thought, my dear, what was to follow this supposed condescension.

And then I ran over with blessings for this good news (and she permitted me so to do by her silence); congratulating myself, that I *thought* my father could not resolve to carry things to the last extremity. —

Hold, niece, said she, at last — you must not give yourself too much joy upon the occasion neither. — Don't be surprised, my dear. — Why look you upon me, child, with so affecting an earnestness? — But you must be Mrs. Solmes for all that.

I was dumb.

She then told me, that they had had undoubted information, that a certain desperate *ruffian* (I must excuse her that word, she said) had prepared armed men to waylay my brother and uncles, and seize me, and carry me off — surely, she said, I was not consenting to a violence that might be followed by murder on one side or the other; perhaps on both.

I was still silent.

That therefore my father (still more exasperated than before) had changed his resolution as to my going to my uncle's; and was determined next Tuesday to set out thither *himself* with my mother; and that (for it was to no purpose to conceal a resolution so soon to be put in execution) I must not dispute it any longer — on Wednesday I must give my hand — as they would have me.

She proceeded; that orders were already given for a licence: that the ceremony was to be performed in my own chamber, in presence of all my friends, except of my father and mother, who would not return, nor see me, till all was over, and till they had a good account of my behaviour.

The very intelligence, my dear! the very intelligence this which Lovelace gave me!

I was still dumb — only sighing as if my heart would break.

She went on, comforting me as she thought. "She laid before me the merit of obedience: and told me, that if it were my desire that my Norton should be present at the ceremony, it would be complied with: that the pleasure I should receive from reconciling all my friends to me, and in their congratulations upon it, must needs overbalance with such a one as me the difference of persons, however preferable I might think the one man to the other: that love was a fleeting thing, little better than a name, where morality and virtue did not distinguish the object of it: that a choice made by its dictates was seldom happy; at least not *durably* so: nor was it to be wondered at, when it naturally exalted the object above its merits, and made the lover blind to faults that were visible to every body else: so that when a nearer intimacy stript it of its imaginary perfections, it left frequently both parties surprised that they could be so grossly cheated; and that then the indifference became stronger than the love ever was. That a woman gave a man great advantages, and inspired him with great vanity, when she avowed her love for him, and preference of him: and was generally requited with insolence and contempt: whereas the confessedly obliged man, it was probable, would be all reverence and gratitude" — and I cannot tell what.

"You, my dear," said she, "believe you shall be unhappy if you have Mr. Solmes: your parents think the contrary; and that you will be undoubtedly so were you to have Mr. Lovelace, whose morals are unquestionably bad: suppose it were your sad lot to be unhappy with either, let me beseech you to consider, what great consolation you will have on one hand, if you pursue your parent's advice, that you did so; what mortification on the other, that, by following your own, you have nobody to blame but yourself."

This, you remember, my dear, was an argument enforced upon me by Mrs. Norton.

These, and other observations which she made, were worthy of my aunt Hervey's good sense and experience, and, applied to almost any young creature who stood in opposition to her parent's will, but one who had offered to make the sacrifices I have offered to make, ought to have had their due weight. But although it was easy to answer some of them in my own particular case; yet having over and over, to my mother, brother and sister, and even to my aunt Hervey, *since*, said what I must now have repeated, I was so much mortified and afflicted at the cruel tidings she brought me, that however attentive I was to what she said, I had neither power nor will to answer one word; and, had she not stopped of herself, she might have gone on an hour longer without interruption from me.

Observing this, and that I only sat weeping, my handkerchief covering my face, and my bosom heaving ready to burst; What! no answer, my dear? — Why so much *silent* grief? You know *I* always loved you. You know that *I* have no interest in the affair. You would not permit Mr. Solmes to acquaint you with some things which would have set your heart against Mr. Lovelace. Shall I tell you some of the matters charged against him? — Shall I, my dear?

Still I answered only by my tears and sighs.

Well, child, you shall be told these things afterwards, when you will be in a better state of mind to hear them; and then you will rejoice in the escape you will have had. It will be some excuse, then, for you to plead for your behaviour to Mr. Solmes, that you could not have believed Mr. Lovelace had been so very vile a man.

My heart fluttered with impatience and anger at being so plainly talked to as the wife of this man; but yet I then chose to be silent. If I had spoken, it would have been with vehemence.

Strange, my dear, such silence! — Your concern is infinitely more on this side the day than it will be on the other. But let me ask you, and do not be displeased, will you choose to see what generous stipulations for you there are in the settlements? — You have knowledge beyond your years — give the writings a perusal: do, my dear: they are engrossed, and ready for signing, and have been for some time. — Excuse me, my love — I mean not to disorder you: — your father would oblige me to bring them up, and to leave them with you. He commands you to read them. But to read them, niece — since they are engrossed, and *were* before you made them absolutely hopeless.

And then, to my great terror, out she drew some parchments from her handkerchief, which she had kept (unobserved by me) under her apron; and, rising, put them in the opposite window. Had she produced a serpent, I could not have been more frighted.

Oh! my dearest aunt, turning away my face, and holding out my hands: hide from my eyes those horrid parchments! — Let me conjure you to tell me — by all the tenderness of near relationship, and upon your honour, and by your love for me, say, are they absolutely resolved, that come what will, I must be that man's?

My dear, you must have Mr. Solmes: indeed you must.

Indeed I never will! This, as I have said over and over, is not originally my father's will. — Indeed I never will — and that is all I will say!

It is your father's will *now*, replied my aunt; and, considering how all the family is threatened by Mr. Lovelace, and the resolution he has certainly taken, to force you out of their hands, I cannot but say they are in the right not to be bullied out of their child.

Well, madam, then nothing remains for me to say. I am made desperate. I care not what becomes of me.

Your piety and your prudence, my dear, and Mr. Lovelace's immoral character, together with his daring insults and threatenings, which ought to incense *you* as much as any body, are every one's dependence. We are sure the time will come, when you'll think very differently of the steps your friends take to disappoint a man who has made himself so justly obnoxious to them all.

She withdrew; leaving me full of grief and indignation: — and as much out of humour with Mr. Lovelace as with any body; who by his conceited contrivances has made things worse for me than before; depriving me of the hopes I had of gaining time to receive your advice, and private assistance to get to town; and leaving me no other choice, in all appearance, than either to throw myself upon his family, or to be made miserable for ever with Mr. Solmes. But I was still resolved to avoid both these evils, if possible.

I sounded Betty in the first place (whom my aunt sent up, not thinking it proper, as Betty told me, that I should be left by myself, and who, I found, knew their designs) whether it were not probable that they would forbear, at my earnest entreaty, to push matters to the threatened extremity.

But she confirmed all my aunt said: rejoicing (as she said they all did) that Mr. Lovelace had given them so good a pretence to save me from him now, and for ever.

She ran on about equipages bespoken; talked of my brother's and sister's exultations that now the whole family would soon be reconciled to each other: of the servants' joy upon it: of the expected licence: of a visit to be paid me by Dr. Lewen, or another clergyman, whom they named not to *her;* which was to crown the work: and of other preparations, so particular, as made me dread that they designed to surprise me into a still nearer day than next Wednesday.

These things made me excessively uneasy. I knew not what to resolve upon.

At one time, what have I to do, thought I, but to throw myself at once into the protection of Lady Betty Lawrence? — But then, in resentment of his *fine* contrivances, which had so abominably disconcerted me, I soon resolved to the contrary: and at last concluded to ask the favour of another half hour's conversation with my aunt.

I sent Betty to her with my request.

She came.

I put it to her, in the most earnest manner, to tell me, whether I might not obtain the favour of a fortnight's respite?

She assured me it would not be granted.

Would a week? Surely a week would.

She believed a week might, if I would promise two things: the first, upon my honour, not to write a line out of the house in that week: for it was still suspected, she said, that I found means to write to *somebody.* And, secondly, to marry Mr. Solmes at the expiration of it.

Impossible! Impossible! I said with passion — what! might not I be obliged with one week, without such a horrid condition as the last?

She would go down, she said, that she might not seem of her own head to put upon me what I thought a hardship so great.

She went down, and came up again.

Did I want, was the answer, to give the vilest of men an opportunity to put his murderous schemes into execution? — It was time for them to put an end to my obstinacy (they were tired out with me) and to his hopes at once. And an end should be put on Tuesday, or Wednesday next at furthest: unless I would give my honour to comply with the condition upon which my aunt had been so good as to allow me a longer time.

I even stamped with impatience! — I called upon her to witness that I was guiltless of the consequence of this compulsion; this *barbarous* compulsion I called it: let that consequence be what it would.

My aunt chid me in a higher strain than ever she did before.

While I, in a half phrensy, insisted upon seeing my father: such usage, I said, set me above fear. I would rejoice to owe my death to him, as I did my life.

I did go down half way of the stairs, resolved to throw myself at his feet wherever he was. — My aunt was frighted: she owned that she feared for my head. — Indeed I was in a perfect phrensy for a few minutes — but hearing my brother's voice, as talking to somebody in my sister's apartment just by, I stopt; and heard the barbarous designer say, speaking to my sister, This works charmingly, my dear Arabella.

It does! it does! said she, in an exulting accent.

Let us keep it up, said my brother. — The villain is caught in his own trap! — Now must she be what we would have her be.

Do you keep my father to it;

I'll take care of my mother, said Bella.

Never fear! said he. — And a laugh of congratulation to each other, and derision of me (as I made it out) quite turned my frantic humour into a vindictive one.

My aunt just then coming down to me, and taking my hand, led me up; and tried to soothe me.

My raving was turned into sullenness.

She preached patience and obedience to me.

I was silent.

At last she desired me to assure her that I would offer no violence to myself.

God, I said, had given me more grace, I hoped, than to permit me to be guilty of so horrid a rashness. I was his creature, and not my own.

She then took leave of me, and I insisted upon her taking down with her the odious parchments.

Seeing me in so ill a humour, and very earnest that she should take them with her, she took them; but said, that my father should not know that she did: and hoped I would better consider of the matter, and be calmer next time they were offered to my perusal.

I revolved after she was gone all that my brother and sister had said. I dwelt upon their triumphings over me, and found rise in my mind a rancour that was new to me, and which I could not withstand. — And putting every thing together, dreading the near day, what could I do? — Am I in any manner excusable for what I did do? — If I shall be condemned by the world who know not my provocations, may I be acquitted by you? — If *not*, I am unhappy indeed! — For this I did.

Having shaken off the impertinent Betty, I wrote to Mr. Lovelace, to let him know, "that all that was threatened at my uncle Antony's was intended to be executed *here*. That I had come to a resolution to throw myself upon the protection *of either of his two aunts*, who would afford it me — in short, that by endeavouring to obtain leave on Monday to dine in the ivy summer-house, I would, if possible, meet him without the garden door, at two, three, four or five o'clock on Monday afternoon, as I should be able. That in the meantime he should acquaint me, *whether I might hope for either of those ladies' protection:* and if I might, I absolutely insisted that *he should leave me with either, and go to London himself, or remain at Lord M.'s: nor offer to visit me till I were satisfied that nothing could be done with my friends in an amicable way; and that I could not obtain possession of my own estate, and leave to live upon it: and particularly, that he should not hint marriage to me till I consented to hear him upon that subject.* — I added, that if he could prevail upon one of the Miss Montagues to *favour me with her company on the road*, it would make me abundantly more easy in the thoughts of carrying into effect a resolution which I had not come to, although so driven, but with the utmost reluctance and concern: and which would throw such a slur upon my reputation in the eye of the world, as perhaps I should never be able to wipe off."

This was the purport of what I wrote: and down into the garden I slid with it in the dark, which at another time I should not have had the courage to do: and deposited it, and came up again unknown to any body.

My mind so dreadfully misgave me when I returned, that to divert in some measure my increasing uneasiness I had recourse to my private pen, and in a very short time ran this length.

And now, that I am come to this part, my uneasy reflections begin again to pour in upon me. Yet what can I do? — I believe I shall take it back again the first thing I do in the morning — yet what can I do?

And who knows but they may have a still earlier day in their intention, than that which will too soon come?

I hope to deposit this early in the morning for you, as I shall return from resuming my letter, if I do resume it as my *inwardest* mind bids me.

Although it is now near two o'clock, I have a good mind to slide down once more, in order to take back my letter. Our doors are always locked and barred up at eleven; but the seats of the lesser hall windows being almost even with the ground without, and the shutters not difficult to open, I could easily get out.

Yet why should I be thus uneasy, since, should the letter go, I can but bear what Mr. Lovelace says to it? His aunts live at too great a distance for him to have an immediate answer from them; so I can scruple going to them till I have invitation. I can *insist* upon one of his cousins meeting me, as I have hinted, and accompanying me in the chariot: and he may not be able to obtain that favour from either of them. Twenty things may happen to afford me a suspension at least: why should I be so very uneasy?— When likewise I can take back my letter early, before it is probable he will have the thought of finding it there. Yet he owns he spends three parts of his days, and has done for this fortnight past, in loitering about, sometimes in one disguise, sometimes in another, besides the attendance given by his trusty servant, when he himself is not *in waiting*, as he calls it.

But, these strange forebodings! — Yet I can, if you advise, cause the chariot he shall bring with him to carry me directly for town, whither in my London scheme, if you were to approve it, I had proposed to go: and this will save you the trouble of procuring for me a vehicle; as well as prevent any suspicion from your mother of your contributing to my escape.

But, solicitous for your advice and approbation too, if I *can* have it, I will put an end to this letter. Adieu, my dearest friend, adieu!

LETTER LXXXIII.

Miss Clarissa Harlowe to Miss Howe.

Friday morning, 7 o'clock (April 7).

My aunt Hervey, who is a very early riser, was walking in the garden (Betty attending her, as I saw from my window this morning) when I arose; for after such a train of fatigue and restless nights, I had unhappily overslept myself: so all I durst venture upon was, to step down to my poultry-yard and deposit mine of yesterday and last night. And I am just come up: for she is still in the garden. This prevents me from going to resume my letter as I think still to do; and hope it will not be too late.

I said I had unhappily overslept myself: I went to bed at about half an hour after two. I told the quarters till five; after which I dropt asleep, and awaked not till past six, and then in great terror, from a dream, which has made such an impression upon me, that slightly as I think of dreams, I cannot help taking this opportunity to relate it to you.

"Methought my brother, my uncle Antony, and Mr. Solmes, had formed a plot to destroy Mr. Lovelace; who discovering it, and believing I had a hand in it, turned all his rage against me. I thought he made them all fly to foreign parts upon it; and afterwards seizing upon me, carried me into a church-yard; and there, notwithstanding all my prayers and tears, and protestations of innocence, stabbed me to the heart, and then tumbled me into a deep grave ready dug, among two or three half dissolved carcases; throwing in the dirt and earth upon me with his hands, and trampling it down with his feet."

I awoke in a cold sweat, trembling, and in agonies; and still the frightful images raised by it remain upon my memory.

But why should I, who have such *real* evils to contend with, regard *imaginary* ones? This, no doubt, was owing to my disturbed imagination; huddling together wildly all the frightful ideas which my aunt's communications and discourse, my letter to Mr. Lovelace, my own uneasiness upon it, and the apprehensions of the dreaded Wednesday, furnished me with.

Eight o'clock.

THE man, my dear, has got the letter! — What a strange diligence! I wish he mean me well, that he takes so much pains! — Yet, to be ingenuous, I must own, that I should be displeased if he took less — I wish, however, he had been an hundred miles off! — What an advantage have I given him over me!

Now the letter is out of my power, I have more uneasiness and regret than I had before. For, till now, I had a doubt whether it should or should not go: and now I think it ought *not* to have gone. And yet is there any other way than to do as I have done, if I would avoid Solmes? But what a giddy creature shall I be thought, if I pursue the course to which this letter must lead me!

My dearest friend, tell me, have I done wrong? — Yet do not *say* I have if you *think* it; for should all the world besides condemn me, I shall have some comfort, if *you* do not. The first time I ever besought you to flatter me. That, of itself, is an indication that I have done wrong, and am afraid of hearing the truth — O tell me (but yet do not tell me) if I have done wrong.

Friday, 11 o'clock.

MY aunt has made me another visit. She began what she had to say with letting me know, that my friends are all persuaded that I still correspond with Mr. Lovelace; as is plain, she said, by hints and menaces he throws out, which shews that he is apprised of several things that have passed between my relations and me, sometimes within a very little while after they have happened.

Although I approve not of the method he stoops to take to come at his intelligence, yet it is not prudent in me to clear myself by the ruin of the corrupted servant (although his vileness has neither my connivance nor approbation), since my doing so might occasion the detection of my own correspondence, and so frustrate all the hopes I have to avoid Mr. Solmes. Yet it is not at all unlikely, that this very agent of Mr. Lovelace acts a double part between my brother and him: how else can our *family* know (so *soon* too) his menaces upon the passages they hint at?

I assured my aunt, that I was too much ashamed of the treatment I met with (and that for every one's sake as well as for my own) to acquaint Mr. Lovelace with the particulars of that treatment, even were the means of corresponding with him afforded me: that I had reason to think, that if he were to know of it from me, we must be upon such terms that he would not scruple making some visits which would give me great apprehensions. They all knew, I said, that I had no communication with any of my father's servants, except my sister's Betty Barnes: for although I had a good opinion of them all, and believed, if left to their own inclinations, that they would be glad to serve me; yet, finding by their shy behaviour, that they were under particular direction, I had forborne, ever since my Hannah had been so disgracefully dismissed, so much as to speak to any of them, for fear I should be the occasion of *their* losing their places too. They must therefore account among *themselves* for the intelligence Mr. Lovelace met with, since neither my brother nor sister (as Betty had frequently, in praise of their open hearts, informed me), nor perhaps their favourite Mr. Solmes, were at all careful before whom they spoke, when they had any thing to throw out against him, or even against *me*, whom they took great pride to join with him on this occasion.

It was but too natural, my aunt said, for my friends to suppose, that he had his intelligence (part of it at least) from me; who, thinking myself hardly treated, might complain of it, if not to him, to Miss Howe; which, perhaps, might be the same thing; for they knew Miss Howe spoke as freely of them as they could do of Mr. Lovelace; and must have the particulars she spoke of from somebody who knew what was done here. That this determined my father to bring the whole matter to a speedy issue, lest fatal consequences should ensue.

I perceive you are going to speak with warmth, proceeded she [*and so I was*]. For my own part, I am sure you would not write any thing, if you *do* write, to inflame so violent a spirit. — But this is not the end of my present visit.

You cannot, my dear, but be convinced, that your father *will* be *obeyed*. The more you contend against his will, the more he thinks himself obliged to assert his authority. Your mother desires me to tell you, that if you will give her the least hopes of a dutiful compliance, she will be willing to see you in her closet just now, while your father is gone to take a walk in the garden.

Astonishing perseverance! said I. I am tired with making declarations and with pleadings on this subject; and had hoped, that my resolution being so well known,

I should not have been further urged upon it.

You mistake the purport of my present visit, miss, [looking gravely] — Heretofore you have been *desired* and *prayed* to obey and oblige your friends. *Entreaty* is at an end: they give it up. Now it is *resolved upon* that your father's will *is to be obeyed;* as it is fit it should. Some things are laid at your door, as if you concurred with Lovelace's threatened violence to carry you off, which your mother will not believe. She will tell you her own good opinion of you. She will tell you how much she still loves you; and what she expects of you on the approaching occasion. But yet, that she may not be exposed to an opposition, which would the more provoke her, she desires that you will first assure her that you go down with a resolution to do that with a grace which must be done with or without a grace. And besides, she wants to give you some advice how to proceed in order to reconcile yourself to your father, and to everybody else. Will you go down, Miss Clary, or will you not?

I said, I should think myself happy, could I be admitted to my mother's presence, after so long a banishment from it; but that I could not wish it upon those terms.

And this is your answer, niece?

It must be my answer, madam. Come what may, I never will have Mr. Solmes. It is cruel to press this matter so often upon me. — I never will have that man.

Down she went with displeasure. I could not help it. I was quite tired with so many attempts, all to the same purpose. I am amazed that they are not! — So little variation! And no concession on either side!

I will go down and deposit this; for Betty has seen I have been writing. The saucy creature took a napkin, and dipped it in water, and with a fleering air, Here, miss; holding the wet corner to me.

What's that for? said I.

Only, miss, one of the fingers of your right-hand, if you please to look at it.

It was inky.

I gave her a look; but said nothing.

But lest I should have another search, I will close here.

CL. HARLOWE.

LETTER LXXXIV.

Miss Clarissa Harlowe to Miss Howe.

Friday, 1 o'clock.

I HAVE a letter from Mr. Lovelace, full of transports, vows, and promises. I will send it to you inclosed. You'll see how "he engages in it for Lady Betty's protection, and for Miss Charlotte Montague's accompanying me. I have nothing to do, but to persevere, he says, and prepare to receive the personal congratulations of his whole family."

But you'll see how he presumes upon my being *his*, as the consequence of throwing myself into that lady's protection.

"The chariot-and-six is to be ready at the place he mentions. You'll see as to the slur upon my reputation about which I am so apprehensive, how boldly he argues. Generously enough, indeed, were I to be *his;* and had given him reason to believe that I would. — But that I have not done.

How one step brings on another with this encroaching sex! How soon may a young creature, who gives a man the least encouragement, be carried beyond her intentions, and out of her own power! You would imagine, by what he writes, that I have given him reason to think that my aversion to Mr. Solmes is all owing to my favour for him.

The dreadful thing is, that, comparing what he writes from his intelligencer of what is designed against me (though he seems not to know the threatened day) with what my aunt and Betty assure me of, there can be no hope for me, but that I must be Solmes's wife, if I stay here.

I had better have gone to my uncle Antony's at this rate. I should have gained time, at least, by it. This is the fruit of his fine contrivances!

"What we are to do, and how good he is to be: how I am to direct all his future steps." All this shews, as I said before, that he is sure of me.

However, I have replied to the following effect: "That although I had given him room to expect, that I would put myself into the protection of one of the ladies of his family; yet as I have three days to come, between this and Monday, and as I still hope that my friends will relent, or that Mr. Solmes will give up a point they will find it impossible to carry; I shall not look upon myself as *absolutely bound by the appointment:* and expect therefore, if I recede, that I shall not again be called to account for it by him. That I think it necessary to acquaint him, that if by throwing myself upon Lady Betty Lawrence's protection, as he proposed, he understands, *that I mean directly to put myself into his power, he is very much mistaken:* for that there are *many points in which I must be satisfied, several matters to be adjusted,* even after I have left this house (if I do leave it) *before I can think of giving him any particular encouragement:* that in the *first place* he must expect that I will do my utmost to *procure my father's reconciliation and approbation of my future steps;* and that *I will govern myself entirely by his commands,* in every reasonable point, *as much as if I had not left his house:* that if he imagines, I shall not reserve to myself this liberty, but that my withdrawing is to give him any advantages which he would *not otherwise have had;* I am determined to stay where I am, and abide the event, in hopes that my friends will still accept of my reiterated promise *never to marry him or any body else, without their consent."*

This I will deposit as soon as I can. And as he thinks things are near their crisis, I dare say it will not be long before I have an answer to it.

Friday, 4 o'clock.

I am really ill. I was used to make the best of any little accidents that befel me, for fear of making my *then* affectionate friends uneasy: but now I shall make the worst of my indisposition, in hopes to obtain a suspension of the threatened evil of Wednesday next. And if I do obtain it, will postpone my appointment with Mr. Lovelace.

Betty has told them that I am very much indisposed. But I have no pity from any body.

I believe, I am become the object of every one's aversion, and that they would all be glad I were dead. Indeed, I believe it. "What ails the perverse creature?" cries one. — "Is she love-sick?" another.

I was in the ivy summer-house, and came out shivering with cold, as if aguishly affected. Betty observed this, and reported it. — "O, no matter! — Let her shiver on! — Cold cannot hurt her. Obstinacy will defend her from harm. Perverseness is a bracer to a love-sick girl, and more effectual than the cold bath to make hardy, although the constitution be ever so tender."

This said by a cruel brother, and heard said by the dearer friends of one, for whom, but a few months ago, every body was apprehensive at the least blast of wind to which she exposed herself!

Betty, it must be owned, has an admirable memory on these occasions. Nothing of this nature is lost by her repetition: even the very air with which she repeats what she hears said, renders it unnecessary to ask, who spoke this or that severe thing.

Friday, 6 o'clock.

My aunt, who again stays all night, has just left me. She came to tell me the result of my friends' deliberations about me. It is this:

Next Wednesday morning they are all to be assembled: to wit, my father, mother, my uncles, herself, and my uncle Hervey; my brother and sister of course: My good Mrs. Norton is likewise to be admitted: and Dr. Lewen is to be at hand, to exhort me, it seems, if there be occasion: but my aunt is not certain whether he is to be among them, or to tarry till called in.

When this awful court is assembled, the poor prisoner is to be brought in, supported by Mrs. Norton; who is to be first tutored to instruct me in the duty of a child; which it seems I have forgotten.

Nor is the success at all doubted, my aunt says: since it is not believed that I can be hardened enough to withstand the expostulations of so venerable a judicature, although I have withstood those of several of them separately. And still the less, as she hints at *extraordinary condescensions from my father*. But what condescensions, from even my father, can induce me to make such a sacrifice as is expected from me?

Yet my spirits will never bear up, I doubt, at such a tribunal — my father presiding in it.

Indeed I expected, that my trials would not be at an end till he had admitted me into his awful presence.

What is hoped from me, she says, is, That I will cheerfully, on Tuesday night, if not before, sign the articles: and so turn the succeeding day's solemn convention into a day of festivity. I am to have the licence sent me up, however, and once more the settlements, that I may see how much in earnest they are.

She further hinted, that my father himself would bring up the settlements for me to sign.

O my dear! what a trial will this be! — How shall I be able to refuse to my father the writing of my name? — To my father, from whose presence I have been so long banished! — He commanding and entreating, perhaps, in a breath! — How shall I be able to refuse this to my father!

They are sure, she says, something is working on Mr. Lovelace's part, and perhaps on mine: and my father would sooner follow me to the grave, than see me *his* wife.

I said, I was not well: that the very apprehensions of these trials were already insupportable to me; and would increase upon me, as the time approached; and I was afraid I should be extremely ill.

They had prepared themselves for such an *artifice* as that, was my aunt's unkind word; and she could assure me, it would stand me in no stead.

Artifice! repeated I: and this from my aunt Hervey?

Why, my dear, said she, do you think people are fools? — Can they not see, how dismally you endeavour to sigh yourself down within doors? — How you hang down your *sweet face* [those were the words she was pleased to use] upon your bosom: — how you totter, as it were, and hold by this chair, and by that door-post, when you know that anybody sees you [This, my dear Miss Howe, is an aspersion to fasten hypocrisy and contempt upon me: my brother's or sister's aspersion! — I am not capable of arts so low]. But the moment you are down with your poultry, or advancing upon your garden walk, and, as you imagine, out of every body's sight, it is seen how nimbly you trip along, and what an alertness governs all your motions.

I should hate myself, said I, were I capable of such poor *artifices* as these. I must be a fool to use them, as well as a mean creature; for have I not had experience enough, that my friends are incapable of being moved in much more *affecting instances?* — But you'll see how I shall be by Tuesday.

My dear, you will not offer any violence to your health? — I hope, God has given you more grace than to do that.

I hope he has, madam. But there

is violence enough offered, and threatened, to affect my health: and so it will be found, without my needing to have recourse to any other, or to *artifice* either.

I'll only tell you one thing, my dear: and that is; ill or well, the ceremony will probably be performed before Wednesday night: — but this, also, I will tell you, although beyond my present commission, that Mr. Solmes will be under an engagement (if you should require it of him as a favour) after the ceremony is passed, and Lovelace's hopes thereby utterly extinguished, to leave you at your father's, and return to his own house every evening, until you are brought to a full sense of your duty, and consent to acknowledge your change of name.

There was no opening of my lips to such a speech as this. I was dumb.

And these, my dear Miss Howe, are they, who, *some* of them at least, have called me a romantic girl! — This is my chimerical brother, and wise sister; both joining their heads together, I dare say. And yet, my aunt told me, that the last part was what took in my mother! who had, till that expedient was found out, insisted, that her child should not be married, if, through grief or opposition, she should be ill, or fall into fits.

This intended violence my aunt often excused, by the certain information they pretended to have, of some plots or machinations, that were ready to break out from Mr Lovelace's:[*] the effects of which were thus cunningly to be frustrated.

Friday, 9 o'clock.

And now, my dear, what shall I conclude upon? You see how determined — but how can I expect your advice will come time enough to stand me in any stead? For here I have been down, and already have another letter from Mr. Lovelace [*The man lives upon the spot, I think:*] and I must write to him, either that I will or will not stand to my first resolution of escaping hence on Monday next. If I let him know, that I will not (appearances so strong *against* him, and *for* Solmes, even stronger than when I made the appointment) will it not be justly deemed my own fault, if I am compelled to marry their odious man? And if any mischief ensue from Mr. Lovelace's rage and disappointment, will it not lie at my door? — Yet, he offers so fair! — Yet, on the other hand, to incur the censure of the world, as a giddy creature — but that, as he hints, I have already incurred — what can I do? — O that my cousin Morden — but what signifies wishing?

I will here give you the substance of Mr. Lovelace's letter. The letter itself I will send, when I have answered it; but that I will defer doing as long as I can, in

[*] It may not be amiss to observe in this place, that Mr. Lovelace artfully contrived to drive the family on, permitting *his* and *their* agent Leman to report machinations, which he had neither intention nor power to execute.

hopes of finding reason to retract an appointment on which so much depends. And yet it is necessary you should have all before you as I go along, that you may be the better able to advise me in this dreadful crisis.

"He begs my pardon for writing with so much assurance; attributing it to his unbounded transport; and entirely acquiesces in my will. He is full of alternatives and proposals. He offers *to attend me directly to Lady Betty's;* or, if I had rather, *to my own estate;* and that my Lord M. shall protect me there" [he knows not, my dear, my reasons for objecting to this inconsiderate advice]. In either case, as soon as he sees me safe, he will go up to London, or whither I please; and not come near me, but by my own permission; and till I am satisfied in every thing I am doubtful of, as well with regard to his reformation, as to settlements, &c.

"To *conduct me to you,* my dear, is another of his proposals, not doubting, he says, but your mother will receive me:* or, if that be not agreeable to you, or to your mother, or to me, he will put me into *Mr. Hickman's* protection: whom, no doubt, he says, you can influence; and that it may be given out, that I am gone to Bath, or Bristol, or abroad; wherever I please.

"Again, if it be more agreeable, he proposes *to attend me privately to London,* where he will procure handsome lodgings for me, and

* See the note on p. 383, of this volume.

both *his cousins Montague to receive me in them, and to accompany me till all shall be adjusted to my mind; and till a reconciliation shall be effected;* which he assures me nothing shall be wanting in him to facilitate; greatly as he has been insulted by all my family.

"These several measures he proposes to my choice; as it was unlikely, he says, that he could procure, *in the time,* a letter from Lady Betty, under her own hand, to invite me in form to her house, unless he had been himself to go to that lady for it; which, at this critical juncture, while he is attending my commands, is impossible.

"He conjures me in the most solemn manner, if I would not throw him into utter despair, to keep to my appointment.

"However, instead of threatening my relations, or Solmes, if I recede, he respectfully says, that he doubts not, but that, if I *do,* it will be upon such reasons as he ought to be satisfied with; upon no slighter, he hopes, than their leaving me at full liberty to pursue my own inclinations: in which (whatever they shall be) he will entirely acquiesce; only endeavouring *to make his future good behaviour the sole ground for his expectation of my favour.*

"In short, he solemnly vows, that his *whole* view at present is, To free me from my imprisonment; and to restore me to my own free will, in a point so absolutely necessary to my future happiness. He declares, that neither the hopes he has of my future favour, nor the consideration of his own and family's honour, will permit him to propose any thing *that shall be inconsistent with my own most scrupulous notions:* and, for my mind's sake, should choose to have the proposed end obtained by my friends declining to compel me. But that nevertheless, as to the world's opinion, it is impossible to imagine, that the behaviour of my relations to me has not already brought upon my family those free censures which they deserve, and caused the step which I am so scrupulous about taking, to be no other than the *natural* and *expected* consequence of their treatment of me."

Indeed, I am afraid all this is true: and it is owing to some little degree of politeness, that Mr. Lovelace does not say all he might say on this subject: for I have no doubt that I am the talk, and perhaps the by-word of half the county. If so, I am afraid I can now do nothing that will give me more disgrace than I have already so causelessly received by their indiscreet persecutions: and let me be whose I will, and do what I will, I shall never wipe off the stain which my confinement, and the rigorous usage I have received, have fixed upon me; at least in my own opinion.

I wish, if ever I am to be considered as one of the eminent family this man is allied to, some of them do not think the worse of me, for the disgrace I have received. In that case, perhaps, I shall be obliged to him, if *he* do not. You see how much this harsh, this cruel treatment from my own family has humbled me! But perhaps I was too much exalted before.

Mr. Lovelace concludes, "with repeatedly begging an interview with me; and that, *this* night, if possible: an honour, he says, he is the more encouraged to solicit for, as I had twice before made him hope for it. But whether he obtain it or not, he beseeches me to choose one of the alternatives he offers to my acceptance; and not to depart from my resolution of escaping on Monday, unless the reason ceases on which I had taken it up; and that I have a prospect of being restored to the favour of my friends; at least to my own liberty, and freedom of choice."

He renews all his vows and promises on this head in so earnest and so solemn a manner, that (his own *interest*, and his family's *honour*, and their *favour* for me, co-operating) I can have no room to doubt of his sincerity.

LETTER LXXXV.

Miss Clarissa Harlowe to Miss Howe.

Sat. morn. 8 o'clock, (April 8.)

WHETHER you will blame me or not, I cannot tell, but I have deposited a letter confirming my resolution to leave this house on Monday next, within the hour mentioned in my former, if possible. I have not kept a copy of it. But this is the substance:

I tell him, "That I have no way to avoid the determined resolution of my friends in behalf of Mr. Solmes, but by abandoning this house by his assistance."

I have not pretended to make a merit with him on this score; for I plainly tell him, "That could I, *without an unpardonable sin*, die when I *would*, I would sooner make death my choice, than take a step, which all the world, if not my own heart, will condemn me for taking."

I tell him, "That I shall not try to bring any other clothes with me, than those I shall have on; and those but my common wearing-apparel; lest I should be suspected. That I must expect to be denied the possession of my estate: but that I am determined never to consent to a litigation with my father, were I to be reduced to ever so low a state: so that the protection I am to be obliged for to any one, must be alone for the distress' sake. That, therefore, he will have nothing to hope for from this step, *that he had not before:* and that in every light I reserve to myself to *accept or refuse his address, as his behaviour and circumspection shall appear to me to deserve.*"

I tell him, "That I think it best to go into a private lodging, in the neighbourhood of Lady Betty Lawrence; and not to her ladyship's house; that it may not appear to the world, *that I have refuged myself in his family;* and that a reconciliation with my friends may not, on that account, be made impracticable: that I will send for thither my faithful Hannah; and apprise only Miss Howe where I am: that *he shall instantly leave me*, and go to London, or to one of Lord M.'s seats; and (as he had promised) not come near me, but by my leave; contenting himself with a correspondence by letter only.

"That if I find myself in danger of being discovered, and carried back by violence, I will then throw myself directly into the protection either of Lady Betty or Lady Sarah: but *this only in case of absolute necessity;* for that it will be more to my reputation, for me, by the best means I can, (taking advantage of my privacy) to enter by a second or third hand *into a treaty of reconciliation with my friends.*

"That I must, however, plainly tell him, that if in this treaty my friends *insist upon my resolving against marrying him, I will engage to comply with them;* provided they will allow me to promise him, *that I will never be the wife of any other man while he remains single, or is living:* that this is a compliment I am willing to pay him in return for the trouble and pains he has taken, and the usage he has met with, on my account: although I intimate, that he may, in a great measure, thank himself (by reason of the little regard he has paid to his reputation) for the slights he has met with."

I tell him, "That I may, in this privacy, write to my cousin

Morden, and, if possible, interest him in my cause.

"I take some brief notice then of his alternatives."

You must think, my dear, that this unhappy force upon me, and this projected flight, make it necessary for me to account to him much sooner than I should otherwise choose to do, for every part of my conduct.

"It is not to be expected, I tell him, that your mother will embroil herself, or suffer you or Mr. Hickman to be embroiled, on my account: and as to his proposal of my going to London, I am such an absolute stranger to every body there, and have such a bad opinion of the place, that I cannot by any means think of going thither: except I should be induced, some time hence, by the ladies of his family to attend them.

"As to the meeting he is desirous of, I think it by no means proper; especially as it is so likely that I may soon see him. But that if any thing occurs to induce me to change my mind, [as to withdrawing, I will *then take the first opportunity to see him, and give him my reasons for that change.*"

This, my dear, I the less scrupled to write, as it might qualify him to bear such a disappointment, should I give it him; he having, besides, behaved so very unexceptionably when he surprised me some time ago in the lonely woodhouse.

Finally, "I commend myself, as a person in distress, and *merely as such*, to *his* honour, and to the protection of the ladies of his family. I repeat [most cordially, I am sure!] my deep concern for being forced to take a step so disagreeable, and so derogatory to my honour. And having told him, that I will endeavour to obtain leave to dine in the ivy summer-house*, and to send Betty of some errand, when there, I leave the rest to him; but imagine, that about four o'clock will be a proper time for him to contrive some signal to let me know he is at hand, and for me to unbolt the garden-door."

I added, by way of postscript, "That their suspicions seeming to increase, I advise him to contrive to send or come to the usual place, as frequently as possible, in the interval of time till Monday morning ten or eleven o'clock; as something may possibly happen to make me alter my mind."

O my dear miss Howe! — what a sad, sad thing is the necessity, forced upon me, for all this pre-

---

* The ivy summer-house (or ivy bower, as it was sometimes called in the family) was a place that from a girl this young lady delighted in. She used in the summer months frequently to sit and work, and read and write, and draw, and (when permitted) to breakfast, and dine, and sometimes to sup in it, especially when Miss Howe, who had an equal liking to it, was her visitor and guest.

She describes it, in another letter, (which appears not) as pointing "to a pretty variegated landscape of wood, water, and hilly country; which had pleased her so much, that she had drawn it, the piece hanging up, in her parlour, among some of her other drawings."

paration and contrivance! — But it is now too late! — But how? — Too late, did I say? — What a word is *that!* — what a dreadful thing, *were* I to repent, to *find* it to be too late to remedy the apprehended evil!

Saturday, 10 o'clock.

Mr. Solmes is here. He is to dine with his new relations, as Betty tells me he already calls them.

He would have thrown himself in my way once more: but I hurried up to my prison, in my return from my garden-walk, to avoid him.

I had when in the garden the curiosity to see if my letter was gone: I cannot say with an intention to take it back again if it were not, because I see not how I could do otherwise than I have done; yet, what a caprice! when I found it gone, I began (as yesterday morning) to wish it had not: for no other reason, I believe, than because it was out of my power.

A strange diligence in this man! — He *says*, he almost lives upon the place; and I think so too.

He mentions, as you will see in his letter, four several disguises, which he put on in one day. It is a wonder, nevertheless, that he has not been seen by some of our tenants: for it is impossible that any disguise can hide the gracefulness of his figure. But this is to be said, that the adjoining grounds being all in our own hands, and no common footpaths near that part of the garden, and through the park and coppice, nothing can be more bye and unfrequented.

Then they are less watchful, I believe, over my garden-walks, and my poultry-visits, depending, as my aunt hinted, upon the bad character they have taken so much pains to fasten upon Mr. Lovelace. This, they think (and *justly* think) must fill me with doubts. And then the regard I have hitherto had for my reputation, is another of their securities. Were it not for these two, they would not surely have used me as they have done, and at the same time left me the opportunities which I have several times had, to get away, had I been disposed to do so*: and indeed their dependence on both these motives would have been well founded had they kept but tolerable measures with me.

Then, perhaps, they have no notion of the back-door; as it is seldom opened, and leads to a place so pathless and lonesome.**

---

* They might, no doubt, make a dependence upon the reasons she gives: but their chief reliance was upon the vigilance of their Joseph Leman; little imagining what an implement he was of Mr. Lovelace.

** This, in another of her letters (which neither is inserted), is thus described: — "A piece of ruins upon it, the remains of an old chapel, now standing in the midst of the coppice; here and there an overgrown oak, surrounded with ivy and misletoe, starting up, to sanctify, as it were, the awful solemness of the place: a spot, too, where a man having been found hanging some years ago, it was

If not, there can be no other way to escape (if one would) unless by the plashy lane, so full of springs, by which your servant reaches the solitary woodhouse; to which lane one must descend from a high bank, that bounds the poultry-yard. For, as to the frontway, you know, one must pass through the house to that, and in sight of the parlours, and the servants' hall; and then have the open court-yard to go through, and, by means of the iron-gate, be full in view, as one passes over the lawn, for a quarter of a mile together; the young plantations of elms and limes affording yet but little shade or covert.

The ivy summer-house is the most convenient for this heart-affecting purpose, of any spot in the garden, as it is not far from the back-door, and yet in another alley, as you may remember. Then it is seldom resorted to by any body else, except in the summer-months, because it is cool. When they loved me, they would often, for this reason, object to my long continuance in it: but now, it is no matter what becomes of me. Besides, *cold is a bracer*, as my brother said yesterday.

Here I will deposit what I have used to be thought of by us when children, and by the maid servants, with a degree of terror (it being actually the habitation of owls, ravens, and other ominous birds) as haunted by ghosts, goblins, spectres: the genuine result of country loneliness and ignorance: notions which, early propagated, are apt to leave impressions even upon minds grown strong enough at the same time to despise the like credulous follies in others."

written. Let me have your prayers, my dear; and your approbation, or your censure, of the steps I have taken: for yet it may not be quite too late to revoke the appointment. I am

Your most affectionate and
faithful,
CL. HARLOWE.

Why will you send your servant empty-handed?

LETTER XLVII.

Miss Howe to Miss Clarissa Harlowe.

Sat. afternoon.

BY your last date of ten o'clock in your letter of this day, you could not long have deposited it before Robin took it. He rode hard, and brought it to me just as I had risen from table.

You may justly blame me for sending my messenger empty-handed, your situation considered; and yet that very situation (so critical!) is partly the reason for it: for indeed I knew not what to write, fit to send you.

I have been inquiring privately, how to procure you a conveyance from Harlowe Place, and yet not appear in it; knowing, that to oblige in the *fact*, and to disoblige in the *manner*, is but obliging by halves: my mother being moreover very suspicious, and very uneasy: made more so by daily visits from your uncle Antony; who tells her, that every thing is now upon the point of being determined; and hopes, that her daughter will not so interfere, as to discourage your compliance with their wills. This I came at by a way that I cannot take notice of, or *both* should hear of it in a manner *neither* would like: and, *without* that, my mother and I have had almost hourly bickerings.

I found more difficulty than I expected (as the time was confined, and secresy required, and as you so earnestly forbid me to accompany you in your enterprise) in procuring you a vehicle. Had you not obliged me to keep measures with my mother, I could have managed it with ease. I could even have taken our own chariot, on one pretence or other, and put two horses extraordinary to it; if I had thought fit; and I could when we had got to London, have sent it back, and nobody the wiser as to the lodgings we might have taken.

I wish to the Lord, you had permitted this. Indeed I think you are too punctilious a great deal for your situation. Would you expect to enjoy yourself with your usual placidness, and not be ruffled, in an hurricane which every moment threatens to blow your house down?

Had your distress sprung from yourself, that would have been another thing. But when all the world knows where to lay the fault, this alters the case.

How can you say I am happy, when my mother, to her power, is as much an abettor of their wickedness to my dearest friend, as your aunt, or any body else? — And this through the instigation of that odd-headed and foolish uncle of yours, who [sorry creature that he is!] keeps her up to resolutions which are unworthy of her, for an example to me, if it please you. Is not this cause enough for me to ground a resentment upon, sufficient to justify me for accompanying you; the friendship between us so well known?

Indeed, my dear, the importance of the case considered, I must repeat that you are too nice. Don't they already think, that your non-compliance with their odious measures is owing a good deal to my advice? Have they not prohibited our correspondence upon that very surmise? And have I, but on *your* account, reason to value *what* they think?

Besides, what discredit have I to fear by such a step? What detriment? Would Hickman, do you believe, refuse me upon it? -- If he did, should I be sorry for that? — Who is it, that has a soul, who would not be affected by such an instance of female friendship?

But I should vex and disorder my mother! — Well, that is something: but not more than she vexes and disorders me, on her being made an implement by such a sorry creature, who ambles hither every day in spite to my dearest friend — woe be to *both*, if it be for a *double end!* — Chide me, if you will: I don't care.

I say, and I insist upon it, such a step would *ennoble* your friend: and if still you will permit it, I will take the office out of Lovelace's hands; and, to-morrow evening, or on Monday before his time of appointment takes place, will come in a chariot, or chaise: and then, my dear, if we get off as I wish, will we make terms (and what terms we please) with them all. My mother will be glad to receive her daughter again I warrant: and Hickman will cry for *joy* on my return; or he shall for *sorrow*.

But you are so very earnestly angry with me for proposing such a step, and have always so much to say for your side of *any* question, that I am afraid to urge it further. — Only be so good (let me add) as to encourage me to resume it, if, upon further consideration, and upon weighing matters well (and in *this* light, whether best to go off with *me*, or with *Lovelace*) you can get over your punctilious regard for my reputation. A woman going away with a *woman* is not so discreditable a thing, surely! and with no view, but to *avoid the fellows!* — I say, only be so good as to *consider* this point; and if you *can* get over your scruples on *my* account, do. And so I will have done with this argument for the present; and apply myself to some of the passages in yours.

A time, I hope, will come, that I shall be able to read your affecting narratives without that impatient bitterness, which now boils over in my heart, and would flow to my pen, were I to enter into the particulars of what you write. And indeed I am afraid of giving you my advice at all, or of telling you what I should do in your case (supposing you will still refuse my offer; finding too, what you have been brought or rather driven to, without it); lest any evil should follow it: in which case, I should never forgive myself. And this consideration has added to my difficulties in writing to you now you are upon such a crisis, and yet refuse the *only* method — but I said, I would not for the present touch any more that string. Yet, one word more, chide me if you please: if any harm betide you I shall for ever blame my mother — indeed I shall — and perhaps yourself, if you do not accept of my offer.

But one thing, in your present situation and prospects, let me advise: it is this, that if you *do* go off with Mr. Lovelace, you take the first opportunity to marry. Why should you *not?* when every body will know by *whose* assistance, and in *whose* company, you leave your father's house, go whithersoever you will? — You may indeed keep him at a distance, until settlements are drawn, and suchlike matters are adjusted to your mind: but even these are matters of less consideration in your particular case, than they would be in that of most others: and first, *because,* be his other faults what they will, nobody thinks him an ungenerous man: next *because* the possession of your estate must be given up to you as soon as your cousin Morden comes; who, as your trustee, will see it done; and done upon proper terms: 3dly, *because* there is no want of fortune on his side: 4thly, *because*, all his family value you, and are extremely desirous that you should be their relation: 5thly, *because* he makes no scruple of accepting you without conditions. You see how he has always defied your relations [I, for my own part, can forgive him for the fault: nor know I, if it be not a noble one]: and I dare say, he would rather call you *his*, without a shilling, than be under obligation to those whom he has full as little reason to love, as they have to love him. You have heard, that his own relations cannot make his proud spirit submit to owe any favour to them.

For all these reasons, I think, you may the less stand upon previous settlements. It is therefore my absolute opinion, that, if you *do* withdraw with him (and in that case you must let *him* be judge, when he can leave you with safety, *you'll observe that*) you should not postpone the ceremony.

Give this matter your most serious consideration. Punctilio is out of doors the moment you are out of your father's house. I know how justly severe you have been upon those inexcusable creatures whose giddiness, and even want of decency, have made them, in the *same hour* as I may say, leap from a parent's window to a husband's bed — but considering Lovelace's character, I repeat my opinion, that your *reputation* in the eye of the world requires that no delay be made in *this* point when once you are in his power.

I need not, I am sure, make a stronger plea to *you*.

You say, in excuse for my mother, (what my fervent love for my friend very ill brooks) that we ought not to blame any one for not doing what she has an option to do, or to let alone. This, in cases of friendship, would admit of very strict discussion. If the thing requested be of *greater* consequence, or even of *equal*, to the person sought to, and it were, as the old phrase has it, *to take a thorn out of one friend's foot to put it into one's own*, something might be said. — Nay, it would be, I will venture to say, a selfish thing in us to ask a favour of a friend which would subject that friend to the *same* or *equal* inconvenience as that from which we wanted to be relieved. The requester would, in this case, teach his friend, by his *own* selfish example, with much *better* reason, to deny him, and despise a friendship so *merely* nominal. But if, by a *less* inconvenience to ourselves, we could relieve our friend from a *greater*, the refusal of such a favour makes the refuser unworthy of the name of friend: nor would I admit such a one, not even into the *outermost* fold of my heart.

I am well aware that this is your opinion of friendship, as well as mine: for I owe the distinction to you, upon a certain occasion; and it saved me from a very great inconvenience, as you must needs remember. But you were always for making excuses for *other* people, in cases wherein you would not have allowed of one for *yourself*.

I must own, that were these excuses for a friend's indifference, or denial, made by any body but *you*, in a case of such *vast* importance to herself, and of so comparative a *small* one to those for whose protection she would be thought to wish; I, who am for ever, as you have often remarked, endeavouring to trace effects to their causes, should be ready to suspect, that there was a latent, unowned inclination, which balancing, or *preponderating* rather, made the issue of the alternative (however important) sit more lightly upon the excuser's mind than she cared to own.

You will understand me, my dear. But if you do not, it may be as well for me; for I am afraid I shall *have it* from you, for but starting such a notion, or giving a hint, which perhaps, as you did once in another case, you will reprimandingly call, "Not being able to forego the ostentation of sagacity, though at the expense of that tenderness which is due to friendship and charity."

What signifies owning a fault without mending it, you'll say? — Very true, my dear. But you know I ever was a saucy creature — ever stood in need of great allowances. — And I remember likewise that I ever had them from my dear Clarissa. Nor do I doubt them now: for you know how much I love you — if it be possible, *more* than *myself* I love you! Believe me, my dear: and, in consequence of that belief, you will be able to judge, how much I am affected by your present distressful and critical situation; which will not suffer me to pass by without a censure even that *philosophy* of temper in your own cause, which you have not in another's, and which all that know you ever admired you for.

From this critical and distressful situation, it shall be my hourly prayers, that you may be delivered without blemish to that fair fame, which has hitherto, like your heart, been unspotted.

With this prayer, twenty times repeated, concludes

Your ever affectionate
ANNA HOWE.

I hurried myself in writing this; and I hurry Robin away with it, that in a situation so very critical, you may have all the time possible to consider what I have written, upon two points so very important. I will repeat them in a very few words:

"Whether you choose not rather to go off with one of *your own sex;* with your ANNA HOWE — than with one of the *other;* with Mr. LOVELACE?"

And if *not*,

"Whether you should not marry him as soon as possible?"

LETTER LXXXVII.
Miss Clarissa Harlowe to Miss Howe.

[*The preceding letter not received.*]
Saturday afternoon.

ALREADY have I an ecstatic answer, as I may call it, to my letter. "He promises compliance with my will in every article: approves of all I propose; particularly of the private lodging: and thinks it a happy expedient to obviate the censures of the busy and the unreflecting: and yet he hopes, that the putting myself into the protection of either of his aunts (treated as I am treated) would be far from being looked upon by any body in a disreputable light. But every thing I enjoin or resolve upon must, he says, be right, not only with respect to my present but future reputation: with regard to which he hopes so to behave himself, as to be *allowed* to be, next to myself, more *properly* solicitous than any body. He will only assure me, that his whole family are extremely desirous to take advantage of the persecutions I labour under, to make their court and endear themselves to me, by their best and most cheerful services: happy, if they can in any measure contribute to my present freedom and future happiness.

"He will this afternoon, he says, write to Lord M. and to Lady Betty and Lady Sarah, that he is now within view of being the happiest man in the world, if it be not his own fault; since the only woman upon earth that can make him so, will be soon out of danger of being another man's; and cannot possibly prescribe any terms to him that he shall not think it his duty to comply with.

"He flatters himself now (my last letter *confirming* my resolution) that he can be in no apprehension of my changing my mind, unless my friends change their manner of acting by me; which he is too sure they will not.* And now will all his relations who take such a kind and generous share in his interests, glory and pride themselves in the prospects he has before him."

Thus artfully does he hold me to it.

"As to fortune, he begs of me not to be solicitous on that score: that his own estate is sufficient for us both: not a *nominal*, but a *real*, two thousand pounds *per annum*, equivalent to some estates reputed a third more: that it never was encumbered: that he is clear of the world, both as to book and bond debts; thanks, perhaps, to his *pride*, more than to his *virtue*: that Lord M. moreover resolves to settle upon him a thousand pounds *per annum* on his nuptials. And to this, he will have it, his Lordship is instigated more by motives of *justice* than of *generosity;* as he must consider it was but an equivalent for an estate which he had got possession of, to which *his* (Mr. Lovelace's) mother had better pretensions. That his Lordship also proposed to give him up either his seat in Hertfordshire, or that in Lancashire, at his own or at his wife's option, especially if I am the person. All which it will be in my power to see done, and proper settlements drawn, *before* I

* Well he might be so sure, when he had the art to play them off, by his corrupted agent, and to make them all join to promote his views unknown to themselves; as is shewn in some of his preceding letters

enter into any further engagements with him; if I will have it so."

He says, "That I need not be under any solicitude as to *apparel*: all *immediate* occasions of that sort will be most cheerfully supplied by the ladies of his family: as my others shall, with the greatest pride and pleasure (if I will allow him that honour) by himself.

He assures me, "That I shall govern him as I please with regard to any thing in *his* power towards effecting a reconciliation with my friends;" A point he knows my heart is set upon.

He is afraid, "That the time will hardly allow of his procuring Miss Charlotte Montague's attendance upon me, at St. Alban's, as he had proposed she should; because, he understands, she keeps her chamber with a violent cold and sore throat. But both she and her sister, the first moment she is able to go abroad, shall visit me at my private lodgings; and introduce me to Lady Sarah and Lady Betty, or those ladies to me, as I shall choose; and accompany me to town, if I please; and stay as long in it with me, as I shall think fit to stay there.

"Lord M. will also, at my own time, and in my own *manner*, (that is to say, either publicly or privately) make me a visit. And, for his own part, when he has seen me in safety, either in their protection, or in the privacy I prefer, he will leave me, and not attempt to visit me but by my own permission.

"He had thoughts once, he says, on hearing of his cousin Charlotte's indisposition, to have engaged his cousin Patty's attendance upon me, either in or about the neighbouring village, or at St. Alban's: but that she is a low-spirited, timorous girl, and would but the more have perplexed us."

So, my dear, the enterprise requires courage and high spirits, you see! — And indeed it does! — What am I about to do!

He himself, it is plain, thinks it necessary that I should be accompanied by one of my own sex. — He might, at least, have proposed the woman of one of the ladies of his family. — Lord bless me! — What am I about to do!

* * *

After all, as far as I have gone, I know not but I may still recede: and if I do, a mortal quarrel I suppose will ensue. — And what if it does? — Could there be any way to escape this Solmes, a breach with Lovelace might make way for the single life to take place, which I so much prefer: and then I would defy the sex. For I see nothing but trouble and vexation that they bring upon ours: and when once entered, one is obliged to go on with them, treading, with tender feet, upon thorns, and sharper thorns, to the end of a painful journey.

What to do I know not. The more I think, the more I am embarrassed! — And the stronger will be my doubts as the appointed time draws near.

But I will go down, and take a little turn in the garden; and deposit this, and his letters, all but the two last, which I will inclose in my next, if I have opportunity to write another.

Meantime, my dear friend — But what can I desire you to pray for? — Adieu then! — Let me only say — adieu!

LETTER LXXXVIII.
Miss Clarissa Harlowe to Miss Howe.

[In answer to letter lxxxvi.]

Sunday morning, April 9.

Do not think, my beloved friend, although you have given me in yours of yesterday a *severer* instance of what, nevertheless, I must call your *impartial* love, than ever yet I received from you, that I will be displeased with you for it. That would be to put myself into the inconvenient situation of royalty: that is to say, *out of the way* of ever being told of my faults; of ever mending them; and *in the way* of making the sincerest and warmest friendship useless to me.

And then how brightly, how nobly glows in your bosom the sacred flame of friendship; since it can make you ready to impute to the unhappy sufferer a *less degree* of warmth in *her own* cause, than *you* have for her, because she endeavours to divest herself of *self* so far as to leave to others the option which they have a right to make! — Ought I, my dear, to blame, ought I not rather to admire you for this ardour?

But nevertheless, lest you should think that there is any foundation for a surmise which (although it owe its rise to *your* friendship) would, if there *were*, leave *me* utterly inexcusable; I must, in justice to myself, declare, that I know not my own heart if I have any of that *latent or unowned inclination*, which you would impute to *any other but me*. Nor does the *important alternative sit lightly on my mind*. And yet I must excuse your mother, were it but on this single consideration that I could not presume to reckon upon *her* favour, as I could upon *her daughter's*, so as to make the claim of friendship upon *her*, to whom, as the mother of my dearest friend, a veneration is owing, which can hardly be compatible with that sweet familiarity which is one of the indispensable requisites of the sacred tie by which your heart and mine are bound in one.

What therefore I might expect from my *Anna Howe*, I *ought not* from her *mother;* for would it not be very strange, that a person of her experience should be reflected upon because she gave not up her own judgment, where the consequence of her doing so would be to embroil herself, as she apprehends, with a family she has lived well with, and in behalf of a child against her parents? — As she has moreover a daughter of her own: — a daughter too, give me leave to say, of whose vivacity and charming spirits she is more apprehensive than she need to be, because her truly maternal cares make her fear more from her *youth*, than she hopes from her *prudence;* which nevertheless she and all the world know to be *beyond* her years.

And here let me add, that whatever you may generously, and as the result of an ardent affection for your unhappy friend, urge on this head, in my behalf, or harshly against any one who may refuse me protection in the extraordinary circumstances I find myself in; I have some pleasure, in being able to curb undue expectations upon my indulgent friends, whatever were to befal myself from those circumstances; for I should be extremely mortified, were I by my selfish forwardness to give occasion for such a check, as to be told that I had encouraged an unreasonable hope; or, according to the phrase you mention, wished to take *a thorn out of my own foot, and to put it into that of my friend.* Nor should I be better pleased with myself, if, having been taught by my good Mrs. Norton, that the best of schools is *that of affliction,* I should rather learn impatience than the contrary, by the lessons I am obliged to get by heart in it; and if I should judge of the *merits of others,* as they were *kind to me;* and that at the expense of their own convenience or peace of mind. For is not this to suppose myself ever in the right; and all who do not act as I would have them act, perpetually in the wrong? In short, to make *my* sake, *God's* sake, in the sense of Mr. Solmes's pitiful plea to me?

How often, my dear, have you and I endeavoured to detect and censure this partial spirit in others?

But I know you do not always content yourself with saying what you think may *justly* be said; but, in order to shew the extent of a penetration which can go to the bottom of any subject, delight to say or to write all that *can be said* or *written,* or even *thought,* on the particular occasion; and this partly perhaps from being desirous [pardon me, my dear!] to be thought mistress of a sagacity that is aforehand with events. But who would wish to drain off or dry up a refreshing current, because it now and then puts us to some little inconvenience by its overflowings? In other words, who would not allow for the liveliness of a spirit which for one painful sensibility gives an hundred pleasurable ones? And the *one* in consequence of the *other?*

But now I come to the two points in your letter, which most sensibly concern me: thus you put them:

"Whether I choose not rather to go off [shocking words!] with one of my *own sex;* with my ANNA HOWE — than with one of the *other*; with Mr. LOVELACE?"

And if *not,*

"Whether I should not marry him as soon as possible?"

You know, my dear, my reasons for rejecting your proposal, and even for being earnest that you should not be *known* to be assisting to me in an enterprise in which a cruel necessity induced *me* to think of engaging; and for which *you* have not the same plea. At this rate, *well* might your mother be uneasy at our correspondence, not knowing to what inconveniences it might subject her and you!— If *I* am hardly excusable to think of withdrawing from my *unkind* friends, what could *you* have to say for yourself, were you to abandon a mother so *indulgent?* Does she suspect that your fervent friendship may lead you to a *small* indiscretion? and does this suspicion offend you? And would you in resentment, shew her and the world, that you can voluntarily rush into the *highest error* that any of our sex can be guilty of?

And is it worthy of your generosity [I ask you, my dear, is it?] to think of taking so undutiful a step, because you believe your mother would be glad to receive you again?

I do assure you, that were I to take this step myself, I would run all risks rather than you should accompany me in it. Have I, do you think, a desire to *double* and treble my own fault in the eye of the world? In the eye of that world, which, cruelly as I am used (not knowing all), would not acquit *me?*

But, my dearest, kindest friend, let me tell you, that we will *neither* of us take such a step. The manner of putting your questions abundantly convinces me, that I ought not, in *your* opinion, to attempt it. You no doubt *intend* that I shall *so* take it; and I thank you for the equally polite and forcible conviction.

It is some satisfaction to me (taking the matter in this light) that I had begun to waver before I received your last. And now I tell you, that it has absolutely determined me not to go off; at least not to-morrow.

If *you*, my dear, think, *the issue of the alternative* (to use your own words) *sits so lightly upon my mind; in short, that my inclination is faulty;* the *world* would treat me much less scrupulously. When therefore, you represent, *that all punctilio must be at an end the moment I am out of my father's house; and hint*, that I must submit it to Mr. Lovelace to judge *when* he can leave me with safety; that is to say, give *him* the option whether he will leave me or not; who can bear these reflections, who can resolve to incur these inconveniences, that has the question still in her own power to decide upon?

While I thought only of an escape from *this house* as an escape from Mr. Solmes; that already my reputation suffered by my confinement; and that it would be still in my own option, either to marry Mr. Lovelace or wholly to renounce him; bold as the step was, I thought, treated as I am treated, something was to be said in excuse of it — if not to the world, to *myself:* and to be *self-acquitted* is a blessing to be preferred to the opinion of all the world. But, after I have censured most severely, as I have ever done, those giddy girls, who have in the same hour, as I may say, that they have fled from their chamber, presented themselves at the altar that is to witness to their undutiful rashness; after I have stipulated with Mr. Lovelace *for time*, and for *an ultimate option whether to accept or refuse him*; and for his *leaving me as soon as I am in a place of safety* (which, as you observe, he must be the judge of); and after he has *signified to me his compliance with these terms*; so that I cannot, if I *would*, recall them, and suddenly marry; — you see, my dear, that I have nothing left me but to resolve *not* to go away with him.

But how, on this revocation of my appointment, shall I be able to pacify him?

How! — Why, assert the privilege of my sex! — Surely, on *this* side of the solemnity he has no right to be displeased. Besides, did I not reserve a power of receding, as I saw fit? To what purpose, as I asked in the case between your mother and you, has any body an option, if the making use of it shall give the refused a right to be disgusted?

Far, very far, would *those*, who, according to the old Law, have a right of *absolving*, or *confirming* a child's promise, be from ratifying mine, had it been ever *so solemn* a one.* But this was rather an appointment than a promise: and suppose it had been the latter! and that I had *not* reserved to myself a liberty of revoking it; was it to preclude *better* or *maturer* consideration? — If so, how unfit to be given! — How ungenerous to be insisted upon! — And how unfitter still to be kept! — Is there a man living who ought to be angry that a woman whom he hopes one day to call his shall refuse to keep a rash promise, when, on the maturest deliberation, she is convinced that it *was* a rash one?

I resolve then, upon the whole, to stand this one trial of Wednes-

---

* See Numb. xxx. where it is declared, whose vows shall be binding, and whose not. The vows of a man, or of a widow, are there pronounced to be indispensable: because they are sole, and subject to no other domestic authority. But the vows of a single woman, and of a wife, if the father of the one, or the husband of the other, disallow of them as soon as they know them, are to be of no force.

A matter highly necessary to be known; by all young ladies especially, whose designing addressers too often endeavour to engage them by vows; and then plead conscience and honour to them to hold them down to the performance.

It cannot be amiss to recite the very words.

Ver. 3. *If a woman vow a vow unto the Lord, and bind herself by a bond, being in her father's house in her youth;*

4. *And her father hear her vow, and her bond wherewith she hath bound her soul, and her father shall hold his peace at her; then all her vows shall stand, and every bond wherewith she hath bound her soul shall stand.*

5. *But if her father disallow her in the day that he heareth: not any of her vows, or of her bonds wherewith she hath bound her soul shall stand: and the Lord shall forgive her, because her father disallowed her.*

The same in the case of a wife, as said above. See ver. 6, 7, 8, &c. — And all is thus solemnly closed.

Ver. 16. *These are the statutes which the Lord commanded Moses between a man and his wife, between the father and his daughter, being yet in her youth in her father's house.*

day next — or, perhaps, I should rather say, of Tuesday evening, if my father hold his purpose, of endeavouring, in person, to make me *read*, or *hear* read, and then *sign*, the settlements. — *That, that* must be the greatest trial of all.

If I am compelled to sign them over-night — then (the lord bless me!) must all I dread follow, as of course, on Wednesday. If I can prevail upon them by my prayers [perhaps I shall fall into fits; for the very first appearance of my father, after having been so long banished his presence, will greatly affect me — if, I say, I can prevail upon them by my prayers] to lay aside their views; or to suspend the day, if but for one week; if not, but for two or three days; still Wednesday will be a lighter day of trial. They will surely give me time to *consider*, to *argue* with myself. This will not be *promising*. As I have made no effort to get away; they have no reason to suspect me; so I may have an opportunity, in the last resort, to withdraw. Mrs. Norton is to be with me: she, although she should be chidden for it, will in my extremity plead for me. My aunt Hervey *may*, in such an extremity, join with her. Perhaps my mother may be brought over. I will kneel to each, one by one, to make a friend. Some of them have been afraid to see me, lest they should be moved in my favour: does not this give me a reasonable hope that I *may* move them? My brother's counsel, heretofore given, to turn me out of doors to my evil destiny, may again be repeated, and may prevail. *Then* shall I be in no *worse* case than *now*, as to the displeasure of my friends; and thus far *better*, that it will not be my fault that I seek another protection: which even *then* ought to be my cousin Morden's rather than Mr. Lovelace's, or any other person's.

My heart, in short, misgives me less, when I resolve *this* way, than when I think of the *other*; and in so strong and involuntary a bias, the *heart* is, as I may say, conscience. And well cautions the wise man: "Let the counsel of thine own heart stand; for there is no man more faithful to thee than it: for a man's mind is sometimes wont to tell him more than seven watchmen, that sit above in a high tower." *

Forgive these indigested self-reasonings. I will close here: and instantly set about a letter of revocation to Mr. Lovelace; take it as he will. It will only be another trial of temper to *him*. To *me* of infinite importance. And has he not promised temper and acquiescence, on the supposition of a change in my mind?

LETTER LXXXIX.

Miss Clarissa Harlowe to Miss Howe.

Sunday morning, (April 9.)

NOBODY it seems will go to church this day. No blessing to be expected perhaps upon views so worldly, and in some so cruel.

* Ecclus. xxxvii. 13, 14.

They have a mistrust that I have some device in my head. Betty has been looking among my clothes. I found her, on coming up from depositing my letter to Lovelace (for I *have* written!) peering among them; for I had left the key in the lock. She coloured, and was confounded to be caught. But I only said, I should be accustomed to any sort of treatment in time. If she had her orders — those were enough for her.

She owned, in her confusion, that a motion had been made to abridge me of my airings; and the report *she* should make would be of no disadvantage to me. One of my friends, she told me, urged in my behalf, that there was no need of laying me under greater restraint, since Mr. Lovelace's threatening to *rescue* me by violence, were I to have been carried to my uncle's, was a conviction that I had no design to go to him voluntarily: and that if I *had*, I should have made preparations of that kind *before now*; and, most probably, been detected in them. — *Hence* it was also inferred, that there was no room to doubt but I would at last comply. And, added the bold creature, If you don't intend to do so, your conduct, miss, seems strange to me. — Only thus she reconciled it: that I had gone so far I knew not how to come off *genteelly:* and she fancied I should, in *full congregation*, on Wednesday, give Mr. Solmes my hand. And, then, said the confident wench, as the learned Dr. Brand took his text last Sunday, *there will be joy in heaven* —

This is the substance of my letter to Mr. Lovelace:

"That I have reasons of the greatest consequence to *myself* (and which, when known, must satisfy *him*) to suspend, for the present, my intention of leaving my father's house: that I have hopes that matters may be brought to a happy conclusion, without taking a step which nothing but the last necessity could justify: and that he may depend upon my promise, that I will die rather than consent to marry Mr. Solmes."

And so I am preparing myself to stand the shock of his exclamatory reply. But be that what it will, it cannot affect me so much as the apprehensions of what may happen to me next Tuesday or Wednesday; for now those apprehensions engage my whole attention, and make me sick at the very heart.

Sunday, four in the afternoon.

My letter is not yet taken away — if he should not send for it, or take it, and come hither on my not meeting him to-morrow, in doubt of what may have befallen me, what shall I do! Why had I any concerns with this sex! — I, that was so happy till I knew this man!

I dined in the ivy summer-house. My request to do so was complied with at the first word. To shew I meant nothing, I went again into the house with Betty, as soon as I had dined. I thought it was not amiss to ask this liberty, the weather seeming to be set in fine. Who knows what Tuesday or Wednesday may produce?

Sunday evening, seven o'clock.

There remains my letter still! — He is busied, I suppose, in his preparations for to-morrow. But then he has servants. Does the man think he is so *secure* of me, that having appointed, he need not give himself any further concern about me till the very moment? He knows how I am beset. He knows not what may happen. I *might* be ill, or still more closely watched or confined than before. The correspondence *might* be discovered. It *might* be necessary to vary the scheme. I *might* be forced into measures which might entirely frustrate my purpose. I *might* have new doubts. I *might* suggest something more convenient, for any thing he knew. What can the man mean, I wonder! — Yet it shall lie; for if he has it any time before the appointed hour, it will save me declaring to him personally my changed purpose, and the trouble of contending with him on that score. If he send for it at all, he will see by the date that he might have had it in time; and if he be put to any inconvenience from shortness of notice, let him take it for his pains.

Sunday night, nine o'clock.

It is determined, it seems, to send for Mrs. Norton to be here on Tuesday to dinner; and she is to stay with me for a whole week. So she is first to endeavour to persuade me to comply; and, when the violence is done, she is to comfort me, and try to reconcile me to my fate. They expect *fits* and *fetches*, Betty insolently tells me, and expostulations and exclamations *without number:* but every body will be prepared for them; and when it's over it's over; and I shall be easy and pacified when I find I can't help it.

Monday morn. (April 10,) seven o'clock.

O my dear! there yet lies the letter, just as I left it! Does he think he is so sure of me? — Perhaps he imagines that I *dare not* alter my purpose. I wish I had never known him! I begin now to see this rashness in the light every one else would have seen it in, had I been guilty of it. But what can I do, if he come to-day at the appointed time! If he receive not the letter, I must see him, or he will think something has befallen me; and certainly will come to the house. As certainly he will be insulted. And what in that case may be the consequence! Then I as good as promised that I would take the first opportunity to see him, if I changed my mind, and to give him my reasons for it. I have no doubt but he will be out of humour upon it: but better, if we meet, that *he* go away dissatisfied with *me*, than that *I* should go away dissatisfied with *myself*.

Yet, short as the time is, he may still perhaps send and get the letter. Something may have happened to prevent him, which, when known, will excuse him.

After I have disappointed him more than once before, on a requested *interview* only, it is impossible he should not have *curiosity* at least to know if something has not happened; and whether my mind hold or not in this more *important case*. And yet, as I rashly confirmed my resolution by a second letter, I begin now to doubt it.

Nine o'clock.

My cousin Dolly Hervey slid the inclosed letter into my hand, as I passed by her coming out of the garden.

DEAREST MADAM,

I HAVE got intelligence from one who pretends to know every thing, that you must be married on Wednesday morning to Mr. Solmes. Perhaps, however, she says this only to vex me; for it is that saucy creature Betty Barnes. A licence is got, as she says: and so far she went as to tell me (bidding me say nothing; but she knew I would) that Mr. Brand is to marry you; for Dr. Lewen, I hear, refuses, unless your consent can be obtained; and they have heard that he does not approve of their proceedings against you. Mr. Brand, I am told, is to have his fortune made by uncle Harlowe and among them.

You will know better than I what to make of all these matters; for sometimes I think Betty tells me things as if I should not tell you, and yet expects that I will.*

For there is great whispering between Miss Harlowe and her; and I have observed that when their whispering is over, Betty comes and tells me something by way of secret. She and all the world know how much I love you: and so I would *have* them. It is an honour to me to love a young lady who is, and ever was, an honour to all her family, let them say what they will.

But from a more certain authority than Betty's I can assure you (but I must beg of you to burn this letter) that you are to be searched once more for letters, and for pen and ink; for they know you write. Something they pretend to have come at from one of Mr. Lovelace's servants, which they hope to make something of. I know not for certain what it is. He must be a very vile and wicked man, who would boast of a lady's favour to him, and reveal secrets. But Mr. Lovelace, I dare say, is too much of a gentleman to be guilty of such ingratitude.

Then they have a notion, from that false Betty I believe, that you intend to take something to make yourself sick; and so they will search for phials and powders, and such like.

* It is easy for such of the readers as have been attentive to Mr. Lovelace's manner of working, to suppose, from this hint of Miss Hervey's, that he had instructed his double faced agent to put his sweetheart Betty upon alarming Miss Hervey, in hopes she would alarm her beloved cousin (as we see she does,) in order to keep her steady to her appointment with him.

If nothing shall be found that will increase their suspicions, you are to be used more kindly by your papa when you appear before them all than he of late has used you.

Yet, sick or well, alas! my dear cousin! you must be married. But your husband is to go home every night without you till you are reconciled to him. And so illness can be no pretence to save you.

They are sure you will make a good wife. So would not I, unless I liked my husband. And Mr. Solmes is always telling them how he will purchase your love by rich presents. — A sycophant man! — I wish he and Betty Barnes were to come together, and he would beat her every day.

After what I have told you, I need not advise you to secure every thing you would not have seen.

Once more let me beg that you will burn this letter: and pray, dearest madam, do not take any thing that may prejudice your health: for that will not do. I am

Your truly loving cousin,
D. H.

When I first read my cousin's letter, I was half inclined to resume my former intention; especially as my countermanding letter was not taken away, and as my heart ached at the thoughts of the conflict I must expect to have with him on my refusal. For, see him for a few moments I doubt I must, lest he should take some rash resolutions; especially as he has reason to expect I will see him. But here your words, *That all punctilio is at an end the moment I am out of my father's house*, added to the still more cogent considerations of duty and reputation, determined me once more against taking the rash step. And it will be very hard (although no seasonable fainting or wished-for fit should stand my friend) if I cannot gain one month, or fortnight' or week. And I have still more hopes that I shall prevail for some delay, from my cousin's intimation that the good Dr. Lewen refuses to give his assistance to their projects, if they have not my consent, and thinks me cruelly used: since, without taking notice that I am apprised of this, I can plead a scruple of conscience, and insist upon having that worthy divine's opinion upon it: in which, enforced as I shall enforce it, my mother will surely second me: my aunt Hervey and Mrs. Norton will support *her*: the suspension must follow: and I can but get away afterwards.

But, if they *will* compel me: if they *will* give me no time: if nobody *will* be moved: if it be resolved that the ceremony shall be read over my constrained hand — why then — alas! what then! — I can but — but what? O my dear! this Solmes shall never have my vows, I am resolved! And I will say nothing but No as long as I shall be able to speak. And who will presume to look upon such an act of violence as a marriage? It is impossible surely, that a father and mother can see such a dreadful compulsion offered to their child — but if mine should withdraw, and leave the task to my brother and sister, they will have no mercy.

I am grieved to be driven to have recourse to the following artifices.

I have given them a clue, by the feather of a pen sticking out, where they will find such of my hidden stores as I intend they shall find.

Two or three little essays I have left easy to be seen, of my own writing.

About a dozen lines also of a letter begun to you, in which I express my hopes (although I say that appearances are against me) that my friends will relent. They know from your mother, by my uncle Antony, that, somehow or other, I now and then get a letter to you. In this piece of a letter I declare renewedly my firm resolution to give up the man so obnoxious to my family, on their releasing me from the address of the other.

Near the essays I have left the copy of my letter to Lady Drayton;* which affording arguments suitable to my case, may chance (thus accidentally to be fallen upon) to incline them to favour me.

I have reserves of pens and ink, you may believe; and one or two in the ivy summer-house; with which I shall amuse myself, in order to lighten, if possible, those apprehensions which more and more affect me, as Wednesday, the day of trial, approaches.

LETTER XC.

Miss Clarissa Harlowe to Miss Howe.

Ivy summer-house, two o'clock.

He has not yet got my letter: and while I was contriving here how to send my officious gaoleress from me, that I might have time for the intended interview, and had hit upon an expedient, which I believe would have done, came my aunt, and furnished me with a much better. She saw my little table covered preparative to my solitary dinner; and hoped, she told me, that this would be the last day that my friends would be deprived of my company at table.

You may believe, my dear, that the thoughts of meeting Mr. Lovelace, for fear of being discovered, together with the contents of my cousin Dolly's letter, gave me great and visible emotions. She took notice of them — Why these sighs, why these heavings here? said she, patting my neck — O my dear niece, who would have thought so much natural sweetness could be so very unpersuadable?

I could not answer her, and she proceeded — I am come, I doubt, upon a very unwelcome errand. Some things that have been told us yesterday, which came from the mouth of one of the most desperate and insolent men in the world, convince your father and all of us, that you still find means

* See p. 80, 81.

to write out of the house. Mr. Lovelace knows every thing that is done here; and that as soon as done; and great mischief is apprehended from him, which you are as much concerned as any body to prevent. Your mother has also some apprehensions concerning yourself, which yet she hopes are groundless; but, however, cannot be easy, nor will be permitted to be easy, if she would, unless (while you remain here in the garden or in this summer-house) you give her the opportunity once more of looking into your closet, your cabinet, and drawers. It will be the better taken, if you give me cheerfully your keys. I hope, my dear, you won't dispute it. Your desire of dining in this place was the more readily complied with for the sake of such an opportunity.

I thought myself very lucky to be so well prepared by my cousin Dolly's means for this search: but yet I artfully made some scruples, and not a few complaints of this treatment: after which, I not only gave her the keys of all, but even officiously emptied my pockets before her, and invited her to put her fingers in my stays, that she might be sure I had no papers there.

This highly obliged her; and she said she would represent my cheerful compliance as it deserved, *let my brother and sister say what they would.* My mother, in particular, she was sure, would rejoice at the opportunity given her to obviate, as she doubted not would be the case, some suspicions that were raised against me.

She then hinted, that there were methods taken to come at all Mr. Lovelace's secrets, and even, from his careless communicativeness, at some of *mine;* it being, she said, his custom boastingly to prate to his very servants of his intentions, in particular cases. She added, that deep as he was thought to be, my brother was as deep as he, and fairly too hard for him at his own weapons — as one day it would be found.

I knew not, I said, the meaning of these dark hints. I thought the cunning she hinted at, on *both* sides, called rather for contempt than applause. I myself might have been put upon artifices which my heart disdained to practise, had I given way to the *resentment* which, I was bold to say, was much more justifiable than the actions that occasioned it: that it was evident to me, from what she had said, that their present suspicions of me were partly owing to this supposed superior cunning of my brother, and partly to the consciousness that the usage I met with might naturally produce a reason for such suspicions: that it was very unhappy for me to be made the butt of my brother's wit: that it would have been more to his praise to have aimed at shewing a kind heart than a cunning head: that, nevertheless, I wished he knew *himself* as well as I imagined *I* knew him, and he would then have less conceit of his abilities; which abilities would, in my opinion, be less thought of, if his power to do ill offices were not much greater than they.

I was vexed. I could not help making this reflection. The dupe the other too probably makes of him, through his own spy, deserved it. But I so little approve of this low art in either, that were I but tolerably used, the vileness of that man, that Joseph Leman, should be inquired into.

She was sorry, she said, to find that I thought so disparagingly of my brother. He was a young man both of learning and parts.

Learning enough, I said, to make him vain of it among us women: but not of *parts* sufficient to make his learning valuable either to himself or to any body else.

She wished, indeed, that he had more good nature: but she feared that I had too great an opinion of somebody else, to think so well of my brother as a sister ought: since between the two there was a sort of rivalry as to abilities that made them hate one another.

Rivalry, madam! said I. — If that be the case, or whether it be or not, I wish they both understood better than either of them seems to do, what it becomes gentlemen, and men of liberal education, to be and to do. — Neither of them, then, would glory in what they ought to be ashamed of.

But waving this subject, it was not impossible, I said, that they might find a little of my writing, and a pen or two, with a little ink [hated art!] — or rather hateful the necessity for it!] as I was not permitted to go up to put them out of the way: but if they did, I must be contented. And I assured her, that, take what time they pleased, I would not go in to disturb them, but would be either in or near the garden, in this summer-house, or in the cedar one, or about my poultry-yard, or near the great cascade, till I was ordered to return to my prison. With like cunning I said, that I supposed the unkind search would not be made till the servants had dined; because I doubted not that the pert Betty Barnes, who knew all the corners of my apartment and closet, would be employed in it.

She hoped, she said, that nothing could be found that would give a handle against me: for, she would assure me, the motives to the search, on my mother's part especially, were, that she hoped to find reason rather to acquit than to blame me; and that my father might be induced to see me to-morrow night, or Wednesday morning, with temper; with *tenderness*, I should rather say, said she; for he is resolved so to do, if no new offence be given.

Ah! madam, said I —

Why that Ah! madam, and shaking your head so significantly.

I wish, madam, that I may not

have more reason to dread my father's continued displeasure than to hope for his returning tenderness.

You don't *know*, my dear! — Things may take a turn — things may not be so bad as you fear —

Dearest madam, have you any consolation to give me? —

Why, my dear, it is possible that *you* may be more compliable than you have been.

Why raised you my hopes, madam! — Don't let me think my dear aunt Hervey cruel to a niece who truly honours her.

I may tell you more, perhaps, said she, (but in confidence, in absolute confidence) if the inquiry within come out in your favour. Do you know of any thing above that can be found to your disadvantage? —

Some papers they will find, I doubt: but I must take consequences. My brother and sister will be at hand with their good-natured constructions. I am made desperate, and care not what is found.

I hope, I *earnestly* hope, said she, that nothing can be found that will impeach your discretion; and then — but I may say too much —

And away she went, having added to my perplexity.

But I now can think of nothing but this interview. — Would to Heaven it were over! — To meet to quarrel — but, let him take what measures he will, I will not stay a *moment* with him, if he be not quite calm and resigned.

Don't you see how crooked some of my lines are? Don't you see how some of the letters stagger more than others? — That is when this interview is more in my head than my subject.

But, after all, should I, *ought* I to meet him? How have I taken it for granted that I should! — I wish there were time to take your advice. Yet you are so loth to speak *quite* out — but *that* I owe, as you own, to the difficulty of my situation.

I should have mentioned, that in the course of this conversation I besought my aunt to stand my friend, and to put in a word for me, on my approaching trial; and to endeavour to procure me *time for consideration*, if I could obtain nothing else.

She told me, that, after the ceremony was performed [*odious confirmation of a hint in my cousin Dolly's letter!*] I should have what time I pleased to reconcile myself to my lot, before cohabitation.

This put me out of all patience. She requested of me in *her* turn, she said, that I would resolve to meet them all with cheerful duty, and with a spirit of absolute acquiescence. It was in my power to make them all happy. And how joyful would it be to her, she said, to see my father, my mother, my uncles, my brother, my sister, all embracing me with raptures, and folding me in turns to their fond hearts, and congratulating each other on their restored happiness! Her own joy, she said, would probably make her motionless and speechless for a time: and for her Dolly — the poor girl, who had suffered in the esteem of some for her *grateful* attachment to me, would have every body love her again.

Will you doubt, my dear, that my next trial will be the most affecting that I have yet had?

My aunt set forth all this in so strong a light, and I was so particularly touched on my cousin Dolly's account, that, impatient as I was just before, I was greatly moved: yet could only shew by my sighs and my tears, how desirable such an event would be to me, could it be brought about upon conditions with which it was possible for me to comply.

Here comes Betty Barnes with my dinner —

* * *

The wench is gone. The time of meeting is at hand. O that he may not come! — But should I, or should I not, meet him? — How I question, without possibility of a timely answer!

Betty, according to my leading hint to my aunt, boasted to me, that she was to be *employed*, as she called it, after she had eat her own dinner.

She should be sorry, she told me, to have me found out. Yet 'twould be all for my good. I should have it in my power to be forgiven for all at once before Wednesday night. The confident creature, then, to stifle a laugh, put a corner of her apron in her mouth, and went to the door: and on her return to take away, as I

angrily bid her, she begged my excuse. — But — but — and then the saucy creature laughed again, she could not help it, to think how I had drawn myself in by my summer-house dinnering; since it had given so fine an opportunity, by way of surprise, to look into all my private hoards. She thought *something was in the wind*, when my brother came into my dining here so readily. Her young master was too hard for every body. Squire Lovelace himself was nothing at all at a quick thought to her young master.

My aunt mentioned Mr. Lovelace's boasting behaviour to *his* servants: perhaps *he may* be so mean. But as to my brother, he always took a pride in making himself appear to be a man of parts and learning to *our* servants. *Pride* and *meanness*, I have often thought, are as nearly allied, and as close borderers upon each other, as the poet tells us *wit* and *madness* are.

But why do I trouble you (and myself, at such a crisis) with these impertinencies? — Yet I would forget, if I could, the nearest evil the interview; because my apprehensions increasing as the hour i at hand, I should, were my atten tion to be engrossed by them, b unfit to see him, if he does com and then he will have too muc advantage over me, as he wi have seeming reason to reproa me with change of resolution.

The *upbraider*, you know, n dear, is in some sense a superic while the *upbraided*, if with rea upbraided, must make a figure as spiritless as conscious.

I know that this wretch will, if he *can*, be his own judge, and *mine* too. But the latter he shall not be.

I dare say we shall be all to pieces. But I don't care for that. It would be hard, if I, who have held it out so sturdily to my father and uncles, should not — but he is at the garden door —

* * *

I was mistaken! — How may noises *un-like*, be made *like* to, what one fears! — Why flutters the fool so! —

* * *

I will hasten to deposit this. Then I will, for the last time, go to the usual place, in hopes to find that he has got my letter. If he *has*, I will not meet him. If he has *not*, I will take it back, and shew him what I have written. That will break the ice, as I may say, and save me much circumlocution and reasoning: and a steady adherence to that my written mind is all that will be necessary. — The interview must be as short as possible; for should it be discovered, it would furnish a new and strong pretence for the intended evil of Wednesday next.

Perhaps I shall not be able to write again one while. Perhaps not, till I am the miserable property of that Solmes! — But that shall never, never be, while I have my senses.

If your servant find nothing from me by Wednesday morning you may conclude that I can neither write to you nor receive your favours.

In that case, pity and pray for me, my beloved friend, and continue to me that place in your affection which is the pride of my life, and the only comfort left to

Your
CL. HARLOWE.

LETTER XCI.

Miss Clarissa Harlowe to Miss Howe.

St. Alban's, Tuesday morn. past one.

O MY DEAREST FRIEND!

AFTER what I had resolved upon, as by my former, what shall I write? What *can* I? With what consciousness, even by *letter*, do I approach you? — You will soon hear (if already you have not heard from the mouth of common fame) that your Clarissa Harlowe is gone off with a man!

I am busying myself to give you the particulars at large. The whole twenty-four hours of each day (to begin the moment I can fix) shall be employed in it till it is finished! every one of the hours, I mean, that will be spared me by this interrupting man, to whom I have made myself so foolishly accountable for too many of them. Rest is departed from me. I have no call for that: and that has no balm for the wounds of my mind. So you'll have all those hours without interruption till the account is ended.

But will you receive, shall you be *permitted* to receive my letters, after what I have done?

O my dearest friend! — But I must make the best of it. I hope that will not be very bad! Yet am I convinced, that I did a rash and inexcusable thing in meeting him; and all his tenderness, all his vows, cannot pacify my inward reproaches on that account.

The bearer comes to you, my dear, for the little parcel of linen which I sent you with far better and more agreeable hopes.

Send not my letters. Send the linen only: except you will favour me with one line, to tell me you love me still; and that you will suspend your censures till you have the whole before you. I am the readier to send thus early, because if you have deposited any thing for me, you may cause it to be taken back, or withhold any thing you had but intended to send.

Adieu, my dearest friend! — I beseech you to love me still — but alas! what will your mother say? — What will mine? — What my other relations? — and what my dear Mrs. Norton? — And how will my brother and sister triumph! —

I cannot at present tell you how, or where, you can direct to me. For very early shall I leave this place; harassed and fatigued to death. But, when I can do nothing else, constant use has made me able to write. Long, very long, has that been all my amusement and pleasure: yet could not *that* have been such to me, had I not had *you*, my best beloved friend, to write to. Once more adieu. Pity and pray for
Your
Cl. Harlowe.

LETTER XCII.

Miss Howe to Miss Clarissa Harlowe.

Tuesday, 9 o'clock.

I write, because you enjoin me to do so. Love you still! — How can I help it, if I would? You may believe how I stand aghast, your letter communicating the first news — good God of heaven and earth! — But what shall I say? — I am all impatience for particulars.

Lord have mercy upon me! — But can it be?

My mother will *indeed* be astonished! — How can I tell it her! — It was but last night (upon some jealousies put into her head by your foolish uncle) that I assured her, and this upon the strength of your *own* assurances, that neither man nor devil would be able to induce you to take a step that was in the least derogatory to the most punctilious honour.

But, once more, can it be? — What woman at this rate! — But, God preserve you!

Let nothing escape you in your letters. Direct them for me however to Mrs. Knollys's, till further notice.

* * *

Observe, my dear, that I don't blame *you* by all this — your relations only are in fault! — Yet how you came to change your mind is the surprising thing.

How to break it to my mother, I know not. Yet if she hear it first from any other, and find I knew it before, she will believe it to be by my connivance! — Yet, as I hope to live, I know not how to break it to her.

But this is teasing you. — I am sure, without intention.

Let me now repeat my former advice — if you are *not* married by this time, be sure delay not the ceremony. Since things are as they are, I wish it were thought that you were privately married before you went away. If these men plead AUTHORITY to our pain, when we are *theirs* — why should we not, in such a case as *this*, make some good out of the hated word, for our reputation, when we are induced to violate a more natural one?

Your brother and sister (that vexes me almost as much as any thing!) have now their ends. Now, I suppose, will go forward alterations of wills, and such-like spiteful doings.

* * *

Miss Lloyd and Miss Biddulph this moment send up their names. They are out of breath, Kitty says, to speak to me — easy to guess their errand! — I must see my mother, before I see them. I have no way but to shew her your letter to clear myself. I shall not be able to say a word, till she has run herself out of her first breath. — Forgive me, my dear — surprise makes me write thus. If your messenger did not wait, and were not those young ladies below, I would write it over again, for fear of afflicting you.

I send what you write for. If there be any thing else you want that is in my power, command without reserve

Your ever affectionate
ANNA HOWE.

LETTER XCIII.

Miss Clarissa Harlowe to Miss Howe.

Tuesday night.

I THINK myself obliged to thank you, my dear Miss Howe, for your condescension, in taking notice of a creature who has occasioned you so much scandal.

I am grieved on this account, as much, I verily think, as for the evil itself.

Tell me — but yet I am afraid to know — what your mother said.

I long, and yet I dread, to be told, what the young ladies, my companions, now never more perhaps to be so, say of me.

They cannot, however, say worse of me than I will of myself. Self-accusation shall flow in every line of my narrative where I think I am justly censurable. If any thing can arise from the account I am going to give you, for extenuation of my fault (for that is all a person can hope for, who cannot excuse herself), I know I may expect it from your friendship, though not from the charity of any other: since by this time I doubt not every mouth is opened against me; and all that know

Clarissa Harlowe condemn the fugitive daughter.

* * *

After I had deposited my letter to you, written down to the last hour, as I may say, I returned to the ivy summer-house; first taking back my letter from the loose bricks: and there I endeavoured, as coolly as my situation would permit, to recollect and lay together several incidents that had passed between my aunt and me; and, comparing them with some of the contents of my cousin Dolly's letter, I began to hope, that I needed not to be so very apprehensive as I have been of next Wednesday. And thus I argued with myself.

"Wednesday cannot possibly be the day they intend, although to intimidate me they may wish me to think it is: for the settlements are unsigned: nor have they been offered me to sign. I can choose whether I will or will not put my hand to them; hard as it will be to refuse if my father tender them to me — besides, did not my father and mother propose, if I made compulsion necessary, to go to my uncle's themselves in order to be out of the way of my appeals? Whereas they intend to be present on Wednesday. And however affecting to me the thought of meeting them and all my friends in full assembly is, perhaps it is the very thing I ought to wish for: since my brother and sister had such an opinion of my interest in them, that they got me excluded from their presence, as a measure which they thought previously necessary to carry on their designs.

"Nor have I reason to doubt, but that (as I had before argued with myself) I shall be able to bring over some of my relations to my party; and, being brought face to face with my brother, that I shall expose his malevolence, and of consequence weaken his power.

"Then supposing the very worst, challenging the minister as I shall challenge him, he will not presume to proceed: nor surely will Mr. Solmes dare to accept my refusing and struggling hand. And finally, if nothing else will do, nor procure me delay, I can plead scruples of conscience, and even pretend prior obligation; for, my dear, I have given Mr. Lovelace room to hope (as you will see in one of my letters in your hands) that I will be no other man's while he is single, and gives me not wilful and premeditated cause of offence against him; and this in order to rein-in his resentment on the declared animosity of my brother and uncles to him. And as I shall appeal, or refer my scruples on this head, to the good Dr. Lewen, it is impossible but that my mother and aunt (if nobody else) must be affected with this plea."

Revolving cursorily these things, I congratulated myself, that I had resolved against going away with Mr. Lovelace.

I told you, my dear, that I

would not spare myself; and I enumerate these particulars as so many arguments to condemn the actions I have been so unhappily betrayed into. An argument that concludes against me with the greater force, as I must acknowledge, that I was apprehensive, that what my cousin Dolly mentions as from Betty, and from my sister was told her, that she should tell *me*, in order to make me desperate, and perhaps *to push me upon some such step as I have been driven to take, as the most effectual means to ruin me with my father and uncles.*

God forgive me if I judge too hardly of their views!— But if I do *not*, it follows, that they laid a wicked snare for me; and that I have been caught in it. — And now may they triumph, if they *can* triumph, in the ruin of a sister, who never wished or intended hurt to them!

As the above kind of reasoning had lessened my apprehensions as to the Wednesday, it added to those I had of meeting Mr. Lovelace — now, as he seemed, not only the nearest, but the heaviest evil; principally indeed because *nearest;* for little did I dream (foolish creature that I was, and every way beset)! of the event proving what it has proved. I expected a contention with him, 'tis true, as he had not my letter: but I thought it would be very strange, as I mentioned in one of my former*, if I, who had so steadily held out against characters so

* See p. 421.

venerable, against authorities so sacred, as I may say, when I thought them unreasonably exerted, should not find myself more equal to such a trial as this; especially as I had so much reason to be displeased with him for not having taken away my letter.

On what a point of time may one's worldly happiness depend! Had I had but two hours more to consider of the matter, and to attend to and improve upon these new lights, as I may call them — but even then, perhaps, I might have given him a meeting.— Fool that I was! what had I to do to give him hope that I would *personally* acquaint him with the reason for my change of mind, if I did change it?

O my dear! an obliging temper is a very dangerous temper!— By endeavouring to gratify others, it is evermore disobliging itself!

When the bell rang to call the servants to dinner, Betty came to me and asked, if I had any commands before she went to hers; repeating her hint, that she should be *employed;* adding, that she believed it was expected, that I should not come up till she came down, or till I saw my aunt or Miss Hervey.

I asked her some questions about the cascade, which had been out of order, and lately mended; and expressed a curiosity to see how it played, in order to induce her [how cunning to cheat myself, as it proved!] to go thither, if she found me not where she left me;

it being at a part of the garden most distant from the ivy summer-house.

She could hardly have got into the house when I heard the first signal — O how my heart fluttered! — But no time was to be lost. I stept to the garden-door! and seeing a clear coast, unbolted the already unlocked door — and there was he, all impatience, waiting for me.

A panic next to fainting seized me when I saw him. My heart seemed convulsed; and I trembled so, that I should hardly have kept my feet, had he not supported me.

Fear nothing, dearest creature, said he — let us hasten away — the chariot is at hand — and by this sweet condescension, you have obliged me beyond expression or return.

Recovering my spirits a little, as he kept drawing me after him, O Mr. Lovelace, said I, I cannot go with you, *indeed* I cannot — I wrote you word so — let go my hand, and you shall see my letter. It has lain there from yesterday morning, till within this half-hour. I bid you watch to the last for a letter from me, lest I should be obliged to revoke the appointment; and had you followed the direction, you would have found it.

I have been watched, my dearest life, said he, half out of breath — I have been watched in every step I took: and my trusty servant has been watched too, ever since Saturday; and dared not to come near your wall. — And here we shall be discovered in a moment. — Speed away, my charmer. — This is the moment of your deliverance — if you neglect this opportunity, you *never* can have such another.

What is it you mean, sir?—Let go my hand; for I tell you [struggling vehemently] that I will sooner die than go with you.

Good God! said he, with a look of wildness and surprise, what is it I hear! — But [still drawing me after him, as he retreated further from the door] it is no time to argue — by all that's good you must go — surely you cannot doubt my honour, nor give me cause to question your own.

As you value me, Mr. Lovelace, urge me no further. I come fixed and resolved. Let me give you the letter I had written. My further reasons shall follow; and they will convince you that I ought not to go.

Nothing, madam, can convince me — by all that's sacred, I will not leave you. To leave you now would be to lose you for ever —

Am I to be thus compelled? interrupted I, with equal indignation and vehemence — let go my hands, — I am resolved not to go with you — and I will convince you that I *ought* not.

All my friends expect you madam — all your own are determined against you — Wednesday next is the day, the important perhaps the fatal day! Would you stay to be Solmes's wife? Can this be your determination last?

No, never, never, will I be that man's — but I will not go with you! [Draw me not thus — how dare you, sir? I would not have seen you, but to tell you so.] I had not met you, but for fear you would have been guilty of some rashness — and, once more, I will not go — what mean you? — Striving with all my force to get from him.

What can have possessed my angel, said he, [quitting my hands, and with a gentler voice] that after so much ill-usage from your relations; vows so solemn on my part; and affection so ardent; you stab me with a refusal to stand by your own appointment?

We have no time to talk, Mr. Lovelace. I will give you my reasons at a better opportunity. I cannot go with you now — and once more, urge me no further — surely, I am not to be compelled by every body!

I see how it is, said he, with a dejected but passionate air — what a severe fate is mine — at length your spirit is subdued! — Your brother and sister have prevailed: and I must give up all my hopes to a wretch so *truly* despicable —

Once more I tell you, interrupted I, I never will be his — all may end on Wednesday differently from what you expect —

And it may *not!* — And then, good heavens!

It is to be their last effort, as I have reason to believe —

And I have reason to believe so too — since if you stay, you will inevitably be Solmes's wife. Not so, interrupted I — I have obliged them in one point. They will be in good humour with me. I shall gain time at least. I am sure I shall. I have several ways to gain time.

And what, madam, will gaining time do? It is plain you have not a hope beyond that — it is plain you have not, by putting all upon that precarious issue. O my dearest, dearest life, let me beseech you not to run a risk of this consequence. I can convince you, that it will be *more* than a risk if you go back, that you will on Wednesday next be Solmes's wife. — Prevent, therefore, now that it is in your power to prevent, the fatal mischiefs that will follow such a dreadful certainty.

While I have any room for hope, it concerns *your* honour, Mr. Lovelace, as well as mine (if you have the value for me you pretend, and wish me to believe you) that my conduct in this great point should justify my prudence.

Your prudence, madam! when has that been questionable? Yet what stead has either your prudence or your duty stood you in, with people so strangely determined?

And then he pathetically enumerated the different instances of the harsh treatment I had met with; imputing all to the malice and caprice of a brother, who set every body against him: and insisting, that I had no other way to bring about a reconciliation with my father and uncles, than by putting myself out of the power of my brother's inveterate malice.

Your brother's whole reliance, proceeded he, has been upon your easiness to bear his insults. Your whole family will seek to *you*, when you have freed yourself from this disgraceful oppression. When they know you are with those who *can* and *will* right you, they will give up to you your own estate. Why then, putting his arms around me, and again drawing me with a gentle force after him, do you hesitate a moment? — Now is the time — fly with me then, I beseech you, my dearest creature! Trust your persecuted adorer. Have we not suffered in the same cause? If any imputations are cast upon you, give me the honour (*as I shall be found to deserve it*) to call you mine; and, when you are so, shall I not be able to protect both your person and character?

Urge me no more, Mr. Lovelace, I conjure you. You yourself have given me a hint, which I will speak plainer to, than prudence, perhaps, on any other occasion, would allow. I am convinced, that Wednesday next (if I had time I would give you my reasons) is not intended to be the day we had both so much dreaded: and if after that day shall be over, I find my friends determined in Mr. Solmes's favour, I will then contrive some way to meet you with Miss Howe, who is not your enemy: and when the solemnity has passed, I shall think that step a duty, which *till* then will be criminal to take: since now my father's authority is unimpeached by any greater. Dearest madam —

Nay, Mr. Lovelace, if you now dispute — if, after this more favourable declaration, than I had the thought of making, you are not satisfied, I shall know what to think both of your gratitude and generosity.

The case, madam, admits not of this alternative. I am all gratitude upon it. I cannot express how much I should be delighted with the charming hope you have given me, were you not next Wednesday, if you stay, to be another man's. Think, dearest creature! what an heightening of my anguish the distant hope you bid me look up to, is, taken in this light!

Depend, depend upon it, I will sooner die than be Mr. Solmes's. If you would have me rely upon *your* honour, why should you doubt of *mine*?

I doubt not your *honour*, madam; your *power* is all I doubt. You never, never can have such another opportunity. — Dearest creature, permit me — and he was again drawing me after him.

Whither, sir, do you draw me? Leave me this moment — do you seek to keep me till my return shall grow dangerous or impracticable? This moment let me go, if you would have me think tolerably of you.

My happiness, madam, both here and hereafter, and the safety of all your implacable family, depend upon this moment.

To Providence, Mr. Lovelace, and to the law, will I leave the safety of my friends. You shall not threaten me into a rashness that my heart condemns! — Shall I, to promote your happiness, as you call it, destroy all my future peace of mind?

You trifle with me, my dear life, just as our better prospects begin to open. The way is clear; just now it is clear; but you may be prevented in a moment. What is it you doubt? — May I perish eternally, if your will shall not be a law to me in every thing! All my relations expect you. Your own appointment calls upon you. Next Wednesday! — Dearest creature! think of next Wednesday! — And to what is it I urge you, but to take a step that sooner than any other will reconcile you to all whom you have most reason to value in your family?

Let me judge for myself, sir. Do not you, who blame my friends for endeavouring to compel me, *yourself* seek to compel me. I won't bear it. Your earnestness gives me greater apprehensions, and greater reluctance. Let me go back, then — let me, before it is too late, go back, that it may not be worse for both. — What mean you by this forcible treatment? Is it thus that I am to judge of the entire submission to my will which you have so often vowed! — Unhand me this moment, or I will cry out for help.

I will obey you, my dearest creature! — And quitted my hand with a look full of tender despondency, that, knowing the violence of his temper, half-concerned me for him. Yet I was hastening from him, when, with a solemn air, looking upon his sword, but catching, as it were, his hand from it, he folded both his arms, as if a sudden thought had recovered him from an intended rashness.

Stay, one moment — but one moment stay, O best beloved of my soul! — Your retreat is secure, if you *will* go; the key lies down at the door. — But, O madam; next *Wednesday*, and you are Mr. Solmes's! — Fly me not so eagerly — hear me but a few words.

When near the garden door I stopped; and was the more satisfied, as I saw the key there, by which I could let myself in again at pleasure. But, being uneasy lest I should be missed, told him, I could stay no longer. I had already staid too long. I would write to him all my reasons. And depend upon it, Mr. Lovelace, said I, [just upon the point of stooping for the key, in order to return] I will die, rather than have that man. You know what I have promised, if I find myself in danger.

One word, madam, however; one word more [approaching me, his arms still folded, as if, as I thought, he would not be tempted to mischief.] Remember only, that I come at your appointment, to redeem you, at the hazard of my life, from your gaolers and persecutors, with a resolution, God is my witness, or may he for ever blast me! [that was his shocking imprecation] to be a father, uncle, brother, and, as I humbly hoped, in your own good time, a *husband* to you, all in one. But since I find you are so ready to cry out for help against me, which must bring down upon me the vengeance of all your family, I am contented to run all risks. I will not ask you to retreat with *me;* I will attend you into the garden, and into the *house,* if I am not intercepted.

Nay, be not surprised, madam. The help you would have called for, I will attend you to; for I will face them all: but not as a revenger, if they provoke me not too much. You shall see what I can further bear for your sake — and let us both see, if expostulation and the behaviour of a gentleman *to* them will not procure me the treatment due to a gentleman *from* them.

Had he offered to draw his sword upon himself, I was prepared to have despised him for supposing me such a poor novice, as to be intimidated by an artifice so common. But this resolution, uttered with so serious an air, of accompanying me in to my friends, made me gasp with terror.

What mean you, Mr. Lovelace? said I. I beseech you, leave me — leave me, sir, I beseech you.

Excuse me, madam! I beg you to excuse me. I have long enough sculked like a thief about these lonely walls — long, too long, have I borne the insults of your brother, and other of your relations. Absence but heightens malice. I am desperate. I have but this one chance for it; for is not the day after to-morrow *Wednesday?* I have encouraged virulence by my tameness — Yet *tame* I will still be. You shall see, madam, what I will bear for your sake. My sword shall be put sheathed into your hands [and he offered it to me in the scabbard] — my heart, if you please, clapping one hand upon his breast, shall afford a sheath for your brother's sword. Life is nothing, if I lose you — Be pleased, madam, to shew me the way into the garden [moving towards the door.] I will attend you, though to my fate! — But too happy, be it what it will, if I receive it in your presence. Lead on dear creature! [putting his sword into his belt] — you shall see what I can bear for you. And he stooped and took up the key; and offered it to the lock; but dropped it again, without opening the door, upon my earnest expostulations.

What can you mean, Mr. Lovelace? — said I — would you thus expose *yourself?* Would you thus expose *me?* — Is this your generosity? Is every body to take advantage thus of the weakness of my temper?

And I wept. I could not help it.

He threw himself upon his knees at my feet — Who can bear, said he [with an ardour that could not be feigned, his own eyes glistening] who can bear to behold such sweet emotion? — O charmer of my heart! [and, respectfully still kneeling, he took my hand with both his, pressing it to his lips] command me *with* you, command me *from* you; in every way I am all implicit obedience — but I appeal to all you know of your relations' cruelty to *you*, their determined malice against *me*, and as determined favour to the *man* you tell me you hate (and, oh! madam, if you did not hate him, I should hardly think there would be a merit in your approbation, place it where you would) — I appeal to every thing you know, to all you have suffered, whether you have not reason to be apprehensive of *that* Wednesday which is my terror! — Whether you can possibly have such another opportunity — the chariot ready: my friends with impatience expecting the result of *your own* appointment: a man whose will shall be entirely your will, imploring you, thus, on his knees, imploring you — to be *your own mistress;* that is all; *nor will I ask for your favour but as upon full proof I shall appear to deserve it.* Fortune, alliance, unobjectible! — O my beloved creature! pressing my hand once more to his lips, let not such an opportunity slip. You never, never, will have such another.

I bid him rise. He arose; and I told him, that were I not thus unaccountably hurried by his impatience, I doubted not to convince him, that both he and I had looked upon next Wednesday with greater apprehension than was necessary. I was proceeding to give him my reasons; but he broke in upon me —

Had I, madam, but the shadow of a probability to hope what *you* hope, I would be all obedience and resignation. But the licence is actually got: the parson is provided: the pedant Brand is the man. O my dearest creature, do these preparations mean only a trial?

You know not, sir, were the worst to be intended, and weak as you think me, what a spirit I have: you know not what I can do, and how I can resist, when I think myself meanly or unreasonably dealt with: nor do you know what I have already suffered, what I have already borne, knowing to whose unbrotherly instigations all is to be ascribed.

I may expect all things, madam, interrupted he, from the nobleness of your mind. But your spirits may fail you — what may not be apprehended from the invincible temper of a father so positive, to a daughter so dutiful? — Fainting will not save you: they will not, perhaps, be sorry for such an effect of their barbarity. What will signify expostulations against a ceremony performed? Must not *all*, the *dreadful all* follow, that is torture to my heart but to think of? Nobody to appeal to, of what avail will your resistance be against the consequences of a rite witnessed to by the imposers of it; and those your nearest relations?

I was sure, I said, of procuring a delay at least; many ways I had to procure delay. Nothing could be so fatal to us both, as for me now to be found with him. My apprehensions on this score, I told him, grew too strong for my heart. I should think very hardly of him, if he sought to detain me longer. But his acquiescence should engage my gratitude.

And then stooping to take up the key to let myself into the garden, he started, and looked as if he had heard somebody near the door, on the inside; clapping his hand on his sword.

This frighted me so, that I thought I should have sunk down at his feet. But he instantly reassured me: he thought, he said, he had heard a rustling against the door: but *had* it been so, the noise would have been stronger. It was only the effect of his apprehension for me.

And then taking up the key, he presented it to me, — If you *will* go, madam, — yet I cannot, cannot leave you! — I must enter the garden with you — forgive me, but I *must* enter the garden with you.

And will you, will you thus ungenerously, Mr. Lovelace, take advantage of my fears? — of my wishes to prevent mischief? I, vain fool, to be concerned for every one; nobody for me!

Dearest creature! interrupted he, holding my hand, as I tremblingly offered to put the key to the lock — let *me*, if you *will* go, open the door. But once more consider, could you possibly obtain that delay which seems to be your only dependence, whether you may not be closer confined? I know they have already had *that* in consideration. Will you not, in this case, be prevented from corresponding either with Miss Howe, or with me? — Who then shall assist you in your escape, if escape you would? — From your chamber-window only permitted to view the garden you must not enter into, how will you wish for the opportunity you now have, if your hatred to Solmes continue! — But, alas! that cannot continue. If you go back, it must be from the impulses of a yielding (which you'll call, a dutiful) heart, tired and teazed out of your own will.

I have no patience, sir, to be thus constrained. Must I never be at liberty to follow my own judgment? Be the consequence what it may, I will not be thus constrained.

And then, freeing my hand, I again offered the key to the door.

Down the ready kneeler dropt between me and that: and can you, madam, once more on my knees let me ask you, look with an indifferent eye upon the evils that may follow? Provoked as I have been, and triumphed over as I shall be, if your brother succeeds, my *own* heart shudders, at times, at the thoughts of what *must* happen; and can yours be unconcerned? Let me beseech you, dearest creature, to consider all these things; and lose not this only opportunity. My intelligence —

Never, Mr. Lovelace, interrupted I, give so much credit to the words of a traitor. Your base intelligencer is but a servant. He may pretend to know more than he has grounds for, in order to earn the wages of corruption. You know not what contrivances I can find out.

I was once more offering the key to the lock, when, starting from his knees, with a voice of affrightment, loudly whispering, and as if out of breath, *They are at the door, my beloved creature!* And taking the key from me, he fluttered with it, as if he would double-lock it. And instantly a voice from within cried out, bursting against the door, as if to break it open, the person repeating his violent pushes, *Are you there? — Come up this moment! — This moment! — Here they are — Here they are both together! — Your pistol this moment! Your gun!* — Then another push, and another. He at the same moment drew his sword, and clapping it naked under his arm, took both my trembling hands in his; and drawing me swiftly after him, *Fly, fly, my charmer; this moment is all you have for it,* said he. — *Your brother! — Your uncles! — Or this Solmes! They will instantly burst the door — fly, my dearest life, if you would not be more cruelly used than ever — if you would not see two or three murders committed at your feet, fly, fly, I beseech you.* — O Lord! — help, help! cried the fool, all in amaze and confusion, frighted beyond the power of controlling.

Now behind me, now before me, now on this side, now on that, turned I my affrighted face, in the same moment; expecting a furious brother here, armed servants there, an enraged sister screaming, and a father armed with terror in his countenance more dreadful than even the drawn sword which I saw, or those I apprehended. I ran as fast as he; yet knew not that I ran; my fears adding wings to my feet, at the same time that they took all power of thinking from me — my fears, which probably would not have suffered me to know what course to take, had I not had him to urge and draw me after him: especially as I beheld a man, who must have come out of the door, keeping us in his eye, running now towards us; then back to the garden, beckoning and calling to others, whom I supposed he saw, although the turning of the wall hindered me from seeing them; and whom, I imagined to be my brother, my father, and their servants.

Thus terrified, I was got out of sight of the door in a very few minutes: and then, although quite breathless between running and apprehension, he put my arm under his, his drawn sword in the other hand, and hurried me on still faster: my voice, however, contradicting my action, crying, No, no, no, all the while; straining my neck to look back, as long as the walls of the garden and park were within sight, and till he brought me to the chariot: where, attending, were two armed servants of his own, and two of Lord M.'s on horseback.

Here I must suspend my relation for a while: for now I am come to this sad period of it, my

Clarissa. I. 28

indiscretion stares me in the face; and my shame and my grief give me a compunction that is more poignant methinks than if I had a dagger in my heart. To have it to reflect, that I should so inconsiderately give in to an interview, which, had I known either myself or him, or in the least considered the circumstances of the case, I might have supposed, would put me into the power of his resolution, and out of that of my own reason.

For, might I not have believed, that *he*, who thought he had cause to apprehend that he was on the point of losing a person who had cost him so much pains and trouble, would not hinder her, if possible, from returning? That he, who knew I had promised to give him up for ever, if insisted on as a condition of reconciliation, would not endeavour to put it out of my power to do so? In short, that he, who had artfully forborne to send for my letter (for he could *not* be watched, my dear) lest he should find in it a countermand to my appointment, (as I myself could apprehend, although I profited not by the apprehension) would want a device to keep me with him till the danger of having our meeting discovered might throw me absolutely into his power, to avoid my own worse usage, and the mischiefs which might have ensued (perhaps in my very sight) had my friends and he met?

But if it shall come out, that the person within the garden was his corrupted implement, employed to frighten me away with him, do you think, my dear, that I shall not have reason to hate him, and myself still more? I hope his heart cannot be so deep and so vile a one: I hope it cannot! But how came it to pass that one man could get out at the garden door, and no more? How that man kept aloof, as it were, and pursued us not; nor ran back to alarm the house? My fright, and my distance, would not let me be certain; but really, this man, as I now recollect, had the air of that vile Joseph Leman.

O why, why, my dear friends!—But wherefore blame I them, when I had argued myself into a hope, not improbable, that even the dreadful trial I was to undergo so soon might turn out better than if I had been directly carried away from the presence of my once indulgent parents, who might possibly intend that trial to be the last I should have had?

Would to heaven, that I had stood it however! Then if I had afterwards done, what now I have been prevailed upon, or perhaps foolishly frightened to do, I should not have been stung so much by inward reproach as now I am: and this would have been a great evil avoided.

You know, my dear, that your Clarissa's mind was ever above justifying her own failings by those of others. God forgive those of my friends who have acted cruelly by me! But their faults *are* their own, and not excuses for mine. And mine began early: for I ought not to have corresponded with him.

O the vile encroacher! how my indignation, at times, rises at him! Thus to lead a young creature (too much indeed relying upon her own strength) from evil to evil! — This last evil, although the *remote*, yet *sure* consequence of my first — my prohibited correspondence! By a father *early* prohibited.

How much more properly had I acted, with regard to that correspondence, had I, once for all, when he was forbidden to visit me, and I to receive his visits, pleaded the authority by which I ought to have been bound, and denied to write to him! — But I thought I could *proceed* or *stop*, as I pleased. I supposed it concerned *me more than any other, to be the arbitress of the quarrels of unruly spirits*. And now I find my presumption punished — punished, as other sins frequently are, by *itself*.

As to this last rashness; now, that it is too late, I plainly see how I ought to have conducted myself. As he knew I had but one way of transmitting to him the knowledge of what befel me; as he knew, that my fate was upon a crisis with my friends; and that I had in my letter to him, reserved the liberty of revocation; I should not have been solicitous whether he had got my letter or not: when he had come, and found I did not answer his signal, he would presently have resorted to the loose bricks, and there been satisfied by the date of my letter, that it was his own fault, that he had it not before. But, *governed by the same pragmatical motives* which induced me to correspond with him at first, I was again afraid, truly, with my foolish and busy prescience, that the disappointment would have thrown him into the way of receiving fresh insults from the same persons, which might have made him guilty of some violence to them. And so to save him an *apprehended* rashness, I have rushed into a *real* one myself. And what vexes me more, is, that it is plain to me now, by all his behaviour, that he had as great a confidence in my weakness, as I had in my own strength. And so, in a point, entirely relative to my honour, he has triumphed; for he has not been mistaken in me, while I have in myself!

Tell me, my dear Miss Howe, tell me truly if your unbiassed heart does not despise me? — It must! for your mind and mine were ever *one;* and I despise *myself!* — And well I may: for could the giddiest and most inconsiderate girl in England have done worse than I shall appear to have done in the eye of the world? Since my crime will be known without the provocations, and without the artifices of the betrayer too; while it will be a high aggravation, that better things were expected from me, than from many others.

You charge me *to marry the first opportunity* — Ah! my dear! another of the blessed effects of my folly—That's as much in my power now as — as I am myself! — And can I besides give a sanction immediately to his deluding arts? — Can I *avoid* being angry with him for tricking me thus, as I may say (and as I have called it to him) out of *myself?* — For compelling me to take a step so contrary to all my resolutions and assurances given to you; a step so dreadfully inconvenient to myself; so disgraceful and so grievous (as it must be) to my dear mother, were I to be less regardful of any other of my family or friends — you don't know, nor can you imagine, my dear, how I am mortified! — How much I am sunk in my own opinion — I, that was proposed for an example, truly, to others! O that I were again in my father's house, stealing down with a letter *to* you; my heart beating with expectation of finding one *from* you.

* * *

This is the Wednesday morning I dreaded so much, that I once thought of it as the day of my doom: but of the Monday, it is plain I ought to have been most apprehensive. Had I stayed, and had the worst I dreaded happened, my friends would then have been answerable for the consequences, if any bad ones had followed: — but now, I have this *only* consolation left me (a very poor one, you'll say!) that I have cleared them of blame, and taken it all upon *myself!*

You will not wonder to see this narrative so dismally scrawled. It is owing to different pens and ink, all bad, and written by snatches of time; my hand trembling too with fatigue and grief.

I will not add to the length of it, by the particulars of his behaviour to me, and of our conversation at St. Alban's, and since; because those will come in course in the continuation of my story; which no doubt you will expect from me.

Only thus much I will say, that he is extremely respectful (even obsequiously so) at present, though I am so much dissatisfied with him and myself, that he has hitherto had no great cause to praise my complaisance to him. Indeed, I can hardly, at times, bear the seducer in my sight.

The lodgings I am in are inconvenient. I shall not stay in them: so it signifies nothing to tell you how to direct to me hither. And where my next may be, as yet I know not.

He knows that I am writing to you; and has offered to send my letter, when finished, by a servant of his. But I thought I could not be too cautious, as I am now situated, in having a letter of this importance conveyed to you. Who knows what such a man may do? So very wicked a contriver. The contrivance, if a contrivance, to get me away, so insolently mean! — But I hope it is not a contrivance neither! — Yet, be that as it will, I must say, that the best of him, and of my prospects with him, are bad: and yet, having enrolled myself among the too-late repenters, who shall pity me?

Nevertheless, I will dare to hope for a continued interest in your affections, [I shall be miserable indeed if I may not!] and to be remembered in your daily prayers. For neither time nor accident shall ever make me cease to be
Your faithful and affectionate
CLARISSA HARLOWE.

LETTER XCIV.

Mr. Lovelace to Joseph Leman.

HONEST JOSEPH,   Sat. April 8.

At length your beloved young lady has consented to free herself from the cruel treatment she has so long borne. She is to meet me without the garden-door, at about four o'clock on Monday afternoon. I told you she had promised to do so. She has confirmed her promise. Thank heaven, she has confirmed her promise.

I shall have a chariot-and-six ready in the byroad fronting the private path to Harlowe Paddock; and several of my friends and servants not far off, armed to protect her, if there be occasion: but every one charged to avoid mischief. That, you know, has always been my principal care.

All my fear is, that when she comes to the point, the over-niceness of her principles will make her waver, and want to go back: although *her* honour is my honour you know, and *mine* is *hers*. If she should, and should I be unable to prevail upon her, all your past services will avail nothing, and she will be lost to me for ever: the prey then to that cursed Solmes, whose vile stinginess will never permit him to do good to any of the servants of the family.

I have no doubt of your fidelity, honest Joseph; nor of your zeal to serve an injured gentleman, and an oppressed young lady. You see by the confidence I repose in you, that I have *not*; more particularly, on this very important occasion, in which your assistance may crown the work: for, if she waver, a little innocent contrivance will be necessary.

Be very mindful therefore of the following directions: take them into your heart. This will probably be your last trouble, until my beloved and I are joined in holy wedlock: and then we will be sure to take care of you. You know what I have promised. No man ever reproached me for breach of word.

These, then, honest Joseph, are they:

Contrive to be in the garden, in *disguise*, if possible, and unseen by your young lady. If you find the garden door unbolted, you will know that she and I are together, although you should not see her go out at it. It will be locked, but my key shall be on the ground just without the door, that you may open it with yours, as it may be needful.

If you hear our voices parleying, keep at the door till I cry hem, hem, twice: but be watchful for this signal; for I must not hem very loud, lest she should take it for a signal. Perhaps, in struggling to prevail upon the dear creature, I may have an opportunity to strike the door hard with my elbow, or heel, to confirm you — then you are to make a violent burst against the door, as if you would break it open, drawing backward and forward the bolt in a hurry: then, with another push, but with more noise than strength, lest the lock give way, cry out (as if you saw some of the family), come up, come up, instantly! — Here they are! Here they are! — Hasten! — This instant! Hasten! And mention swords, pistols, guns, with as terrible a voice as you can cry out with. Then shall I prevail upon her, no doubt, if loth before, to fly. If I cannot, I will enter the garden with her, and the house too, be the consequence what it will. But so affrighted, there is no question but she will fly.

When you think us at a sufficient distance [and I shall raise my voice urging her swifter flight, that you may guess at *that*] then open the door with your key: but you must be sure to open it very cautiously, lest we should not be far enough off. I would not have her know you have a hand in this matter, out of my great regard to you.

When you have opened the door, take your key out of the lock, and put it in your pocket: then, stooping for mine, put it in the lock on the *inside*, that it may appear as if the door was opened by herself with a key, which they will suppose of my procuring (it being new) and left open by us.

They *should* conclude she is gone off by her own consent, that they may not pursue us: that they may see no hopes of tempting her back again. In either case, mischief might happen, you know.

But you must take notice, that you are only to open the door with your key, in case none of the family come up to interrupt us, and before we are quite gone: for, if they do, you'll find by what follows, that you must not open the door at all. Let them, on breaking it open, or by getting over the wall, find my key on the ground, if they will.

If they do not come to interrupt us, and if you, by help of your key, come out, follow us at a distance; and, with uplifted hands, and wild and impatient gestures (running backward and forward, for fear you should come too near us; and as if you saw somebody coming to your assistance) cry out for help, help, and to hasten. Then shall we be soon at the chariot.

Tell the family, that you saw me enter a chariot with her: a dozen, or more, men on horseback, attending us; all armed; some with blunderbusses, as you believe; and that we took the quite contrary way to that we shall take.

You see, honest Joseph, how careful I am, as well as you, to avoid mischief.

Observe to keep at such a

distance that she may not discover who you are. Take long strides, to alter your gait; and hold up your head, honest Joseph; and she'll not know it to be you. Men's airs and gaits are as various and as peculiar as their faces. Pluck a stake out of one of the hedges; and tug at it, though it may come easy: this, if she turn back, will look terrible, and account for your not following us faster. Then, returning with it, shouldered, brag to the family what you would have done, could you have overtaken us, rather than your young lady should have been carried off by such a — and you may call me names, and curse me. And these airs will make you look valiant, and in earnest. You see, honest Joseph, I am always contriving to give you reputation. No man suffers by serving me.

But, if our parley should last longer than I wish; and if any of her friends miss her before I cry, hem, hem, twice; then, in order to save yourself (which is a very great point with me, I assure you) make the same noise as above: but as I directed before, open not the door with your key. On the contrary, wish for a key with all your heart; but for fear any of them should by accident have a key about them, keep in readiness half a dozen little gravel-stones, no bigger than peas, and thrust two or three slily into the key-hole; which will hinder their key from turning round. It is good, you know, Joseph, to provide against every accident in such an important case as this. And let this be your cry instead of the other, if any of my enemies come in your sight, as you seem to be trying to burst the door open, Sir! sir! or Madam! madam! O Lord, hasten! Mr. Lovelace! — Mr. Lovelace! — And very loud — and that shall quicken me more than it shall those you call to. — If it be Betty, and only Betty, I shall think worse of your art of making love,* than of your fidelity, if you can't find a way to amuse her, and put her upon a false scent.

You must tell them, that your young lady seemed to run as fast off with me, as I with her. This will also confirm to them that all pursuit is in vain. An end will hereby be put to Solmes's hopes: and her friends, after a while, will be more studious to be reconciled to her, than to get her back. So you will be an happy instrument of great good to all round. And this will one day be acknowledged by both families. You will then be every one's favourite; and every good servant, for the future, will be proud to be likened to honest Joseph Leman.

If she should guess at you, or find you out, I have it already in my head to write a letter for you to copy;** which occasionally produced, will set you right with her.

This one time be diligent, be careful: this will be the crown of

* See p. 320.
** See Vol. II. letter xvii.

all: and once more, depend for a recompense upon the honour of
Your assured friend,
R. LOVELACE.

You need not be so much afraid of going too far with Betty. 'If you *should* make a match with her, she is a very likely creature, though a vixen; as you say. I have an admirable receipt to cure a termagant wife. — Never fear, Joseph, but thou shalt be master of thine house. If she be very troublesome, I can teach thee how to break her heart in a twelvemonth; and *honestly* too; — or the precept would not be mine.

I inclose a new earnest of my future favour.

LETTER XCV.
To Robert Lovelace, Esquire, his Honner.

Sunday morning, April 9.
HONNERED SIR,

I MUST confesse I am infinnitely oblidged to your Honner's bounty. But this last command! — It seems so intricket! Lord be merciful to me, how have I been led from littel stepps to grate stepps! — And if I should be found out! — But your honner says, you will take me into your honner's sarvise, and proteckt me, if as I should at any time be found out; and raise my wages besides; or set me upp in a good inne; which is my ambishiou. And you will be honerable and kind to my dearest young lady, God love her — But who can be unkind to she?

I will do the best I am able, since your honner will be apt to lose her, as your honner says, if I do not; and a man so stingie will be apt to gain her. But mayhap my dearesste young lady will not make all this trubble needful. If she has promissed, she will stand to it, I dare to say.

I love your honner for contriveing to save miscbiff so well. I thought till I know'd your honner, that you was verry mischevous, and plese your honner: but find it to be clene contrary. Your honner, it is plane, means mighty well by everybody, as far as I see. As I am sure I do myself; for I am, althoff a very plane man, and all that, a verry honnest one, I thank my God. And have good principels, and have kept my young lady's pressepts always in mind: for she goes no-where, but saves a soul or two, more or less.

So commending myself to your honner's further favour, not forgetting the inne, when your honner shall so please, and a good one offers; for planes are no inherritanses now-a-days. And, I hope, your honner will not think me a dishoncst man for sarvinge your honner agenst my duty, as it may look; but only as my consbence clears me.

Be pleased, howsomever, if it like your honner, not to call me, *honnest Joseph*, and *honnest Joseph*, so often. For, althoff I think myself verry honnest, and all that;

yet I am touched a littel, for fear I should not do the quite right thing: and too-besides, your honner has such a fesseshious way with you, as that I hardly know whether you are in jest or earnest, when your honner calls me honnest so often.

I am a verry plane man, and seldom have writ to such honnerable gentlemen; so you will be good enuff to pass by every-thing, as I have often said, and need not now say over again.

As to Mrs. Betty; I tho'te, indeed, she looked above me. But she comes on verry well, nathelesse. I could like her better, iff she was better to my young lady. But she has too much wit for so plane a man. Natheless, if she was to angre me, althoff it is a shame to bete a woman; yet I colde make a shift to throe my hat at her, or so, your honner.

But that same reseit, iff your honner so please, to cure a shrowish wife. It would more encurrege to wed, iff so be one know'd it before-hand, as one may say. So likewise, if one knoed one could *honnestly*, as your honner says, and as of the handy-work of God, in one twelve-month —

But I shall grow impartinent to such a grate man: — and *hereafter* may do for that, as she turns out: for one mought be loth to part with her, mayhap, so *verry* soon too; espessially if she was to make the notable lanlady your honner put into my head.

Butt wonce moer, begging your honner's parden, and promissing all dilligence and exsacknesse, I reste,

Your honner's dewtiful sarvant to command,

JOSEPH LEMAN.

END OF VOL. I.

www.ingramcontent.com/pod-product-compliance
Lightning Source LLC
Chambersburg PA
CBHW051721300426
44115CB00007B/414